W9-ARY-991

PRAISE FOR THE SECOND EDITION

Public Health Management of Disasters: The Practice Guide is a scholarly addition to the evolving body of disaster medicine literature. This comprehensive text explores disasters from a public health perspective, examining systems and populations. The text's marriage of the public health and emergency management communities will aid the reader in tackling the myriad of disasters, irrespective of type or scope.

Kristi L. Koenig, MD, FACEP
Director of Public Health Preparedness
Department of Emergency Medicine
University of California at Irvine

Public Health Management of Disasters: The Practice Guide will serve as the essential desk reference not only for health professionals responsible for preparing for and responding to disasters, but for emergency managers, government officials and other decision-makers charged with ensuring that limited resources of the affected community are well managed.

Eric K. Noji, MD, MPH
Senior Policy Advisor
Office of Terrorism Preparedness and Emergency Response
Centers for Disease Control and Prevention (CDC)

Public Health Management of Disasters

THE PRACTICE GUIDE *THIRD EDITION*

Public Health Management of Disasters

THE PRACTICE GUIDE *THIRD EDITION*

Linda Young Landesman

American
Public Health
Association

www.aphabookstore.org

American Public Health Association
800 I Street, NW
Washington, DC 20001-3710
www.apha.org

Georges C. Benjamin, M.D., F.A.C.P., F.A.C.E.P. (Emeritus), Executive Director
Howard Spivak, M.D., Publications Board Liaison
Printed and bound in the United States of America
Typesetting: The Charlesworth Group
Cover design: Alan Giarcanella
Front cover illustration: A 66-year-old man, Yoshikatsu Hiratsuka, cries in front of his collapsed house with his mother still missing, possibly buried in the rubble, at Onagawa town in Miyagi prefecture on March 17, 2011. (YOMIURI SHIMBUN/AFP/Getty Images)
Back cover illustration: Volunteers race to raise the levees to 24 feet as the Sheyenne River is expected to crest at a all-time high of 22.5 feet in Valley City, North Dakota, on April 16, 2011. (Michael Rieger/FEMA)
Printing and Binding: Sheridan Press

Library of Congress Cataloging-in-Publication Data

Landesman, Linda Young.
  Public health management of disasters : the practice guide / Linda Young Landesman ; foreword by Eric Noji. -- 3rd ed.
       p. ; cm.
  Includes bibliographical references and index.
  ISBN-13: 978-0-87553-004-8 (alk. paper)
  ISBN-10: 0-87553-004-4 (alk. paper)
  1. Disasters--Health aspects. 2. Disaster medicine. 3. Crisis management. 4. Disaster relief. I. American Public Health Association. II. Title.
  [DNLM: 1. Disaster Planning. 2. Disasters. 3. Public Health Administration. WA 295]
  RA645.9.L36 2011
  363.34'8--dc23

                              2011018914

07/2011

Dedicated to those who make our world a safer and healthier place.

TABLE OF CONTENTS

TABLES AND FIGURES

Chapter 11

Chapter 12

Chapter 14

Foreword

Recent history has shaped our understanding of the health and medical impact of natural disasters, especially lessons learned from the December 2004 Indian Ocean Southeast Asian tsunami event and the powerful 9.0-magnitude earthquake that hit Japan on March 11, 2011, at 2:46 p.m. local time (0546 GMT), unleashing massive tsunami waves that crashed into the northeastern coast of Honshu—the largest and main island of Japan, resulting in widespread damage and destruction—then raced across the Pacific at 800 miles per hour before hitting Hawaii and the West Coast of the United States. According to the government of Japan, at least 25,000 people are confirmed dead. All search, rescue, and relief operations, evacuations, and international humanitarian assistance were conducted within the framework of the possibility of significant radiation release and a nuclear meltdown resulting from the fires and explosions at a coastal nuclear facility.

This past spring, in the United States, we have had record flooding along the Mississippi River, with displacement of tens of thousands, and the worst year on record for tornado-related deaths (both for an outbreak [375 deaths] and for a single event [130 deaths]), with most of the tornado season yet to come. With the incidence of such catastrophes of nature—and the number of people affected by such events—on the increase, the importance of disasters as a public health problem has captured the attention of the world.

This situation represents an unprecedented challenge to public health practitioners.

Ten years have now passed since the landmark first edition of *Public Health Management of Disasters: A Practice Guide* was published by the American Public Health Association in the wake of the catastrophic events of September 11, 2001. The first edition was so successful in part because it was able to serve as a quick reference for public health practitioners or public safety personnel who required quickly available information in an easy to access "practice guide" format. The third edition of *Public Health Management of Disasters: The Practice Guide* was confronted with the daunting task of both summarizing the many important new findings that have now become available through extensive research and the experience of public health practitioners and yet maintain the convenience of a manual. Dr. Landesman has succeeded in accomplishing this magnificently.

The third edition of *Public Health Management of Disasters* has increased the number of pages, with the addition of both new chapters and appendices that summarize in tabular form all of the new elements included in the Centers for

Disease Control and Prevention standards for public health capabilities in preparedness and planning, as well as the important changes at the federal level that have occurred since 9/11 and Hurricane Katrina, such as those resulting from Presidential Decision Directive-8, the National Response Framework (NRF), National Incident Management System, and key elements of emergency planning: disaster prevention, mitigation, preparedness, response, recovery, reconstruction, and community resiliency. The influenza section has been expanded to include our experience with the 2009 novel H1N1 influenza response and includes global considerations, including World Health Organization guidance. Chapters on surveillance have been updated to include global positioning system technology, social media, smartphones, and all of the new alerting systems the U.S. government has put in place; updated and expanded occupational and health guidance; cultural considerations; all of the new functional needs as outlined in NRF, community planning networks for vulnerable population groups, standards and indicators for disaster shelter care for children, ethical issues in disaster response; and the evolving priorities of the U.S. Department of Homeland Security.

As this book goes to print, Japan's social, technical, administrative, political, legal, health care, and economic systems are being tested to their limits by the nature, degree, and extent of the socioeconomic impacts of the earthquake, the tsunami, and the looming possibility of a "nightmare nuclear disaster." This unfolding tragedy more than ever illustrates the enduring value of this publication by the American Public Health Association. *Public Health Management of Disasters: A Practice Guide* will continue to serve as both a timely and comprehensive text for public health officials and for educating the next generation of public health practitioners.

Eric K. Noji, MD, MPH
Centers for Disease Control and Prevention (Retired)

Foreword to the Second Edition

With both disasters and the number of people affected by such events on the increase, the importance of disasters as a public health problem is now widely recognized. The last quarter century has witnessed a heightened recognition of the role of the health professional in managing disasters. For example, in the early 1970s, health personnel working in disaster situations observed that the effects of disasters on the health of populations were amenable to study by epidemiological methods and that certain common patterns of morbidity and mortality following certain disasters could be identified. Subsequently, post-disaster evaluations of the effectiveness of the health management of disasters have provided critical lessons for improving preparedness and mitigating the human impact of these events. Furthermore, government officials and other decision-makers have increasingly acknowledged the importance of collecting relevant health data that can be used as a scientific basis for taking action on a myriad of problems facing a disaster-affected community (i.e., recovery and reconstruction).

During the past 15 years, the medical and public health impact of disasters have been reviewed in a number of publications with periodic updates on the "state of the art" appearing every few years. As a result, a considerable body of knowledge and experience related to the adverse health effects of disasters is now accumulating that requires regular updating so that we can apply the lessons learned during one disaster to the management of the next. This book, Public Health Management of Disasters: The Practice Guide, does exactly that and more. With years of experience, Dr. Landesman gives the reader ample technical descriptions of each kind of disaster, the structural and organizational makeup of emergency management particularly those related to the role and responsibilities of health professionals, and copious information useful for management practices in the disaster setting (e.g., risk assessment, surveillance, communications and environmental issues). In addition, always emphasizing the use of proven management methods and practices, Dr. Landesman challenges public health professions with questions that must still be answered to respond effectively in emergency situations.

All disasters are unique because each affected region of the world has different social, economic, and baseline health conditions. Public Health Management of Disasters: The Practice Guide will serve as the essential desk reference not only for health professionals responsible for preparing for and responding to disasters, but for emergency managers, government officials and other decision-makers charged with ensuring that limited resources of the affected community are well managed.

Eric K. Noji, MD, MPH
Centers for Disease Control and Prevention

Author's Reflections and Acknowledgments

Evolution of the Field

Public health preparedness is now a recognized field—far different from the early 1980s to mid-1990s when I frequently was asked, "What does public health have to do with disasters?" Now, as in any established field, there is a large body of specialized technical information critical to this function. The preparedness practitioner must know where to gather information about a broad range of public health problems to make decisions quickly. When I wrote the first edition of *The Practice Guide*, my goal was to consolidate important information into one source. This book continues to bring together that essential knowledge.

Along with the evolution of the field, the concept of *preparedness* is also changing. Being prepared is now the responsibility of everyone—government at all levels, the private sector, nonprofit organizations, and residents of communities across the United States. In catastrophic events we have seen that preparedness was insufficient when it was only focused on what government can provide. We know that people are more likely to take actions that will help them mitigate risks if they see others taking similar actions. To be prepared, our country must build a culture of preparedness that starts with kindergarten through 12th-grade education. For our part, public health professionals can use the models of community-based participation to engage collective participation and advance preparedness. We learned from Hurricane Katrina that services must be provided for the entire community, and guidance to carry out those responsibilities is detailed in this edition.

Lessons Learned

As I was writing this book, we experienced 15 months of notable disasters worldwide: the deadly earthquakes in Chile and Haiti, the oil spill in the Gulf of Mexico, a triple hitter in Japan, devastating tornadoes in the southeastern United States, and massive flooding along the Mississippi River. In addition, Britain experienced shortages of vaccine for influenza, forcing them to look at their preparedness efforts in the winter of 2010–2011. The triple catastrophe suffered by Japan in March 2011—the severest possible earthquake, historic tsunami, and highest level of radiation accident—was also a powerful reminder that major disasters have global impacts.

There is much to learn from the Japanese experience, as similar hazards exist in the United States and worldwide. In the United States, population density is high in areas known for flooding, earthquakes, hurricanes, tornadoes, and location of nuclear power plants, placing millions at heightened exposure to hazardous risks. Furthermore, the Japanese experienced behavioral reactions and exacerbations to chronic disease similar to those seen after Hurricane Katrina and other devastating disasters.

To apply the lessons, we first have to believe that catastrophic events can happen to *us*. We have thought of catastrophic events as the *perfect storm*, where a rare combination of conditions results in catastrophic events. Another term—*Black Swan* events—is used to characterize the rare events that have a significant impact upon society. Many think of the Black Swans as the low-probability, high-consequence events that happened to another generation. Thinking that catastrophes are rare prevents us from taking the kinds of actions needed to be better prepared. Despite the ancient markers along the Japanese coastline warning generations about the dangers of tsunamis, high-risk areas were highly developed. The Japanese government had anticipated that similar catastrophic events would occur in their country, though in another location, and had taken steps to mitigate and manage them. Despite being well prepared, they didn't do enough to protect the population along the coastline and failed to heed the message of the markers: "Remember the calamity of great tsunamis." Furthermore, they failed to recognize and communicate the severity of the nuclear accident in a timely manner.

How to Use the Book

This book has two purposes: to educate public health workers and students about the areas where they will intervene as professionals, and to be a resource for anyone involved in preparing for or responding to disasters where public health problems are confronted. Using the material in this book, public health professionals will be better able to carry out the capabilities expected of them.

The principles in this book are applicable to disasters around the world. Although governmental systems may vary, similar disasters have common problems and similar outcomes—only more dramatic in countries lacking a robust infrastructure. All large-scale catastrophes require a coordinated response across many professional agencies and disciplines. This book includes guidance from both the American and world health experience.

As this edition was going to press, President Obama signed the Presidential Decision Directive-8 (PDD-8). Although the thrust of PDD-8 is discussed in Chapter 3, the final implementation may alter some of the information in this book, such as the Preparedness Goal. The implementation of PDD-8 is expected to build upon the improvements made since the passage of the Post-Katrina Emergency Management Reform Act of 2006. These improvements are included in this edition. The public health profession has been ahead of this new effort with the publication of national standards for the preparedness capabilities of public health agencies (see Appendix E). The reader should follow federal policy guidance as it is released in late 2011.

In addition, emerging technologies are being developed that will transform the field of emergency management. People have revolutionized disaster communication by finding creative uses for social media. At present, the use of social media in disaster operations is not fully realized. There are no data standards or guidance for triaging the information that comes from social media. This is an area where public health agencies can make an important contribution.

The chapters of the book, although organized by general content area, have some overlap and the reader will see references to relevant chapters. The appendices have grown in importance in the third edition, as more technical resources have become available. The appendices are grouped as follows:

- Basics: terms, acronyms, the language of disasters
- Key concepts of a public health preparedness program, Centers for Disease Control and Prevention capabilities standards
- Federal responsibilities and capabilities for medical/public health
- The Joint Commission and National Fire Protection Association standards
- Reducing morbidity
- First aid
- At-risk populations
- Infectious disease and Chemical/Biological/Radiological/Nuclear/Explosive events
- Resources and References

Appreciation

My colleagues have been a wonderful source of knowledge, resources, and tips. As always, I am indebted to them for their help and guidance:

Kevin Yeskey, Director of the Office of Preparedness and Emergency Operations, Assistant Secretary for Preparedness and Response, generously brought me up to date on the National Disaster Medical System and provided immensely helpful comments on Chapter 3.

June Kailes, the pioneer in disabilities and disaster, shared the latest guidance for vulnerable populations and helped me understand both the concept of functional needs and the implementation actions required by the new federal guidance.

My sister Pam Holmes, member of the National Council on Disability, provided insightful comments for the chapter on vulnerable populations and ensured that the content was current on services for those who are deaf or hard of hearing.

Scott Becker, a partner in developing the first national curriculum for public health preparedness published in 2001, continues to share valuable guidance. Thanks to Scott and Chris Mangal for the latest on public health laboratories.

Katherine Galifianakis provided a valuable perspective from the national office of the American Red Cross on functional needs and medical shelters.

My HHC colleagues, Caroline Jacobs and JoAnn Liburd, graciously directed me to the latest The Joint Commission standards for hospital preparedness and helped me understand how the revised standards are used. Joyce Wale provided perceptive and helpful comments on the behavioral health chapter.

Isaac Weisfuse and the dedicated professionals at the New York City Department of Health and Mental Health have provided national leadership in health department preparedness and were a great help with technical questions.

Eric Noji, a world leader in public health preparedness, wrote a thoughtful review and Foreword, as always.

Many thanks to Georges Benjamin, Nina Tristani, Howard Spivak, Brian Selzer, Dave Hartogs, Vivian Tinsley, and especially Dave Stockhoff for their roles in making the third edition the book that it is.

About the Author

Dr. Linda Young Landesman is a nationally recognized expert in emergency preparedness who has a long and distinguished career in public health working as a clinician, administrator, educator, policymaker, and author. She has worked as Assistant Vice President, Office of Professional Services and Affiliations, at the New York City Health and Hospitals Corporation (HHC) since 1996. At HHC, Dr. Landesman is responsible for over $850 million in workforce contracts between HHC and medical schools and professional medical groups, and has been responsible for the oversight, restructuring, negotiation, implementation, monitoring, and evaluation of these affiliation contracts. While at HHC, Dr. Landesman was recognized for innovative work when she received an award for Business Process Improvement from the Technology Managers Forum.

At the onset of her career, Dr. Landesman practiced clinical social work in academic medical centers in southern California. She worked with women alcoholics, families and children who had cystic fibrosis, women with high-risk pregnancies, and families whose babies required care in the neonatal intensive care unit. Dr. Landesman was the Principal Investigator for the first national curriculum on the public health management of disasters, developed through a cooperative agreement with the Association of Schools of Public Health and sponsored by the Centers for Disease Control and Prevention. She also developed national standards for Emergency Medical Services response.

Appointments to numerous committees and community boards included the Masters of Public Health Program Community Advisory Board at Long Island University; Regional Advisory Committee for the New York State Commission on Health Care Facilities for the Twenty-First Century; Commissioners' Advisory Committee, New York City Department of Health and Mental Hygiene; Advisory Committee, World Trade Center (WTC) Evacuation Study; Weapons of Mass Destruction Advisory Council, New York City Department of Public Health; Emergency Preparedness Council, New York City Health and Hospitals Corporation; Research Subcommittee, Advisory Group Subcommittee, Office of Emergency Management Subcommittee, Curriculum Subcommittee, and WTC Subcommittee, Center for Public Health Preparedness, Mailman School of Public Health of Columbia University; Violence Prevention Subcommittee, Albert Einstein College of Medicine; Environmental Subcommittee, New York Academy of Medicine; F30 accelerated writing groups and content expert, ASTM International; and the Disabled in Disaster Advisory Group, Orange County, CA.

Dr. Landesman is a member of the Public Health Association of New York City, the New York State Public Health Association and Hermann Biggs Society, and a Fellow at the New York Academy of Medicine. She has edited or authored eight books, including the landmark book, *Public Health Management of Disasters: The Practice Guide*, now in its third edition. She has written dozens of journal articles and book chapters. Dr. Landesman earned her BA and MSW degrees from the University of Michigan. She received her DrPH in health policy and management from the Columbia University Mailman School of Public Health. Her doctoral dissertation focused on hospital preparedness for chemical accidents and won the Doctoral Dissertation Award from the Health Services Improvement Fund in 1990. Dr. Landesman is currently on the faculty of the Public Health Practice Program at the University of Massachusetts–Amherst, where she teaches research methods and public health emergency management online.

Publisher's Note

D isasters are unpredictable and increasingly complex. In 1982, in our nation's capital, Air Florida flight 90 crashed into the Potomac River, killing more than 70 people. Rescue and response efforts were complicated by ice-covered roads and gridlocked traffic as a result of that day's blizzard. In addition, a Metro subway train derailed within thirty minutes of the crash, killing three passengers and further stretching emergency resources. In September 2005, Hurricane Katrina's impact was deadly, but then came the broken levee that left much of New Orleans under water, resulting in a more complicated rescue operation in the city. In Japan, one of the world's leaders in emergency preparedness, officials found themselves struggling to respond to multiple disasters in early 2011: earthquake, tsunami, and nuclear meltdown. Disasters happen; and as we have seen in recent years, they can be complex. Although we often hope for the best, we must prepare for the worst.

A decade after the September 11, 2001, terror attacks and the subsequent anthrax letters, this updated edition is being released to help public health professionals strengthen our disaster response. It is a practical guide, one that provides the core approach to disaster management. It also is a reminder that we in the public health community play an important role in preparing individuals, families, and communities in ways that make them resilient. Resiliency is the essential capacity that helps with recovery and reconstruction.

In this edition, public health professionals can learn not only about the structure of health management in disasters but also about hazard assessment, delivery of care under extreme conditions, and how to put a preparedness plan into practice. They can explore environmental and occupational health issues as well as behavioral health strategies, another often overlooked area during crises. Yet those are the times behavioral health needs cannot be ignored. Here we find key information on disaster-related surveillance, vulnerability analysis, key considerations in surge capacity, and other important ways we can prepare.

The text also addresses the ethical issues in disaster management. Although emergency responders make many life and death decisions during a disaster, none are as sensitive as those around changing the standard of care from the norm. This often occurs when decisions have to be made concerning who should get limited resources such as ventilators or medications. Those ethical considerations are explored in this new edition.

This book is an essential read and resource for those who practice public health and want a core understanding of how to protect our health when disaster strikes.

Georges C. Benjamin, MD, FACP, FACEP (Emeritus)
Executive Director, American Public Health Association
Washington, DC

Chapter 1

Types of Disasters and Their Consequences

A disaster can be defined as an emergency of such severity and magnitude that the combination of deaths, injuries, illness, and property damage cannot be effectively managed with routine procedures or resources. These events can be caused by nature, equipment malfunction, human error, or biological hazards and disease. Public health agencies must be concerned about the universal risk for disaster, the increase in natural disasters across the United States, the negative impact of disasters on public health, and the likely increase of actual and potential effects of man-made disasters.[1]

A significant proportion of Americans are at risk from only three classes of natural disasters: floods, earthquakes, and hurricanes. Twenty-five to 50 million people live in floodplains that have been highly developed as living and working environments. More than 110 million people live in coastal areas of the United States, including the Great Lakes region. A category 4 hurricane has an 80% chance of hitting the coastal area from Maine to Texas. Population in America's ten largest cities is growing faster than in nonurban areas, putting more people at risk if disaster strikes those urban centers. Further, using the definition of "at-risk" individuals discussed later in Chapter 10, more than 50% of the U.S. population is vulnerable to the effects of disaster. Of the 308.2 million people (2009) living in the United States, 54 million (17.5%) have a disability, 74.5 million are children (24%), and 34.7 million (11%) are 65 years old or older.

Disasters pose a number of unique problems not encountered in the routine practice of emergency health care. Examples include the need for warning and evacuation, widespread urban search and rescue, triage and casualty distribution, and coordination among multiple jurisdictions, government offices, and private sector organizations. The effective management of these concerns requires special expertise. However, hospitals and other health care agencies must be able to address these situations quickly and effectively to meet the standards of The Joint Commission and the regulations of the Occupational Safety and Health Administration.

Natural and Technological Disasters

Natural disasters can be categorized as either acute or gradual in their onset. They are predictable because they cluster in geographic areas. Natural hazards are

---

[1]The National Response Framework uses the term "incident." See Appendix A for an explanation of the different terms used.

unpreventable and, for the most part, uncontrollable. Even if quick recovery occurs, natural disasters can have long-term effects. Natural disasters with acute onsets include events such as earthquake, flood, hurricane or typhoon, tornado, fire, tsunami or storm surge, avalanche, volcanic eruption, extreme cold or blizzard, and heat wave. Natural hazards with a slow or gradual onset include drought, famine, desertification, deforestation, and pest infestation. The most important natural disasters and examples of their environmental effects are listed in Table 1.

Technological or man-made disasters include nuclear accidents, bombings, and bioterrorism. Increasingly, agencies involved in disasters and their management are concerned with the interactions between man and nature, which can be complex and can aggravate disasters. The severity of damage caused by natural or technological disasters is affected by population density in disaster-prone areas, local building codes, community preparedness, and the use of public safety announcements and education on how to respond correctly at the first signs of danger. Recovery following a disaster varies according to the public's access to pertinent information (such as sources of government and private aid), preexisting conditions that increase or reduce vulnerability (such as economic or biological factors), prior experience with stressful situations, and availability of sufficient savings and insurance.

Table 1. Natural Disasters and Their Environmental Effects

Disaster	Environmental Effects
Blizzard/cold wave/heavy snowfall	Avalanche, erosion, snow melt (flooding), loss of plants and animals, river ice jams (flooding)
Cyclone	Flooding, landslide, erosion, loss of plant and animal life
Drought	Fire, depletion of water resources, deterioration of soil, loss of plant and animal life
Earthquake	Landslide, rock fall, avalanche
Flood/thunderstorm	Heavy rainfall, fire, landslide, erosion, destruction of plant life
Heat wave	Fire, loss of plants and animals, depletion of water resources, deterioration of soil, snow melt (flooding)
Tornado	Loss of plant and animal life, erosion, water disturbance
Tsunami	Flooding, erosion, loss of plant and animal life
Volcanic eruption	Loss of plant and animal life, deterioration of soil, air and water pollution
Wildfires	Destruction of ground cover, erosion, flooding, mudslides, long-term smog, and tainted soil

Blizzard/Cold Wave/Heavy Snowfall

A major winter storm can be lethal. Winter storms bring ice, snow, cold temperatures, and often dangerous driving conditions in the northern parts of the United States. Even small amounts of snow and ice can cause severe problems for southern states where storms are infrequent. Familiarity with winter storm warning messages such as *windchill, winter storm watch, winter storm warning,* and *blizzard warning* can facilitate quick action by public health professionals. Windchill is a calculation of how cold it feels outside when the effects of temperature and wind speed are combined. The National Weather Service (NWS) uses the Windchill Temperature (WCT) index to calculate potential dangers from winter winds and freezing temperatures. The WCT uses meteorology, biometeorology, and computer modeling as the basis of the predictions.

A winter storm watch indicates that severe winter weather may affect an area. A winter storm warning indicates that severe winter weather conditions are definitely on the way and emergency preparedness plans should be activated. A blizzard warning means that large amounts of falling or blowing snow and sustained winds of at least 35 miles per hour are expected for several hours.

Risk of Morbidity and Mortality

Transportation accidents are the leading cause of death during winter storms. Preparing vehicles for the winter season and knowing how to react if stranded or lost on the road are the keys to safe winter driving. Morbidity and mortality associated with winter storms includes frostbite and hypothermia, carbon monoxide (CO) poisoning, blunt trauma from falling objects, penetrating trauma from the use of mechanical snowblowers, and cardiovascular events usually associated with snow removal. Frostbite is a severe reaction to cold exposure that can permanently damage its victims. A loss of feeling and a white or pale appearance in fingers, toes, or nose and ear lobes are symptoms of frostbite. Hypothermia is a condition brought on when the body temperature drops to less than 90°F. Symptoms of hypothermia include uncontrollable shivering, slow speech, memory lapses, frequent stumbling, drowsiness, and exhaustion.

Water has a unique property in that it expands as it freezes. This expansion puts tremendous pressure on whatever contains it, including metal or plastic pipes. No matter the "strength" of a container, expanding water can cause pipes to break, causing flooding. Flooding creates a risk for drowning and electrocution. Pipes that freeze most frequently are those that are exposed to severe cold, like outdoor hose bibs, swimming pool supply lines, water sprinkler lines, and water supply pipes in unheated interior areas like basements and crawl spaces, attics, garages, or kitchen cabinets. Pipes that run against exterior walls that have little or no insulation are also subject to freezing. Pipe freezing is a particular problem in warmer climates, where pipes often run through uninsulated or under-insulated attics or crawl spaces. A secondary risk is the loss of heat as a result of frozen pipes.

Individuals who are particularly vulnerable to exposure from freezing temperatures, such as the elderly and those with disabilities, should organize activities outside of their home so that they go out during the warmest part of the day (usually noon to 2:00 PM). Those paralyzed from the chest or waist down and individuals who have difficulty sensing and maintaining heat in their extremities are at risk for severe frostbite and need to protect their feet, pelvic areas, and hands because of circulation problems. It is important to dress for the weather by wearing several layers of clothing, keeping one's head, neck, and chest covered with scarves, and wearing two pairs of thick socks inside lined boots. Wheelchair users should wrap a blanket over their pelvic regions and limit the amount of time outside.

To enable the full functioning of driving adaptation equipment in motor vehicles, these vehicles have to warm up before the person gets in them. Service animals should wear a coat or cape underneath their regular harness and should sit or lie on a blanket in the vehicle. Dogs' paws should be protected with boots.

Pneumatic tires provide better traction for wheelchairs on icy surfaces. Tires for dirt bikes (sold in bicycle shops) can be used as an alternative on icy surfaces. Ramps should be cleared of ice by using standard table salt, cat litter, or ice melters that are safe for pets, as rock salt is poisonous to service dogs. Rock salt can also be slippery for certain types of mobility aides. Freezing rain will stick to canes, walkers, forearm cuffs, and wheelchairs, making metal parts slippery and cold to the touch. Driving gloves that grip can be helpful. When returning wheelchairs to vehicles, it is important to first remove the tires and shake the debris and ice from them. Tire rims and other metal parts that may have any salt or other deicing chemicals on them need to be wiped off to avoid rust on the metal parts.

Public Health Interventions

Educating communities about preventive steps that can be taken, both in advance of winter and once a storm has begun, will help reduce the impact. Winter storm preparation activities should include the following:

- Home winterization activities (insulating pipes, installing storm windows)
- Collect winter clothing and supplies such as extra blankets, warm coats and clothes, water-resistant boots, hats, and mittens
- Assemble a disaster supplies kit containing a first aid kit, battery-powered weather radio, flashlight, and extra batteries
- Stock canned food, a nonelectric can opener, and bottled water
- Winterize vehicles, keep gas tank full, and assemble a disaster supplies car kit
- Stay away from downed power lines in heavy snow

Cyclone, Hurricane, and Typhoon

Cyclones are large-scale storms characterized by low pressure in the center surrounded by circular wind motion (counterclockwise in the Northern Hemisphere, clockwise in the Southern Hemisphere). Severe storms arising in the

Atlantic waters are known as hurricanes, and those developing in the Pacific Ocean and the China Seas are called typhoons. The precise classification (e.g., tropical depression, tropical storm, hurricane) depends on the wind force (Beaufort Scale), wind speed, and manner of creation.

Hurricanes are powerful storms that form at sea with wind speeds of 74 miles per hour or greater. They are tracked by satellites from the moment they begin to form, so warnings can be issued 3 to 4 days before a storm strikes. A hurricane covers a circular area between 200 and 480 miles in diameter. In the storm, strong winds and rain surround a central, calm "eye," which is about 15 miles across. Winds in a hurricane can sometimes reach 200 miles per hour. However, the greatest damage to life and property is not from the wind but from tidal surges and flash flooding. Hurricanes are rated on a 1 to 5 scale, known as the Saffir-Simpson Hurricane Wind Scale. Category 3, 4, and 5 hurricanes are considered major storms. See Table 2 for the Saffir-Simpson Hurricane Wind Scale.

Owing to its violent nature, its potentially prolonged duration, and the extensive area that could be affected, the hurricane is the most devastating of all storms. The hurricane season lasts from June 1 through November 30, but most occur in August and September. Scientists have developed a relatively good understanding of the nature of hurricanes through observation, radar, weather satellites, and computer models.

A distinctive characteristic of hurricanes is the increase in sea level, often referred to as the storm surge. This increase in sea level is the result of the low-pressure central area of the storm creating a vacuum, the storm winds piling up water, and the tremendous speed of the storm. Rare storm surges have risen as much as 14 meters (almost 46 feet) above normal sea level. This phenomenon can be experienced as a large mass of seawater pushed along by the storm with great force. When it reaches land, the impact of the storm surge can be exacerbated by high tide, a low-lying coastal area with a gently sloping seabed, or a semi-enclosed bay facing the ocean.

The severity of a storm's impact on humans is exacerbated by deforestation, which often occurs as the result of population pressure. When trees disappear along the coastlines, the winds and the storm surges can enter the land with greater force. Deforestation on the slopes of hills and mountains increases the risk of violent flash

Table 2. Saffir-Simpson Hurricane Wind Scale

Category	Damage	Winds	Storm Surge
1	Minimal	74-95 mph	4-5 feet
2	Moderate	96-110 mph	6-8 feet
3	Extensive	111-130 mph	9-12 feet
4	Extreme	131-155 mph	13-18 feet
5	Catastrophic	156 mph	18 feet +

floods and landslides caused by the heavy rain associated with tropical cyclones. At the same time, the beneficial effects of the rainfall—replenishment of the water resources—may be negated because of the inability of a forest ecosystem to absorb and retain water.

Risk of Morbidity and Mortality

Deaths and injuries from hurricanes occur because victims fail to evacuate or take shelter, do not take precautions in securing their property despite adequate warning, and do not follow guidelines on food and water safety or injury prevention during recovery. Morbidity during the storm itself results from drowning, electrocution, lacerations or punctures from flying debris, and blunt trauma from falling trees or other objects. Heart attacks and stress-related disorders can arise during the storm or its aftermath. Gastrointestinal, respiratory, vector-borne, and skin disease as well as accidental pediatric poisoning can all occur during the period immediately following the cyclone. Injuries from improper use of chain saws or other power equipment, disrupted wildlife (e.g., bites from animals, snakes, or insects), and fires are common. Fortunately, the ability to detect and track storms has helped reduce morbidity and mortality in many countries.

Injury Prevention

Public health professionals work with local emergency management agencies to prepare people to evacuate and to turn off their utilities. To avoid injury, residents should be advised to use common sense and wear proper clothing, including long-sleeved shirts, pants, and safety shoes or boots. Furthermore, they should learn proper safety precautions and operating instructions before operating gas-powered or electric chain saws. People should use extreme caution when using electric chain saws to avoid electrical shock and should always wear gloves and a safety face shield or eyeglasses when using any chain saw. Evacuees should be advised against wading in water as there may be downed power lines, broken glass, metal fragments, or other debris beneath the surface.

When returning to their dwellings after a disaster, residents should check for structural damage and electrical or natural gas or propane tank hazards. They should return to homes during the daytime and only use battery-powered flashlights and lanterns to provide light rather than candles, gas lanterns, or torches.

During the recovery period, public health and local emergency management officials must ensure an adequate supply of safe water and food for the displaced population. In addition to offering acute emergency care, community plans should provide for the continuity of care for homeless residents with chronic medical conditions.

Public Health Interventions

- Conduct needs assessment for affected communities, including a review of public health infrastructure

- Establish active and passive surveillance systems for deaths, illness, and injuries
- Educate the public about maintaining safe and adequate supplies of food and water
- Establish environmental controls
- Monitor infectious disease and make determinations about needed immunizations (e.g., tetanus)
- Institute multifaceted injury control programs
- Establish protective measures against potential disease vectors
- Monitor potential release of hazardous materials
- Assure evacuation plans for people with functional needs in nursing homes, hospitals, and home care
- Work with local communities to improve building codes (e.g., developing improved designs for wind safety)

Drought

Drought affects more people than any other environmental hazard, yet it is perhaps the most complex and least understood type of all environmental hazards. Drought is often seen as the result of too little rain and used synonymously with famine. However, fluctuation in rainfall alone does not cause a famine. Drought often triggers a crisis in the arid and semiarid areas, since rain is sparse and irregular, but alone does not cause desertification. The ecosystem changes leading to desertification are all attributed to human activities, such as over-cultivation, deforestation, overgrazing, and unskilled irrigation. Each of these activities is exacerbated by increasing human populations. The first three activities strip the soil of vegetation and deplete its organic and nutrient content. This leaves the soil exposed to the eroding forces of the sun and the wind. The subsoil that is left can become so hard that it no longer absorbs rain, and the water flows over the surface, carrying away the little topsoil that might have remained.

Risk of Morbidity and Mortality

Displaced populations suffer high rates of disease caused by the stress of migration, crowding, and unsanitary conditions of relocation sites. Morbidity and mortality can result from diarrheal disease, respiratory disease, and malnutrition. Malnutrition retards normal growth and is a risk factor for illness and death. Low weight-to-height is identified through the percentage of children two or more standard deviations (z-score) from the reference median compared with mean z-scores; children with edema are severely malnourished. Mortality exceeding a baseline rate of 1 death per 10,000 people per day is the index of concern.

Public Health Interventions

- Monitor health and nutritional status by assessing weights and heights
- Assess and ensure food security, including availability, accessibility, and consumption patterns
- Monitor death rate
- Ensure safe water, sanitation, and disease control

Earthquake

Earthquakes are sudden slippages or movements in a portion of the earth's crust accompanied by a series of vibrations. Aftershocks of similar or lesser intensity can follow the main quake. Earthquakes can occur at any time of the year. An earthquake is generally considered to be the most destructive and frightening of all forces of nature. Earthquake losses, like those of other disasters, tend to cause more financial impacts in industrialized countries and more injuries and deaths in undeveloped countries. In fact, more than 200,000 people died in the earthquake that struck Haiti in 2010, but less than 30,000 were dead or missing following the massive 9.0 magnitude earthquake and subsequent tsunami that devastated northern Japan in early 2011.

The Richter magnitude, used as an indication of the force of an earthquake, measures the magnitude and intensity or energy released by the quake. This value is calculated based on data recordings from a single observation point for events anywhere on earth, but it does not address the possible damaging effects of the earthquake. According to global observations, an average of two earthquakes of a Richter magnitude 8 or slightly more occur every year. A one-digit drop in magnitude equates with a tenfold increase in frequency. Therefore, earthquakes of magnitude 7 or more generally occur 20 times in a year, and those with a magnitude 6 or more occur approximately 200 times.

Earthquakes can result in a secondary disaster, catastrophic tsunami. Tsunami, a series of waves of very great length and period, are usually generated by large earthquakes under or near the oceans, close to the edges of the tectonic plates. These waves may travel long distances, increase in height abruptly when they reach shallow water, and cause great devastation far away from the source. Submarine landslides and volcanic eruptions beneath the sea or on small islands can also be responsible for tsunami, but their effects are usually limited to smaller areas. Volcanic tsunami are usually of greater magnitude than are seismic ones; waves of more than 40 meters (131.2 feet) in height have been witnessed.

Geologists have identified regions where earthquakes are likely to occur. With the increasing population worldwide and urban migration trends, higher death tolls and greater property losses are more likely in many areas prone to earthquakes. At least 70 million people face significant risk of death or injury from earthquakes because they live in the 39 states that are seismically active. In addition to the significant risks in California, the Pacific Northwest, Utah, and Idaho, six Midwestern cities with populations greater than 100,000 are located within the seismic area of the New Madrid fault. Major South American cities in which large numbers are forced to live on earthquake-prone land in structures unable to withstand damage include Lima, Peru; Santiago, Chile; Quito, Ecuador; and Caracas, Venezuela.

Risk of Morbidity and Mortality

Deaths and injuries from earthquakes vary according to the type of housing available, time of day of occurrence, and population density. Common injuries include cuts, broken bones, crush injuries, and dehydration from being trapped in rubble. Stress reactions are also common. Morbidity and mortality can occur during the actual quake, the delayed collapse of unsound structures, or cleanup activity.

Injury Prevention

Public health officials can intervene both in advance of and after earthquakes to prevent post-earthquake injuries. The safety of homes and the work environment can be improved by building standards that require stricter codes and use of safer materials. Measures to prevent injuries include securing appliances, securing hanging items on walls or overhead, turning off utilities, storing hazardous materials in safe, well-ventilated areas, and checking homes for hazards such as windows and glass that might shatter.

Public health workers should follow the recommendations listed previously for cyclone.

Public Health Interventions

- Encourage earthquake drills to practice emergency procedures
- Recommend items for inclusion in an extensive first aid kit and a survival kit for home and automobile
- Teach basic precautions regarding safe water and safe food
- Ensure the provision of emergency medical care to those who seek acute care in the first 3 to 5 days after an earthquake
- Ensure continuity of care for those who have lost access to prescriptions, home care, and other medical necessities
- Conduct surveillance for communicable disease and injuries, including location and severity of injury, disposition of patient, and follow-up contact information
- Prepare media advisories with appropriate warnings and advice for injury prevention
- Establish environmental controls
- Facilitate use of surveillance forms by search and rescue teams to record type of building, address of site, type of collapse, amount of dust, fire or toxic hazards, location of victims, and nature and severity of injuries

Flood

Global statistics show that floods are the most frequently recorded destructive events, accounting for about 30% of the world's disasters each year. The frequency of floods is increasing faster than any other type of disaster. Much of this rise in incidence can be attributed to uncontrolled urbanization, deforestation, and the effects of the El Niño and La Niña climate patterns. Floods may also accompany other natural disasters, such as sea surges during hurricanes and tsunami following earthquakes.

Except for flash floods, flooding causes few deaths. Instead, widespread and long-lasting detrimental effects include mass homelessness, disruption of communications and health care systems, and heavy loss of business, livestock, crops, and grain, particularly in densely populated, low-lying areas. The frequent repetition of flooding means a constant, or even increasing, drain on the economy for rural populations.

Risk of Morbidity and Mortality

Flood-related mortality varies from country to country. Flash flooding, such as from excessive rainfall or sudden release of water from a dam, is the cause of most flood-related deaths. Most flood victims become trapped in their cars and drown when attempting to drive through rising or swiftly moving water. Other deaths have been caused by wading, bicycling, or other recreational activities in flooded areas.

The stress and exertion required for cleanup following a flood also cause significant morbidity (mental and physical) and mortality (e.g., myocardial infarction). Fires, explosions from gas leaks, downed live wires, and debris can all cause significant injury. Waterborne diseases (e.g., enterotoxigenic *Escherichia coli*, *Shigella*, hepatitis A, leptospirosis, giardiasis) become a significant hazard, as do other vector-borne disease and skin disorders. Injured and frightened animals, hazardous waste contamination, disruption of sewer and solid waste collection systems, molds and mildew, and dislodging of graves pose additional risks in the period following a flood. Flooding and sea surges may result in food shortages caused by water-damaged stocks.

Injury Prevention

Educating the public about the dangers of floods and about avoiding risky behaviors may prevent deaths. Since most flood-related deaths are caused by drowning in motor vehicles, educational campaigns can discuss how cars do not provide protection from moving water and that as little as 2 feet of water is capable of carrying vehicles away.

Even more important to injury and disease prevention is education regarding cleanup procedures and precautions. Rubber boots and waterproof gloves should be worn during cleanup. Walls, hard-surfaced floors, and many other household surfaces should be cleaned with soap and water and disinfected with a solution of 1 cup of bleach to 5 gallons of water. Surfaces on which food may be stored or prepared and areas in which small children play must be thoroughly disinfected. Children's toys must be disinfected prior to use or discarded. All linens and clothing must be washed in hot water or dry-cleaned. Items that cannot be washed or dry-cleaned, such as mattresses and upholstered furniture, should be air-dried in the sun and then sprayed thoroughly with a disinfectant. All carpeting must be steam-cleaned. Household materials that cannot be disinfected should be discarded.

Residents must understand that floodwater may contain fecal material from overflowing sewage systems as well as agricultural and industrial by-products. Although skin contact with floodwater does not by itself pose a serious health risk, there is some risk of disease from eating or drinking anything contaminated with floodwater. Anyone with open cuts or sores who could be exposed to floodwater must keep these areas as clean as possible by washing with soap to control infection. Wounds that develop redness, swelling, or drainage require immediate medical attention.

Routine sanitary procedures are essential for disease prevention. Hands must be washed with soap and water that has been boiled or disinfected before preparing or eating food, after toilet use, after participating in flood cleanup activities, and after handling articles contaminated with floodwater or sewage. Children's hands should be washed frequently, and children should not be allowed to play in previously flooded areas.

Public Health Interventions

- Conduct needs assessment to determine the status of public health infrastructure, utilities (water, sewage, electricity), and health, medical, and pharmaceutical needs
- Conduct surveillance of drinking water sources, injuries, increases in vector populations, and endemic, waterborne, and vector–borne disease
- Organize delivery of health care services and supplies and continuity of care
- Educate public regarding proper sanitation and hygiene
- Educate public regarding proper cleanup

Heat Wave

Over time, populations can acclimatize to hot weather. However, mortality and morbidity rise when daytime temperatures remain unusually high for several days in a row and nighttime temperatures do not drop significantly. Because populations acclimatize to summer temperatures, heat waves in June and July in the United States and Europe have more of an impact than do those in August and September. There is often a delay between the onset of a heat wave and adverse health effects. Deaths occur more commonly during heat waves where there is little cooling at night and taper off to baseline levels if a heat wave is sustained. Table 3 lists common terms associated with heat-related conditions.

Risk of Morbidity and Mortality

Heat waves result in adverse health effects in cities more than in rural areas. Those at greatest risk of adverse health outcomes include older adults, infants, those with a history of prior heatstroke, and those who are obese. Drugs that may predispose users to heatstroke include neuroleptics and anticholinergics. Heat-related morbidity and mortality come from heat cramps, heatstroke, heat exhaustion, heat syncope, myocardial infarction, loss of consciousness, dizziness, cramps, and stroke.

Injury Prevention

Residents at greatest risk must be moved to air-conditioned buildings for at least a few hours each day. All residents must maintain adequate hydration and reduce outdoor activity levels. Education campaigns should concentrate on protecting older adults and helping parents of children younger than 5 years of age understand how to protect their children from heat and prevent heat disorders.

Table 3. Heat Wave Terms

Heat Wave: A prolonged period of humidity. The NWS steps up its procedures to alert the public during heat and humidity.

Heat Index: A number in degrees Fahrenheit that tells how hot it really feels when relative humidity is added to the actual air temperature. Exposure to full sunshine can increase the heat index.

Heat Cramps: Heat cramps are muscular pains and spasms caused by heavy exertion, usually involving the abdominal muscles or legs. It is generally thought that the loss of water from heavy sweating causes the cramps.

Heat Exhaustion: Heat exhaustion typically occurs when people exercise heavily or work in a warm place where body fluids are lost through heavy sweating. Blood flow to the skin increases, causing blood flow to decrease to vital organs. This results in a form of mild shock. If not treated, the victim's condition will worsen. Body temperature will keep rising and the victim may suffer heatstroke.

Heatstroke: Heatstroke is life-threatening. The victim's temperature control system, which produces sweating to cool the body, stops working. The body temperature can rise so high that brain damage and death may result if the body is not cooled quickly.

Sunstroke: Another term for heatstroke.

Public Health Interventions

- Develop an early warning surveillance system that triggers the mobilization of prevention and intervention activities
- Identify the location of residents who might be at risk as a result of age, preexisting conditions, lack of air-conditioning, and other environmental or health factors
- Work with utilities to educate the public about preventive actions when energy blackouts might be anticipated

Thunderstorm

A thunderstorm is formed from a combination of moisture, rapidly rising warm air, and a force capable of lifting air such as a warm and cold front, a sea breeze, or a mountain. All thunderstorms contain lightning. Thunderstorms may occur singly, in clusters, or in lines. Thus, it is possible for several thunderstorms to affect one location in the course of a few hours. Some of the most severe weather occurs when a single thunderstorm affects one location for an extended time. Thunderstorms can bring heavy rains (which can cause flash flooding), strong winds, hail, lightning, and tornadoes. Severe thunderstorms can cause extensive damage to homes and property.

Lightning is a major threat during a thunderstorm. Lightning is an electrical discharge that results from the buildup of positive and negative charges within a thunderstorm. When the buildup becomes strong enough, lightning appears as a "bolt." This flash of light usually occurs within the clouds or between the clouds and the ground. A bolt of lightning reaches a temperature approaching 50,000°F in a split second. The rapid heating and cooling of air near the lightning causes thunder.

Risk of Morbidity and Mortality

In the United States, between 75 and 100 persons are hit and killed each year by lightning. Morbidity is reduced if, when caught outdoors, individuals avoid items which act as natural lightning rods, such as tall isolated trees in an open area or the top of a hill, and metal objects such as wire fences, golf clubs, and metal tools. It is a myth that lightning never strikes twice in the same place. In fact, lightning may strike several times in the same place during the course of one discharge.

Although thunderstorms and lightning can be found throughout the United States, they are most likely to occur in the central and southern states. The state with the highest number of thunderstorm days is Florida. Table 4 identifies the terms used to alert the public about weather conditions and defines each condition.

Tornado

Tornadoes are rapidly whirling, funnel-shaped air spirals that emerge from a violent thunderstorm and reach the ground. Tornadoes can have a wind velocity of up to 200 miles per hour and generate sufficient force to destroy even massive buildings. The average circumference of a tornado is a few hundred meters, and it is usually exhausted before it has traveled as far as 20 kilometers (12.4 miles). Severity is rated on the Fujita Scale according to wind speed. The Fujita Scale uses a scoring system of F0 (no damage) to F5 (total destruction). The extent of damage depends on updrafts within the tornado funnel, the tornado's atmospheric pressure (which is often lower than the surrounding barometric pressure), and the effects of flying debris.

Risk of Morbidity and Mortality

Approximately 1000 tornadoes occur annually in the United States, and none of the lower 48 states is immune. Certain geographic areas are at greater risk as a result of their recurrent weather patterns; tornadoes most frequently occur in the midwestern and southeastern states. Although tornadoes often develop in the late afternoon and more often from March through May, they can arise at any hour of the day and during any month of the year.

Injuries from tornadoes occur because of flying debris or people being thrown by the high winds (i.e., head injuries, soft tissue injury, secondary wound infection). Stress-related disorders are more common, as is disease related to loss of utilities, potable water, or shelter.

Injury Prevention

Because tornadoes can occur so quickly, communities should develop redundant warning systems (such as media alerts and automated telephone warnings), establish

Table 4. Severe Weather Watches and Warnings: Definitions

Flood Watch: High flow or overflow of water from a river is possible in the given time period. It can also apply to heavy runoff or drainage of water into low-lying areas. These watches are generally issued for flooding that is expected to occur at least 6 hours after heavy rains have ended.

Flood Warning: Flooding conditions are actually occurring or are imminent in the warning area.

Flash Flood Watch: Flash flooding is possible in or close to the watch area. Flash flood watches are generally issued for flooding that is expected to occur within 6 hours after heavy rains have ended.

Flash Flood Warning: Flash flooding is actually occurring or imminent in the warning area. It can be issued as a result of torrential rains, a dam failure, or ice jam.

Tornado Watch: Conditions are conducive to the development of tornadoes in and close to the watch area.

Tornado Warning: A tornado has actually been sighted by spotters or indicated on radar and is occurring or imminent in the warning area.

Severe Thunderstorm Watch: Conditions are conducive to the development of severe thunderstorms in and close to the watch area.

Severe Thunderstorm Warning: A severe thunderstorm has actually been observed by spotters or indicated on radar, and is occurring or imminent in the warning area.

Tropical Storm Watch: Tropical storm conditions with sustained winds from 39 to 73 miles per hour are possible in the watch area within the next 36 hours.

Tropical Storm Warning: Tropical storm conditions are expected in the warning area within the next 24 hours.

Hurricane Watch: Hurricane conditions (sustained winds greater than 73 miles per hour) are possible in the watch area within 36 hours.

Hurricane Warning: Hurricane conditions are expected in the warning area in 24 hours or less.

---

protective shelter to reduce tornado-related injuries, and practice tornado-shelter drills. In the event of a tornado, the residents should take shelter in a basement if possible, away from windows, while protecting their heads. Special outreach should be made to people with functional needs who can make a list of their limitations, capabilities, and medications and have ready an emergency box of needed supplies. People with functional needs should have a "buddy" who has a copy of the list and who knows of the emergency box.

Other precautions include those listed under Cyclone.

Public Health Interventions

- Work with emergency management on tornado shelter drills for vulnerable communities
- Conduct needs assessment using maps that detail preexisting neighborhoods, including landmarks, and aerial reconnaissance
- Ensure the provision of medical care, shelter, food, and water
- Establish environmental controls
- Establish a surveillance system based at both clinical sites and shelters

Volcanic Eruption

Volcanic activity involves the explosive eruption or flow of rock fragments and molten rock in various combinations of hot or cold, wet or dry, and fast or slow. Extremely high temperature and pressure cause the mantle, located deep inside the earth between the molten iron core and the thin crust at the surface, to melt and become liquid rock or magma. When a large amount of magma is formed, it rises through the denser rock layers toward the earth's surface. Magma that has reached the surface is called lava. Volcanic hazards vary in severity depending on the size and extent of the eruption and whether the eruption is occurring in a populated area. Volcanoes are classified by similar characteristic behavior, and have been called "Strombolian," "Vulcanian," "Vesuvian," "Pelean," "Hawaiian," and others. When active, volcanoes may exhibit only one characteristic type of eruption or a sequence of types.

A volcano may begin to show signs of unrest several months to a few years before an eruption. Accurate long-term predictions, specifying when and where an eruption is most likely to occur and what type and size eruption should be expected are not possible. Warnings that an eruption is hours to days away are possible because eruptions are preceded by such changes in a volcano's earthquake activity, ground deformation, and gas emissions over a period of days to weeks.

In the United States, volcano warnings are made through a series of alert levels that correspond generally to increasing levels of volcanic activity. Each increase in the alert level helps authorities gauge and coordinate their response to a developing volcano emergency.

Depending on the location of the volcano (California, Alaska, Pacific Northwest, or Hawaii), different alert levels[2] are used to provide volcano warnings and emergency information regarding volcanic unrest and eruptions. Different alert levels are used because volcanoes exhibit different patterns of unrest in the weeks to hours before they erupt, volcano hazards differ requiring a warning scheme that addresses specific volcano hazards, and there is variability in the intensity of monitoring U.S. volcanoes. The Volcanic Explosivity Index or VEI is the eruption magnitude scale used to rate the eruption. The VEI considers the plume height, volume of magma, classification, and how often the volcano in question erupts. The VEI ranges from VEI 0 to VEI 8. Any eruption that occurs anywhere will rate at least

[2]Also referred to as status levels, condition levels, or color code.

a VEI 0 on the scale, which is defined as having less than 10,000 cubic meters of ejecta, the combination of lava and ash. VEI 3 volcanoes have as much as 100 million cubic meters of ejecta. A VEI 8 volcano must spew out a minimum of one trillion cubic meters of ejecta.

Risk of Morbidity and Mortality

Many kinds of volcanic activity can endanger the lives of people and property located both close to and far away from a volcano. The range of adverse health effects is quite broad and extensive. Immediate, acute, and nonspecific irritant effects have been reported in the eyes, including corneal abrasions, nose, skin, and upper airways of persons exposed to volcanic dusts and ash particles. Victims can experience exacerbation of their asthma symptoms and can asphyxiate as a result of inhalation of ash or gases. There is the potential of injuries from blasts and projectile of rock fragments. Lacerations can occur if sound waves shatter windows and break glass. Volcanic flow can set homes on fire causing thermal injuries including death. Victims can experience trauma from fallen trees or rocks or the collapse of buildings under weight of the ash. Foraging animals may be unable to find adequate supply of food or water. Indoor air radon levels may be elevated. Flooding and pooling of water secondary to debris or obstruction of waterways can lead to spread of infectious disease. Finally, victims can experience anxiety, depression, or post-traumatic stress disorder.

Public Health Interventions

- Collaborate with emergency management specialists to develop effective warning schemes
- Participate in volcano emergency planning workshops and emergency response exercises
- Prepare educational materials, including fact sheets, booklets, video programs, and maps
- Designate areas for evacuation and evacuate when indicated
- Provide emergency air monitoring equipment for detecting toxic gases
- Stockpile and distribute masks and eye shields or goggles where indicated
- Prepare for breakdown of water systems
- Encourage protection by remaining inside sturdy houses with shuttered windows when evacuation is not indicated or possible
- Strengthen roofs of building with supports or take shelter in most resistant part of building
- Stay indoors during worst conditions

Wildfires

More and more people are building their homes in woodland settings in or near forests, rural areas, or remote mountain sites. As residential areas expand into relatively untouched wildlands, these communities are increasingly threatened by forest fires. Protecting structures in the wildlands from fire poses special problems, and can stretch firefighting resources to the limit. Wildfires often begin unnoticed and can spread quickly, igniting brush, trees, and homes.

There are three different classes of wildfires. A *surface fire* is the most common type and burns along the floor of a forest, moving slowly and killing or damaging trees. A *ground fire* is usually started by lightning and burns on or below the forest floor in the human layer down to the mineral soil. *Crown fires* spread rapidly by wind and move quickly by jumping along the tops of trees. Depending on prevailing winds and the amount of water in the environment, wildfires can quickly spread out of control, causing extensive damage to personal property and human life. If heavy rains follow a fire, other natural disasters can occur, including landslides, mudflows, and floods. Once ground cover has been burned away, little is left to hold soil in place on steep slopes and hillsides, and erosion becomes one of several potential problems. A major wildland fire can leave a large amount of scorched and barren land, and these areas often do not return to prefire conditions for decades. Danger zones include all wooded, brush, and grassy areas—especially those in Kansas, Mississippi, Louisiana, Georgia, Florida, the Carolinas, Tennessee, California, Massachusetts, and the national forests of the western United States.

Risk of Morbidity and Mortality

Morbidity and mortality associated with wildfires include burns, inhalation injuries, respiratory complications, and stress-related cardiovascular events (exhaustion and myocardial infarction from fighting or fleeing the fire).

Public Health Interventions

More than four out of every five wildfires are started by people. Negligent human behavior, such as smoking in forested areas or improperly extinguishing campfires, is the cause of many forest fires. Another cause of forest fires is lightning. Prevention efforts include working with the fire service to educate people to

- Build fires away from nearby trees or bushes. Ash and cinders lighter than air float and may be blown into areas with heavy fuel load, starting wildfires
- Be prepared to extinguish fires quickly and completely. If a fire becomes threatening, someone will need to extinguish it immediately
- Never leave a fire—even a cigarette—burning unattended. Fire can quickly spread out of control
- Encourage the development of a family wildfire evacuation plan if the area in your community is at risk for wildfire

Summary of Effects

Table 5 summarizes the types of short-term effects that occur following major natural disasters, and Table 6 identifies common environmental impacts caused by natural disasters.

Table 5. Short-Term Effects of Major Natural Disasters

Effect	Earthquakes	High Winds (Without Flooding)	Tidal Waves/Flash Floods	Slow-Onset Floods	Landslides	Volcanoes
Deaths*	Many	Few	Many	Few	Many	Many
Severe injuries requiring extensive treatment	Many	Moderate	Few	Few	Few	Few
Increased risk of communicable diseases	Potential risk following all major disasters (probability rising with overcrowding and deteriorating sanitation)					
Damage to health facilities	Severe (structure and equipment)	Severe	Severe but localized	Severe (equipment only)	Severe but localized	Severe (structure and equipment)
Damage to water systems	Severe	Light	Severe	Light	Severe but localized	Severe
Food shortage	Rare (may occur due to economic and logistic factors)		Common	Common	Rare	Rare
Major population movements	Rare (may occur in heavily damaged urban areas)		Common (generally limited)			

*Potential lethal impact in absence of preventive measures.

Reprinted with permission from Pan American Health Organization (PAHO). 2000. *Natural Disasters: Protecting the Public's Health.* Table 1.1. Washington, DC: PAHO.

Table 6. Most Common Effects of Specific Events on Environmental Health

	Earthquake	Hurricane	Flood	Tsunami	Volcanic Eruption
Water Supply and Wastewater Disposal					
Damage to civil engineering structures	1	1	1	3	1
Broken mains	1	2	2	1	1
Damage to water sources	1	2	2	3	1
Power outages	1	1	2	2	1
Contamination (biological or chemical)	2	1	1	1	1
Transportation failures	1	1	1	2	1
Personnel shortages	1	2	2	3	1
System overload (due to population shifts)	3	1	1	3	1
Equipment, parts, and supply shortage	1	1	1	2	1
Solid Waste Handling					
Damage to civil engineering structures	1	2	2	3	1
Transportation failures	1	1	1	2	1
Equipment shortages	1	1	1	2	1
Personnel shortages	1	1	1	3	1
Water, soil, and air pollution	1	1	1	2	1
Food Handling					
Spoilage of refrigerated food	1	1	2	2	1
Damage to food preparation facilities	1	1	2	3	1

(continued on next page)

Table 6. (*continued*)

	Earthquake	Hurricane	Flood	Tsunami	Volcanic Eruption
Transportation failures	1	1	1	2	1
Power outages	1	1	1	3	1
Flooding of facilities	3	1	1	1	3
Contamination/degradation of relief supplies	2	1	1	2	1
Vector Control					
Proliferation of vector breeding sites	1	1	1	1	3
Increase in human/vector contacts	1	1	1	2	1
Disruption in vector-borne disease control programs	1	1	1	1	1
Home Sanitation					
Destruction or damage to structures	1	1	1	1	1
Contamination of water and food	2	2	1	2	1
Disruption of power, heating, fuel, water, or supply waste disposal services	1	1	1	2	1
Overcrowding	3	3	3	3	2

1 = severe possible effect; 2 = less severe possible effect; 3 = least or no possible effect.

Reprinted with permission from Pan-American Health Organization (PAHO). 2000. *Natural Disasters: Protecting the Public's Health*. Table 8.1. Washington, DC: PAHO.

Man-Made and Technological Disasters

Man-made and technological disasters are unpredictable, can spread across geographic boundaries, may be unpreventable, and may have limited physical damage but long-term effects. Some disasters in this class are entirely man-made, such as terrorism. Other technological disasters occur because industrial sites are located in communities affected by natural disasters, equipment failures occur, or workers have inadequate training or fatigue and make errors. The threat of terrorism is categorized as a potential technological disaster and includes bombings, civil and political disorders, economic emergencies, and riots.

Technological disasters include a broad range of incidents. Some are accidental and unintentional such as airplane crashes, hazardous materials spills, nuclear accidents, oil spills, and train derailments. Others are intentional and deliberate, such as terrorist acts. Intentional disasters include biological, chemical, explosives, nuclear, and radiological attacks. Routes of exposure are through water, food and drink, airborne releases, fires and explosions, and hazardous materials or waste released into the environment from a fixed facility or during transport. Building or bridge collapse, transportation crashes, dam or levee failure, nuclear reactor accidents, and breaks in water, gas, or sewer lines are other examples of unintentional technological disasters.

Risk of Morbidity and Mortality

Communities in which industrial sites are located or through which hazardous materials pass via highway, rail, or pipeline are at risk for technological disasters. Injuries can occur to workers at the site, responders bringing the incident under control and providing emergency medical care, and residents in the community. Those with preexisting medical conditions, such as lung or heart disease, could be at increased risk for negative health outcomes if exposed to toxic releases. Burns, skin disorders, and lung damage can result from exposure to specific agents. Table 7 lists the health consequences of several classes of toxins.

Injury Prevention

Ensuring that local industry implements basic safety procedures can significantly reduce negative health outcomes from accidental releases of toxins. Emergency preparedness—including the ability of prehospital and hospital systems to care for patients exposed to industrial agents, the training of medical personnel to work in

Table 7. Health Consequences of Exposure to Chemical Agents

Chemical Agent	Health Effects
Nerve agents	Miosis, rhinorrhea, dyspnea
Vesicants	Erythema, blisters, eye irritation, cough, dyspnea
Cyanide	Loss of consciousness, seizures, apnea
Pulmonary CG (phosgene)	Dyspnea, coughing

contaminated environments, and the stockpiling of personal protective equipment for responders—is key to providing care following industrial accidents or acts of bioterrorism. Government agencies, in coordination with hospitals and public health, should conduct computer simulations or field exercises to test the community's ability to evacuate those at risk and the ability of the health sector to provide care to those exposed to accidental releases. Information about the clinical management of exposure to toxins can be provided by poison control centers, the Chemical Transportation Emergency Center (CHEMTREC), and industry databases.

Public Health Interventions

- Take a visible role in community planning
- Conduct hazard assessments
- Review material safety data sheets for agents produced, stored, or used locally and regionally to evaluate range of potential adverse health effects
- Conduct vulnerability analyses to identify target populations and potential adverse public health consequences
- Conduct risk assessment to determine if specific agents will reach toxic levels in the vicinity of vulnerable populations
- Determine minimal thresholds of exposure for specific agents that would trigger evacuation
- Gather information on chemical neutralization, estimation models of plume dispersion, and appropriate antidotes
- Work with local hospitals to stockpile appropriate antidotes, medications, and supplies
- Stockpile two pills per person of potassium iodide in communities located within 10 miles of nuclear reactor sites
- Provide emergency services and medical care to victims
- Activate the health alert network

Blasts and Explosions

Explosions can inflict multisystem life-threatening injuries on many persons simultaneously. Multiple factors contribute to the injury patterns which result from blasts. Contributing factors include the composition and amount of the materials involved, the environment in which the event occurs, the method of delivery, such as a bomb, the distance between the victim and the blast, and the absence or presence of protective barriers or environmental hazards in the area of the blast. To predict subsequent demand for medical care and resources needed, it is useful to remember that post-blast, half of the initial casualties will seek medical care during the first hour. Those with minor injuries often arrive before the most severely injured, because they go directly to the closest hospitals using whatever transportation is available. Furthermore, when the explosion has resulted in a structural collapse, victims will be more severely injured and their rescue can occur over prolonged time periods.

The two types of explosives, high-order explosives (HEs) and low-order explosives (LEs), cause different injury patterns. Injury patterns also differ whether the bombs are manufactured or improvised. HE devices, such as TNT, C–4, Semtex, nitroglycerin, dynamite, and ammonium nitrate fuel oil, produce a defining supersonic overpressurization shock wave. LE devices, such as pipe bombs, gunpowder, and pure petroleum-based bombs (aka Molotov cocktails), create a subsonic explosion and lack the overpressurization wave. Manufactured explosives are usually those used by the military, mass produced, and quality tested as weapons. Improvised explosives and incendiary (fire) bombs are often individually produced in small quantities and include devices used differently from their initial purpose.

Risk of Morbidity and Mortality

The most common injury for survivors of explosions is penetrating and blunt trauma. Blast lung is the most common fatal injury among initial survivors. Explosions in confined spaces (mines, buildings, or large vehicles) and structural collapse are associated with the greatest morbidity and mortality. Blast injuries can occur to any body system: auditory, digestive, circulatory, central nervous system, extremities, renal, and respiratory. Up to 10% of all blast survivors have significant eye injuries. These injuries can occur with minimal discomfort initially and patients can come for care days, weeks, or even months after the event. Symptoms can include eye pain or irritation, foreign body sensation, altered vision, periorbital swelling, or contusions. Clinical findings in the gastrointestinal tract may be absent until the onset of complications. Victims can also experience tinnitus or temporary or permanent deafness from blasts.

Table 8 describes the four basic mechanisms of blast injury and Table 9 provides an overview of explosive-related injuries.

Public Health Interventions

- As part of a community preparedness plan, identify the medical institutions and personnel who can provide the emergency care that will be required, including otologic assessment and audiometry, burn and trauma centers, hyperbaric oxygen chamber, and so forth
- Ensure that the community preparedness plan includes structure for surge capacity. To estimate the "first wave" of casualties, double the number appearing for care in the first hour. Prepare written communications and instructions for victims who may experience temporary or permanent deafness
- Work with the regional emergency management organization, police, fire, and Emergency Medical Services to have a plan in place to identify potential toxic exposures and environmental hazards for which the health department will need to help protect responders in the field and the community
- With the hospital community, establish a victim identification registry
- With the mental health community, plan for the reception and intervention with family and friends

Table 8. Mechanisms of Blast Injury

Category	Characteristics	Body Part Affected	Types of Injuries
Primary	Unique to HE, results from the impact of the overpressurization wave with body surfaces	Gas-filled structures are most susceptible—lungs, gastrointestinal tract, and middle ear	Blast lung (pulmonary barotrauma) Tympanic membrane rupture and middle ear damage Abdominal hemorrhage and perforation Globe (eye) rupture Concussion (traumatic brain injury without physical signs of head injury)
Secondary	Results from flying debris and bomb fragments	Any body part may be affected	Penetrating ballistic (fragmentation) or blunt injuries Eye penetration (can be occult)
Tertiary	Results from individuals being thrown by the blast wind	Any body part may be affected	Fracture and traumatic amputation Closed and open brain injury
Quaternary	All explosion-related injuries, illnesses, or diseases not due to primary, secondary, or tertiary mechanisms Includes exacerbation or complications of existing conditions	Any body part may be affected	Burns (flash, partial, and full thickness) Crush injuries Closed and open brain injury Asthma, chronic obstructive pulmonary disease, or other breathing problems from dust, smoke, or toxic fumes Angina, hyperglycemia, hypertension

From Centers for Disease Control and Prevention (CDC). 2006. Explosions and blast injuries: a primer for clinicians. Table 1. Mechanisms of blast injury. Atlanta, GA: CDC. Available at: http://www.bt.cdc.gov/masscasualties/explosions.asp.

Epidemics

The spread of infectious disease depends on preexisting levels of the disease, ecological changes resulting from disaster, population displacement, changes in density of population, disruption of public utilities, interruption of basic public health services, and compromises to sanitation and hygiene. The risk that epidemics of infectious diseases will occur is proportional to the population density and

Table 9. Overview of Explosive-Related Injuries

System or Area	Injury or Condition
Auditory	Tympanic membrane rupture, ossicular disruption, cochlear damage, foreign body
Eyes, orbits, face	Perforated globe, foreign body, air embolism, fractures
Respiratory	Blast lung, hemothorax, pneumothorax, pulmonary contusion and hemorrhage, arterioventricular fistulas (source of air embolism), airway epithelial damage, aspiration pneumonitis, sepsis
Digestive	Bowel perforation, hemorrhage, ruptured liver or spleen, sepsis, mesenteric ischemia from air embolism
Circulatory	Cardiac contusion, myocardial infarction from air embolism, shock, vasovagal hypotension, peripheral vascular injury, air embolism-induced injury
Central nervous system	Concussion, closed and open brain injury, stroke, spinal cord injury, air embolism-induced injury
Renal	Renal contusion, laceration, acute renal failure due to rhabdomyolysis, hypotension, and hypovolemia
Extremities	Traumatic amputation, fractures, crush injuries, compartment syndrome, burns, cuts, lacerations, acute arterial occlusion, air embolism-induced injury

From Centers for Disease Control and Prevention (CDC). 2006. Explosions and blast injuries: a primer for clinicians. Table 2. Overview of explosive-related injuries. Atlanta, GA: CDC. Available at: http://www.bt.cdc.gov/masscasualties/explosions.asp.

displacement. A true epidemic can occur in susceptible populations in the presence or impending introduction of a disease agent compounded by the presence of a mechanism that facilitates large-scale transmission (e.g., contaminated water supply or vector population).

Quick response is essential because epidemics, which result in human and economic losses and political difficulties, often arise rapidly. An epidemic or threatened epidemic can become an emergency when the following characteristics of the events are present:

- Risk of introduction to and spread of the disease in the population
- Large number of cases may reasonably be expected to occur
- Disease involved is of such severity as to lead to serious disability or death
- Risk of social or economic disruption resulting from the presence of the disease
- Authorities are unable to cope adequately with the situation because of insufficient technical or professional personnel, organizational experience, and necessary

supplies or equipment (e.g., drugs, vaccines, laboratory diagnostic materials, vector-control materials)
- Risk of international transmission

Not all of these characteristics need be present and must be assessed with regard to relative importance locally.

The categorization of "emergency" differs from country to country, depending on two local factors: whether the disease is endemic and a means of transmitting the agent exists. Table 10 describes epidemic emergencies for particular diseases listed in nonendemic areas.

Table 10. Epidemic Emergencies Defined

Disease	Nonendemic Areas	Endemic Areas
Cholera	One confirmed indigenous case	Significant increase in incidence over and above what is normal for the season, particularly if multifocal and accompanied by deaths in children younger than 10 years old
Giardiasis	A cluster of cases in a group of tourists returning from an endemic area	A discrete increase in incidence linked to a specific endemic place
Malaria	A cluster of cases, with an increase in incidence in a defined geographic area	Rarely an emergency; increased incidence requires program strengthening
Meningococcal meningitis	An incidence rate of 1 per 1000 in 1 week in a defined geographic area	The same rate for 2 consecutive weeks is an emergency
Plague	One confirmed case apparently linked by domestic rodent or respiratory transmission or by a rodent epizootic	A cluster of cases
Rabies	One confirmed case of animal rabies in a previously rabies-free locale	Significant increases in animal and human cases
Salmonellosis	A large cluster of cases in a limited area, with a single or predominant stereotype (e.g., specific event or restaurant), or a significant number of cases occurring in multiple foci, apparently related by a common source (such as a specific food product)	

(continued on next page)

Table 10. (*continued*)

Disease	Nonendemic Areas	Endemic Areas
Smallpox	Any strongly suspected case	Not applicable
Typhus fever/rickettsia	One confirmed case in a louse-infested, nonimmune population	Significant increase in number of cases in a limited period of time
Viral encephalitis	Cluster of time- and space-related cases in a nonimmune population (a single case should be regarded as a warning)	Significant increase in the number of cases with a mosquito-borne single, identified etiological agent in a limited period
Viral hemorrhagic fever	One confirmed indigenous or imported case with an etiological single agent with which person-to-person transmission may occur in a limited period of time	Significant increase in the number of cases with an identified etiological agent
Yellow fever	One confirmed case in a community	Significant increase in the number of cases in a population and an adequate/limited period of time for vector population to increase

Public Health Interventions

- Control or prevent epidemic situations
- Conduct surveillance to identify when an epidemic is likely to occur
- Ensure that items requiring refrigeration, such as vaccines, are kept refrigerated throughout the chain of distribution
- Monitor the maintenance of immunization programs against childhood infectious disease (measles, mumps, polio)

Chapter 2

Role and Responsibility of Public Health

P ublic health professionals must take responsibility for community health in both disaster preparedness and response. This chapter outlines in detail roles, action plans, personnel requirements, applicable laws, and the functional model of public health response.

Public Health Role

- Coordinate, plan, and administer public health response
- Develop an all-hazards public health emergency response plan
- Consult with health care systems and facilities to determine the magnitude and extent of public health and medical problems and the assistance needed
- Identify community resources applicable to the physical, social, and psychosocial effects of disaster
- Identify groups most at risk from disaster (i.e., children, older adults, homeless, chronically ill, homebound, physically or mentally disabled)
- Communicate with government officials about the public health effects of potential disasters and provide expert assistance during and after disasters
- Provide disaster education both in advance of (i.e., what to expect in a disaster) and after (i.e., how to deal with effects) an event
- Take responsibility for the health of a community following a disaster:

  - Prevent disease by providing health advisories on injury prevention, food and water safety, and vector control
  - Coordinate public health interventions including dispensing of antibiotics, vaccination, and issuing social distancing requirements
  - Use such resources as assessment, epidemiology, and data analysis to make and implement recommendations for limiting morbidity and mortality following a disaster
  - Use public health laboratories to assess biological, chemical, and radiation samples and determine threats
  - Assure that health services continue postimpact, including acute care, continuity of care, primary care, and emergency care
  - Conduct and oversee necessary public health investigation including surveillance, epidemiological, and environmental investigation
  - Provide information on cleanup and contamination

- Cooperate and collaborate with the broadest range of community agencies to ensure that primary health, public health, mental health, and social impacts are adequately addressed in disaster planning
- Inspect Red Cross shelters and feeding operations
- Request, recruit, and credential volunteers through established programs
- Request volunteers from the Red Cross to supplement medical and nursing needs
- Become National Incident Management System (NIMS) compliant
- Develop and advocate public policies designed to reduce the public health impact of potential disasters
- Collaborate with other health and human service professionals to rigorously evaluate intervention outcomes

Local public health authorities have the primary responsibility for the health of a community following a disaster. These professionals bring unique resources to the emergency management community that can limit morbidity and mortality caused by both natural and technological disasters. In fact, the contributions of public health authorities to community disaster preparations and response represent an extension of their normal activities. Public health officials are knowledgeable about the prevention of infectious disease and injury, routinely conduct surveillance for infectious disease, maintain working relationships with other agencies within the health sector, have governmental jurisdiction for overseeing the public's health, can draw from the expertise of multidisciplinary members, and use triage skills that can easily be adapted for use following a disaster.

The responsibilities of public health agencies in disaster preparedness and response are more complicated than in a typical public health activity. In preparedness activities, public health professionals must participate as part of a multiagency team, some members of which have little or no knowledge of public health. Public health and other human service departments (e.g., aging, disability, behavioral health) are often organized as separate governmental units. As such, careful advance coordination of preparedness efforts is an essential part of community planning. Further, public health practitioners must work with multiple bureaucratic layers of infrastructure in a condensed time frame and interact with personnel with whom they normally do not have contact, and whose lexicon and methods may be different. Since the sectors involved in the Incident Command System have already trained together, public health must integrate itself into this established response, particularly where there is a unified command.

Public health workers can conduct assessments and epidemiological studies and can make and implement appropriate recommendations based on data analysis. Such data collection is critical before disaster occurs to ensure that potential social impacts are adequately addressed in disaster planning and that emergency, public, and mental health needs are met in the community. Maintenance of continuity of care is especially important for older adults, those with chronic disease, and those in long-term care facilities. Health advisories on injury prevention, food and water safety, and disaster-specific precautions should be developed in advance and available for immediate distribution when needed. Public health officials should regularly communicate with elected officials about the likely impact of potential disasters for which the community is at risk and help develop policies and regulations that can prevent or reduce morbidity and mortality following disaster.

Action Plan

The health sector is responsible for ensuring the continuity of health care services. Resource problems following disasters in the United States have resulted from poor planning in the use or distribution of assets rather than a deficiency of those assets. The public health system works with health sector agencies in the community to coordinate planning for the continued delivery of services both during and after the disaster. This interagency coordination includes the development of an action plan to address community health needs. Components of the plan include the following:

- Ensuring continuity of health care services (acute emergency care, continuity of care, primary care, and preventive care)
- Monitoring environmental infrastructure (water, sanitation, and vector control)
- Assessing the needs of the elderly and other special populations
- Initiating injury prevention programs and surveillance
- Ensuring that essential public health sector facilities will be able to function postimpact (ambulatory care centers, hospitals, health departments, pharmacies, physicians' offices, storage sites for health care supplies, dispatch centers, paging services, and ambulance stations)
- Allocating resources to ensure that the above responsibilities can be accomplished

Personnel

The responsibility of disaster preparedness should be assigned to someone who has the organizational authority to ensure an adequate level of preparation. Otherwise, the effort may be less than optimal, because the designated individual lacks authority to delegate tasks to the proper offices and personnel. In addition, such a decision creates the false impression that an effective program exists because someone has been assigned to disaster preparedness.

Both the lead individual and all those involved in disaster preparedness and response must have a well-grounded understanding of the public health consequences of disaster and human response to disaster on the part of both victims and responders. Public health practitioners must recognize how the health sector fits into the emergency management model of disaster preparedness and response, including components of a typical response and team-based, interdisciplinary problem-solving. Those involved in disaster response must have both the expertise and ability to access state-of-the-art resources to provide technical assistance to communities and to collect and analyze data as quickly as possible. Through such data collection, epidemiological methods can be applied to develop the best disaster response both to prevent morbidity and mortality and to mitigate medical or public health problems. Public health officials also help blend public health approaches with clinical practice. Likewise, they provide direction to the Red Cross to ensure the provision of appropriate care and resources and inspect Red Cross shelters and feeding operations.

Public Health Law and Emergencies

As part of public health disaster preparedness, health departments must review state and local laws to understand the nuances of their authority in these circumstances and to prepare a legal plan of action for times of emergency. Although universal generalities form the underpinnings of emergency authority, operational authority will vary among jurisdictions. Indeed, the Centers for Disease Control and Prevention have developed a public health law program whose mission is to articulate the connection between law and public health for public health practitioners, including during emergencies.

The authority to protect the health of the public in emergencies is not assigned in a single law, but generally requires a chain of events. For example, a Board of Health could declare an emergency, allowing the commissioner of health to modify requirements set forth in the health code. A mayor could declare an emergency, which would in turn allow the mayor's office to modify provisions of local laws and regulations or the health code. Similarly, if a governor declares an emergency, the governor can modify applicable provisions of state and local laws and regulations, including the health code. However, again, each public health department must research in advance which procedures for declaring emergencies and altering health codes apply to each jurisdiction.

Functional Model of Public Health Response

The functional model summarizes a typical disaster response within the public health field and categorizes the cycle of activities. The model identifies tasks assigned to each of the core areas of public health in the context of emergency management activities. The functional model expands traditional public health partnerships with other disciplines and agencies and emphasizes collaboration to ensure competence in disaster preparedness and response.

The functional model outlined below and on the pages following comprises six phases that correspond to the type of activities involved in preparing for and responding to a disaster: planning, prevention, assessment, response, surveillance, recovery, and evaluation. The model additionally delineates the responsibilities of the various disciplines of public health.

Planning

- Apply basic concepts of local public health to disaster management
- Conduct hospital disaster planning and coordinate with hospitals
- Help community develop plan with public health focus
- Develop health promotion and disease prevention protocols and motivate use through education campaign

- Conduct needs assessments and analyze hazards and vulnerability
- Work with other health professionals to write a disaster plan specifically for public health and health concerns
- Train workforce on public health responsibilities
- Inventory supplies, equipment, communications, and people available for response
- Develop mutual aid agreements in advance
- Conduct facility-wide/agency-wide exercises to stress organizational mobilization, coordination, and communication

Prevention

Primary prevention (before event):

- Immunization
- Control and prevent outbreaks
- Protect against risks identified in hazards, vulnerability, and needs assessments
- Conduct community education in first aid, personal hygiene, and injury prevention
- Protect and distribute safe food and water
- Protect or reestablish sanitation systems

Secondary prevention (response to event):

- Organize and deploy teams for immunization of the general public or selected populations
- Coordinate public health interventions including dispensing of antibiotics or vaccines and ordering social distancing
- Provide advice to the public regarding personal protection
- Determine need for and coordinate the delivery of medical and pharmaceutical supplies
- Detect and extricate victims
- Provide emergency medical care
- Organize services and treatment
- Conduct case identification and surveillance
- Establish infectious disease control
- Conduct short-term counseling and intervention
- Manage bystander response

Tertiary prevention (recovery from event):

- Provide long-term counseling and mental health intervention
- Manage emergency services
- Manage injuries and cleanup behavior
- Reestablish health services
- Use records from response to update action plan

Assessment

- Identify potential outbreaks
- Identify potential medical, behavioral, social, and political effects of event
- Assess potential effect of loss of infrastructure on health and mental health
- Identify potential hazards and levels of acceptable exposure
- Determine incidence of disease and causal factors
- Understand mechanics of hazardous agents (i.e., radiation, toxins, thermal and water pollution, land mines, weapons)
- Determine vulnerability, level of risk, and requirement for rapid needs assessment
- Identify appropriate data to collect for decision-making
- Summarize damage to health care infrastructure
- Establish continuous data monitoring

Response

Service:

- Staff the local/state Emergency Operations Center, Disaster Recovery Centers, and Disaster Field Offices as requested
- Determine the magnitude and extent of public health and medical problems associated with the disaster

    ○ Conduct "quick and dirty" assessments on which to base initial decisions

- Develop specific requests for assistance under Emergency Support Function (ESF) 8 (where federal assistance is being requested or has been approved), including medical personnel, equipment, and supplies
- Determine assistance needed to move patients to definitive care facilities that are part of the National Disaster Medical System
- Administer logistics
- Organize services (casualty management and behavioral health)
- Communicate plans and needs (internal and external)
- Identify need for and provide emergency treatment, resources, and equipment
- Institute unified command and control
- Continue provision of primary care
- Coordinate with emergency management response structures (incident command system, federal response, international disaster relief, United Nations agencies, International Committee of the Red Cross, nongovernmental organizations)
- Assist officials by providing information on public health matters

Education:

- How long foods can be stored in a refrigerator or freezer after the power goes off
- When water is or is not safe to drink
- How long water should be boiled before drinking

- Whether mass immunizations are needed
- When it is safe to reenter homes or eat food after a toxic cloud has dissipated
- What the risks are of delayed effects (i.e., cancer, birth defects) from a chemical or nuclear mishap to the average citizen and to those who are pregnant

Management:

- Dispose of waste, debris, human and animal bodies, and biologic hazards
- Control disease vectors
- Monitor and provide information on water, sanitation, food, and shelter
- Control infection
- Control cleanup injuries (i.e., chain saw accidents, electrocution, fire, unsafe structures)
- Coordinate delivery of mental health services
- Communicate health information and risks via media outlets
- Control disease and issue quarantines where necessary
- Provide interventions to large groups

Surveillance

- Establish syndromic information systems for disaster
- Conduct sentinel surveillance, using active or passive systems, of disease and public health conditions
- Use data to recognize acute disease states and high-risk groups

Recovery

- Determine present level and extent of patient care capability
- Interpret data to influence deployment of resources
- Work with community agencies to mitigate long-term impact on public health
- Conduct evaluations (structured, semistructured, qualitative)
- Plan and direct field studies
- Manage media
- Use principles of capacity building
- Mobilize resources
- Use techniques for supplemental and therapeutic food distribution and feeding
- Organize and conduct large-scale immunization and primary health care
- Ensure maintenance of mental health program
- Work with Red Cross to incorporate functional needs services in shelters
- Provide basic medical care and referral services for those requiring medical attention in shelters, through 24-hour staff
- Set up emergency public health hotline staffed 24 hours a day for medical issues and another one for mental health issues with workers speaking the major languages of the community

Evaluation

- Use information revealed through evaluation to make decisions about a community's emergency management needs or improving future response
- Conduct assessments of planning and emergency response to provide continuing feedback which can improve an organization or community's preparedness
- Determine whether emergency plans and disaster response are effective and efficient

Chapter **3**

Structure and Organization of Health Management in Disaster Response

T he public health profession has become increasingly involved in national emergency management since the 1980s. The recognition of health effects from the volcanic eruption at Mount St. Helens motivated the beginning of formal public health and medical sector participation in preparedness and response activities. The catastrophic tragedies that resulted from the terrorist attacks in 2001 and Hurricane Katrina in 2005 led to the transformation of emergency preparedness and response from a mostly volunteer service to a highly professional corps, and solidified the public health profession's inclusion as a permanent member of the emergency management team in the United States.

The requirements for preparedness and response in the United States have come from presidential policies and congressional action. The response to disasters is organized though multiple jurisdictions, agencies, and authorities. As a result, local response to disaster situations requires extensive planning, organization, and coordination with other regional, state, and federal officials. The term *comprehensive emergency management* is used to refer to these activities.

This chapter discusses the guidelines, framework, and structure of the federal response, the process of declaring disasters and requesting federal resources, how the federal response is conducted, the responsibilities of local responders and health providers (including public health incident command), interactions with other responders through mutual aid and deployment of volunteers, and costs and reimbursement sources for disaster response and relief.

Public Health Role

- Participate with other professionals who engage in emergency preparedness and response
- Activate public health emergency operations centers (EOCs) and participate in communitywide EOCs
- Assess medical, public health, and mental health needs, prepare recommendations on clinical aspects of emergency, and assure provision of services
- Assess viability of health care infrastructure
- Conduct health surveillance, detect, identify, and verify individual cases through laboratory sciences, and institute measures to control infectious disease
- Provide expert assistance in responding to chemical, radiological, or biological hazards

- Staff public health clinics involved in emergencies
- Supplement clinical backup to school health program sheltering activities
- Assure potable water supply, food safety, and sanitation
- Assure worker safety
- Educate about vector control and implement appropriate measures
- Provide public health information
- Work with voluntary organizations (such as Red Cross) to provide emergency shelter
- Identify victims and manage corpses
- Be able to respond 24 hours a day, 7 days a week
- Coordinate with other sectors on long-term consequence management

Structure of the Federal Response

The president has issued executive orders, known as Presidential Directives (PDs) or Presidential Decision Directives (PDDs), that established national policy regarding disasters. PDD-39 (January 21, 1995) defined federal actions to be taken in response to threats or acts of terrorism, and PDD-62 (May 22, 1998) established the fight against terrorism as a top national security priority. Homeland Security Presidential Directive (HSPD) 5 (February 28, 2003) required that all responses to emergencies be conducted using a comprehensive National Incident Management System (NIMS) with a unified command. HSPD-8 (December 17, 2003) required the development of a national domestic all-hazards preparedness goal, with mechanisms for improving federal assistance to state and local governments and for strengthening the capabilities of all jurisdictional entities. The methods in which these policies were implemented are described in this chapter.

On March 30, 2011, President Obama issued PDD-8, which replaced HSPD-8. When fully implemented, PDD-8 will advance some principles discussed in this chapter and alter others. The reader should watch for final guidance from the U.S. Department of Homeland Security (DHS) in early 2012.

Presidential Decision Directive 8

The goal of PDD-8 is to enhance preparedness by focusing on key capabilities (operational capacity and ability to execute preparedness tasks) needed to prepare for any emergency, especially those that pose the greatest risk to a region. PDD-8 calls for building key capabilities to carry out a preparedness plan that is flexible, robust, and adaptable enough to respond to a wide range of incidents, including the most catastrophic. NIMS, discussed later in the chapter, is built upon this principle.

As provided for in the PDD-8, DHS is leading the development of a national preparedness goal, a national preparedness system, and an evaluation system in which a report will be compiled annually to address (1) how we know whether we are prepared and (2) whether we are better prepared than we were the previous year.

By October 2011, the secretary of DHS will develop the national preparedness goal which will build upon existing strategies and directives. The new goal will identify the core capabilities needed for all levels of government to be prepared based on regional variations in the risk of specific threats and vulnerabilities. The process of developing a national preparedness goal and capabilities will be inclusive, with DHS seeking input from all levels of government, the private and nonprofit sectors, and the public. In March 2011, the Centers for Disease Control and Prevention (CDC) published standards for 15 capabilities that apply to public health agencies (see Chapter 7 and Appendix E).

DHS will develop a description of the national preparedness system to guide the achievement and maintenance of capabilities in planning, organization, equipment, and training and exercises by December 2011. This system will include many of the concepts discussed in this chapter:

- Integrated national planning frameworks
- Frameworks built upon scalable, flexible, and adaptable coordinating structures to align key roles and responsibilities
- Frameworks coordinated under a unified system with a common terminology and approach, built around basic plans that support the all-hazards approach to preparedness
- Interagency operational plan to support each national planning framework
- Guidance for resources (arrangements to share personnel), equipment (nationwide interoperability), and national training and exercise programs

This directive calls for a "whole-of-nation" approach in which all sectors of society are involved in ensuring a community's preparedness by shoring up identified capabilities. The Federal Emergency Management Agency (FEMA) currently follows this "whole community" approach which involves partnering with institutions, groups and individuals actively engaged in preparedness and with communities dealing with the effects of a disaster. In addition, enhanced capability-based planning will focus on the key principles discussed in this book: prevention, mitigation, response, and recovery.

The implementation of whole community preparedness will fundamentally change how the United States carries out disaster preparedness, response, recovery and mitigation. The current approach to disaster response is centered on government action. Whole community preparedness will involve all parts of a community (community and faith-based organizations, private sector, residents, volunteers) in a unified approach to preparedness and response. This approach involves knowing and meeting the preparedness needs of the entire community, engaging the entire community in identifying those needs and arranging to fulfill them, and strengthening what works well in communities to improve their resilience (see Chapter 9 for a discussion of resilience).

National Preparedness Guidelines

The development of the National Preparedness Guidelines to target the country's comprehensive efforts in emergency preparedness was directed through HSPD-8. The guidelines include a national all-hazards preparedness goal and the tools needed for organizing a national preparedness system.[1] The two key elements relevant to public health practice are the National Planning Scenarios and the Target Capabilities List (TCL). The National Planning Scenarios focus contingency planning and operational and tactical coordination carried out by all federal-level agencies. The scenarios identify 15 types of emergencies that could cause great harm to people or property for which coordinated investments are needed in planning, training, exercises, and grants. Table 11 lists the 15 National Planning Scenarios. The TCL defines 37 specific skills that workers at all levels of government should possess to respond effectively to disasters. Although the comprehensive capabilities identified in the TCL cannot be met by any single professional group, the list is an essential reference allowing jurisdictions to understand how to focus their preparedness activities. The original TCL (2007) is presented in Appendix G.

Homeland Security

DHS was established by the president and Congress (in the Homeland Security Act of 2002) to coordinate federal programs and to assist state and local governments in responding to the full range of emergencies, disasters, and catastrophes. By assuming primary responsibility in the event of a terrorist attack, natural disaster, or other large-scale emergency, DHS provides a unifying core for the vast national network of organizations and institutions involved in preparedness efforts. DHS is responsible for developing and implementing preparedness plans; developing procedures and policies to guide response to a terrorist attack; conducting training and exercises for first responders; enhancing partnerships with state and local governments, private sector institutions, and other organizations; and funding the purchase of equipment for first responders, states, cities, and towns.

To provide direction for the national preparation and response to all hazards, the DHS created the National Response Framework (NRF), which replaced the National Response Plan in 2008, and NIMS. Whereas the NRF provides the structure and mechanisms which guide national policy for emergency response, NIMS provides the template for managing emergencies regardless of size, scope, or cause. Together, these guidelines provide methods to implement and coordinate a comprehensive, unified, and consistent federal response in support of state and local officials. The lead department for federal emergency management is the DHS, with much of the strategic planning and response activities delegated to FEMA. FEMA's National Preparedness Division helps states, tribes, and localities conform plans and training based on the previous National Response Plan to the new NRF. FEMA is discussed later in the chapter.

State and local resources are the first line of support in response to a disaster. This principle drives all preparedness at the state and local level, since states must pay a share of the costs of federal response and recovery, and an efficient use of local resources can reduce that additional cost. Once state resources and capabilities are exhausted, federal assistance may be provided to supplement state operations.

---

[1]Check for proposed changes to these guidelines from activities under PDD-8 in December 2011.

Table 11. National Planning Scenarios

Scenario	Description
1	Nuclear detonation—10-kiloton improvised nuclear device
2	Biological attack—aerosol anthrax
3	Biological disease outbreak—pandemic influenza
4	Biological attack—plague
5	Chemical attack—blister agent
6	Chemical attack—toxic industrial chemicals
7	Chemical attack—nerve agent
8	Chemical attack—chlorine tank explosion
9	Natural disaster—major earthquake
10	Natural disaster—major hurricane
11	Radiological attack—radiological dispersal devices
12	Explosives attack—bombing using improvised explosive devices
13	Biological attack—food contamination
14	Biological attack—foreign animal disease (foot and mouth disease)
15	Cyber attack—computer-to-computer

Adapted from Department of Homeland Security (DHS). 2007. National Preparedness Guidelines. Washington, DC: DHS. Available at: http://www.dhs.gov/xlibrary/assets/National_Preparedness_Guidelines.pdf; and Federal Emergency Management Agency (FEMA). 2009. National Planning Scenarios. FEMA Fact Sheet. Washington, DC: FEMA. Available at: http://www.fema.gov/pdf/media/factsheets/2009/npd_natl_plan_scenario.pdf.

The Pandemic and All-Hazards Preparedness Act

The Pandemic and All-Hazards Preparedness Act (PAHPA, Public Law 109-417) amended the Public Service Health Act and became law in December 2006. PAHPA created mechanisms to improve public health preparedness and response at all levels of government and created clear lines of authority and accountability when responding to public health emergencies and incidents covered by the NRF.

PAHPA seeks to ensure that state and local public health departments have met established standards in preparedness. PAHPA establishes numerous approaches to create surge capacity at the federal, state, and local levels. The approaches include enhancing the training of health care providers and volunteers, making it easier for qualified health care providers to volunteer during emergency situations, allowing treatment to be delivered at alternative health care facilities and mobile hospitals, providing liability protections as incentives for service, and funding grants to hospitals and other health care facilities. Through these initiatives, Congress expects that communities will be better prepared when the number of health professionals available during an emergency increases and the capacity for response by medical and public health professionals improves.

PAHPA also reinforces preparedness efforts for at-risk individuals. Implementation of the National Preparedness goal, state and local grant activities, and the Strategic National Stockpile (SNS; discussed later in this chapter) must incorporate the public health and medical needs of at-risk individuals. Further, best practices must be disseminated on outreach to and caring for at-risk individuals during any phase of a disaster (see Chapter 10 for discussion of vulnerable populations).

The HHS is responsible for achieving the goals of this act. Within HHS, the Office of the Assistant Secretary for Preparedness and Response (ASPR) was created to lead national efforts to prevent, prepare for, and respond to emergencies and disasters affecting public health. This office provides federal support to augment state and local capabilities during a disaster and is discussed later in this chapter. Key components of the PAHPA legislation include the creation of a National Health Security Strategy (NHSS) and enhanced surge capacity (also see Chapter 7). The NHSS establishes a vision to focus national preparedness and response efforts to protect against threats or emergencies that could negatively affect health. The goals of the NHSS, released in January 2010, are building community resilience and strengthening and sustaining health and emergency response systems. These strategic goals are met through defined operational tasks, or capabilities.

At the state level, PAHPA established funding for the Medical Reserve Corps (MRC) and Emergency System for Advance Registration of Volunteer Health Professionals (ESAR-VHP). MRC is a state-administered, locally run program for medical volunteers who train together so they are ready to augment a medical response in the event of disasters involving many serious injuries, known as mass casualty incidents, in their community. For ESAR-VHP, a state registers health care volunteers before an incident to ensure that they are properly licensed and credentialed. Both are discussed in the section on volunteers later in this chapter.

National Response Framework

The NRF defines the unifying principles, roles, and structures that organize how we respond as a nation to disasters and emergencies. It provides the mechanism for coordinating the delivery of federal assistance and resources to augment efforts of state and local governments in support of the Robert T. Stafford Disaster Relief and Emergency Assistance Act of 1988 (Stafford Act; discussed later in this chapter) or a federal response managed under the Economy Act of 1932.[2] Rather than detailing a specific plan for response, the NRF describes the planning process and directs federal agencies to participate in the entire spectrum of emergency management from preparedness to recovery. The NRF

- Describes how communities, tribes, states, the federal government, private sectors, and nongovernmental partners work together to coordinate the national response.
- Describes specific authorities and best practices for managing incidents.
- Builds upon NIMS; provides a common template and an operational structure based on the principles and standard methodology of the Incident Command System (ICS) for managing incidents. ICS is used because disasters, regardless of magnitude, require a coordinated response from a number of different agencies for organizing the delivery of services in disaster response. ICS is discussed later in the chapter.

It should be noted that some types of responses are generated by authorities other than the Stafford Act and are managed outside of the NRF. The 2010 Gulf of Mexico oil spill, the response to the earthquake in Haiti, and the 2009–2010 influenza pandemic exemplify disasters in which the national responses included a significant medical component yet were not managed through the NRF. As an example, the oil spill was managed through the authority of the National Contingency Plan. Authorization to respond to international incidents is provided through treaties and arrangements with the U.S. Department of State. Although these are the exceptions, they are not that uncommon. The key is that without a presidential declaration and the resources of the Stafford Act (discussed later in the chapter), funding for federal support is limited and unorganized.

Information on the NRF, including documents, annexes, references, and briefings and training courses, can be obtained from the NRF Resource Center (available at http://www.fema.gov/emergency/nrf).

National Incident Management System

The goal of HSPD-5 is to enhance the ability of the United States to oversee a coordinated response by establishing a single, comprehensive model for the national management of major domestic emergencies. The comprehensive model which provides the template for managing all emergencies is the NIMS. The NIMS is built upon the principle that effective preparedness involves many groups who work together, including preparedness organizations, elected and appointed officials, nongovernmental organizations, and the private sector. Further, everyone directly involved in managing an emergency should understand the command reporting structures, common terminology, and roles and responsibilities inherent in a response operation.

---

[2]The Economy Act provides a mechanism to avoid duplication of work by governmental agencies. It allows for interdepartmental procurement where one federal agency can request the assistance of another agency, with the transfer of funds between agencies for the provision of goods and services.

NIMS is relevant to all jurisdictions and functional disciplines and is applicable across all emergencies, regardless of size, location, or complexity. NIMS was designed to improve coordination and cooperation and to provide a common standard for the broad range of personnel who interact to manage emergencies. Using NIMS principles, a diverse group of professionals can develop a shared understanding of the procedures and protocols that will be used and how equipment and personnel will be deployed. All involved in emergency response, whether career professionals, volunteers, or government officials, are required to complete federally approved NIMS training. Further, all recipients of federal funding for preparedness and response activities must be NIMS compliant. Finally, hospitals and health care systems receiving federal funds for preparedness must implement NIMS.

Key features of NIMS include the following:

Preparedness: To enhance a responder's readiness to carry out his or her functions, NIMS defines activities of advance preparedness such as planning, training, exercises, qualification and certification, equipment acquisition and certification, and publication management. Preparedness also incorporates mitigation, or preventive activities such as public education, enforcement of building standards and codes, and measures to deter or lessen the loss of life or property.

Communications and information management: To standardize communications during an incident, NIMS prescribes interoperable communications systems including standards for equipment and training. Interoperable communication is described in Chapter 6.

Resource management: NIMS defines the steps necessary to be prepared and to manage assets during an emergency.

Incident Command System: NIMS establishes ICS as the standard incident management model with five functional areas—command, operations, planning, logistics, and finance/administration. NIMS operates through unified command to coordinate the efforts of many jurisdictions, and to provide for and assure joint decisions on objectives, strategies, plans, priorities, and public communications. An example of public health incident command is described later in this chapter.

Multiagency Coordination System: MACS is used to coordinate activities above the field level and to prioritize the allocation of critical or competing resources. MACS integrates the personnel, procedures, protocols, business practices, and communications which are deployed from numerous agencies, into a common system. EOCs, one of several components, provide support to those in charge of the response.

Joint Information System (JIS): To ensure that all levels of government are releasing the same information during an incident, the JIS provides unified messages with timely and accurate information, including messages over the Internet, about the incident. Those who will communicate about the incident are brought together to develop, coordinate, and deliver a unified message in a Joint Information Center (JIC),

NIMS Integration Center (NIC): The NIC provides strategic direction and oversight of NIMS, administers its program to determine compliance with NIMS requirements, and supports training and exercises.

Emergency Support Functions

The emergency management community uses the term *function* to describe the responsibilities within the NRF that must typically be addressed in a disaster response. These responsibilities are grouped into 15 Emergency Support Functions (ESFs), each headed by a federal agency with the support of the others. Many ESFs directly or indirectly affect efforts to protect the health and welfare of disaster victims. The federal response to the specific health needs of disaster victims is primarily contained in ESF-8: Public Health and Medical Services Annex. The federal response of HHS is organized to meet the functions defined in ESF-8. The public health and medical responsibilities include the following:

- Assessment of public health/medical needs
- Health surveillance
- Medical care personnel
- Health/medical/veterinary equipment and supplies
- Patient evacuation
- Patient care
- Safety and security of drugs, biologics, and medical devices
- Food safety and security
- Agriculture safety and security
- All-hazard public health and medical consultation, technical assistance, and support
- Behavioral health care
- Public health and medical information
- Vector control
- Potable water/wastewater and solid waste disposal
- Mass fatality management, victim identification, and decontaminating remains
- Veterinary medical support

The 15 ESFs and their responsible lead federal agencies are shown in Table 12.

Health and Human Services

In disasters of the magnitude requiring a presidential declaration, the U.S. Department of Health and Human Services (HHS) has lead responsibility for supporting local officials in their response to medical and public health needs. PAHPA provides that public health resources may also be deployed by HHS through its executive agent, the ASPR (formerly the Office of Public Health Emergency Preparedness).

In a health emergency or public health event, the secretary of HHS delegates to the ASPR the leadership role in carrying out the support function for health and medical services. The ASPR works with other federal agencies and with state and local governments to coordinate the planning and response; provides logistical support for any federal response, and oversees the development and procurement of medical countermeasures to pandemics and other hazards.

Table 12. Emergency Support Functions (ESFs) and Responsible Lead Federal Agency

ESF	ESF Title and Function	Lead Federal Agency
1	Transportation—aviation/airspace management and control, transportation safety, restoring transportation infrastructure	Department of Transportation
2	Communications—coordinating telecommunications and information technology industries, restoring telecommunications infrastructure, protect and sustain national cyber and information technology resources	Department of Homeland Security (DHS)/National Communications System
3	Public Works and Engineering—infrastructure repair, restoration, and protection, emergency contracting services for repair	Army Corps of Engineers
4	Firefighting—coordination of support to firefighting operations	Department of Agriculture/Forest Service
5	General Support—coordination of incident management and response activities including human resource management and incident action planning	DHS/Federal Emergency Management Agency (FEMA)
6	Mass Care—coordinates mass care, emergency assistance, housing, and human services	DHS/FEMA
7	Logistics Management and Resource Support—comprehensive logistical planning and support	General Services Administration and DHS/FEMA
8	Public Health and Medical Services—public health, health care delivery, mental health, and mass fatality management	HHS
9	Search and Rescue—lifesaving and search and rescue operations	DHS/FEMA
10	Hazardous Materials and Oil Spill Response—hazardous materials response and coordination of short- and long-term restoration	Environmental Protection Agency
11	Agriculture and Natural Resources—provide nutrition assistance; control and eradicate outbreaks of contagious or economically devastating animal/zoonotic disease, or any outbreak of an economically devastating plant pest or disease; ensure the safety and security of the commercial food supply; and provide for the safety and well-being of household pets during an emergency response or evacuation situation	Department of Agriculture

(continued on next page)

Table 12. (*continued*)

ESF	ESF Title and Function	Lead Federal Agency
12	Energy—coordination of energy companies, energy infrastructure assessment, repair, and restoration	Department of Energy
13	Public Safety and Security—facility and resource security, security planning, response, and assistance	Department of Justice
14	Long-Term Community Recovery—provision of long-term recovery assistance and aid to state, local, and tribal governments	DHS/FEMA
15	External Affairs—coordination of public information and risk communications, Congressional liaison, tribal, and insular affairs	DHS

Adapted from Federal Emergency Management Agency (FEMA). 2008. Emergency Support Function Annexes. Table 1. Roles and responsibilities of the ESFs; and Table 2. Designation of ESF coordinator and primary and support agencies. Washington, DC: FEMA. Available at: http://www.fema.gov/pdf/emergency/nrf/nrf-esf-all.pdf.

Six offices are part of ASPR, as follows:

Biomedical Advanced Research and Development Authority (BARDA): BARDA provides coordination and helps develop and procure medical countermeasures to speed the development and availability of vaccines and pharmaceuticals to treat highly infectious diseases in public health emergencies. BARDA has responsibility for establishing strategies for the deployment and use of medical countermeasures supplied through the SNS. BARDA acquires medical countermeasures for at-risk populations, such as vaccines for immunocompromised populations. The Public Health Emergency Countermeasure Enterprise (PHEMCE) provides funding for pandemic influenza vaccine development, alternative techniques for vaccine production, and novel testing and treatments for bioterrorism agents. BARDA provides expertise and leadership on PHEMCE.

Office of Preparedness and Emergency Operations (OPEO): To ensure federal preparedness, OPEO develops operational plans, participates in training and exercises, and secures the systems and logistical support necessary for the ASPR to coordinate HHS's operational response.

Office of Acquisition Management, Contracts and Grants (OAMCG): OAMCG guides ASPR program offices through the federal procurement process and assists in drafting acquisition strategies and plans and refining their requirements. A key function is to support the acquisition of supplies and pharmaceuticals for the chemical, biological, radiological, and nuclear and influenza programs.

Office of Policy and Planning (OPP): OPP is responsible for strategic planning and develops and analyzes policy for the ASPR.

Office of Financial Planning and Analysis (OFPA): OFPA helps formulate and implement fiscal policies and procedures for the allocation and utilization of program resources.

Office of the Chief of Staff: The Office of the Chief of Staff is responsible for external communications and agency operations.

National Terrorism Advisory System

Following HSPD-3 (March 11, 2002), DHS established the Homeland Security Advisory System (HSAS) to guide preventive actions taken in response to information about threats and vulnerability assessments. Most remember the color-coding alerts as key to the HSAS. In 2011, the National Terrorism Advisory System (NTAS) replaced the HSAS. The NTAS is also designed to communicate information about terrorist threats so that preventive actions can be taken. Under the new system, DHS with other federal entities will issue alerts when the federal government receives information about a specific or credible terrorist threat. These alerts will include a clear statement that there is an *imminent* or *elevated* threat. The alerts will provide a summary of the potential threat, information about actions being taken to ensure public safety, and recommended steps that individuals and communities, businesses and governments can take. Alerts will be sent directly to the affected groups, such as law enforcement, the private sector, or to the general population. Multiple communication channels will be used including a designated DHS Web page (available at http://www.dhs.gov/alerts), and social media (Facebook and Twitter @NTASAlerts). Individual threat alerts will be issued with a specified end date but can be extended if needed.

As the NTAS evolves, public health agencies should develop a checklist of activities that they would undertake with changing levels of threat. The checklist should include:

1. Informational gathering. Check information from the Centers for Disease Control and Prevention (CDC), state Departments of Health, Offices of Emergency Management, and others.
2. Surveillance system. Check emergency and ambulatory admissions for patients who may have conditions or illness suggestive of chemical, biological, nuclear, or radiological exposures.
3. Security. Enhance security measures with an increased level of threat.
4. Staffing. Assess staffing patterns and determine what to do for coverage.
5. Communications. Check availability of systems, including state information systems.
6. Supplies and equipment. Assure availability and functionality.

Federal Emergency Management Agency

FEMA has seven main directorates to carry out the mission of emergency management:

Recovery Directorate: Helps individuals and communities affected by disasters return to normal functioning quickly; provides individual assistance (housing, financial assistance, unemployment assistance); and public assistance (helps communities to rebuild public systems and facilities).

Response Division: Provides coordinated federal operational and logistical response to disaster-affected communities; coordinates all response operations, planning, logistics, and the integration of federal, state, tribal, and local disaster programs.

Logistics Management Directorate: Plans for, manages, and sustains the national logistics response and recovery operations, including logistics operations, plans, and exercises; distribution; and property management.

Mitigation Directorate: Manages the National Flood Insurance Program and other programs designed to reduce future losses to homes, businesses, schools, public buildings, and critical facilities from floods, earthquakes, tornadoes, and other natural disasters.

National Continuity Programs Directorate: Is the lead Federal Agent for the continuity of national essential functions, the development and promulgation of the Continuity of Operations, and manages the Integrated Public Alert and Warning System.

National Preparedness Directorate: The 2006 Post-Katrina Emergency Management Reform Act mandated the creation of the NPD. The NPD oversees the coordination and development of the capabilities and tools necessary to prepare for terrorist incidents and natural disasters, and provides guidance in building prevention, response, and recovery capabilities.

U.S. Fire Administration: Oversees the coordination and directing of national efforts to prevent fires and to improve fire response; trains emergency managers, firefighters, elected officials, and other emergency responders through a variety of courses in all-hazards emergency.

In addition to their Washington, DC, headquarters, FEMA operates a number of regional offices (see Appendix Z for a list of offices and locations). Other agencies, such as HHS and its National Disaster Medical System (NDMS) described later in the chapter, use the same geographic zones to organize personnel and resources throughout the nation.

Disaster Declarations and Federal Assistance

In the event of a natural disaster, the Robert T. Stafford Disaster Relief and Emergency Assistance Act, PL 92–388 amended by Disaster Mitigation Act 2000 PL 106–34042 (42 U.S.C. 5121 et seq.) and by the Post-Katrina Emergency Management Reform Act of 2006 (PKEMRA; S. 3721), provides for "an orderly and continuing means of assistance by the federal government to state and local governments in carrying out their responsibilities to alleviate the suffering and damage which result from major disasters and emergencies." Under the Stafford Act, the president may provide federal resources, financial assistance, services, medicine, food, and other consumables through what is known as a presidential declaration. In a major disaster, PKEMRA authorized the president to order precautionary evacuations and provide accelerated federal support even before state and local governments have made a specific request.

Before the passage of the Homeland Security Act of 2002, federal assistance was initiated in one of three ways: states request federal assistance in advance of the disaster to activate a declaration when the threat is imminent and warrants limited predeployment actions to lessen or avert a catastrophe; governors submit requests after the disaster has struck; or the president exercises primary authority, as was done following the bombing at Oklahoma City. With the passage of the Homeland Security Act, the secretary of Homeland Security has a lot of discretion in the deployment of federal resources. Homeland Security can activate the federal government's resources if and when any of the following four conditions applies:

- A federal department or agency, acting under its own authority, has requested the assistance of the secretary
- The resources of state and local authorities are overwhelmed and federal assistance has been requested by the appropriate state or local authorities (i.e., through the Stafford Act)
- More than one federal department or agency has become substantially involved in responding to the incident
- The secretary has been directed to assume responsibility for managing the incident by the president

When there is a declaration, each affected state must take the initiative in requesting a declaration. States must individually request a separate declaration, even when affected by the same disaster. FEMA assigns a sequential number to each major disaster (DR) or emergency (EM). For the small number of declared disasters or emergencies, the events are of such magnitude that a subsequent "major disaster declaration" is requested (e.g., Hurricane Katrina).

Once there has been a presidential declaration, FEMA is responsible for coordinating the federal response for emergency management. FEMA performs many of the same functions as a local emergency management agency, but can also direct federal resources and money toward the preparation for, response to, and recovery from larger emergencies and disasters. If communities and agencies provide mutual aid to one another and there is no presidential declaration, it is important that they execute interagency agreements. Mutual aid in response to a disaster will be voluntary without authorization under the Stafford Act. Table 13 outlines the declarations and assessment process.

Organization of Response

When a governor, or designee, of an affected state has requested a presidential declaration under the Stafford Act, the NRF is activated. In anticipation of a catastrophic event, federal assets may also be mobilized and deployed in advance of a formal request for assistance. The Catastrophic Incident Supplement of the NRF establishes the procedures and mechanisms by which this occurs.

Table 13. Disaster Declaration Process

Declaration Process/Action	Preliminary Damage Assessments (PDAs)	Primary Considerations for Declarations
After initial response by local groups, governor consults with local government officials and determines that combined resources of both the state and local governments are not sufficient	PDAs, conducted in affected counties, assist governor in determining if request for assistance is needed	Criteria used by Federal Emergency Management Agency (FEMA): Amount and type of damage (number of homes destroyed/major damage) Impact on infrastructure or on critical facilities Imminent threats to public health and safety Impacts on essential government services and functions Unique capability of federal government Dispersion or concentration of damage Level of insurance coverage in place Other available assistance Previous state and local commitments for resources Frequency of disaster events over recent time period
Governor declares a state of emergency and invokes the state's emergency plan	FEMA, state's emergency management agency, county and local officials, and the U.S. Small Business Administration conduct assessments	

(continued on next page)

Table 13. (*continued*)

Declaration Process/Action	Preliminary Damage Assessments (PDAs)	Primary Considerations for Declarations

Governor:
  Submits written request to the president through FEMA regional office
  Requests supplemental federal assistance under the Robert T. Stafford Disaster Relief and Emergency Assistance Act, 42 U.S.C. §§ 5121-5206
  Certifies that severity and magnitude of disaster exceed state and local capabilities
  Certifies federal assistance is necessary to supplement state and local governments, disaster relief organizations, and compensation by insurance companies for disaster-related losses
  Confirms execution of the state's emergency plan
  Certifies adherence to cost sharing
	Team reviews:
	  Types of damage
	  Emergency costs incurred
	  Impact to critical facilities
	  Affect on individuals and businesses
	  Number of people displaced
	  Threats to health and safety
	  Any additional data from the Red Cross	

Request and findings of the PDAs are reviewed by FEMA regional and national offices FEMA provides an analysis of the situation and recommends a course of action to the president	Team collects estimates of the expenses and damages	
	Governor uses information to support declaration request, identify cost of response, and certify that damage exceeds state and local resources	

Adapted from Federal Emergency Management Agency (FEMA). 2010. Declaration Process Fact Sheet: The Emergency Response Process. Washington, DC: FEMA. Available at http://www.fema.gov/media/fact_sheets/declaration_process.shtm.

More than 28 federal agencies and the Red Cross provide personnel, technical expertise, equipment, and other resources to state and local governments, and assume an active role in managing a national response. Within HHS, the lead federal agency, the CDC and National Institute of Occupational Safety and Health provide technical personnel and logistical support, such as epidemiologists, environmental sampling equipment, and laboratory assistance. The Departments of Defense (DOD) and Veterans Affairs (VA) provide support in the event of a catastrophic disaster where many people require hospitalization. Agencies issue mission assignments, or work orders, which direct the agency to carry out and fund specified tasks in response to the disaster.

Emergency Management Response

As the nation saw in the response to Hurricane Katrina, a catastrophic disaster requires resources at every level of government and from every agency. The coordination of such an immense response is complicated and involves numerous levels of bureaucracy. After Katrina, significant improvements have been made in the organization of response, with a specific designation for the various levels of responsibility. This section describes the key federal roles and how these personnel generally interact with state and local officials.

Federal Agencies and Staff

Under the NRF and NIMS, the president designates a Principal Federal Official (PFO) to coordinate the activities of all federal agencies during a catastrophic disaster and to serve as the secretary of Homeland Security's direct representative to the response. The PFO interfaces with all jurisdictional officials regarding the management of the incident and is the primary federal spokesperson. For major disasters, the president appoints a Federal Coordinating Officer (FCO) who is responsible for coordinating the timely delivery of federal disaster assistance to the affected state and local governments, and disaster victims. The FCO oversees the commitment of FEMA resources and the assignment of other federal departments or agencies. In many cases, the FCO also serves as the Disaster Recovery Manager and administers the financial aspects of assistance authorized under the Stafford Act. Different individuals will serve as the PFO and FCO for a given response.

Federal and state personnel work together to carry out their response and recovery responsibilities. The FCO works closely with both the State Coordinating Officer (SCO), appointed by the governor to oversee disaster operations for the state, and the Governor's Authorized Representative, empowered by the governor to execute all necessary documents for disaster assistance on behalf of a state. In accordance with the state's emergency operations plan, requests for assistance from local jurisdictions are channeled first to the SCO through the designated state agencies, and then to the FCO or designee for consideration. When resources from the federal government are required, states must complete a purchase order, blanket purchase agreement, contract, or cooperative agreement to formalize the request.

Additionally, DHS may use a mission assignment as discussed above. The Financial Management Support Annex of the NRF provides additional information about this process (available at http://www.au.af.mil/au/awc/awcgate/frp/frpfm.htm).

FEMA maintains both a National Response Coordination Center (NRCC) and ten Regional Response Coordination Centers (RRCCs) in the event that incidents require federal-level resources. Both the NRCC and the RRCCs are staffed to provide all necessary coordination. In the event of an incident requiring extensive federal support, both coordinating centers can augment their staffing with additional personnel from FEMA and other relevant federal agencies.

In the Field

For the response in the field, a federal Joint Field Office (JFO) coordinates federal and state activities and provides tactical-level direction. Before the establishment of a JFO, an Emergency Response Team–Advance (ERT-A) will go to the affected area to assess the requests for assistance and the capacity of the local and state agencies to meet the requirements of a response. The JFO, led by a Unified Coordination Group (UCG), uses a unified incident command structure. The UCG includes senior state and federal leaders who work with all of the potential stakeholders in a coordinated federal response. The UCG can also include a Senior Federal Official from HHS when the events involve health care delivery or public health concerns. In the event of a terrorist act, the UCG will include a Senior Federal Law Enforcement Officer. Liaisons from the affected governments, businesses, and the JIC are assigned to work with the coordinating staff.

Officials responsible for four functional areas within NIMS—planning, operations, logistics, and finance and administration—report to the coordinating staff. Planning and operations activities are closely coordinated with the same functional units at the state level. Figure 1 lists the participants and shows the reporting structure for the JFO.

Local and state officials will activate an Emergency Operations Center (EOC). The EOC is the physical location where numerous agencies (e.g., emergency management, public health, and hospital groups) gather to manage the response. EOCs are staffed 24 hours a day while in operation. Depending on the scale of the disaster, the JFO will coordinate with the EOC and report to either the NRCC or RRCC.

Deployment and Operations

Requests for assistance (RFAs) from the federal government come through either the ERT-A or the JFO. RFAs can be submitted to the SCO, who sends the RFA to the ERT-A or to the JFO. Requests can also be submitted directly by the governor to senior DHS leadership or to the president. The FCO reviews RFAs and can approve all appropriate requests. Once approved, the JFO identifies what is required to meet the needs of the RFA. The federal agency with the identified capability validates the requirement and assigns a unit to meet the request. The funding for the assigned unit is provided through the Stafford or Economy Acts.

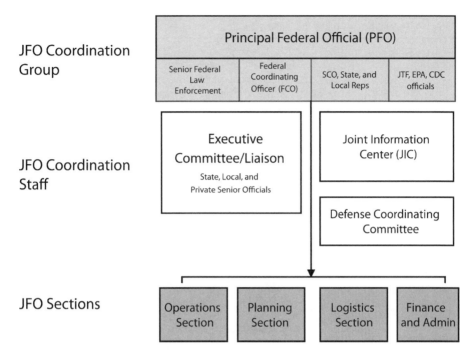

Figure 1. Joint Field Office Organizational Chart

SCO = State Coordinating Officer; **JTF** = Joint Task Force; **EPA** = Environmental Protection Agency; **CDC** = Centers for Disease Control and Prevention.

Adapted from Department of Homeland Security (DHS). 2006. Joint Field Office, Activation and Operations, Interagency Integrated Standard Operating Procedures. Table 2 to Annex H: Sample JFO Organization for Terrorism Incidents. Washington, DC: DHS. Available at http://www.fema.gov/pdf/emergency/nrf/NRP_JFO_SOPAnnexes.pdf.

Once deployed, the assigned unit works either directly for a local or state agency or as part of a larger federal response. Regardless of assignment, response activities are conducted using the principles of NIMS. Coordination occurs among the local, state and federal responders and each level develops and implements what is called an *incident action plan* (IAP). An IAP contains the specific action steps that will be taken to respond to the emergency. Federal involvement decreases when the incident no longer requires the most intensive level of response. Eventually, all resources are returned to their original location and are readied for future needs.

As the lead agency for ESF 8, HHS has developed a Concept of Operations Plan (CONOPS) to provide a framework for its management of the public health and medical response. CONOPS, consistent with HSPD-5 and the NRF, provides strategies to ensure that there is a unified approach to all activities carried out by HHS. Table 14 describes federal actions that can be initiated under the provisions of the Stafford Act.

Figure 2 graphically shows the flow of activities following an incident.

Table 14. Federal Actions Under the Stafford Act

Pre-event	U.S. Department of Homeland Security (DHS) National Operations Center monitors potential disasters
	With advance warning, DHS may deploy liaisons to state emergency operations centers
	A Regional Response Coordination Center (RRCC) may be fully or partially activated
	Mobilization centers may be established
Immediately after	Local emergency personnel respond and assess
	Locals seek help through mutual aid and from state
	State reviews situation, mobilizes state resources, requests assistance through Emergency Management Assistance Compacts (EMACs), and provides assessments to Federal Emergency Management Agency (FEMA) regional office
	Governor activates state emergency operations plan, declares state of emergency, and requests state/DHS preliminary damage assessment (PDA)
	PDA conducted
	Governor requests presidential declaration based on PDA
Post-disaster declaration	The RRCC coordinates regional and field activities until the Joint Field Office (JFO) is in place
	Regional teams assess needs and start setting up field facilities
	National-level Incident Management Assistance Team is deployed when regional resources are overwhelmed
Response activities	The National Response Coordination Center supports the RRCC
	Governor appoints State Coordinating Officer to coordinate state activities
	President appoints Federal Coordinating Officer to coordinate federal activities
	JFO established
	Unified Coordination Group (UCG) leads JFO
	UCG develops objectives and action plan
	UCG coordinates field operations from JFO
	Emergency Support Functions assess and identify needs
	Federal agencies provide support under DHS/FEMA mission assignments or own authorities
	Stafford Act public assistance program provides assistance
	UCG releases federal resources as need indicates

Adapted from Federal Emergency Management Agency (FEMA). 2008. National Response Framework: Overview of Stafford Act Support to States. Washington, DC: FEMA. Available at http://www.fema. gov/pdf/emergency/nrf/nrf-stafford.pdf.

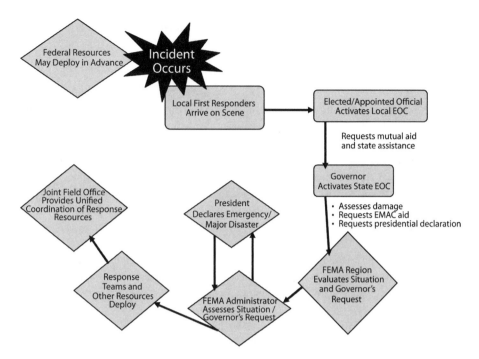

Figure 2. Federal Actions in Disaster Response

EOC = Emergency Operations Center; EMAC = Emergency Management Assistance Compact; FEMA = Federal Emergency Management Agency.

Adapted from Federal Emergency Management Agency (FEMA). 2008. National Response Framework: Overview of Stafford Act Support to States. Washington, DC: FEMA. Available at http://www.fema.gov/pdf/emergency/nrf/nrf-stafford.pdf.

Public Health and Medical Response

At the national level, the management of information and strategic-level command and control for ESF-8 occur in the HHS Secretary's Operations Center (SOC). During an emergency, the HHS Emergency Management Group (EMG) coordinates the ESF-8 response out of this operations center. Their goals for the response are communicated through the distribution of a plan called an *Incident Coordination Plan.*

Many resources are available to the ASPR in the coordination of public health and medical assistance under ESF-8. An Incident Response Coordination Team (IRCT) is mobilized by the ASPR to coordinate all deployed ESF-8 assets. The IRCT, usually led by a Regional Emergency Coordinator, serves as the link between the SOC/EMG and those responding in the field. The IRCT team leader is accountable for executing field activities for the ASPR. Other federal resources include the National Disaster Medical System (NDMS), the U.S. Public Health Service (USPHS) Office of Force Readiness and Deployment (OFRD), volunteers registered with the MRC or ESAR-VHP, and the Red Cross. Through the federal programs, volunteer clinicians can be activated to augment federal assets and practice as federal providers.

National Disaster Medical System

NDMS, operating within the office of the ASPR, manages and coordinates the federal medical response to major emergencies and federally declared disasters under the NRF. NDMS works in partnership with the USPHS, FEMA, DOD, and VA.

NDMS provides a nationally integrated medical response to (1) help state and local authorities address the medical and health effects of major peacetime disasters, and (2) provide support to the military and medical systems of the VA in caring for casualties evacuated to the United States from overseas armed conflicts.

NDMS has three components:

- Medical response to a disaster area in the form of teams, supplies, and equipment
- Patient movement from a disaster site to unaffected areas of the nation
- Definitive medical care at participating hospitals located in unaffected areas

When the mission assignment is received by NDMS headquarters, an Incident Management Team determines how best to meet the tasks and what resources are required. An operations group, assembled from an on-call list, works with the affected state(s) as they articulate what they need and will be requesting. Health care at the site of the disaster is provided by NDMS and USPHS teams with NDMS headquarters supporting the team coordination. NDMS also interacts with the JFO to meet the responsibilities of ESF 8.

Federal Coordinating Centers and Patient Movement

Federal Coordinating Centers (FCCs) recruit hospitals and maintain local nonfederal hospital participation in NDMS; assist in the recruitment, training, and support of Disaster Medical Assistance Teams (DMATs); coordinate exercises and emergency plans with participating hospitals and other local authorities to develop patient reception, transportation, and communication plans; and coordinate the reception and distribution of patients being evacuated to the area. FCCs are managed by the DOD and the VA.

Hospitals become part of NDMS by signing a memorandum of agreement between the chief executive of the hospital and the director of the FCC in their locale. As of this printing, NDMS reimburses participating hospitals up to 110% of Medicare and is the third-level payer after private insurance and Medicare. Hospitals should assume that comprehensive and complete documentation will be required to receive reimbursement and must establish the information systems necessary to comply.

FCCs contract with local Emergency Medical Services (EMS) to transport patients in the communities where NDMS member hospitals are located. The contracts facilitate the availability of ambulances from outside the affected region, to be able to transport patients from the disaster within 24 hours. Contracts are in place for 300 ambulances, 3000 paratransit seats, and 25 air ambulances. The FEMA regional ambulance contract also provides medical transport resources for deployment.

In the event of a federally declared natural or technological disaster, the DOD sets up a tracking system, the Global Patient Movement Requirements Center (GPMRC), to determine if patients need to be evacuated. When a mission assignment is issued to the DOD, the FCCs are activated. The FCCs partner with NDMS and NDMS member hospitals to identify and report available beds. While the number of beds is being assessed, patient information is being gathered at the disaster site and forwarded to the GPMRC. The GPMRC determines the movement of patients to specific FCCs based on both the victims' needs and the availability of beds and transportation. In addition to the tracking done by the DOD tracking, NDMS tracks patients through the Joint Patient Assessment Tracking System from the time that the status of patients is known at the FCCs until they are discharged.

Where the need for hospital beds exceeds local capacity, patients are stabilized at the site of the disaster by DMATs or other specialty teams and then evacuated by the DOD aeromedical system to hospitals that are part of NDMS. At the airport of the NDMS reception area, patients are met by a team from the local EMS. EMS assesses patients and transports them to participating hospitals according to procedures developed by local authorities and the local area's FCC.

National Disaster Medical System Teams

There are multiple teams within NDMS including the DMATs, Disaster Mortuary Operational Response Teams (DMORTs), National Veterinary Response Teams (NVRTs), Logistical Response Assistance Teams (LRATs), and the International Medical Surgical Teams (IMSurTs). In addition, a specialty team is available to provide supplemental skills when needed. Members of these teams are required to maintain appropriate certifications and licensure within their discipline and are activated as federal employees with their licensure and certification recognized by all states. When activated, team members are paid as intermittent federal employees, retain rights to return to their full-time employment, are protected with workers' compensation insurance, and have the protection of the Federal Tort Claims Act in which the federal government becomes the defendant in the event of a malpractice claim. As federal employees, NDMS team members also have to comply with federal ethics and conflict of interest regulations.

Disaster Medical Assistance Teams. DMATs are squads of licensed, actively practicing multidisciplinary medical personnel who function as rapid-response medical teams to supplement local medical care during a disaster or other event. DMAT personnel include physicians, nurses, nurse practitioners, emergency medical technicians (EMTs), paramedics, pharmacists and pharmacy technicians, dentists, respiratory therapists, communication specialists, social workers, and other allied health personnel. During mass casualty incidents, their responsibilities include triaging patients, providing austere medical care, and preparing patients for evacuation. In other situations, they may provide primary health care or assist overloaded medical staffs. Additionally, they are prepared to provide patient care during evacuation to definitive care sites.

The federal government now sponsors each team; thus, outside sponsorship is no longer needed. NDMS organizes reservists, recruits members, arranges training, and coordinates the dispatch of the team. NDMS registers and verifies the credentials of the members of DMATs in advance of activation.

Logistical Response Assistance Teams. LRATs are new teams responsible for being on-site with the equipment and supplies necessary to support NDMS teams within 12 hours of notification. In the event of a national deployment, the team will be assembled from the regional LRAT teams and team composition will be determined by the ASPR Logistics Unit, the LRAT Commander, and the chief of logistics.

Each LRAT consists of 12 logistics and administrative staff from throughout the NDMS system and is directed by the logistics division of ASPR. LRATs are responsible for receiving the teams, providing ground transportation, arranging for lodging and food, providing the equipment needed to set up ambulatory clinics, and maintaining and deploying the equipment and pharmaceutical caches for all NDMS teams so that the teams remain self-sustaining for at least 72 hours. The deployment of morgue supplies to a disaster site is now carried out by LRATs.

Disaster Mortuary Assistant Teams. DMORTs were developed to fulfill the responsibilities outlined for NDMS in ESF-8. DMORTs are composed of private citizens who, when activated into federal service, work under the guidance of local authorities and whose function is to augment the capacity of the local coroner. They provide technical assistance and personnel in the recovery, identification, and processing of deceased victims during an emergency response. Teams are composed of funeral directors, medical examiners, coroners, pathologists, forensic anthropologists, medical records technicians and transcribers, fingerprint specialists, forensic odontologists, dental assistants, X-ray technicians, mental health specialists, computer professionals, administrative support staff, and security and investigative personnel. The team members are skilled in identifying victims and working with relatives of victims.

These responsibilities include the following:

- Temporary morgue facilities
- Victim identification
- Forensic dental pathology
- Forensic anthropology methods
- Processing
- Preparation
- Disposition of remains

Family Assistance Center Teams work with family members to gather information about identifying features such as jewelry, dental work, or tattoos and to collect items that may carry genetic markers, such as tooth or hair brushes. The DMORTs work to match up the antemortem materials with the human remains for victim identification.

National Veterinary Response Teams. The NRF requires that NVRTs deliver veterinary medical treatment and address animal and public health issues resulting from disasters when the local veterinary community is overwhelmed. NVRTs are teams of veterinarians, technicians, toxicologists, and support personnel. NVRTs can be deployed only if a state or the federal government requests a NVRT following a presidential disaster declaration. Once the state determines that its local veterinary community is overwhelmed, the state submits a request for federal assistance through FEMA and, once approved, the request is forwarded to USPHS for approval. If a state alone requests a NVRT, the state may be required to fund the response. If a federal disaster is declared, the federal government covers a large part of the cost.

NVRT team members triage and stabilize animals such as search and rescue dogs at a disaster site and provide austere veterinary medical care. These teams are mobile units that can deploy within 12 to 24 hours when their assistance is requested by the state officials from the affected state. NVRT responsibilities during disasters include the following:

- Humane euthanasia
- Epidemiology
- Assessment of medical needs of animals
- Medical treatment and stabilization of animals
- Animal disease surveillance
- Zoonotic disease surveillance and public health assessment
- Technical assistance to assure food and water quality
- Hazard mitigation
- Biological and chemical terrorism surveillance
- Animal decontamination

Specialty Teams. The previous teams with specific skills—pharmacists, nurses, mental health providers, and experts on medical conditions such as crush injury and burn—are now organized into multidisciplinary specialty teams. Members of the team remain on the NDMS roster and are called up to provide additional services within DMATs when their specific skills are needed.

Federal Medical Stations. In addition to the teams described above, NDMS can deploy medical facilities called *federal medical stations* (FMS). Using buildings of opportunity (i.e., those which are readily available), an FMS contains equipment, up to 250 patient beds, medical supplies and pharmaceuticals to provide primary care, distribute medications, or hospitalize patients including those needing intensive care. These medical stations are staffed by the Rapid Deployment Force team described in the next section.

U.S. Public Health Service Commissioned Corps

The U.S. Public Health Service Commissioned Corps is composed of more than 6500 full-time officers and is one of the United States' seven uniformed services. Commissioned Corps officers come from many professional backgrounds, including physicians, nurses, pharmacists, dentists, dietitians, engineers, environmental health officers, health service officers, scientists, therapists, and veterinarians. As part of their duties, Commissioned Corps officers are trained and equipped to respond to public health crises, natural disasters, disease outbreaks, and terrorist attacks and also to serve on humanitarian assistance missions. Strategic and policy direction for the Commissioned Corps is provided by the Assistant Secretary for Health and the Office of the Surgeon General (OSG) oversees its operations. Commissioned Corps emergency response teams are managed by the OSG.

The Patient Protection and Affordable Care Act (PPACA), enacted March 23, 2010, created the Ready Reserve Corps (RRC), a new component of the Commissioned Corps. The RRC was established to enable part-time personnel to volunteer on short notice to assist regular Commissioned Corps personnel during times of public health emergencies. When called up, RRC members perform duties for assigned periods of time. During these same emergencies, full-time Commissioned Corps members may be on extended active duty.

RRC officers participate in routine training, are available and ready for calls to active duty during national emergencies and public health crises or to backfill critical positions left vacant during deployment of regular Corps members, and are available for service assignments in isolated and medically underserved communities. The PPACA law eliminated the previous Reserve Corps and now all officers called to extended active duty are part of the regular Commissioned Corps. (For more information about the RRC, check the U.S. Public Health Service Web site at http://www.usphs.gov.)

Office of Force Readiness and Deployment

Within the OSG, the OFRD has six teams that can be deployed to carry out responsibilities under ESF-8. These teams, created as part of the public health and medical assets under the NRF, are defined as follows:

Rapid Deployment Forces (RDFs): 105-member teams that staff the FMS and provide mass care, point of distribution operations, medical surge capacity, isolation and quarantine, prehospital triage and treatment, medical supply management and distribution, epidemiological investigations, worker health and safety, and animal health support. RDF teams are deployed within 24 hours.

Applied Public Health Teams: 40-member teams that function as public health departments in the field and provide epidemiology and surveillance, deliver preventive medical services, and monitor environmental concerns.

Mental Health Teams: 27-person teams that screen for suicide risk, stress reactions, substance abuse, and mental health disorders; diagnose and treat; and provide psychological first aid, crisis intervention, and limited counseling. The mental health teams are deployed within 48 hours.

Service Access Teams: Respond to the many needs following a major disaster. They can conduct needs assessments, develop plans with cultural sensitivity, advocate, and manage continuity, transition, psychosocial issues, and reintegration.

National Incident Support Teams: Provide continual needs assessments; support, provide direction and coordinate the distribution of assets deployed to the field; serve as liaison with state, tribal, and local officials; provide on-site incident management; respond to health and safety issues; and provide demobilization support.

Regional Incident Support Teams: Recruited from people who live and work in the affected region. Respond short term by conducting rapid needs assessments, support and direct response assets, serve as liaison with officials, provide on-site incident management, and respond to health and safety issues.

In addition, a Capital Area Provider Team has been organized to provide emergency medical care for events at the United States Capitol.

Operations/Deployment

Whereas USPHS has preexisting agreements, the surgeon general considers requests for RRC assistance. Once the mission requirements and the category, discipline, and specialty of RRC members are determined, OFRD will match the requirements against the qualifications of officers on that month's rotational "ready roster." Table 15 summarizes the activation and deployment process.

Centers for Disease Control and Prevention

At the CDC, the Office of Public Health Preparedness and Response (OPHPR) reports directly to the Director. OPHPR provides strategic direction, coordination,

Table 15. Ready Reserve Corps (RRC) Activation and Deployment Process

Activation Process	Request for Activation	Identification of Assets	Deployment
Office of Force Readiness and Deployment (OFRD) staff receive request for assistance	OFRD staff submits formal request for RRC activation to the surgeon general	Needs of the mission are matched with the skills and qualifications on the rotational ready roster	Agencies are informed officers from the roster are needed
RRC staff receive request	The surgeon general is briefed regarding the situation	Officers are identified	Officers are contacted
Evaluation of need— appropriate utilization of RRC	If the surgeon general concurs; RRC is activated		Supervisory release is obtained
			Travel orders and arrangements prepared; officer is deployed

and support for all of the CDC's terrorism preparedness and emergency response activities. The four divisions of OPHPR are as follows:

Division of Emergency Operations: Responsible for the overall coordination of CDC activities before and during public health emergencies; responsible for the CDC EOC, which maintains situational awareness of potential health threats round the clock, every day of the year; and is the centralized location for managing events when activated.

Division of State and Local Readiness: Administers the Public Health Emergency Preparedness (PHEP) cooperative agreement, which supports upgrading the ability of state and local health departments to effectively respond to all hazards with public health consequences.

Division of Strategic National Stockpile: Manages the SNS in the delivery of critical medical assets to the site of a national emergency.

Division of Select Agents and Toxins: Regulates the possession, use, and transfer of biological agents and select toxins that have the potential to pose a severe threat to public health and safety.

In close interaction with partners in the public health and health care communities, the CDC coordinates among multiple professions and the breadth of federal and state agencies involved in preparedness and response, including law, forensics, public safety, and national security. The CDC program focuses on a number of critical aspects of public health infrastructure. It seeks to improve disease surveillance and epidemiology, assure and support readiness at the state and local level, provide for the availability of key medical supplies including pharmaceuticals and vaccines, expand laboratory capacity, strengthen the ability for risk and emergency communication, protect vulnerable populations, improve the surge capacity of the public health workforce, enhance education and training programs, and support planning for infectious disease, such as smallpox or pandemic influenza. During an emergency, the CDC provides information for clinical diagnosis and medical management; as guidance to first responders; to inform the public health response; to facilitate the utilization of clinical and reference laboratory protocols; and to educate the public. Federal assistance may be provided directly to the states by the Epidemic Intelligence Service officers from the CDC or by experts from the Agency for Toxic Substances Disease Registry (ATSDR), among others. These federal public health personnel, stationed at regional offices of HHS, can quickly enter the field to conduct surveillance and rapid needs assessments.

Strategic National Stockpile

The SNS Program is managed by the CDC. The SNS Program maintains a national repository of antibiotics and life-support medications, antitoxins, chemical antidotes, vaccines, and medical supplies and equipment used to supplement state and local resources during a large-scale public health emergency. The materials in the SNS are intended to be drawn upon after states and localities have used their own supplies.

Each state's Emergency Management Office (SEMO), in partnership with the state DOH, is responsible for both the warehousing and logistics of the SNS distribution. Each state has a stockpile officer who is responsible for coordination with SEMO. Relationships have also been worked out with private companies regarding warehousing and distribution. Requests for predeployment of full or modified "push packs" can be considered in advance if a community is anticipating a major event, such as the requests made by Denver, Colorado, and St. Paul, Minnesota, respectively, in advance of the Democratic and Republican National Conventions in 2008.

The push packs are located in secure locations around the United States so that they can be delivered upon request within 12 or fewer hours. Each one weighs more than 50 tons and fills seven 53-foot trucks. The contents occupy 130 cargo containers and include pharmaceuticals, antibiotics, antitoxins, nerve agent antidotes, and other emergency medications, intravenous supplies, airway equipment, and so forth. Additional vendor-managed inventory is stored at pharmaceutical companies, which have the experience and manpower to deliver supplies quickly, and can be delivered within 24 to 36 hours. In addition, a state DOH can contact the CDC and request that only certain medications be delivered. In an emergency, responsible personnel at the state DOH should refer to the CDC's response program for guidance.

Structure and Operation of the State and Local Response

Every state has an emergency management agency, alternately called an *office of emergency preparedness.* Under the authority of the governor's office, the emergency management agency coordinates the deployment of state resources used in an emergency or disaster. This includes the resources of the many agencies of state government, such as health, public safety, and social services.

Mutual Aid

When the resources of a local jurisdiction are insufficient to respond to a given disaster, additional resources are requested from the surrounding region, a process commonly referred to as *mutual aid.* States can receive aid from neighbors through regional mutual aid compacts, or they can request federal resources, as described earlier in this chapter. The request of additional resources from the state or federal governments is called *escalating a response.*

States in many regions of the country have formed regional agreements through the Emergency Management Assistance Compact (EMAC). EMAC is a nonfederal, interstate agreement for mutual aid. Member states who are geographically close to disaster sites can respond rapidly through EMAC. The deployment of assets, including expertise, services, and goods, is coordinated in conjunction with the NRF. In an emergency, a member state uses EMAC's procedures to formally request assistance. Member states negotiate the costs and terms of providing assistance with the requesting state in formal written agreements. Intrastate and interstate mutual aid can be executed before a presidential disaster declaration or when a declaration is not necessary, providing both timely and cost-effective support.

A key lesson from the response to Hurricane Katrina and the subsequent flooding was that although collaboration with one's neighbors is necessary, it may not be sufficient to respond to the most far-reaching disasters. Communities need to increase mutual aid by broadening their geographic and traditional partnerships through cross-jurisdictional collaboration and regional consortia extending to agencies and organizations that were not previously linked. In some communities, there may be multiple agreements for mutual aid within the public health and medical community. Working with the local office of emergency management (OEM), public health agencies can serve as a clearinghouse and help coordinate the mutual aid pacts which affect the health of the community.

Emergency and Disaster Response Components

Based on response requirements identified by the state and approval by the FCO or designee, those responsible for ESF-8 coordinate with their counterpart state agencies. If directed, they may also coordinate with local agencies to provide the assistance required. Federal fire, rescue, and emergency medical responders arriving on the scene are integrated into the local response.

Although public safety agencies (e.g., emergency management, sheriff's office/ police department, fire department) are usually the local lead for the overall disaster response, optimally local health departments coordinate the many health-related agencies. The health department plans in advance how personnel will carry out their emergency response functions and assigns tasks to appropriate divisions within each department. Health departments work with the emergency management sectors, local hospitals, and other health care providers to develop an emergency response plan for public health systems. A well-designed preparedness program will include a hazard and vulnerability analysis, a risk assessment, a forecast of the probable health effects, a list of the resources needed, an analysis of resource availability, and the identification of vulnerable individuals in the community who will require additional assistance (e.g., children, the elderly, homebound, or disabled).

Public health professionals work with many community agencies in a multidisciplinary effort. In a local operation, the Red Cross has a credentialing system for those who respond in the field. The Red Cross provides sheltering, feeding, emergency first aid, family reunification, and distribution of emergency relief supplies to disaster victims. They also feed emergency workers, handle inquiries from concerned family members outside the disaster area, provide blood and blood products to disaster victims, and help those affected connect with other resources. Faith-based affiliated groups provide meals, clothing, or assistance during recovery and reconstruction efforts. Public works departments manage the water supply and cleanup. Social services agencies work with the displaced, deliver psychosocial services, and assure that vulnerable populations receive needed care. Importantly, if an agency's staff is not prepared, they will not be able to perform optimally. As part of any agency's preparedness, all staff should develop a preparedness plan for themselves and their families, so when they function as part of an organization's response during an emergency they will not need to begin putting personal plans in place.

Emergency Medical Services

Throughout most of the United States, EMS is provided by local agencies with oversight at the regional or state level. In most states, EMS is not provided directly by the state health department but is under its authority. The health department or other duly appointed governmental agency has training and regulatory jurisdiction over all EMS personnel regardless of their organizational affiliation. Some EMS systems are based in local fire departments, with ambulance and fire services operated side by side. Medics based in fire departments are often cross-trained in both firefighting and victim extrication. Some cities and counties operate independent EMS systems. In some parts of the United States, particularly the East Coast and in many rural areas, EMS is provided by volunteer independent rescue squads or volunteer ambulance squads, which may be connected with a volunteer fire department. Finally, some EMS services are operated from local hospitals.

The EMS system includes both prehospital and in-hospital components. The prehospital components start with a public access system through which a resident notifies authorities that a medical emergency exists. Where available, the 911 emergency telephone system is used for this access. A dispatch communications system is then used to send ambulance personnel or other emergency first responders in response to the person(s) in need.

EMTs and paramedics, trained to identify and treat medical emergencies and injuries, provide medical support while transporting patients to hospitals or other sources of definitive care. The medical care delivered by EMS is classified as basic or advanced life support. Most EMS providers are trained to provide care at the basic life support level (e.g., noninvasive first aid, stabilization for a broad variety of emergency conditions, and defibrillation for cardiac arrest victims). Paramedics provide more sophisticated diagnosis through advanced life support, with treatment following medical protocols both in the field and while being transferred to the hospital. Ground ambulances are the vehicle of choice for most transports, but helicopters, boats, or snow cats may be used under specific circumstances.

When planning for the delivery of disaster care through EMS, officials must consider response patterns that commonly occur. Initially, units can be dispatched in an atypical fashion. Often they will hear about the disaster on police scanners or via the news media rather than through normal dispatch. Assuming that too much help is better than too little, emergency units may respond on an unsolicited basis, sometimes from tens or even hundreds of miles away. In widespread disasters such as earthquakes, floods, tornadoes, and hurricanes, there may be no single site to which trained emergency units can be sent. Similarly, hospitals may obtain their initial information about what has happened in an unplanned way from the first arriving casualties or the news media.

Incident Command Systems

The emergency management field organizes its activities by sectors, such as fire, police, EMS, and health. All sectors use ICS for organizing their response to emergencies. Although ICS was originally developed in the 1970s as a way of responding to wildfires throughout California, this methodology now applies to all types of incidents, including hazardous material incidents, fires, transportation accidents, mass casualty incidents, search and rescue operations, and natural or technological disasters. ICS organizes its responses with a single person in charge and divides the tasks, functions, and resources into manageable components. Table 16 identifies some of the agencies involved in ICS and the resources that they bring.

The ICS organization is constructed with five major components: command, planning, operations, logistics, and finance/administration. Whether there is a routine emergency, a major event, or a catastrophic disaster, the management system employs all five components. The management system expands or contracts depending on the size of the event. An incident commander is responsible for

Table 16. Agencies Involved in the Incident Command System

Agency	Resources
Red Cross	Shelter personnel Communications equipment
Electric company	Repair personnel Trucks Repair equipment Communications equipment
Emergency management	Emergency Operations Center Equipment
Fire	Firefighters Fire apparatus
Law enforcement	Police officers Flares, blockades Communications equipment
Public health	Surveillance systems Public health personnel
Public works/highway department	Repair personnel Trucks Repair equipment Communications equipment

on-scene management, regardless of the size or complexity of the event. Incident management encompasses the following:

- Establishing command
- Ensuring responder safety
- Assessing incident priorities
- Determining operational objectives
- Developing and implementing an IAP
- Developing an appropriate organizational structure
- Maintaining a manageable span of control
- Managing incident resources
- Coordinating overall emergency activities
- Coordinating the activities of outside agencies
- Authorizing the release of information to the media
- Monitoring and recording costs

The sector responsible for public health services (including non-EMS health care providers, such as hospitals, urgent care centers, and health departments) faces several challenges when integrating their efforts into this coordinated response. Although NIMS requires all agencies to use ICS, until recently in the evolution of emergency management, ICS was a preexisting management structure that may have planned and practiced for incidents without any input from the broader public health community. Public health agencies must continue to find a "fit" with this preexisting response structure. Second, health care systems draw patients from broader geographic areas than the political jurisdiction in which they are located. As a result, coordination is required between the prehospital system and the public health delivery system, which may have a broader jurisdictional authority in its day-to-day practice.

Incident Command System Concepts and Principles

Many jurisdictions establish and maintain an EOC as part of their community's emergency preparedness program. ICS and EOC function together but at different levels of responsibility. ICS is responsible for on-scene activities, whereas the operations center is responsible for the communitywide response.

The organization of ICS response is modular and develops from a top-down structure at any incident. Several communications networks may be established, depending on the size of the incident, but all communication is integrated. ICS employs a unified command whereby all agencies with responsibility for the incident, including public health, establish a common set of objectives and strategies. All involved agencies help to determine overall objectives, plan for joint operational activities, and maximize the use of assigned resources. Under unified command, the incident functions under a single, coordinated plan.

Effective response depends on all personnel using common terminology, as defined by ICS. The incident commander will give a specific name to the incident (such as "Ground Zero" for the bombing at this location). All response personnel use the same name for all personnel, equipment, and facilities. Radio transmissions should not use agency specific codes or terms but rather the language that everyone will understand.

An IAP for the local response to the emergency is organized by the Planning Section Chief with tactical input from the Operations Section Chief. In presidentially declared disasters where ESF-8 is being implemented, the IRCT described previously communicates the federal goals for the deployment of health and medical resources through a federal IAP.

Public Health Incident Command

Departments of health organize their internal emergency response structure using incident command principles. The cornerstone of a Public Health Incident Command System (PHICS) is to define the role, responsibility, chain of command, and job title of the person(s) carrying out each function that will be necessary to manage an incident. Table 17 lists the types of roles and responsibilities that might be predefined in departments of health. The goals are to (1) provide direct public health services as required by the emergency; (2) support the response of federal, state, local, and international health systems in public health emergencies; (3) support the deployment of health assets in response to or anticipation of a public health emergency; and (4) provide real-time situational information to and from

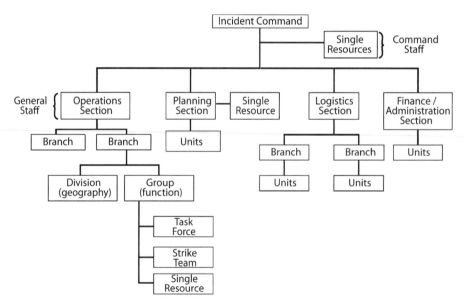

Figure 3. The Incident Command System

From Federal Emergency Management Agency (FEMA). Incident Command System: Introduction and Overview. Washington, DC: FEMA. Available at: http://water.epa.gov/infrastructure/watersecurity/upload/ICS.ppt#256,1,Incident Command System.

Table 17. Function, Roles, Responsibilities, and Chain of Command for Departments of Health

Function	Role	Responsibility	Chain of Command
Health commissioner ("Commissioner") or departmental director	Incident commander responsible for overall agency response	Declares emergency Authorizes department of health (DOH) emergency operations center (EOC) activation Authorizes allocation of resources Communicates with mayor/governor and office of emergency management (OEM) EOC coordinator Principal departmental spokesperson to media Identifies need for consultants on technical issues Authorizes requests to the Centers for Disease Control and Prevention (CDC) for assistance Authorizes requests for mutual aid from other DOH jurisdictions	Reports to mayor/governor Reports to Commissioner
Senior managers	Counsel and assist Commissioner and/or DOH EOC members	Responds to request for assistance from Commissioner and DOH EOC	
Deputy commissioner		Senior advisor to Commissioner on policy decisions	Reports to Commissioner
	Senior advisor to EOC coordinator on operational decisions		
		Assumes Commissioner's role in Commissioner's absence	

(continued on next page)

Table 17. (*continued*)

Function	Role	Responsibility	Chain of Command
Public affairs		Liaison with press offices of mayor, OEM, and other agencies Coordinates press and public requests for information Drafts press releases Assists in creating and disseminating public information and educational messages Monitors press coverage of emergency Compiles/prepares material for Web site posting	Reports to Commissioner or deputy commissioner
Governmental and community affairs		Liaison with non-DOH governmental and community agencies/parties Notifies these agencies/parties of new developments or responses to emergency Assists in gaining cooperation of local officials for DOH activities	Reports to Commissioner or deputy commissioner
Legal affairs		Monitors departmental activities and advises regarding legal issues Reviews documents related to emergency activities (e.g., declaration by Commissioner)	Reports to Commissioner
Incident-specific experts		Provide expertise and advice to guide policymaking around emergencies: —Exposure, vector. and disease-specific knowledge —Training —Health and safety —Mental health	Reports to Commissioner or deputy commissioner

(*continued on next page*)

Table 17. (*continued*)

Function	Role	Responsibility	Chain of Command
DOH EOC coordinator	Coordinates DOH response during emergency Responsible for all operational aspects of the response Oversees EOC during activation	Directs the DOH EOC Oversees emergency committees Oversees response to OEM activity requests Maintains documentation of key elements of the response and compiles final report Assesses need to request outside assistance (e.g., from the CDC) Responds to requests and needs of senior managers Synthesizes data from all sources Raises policy issues to Commissioner	Reports to Commissioner Receives input from senior emergency managers, committee representatives and senior managers
Senior emergency manager	Coordinates administrative and logistical operations of the DOH EOC	Communicates with DOH EOC coordinator Coordinates committee activities Communicates with DOH liaison at OEM EOC (report and job requests, transmits information and dispositions) Assures ongoing rotation of staff at DOH EOC and OEM EOC Assists/coordinates mobilization of staff to carry out committee activities Compiles and distributes manual of operations to EOC participants (staffing schedule, contact numbers, protocols)	Reports to EOC coordinator Receives input from committee representatives and EOC liaison

(*continued on next page*)

Table 17. (*continued*)

Function	Role	Responsibility	Chain of Command
EOC liaison	DOH representative at OEM EOC Liaison between OEM EOC and DOH EOC	Staffs DOH workstation at OEM EOC Follows developments in emergency situation and in citywide response and provides briefing to DOH EOC Receives OEM requests for DOH activities and transmits to senior emergency manager (at DOH EOC) Informs OEM of DOH activities, responses, and recommendations Interacts with other agency representatives at OEM	Reports to senior emergency manager Receives input from OEM and senior emergency managers
Emergency committee representatives	Represent emergency committees at DOH EOC	Staff DOH EOC Provide policy guidance from OEM via senior emergency manager Accept action requests from OEM via senior emergency manager Accept request for data or activity orders from EOC coordinator Transmit information and requests for data or activity orders from EOC coordinator Report committee activities and information to EOC coordinator and senior emergency manager	Report to EOC coordinator and senior emergency manager Receive input from committee response coordinators
Committee response coordinators	Coordinate the emergency committee activities that comprise the DOH response to emergencies	Oversee activities of emergency committees Mobilize necessary workforce Receive information and job requests from committee representatives at DOH EOC Regularly report data and developments to committee representatives at DOH EOC Report needs to committee representatives at DOH EOC	Report to committee representatives at DOH EOC Receive input from committee members

(*continued on next page*)

Table 17. (*continued*)

Function	Role	Responsibility	Chain of Command
Epidemiology surveillance		Research specific topic	
		Provide background information	
		Conduct field epidemiological investigations	
		Identify and monitor existing surveillance and data systems	
		Establish new surveillance systems	
		Assemble field teams	
		Develop questionnaires/ abstraction forms/ information sheets	
		Liaison with hospital or other field personnel	
		Collect data; establish databases; analyze data; develop recommendations for policy	
Medical clinical		Research specific topic	
		Provide background information	
		Prepare recommendations/ advice on clinical aspects of emergency:	
		—Public safety issues	
		—Worker safety issues	
		—Disinfection or decontamination issues	
		—Clinical information and training of community physicians	
		—Development of prevention and treatment messages	
		Establish and staff prophylaxis or treatment distribution centers	
		Staff DOH clinics engaged in clinical activities related to emergency	
		Liaison with Office of Chief Medical Examiner	
		Provide clinical backup to shelter committee activities	

(continued on next page)

Table 17. (*continued*)

Function	Role	Responsibility	Chain of Command
Environmental		Research specific topic	
		Provide background information	
		Prepare advice/recommenda-tions regarding public health threat, sample collection, evacuation, reoccupation	
		Collect samples	
		Collaborate with fire, HAZMAT, Department of Environmental Protection	
Shelter		Mobilize nurses to staff Red Cross clinics	
		Provide medical backup to clinics	
Operations		Provide resources to facilitate emergency committee activities:	
		—Transportation	
		—Communication	
		—Facility issues	
		—Security	
		—Human resources regarding mobilizing workforce	
		—Printing	
		Coordinate telephone hotlines for public and provider information	
Information management		Facilitate computing issues during emergency:	
		—Web site posting	
		—Field-to-HQ data transmission	
		—Database management	
		—Mapping and geographic information systems	

(*continued on next page*)

Table 17. (*continued*)

Function	Role	Responsibility	Chain of Command
Laboratories		Provide recommendations regarding specimen types and handling Accept specimens for testing Ensure rapid transport to reference labs if testing not available at DOH lab Perform testing Coordinate with epidemiology/surveillance regarding data entry Liaison with outside labs regarding testing and data reporting	
DOH EOC	Integrated operations center for organizing and facilitating DOH response activities during emergencies	Provides accurate, timely information concerning the emergency to policymakers and public affairs officials Mobilizes DOH resources to respond to emergencies Communicates with and receives requests from OEM regarding data and activities Serves as a forum for integrating and synthesizing data as they come in from the emergency committees, OEM, EOC, senior managers	Staff: EOC coordinator, senior managers, emergency committee representatives Support staff as needed Senior managers and consultants as needed

federal, state, local, and international agencies, organizations, and field teams. The operationalization of PHICS includes the establishment of an agency EOC and each of the supporting units. The specific components of the EOC may vary from agency to agency. On a local level, typical units may include operations (including alert, notification, and escalation), epidemiology and surveillance, medical/clinical response teams, specialized laboratories and subject matter experts, environmental consultation and response, management information services, and administration.

When a PHICS is activated, personnel must know what their role is and what they will be asked to do. Often, much of a disaster response is maintaining the daily functions of an agency. Most personnel will be doing their usual job, though possibly at a different time of day, in a different location, and with different people. The tasks and required skills will be more specific as the responsibilities become more administrative. Agency administration should ensure that each staff knows the task group they are assigned to and the responsibilities of that group, and how and where they get information about their responsibilities during an emergency. Although many skills are translatable (for example, clerical personnel can answer phones and provide directions as instructed and drivers can transport people and materials), some require additional training (such as chart abstractors who need specific skills in identifying disease-specific indicators).

Hospital Incident Command System

Hospital Preparedness

Earlier, we discussed the prehospital component of an emergency medical system. The in-hospital system components include definitive care, usually delivered in the emergency department of a hospital, often by emergency physicians and certified emergency nurses who specialize in emergency medical care. Hospitals face challenges similar to public health in becoming integrated within the community's ICS.

Hospitals must meet explicit standards for comprehensive emergency management as part of their accreditation by The Joint Commission. The Joint Commission standards mandate that hospitals marry the range of activities regularly conducted by the emergency management community with the traditional tasks of providing health care. Hospital disaster plans must be applicable to all hazards. Because The Joint Commission has deeming authority, or the ability to determine compliance with regulations, for the Centers for Medicare and Medicaid Services (CMS), all of their standards are consistent with CMS requirements.

As of 2009, emergency management is a key standard for Joint Commission accreditation and is now structured as a discrete chapter in the accreditation manual with 12 standards. All previous standards have been reorganized and renumbered as follows:

- Foundation for the Emergency Operations Plan (EM.01.01.01)
- The Plan for Response and Recovery

  ○ General Requirements (EM.02.01.01)
  ○ Specific Requirements

    - Communications (EM.02.02.01)
    - Resources and Assets (EM.02.02.03)
    - Security and Safety (EM.02.02.05)
    - Staff (EM.02.02.07)
    - Utilities (EM.02.02.09)
    - Patients (EM.02.02.11)
    - Disaster Volunteers

      ◇ Volunteer Licensed Independent Practitioners (EM.02.02.13)
      ◇ Volunteer Practitioners (EM.02.02.15)

- Evaluation (EM.03.01.01, EM.03.01.03)

In addition, NIMS establishes 17 elements that hospitals must comply with, including a functioning ICS structure. Hospitals establish a system of incident command specific for their organizational structure known as HICS. Use of incident command improves a facility's ability to plan, respond, and recover from emergencies. HICS focuses on how a hospital organizes internally by establishing a chain of command with one person in charge and using job action sheets with predefined responsibilities. HICS requires that hospitals conduct a hazard analysis (as discussed in Chapter 5 and Appendix I); establish mutual aid; coordinate with the local OEM; and maintain comprehensive documentation on how decisions were made, where patients went, how patients were tracked, and how reimbursement was obtained. These standards help to protect hospitals from claims of liability after a disaster.

The National Fire Protection Association (NFPA) 99 and 1600 establish minimum criteria for health care facilities and standardize the coordination of disaster management and business continuity within communities. The NFPA standards were updated in 2010 to ensure NIMS compliance. Hospitals must follow federal procedures to be reimbursed for disaster-related response, and administrators should review the requirements of the Stafford Act, The Joint Commission, and NFPA 1600. The applicable 2010 The Joint Commission standards are provided in full in Appendix H.

Hospitals have to meet other regulations to be prepared. To fulfill requirements of the U.S. Occupational Safety and Health Administration (OSHA), hospitals have to develop and implement an emergency action plan (EAP) to report fires and other emergencies. An EAP must include (1) evacuation policy and procedures, including emergency escape procedures and routes (floor plans, maps, and areas of refuge) and an alarm system to alert employees of emergencies; (2) name, title, and contacts for additional information; (3) procedures to shut down the clinical operation; (4) firefighting or other essential services; and (5) rescue and medical duties. OSHA also recommends the assignment of an area to assemble, procedures for accountability, establishing an alternative communications center and system for document management and data backup. OSHA recommends that hospital staff be trained on the types of emergencies that could occur and the proper course of action; a review of who is in charge and the process of incident command; staff roles and responsibilities; the process of notification, warning and communication; emergency response procedures; evacuation, shelter, and accountability; the location and use of emergency equipment; emergency shutdown procedures; first aid and cardiopulmonary resuscitation; respiratory protection; and methods to prevent unauthorized access.

OSHA has issued a best practices document to guide hospitals who are receiving victims of incidents involving hazardous materials. It is assumed that hospitals will have little or no warning before patients who have been exposed to toxic materials will arrive in emergency departments. OSHA requires Level B protection or self-contained breathing apparatus when patients may be exposed to unknown substances. (This detailed program can be found at http://www.osha.gov/dts/osta/bestpractices/html/hospital_firrstreceivers.html.)

When patients go directly to hospitals, rather than being evaluated by first providers in the field, hospitals have to consider decontamination of patients (gross or secondary) in the event that the incident involves hazardous materials or biological or radiological exposures. Preparedness requires the purchase and stocking of personal protective equipment (PPE) so that providers can perform patient care. PPE must be appropriate to the risk and be accepted by the users, and hospitals have to provide training on the use of PPE so that providers are familiar with it in advance. Hospitals have to establish a mechanism for medical surveillance and fit testing so that all personnel are ready to use PPE quickly in an emergency.

The ability to respond to a large influx of patients is a challenging one for U.S. hospitals, most of which operate daily with a thin margin of staff and supplies. The Agency for HealthCare Research and Quality (AHRQ) has developed models for Personal Protective Equipment, Decontamination, Isolation/Quarantine, and Laboratory Capacity (models are available at http://www.ahrq.gov/research/ devmodels). AHRQ has other tools and resources that can be used in response and recovery efforts, such as a computer model to aid the planning for antibiotic dispensing and vaccination campaigns. Based on the number of staff and the estimated number of patients to be treated, this resource can be used to calculate the specific needs of local health care systems.

Volunteers

The Citizen Corps is a national volunteer network that improves a community's resilience by involving citizens in all-hazards emergency preparedness. The Citizen Corps works to make communities better prepared by training and involving volunteers for response to public health disasters. One specialized component of the Citizens Corps is the Medical Reserve Corps (MRC).

Medical Reserve Corps

The MRC is a federally sponsored program of the OSG. The MRC provides an organized way for medical and public health volunteers from a community to supplement the manpower of existing local health and medical personnel by offering their skills and expertise during local emergencies. The MRC is designed to provide the appropriate training of these community volunteers and the needed organizational structure for deployment. The MRC can also be activated for nonemergency public health services, such as immunization or blood drives. MRC units have been organized through governmental offices, faith-based groups, public health offices, hospitals, and other nongovernmental organizations.

There are ten MRC regions in the United States, each with a variable number of local MRC units. Coordination occurs between the state and local MRCs and MRC regions. MRC units at the local level are responsible for recruiting and training volunteers to match specific community needs. Although MRC units are organized to supplement local response, they have been deployed outside their home areas in recent disasters.

Most MRCs are integrated with local health care, public health, or emergency management organizations. In communities which have established Citizen Corps Councils (which organize programs of volunteerism at a community level) it is important that the planners and managers of a local MRC unit have a working relationship with this council.

Nationally established criteria that guide the registration of MRC units include the following:

- Affiliation with an appropriate local organization
- Identification of MRC unit leader(s)
- Partnership with local and community stakeholder groups
- Verification of members' credential(s) (i.e., professional licenses/certificates)
- Plans for establishing, implementing, and sustaining unit
- Participation in public health, preparedness, and emergency response activities
- Active involvement in the local, state, regional, and national MRC network

MRC units are funded from local and state resources, federal agencies such as the DHS Office of Domestic Preparedness and Citizen Corps, and through the CDC and the Health Resources and Services Administration.

Emergency System for Advance Registration of Volunteer Health Professionals

ESAR-VHP is a federal program created to establish standardized volunteer registration programs for disasters and public health emergencies for national deployment. Each local organization verifies the identity and credentials of health professionals in advance so that they are ready to volunteer during disasters and public health emergencies. Once verified, ESAR-VHP volunteers are available to be deployed nationally through mutual aid mechanisms.

Currently licensed and credentialed health professionals can volunteer with ESAR-VHP. Registration varies from state to state. Some states use an online, electronic registration system whereas other states may require volunteers to register via paper applications. Some states may accept both electronic and paper registrations. Volunteers may be entitled to workers' compensation if injured while participating in an emergency response and liability protections will vary by state. Check your state's ESAR-VHP Web site for information about the protections available in your state.

Liability

Liability is an issue that each locality must investigate thoroughly. Participation in a local MRC or registration with a state ESAR-VHP program does not result in the recognition of professional licensure by other states. All states have some form of "good Samaritan" legislation, although this legislation may be limited in its protections. Protection is also found through the Volunteer Protection Act (VPA; codified at 42 U.S.C. § 14501 et seq.). VPA, which provides qualified immunity from liability for volunteers, is helpful because it provides baseline legal protection where there is a wide variety of state laws. Further, the Uniform Emergency Volunteer Health Practitioners Act (UEVHPA) facilitates the registration, deployment and recognition of licensed health professionals during emergencies. As of this writing, 11 states had enacted UEVHPA: Arkansas, Colorado, District of Columbia, Indiana, Kentucky, Louisiana, New Mexico, North Dakota, Tennessee, Oklahoma, and the U.S. Virgin Islands.

Hospital Credentialing of Volunteers

The RRC and DMATs are two systems in which the process of credentialing medical volunteers is "federalized," whereby the federal government waives state licensing procedures and also assumes liability. However, until those resources are in place, hospitals and public health agencies might have to credential staff in a rapid manner. Experience shows that following a disaster, the community is deluged with calls from volunteers, many of whom are physicians and nurses looking to help. As part of their overall disaster plan, hospitals and public health agencies should have a procedure to manage and verify the credentials of professional volunteer staff. (Coordinate planning with your state licensing boards, professional societies, and regional hospitals, as they may have developed a uniform way to verify current licensure, specialty, and hospital status of professionals.) Medical staff bylaws should also be amended to allow for emergency credentialing in disaster situations, and should designate who will be responsible for credentialing and overall clinical direction and supervision of volunteers. Practitioners should not be granted emergency privileges for procedures that they are not credentialed to perform at the hospitals where they are fully credentialed, and that emergency privileges terminate on their own when the disaster is under control and the hospital's emergency management plan is no longer activated. The 2009 Joint Commission standards (Volunteer Licensed Independent Practitioners, EM.02.02.13, and Volunteer Practitioners, EM.02.02.15) define the process for granting of emergency privileges when a hospital's emergency operations plan has been activated and the organization is unable to handle patient needs.

    To grant emergency (or disaster) privileges to licensed independent practitioners who are not members of that hospital's medical staff, the following are necessary:

- The emergency operations plan has been activated
- The hospital is unable to manage its patients' immediate needs
- The individual(s) responsible and alternatives for granting emergency privileges are identified (chief executive officer or medical staff president or his or her designee[s]), as are the responsibilities of the individual(s) accountable for granting emergency privileges
- Mechanisms to manage the activities of individuals who receive emergency privileges and to allow staff to readily identify these individuals are developed
- A privileging process, identical to the process established under the medical staff bylaws for granting temporary privileges, is established with a verification procedure

- The chief executive officer or president of the medical staff or his or her designee(s) may grant emergency privileges upon presentation of a current valid photo identification issued by a state, federal, or regulatory agency and any of the following:

  - A current picture identification card from a health care organization that clearly identifies professional designation
  - Identification indicating that the individual is a member of DMAT, MRC, ESAR-VHP, or other recognized state or federal response organization or group
  - Identification indicating that the individual has been granted authority to render patient care in emergency circumstances, such authority having been granted by a federal, state, or municipal entity
  - Confirmation by a licensed independent practitioner currently privileged by the hospital or by a staff member with personal knowledge of the volunteer practitioner's ability to act as a licensed independent practitioner during a disaster

The plan for credentialing physicians in an emergency should provide for clear identification of these practitioners. Identification should be easily legible, including a picture, their name and service, and the words "Disaster Privileges" in a different color. In the event of a power outage, a Polaroid camera and a label maker can be used, as can wrist bands.

The management plan should provide precise recordkeeping of who was credentialed and their profession and specialty. Employees from the medical staff office should be identified to manage the emergency credentialing, and to orient the volunteers and familiarize them with hospital operations and the nature of the emergency services needed.

Verify and check the following, or check similar agencies and databases that operate in your state:

- National Practitioner Data Bank
- State medical license
- Office of Professional Medical Conduct
- Office of Inspector General
- Photo identification

Finally, request the hospital where current privileges are held to confirm current active membership and privileges, check the American Medical Association or medical specialty profile, and require a signed statement from the non–staff physician attesting to the facts and allowing the hospital to obtain the necessary documents.

Costs, Funding, Reimbursement for Disaster Preparedness and Response

For public and nonprofit entities, the Stafford Act provides for federal reimbursement of some expenses associated with the effects of the disaster and disaster response. This funding is known as public assistance. FEMA's public assistance grant program provides assistance to state, tribal, and local governments and some nonprofit organizations to enable communities to respond and recover quickly from disasters receiving a presidential declaration. Through the public assistance program, FEMA provides disaster grants for removal of debris, emergency protective measures, and the repair, replacement, or restoration of disaster-damaged public or certain nonprofit facilities. The public assistance program also provides aid for hazard mitigation measures during the recovery process. These federal grants will pay at least 75% of the eligible cost and the grantee (usually the state) determines how the remaining share (up to 25%) is split among the subgrantees.

Disaster Assistance

Individuals, families, and businesses can receive direct assistance where property has been damaged or destroyed and losses are not covered by insurance. This money is intended to help pay for critical expenses that cannot be covered in other ways. Disaster assistance will provide money for temporary housing, to repair damage to a primary residence, or replace a destroyed home where these costs are not covered by insurance, or in remote locations specified by FEMA where no other type of housing assistance is possible, provide money for the construction of a home. Some housing assistance funds are available through FEMA's Individuals and Households Program. However, most disaster assistance from the federal government is in the form of loans administered by the Small Business Administration. In addition, money is also available for necessary expenses or serious needs as determined by FEMA such as disaster-related medical, dental, funeral, and burial costs.

Title 44 of the Code of Federal Regulations (CFR; Emergency Management and Assistance) contains the rules, policies, and procedures regarding the administration of federal disaster assistance programs by FEMA. Part 206 of the 44 CFR, Subparts C, and G-L, contain most of the regulations applicable to FEMA's disaster assistance program. FEMA coordinates that process and provides the forms that must be submitted for reimbursement. When local governments receive the support of any federal assets, the federal government absorbs the costs in the initial hours of the response. However, local governments are expected to reimburse the federal government for assets provided thereafter through a cost-sharing formula. In extraordinary cases, the president may choose to adjust the cost share or waive it for a specified time period. The presidential declaration notes any cost-share waiver, and a DHS–State Agreement is signed further stipulating the division of costs among federal, state, and local governments and other conditions for receiving assistance.

The public assistance program will reimburse for damage to infrastructure, for equipment, and for overtime for personnel. It will not reimburse for providing patient care as part of the normal course of doing business. The public assistance program will not reimburse for service eligible for funding under another federal program, such as the VA. All public health agencies should obtain a copy of the rules, including the details of documentation necessary for reimbursement. Local agencies should identify what aid is available through their state. Some have a state-funded reimbursement mechanism, similar to the federal assistance program, which may reimburse local health departments for a percentage of costs for medical emergencies through public health law. However, total reimbursement from state and federal sources cannot exceed 100%. It is important to ensure that there is no duplication, as disaster victims are responsible for repayment of federal assistance duplicated by private insurance or other federal programs. Finally, if an event is declared a terrorist attack, localities should realize that commercial insurance policies may deny reimbursement because care was required because of "an act of war."

Currently, there are a variety of funding opportunities to help communities prepare for disasters. Grant listings have been integrated at a DHS Web site (available at http://www.dhs.gov/grants) and the application process has been streamlined. PAHPA provides for cooperative agreements and grants to state and local governments to improve health security. Grants can also be awarded to hospitals, clinical laboratories, and universities for improvements in real-time disease detection. The Catalogue of Federal Domestic Assistance (available at https://www.cfda.gov) links to a variety of federal funding programs. Table 18 summarizes other federal funding opportunities.

Table 18. Federal Funding Opportunities

Source	Web Site
Government funding	http://www.grants.gov
CDC	http://www.cdc.gov/od/pgo/funding/grantmain.htm
CDC ATSDR Federal Assistance Funding Book	http://www.atsdr.cdc.gov/funding.html
FEMA Fire Service	http://www.usfa.fema.gov/fire-service/grants/federal/g_assist.shtm
Hospital Preparedness Program	http://www.phe.gov/preparedness/planning/hpp/Pages/default.aspx

Chapter 4

Disaster-Related Surveillance and Emergency Information Systems

S urveillance and exchange of gathered information guides emergency response as well as long-term planning. This chapter examines disaster epidemiology, emergency information systems (EIS) throughout the disaster event, public health surveillance, and geographic information systems (GIS) in preparing for and responding to disaster.

Public Health Role

Develop, apply, and evaluate tools, methods, guidance, and protocols to improve investigation of public health emergencies at the federal, state, and local levels:

- Describe and monitor medical, public health, and psychosocial effects of disaster
- Identify changes in agents and host factors
- Detect changes in health practices
- Detect illness or injuries, including sudden changes in disease occurrence
- Detect, investigate, and analyze collected data to identify necessary interventions
- Monitor long-term disease trends
- Provide evidence for establishment of response protocols
- Provide information about probable adverse health effects for decision-making
- Investigate rumors
- Determine needs and match resources in affected communities
- Evaluate how personnel and partners are conducting surveillance activities for effective practice and the improvement of surveillance activities
- Inform evaluation of the effectiveness of response activities

Disaster Epidemiology and Surveillance

Epidemiology can be used to investigate the public health and medical consequences of disasters. The aim of disaster epidemiology is to ascertain strategies for the prevention of both acute and chronic health events as a result of the occurrence of natural or technological hazards. Primary prevention seeks to prevent disaster-related deaths, injuries, or illness before they occur (for example, to evacuate residents prior to landfall of a hurricane). With secondary prevention, the goal is to mitigate the health consequences of a disaster (such as by providing education about injury control during the cleanup and recovery period). Tertiary prevention minimizes the effects of disease and disability among those already ill (for example, by setting up evaluation units where the chronically ill can obtain access to short-term pharmaceuticals when their usual source of care has been disrupted).

Disaster epidemiology includes rapid needs assessment, disease control strategies, assessment of the availability and use of health services, surveillance systems for both descriptive and analytic investigations of disease and injury, and research on risk factors contributing to disease, injury, or death. Although this chapter focuses on surveillance and the tools used to conduct it, some of the systems discussed are used in other epidemiology tasks.

In disasters, surveillance concentrates on the incidence, prevalence, and severity of illness or injury as a result of ecological changes, changes in endemic levels of disease, population displacement, loss of usual source of health care, overcrowding, breakdowns in sanitation, and disruption of public utilities. Surveillance also monitors increases in communicable diseases, including vector-borne, waterborne, and person-to-person transmission. Data for disaster surveillance are collected through EIS. EIS are a form of active surveillance and complement traditional reporting mechanisms that may not be fully functional following a disaster.

Emergency Information Systems

EIS amass data about the effects of a disaster during the impact phase, response phase, and early stages of recovery. EIS consist of integrated sets of files, procedures, and equipment for the storage, manipulation, and retrieval of information. The data collected through EIS are used to make decisions about the services that are needed postimpact, such as emergency and short-term relief, as well as long-term planning for recovery and reconstruction. EIS personnel examine how the everyday relationship between people and their physical and social environments has been disrupted by disasters, such as by lost productivity, as well as emerging problems or problems under control.

Data must be collected rapidly, sometimes under adverse circumstances. The quick processing, analysis and interpretation ensures a timely flow of information to inform an appropriate response. To enhance the ability to analyze the information, surveillance activities must be based on standardized data with the procedures established and teams trained in advance. Table 19 summarizes the types and uses of data collected through EIS.

Disaster Surveillance

To determine actions important for a public health response, managers assess concern about public health issues and the necessity of monitoring disaster-related morbidity and mortality before initiating EIS. Considerations include whether existing systems could be used (preferable as a result of the level of resources required for active surveillance, though often not possible because of lost infrastructure); sufficient personnel are available, including volunteers such as medical, nursing, or public health students; the data are needed to influence the public health response;

Table 19. Emergency Information Systems Data Collection

Type of Data	Uses of Data
Deaths	Assess the magnitude of disaster Evaluate effectiveness of disaster preparedness Evaluate adequacy of warning system
Casualties	Estimate needs for emergency care Evaluate preimpact planning and preparedness Evaluate adequacy of warning systems
Morbidity	Estimate type and volume of immediate medical relief needed Evaluate appropriateness of relief Identify populations at risk Assess needs for further planning
Health needs	Prioritize services delivered Prioritize groups most affected Evaluate adequacy of resources
Public health resources	Estimate the type and volume of needed supplies, equipment, and services Evaluate appropriateness of relief Assess needs for further planning
Donated goods	Estimate the type and volume of needed supplies, equipment, and services Evaluate appropriateness of relief Assess needs for further planning
Hazards	Monitor health events, disease, injuries, hazards, exposures, or risk factors Support early warning system to forecast occurrence of a disaster event by monitoring conditions that may signal the event

and data collection can be funded, either by the participating institutions or externally, such as support through the Robert T. Stafford Disaster Relief and Emergency Assistance Act of 1988 (Stafford Act).

When using existing systems, such as those established to track reportable diseases, EIS personnel must ensure they have the capacity to provide information that is both adequate and timely. Existing hospital-based data may provide an accurate representation of morbidity attributable to the disaster. Data can be obtained from mobile care sites and clinics. All health care facilities may be asked to participate in a syndromic surveillance system, or, given finite resources, selected sites may be chosen to provide a reasonable representation of the health effects being monitored. At a minimum, hospitals should report on surge capacity (beds, staffing, supply needs, availability), event-related data (e.g., numbers of patients seen, waiting to be seen, unidentified, deceased), and patient locator information (for example, name, sex, and date of service for patients seen as a result of the disaster). When there are concerns about infectious disease, syndrome-specific morbidity data may be requested from all sites providing care.

Community clinicians play a key role in identifying and reporting cases, educating patients about infectious risks, and preventing the spread of infections. Interventions to improve detection and to ensure that information is reported quickly and correctly include outreach to both hospital-based and community providers through educational forums for clinicians, laboratorians, and trainees; health department mailings; health alerts by broadcast fax and e-mail; a provider portal, the Health Alert Network; and a public Web site. Although the ability to collect surveillance information has expanded tremendously in the past few years, if existing systems do not meet the adequate and timely standard, temporary sentinel surveillance systems can be organized for the duration of the emergency period or at any point before, during, or after the disaster. To expedite EIS, epidemiologists need portable computers with access to other data reporting systems, such as the National Electronic Disease Surveillance System (NEDSS), and existing electronic disease reporting. Data should be collected using the standardized protocols established by the Centers for Disease Control and Prevention (CDC), including veterinary inputs. The information should be presented in a simple format, in a manner easily understood by both public and emergency management officials. Table 20 lists some of the numerous surveillance systems in operation.

Establishing a Postimpact Surveillance System

Outcomes anticipated from a specific disaster must be identified initially (e.g., crush injuries from earthquakes, diarrheal diseases from floods). From a sample of the disaster-affected population, epidemiologists determine associations between exposure and outcome (disease variables) by identifying demographic, biological, chemical, physical, or behavioral factors associated with outcomes of death, illness, or injury. The incidence of diseases endemic to an area prior to the disaster event would be expected to rise as a result of population displacement, increased population density, the interruption of existing public health programs, and breakdown in sanitation and hygiene. Examples of such exposure-outcome relationships in disaster settings are included in Table 21.

To ensure uniformity, case definitions must be established in advance for the outcomes that will be measured. Without standard case definitions and data, unusual occurrences of diseases might not be detected, trends cannot be accurately monitored, and the effectiveness of intervention activities cannot be easily evaluated. Within the definitions, detection thresholds must be flexible enough to respond to changing risk levels and priorities of detection. Criteria for evaluating morbidity include clinical signs and symptoms, results from laboratory tests that confirm a diagnosis, and epidemiological limits on person, place, and time. Four case classifications are used: confirmed, probable, suspect, or not a case because it failed to fulfill the criteria for confirmed, probable, or suspect cases. In addition, sources of comparison data, such as incidence of a disease in the same month or time period during prior years, should be identified for use in the epidemiological analysis. The

Table 20. Surveillance Systems

System	Sponsor	Function
BioSense	Centers for Disease Control and Prevention (CDC)	Monitors and rapidly identifies possible health emergencies through continuous scanning of medical information from hospital emergency rooms and pharmacies
Biowatch	Laboratory Response Network	Uses air samplers to test for threat agents
Electronic Surveillance System for Early Notification of Community-Based Epidemics (ESSENCE)	Department of Defense (DOD)	Early notification of epidemics by monitoring health data to identify and control epidemics
EMERGency IDNET	CDC	Multicenter emergency department based network for research of infectious diseases; a goal is to identify emerging infections in emergency department patients
Geosentinel	International Society of Travel Medicine and the CDC	Conduct syndromic surveillance in international travel medicine clinics
Global Emerging Infections Surveillance (GEIS)	DOD	Protects DOD health care beneficiaries through domestic and international surveillance of respiratory infections, gastrointestinal infections, febrile illness syndromes, antimicrobial resistance, and sexually transmitted infections
Global Public Health Intelligence Network (GPHIN)	Public Health Agency of Canada	Monitors global media sources (news wires, Web sites) as Web-based "early warning" system of public health events in seven languages in real time around the clock
Global Outbreak Alert and Response Network (GOARN)	World Health Organization	Technical collaborative network where human and technical resources are pooled for rapid identification, confirmation and response to international outbreaks

(continued on next page)

Table 20. (*continued*)

System	Sponsor	Function
Infectious Diseases Society of America Epidemic Intelligence Network (IDSA EIN)	Infectious Diseases Society of American	Provider-based emerging infections sentinel network
International Emerging Infections Program (IEIP)	CDC Global Disease Detection Program	IEIP sites track global diseases to detect unusual changes in trends that may signal an outbreak
NEDSS	CDC	Integrated and interoperable surveillance systems for all levels of government to detect outbreaks rapidly
National Notifiable Infectious Conditions	CDC	Voluntary national collection and pub-lication of data for notifiable diseases
National Outbreak Reporting System	CDC	Web-based system for reporting of waterborne, food-borne, enteric per-son-to-person, and enteric zoonotic (animal-to-person) disease outbreaks
Program for Monitoring Emerging Diseases (PROMED)	International Society of Infectious Diseases	Global electronic reporting system for outbreaks of emerging infectious diseases and toxins
PulseNet	CDC	Facilitate early identification of common source outbreaks
Real-Time Outbreak Disease Surveillance (RODS)	University of Pittsburgh	Biosurveillance research laboratory
Syndromic Reporting Information System (SYRIS)	Universities of New Mexico and Arizona	Real-time, Web-based early warning system to prevent the spread of infectious disease, and limit the effectiveness of bioterrorism attacks

CDC/Agency for Toxic Substances and Disease Registry (ATSDR), collaborating with the Council of State and Territorial Epidemiologists, has published and distributed standard case definitions to states and jurisdiction enabling the collection of uniform national data sets.

Appropriate methods for analysis must be considered and applied. Examples include descriptive (age, gender, ethnic group), geographic location, rates of disease or death, secular trends, and an analytic time series defining the total number of cases and trends over time.

Table 21. Exposure–Outcome Relationships in Disaster Settings

Timing	Disaster	Exposure	Outcome
Preimpact	Cyclone	High winds	Injury, death
		Presence of functioning warning system	Evacuation or not
	Tornado	High winds	Injury, death
		Presence of functioning warning system	Evacuation or not
Impact	Flash flood	Motor vehicle occupancy	Death by drowning
	Volcanic eruption	Ash particulate or respirable size	Silicosis
Postimpact	Earthquake	Building type, age, indoor cleanup	Injury, death
	Cyclone	Flood level	Death by electrocution
		Outdoor cleanup	Injury during cleanup

Possible reporting units for data collection include all the institutions that provide information for the surveillance system (e.g., hospital, clinic, health post, mobile health unit, nongovernmental organizations, health care facility, temporary shelters, first responder logs).

Data Collection Used for Decision-Making

To enhance data collection during a disaster, it is important to identify the elements in advance. The public health and responder community will be interested in hospital capacity, such as bed, staffing and supply needs, and availability; event related visits; and information from the patient locator system. A Web-based collection system is best, but alternative collection through fax and phone should be established. If a preexisting system is not in place when a disaster hits, an interim system should be developed. Finally, business rules need to be defined, such as who gets access to hospital-specific, aggregate information.

Since response activities and planning for relief and recovery are based on the data collected, the information should reflect as accurate and reliable a picture of the public health needs as possible. Hazard mapping and vulnerability assessments (discussed in Chapter 5) provide useful background information about the disaster event that can be used both for planning programs for disaster preparedness, and for determining response activities and evacuation plans. Although this information is usually available from the local emergency management office, geological institutions, or departments related to natural resources and the environment, public health professionals can work with these groups to create assessments which highlight public health concerns.

Information about the incident itself includes the following:

- Demographic characteristics of affected areas

- Assessment of casualties, injuries, and selected illness
- Numbers and characteristics of displaced populations
- Type of volunteers needed (e.g., medical, mental health, search and rescue) for coordination of deployment
- Management of health care infrastructure
- Storage and distribution of relief materials, including food, water, and medical supplies
- Public information and rumor control

Information can often be obtained from existing data sets (census, state hospitalization data), hospitals and clinics (emergency departments, patient medical records, electronic health records, e-codes), health maintenance organizations and insurance companies, private providers, temporary shelters (daily shelter census, logs at medical facility in shelter), first responder or Disaster Medical Assistance Team (DMAT) patient logs, and mobile health clinics, such as those run by the military, nongovernmental organizations, and volunteer medical groups (patient logs, records of prescription medications dispensed).

Where hospitals are using radio-frequency identification (RFID) chips (placed inside patient wristbands) in lieu of traditional medical records, health departments can have instant access to hospital databases that can be uploaded through the use of smartphones, personal data assistants or notebooks with RFID readers.

Due to time constraints and adverse environmental conditions, use of rigorous epidemiological methods may not be feasible in the postimpact phase. In disaster situations, assessment team members often use "quick and dirty" methods; "quick" in that they are simple, flexible, and can be used under difficult circumstances; "dirty" in that numerator and denominator data may be rough estimates that are subject to bias, although they serve to answer immediate questions whose answers are needed for the response.

Uniformity in Data Collection

Traditional public health surveillance is dependent on medical providers reporting unusual diseases or patterns of disease and laboratorians reporting unusual clinical isolates or patterns of routine isolates. The establishment of national standards for electronic data interchange can facilitate communication and integration with a breadth of information systems if the data definitions, coding conventions, and other specifications are identical. To ensure that data can be compared across jurisdictions by reducing incompatibilities across data, a number of efforts are being made to establish uniform definitions for data capture.

Examples of Emergency Information Systems

The availability of preexisting EIS has expanded greatly as the need has become better understood across the country. During the response to Hurricane Katrina, the CDC collaborated with many agencies, including the DMATs, the U.S. Public

Health Service, and the Red Cross. DMATs provided triage and medical care and assisted with evacuation while providing information used for surveillance. Many epidemiology and surveillance team members were activated from within the Public Health Service. The Red Cross provided shelter, food, and health and mental health services while gathering information used for surveillance. Coordinating with these agencies, the CDC conducted ongoing surveillance in 12 states. Data sources included hospitals, emergency departments, clinics, DMATS, military treatment units, and evacuation centers. Table 22 identifies key steps in surveillance conducted in the Gulf Coast area following Hurricane Katina and the subsequent flooding.

Table 22. Sentinel Surveillance Post-Katrina

- Louisiana Health Department (LHD) suffered loss of infrastructure

- Concern for outbreaks

- Sentinel (enhanced) surveillance implemented in New Orleans

- Captured data on every patient that accessed care in a New Orleans health care facility

    ○ 8 hospitals

    ○ 6 DMATs

    ○ 5 clinics

    ○ 10 military facilities

- Form captured

    ○ 30 disease syndromes

    ○ 4 mental health conditions

    ○ 15 trauma conditions

    ○ Medication refills

    ○ Severity

    ○ Disposition

- Clinical encounter forms collected every 24 hours

- Forms completed by facility or CDC staff through record review

- Data collection was labor intensive

- Paper form had to be transferred to electronic database

- Identified cases reported to LHD and the CDC

- Transitioned to automated syndromic surveillance after 6 weeks

Although in the United States multiple systems support the collection and reporting of information to public health labs, the clinical community, and state and local health departments, many of these systems operate in isolation without a mechanism to exchange consistent response, health, and disease tracking data between systems. On the federal level, the CDC and ATSDR have developed an ensemble of data collection systems that build on common technical standards and infrastructure. These initiatives include surveillance capacity, email and message centers, and communication networks. On the state and local level, systems have been built which function both in unique ways suitable for the locality and in ways that interface with the federal architecture.

Syndromic Surveillance

One surveillance tool that can be useful in identifying emerging infections and outbreaks is called *syndromic surveillance*. Syndromic surveillance systems collect data describing actions that precede diagnosis such as laboratory test requests, emergency department chief complaints, ambulance run sheets, prescription and over-the-counter drug use, school or work absenteeism. Clusters of medical signs and symptoms may signal a sufficient probability of an outbreak to warrant further public health response.

Syndromic surveillance data are usually collected at the point of medical care and from existing data streams that can monitor disease patterns. Syndromic surveillance has five characteristics which make it ideal for identifying outbreaks. The data are routinely collected and do not rely on physician reporting. The data are immediately computerized, are population-based, and are categorized by syndrome. This EIS is further distinguished from surveillance of mandated notifiable disease in that standard case definitions may not have been established and detection thresholds are flexible.

Hospital-based syndromic surveillance systems often report data from emergency departments. Daily or twice daily transfer of electronic data about patients with fever, respiratory, and gastrointestinal illness allows for analysis and identification of increases 7 days per week. Data can be analyzed by hospital and by zip code and should be examined as close to the time it is collected as possible.

When an alarm is sounded, it is necessary to distinguish between natural variability in the data (e.g., seasonal events, true outbreaks of an expected illness) or an event involving a biological agent or infectious disease. In evaluating the data, public health should be more concerned if there is a sustained or increasing visit rate, if multiple hospitals are involved, if there are dual syndromes in the same area, if other surveillance systems are sounding an alarm and if there is a strong geographic clustering. Of less concern would be a 1-day increase, only a single hospital involved, no other evidence of an outbreak, or a diffuse increase across the city or region.

Two methods of analyzing the data require baseline data. With the first, the analyst looks back for 2 weeks to assess retrospective data trends through a regression analysis which adjusts each day's data for seasonality. In the second, the analyst establishes an expected threshold for each day's statistic by using dual cyclical regression to account for seasonal variation through the Serfling method. A third method would be to look back at the data for the 2 preceding weeks without baseline data.

Sources of data for syndromic surveillance include the following examples:

- Epidemiologists
- Doctors
- Emergency Medical Services workers
- Laboratory scientists
- Medical examiners
- Nurses
- Pharmacists
- Schools
- Veterinarians
- Workplaces

Disaster Surveillance Work Group

In 2006, the CDC established the Disaster Surveillance Work Group (DSWG) to coordinate surveillance activities following a natural disaster. DSWG partners with state and local health departments and the agencies with response authority for emergency support functions (ESFs) 6 and 8. In the event of a disaster, DSWG provides technical resources to its partners and facilitates the methodology for capturing data used for surveillance. To standardize data collection, DSWG has created surveillance forms for individuals and for organizing and reporting the data (available at http://www.bt.cdc.gov/disasters/surveillance).

Public Health Information Network

In order to enhance early detection of public health emergencies and to facilitate gathering, storage, and dissemination of electronic information, a framework called the Public Health Information Network (PHIN) was established by the CDC. Facilitated by the CDC's National Center for Public Health Informatics, the PHIN is a portal which provides for interoperable use of information technology by establishing and promoting technical standards and functions. The PHIN supports the exchange of key health data by defining common data and vocabulary standards and by requiring collaborative partnerships in the collection of data.

Within the PHIN, several key CDC programs have been established or enhanced which facilitate public health operations during a disaster. These include the following programs and their components:

- Directing, Alerting, and Emergency Operations

    Public Health Directory: Lists more than 500,000 people and organizations needed by any CDC program.
    CDC Alerting Service: Sends alerts via phone, text message, e-mail, Web, or fax.

Health Alert Network: National, integrated electronic information and communications system which the CDC uses for the distribution of health alerts, prevention guidelines, national disease surveillance, and laboratory reporting.

Epidemic Information Exchange (EPI-X): EPI-X is the CDC's secure encrypted Web-based communications network which shares real-time health surveillance information with designated public health professionals across the country during an emergency.

- National Notifiable Diseases Surveillance (NNDS)

   National Electronic Disease Surveillance System: NEDSS was designed to advance the development of integrated and interoperable surveillance systems to enable all levels of government to detect outbreaks rapidly.

   National Notifiable Diseases Surveillance System (NNDSS): Collects information for the diseases which require national notification.

- Outbreak Management

   Outbreak Management: Enables the capture of data (demographics, case investigations, laboratory results, exposures), case follow-up, and contact tracing.

   Countermeasure and Response Administration (CRA): Web-based tool to manage CRA activities at state or local level; provides information on recommended countermeasures, and tracks and manages information on vaccinations, prophylaxes, treatments, and quarantine.

   Laboratory Systems: Provides oversight and expertise on informatics and laboratory information management.

   Biosense: Biosurveillance program that enables real-time disease detection and monitoring through the secure transmissions of clinical data from hospitals to the CDC or a state or local system.

National Electronic Disease Surveillance System

NEDSS is a major component of the PHIN. A primary goal of NEDSS is to facilitate the ongoing, automatic capture and analysis of data already available electronically. By integrating surveillance systems, NEDSS facilitates the efficient entry, updating, and electronic transfer of demographic and notifiable disease data from clinical information systems located in health care settings to public health departments at local, state, and federal levels. To ensure uniformity, NEDSS recommends a minimum set of data elements to be collected as part of routine surveillance coupled with standards that facilitate data collection, management, transmission, analyses, access, and dissemination.

In addition to being an effective tool for analysis, NEDSS reduces the provider burden and ensures the timeliness and quality of the information provided. When the data are entered locally, at hospitals or labs, the user only enters the data once. When the provider enters the data into the system, they automatically roll into the NEDSS back end. The state receives the data regularly, enabling state-level reporting, while the hospital or laboratory maintains their local database. Further, data are shipped to the CDC on a routine basis, providing a robust data set which enables the CDC to more accurately and more quickly identify outbreaks.

NEDSS is compliant with the Health Insurance Portability and Accountability Act of 1996 (HIPAA) Privacy Rule which governs the use and disclosure of protected health information. HIPAA permits health care providers to share individually identifiable information with legally authorized public health entities for public health activities, including surveillance, investigation, and intervention.

National Electronic Disease Surveillance System and Geographic Information Systems

When combined with GIS, NEDSS can be a powerful tool for analysis. As data are loaded into the system, it goes through geocoding, which provides the latitude and longitude of the information so that the user can see the mapping both visually and in a tabular report. Seeing the data visually is like viewing a series of transparencies overlaid on top of one another, each with a new set of information. The ability to visualize the data permits modeling of activity based on parameters that the user will set. RISKMAP and WebFOCUS are two commercially available software programs that build a tunnel and provide an interface between the GIS and NEDSS databases. (RISKMAP is available at http://riskmapsoftware.com; WebFOCUS is available at http://www.workflowdownload.com/businessintelligence/download-webfocus.htm.)

To understand the advantages that this technology offers, it is worthwhile to describe how GIS operate and the opportunities for public health response and preparedness in emergencies.

GIS can be a useful tool to support epidemiology and surveillance in preparation for and in response to disasters. GIS technology allows the user to digitally link data, spatial information, and geography and display the information in an easy-to-understand visual medium. GIS data combine information about *where* things are with information about *what* things are so that we can identify which groups with different features are located together. Using spatial database management, visualization and mapping, and spatial analyses, this technology allows us to see spatial and temporal relationships among data. These systems allow researchers, public health professionals, and policymakers to better understand geographic relationships that affect health outcomes, public health risks, disease transmission, access to health care, and other public health concerns as they relate to all emergencies. GIS data are accurate to 15 centimeters and can show buildings shifting after a disaster. GIS maps allow departments to switch from an overview of sections of a city to the location of individual objects. For example, if a hospital needs to bring nurses from home following an emergency, using MapPoint software, GIS can provide information about transporting them to your hospital, department, and so forth by identifying safe passageways. Further, a process available through GIS, Geographic Allocation Process analysis, helps determine where gaps in service exist. GIS can be supported in a network environment. Table 23 identifies the many public health uses of GIS data in emergencies.

Table 23. Public Health Uses of Geographic Information Systems Data in Emergency Preparedness

Community Preparedness Efforts

- Assess community risks

- Identify high concentrations of vulnerable populations

- Estimate populations in hazard zones

- Map demographic factors (e.g., housing type, age, those needing special assistance) to target preventive activities for specific populations

- Develop treatment profiles of physicians so officials know how to target education (for example, large number of physicians prescribed three pills of ciproflaxin as prophylaxis for anthrax following the anthrax mailings in 2001)

- Predict location of disease-transmitting vectors (e.g., mosquitoes)

- Predict, by model, demand for a service for known emergencies (e.g., in regions with frequent flooding, earthquake, or hurricane) both before and after event

- Identify capacity of the health care system:

  ○ Identify the market/treatment area for health care systems

  ○ Locate specialty physicians and specialized services in a community

  ○ Conduct small-area analysis to see how services are used by defined population

- Better distribute services in future disasters or reallocate preventive services in advance of emergency by analyzing both residence and treatment zip codes to identify where victims sought services

- Develop training scenarios

Response Capabilities

- Infection surveillance by identifying geographic spread of disease

  ○ Monitor and track spread of infectious disease and predict path of disease by searching for spatial relationships

- Inform establishment of medical care sites (e.g., points of distribution) or shelters by locating injuries/illness by zip code in relation to existing health care services

- Produce accurate maps for urban search and rescue

- Monitor asset management

- Manage field data in real time

- Improve data-sharing capabilities

- Locate resources

(continued on next page)

Table 23. (*continued*)

- Notify and update residents on status of basic services, utilities, transportation

- Track location and real-time capacity of shelters

- Risk and vulnerability assessments

  - Estimate extent and location of potential damage

  - Identify where centers delivering services are to identify gaps

  - Map patterns of destruction, targeting recovery and reconstruction efforts

  - Track plumes of chemicals to see how they spread through air, soil, or water and who and what will be affected

  - Determine evacuation zone

- Evaluate response

How to Use Data in Geographic Information Systems

The purpose of a geospatial system is to combine data with the questions that are asked administratively. GIS provides spatial information in response to the query, *what should I look at next?* While analyses from relational databases present tabular data in tables and charts, GIS provides a more descriptive view of the information and expands what can be done beyond traditional aggregate reports. Built upon an underlying data model, GIS presents data about locations and attributes by looking spatially at layers of information.

The development of GIS as a management tool for public health as part of the larger community is best achieved through collaboration among several agencies. Establishing a team of GIS personnel often requires volunteers from many disciplines. A GIS volunteer list should include professionals or students who are vetted and credentialed in advance like other public health and mental health personnel. GIS volunteers need to be oriented in advance to the current GIS being used in the community, the configuration of the files, and so forth, so they can quickly help in the event of disaster.

Traditionally, communities collect and use their data in stovepipes, where each agency creates and analyzes its own databases, often without sharing information with sister agencies. The National Spatial Data Infrastructure[1] Executive Order encouraged geospatial data acquisition and access throughout all levels of government, the private and nonprofit sectors, and the academic community.

---

[1]Executive Order 12906. April 13, 1994. *Fed Regist.* 59:17671-17674. Amended by Executive Order 13286. March 5, 2003. *Fed Regist.* 68:10619-10633.

Importantly, the order targeted data needed for emergency response efforts. An enterprise GIS solution, where all agencies have access to a centralized data set of geographic data layers, reduces redundancies of data collection, maintenance, and processing. GIS applications such as ESRI (information available at http://www.esri. com) and ArcPad (information available at http://www.esri.com/software/arcgis/arcpad/ index.html) can be used in the field on smartphones and personal data assistants, allowing field-level assessments in real time and the transmission of information back to the Emergency Operations Center. Interactive mapping applications, such as GEOMAC (information available at http://www.geomac.gov/index.shtml) can be used to assess disaster conditions from anywhere in the United States.

Through GIS, we can map case distributions and variability in disease agents, and analyze temporal and geographic trends in disease outbreaks, all of which can inform our decisions on targeting interventions and preventive activities. By matching addresses through geocoding we can convert each address to a point on a map. For example, by creating a zip code map of high risk (e.g., areas of outbreaks and areas with large numbers of non–English-speaking residents) public health can identify where the development of educational materials in multiple languages is needed. By mapping the areas which lack accessible services, have high-density residential housing, and the historical sites where injuries occurred in a previous disaster, public health may be better able to plan the locations for temporary treatment centers or DMATs. By mapping data from syndromic surveillance systems with GIS, we can predict where infections or outbreaks will spread. We can use a GIS-based application coupled with an automated telephone dialing system to communicate an emergency message, such as warning citizens about impending or ongoing disasters. As an example, NEDSS data are collected and entered at the hospital, are automatically shipped to the state, which customizes the data by setting the parameters for analysis. When analyses are run and maps created that identify a community at risk, the system can trigger an automatic telephone notification, in which a series of phones ring automatically and prerecorded messages tell people to do X, Y, or Z depending on their address and its proximity to the emergency.

Using GIS, departments of health working with the state or local offices of emergency management have overlaid census data with information about power outages and roadmaps to see which major populations were being impacted. GIS has been used to map sites of dead crows and locate pockets of breeding mosquitoes, helping identify where West Nile virus was spreading. In the response to the World Trade Center attacks of 2001, officials used GIS to create a frame of reference for understanding where the buildings had been. They used GIS to see if buildings next to the site were shifting dangerously. Furthermore, thermal maps were overlaid on orthoimagery to identify where fire suppression was necessary and where to avoid sending workers.

Where to Get Data

The potential sources for locating data are limitless and any data describing a characteristic of a community can better inform decision-makers. Some data are available without cost, while some must be purchased. For example, ArcGIS (available at http://www.esri.com/software/arcgis/index.html) has many links that permit the download of state level information (available at http://www.esri.com/industries/stategov/index.html). The Web site Geodata.gov (available at http://gos2.geodata.gov/wps/portal/gos) hosts geographic maps for all levels of jurisdiction and serves as a GIS data clearinghouse. The site includes many data sets and services that were formerly published by ESRI. In addition, GIS departments have parcel maps available for sale.

When locating or purchasing GIS data, it is important to use managed (vs unmanaged) data if they are available. Managed data are a potentially more reliable source that will reduce error in notification of emergencies or other public service announcements, determining evacuation routes or issuing shelter-in-place instructions, or responding to the correct location.

Let's suppose that you, the reader, are interested in building a GIS database for public use during an emergency. When looking for data to create a database for your community, the local zoning and planning commission and local tax commission are the best source of data. Since they make money from tracking activities of daily living, they could be depended on to track such activities accurately. Property tax databases contain the names and phone numbers of homeowners (information that can be imported into an emergency telephone notification application). Information is available from the Department of Transportation, federal railways, census bureau, schools, the White Pages phone book, and so forth. To obtain additional data, search "Google" by entering the search term "GIS data." Locating a GIS user network in your area is an important place to get started, as these groups will know where data sets are "buried."

Furthermore, research and nonprofit institutions may have data sets that will be valuable to your community. Rich data sets are possible in locales where land is owned by state or federal governments, county governments, other public agencies, or public-interest organizations. To expand data and improve resource and facility management, electronic blueprints can be created by zooming in on individual hospitals and getting a detailed map of which facilities are operational by tying hospital floor plans to the community's disaster plans. Two publicly available software packages, CATS (Consequences Assessment Tool Set) and HAZUS (Hazards U.S.), use GIS (ArcView and ArcGIS) and include extensive national data sets of assets necessary in disaster response. The assets include hospitals, pharmacies, and nuclear plants that can be mapped by GIS. The following are types of data sets that are useful when public health professionals work with GIS:

- Airports
- Community-based organizations
- Community centers
- Demographics of the community
- Doctors' offices at which patients have signed HIPAA authorization
- Fire and other emergency services
- Government buildings

- Hospitals
- Hospital surveillance
- Law enforcement facilities
- Long-term care facilities
- Major highways and railways
- Pharmacies
- Phone lines
- Power-generating plants
- Schools and school surveillance
- Sentinel reporting systems
- Toxics Release Inventory
- Veterinary clinics
- Vital statistics

It is very important that complete and current data be obtained about both the assets available to the community and the potential hazards when planning a GIS-focused disaster management program,. It is also useful to collate and regularly update the contact names, current mobile telephone numbers, and e-mail addresses of GIS personnel and current emergency management contacts.

Because it is difficult to know what data will be needed postdisaster, the goal should be to create as rich a data set as possible, including as many types of information as available. Once the data sets have been located, it should be ensured that they will be immediately available following a disaster by negotiating data-sharing agreements before the data are needed. Sharing data facilitates a community's coordinated planning and response through public-private partnerships. The directory structure of your GIS data set should be logical, because many people may use it. For naming conventions, use simple, descriptive labels that will be easily recognizable.

Planning With Geographic Information System Data

Once the data sets have been assembled, the analysis should begin with identification of vulnerable assets, including critically important facilities. Examples include the following:

- Structures used for communication
- Fire and rescue
- Hospital and nursing facilities
- Pharmacies
- Police
- Schools and day care facilities
- Shelter
- Transportation
- Utilities

Facilities whose destruction could result in severe public health problems for one's community should also be examined, such as hazardous material storage sites, food and water sources, and sanitation centers.

Developing the Data Set

An initial step is to identify the historical events that have been hazardous to a community and prioritize those events according to frequency, magnitude, and area of impact. High-risk areas get assigned a risk level based on probability and historic occurrence. Because critical decisions will be made based on the data, it is important to keep a log of the pedigree of the data one is using, such as summaries of origin, update schedules, and contact numbers for data librarians. The pedigree of the data may influence some decision-making about public health interventions. Some data, such as those collected through active short-term surveillance systems, may be incomplete and require follow-up data cleaning. For example, corrections to the record of reportable disease can be made by utilizing address data as geographic identifiers. Furthermore, when data are obtained from a variety of data sources, it is often necessary to convert the data to make them usable and compatible. Finally, although specific data sets can be established as shapefiles for each hazard, another robust format is the Spatial Data Transfer Standard, which was designed so that spatial data could be easily used on different computer platforms.

Social Vulnerability and Community Preparedness

GIS is useful to identify people or neighborhoods most at risk of suffering adverse outcomes as a result of their social vulnerability, enhancing a community's preparedness efforts and targeted response and recovery. Although vulnerability is discussed at greater length in Chapter 10, it is sufficient here to define socially vulnerable individuals as those with functional needs or language barriers and those without financial resources, women, children, and the elderly. Entire communities may also be vulnerable.

A tool called the Social Vulnerability Index (SOVI) measures the social vulnerability of U.S. counties to various hazards. The index combines 32 socioeconomic variables that predict a community's inability to prepare for, respond to, and recover from hazards. SOVI highlights the geographic variation in social vulnerability and enables the planner to identify which communities might not have the capacity to prepare or respond and where resources might be used most effectively to reduce the preexisting vulnerability. SOVI can also be used to indicate different rates in the recovery of communities. (More information is available at http://www.222.sovius.org.)

The process of determining who is vulnerable in a community can be straightforward. As an example, start with a single agency by gathering the addresses of the individuals of interest. After collecting the addresses of clients who are served, service providers, facilities, and staff, geocode each of these addresses. Overlay the addresses onto the potential hazardous area (for example, a known flood zone). Finally, prepare the maps and discuss the results with the planners.

HIPAA compliance can be ensured by establishing data-sharing agreements with designated public health authorities, obtaining authorizations from the individuals involved, or using registries of individuals who want to be notified about emergencies. In addition, guidelines should be established between emergency management and public health agencies about data-sharing for vulnerable populations and those with functional needs.

Use of Geographic Information Systems in Mitigation

GIS products and spatial analysis allow the user to precisely map where hazards exist and to visualize that information so that decisions can be made about possible preventive activities. GIS can be used to combine areas of high risk with areas where many high-value assets or vulnerable populations are found. An example is wildfire-prone areas where brush could be cut back. Once a community determines the areas and populations at risk, public health can work with emergency management and community leaders to target areas where preventive or mitigation activities would be beneficial.

Since many communities use GIS to create assessment maps of economic damage, the foundation has been set to create assessment maps for public health. Public health planners can focus mitigation efforts where calculations show a probability that a hazard common to the community would cause an unacceptable level of morbidity and mortality.

Maps

Following an emergency, there will be a high demand for spatial information by many sectors. Where a disaster has destroyed a neighborhood or a community's landmarks, a geographic visualization of the area can help with reorientation and stabilization of the site. Maps provide a common platform for everyone to visualize needed information about the location of events, resources, transportation, emergency networks, and so forth, facilitating communication and decision-making. Further, through social networking sites on the Internet and interactive mapping programs, public health workers can inform a community about interventions and recovery progress, enabling real-time online changes.

GIS can create individualized maps, customized to the features needed in the user's tasks. As a start, it is necessary to create what are known as *basemaps*, basic generic maps used as a reference to the location of preexisting community data. The attributes of basemaps will vary according to the risks of the community. Because disasters aren't confined to jurisdictional boundaries, basemaps often cross territorial lines. Multiple basemaps with differing attributes may be needed. As an example, for responders who traveled from out of the area, to become oriented to their surroundings the basemaps need to be very specific about landmarks that may still be standing. Basic operational field maps would be valuable for directing off-site support teams in the field, in identifying where supplies are needed, and so forth. One basemap may be needed that locates pet shelters, and others to show the preexisting locations of hospitals and schools.

Part of the implementation of GIS is the establishment of a system to create and distribute maps. OEM is often the agency responsible for the distribution of the maps. Three types of maps should be distinguished: standard, templates, and special needs. Maps can be created by using desktop mapping products such as ArcGIS and a relational database such as SQL Server. By permitting online requests for maps, one can establish and track the parameters of map requests. This online site can also provide the complex array of Incident Command System forms that are so often requested by responders and agencies.

As maps can undergo numerous changes, users of GIS should develop a log which tracks the history of each map and the data used to build each one. It is important to keep a record of earlier maps and the data used because, as was the case at the World Trade Center site, officials may not know the types of hazardous substances at the site until some time later. Public health will want to trace exposures over time, especially as new information is added or if stations for decontamination are moved.

The National Oceanic and Atmospheric Administration's (NOAA's) Office of Response and Restoration provides comprehensive modeling programs and data sets (available at http://www.response.restoration.noaa.gov/type_catalog.php?RECORD_KEY(type_chosen)=type_id&type_id(type_chosen)=3). Table 24 describes some of the modeling programs available.

Evaluating Disaster Surveillance

Finally, an EIS must be evaluated within the disaster setting to know when the system is no longer needed. This endpoint is often determined by assessing both the resources and personnel available to run the system and the ability to merge the emergency system into routine surveillance. In addition to describing the attributes, usefulness, and cost of EIS, evaluations can lead to recommendations on the initiation and conclusion of future surveillance related to disasters. See Chapter 13 for more information on such evaluation methods.

If you are concerned about risks in your area, check the assessment systems identified in Table 25.

Table 24. Representative Modeling Programs

Source	Program	Tool	Function	Source
National Oceanic and Atmospheric Administration (NOAA)	**Assessing Risk to Ecological Resources**		Assessing hazardous waste sites	
		Environmental Sensitivity Index (ESI) map	Summary of coastal resources that are at risk if an oil spill occurs nearby	Office of Response and Restoration, NOAA's National Ocean Service; ESI Metadata, Emergency Response Software and Data Sets page (http://www.response.restoration.noaa.gov)
		Community Vulnerability Assessment Tool (CVAT)	Compact disc tool that consists of software, data, and tutorials Can be used to identify a community's hazards Requires customizing to a given environment where there is a unique set of hazards	Can be ordered for free (http://www.csc.noaa.gov/products/nchaz/htm/about.htm)
	Emergency Response Program		Build and sustain NOAA's ability to respond effectively to emergencies	
		Environmental Response Management Application (ERMA)	Assists in response planning Accessible to both the command post and to assets in the field during an actual response incident, such as an oil spill or hurricane	Office of Response and Restoration, NOAA's National Ocean Service; ERMA Web Portal page (http://www.response.restoration.noaa.gov)

(continued on next page)

Table 24. (*continued*)

Source	Program	Tool	Function	Source
		Mapping Application for Response, Planning, and Local Operational Tasks (MARPLOT)	Simple mapping application allowing download of maps of any area of the country	Emergency Management, U.S. EPA (http://www.epa.gov/oem/content/cameo/marplot.htm)
		Aerial Locations of Hazardous Atmospheres (ALOHA)	Gas-dispersion modeling software that uses information the user provides, along with physical property data from its extensive chemical library, to predict how a hazardous gas cloud might disperse in the atmosphere after an accidental chemical release	Emergency Management, U.S. EPA (http://www.epa.gov/osweroe1/content/cameo/aloha.htm)
	Responding to Oil Spills		Support effective and safe responses to oil spills in the coastal environment	
		Automated Data Inquiry for Oil Spills (ADIOS)	Designed to help answer typical questions during oil spill response and cleanup. Used to help assess where the oil was going from the Deepwater Horizon spill	Office of Response and Restoration, NOAA's National Ocean Service; ADOIS2, NOAA's Emergency Response Program page (http://www.response.restoration.noaa.gov)

(*continued on next page*)

Table 24. (*continued*)

Source	Program	Tool	Function	Source
		General (NOAA) Operational Modeling Environment (GNOME)	Oil spill trajectory model	Office of Response and Restoration, NOAA's National Ocean Service; GNOME, Emergency Response Software and Data Sets page (http://www.response.restoration.noaa.gov)
Federal Emergency Management Agency (FEMA)		HAZUS (Hazards U.S.)	Loss-estimation modeling which allows users to forecast most probable physical and economic damage to a community. Models earthquakes, floods, and hurricanes. Bundled with federal data sets, but can be customized with local data. FEMA offers a training course on HAZUS	HAZUS: FEMA's Methodology for Estimating Potential Losses from Disasters (http://www.fema.gov/plan/prevent/hazus)
National Hurricane Center		Sea, Lake, and Overland Surges from Hurricanes (SLOSH)	Evaluate storm surge threat from hurricanes and tropical cyclones. Emergency managers use these data to determine which areas must be evacuated	National Weather Service Meteorological Development Laboratory page (http://www.nws.noaa.gov/mdl)

Table 25. Hazard-Specific Geographic Information Systems Tools

Hazard	Digital Mapping Projects/Tools	Web Resource
Earthquakes	California Geology Survey	http://www.conservation.ca.gov/cgs/information/geologic_mapping/Pages/Index.aspx
	U.S. Geological Survey (USGS) Earthquake Hazards Program, national seismic hazard maps	http://earthquake.usgs.gov/hazards
Fires	U.S. Wildland Fire Assessment System, fire danger rating maps	http://www.wfas.net
	California Department of Forestry and Fire Prevention, Fire and Resource Assessment Program, maps of fire hazard severity zones	http://frap.cdf.ca.gov/data/frapgismaps/select.asp
Floods	Federal Emergency Management Agency (FEMA) National Flood Insurance Program, Flood Hazard Mapping, flood insurance rate maps	http://www.fema.gov/plan/prevent/fhm
	Sea, Lake, and Overland Surges from Hurricanes (SLOSH), hurricane storm surge inundation area maps	http://www.fema.gov/plan/prevent/nhp/slosh_link.shtm
Hurricanes	CATS (Consequences Assessment Tool Set) page	http://gis.esri.com/library/userconf/proc00/professional/papers/PAP722/p722.htm
	USGS Center for Integration of Natural Disaster Information (CINDI) page	http://egsc.usgs.gov/isb/pubs/factsheets/fs00301.html
Landslides	Association of Bay Area Governments, Earthquake and Hazards Program page	http://quake.abag.ca.gov/landslides
Toxic spills, explosions, and fires	HAZUS (Hazards U.S.)	http://www.fema.gov/plan/prevent/hazus
Tsunamis	California Department of Conservation, Tsunami Inundation Map	http://www.consrv.ca.gov/cgs/geologic_hazards/Tsunami/Inundation_Maps/Pages/Statewide_Maps.aspx
	University of Southern California Tsunami Research Center page	http://www.usc.edu/dept/tsunamis/2005/index.php

Hazard Assessment, Vulnerability Analysis, Risk Assessment, and Rapid Health Assessment

R isk and needs assessments must be tailored to the timing, size, and impact of a specific disaster. Key steps to assessing risks are identifying the hazards, determining who is at risk of being harmed, and assessing the probability of the hazard actually occurring. Once risk is determined, decisions can be made on preventive action. This chapter reviews both background information on community vulnerability that can be assembled both before a disaster (including acute needs assessment, longer-term data collection, surveillance, and examination of methods and limitations of data collection) and during the impact and postimpact phases, and the methods that can be used to assess risk from hazards.

Public Health Role

- Identify disaster-related hazards and associated vulnerability in a community
- Determine risk of public health needs likely to be created should such disasters occur
- Prioritize necessary health and public health postimpact requirements based on information from community needs assessment
- Provide decision-makers with objective information to guide prevention, mitigation, and response to disease

Rationale for Assessing Risk

Different types of disasters are associated with distinct patterns of morbidity and mortality. To develop location-specific strategies for reducing negative health outcomes, public health officials and disaster managers must be aware of the types of hazards most likely to affect specific communities. Although all-hazards planning is efficient for the utilization of resources, health planners in Florida, for example, might prepare primarily for hurricanes, whereas those in California would prepare for earthquakes and wildfires.

Six categories of disaster prevention measures can be implemented following the analysis of hazards, vulnerability, and risk:

- Prevention or removal of hazard (e.g., closing down an aging industrial facility that cannot implement safety regulations)

- Moving those at risk away from the hazard (e.g., evacuating populations prior to the impact of a hurricane, resettling communities away from flood-prone areas)
- Providing public information and education (e.g., providing information concerning measures that the public can take to protect itself during a tornado)
- Establishing early warning systems (e.g., using satellite data about an approaching hurricane to inform public service announcements)
- Reducing the impact of the disaster (e.g., enforcing strict building regulations in an earthquake-prone zone)
- Increasing local capacity to respond (e.g., coordinating a plan utilizing the resources of the entire health community, including health departments, hospitals, community clinics and home care agencies)

Hazard Identification and Analysis

Hazard identification is used to determine which events are most likely to affect a community. This assessment of community risk has four steps:

1. Identifying hazardous sites and transport routes
2. Identifying potential incident scenarios and their exposure pathways
3. Identifying vulnerable populations, facilities, and environments
4. Estimating the health impact of potential incidents and the requirements for health care facilities and public health intervention

The National Fire Protection Association 1600 Standard requires that a community's hazard identification include natural events, technological events, and human events (see Appendix I). Decisions about which mitigation steps to take frequently require a cost–benefit analysis and a prioritization of the assets being protected.

Data Collection

Information from several sources, including data from previous hazards, is needed to predict future events. This information can assist in the development of appropriate mitigation measures. Historical data include the nature of previous hazards, the direct causes or contributing factors of previous events (e.g., where failure to observe industrial regulations led to chemical release), the frequency and intensity of past disasters, the magnitude or power of past hazards (as measured with established standards, such as the Richter Scale for earthquakes or the Saffir-Simpson Wind Scale for hurricanes), and the reported effects of an event at a given location (e.g., number of homes destroyed by tornado, number of people displaced by flood).

Baseline data should be collected to assess current potential hazards in a community, including:

- Agricultural facilities
- Chemical manufacturing and storage
- Dams, levies, and other flood control mechanisms
- Facilities for storage of infectious waste

- Firework factories
- Laboratories located in academic or other research institutions
- Military installations
- Munitions factories or depots
- Pesticide manufacturers or storage
- Petrochemical refineries or storage facilities
- Pharmaceutical companies
- Plants for food production or storage
- Radiological power plants or fuel processing facilities
- Ventilation systems for high occupancy buildings
- Water treatment and distribution centers

Scientific Resources

Data from meteorology, seismology, volcanology, and hydrology should be used to provide important predictive information concerning hazards. These data can be obtained from a variety of government agencies and private institutions, including the National Oceanic and Atmospheric Administration, the National Weather Service, the U.S. Geological Survey, and the Natural Hazards Center at the University of Colorado. In addition, decision-support systems can analyze data from several core databases, such as data on building inventories, infrastructure, demographics, and risk. These systems can simulate "what if" scenarios to aid in planning.

Hazardous Materials Documentation

In the United States, the Superfund Amendment and Reauthorization Act requires that all hazardous materials manufactured, stored, or transported by local industry that could affect the surrounding community be identified and reported to health officials. In most communities, gasoline and liquid petroleum gas are the most common hazardous materials, but other potential hazards include chlorine, ammonia, and explosives. Material safety data sheets (MSDS) provide a standardized method of communicating relevant information about each material, including its toxicity, flammability, and known acute and chronic health effects. MSDS are provided by the manufacturers of individual chemicals and can be searched via databases available on the Internet, such as CHEMTREC (available at http://www.chemtrec.com).

Hazard Assessment

Following compilation, the information is analyzed to determine which hazards are most likely to affect a given community and to make decisions about who or what to protect. Data analysis attempts to predict the nature, frequency, and intensity of future hazards; the area(s) most likely to be affected; and the onset time and duration of future events. This assessment becomes the basis of establishing measures for prevention, mitigation, and response. The hazard assessment and data analysis should be conducted at a level appropriate to both the perceived risk and the availability of resources.

Hazard Mapping

With the wealth of gathered data, the location of both previous and potential hazards can be mapped. Aerial photography, satellite imagery, remote sensing, and geographic information systems (GIS) technology can all provide information through hazard mapping. Remote sensing can show changes to land-use maps over time. GIS models enable managers to develop plans with information consolidated from numerous disciplines, including engineering, natural sciences, and public health. Various types of maps are available for different hazards both macro or micro in scale, including inundation maps for floods and seismic zoning maps for earthquakes. Maps detailing the location of industrial sites and hazardous material storage facilities can also be used. Multihazard maps are available from the scientific community, industry, the media, and governmental jurisdictions.

Vulnerability Analysis

A vulnerability analysis is used to obtain information about the susceptibility of individuals, property, and the environment to the adverse effects of a given hazard for developing appropriate prevention strategies. The analysis of this information helps determine who is most likely to be affected, what is most likely to be destroyed or damaged, and what capacities exist to cope with the effects of the disaster. A separate vulnerability analysis should be conducted for each identified hazard. The five categories of vulnerability are described in Table 26.

A community's capacity to withstand the effects of a disaster is determined by collecting data on numerous variables. (See Chapter 9 for information on psychological resilience.) Information on the size, density, location, and socio-economic status of the at-risk community can be obtained from local government officials. Public utility companies, health departments, hospital associations, and school authorities can provide data on the location and structural integrity of lifeline structures (i.e., electricity, gas, water, and sewer) as well as buildings with high occupancy. Information on the location and structural integrity of private dwellings is also useful. A structural engineer may be required to review these data. Additional community capacity elements to be assessed include the presence of early warning systems, the number of available emergency responders and medical personnel, the level of technical expertise among emergency responders, the availability of supplies, and the status of emergency transportation and communication systems.

Probability Estimate

The probability estimate attempts to determine the likelihood of an event of a given magnitude occurring in a certain area over a specified time interval. Several statistical formulations can be used to determine the probabilities. More complicated

Table 26. Categories of Vulnerability

Category	Measures
Proximity and exposure	Identify population(s) vulnerable because they live or work near a given hazard
Physical	Assess vulnerability of buildings, infrastructure, agriculture, and other aspects of the physical environment as a result of factors such as site, materials used, construction technique, and maintenance
	Evaluate transportation systems, communication systems, public utilities (water, sewage, power), and critical facilities (hospitals) for weaknesses
	Estimate potential short- and long-term impact of hazard on crops, food, livestock, trees, and fisheries
Social	Identify population most vulnerable to the effects of disaster who require targeted planning (older adults, children, single-parent families, the economically disadvantaged, those with functional needs)
	Estimate the level of poverty, jobs that are at risk, and the availability of local institutions that may provide social support
Economic	Determine the community's potential for economic loss and recovery following a disaster
Capacity	Evaluate the availability of human resources, material resources, and the presence of mutual aid agreements with neighboring communities
	Review the existence and enforcement of government regulations that mitigate the effects of certain disasters (e.g., building codes)

formulations take into account not only the hazard and vulnerability estimates, but also mitigation efforts to reduce vulnerability and disaster management issues. Although these estimates cannot predict the exact timing of an event, they can be used to guide the allocation of resources in preparing for likely hazards.

Risk Assessment

Risk assessment is used during the prevention and preparedness phases as a diagnostic and planning tool. As an example, one might ask, *how many excess cases of outcome A will occur in a population of size B, due to a hazard event C of severity D?* Key lessons learned from the risk assessment can be used in the development of local and regional disaster plans. Major objectives and examples of risk assessment include the following:

- Identifying major hazards facing the community and their sources (e.g., earthquakes, floods, industrial accidents)
- Determining a community's risk of adverse health effects caused by a specified disaster (e.g., traumatic deaths and injuries following an earthquake)

- Identifying those sections of the community most likely to be affected by a particular hazard (e.g., individuals living in or near flood plains)
- Determining existing measures and resources that reduce the impact of a given hazard (e.g., building codes and regulations for earthquake mitigation)
- Determining areas that require strengthening to prevent or mitigate the effects of the hazard (e.g., constructing levees to protect the community from floodwaters)

Modeling in Risk Assessment

Risk assessment uses the results of the hazard identification and vulnerability analysis to determine the probability of a specified outcome from a given hazard that affects a community with known vulnerabilities and coping mechanisms (risk = hazard × vulnerability). The probability may be presented as a numeric range (e.g., 30 to 40% probability) or in relative terms (e.g., low, moderate, or high risk). A good example of how such models are used is the environmental and climate prediction services provided by the National Weather Service. The results of this modeling are broadcast by the media to warn communities of the risks of thunderstorms, blizzards, tornadoes, and hurricanes.

Models can also be used to guide appropriate responses to disasters. For example, plume dispersion modeling has shown that the most appropriate response to a major chemical release is evacuation of the surrounding community. Other strategies, such as "sheltering in place" (i.e., remaining indoors with windows and doors closed), provide less protection to the population. Similar dispersion models are also used to determine the risks of other technological hazards, including releases from nuclear installations. Table 27 lists some resources for risk assessment modeling.

Rapid Health Assessment

Rapid health assessments are used in the early stages of disaster response, often simultaneously with emergency response, to characterize the health impact of the disaster on the affected community. The primary task of the assessment team is to collect, analyze, and disseminate timely, accurate health data. These data assist public health professionals in determining health needs, prioritizing response activities, initiating an appropriate emergency response, and evaluating the effectiveness of the response. Even if the rapid health assessment is only a basic estimate, it facilitates the rational allocation of available resources according to the true needs of the emergency.

Community plans for disaster response should include teams to provide medical care that are functionally separate from the team(s) conducting the rapid health assessment. Appropriate medical responses can be planned in advance since specific disasters are associated with predictable patterns of morbidity and mortality. Although rapid health assessments provide for the early collection of health data, emergency response activities to save life and limb and to rescue trapped or isolated individuals may

Table 27. Risk Assessment Modeling Resources

Tools	Function	Web Resource
U.S. Environmental Protection Agency (EPA) Ecological risk assessment modeling	Modeling tools to evaluate potential risks from environmental contamination	http://www.epa.gov/superfund/programs/ nrd/era.htm; another site provides detailed information about ecological risk assessments: http://www.evs.anl.gov/project/dsp_ fsdetail_new.cfm?id=52
EPA risk assessment modeling	Determine compliance with National Emissions Standards for Hazardous Air Pollutants for Radionuclides	http://www.epa.gov/rpdweb00/assessment
Adaptive Risk Assessment Modeling System	Determine safe and cleanup target levels for military-relevant compounds and evaluate remediation alternatives	http://el.erdc.usace.army.mil/arams
HAZUS (Hazards U.S.)	Analyze potential losses from floods, hurricane winds, and earthquakes	http://www.fema.gov/plan/prevent/hazus
Environmental Health Shelter Assessment Tool	Conduct rapid assessment of shelter conditions; assessment form covers 14 general areas of environmental health, documents immediate needs in shelters	http://www.bt.cdc.gov/shelterassessment

be initiated before the results of the rapid health assessment are available. Subsequent detailed needs assessments are often conducted during the recovery and rehabilitation phases of the disaster cycle to provide information over time.

Objectives and Methods

The primary objectives of rapid health assessments are to assess the following:

- Presence of ongoing hazards (e.g., a persistent toxic plume following a major chemical release)
- Nature and magnitude of the disaster (number of people affected or geographic area involved)
- Major medical and public health problems of the community (risk of further morbidity and mortality; observed patterns of injury, illness, and death; need for food, water, shelter, and sanitation)

- Availability of resources within the local community and the impact of the disaster on those resources
- Community need for external assistance
- Augmentation of existing public health surveillance to monitor the ongoing health impact of the disaster

Before field visits and preliminary data collection can begin, a team must be assembled. Members of this multidisciplinary team could include an epidemiologist, a clinician, an environmental engineer, and a logistician. If the area affected by the disaster is large and crosses jurisdictions, several assessment teams may be required, as might specialty teams to concentrate on transportation, communications, and infrastructure. It is important to coordinate with local agencies to ensure that each assessment will yield new information and that the information is shared with those who need it. If more than one assessment team is required, all teams should use the same standardized assessment form. Data forms can be developed in advance using existing protocols, such as the rapid health assessment protocols developed by the World Health Organization for various events, including sudden impact natural disasters, chemical emergencies, and sudden population displacements.

Baseline data gathered prior to the field assessment are essential. This information includes background on the population size and demographics, including the presence of vulnerable groups such as older adults, children, and people with functional needs. Census data can provide an accurate estimate of the number of people affected by the disaster, though estimating the actual number of individuals present in the disaster area at the time of impact (e.g., after evacuation following hurricane warnings) can be difficult.

Advanced information on the health care infrastructure is also critical. The location, bed capacity, and capabilities of local and regional health facilities must be documented. The status of local Emergency Medical Services (EMS) must be assessed as well, including search and rescue capabilities. This determination of available EMS resources, can serve as a surrogate measure of likely response in case of disaster. Similar information on the location and status of public utilities (i.e., provision of water, sanitation, and electricity) will also assist assessment efforts.

Detailed maps are essential for rapid health assessments. These maps should show high-risk areas (including vulnerable populations); major transport routes; main utility lines; locations of health facilities and water sources; and concentrations of residential, office, shopping, and industrial areas. These maps are often available from government departments, academic institutions, and utility companies. (See Chapter 4 on GIS maps.)

All these data will be wasted if not supplied to decision-makers with authority to shape the disaster plan. The rapid health assessment should be an integral component of emergency response planning.

Timeline

For acute onset disasters, such as transportation crashes and hazardous material incidents, the initial on-scene assessments should be conducted within minutes if possible, but might not occur for a few hours. When multiple casualties are suspected, such as following an earthquake or tornado, the initial assessment should be completed within several hours of impact. Any assessment should be completed as soon as possible as the majority of deaths will occur within the first 24 to 48 hours. This early information will be critical in identifying the need for Emergency Medical Services and urban search and rescue teams.

For slower-onset disasters, information can be collected during the first 2 to 4 days (e.g., floods, epidemics, population displacements). An even longer time frame may be used for assessments of droughts and famines. In these settings, it is often more appropriate for health officials and disaster managers to collect baseline data and then follow trends with ongoing public health surveillance.

Categories of Data and Priorities for Collection

Data collection priorities differ for sudden impact disasters (e.g., earthquake, tornado) and gradual onset disasters (e.g.., famine, complex humanitarian emergency). Teams often have limited time in which to collect data for a rapid health assessment. In these situations, only the most relevant health-related information should be collected. The specific elements of data will vary according to the type of disaster and the stage of the response. A concise checklist, developed prior to the field visit will ensure that the most critical health issues are assessed.

Sudden Impact Disaster

Days 1 to 2: Baseline information should be gathered as discussed previously. The sole objective is to collect information needed for immediate relief. The priority at this stage is the emergency medical response to save life and limb. Since obtaining accurate data can be difficult directly after impact, initial relief efforts are frequently guided by rough estimates. Key data include the following:

- Ongoing hazards, since persistent hazards that pose a risk to rescue personnel must be eliminated or controlled prior to initiating relief efforts
- Injuries, since the number, categories, and severity of injuries help characterize the impact of the disaster and prioritize relief activities
- Deaths, since the number and causes of death help characterize the impact of the disaster (However, information about deaths is not as important in guiding relief efforts as injury data)
- Environmental health and the status of community lifelines (e.g., water, sewer, power), since an early estimate of the population's needs for shelter, food, water, and sanitation may prevent secondary disaster-related health problems
- Health facilities, since the impact of the disaster on the physical integrity and functioning of the health infrastructure may indicate the need for temporary medical shelters and external medical assistance

Days 3 to 6: At this stage, information will be needed to guide secondary relief. Emergency medical interventions and search and rescue activities may be less important, as more than 96% of critically injured patients will already have received medical care in the event of an earthquake or building collapse. However, flood or hurricane disasters may destroy the health care infrastructure, and assessments should identify the need for care of chronic conditions and other problems, such as loss of medication or medical supplies. If disaster-related deaths are still occurring, any persistent hazards causing or contributing to these deaths must be identified. Injuries as a result of cleanup activities and secondary impact from the disaster (e.g., fire, electrocution, hazardous material release) must be monitored carefully to optimize recovery efforts. Ensuring the availability of and access to primary health care becomes more important at this point than emergency care since disaster-affected populations still require routine medical services. Assessment of environmental health and utilities must clarify the longer-term needs related to food, water, sanitation, shelter, and energy.

Day 6+: During the recovery stage, disaster plans should be fully implemented and resources made available for all sectors. Surveillance should concentrate on both rates of illness and injuries determined from information available from all health facilities and the occurrence of infectious disease, since outbreaks are uncommon after sudden impact disasters unless major population displacement or disruptions of the public health system occur. The surveillance system should track diarrheal disease and acute respiratory infections if people are displaced into overcrowded shelters or if there is a disruption of environmental health services. The status of health facilities, the number of health personnel, and the availability of medical and pharmaceutical supplies should be accurately tracked. Environmental health (water quantity and quality, sanitation, shelter, solid waste disposal) and vector populations must be monitored carefully. Floods are often associated with swells in mosquito populations, increasing the risk of arboviral infections, such as St. Louis encephalitis. Surveillance for arboviruses can assist in determining the need for vector control following flooding.

Gradual Onset Disaster

Baseline assessments are conducted and a surveillance system established. Background information must include population size and demographics, major causes of morbidity and mortality, sources of health care, and the status of preexisting public health programs, such as immunizations. Key health indicators address both morbidity and mortality. For mortality, the crude mortality rate (deaths/10,000/day) is the most sensitive indicator of the population's health. Age- and sex-specific rates should be collected. The under-6 mortality rate is used to assess the health status of one of the most vulnerable groups in the population. For morbidity, information must be collected on rates of disease with public health importance, including diarrheal disease, respiratory infection, measles, malaria, and hepatitis. Rate of malnutrition in children younger than 6 years of age is the second most important indicator of the population's health. Data on environmental health should be collected and compared with the standards of 16 to 20 liters of water per person per day and one pit latrine per family.

The disaster impact on the health system can be assessed by measuring loss of staff, since major population displacements and complex humanitarian emergencies are frequently associated with health professionals not being available to communities; the status of health infrastructure, as populations may no longer have ready access to health facilities, and hospitals and clinics are frequently damaged or destroyed; and the status of public health programs, as immunization programs, maternal and child health services, and vector control programs may all have been disrupted.

Sources and Methods of Data Collection

Data collection methods may be classified as primary (direct observation or surveys) or secondary (interviews with key informants or review of existing records).

Direct observation can be completed on the ground or from the air. Direct on-the-ground observations can provide team members with a firsthand view of the impact and extent of the disaster. Major health problems in the observed area may be identified but may not be generalizable to other sites. Where possible, team members should conduct informal interviews with victims and responders. Aerial observation allows team members to confirm the geographic extent of the disaster and to view the impact in inaccessible areas. In addition, by viewing the entire geographic region, the most severely affected areas may be identified so that relief efforts can be more appropriately targeted.

Four types of surveys can be conducted. First, focused surveys may be used to collect health data. These are relatively resource-intensive and should therefore be reserved for data that are necessary but are not available through other sources. Second, surveys based on convenience samples may be conducted relatively rapidly and provide a gross estimate of the health care needs of the affected community. However, convenience samples do not provide population-based information, so are likely to be sources of bias. Third, telephone surveys using randomly selected telephone numbers may be useful in determining the impact of the disaster and the health care needs of the community. Phone surveys require an intact communications system and may not provide a representative sample. People who are at home during the time of calling (e.g., elderly) may be overrepresented, introducing a potential source of bias. Fourth, surveys based on cluster-sampling methods are being used more frequently in disaster settings. Sampling methods such as simple random sampling, stratified random sampling, and systematic random sampling are time- and resource-intensive, making them impractical for the purposes of a rapid health assessment. Cluster-sampling methods for natural disasters are based on the World Health Organization's Expanded Programme on Immunization method for estimating immunization coverage.

Cluster-sampling techniques provide population-based information to both guide and evaluate relief operations. Modified cluster-sampling methods can be used to estimate the size of the population in the disaster-affected area, the number of people with specific health care needs, the number of damaged or destroyed buildings, and the availability of water, sanitation, food, and power in the community. Cluster surveys can usually be conducted rapidly, and the results made available within 24 hours. Follow-up surveys can be repeated in the same area over the following 3 to 14 days. Cluster surveys are particularly useful when the area of damage is generally uniform, such as after a hurricane. They have been less useful following earthquakes, where the distribution of damage may vary widely between locations. Among displaced and famine-affected populations, such as large refugee settlements, cluster surveys have been used to estimate the prevalence of acute malnutrition, disease rates, the major causes of mortality, and access to health care services.

For secondary data collection, interviews with key health and emergency personnel can be useful in obtaining qualitative data concerning the disaster. Gross estimates of the impact and population needs may also be available. Attempts should be made to corroborate these data with those collected through primary methods. Interviews may be conducted with hospital emergency room staff, medical personnel at temporary health facilities, community providers, public health officials, incident commanders, paramedics, police and fire department officials, Red Cross representatives, and coroners. To augment and confirm these interviews, an effort should be made to review documented medical records from health facilities. Health data may be available from hospital emergency rooms and inpatient units, temporary health facilities, community providers, public health officials, and coroners' offices.

Limitations of Data Assessment

Health officials and disaster managers should be aware of the limitations of data that are collected during the rapid health assessment. Assessment team members must balance their preferences for sound epidemiological methodology against the time constraints and other limitations of the data collection process. Inaccuracies may result from logistical, technical, and organizational problems. Potential limitations include incomplete data, poor internal or external validity, and reliance on secondary sources of information. Unless population-based methodologies are used, data collected may not be representative of the community being assessed, and data collected from one population may not be generalizable to those in other regions. Further, information may not be available from certain disaster-affected areas as a result of poor access and communications. Finally, underreporting of health events by rescue and medical personnel may occur because accurate documentation ranks as a low priority during the initial disaster response, particularly during sudden impact disasters.

Community Assessment for Public Health Emergency Response

The CDC's Community Assessment for Public Health Emergency Response (CASPER) is used to conduct rapid need and rapid health assessments. Based on statistical methods, CASPER standardizes the assessment procedures and assists public health and emergency management officials in determining the health status and basic needs of a community following a disaster. This tool was designed to guide public health in prioritizing their response and to create a basis for distributing resources.

A CASPER toolkit has been developed to provide specific guidelines on developing an instrument for data collection, methodology for conducting a rapid assessment, selecting a sample, steps for data collection, and training those carrying out the assessment, conducting the analysis, and writing the report. CASPER collects information at the housing unit level to determine the population affected by a disaster. Any community considering the use of CASPER should evaluate both the available resources and recommended timeline to determine whether CASPER is the appropriate sampling methodology. (The CASPER toolkit can be found at http://www.bt.cdc.gov/disasters/surveillance/pdf/CASPER_toolkit_508%20COMPLIANT.pdf.)

Chapter 6

Disaster Communications

C ommunications before, during, and after disaster strikes dictate the success of prevention and relief efforts. This chapter reviews both the strategies and methods of communicating with other responding agencies and the public during a disaster and the equipment and systems that public health officials and responders will rely on or use. Specific chapter units include the communication of risk, who is the audience, internal and external communications, communicating warnings and response needs, working with the media, types of communications systems, and the specific communication systems used by public health officials.

Public Health Role

- Communicate about health and public health matters with the following:

  ○ Those providing medical care (hospitals and their emergency departments, community providers, and other public health and social service agencies)
  ○ First responders (fire, police, emergency medical services) and other responders (national guard)
  ○ Local and regional laboratories
  ○ General public
  ○ Officials, mayors, governor(s)
  ○ Partners (emergency management, Red Cross, public works)

- Set up communication network with health-related agencies, the media, and the public by providing public health reports to the media on regular basis
- Share information and conduct data analysis across agencies and organizations

Communicating About Threats Related to Emergencies

Historically, communicating about threats or risks has been part of the responsibility of professionals working in environmental areas. Now, the evolution of practice is requiring all public health leaders to effectively communicate information about potential dangers. Not only does our community look to us for information and guidance, but our colleagues, especially those in governmental agencies, seek our assistance in evaluating and informing them and the public about health risks.

When communicating in emergencies, strategies used in environmental practice can be applied. These strategies incorporate principles that influence people's perception of risk. The principles established by Fischhoff et al. in 1981, are likely to have direct application to our communication practice in the threat of or following disasters. Individuals are less willing to accept risks they perceive as imposed on them or controlled by others, having little or no benefit, unevenly distributed among different groups, created by humans, catastrophic or exotic in occurrence, generated by an untrusted source, and mostly affecting children. By contrast, individuals are more willing to accept risks perceived as voluntary and under an individual's control, having clear benefits, fairly distributed or of natural causation, generated by a trusted source, mostly affecting adults, and whose occurrence is a statistical probability.

Who Is the Audience?

Communication is a task carried out by every person involved in disaster response. The purposes of each communication will vary, depending on whether the person has primary responsibility for communicating (such as an agency official or communications director) or simply considers communications to be part of one's job as an agency employee. The more you know about those with whom you are communicating—what their concerns are, how they perceive the emergent threat, and whom they trust—the greater the likelihood that you will successfully communicate with the people who make up your audience. The characteristics of audiences will vary, and this variance may affect how and what you communicate, such as the nature of their concerns, attitudes, level of involvement, level of knowledge, and experience. Depending on what the individuals experienced and what they were exposed to in the emergency, or their responsibility in responding to the emergency, the audience may be concerned about health and safety, impacts on the environment, economic implications, fairness as to exposure to the health risks, the process of responding, or the legalities of the process. In the response phase of an emergency, health and safety are likely to be the chief concerns. Finally, those responsible for communicating must be sure that the information gets out to the intended audience, a process referred to here as *transmission,* and that the intended audience has received and understood the information, here called *reception.*

Internal and External Disaster Communications

During the impact and postimpact phases of a disaster, communications occur both internally and externally. Public health agencies communicate internally to provide information to other responders and to solve problems. Internal communications also occur among an organization's staff and includes call-up and notification of the emergency, assignments to work, sharing of information, status reporting, monitoring and tracking of public health concerns, and so forth. Internally, a first step in preparing to communicate during an emergency is to compile a 24-hour contact directory so that supervisors can reach staff at any time. External communication occurs among health departments, hospitals, community providers, ambulatory care facilities, emergency management and first responders, laboratories, pharmacies, veterinarians, community decision-makers, community-based organizations, other responders, volunteers, the media, area residents, and the general public.

External communication to the media and area residents must provide factual information that the public finds credible. Information being communicated is referred to as the "message."

Initially, a spokesperson has 15 to 30 seconds to get an agency's message across to those responding to an emergency, who are likely to have an "adrenaline high." Thus, it is important to develop strategies in advance for communicating immediately after the event occurs and during the response phase. There will be more time to plan communications during recovery. Strategies may be different in each phase. Further, when communicating about preparedness and threats such as terrorism or releases of toxic agents, governmental spokespersons should deliver consistent messages that motivate protective actions by those who hear the message.

Three actions are critical to communicating during an emergency: advance planning, collaboration, and updating the message as needed. When planning for your agency's overall response, include communication as a section in the plan. This component should describe how you will communicate information about the emergency and who will deliver the message. Identify what information could be needed for different emergencies and establish ways to gather that information as quickly as possible. Prepare communication messages to have on file or locate how you will access them through federal agencies. Be sure that hard copies of the messages are readily available, in case there is a loss of power and computer files cannot be accessed.

Collaborate with other agencies responsible for communicating in an emergency. Arrangements for release of public information should be worked out in advance, including how you will communicate with community leaders and build on their views that public health professionals are the "go-to" source for health information.

It is important to build vertical connections among the local, state, and federal levels and across response sectors. To create efficiencies in these networks, the channels of communication need to be interoperable. As neither natural nor technological disasters respect borders and boundaries, regions should try in advance to agree on best strategies for handling information about hazards and threats. The development of inter- and intra-agency procedures may involve cross-state cooperative agreements. A broad range of media can be used for communicating to both the press and the public. It is important to involve the stakeholders (public, responders, government officials) and incorporate their views into your message. Finally, during an event, you should track the publics' perceptions and alter the message when needed.

Communicating Warnings and Response Needs

With improved forecast technology, such as the tracking of storms through satellite imagery from government and commercial sources, we can issue advance warnings to allow timely evacuation before hurricanes, taking shelter against tornadoes, and taking active steps toward vector control. Messages communicated to the public should be positive and reassuring yet factual. These bulletins must translate technical information into lay language that will result in the average person taking action. The messages must be accurate, timely, and congruent for both the internal and external audiences so that consistency exists between the actions of the response agencies and the actions requested of the public. Messages should be clear, concise, and credible and include information about the nature of the expected hazards, specific step-by-step actions regarding safety precautions, where to go and what to bring if evacuating, and requirements for sheltering in place, when necessary. When possible, warnings should give sufficient time to enable everyone to take whatever preventive actions are required.

Public health leaders in the stricken community are often inundated with requests for information, and these requests interfere with the more urgent need to educate the public about injury prevention and food and water safety, request supplies, and share surveillance information with community officials. Knowing that this is likely to happen, part of the initial organizational response should be the establishment of and notification about a victim locator service. More information about victim locator services can be found in Chapter 9.

Communication can be a weak aspect of a disaster response without safeguards to ensure both the transmission and reception of information. Senders of all messages must request and receivers supply verification that the transmission was both received and understood. Validation that the intent of the message was understood is evident by observation of safety responses by citizens, use of shelters, and other appropriate actions.

Frequently residents do not want to evacuate areas threatened by impending disasters. In disasters for which adequate warning is available, such as hurricanes, communities can prevent morbidity and mortality by making appropriate decisions, disseminating information, coordinating warnings, and posting messages that are easily understood and motivate evacuation. In disasters such as earthquakes and tornadoes, for which advanced warning is rare, the risk of injury and death increases. However, even with tornadoes, morbidity and mortality can be lessened by warning through a variety of media as soon as conducive weather conditions are identified or the funnel cloud itself is spotted. Nocturnal tornadoes result in the most injuries because people do not hear the warnings.

Unfortunately, some officials withhold warnings until the last possible moment, sometimes until it is too late to take effective protective action. This has been attributed to the disaster myth that panic is a likely response and that panic following a call for evacuation might cause more deaths and injuries than would the disaster itself.

Requests for aid following a disaster require the same clarity as warnings issued in advance. Otherwise, donations may be inappropriate (e.g., wool blankets shipped to hurricane victims in the Caribbean, shipment of outdated medications) and cause additional problems on the receiving end. The management of donations is one of the most time-consuming and difficult response activities in both large domestic and international disasters. The Pan American Health Organization has developed a supply management system known as SUMA that facilitates the sorting, classifying, and inventorying of the supplies sent to a disaster-stricken area. However, the stricken locale has to sort and distribute what is sent, which takes manpower away from the disaster response. Monetary donations can be used more flexibly. Preventing the broadcast of broad appeals for help and volunteers often requires advance education of the media, local government officials, and even disaster relief organizations.

Channels for Communication

Effective communication depends on utilizing specific methods appropriate for both the message and the audience. Different messages are required for different audiences and media. Table 28 describes channels of communication that are mapped for delivery to different audiences.

Working With the Media

A strategically planned campaign, worked out well in advance, will most likely lead to success in working with the media. Designate either a spokesperson or public information officer who can guide the implementation of a comprehensive communications plan, and through whom all information is provided to the media. A designated spokesperson coordinates messages so that the organization speaks with a single voice, and provides a consistent point of contact for media representatives. It is also important to assign an alternate or two, because the designated spokesperson may not always be available. The spokesperson will establish relationships with media professionals in advance and prepare advance protocols for the release of information, including situation-specific messages. Part of a communications campaign will include media training for public health leaders.

The establishment of a Joint Information Center (JIC) as part of the community's response plan is critical to the success of communicating a uniform message. The JIC should provide information consistent with information provided by the state JIC in a statewide emergency. The local JIC must have multiple-line phone banks for answering calls from the public and redundant communication systems in case the phone lines are down.

Preparing for an Interview

This section provides some specific tips about interviewing with the media. When the press calls, remember that reporters are usually working on a deadline. Call back right away. Since reporters' schedules may change if events create "breaking" news, interviews may get canceled or rescheduled for a more urgent story. However, in emergencies, your story is most likely the urgent one.

Ask for the reporter's name and the media organization for which he or she is reporting. Ask the subject, format, and duration of the interview, some sample questions, and who else will be interviewed. If you need time to prepare and the deadline allows, offer to call back at a specific time and follow up. If a reporter arrives in your office or calls at a time when you are unprepared, try to schedule the interview for later in the day so you can prepare. If you are not the best person to interview because you lack the necessary knowledge, let the reporter know that.

Table 28. Audience and Communication Channels

Audience	Communication Channels
Colleagues	Blogs Hotlines Internet forums Meetings to address questions and concerns Microblogs News releases and fact sheets Site tours Social networking sites Podcasts RSS feeds Text messaging Unit newspaper articles
Area residents	Community meetings Direct mailings Fliers Image/video sharing (Flickr, YouTube) Internet forums Films, videos, and other materials at libraries Newspaper articles and ads Microblogs (Twitter) Mobile Web sites Podcasts Radio and TV talk shows RSS feeds Social marketing Social networking sites Text messaging Widgets
Elected officials, agency leaders	Advance notices Fact sheets Frequent telephone calls Invitations to community meetings Microblogs (Twitter) Mobile Web sites News releases Personal visits RSS feeds Widgets

(continued on next page)

Table 28. (*continued*)

Audience	Communication Channels
Media	Blogs
	Clear, informative fact sheets
	Microblogs (Twitter)
	Mobile Web sites
	News releases that focus on your message
	News conferences
	Podcasts
	RSS feeds
	Site visits
	Text messaging
	Widgets

Adapted from Agency for Toxic Substances and Disease Registry. 1994. *A Primer on Health Risk Communication: Principles and Practices.* Rockville, MD: U.S. Public Health Service. Available at: http://www.au.af.mil/au/awc/awcgate/cdc/primer_health_risk_comm.htm. Accessed March 3, 2011; and American Public Health Association (APHA) et al. 2009. Expert Round Table on Social Media and Risk Communication During Times of Crisis: Strategic Challenges and Opportunities. Special Report. Washington, DC: APHA. Available at: http://www.apha.org/NR/rdonlyres/47910BED-3371-46B3-85C2-67EFB80D88F8/0/socialmedreport.pdf. Accessed March 3, 2011.

Prepare by thinking through the interview in advance. The media will be seeking information on who, what, when, where, why, and how. For broadcast media, prepare a 10- to 12-word "sound bite," and for print media prepare a one- to three-line quote for each of two or three main points about your subject. To support your ideas, gather facts and figures presented in printed material that can be given to the reporter to help minimize errors. If time allows, offer to fax or mail the reporter the printed information in advance of the interview. Anecdotes can also be useful in connecting your information to the experience of the reporter's audience. Prepare responses to other questions that the reporter might ask.

Choose a location where you can screen out extraneous noises such as background hums from air conditioning or heating units, phones, computers, or printers. Find out in advance whether the interview is edited or will be live. In a live interview, be prepared to think on your feet and respond "off the cuff." In edited interviews, pause briefly before answering a question to give yourself time to think out your answer and to give the reporter a "clean" sound bite. In a TV interview, look at the reporter and not the camera. The only exception is for a satellite interview, for which the reporter or anchor may not be on location. If you are uncertain where to look, ask.

For television interviews, dress in a subtle manner. Wear solid-colored clothing and simple accessories. Stripes, plaids, or other designs can cause problems with the picture on color televisions. Before you go on the air, practice how you will deliver your key points. If possible, look in a mirror before going on camera. Television magnifies images, so be sensitive to nonverbal messages that you may communicate. Do not allow your body language, position in the room, or dress to be inconsistent with your message. Be aware of your nonverbal communication, particularly gestures or nervous habits. Assume you are on camera at all times, from all angles. Make an effort to appear to be a good listener when other people are speaking.

Sit or stand stationary in front of the radio or TV microphones and avoid moving from the microphone. Moving to and from the microphone can cause the recorded volume to rise and fall.

During the Interview

If you are being interviewed by phone, the reporter is required by law to tell you when you are being recorded. Ask whether the interview is being taped if you are uncertain. Be brief in your responses. Television and radio stories may use only a 10- to 30-second sound bite. The shorter your comments, the less likely they are to be edited.

State your conclusions first and then provide supporting data. Stick to your key message(s) and main points. Provide information on what your agency is doing to respond to the emergency or issue. Emphasize achievements made and ongoing efforts to respond. Don't talk too much and try not to raise other issues. Assume that everything you say and do is part of the public record. Repeat your points if necessary if you have wandered onto a tangential issue. Since you want your response to be understood on its own if the reporter's question is edited out, speak in complete thoughts.

Don't overestimate a reporter's knowledge of your subject and don't assume the facts speak for themselves. Offer background information where necessary. Explain the subject and content by beginning at a basic level using positive or neutral terms. Avoid academic or technical jargon and explain all terms and acronyms. Don't rely on words alone; visuals can be helpful to emphasize key points if the interview is in person. If you do not understand a question, ask for clarification rather than talking around it. Do not assume that you have been understood. Ask whether you have made yourself clear. It's acceptable to say, *This is an important issue and I want to be sure I convey our position precisely. Would you mind reading back what you just heard me say?* If you do not have the answer, say so. Offer to get the information or tell the reporter where to find the information.

Rather than say, *No comment,* tell the reporter if you cannot discuss a subject. For example, *I can't answer that because I haven't seen the research you are referring to.* Be honest and accurate. Don't try to conceal negative information. Let the reporter know what you are doing to solve a problem. If you make a mistake, correct yourself by stating that you would like an opportunity to clarify.

Finally, do not assume the interview is over or the recording equipment is turned off until you are sure that it is off.

After the Interview

Specify for the reporter how you would like to be identified. You will probably not be able to check the reporter's story before it appears. However, you can ask questions at the end of an interview. For example, you might inquire, *What do you think is the main story?*

Most reporters will be able to tell you when the story will appear. If you feel that you misspoke or gave incorrect information, call the reporter as soon as possible and let him or her know. Similarly, you can call with additional information if you forgot to make an important point. If an error appears, let the reporter know right away. Sometimes a correction can be printed or aired. You also will want to prevent the incorrect information from being used as background for future stories.

Watch for and read the resulting report. Thank the reporter if the story is even fairly good. If you are unhappy with a story, share your concerns with the reporter only if the story is factually wrong. For radio and TV stories, obtain a tape of the final broadcast if possible and critique your own performance, looking for ways you might improve in the future.

Communication Systems

Communication during disasters involves the ability to notify authorities and for authorities to notify members of the community that there is an emergency. For citizens to notify authorities, 911 emergency calling and reverse 911 must be accessible to persons with hearing, speech, and vision disabilities. The systems used to notify communities are varied.

Alerting and Warning Systems

Communities are alerted to impending hazards through the Emergency Alert System (EAS) and the National Oceanic and Atmospheric Administration's Weather Radio All-Hazards Network (NWR). Initiated in 1997, EAS superseded the Emergency Broadcast System (and the Control of Electromagnetic Radiation System, commonly known as CONELRAD). Most emergency warnings in the United States are issued through EAS and are generated by the National Weather Service. EAS can be activated by authorities at all levels, including police, fire, weather, and other governmental authorities. Each state and several territories have their own EAS plans.

Working with the EAS, the NWR is a nationwide network of radio stations that broadcast comprehensive weather and emergency information for natural, environmental, and public safety hazards 24 hours a day, 7 days a week. NWR requires a special radio receiver or scanner capable of picking up its signal. Broadcasts are found in the VHF public service band at seven frequencies (MHz): 162.400, 162.425, 162.450, 162.475, 162.500, 162.525, and 162.550.

The national EAS broadcasts alerts over television, radio, cable, and satellite. With the growth of electronic media, Congress passed the Warning, Alert, and Response Network (WARN) Act in 2006 to establish a voluntary, national notification network that would modernize and expand EAS by providing geographically targeted alerts to wireless phones, Web browsers, and other electronic devices. As required in WARN, the Federal Communications Commission (FCC), Federal Emergency Management Agency (FEMA), and mobile phone providers are developing a Commercial Mobile Alert System (CMAS) so that alerts can be received through cellular telephones (cell phones) and other electronic devices by 2012.

Governments at all levels already operate notification services which provide emergency alerts and information on mobile devices. With CMAS, cell phone subscribers will automatically receive information about disasters without having to subscribe. Emergency managers can develop alerts, send them to a national center where alerts are authenticated, and then the national center will aggregate the alerts and send them to CMAS for distribution in the affected area.

FEMA has created a standard for formatting messages so a single message can activate multiple warning systems over various media using numerous applications. This common data format is called the *common alerting protocol*. With CMAS, FEMA will be able to send emergency information that is aggregated from federal, state, and local officials.

The California Emergency Management Agency initiated a CMAS alerting system in the fall of 2010. Similar to emergency alert broadcasts delivered through television or landline phones, the California CMAS alerts will send emergency text messages to cell phones in a defined geographic area, such as a city, county, or segment of a community.

System of Systems

The Department of Homeland Security is leading the development of an Integrated Public Alert and Warning System (IPAWS) to improve, expand, and integrate the existing notification structure. Systems targeted for inclusion in IPAWS include EAS, CMAS, and NWR. IPAWS will use digital media to send emergency alerts. A system-of-systems approach facilitates the delivery of information quickly and efficiently to a diverse population who use a variety of tools to communicate. Rather than depending on a single mode, this aggregated system of communication methodologies will provide for redundancy. Where one communication system may fail to reach the intended audience, another may be successful. A system-of-systems structure is the foundation for creating statewide warning systems. Local systems, regardless of the modes of communication, can tie into the statewide system.

Examples of the potential components of a system-of-systems include the following:

- Landline or cell phone calls based on geography or special groups
- Sirens or other mass notification for communities or buildings
- Messages on social media sites
- Pop-up or instant messages on desktops
- Text messages on smartphones
- E-mail with links to a multimedia system for the deaf
- Messages on digital signs (e.g., Amber Alerts)
- Messages to encoded receivers via FM radio
- Messages to Web media

Notification systems utilizing electronic media have been used for hurricane warnings. Communities can develop lists of phone numbers and e-mail addresses with priority messages sent to the entire list. Before and after Hurricane Ike struck land in September 2008, a Texas community sent messages to warn of the storm's approach and to notify about the availability of emergency supplies and FEMA aid. These systems have been used to instruct residents to shelter in place after a chemical plant explosion spread a plume of black smoke across nearby communities.

Social Media in Emergency Preparedness and Response

Communication in emergencies requires reaching all audiences, whether they use traditional or the latest communication modes, e-mail or text messaging, landline or cell phone, or are individuals who are disabled or are non-English speaking. Throughout history societies have used available technology, such as the teletype during World War II, to broadcast information about emergencies. More recently, communication relied on traditional mediums: radio, telephone, television, handouts, and posters. Technological innovation has exponentially expanded the pathways and today emergency communication occurs through a wide variety of tools.

Web-based and other electronic technologies used for interaction are known as social media. Public health agencies can leverage the networks created by social media to convey alerts and create dialogues that result in speedy community response to emergencies. Alerts can be sent and received in real time and anywhere there is a cell tower or satellite reception. Using social media brings the message directly to the user audience. Social media can reach groups who don't depend on or who may be hard to reach through traditional channels. Importantly, Web-enabled technologies address the problem of interoperability that has plagued traditional communication systems.

Social media are useful in the breadth of emergencies—an expert can supply guidance about an emerging infectious disease or a governmental agency can direct communities to take preventive actions. Emergency broadcasts through social media can help governmental agencies deliver a unified message about an emergency, direct traffic in evacuations, or issue shelter-in-place or other advice to minimize injury and illness. Using networks as a pathway for notification, social media can educate the public and promote preparedness before a disaster strikes. Officials can monitor what is happening on the ground in real time so they have a better understanding of the situation. Through social media, the many people who want to help can form a *crisis crowd*, where the people in the community provide information about events. Collaboration in sharing information and best practices during an emergency is improved using social media. Communication plans that are activated during a disaster should include social media as one of the channels of communication.

How Social Media Can Be Used

In an emergency, it is critical to notify the public and to reach a broad audience as soon as possible. To do this, people must be reached at work, at school, at home, at play, or in transit. People could be on their computers, surfing the Internet, watching television, listening to the radio, talking or texting on their cell phone, using a social networking site, receiving updates from a Web site such as Twitter, or not near a media outlet at all. Communication strategies need to be all encompassing.

The range of media is vast and reshaping the dissemination of emergency information. Services such as Twitter or text messages are used to quickly broadcast alerts and announcements. Blogs and podcasts broadcast messages and encourage a conversation with the audience. Social networking sites, like Facebook, are connected to National Weather Service feeds and are used to disseminate real-time weather alerts, warnings, and other preparedness information. Internet forums generate public participation or comment. Staying current with quickly changing events is effortlessly possible through a Web format known as RSS (Really Simple Syndication). By aggregating multiple data feeds into one location, RSS provides timely updates about a topic without visiting many sites individually and without needing to join multiple newsletters. RSS can be used to notify users that a site has new information.

Our government and other public safety authorities are disseminating information through social media to help citizens understand what it means to be ready or prepared for responding to emergencies. FEMA has initiated a readiness campaign which provides practical advice on preparing for and surviving a disaster. The Centers for Disease Control and Prevention (CDC) has a Twitter account on which they post instant updates on the status of a variety of public health topics. The CDC provides information accessible from smartphones (available at http://m.cdc.gov) on seasonal flu, H1N1 flu, public health emergencies, and more. State agencies are working with YouTube and Google to develop their own social networks. The National Weather Service uses Skype to talk to the local media during a weather event. Medical Reserve Corps chapters use Facebook to improve recruitment. Finally, it is now possible to reach people around the world using social media and current technology. People trapped in rubble after the earthquake in Haiti used their cell phones to call relatives in the United States to ask them to send help.

One of the limitations of social media is that the deluge of posts and texts can overwhelm the system; thus, proper technical planning is critical. When a survivor tweeted about the need for water after tornadoes struck Alabama in April, 2011, more than 20 voluntary agencies responded, because there was no coordination and therefore no feedback that the request was fulfilled. In addition, where there is a limited amount of bandwidth, neighboring communities may need to provide the emergency information. With social media fully integrated into basic emergency preparedness and response, community groups, faith-based organizations, and local public health officials can effectively communicate with more people before, during, and after disasters. By being integrated into social media, public health agencies ensure that accurate information is available to the public as quickly as possible.

Examples of Social Media

Social media have dramatically changed the way communities handle emergency response and has facilitated better decision-making based on more accurate and timely information. Broader audiences can receive the critical information needed to take protective action during and after emergencies through these interactive channels.

The National Weather Service, FEMA, and the National Hurricane Center all provide RSS feeds. Many news-related sites, Weblogs, and other online publishers syndicate their content as an RSS feed. When preparing or posting RSS feeds, it is advisable to include the full date and time in the heading or title of the updated post or press release. The viewer saves time by knowing when the event occurred and whether the report is an update without clicking on the feed. Feed Reader or News Aggregator software, available for different platforms, is needed to read an RSS feed. My Yahoo, Bloglines, and Google Reader are popular Web-based feed readers. Many sites display a small icon with the acronyms RSS, XML, or RDF to indicate that a feed is available. Crisis Commons (available at http://crisiscommons.org and at http://wiki.crisiscommons.org/wiki/Main_Page) is a community that has used technology to share best practices and lessons learned in response to disasters. Through CrisisCamp, an international network supported by Crisis Commons, volunteer users solve problems through technology to help people and communities in crisis. Table 29 describes social media techniques being used by emergency management or in development.

Twitter, Facebook, and YouTube

When landlines are not functioning but cell phone coverage is still intact, Twitter and Facebook are available. Twitter and Facebook are now widely used for the rapid mobilization of equipment, supplies, and people and for fundraising after a disaster. Communities use Twitter, with its 140-character limit, to communicate the broadest range of short messages—traffic delays to bomb threats. Twitter has provided on-the-ground information used for rapid damage assessments, individual requests for help, anecdotal information about relief efforts, even messages of hope for those affected by a disaster. Twitter is used in Southern California to track a wildfire, assess the fire from multiple locations, and inform all about the progression of the fire. By creating graphs of the data streams of a given topic among tweets, it may be possible to use the information for decision-making. As an example, graphing keywords in tweets, such as cough or diarrhea, may serve as a surveillance tool (see Chapter 4). Finally, Social Media for Emergency Management (#SMEMchat) is a community of emergency managers who share valuable information about using social media as part of preparedness.

State and federal agencies, including FEMA, have Facebook pages. Those in the community who are signed up as friends have access to real-time updates and can post relevant information for a broad audience. Nonprofits have organized relief efforts through Facebook. After the earthquake in Haiti, the Global Disaster Relief page utilized the technical infrastructure of Facebook to facilitate a quick response of dollars and resources.

Many governmental departments and nonprofits are utilizing YouTube. Government agencies take advantage of media advertising policies and expand their market by running informational videos before the entertainment on YouTube or

Table 29. Examples of Social Media Techniques for Emergency Management

Location or Agency	Tool	Use
San Francisco, CA	• Facebook, Twitter, YouTube	• Disseminate information about emergency preparedness • Issue public warnings
San Francisco, CA	• AlertSF	• Text-based notification system for emergencies
Manor, TX	• CiviGuard • Smartphones	• Location-specific emergency alerts • Send response data from field to emergency responders
U.S. Geological Service	• Twitter Earthquake Detector • Twitter Associated Press International	• Monitor feeds to rapidly detect earthquakes • Conduct search for earthquake and aggregate information based on number of tweets
Virginia Department of Emergency Management	• Virginia Interoperability Picture for Emergency Response	• Geographic Information System platform that integrates feeds from 250 sources • Emergency response personnel can use single source of information to understand events
U.S. Department of Defense	• All Partners Access Network	• 380,000-user network • Community of communities Web site using wikis, blogs, forums, and file sharing • Exchange of information with authorized mission partners • In Haiti response, posted that fully functioning hospital had no patients and hospital reached capacity the next day
Department of Homeland Security (DHS)	• DHS First Responders Community of Practice	• Online network of emergency response professionals • Share best practices

Adapted from Yasin R. 2010. 5 ways social media improves emergency management. *Government Computer News.* September 6:18–23.

other video hosting sites, like Hulu. FEMA's Ready Campaign (available at http://www.ready.gov) is one example of the use of this strategy. WorkSafeBC, a Canadian organization committed to promoting health and safety for workers, has a dedicated channel on YouTube. WorkSafe posts public service announcements and provides training videos, including during a disaster or large-scale incident.

Smartphones and Other Communication Devices

Smartphones have redundant communication options—voice, short message service, text messaging, e-mail over cellular, Wi-Fi and satellite capability—which enable communication and information access when any one network is not working. Smartphones, with easy access to the resources of the Internet, have software that enables the user to access pictures, maps, and allows the download of health, safety, and preparedness applications before and during an emergency. Personnel can access information from the field as if they were at their desks. Door-to-door field assessments are made easier when assessment forms can be readily completed on the screen of a cell phone with the data automatically loading to a centralized database. Rapid health assessments can be completed in hours. Financial software can be preloaded to track all expenses as they occur, improving on-the-ground financial accounting. Rescue and medical care are also made easier. Phones with global positioning system (GPS) capability have been used to locate people who are trapped in rubble. In Haiti, responders placed cell phones on the chests of the injured and transferred electrocardiogram readings to medical units. Crisis Mappers (available at http://www.crisismappers.net) facilitate a rapid response by combining GPS, mobile phones, statistical modeling, and visual analytics to map needs and requests following a disaster.

Smartphones are also used to provide guidance to those directly impacted. Tsunami warnings via text messaging and e-mails were sent to alert the deaf community. FEMA's Mobile Web site, accessible from any cell phone with a Web browser, provides information on what to do before, during, and after a disaster (available at http://www.m.fema.gov). Being able to access the FEMA Web page from a cell phone makes it easier to know how to take preventive actions. FEMA is establishing systems so that individuals will eventually apply for assistance following a presidential disaster declaration, check on the status of their application, and update an existing application from their phones.

Using Communication Devices

Laptops and cell phones have limitations during emergencies. Although laptops allow work to be done outside of the traditional on-site work environment by accessing information from any location, their bulk and weight make them impractical for emergency workers in the field. Laptops also have relatively short battery lives and require connectivity within the range of a Wi-Fi network. To send an e-mail from a laptop, it has to be turned on and connected to a virtual private network, which may take several minutes. Traditional cell phones allow communication from the field but don't have adequate storage to handle data-enabled applications.

Smartphones are small and lightweight and have increased reliability as a result of recent advances in cellular networks. A user can send an e-mail from a smartphone instantaneously. Smartphones converge voice, database access, productivity applications, and multimedia on a single device.

With a wireless connection, responders can do the following:

- Manage incidents and emergency alerts
- Report on an incident
- Disseminate emergency procedures within seconds on an incident report
- Access preformatted messages, such as "shelter in place" or "evacuate immediately"
- Send message blasts without having to use multiple methods
- Receive confirmation that the message was received
- Send messages within and between agencies
- Use streaming video to enhance situational awareness
- Store documents
- Carry out tasks even if roads are impassable

Many emergencies require a multiagency response. Smartphones can be preprogrammed with contact information so that interagency communication is facilitated. Smartphones can be used to exchange text messages so that information that might otherwise be communicated over a radio is not misunderstood. Since available dedicated channels on two-way radios can be quickly used up during a disaster, communication is quicker, because text messages are not affected by heavy traffic in wireless networks.

Databases can be stored on smartphones using a removable SD ("secure digital") card. Wireless Information System for Emergency Responders (WISER), a free database which contains information from the Hazardous Substances Data Bank, a data file from the National Library of Medicine, can be installed or accessed over the Internet. Responders in the field can find out whether they need to take protective action against hazardous materials by checking WISER (available at http://wiser.nlm.nih.gov).

Employees can access their organization's disaster response plan from their smartphones. They can look up directives, management and inventory records, and emergency medical procedures. Specialized calculators can be used to determine wind speed and direction, radioactive fallout zones, and so forth. Smartphones can even become tactical tools through use of specialized mapping software. Maps of an incident area can show the location, identity, and status of other responders or the location of individuals needing rescue.

The capability of smartphones will be enhanced even more when the next generation of wireless technology, called *long-term evolution* (LTE), is fully developed. LTE is a new standard that increases the mobile bandwidth available to networks, which dramatically increases the flow of information. Using LTE, users in the field can send real-time data, such as high-definition video, in seconds rather than minutes.

Examples of smartphone applications available for better preparation and better management of communications during a crisis include the following:

Google Maps: Used by nongovernmental organizations to map operations.

Emicus: Aims to facilitate the receipt and sharing of disaster information within communities. An iPhone application that can be downloaded from Apple Computer via iTunes, Emicus has mapping tools and provides the location of critical services such as gas stations, building supplies, and pharmacies; allows users to upload photos and eyewitness reports and view real-time reports on Twitter and YouTube; uses a Short Message System for text alerts; and tracks the current status of weather events, such as hurricanes.

IGLOO is a template for PlayBook and BlackBerry that enables users to create and manage an online community directly from the user's tablet. IGLOO has been used to collaborate in disaster response. One example is the Crisis Kitchen, designed to enable and support humanitarian relief in response to the earthquake and recovery in Haiti (available at http://haitiresponse.igloocommunities.com).

Podcasting: Delivers audio and video content to subscribers via RSS.

Smart ICE: ICE (*in case of emergency*) information is programmed into cell phones so that emergency responders can locate next of kin if needed. Smart ICE expands that data to include personal and medical information. Smart ICE has an automatic emergency tone that rings every 2 minutes after calling 911 so that if a caller is incapacitated, responders can look for the iPhone and ICE information.

Xora: The Xora software company developed a location-based application that tracks damage during a disaster. Used to track the 2010 British Petroleum oil spill, responders knew where the damage was and could make real-time decisions on response as on-site teams took pictures of the damage, provided details, and captured the GPS coordinates.

iPhone: Has additional applications for emergency preparedness and response:

- *Hurricane* tracks violent storms and projects their path
- *Outbreaks Near Me* tracks H1N1 flu outbreaks
- The *Daily FEMA Insider* sends out daily bulletins about terror activity, homeland security information, threatening weather, etc.
- *ResQr First Aid* and *CPR Coach*, from Think Safe, provides first aid and CPR advice during emergencies
- *Emergency Medical Spanish Guide*, from Mavro, helps non–Spanish-speaking health care professionals communicate medical information to and from Spanish-speaking patients

As part of disaster preparations, agencies can ask staff to preprogram their phones. Some of the most basic information to program includes the following:

- Nonemergency numbers for police and fire
- Emergency contact information

- Medicines, medical conditions, and medical practitioners
- Emergency phone numbers for other staff and volunteers
- Meeting location where you will reconvene after an emergency
- Phone number to call to check "report to work" status

Communications Systems

Because multiple agencies must be able to share information and communicate without interruption during the impact and postimpact phases of a disaster, responding agencies should prepare to use interoperable information and communication systems. Communication lines must also be available between fixed and mobile locations. It is essential to build redundancy in communication systems as a result of technological limitations and the vulnerability of public networks.

Plans for communicating in emergencies need to ensure interoperability in three conditions: when technology is totally intact; when some technology is intact (e.g., wind or snowstorm); and in spartan conditions when no or little technology is intact (e.g., electrical blackout). The building of compatible systems that do not operate as silos requires careful interagency planning, partnering with the private sector and the implementation of integrated systems and policies based on industry standards. Public health officials must have alternative systems for communication and must be able to establish a link to the community's EAS. Radio systems and radio frequencies must be established, with staff trained on the use of these systems. Protocols should be developed between the 911 system, hospitals, and health departments so that public health agencies are among the parties regularly notified as part of the community's emergency response. Users of cellular, analog, and radio communications must recognize that these networks are not secure and that anyone with a receiver can hear the conversations.

Following both natural disasters (e.g., earthquakes, hurricanes, and tornadoes) and technological disasters (e.g., power blackouts), telephone landline services and data systems are likely to be nonfunctional. Arrangements must be made to receive calls through an emergency telecommunications system if the landline circuits are overloaded or not operational. A redundant, robust phone and data network would include landlines with phone-only units that plug directly into a wall jack, cell phones, Wi-Fi, or wireless Internet devices, beepers, and "walkie-talkies" (e.g., Nextel). Cell phones, one solution for telecommunications during disaster response, depend on the existence of relay stations or cells. Each cell has a limited capacity for simultaneous communications and covers only a defined radius. If too many people are using their cell phones, these systems will crash. Further, it may not be possible to guarantee security or privacy on cell phones. More importantly, cells are usually located in urban areas and along major traffic routes. Rural areas, where disasters are as likely to occur, may not be covered by such systems.

An alternative wireless model is available without a fixed infrastructure. Called *MANET* (mobile ad hoc network), this technology establishes high-speed communications among mobile devices, which double as routers. MANETs can carry all types of digital information, including text, voice, graphics, and video. To send information from one device to another, low-powered radio signals relay the data in short hops from one node to the next until the data reach their destination. MANETs can extend the range beyond that of traditional radios and can penetrate tall buildings. If a mobile computing device can accept the required communications card, it can serve as a node on a MANET. Other models include using a fixed communications station, such as a computer in a vehicle, linked to the Internet via satellite. A *vehicular ad hoc* network (VANET) is a form of MANET that provides communications between nearby vehicles and nearby fixed (usually described as roadside) equipment.

In all cases, the system must have off-site data backup. Some organizations will establish access to duplicate or triplicate networks. These might include separate access cables coming into a building with cable connections that are physically distant from each other. Further protection is provided by upgrading from basic straight-line links to more modern systems. Consider upgrading systems so they can route calls by firing signals through the air in light beams or radio signals. Such systems shoot invisible beams capable of transmitting volumes of data between building rooftops. Some high-speed Internet providers can support voice service, thus enabling multiple functions. Although some cable television systems offer redundancy, with cables run separately from phone lines, the downside is that transmission can slow down as the number of users increases, because cable lines are shared. Fixed facilities (hospitals and health departments) should also have standby sources of power to support communications equipment in addition to lighting, ventilation, heating, and air-conditioning.

Health departments and hospitals should have several unlisted phone numbers so that they can more easily make outgoing phone calls. Telephone lines coming into communication centers should be buried, clearly marked, and protected from damage. Records of the location of telephone lines must be maintained and updated so they can be located quickly postimpact.

For office-based communication about disaster-related activities, public health officials need basic computer equipment. Computers must have a CD-ROM drive, continuous Internet e-mail capacity, and sufficient security (e.g., firewall, password protection, virus scanning) to protect data and prevent against intrusion. Backup power supplies are essential, as is off-site data backup and storage. A system for broadcasting health alerts 24 hours a day, 7 days a week, must also be maintained.

Radio Operations

The emergency management sector will have radio networks available, and public health agencies should be linked as part of a community's emergency communication network. Communities use a variety of radio frequencies to communicate during emergencies. These include Lo Band, Very High Frequency (VHF), Ultra High Frequency (UHF), and 800 megahertz (digital). Both professional and amateur radio operators facilitate communication during emergencies.

Ideally, your community will establish a multichannel, multisite trunked 800-megahertz radio system to provide two-way radio communications. Such a system has dual use: it can provide day-to-day communications in support of public safety and intra/interagency communications in the event of an emergency. Manufacturers recommend that the batteries of these radios be changed every 2 years.

To avoid overload on radio frequencies, protocols should be established to limit the length of conversations and to establish several radio transmitter-receivers operating on multiple frequencies. Radio transmissions should not last more than 30 seconds. If, while using a portable radio, the listener is unable to hear a transmission, the user should relocate his or her position. If poor reception is not corrected by relocating, portable users may need to spell out their message using the phonetic alphabet (Table 30). All times should be denoted as military time (e.g., 1:00 P.M. is 1300 hours). An institution should designate persons responsible for carrying the radio and ensure that they are trained in its use.

It is important to follow the rules of etiquette established in your community when using the radios. Often these rules include identifying yourself and using the full name of your institution so that other users are aware of who is on the system at all times. If one party is transmitting and another party attempts to transmit, the second party's communication will not be received and the second party will hear a tone.

In order to test that the system is transmitting, most communities conduct a daily roll call of radio users. The response to the daily roll call is a simple "10–4" or "5 by 5." Table 31 identifies communication systems available to agencies and facilities.

Table 30. Phonetic Alphabet

A= Adam	L = Lincoln	W = William
B = Boy	M = Michael	X = X-Ray
C = Charlie	N = Nora	Y = Young
D = David	O = Oscar	Z = Zebra
E = Eddie	P = Paul	
F = Frank	Q = Queen	
G = George	R = Robert	
H = Henry	S = Sam	
I = Ida	T = Thomas	
J = John	U = Union	
K = King	V = Victor	

Table 31. Communication Systems

Phone Service	Radios	Internal Communication Methods	External Information Systems	Contact Directories	Social Media
PBX (Private Branch Exchange)	Radio link to local emergency management agency (800-MHz radio)	Walkie-talkies	Stand-alone computer and Internet access through dial-up modems and cable modems	Updated directories for internal and external contacts	Blogs
Analog phone lines	Ham radio (Radio Amateur Civil Emergency Service [RACES])	Overhead speaker and paging systems	Staff have access rights to the Health Alert Network (HAN)	Alert facility operator when Emergency Operations Center (EOC) activated	E-mail alerts and instant messages
Long-distance service provider trunks		Runner system		Vendor contact numbers	Podcasts
Cell phones					Online and streaming video
Satellite phones					Microblogs (Twitter)
Smartphones					Social networking sites (Facebook)
Skype					Mobile Web sites
					Widgets
					RSS feeds

Radio Amateur Civil Emergency Service

The Radio Amateur Civil Emergency Service (RACES) was founded in 1952 as a public service to provide a reserve communications group within government agencies in times of extraordinary need. The FCC regulates RACES operations; the amateur radio regulations (Part 97, Subpart E, §§ 97.407) were created by the FCC to describe RACES operations in detail.

Each RACES group of licensed amateurs is administrated by a local, county, or state agency responsible for disaster services, such as emergency management, police, or fire and rescue services. In some parts of the United States, RACES may be part of an agency's Auxiliary Communications Service. Some RACES groups refer to themselves by other names such as *Disaster Communications Service* or *Emergency Communications Service.* FEMA provides planning guidance, technical assistance, and funding for establishing RACES organizations at the state or local government level. Citizen band radio operators run the General Mobile Radio Service (GMRS). By sharing repeaters, GMRS users can communicate over a much wider area.

RACES provides a pool of emergency communications personnel prepared for immediate deployment in time of need. At the local level, hams may participate in local emergency organizations or organize local "traffic nets" using VHF and UHF. At the state level, hams are often involved with state emergency management operations. Local, county, or state government agencies activate their RACES group. Traditional RACES operations involve the handling of emergency messages on amateur radio frequencies. These operations typically involve messages between critical locations such as hospitals, emergency services, shelters, and other locations where communication is needed. RACES communicators may become involved in communications about public safety, EOC staffing, and emergency equipment repair. RACES groups develop and maintain their communications ability by training throughout the year with special exercises and public service events. (A comprehensive RACES manual, Guidance for Radio Amateur Civil Emergency Service, is available online at http://www.seattleyachtclub.org/files/FEMA%20Amateur%20Radio%20Guidance%20for%20Civil%20Emergencies.pdf.)

Hams also operate on the same radio wavelength through the Amateur Radio Emergency Service (ARES), which is coordinated through the American Radio Relay League and its field volunteers. In addition, in areas that are prone to tornadoes and hurricanes many hams are involved in SKYWARN, operating under the National Weather Service. Many national organizations have other formal agreements with ARES and other amateur radio groups including the National Communications System, the Red Cross, the Salvation Army, and the Association of Public Safety Communications Officials.

In July 2010, the FCC amended the amateur radio services rules to permit amateur radio operators to also transmit messages, under limited circumstances, during emergency disaster drills.

Public Health Emergency Communications Systems

Emergency Communications Systems (ECS) are Web-based systems that ensure rapid, effective and consistent communication to the news media, the public, and key stakeholders during public health emergencies, including terrorism events. Federal ECS facilitate an ongoing two-way dialogue with state and local health officers, public health information officers, clinician associations, policymakers, and other key stakeholders in all 50 states. Federal ECS have been used to respond to public inquiries, media telebriefings, press releases and interviews, and daily Web-based updates.

There are two major components to ECS, the portal and the content. The portal serves as a single gateway to an organization's Web-based information. Portals create efficiencies, facilitate the categorization of groups of information, and integrate applications while ensuring security. Structured levels of access can be granted for employees, public health professionals and community providers, the emergency management community, and the general public as well. By establishing a portal and by setting individualized security levels, organizations are able to control access to their Web-based systems with a single username and password. When a user logs onto a portal, the system looks at his or her credentials and allows the person to access those areas for which they have authorization. The Public Health Information Network (discussed in Chapter 4) is an example of a portal, as are many of the health information networks established at the state Department of Health level.

Epidemic Information Exchange

During an emergency, the Epidemic Information Exchange (EPI-X) links the U.S. Department of Health and Human Services (HHS) and the CDC/ATSDR command centers with state surveillance and response programs, provides 24 hours a day, 7 days a week (24/7) emergency alerts and creates a secure forum to share important disease information nationwide. Participation in EPI-X is limited to designated public health officials who are engaged in identifying, investigating, and responding to health threats. This secured listserv has been used to communicate with colleagues and experts about urgent public health events, to track information and create reports about outbreaks, create online conferences, alert health officials of urgent events by pager, phone, and e-mail, post and discuss newly emerging information from the CDC, and to communicate simultaneously with command centers at HHS, CDC, and all state and large metropolitan bioterrorism response programs. Available to its users in the field, in the laboratory, at the office, or at home, EPI-X was used to notify state epidemiologists by pager and phone of the first anthrax case in New York City and to track and notify new West Nile Virus activity throughout the United States. Other EPI-X reports included food-borne outbreaks, SARS activity, influenza surveillance, and pandemic preparation.

Health Alert Network

The most prevalent content-based ECS is the Health Alert Network, commonly referred to as the *HAN*. HAN, established to strengthen the public health infrastructure nationwide, is a subscription service for providers. HAN is used to ensure communications capacity at all local and state health departments and to update on the presence of disease as often as needed. Locally, HAN has daily practicality, including online dialogues where clinicians can confer with each other about syndromes presenting in their offices, emergency departments, and hospitals.

The numerous HANs—one in each state, the three largest city departments of health, and others—provide an alerting mechanism to pass on alerts that the CDC issues. The CDC established three categories of alerts: alert (do something now), advisory (important, may not require immediate action), and update (no action, information only). The alerting function uses various communication modalities to notify its user base: e-mail, fax, cell phone, and pager. There are both general (routine) and specific (emergency) alerts.

There is variability among the HANS as to their functionality. The most extensive Web-based systems allow access to general and personalized information to the broadest community of users and access to more secure information to a more selected group. HAN utilizes both a *pull* and a *push* method of disseminating information. These HANs are multifunctional. HANs send out e-mails to all subscribers to notify them that a new alert has been posted through a multichannel broadcast. HANs also post health alerts, archive all alerts, have a document library, a bulletin board for posting and threaded discussions, multiple levels of security, and can conduct online conferences supplemented with visuals, such as Microsoft PowerPoint presentations.

Each HAN administrator determines the list of authorized users and their security level. Most users require a one-factor authentication, where the user name and password are linked with a professional license number or other identifier and a third-party certifying authority. Key health care, public health, and emergency response personnel undergo a two-factor authentication (they are issued a username and password with a token or digital certificate that is stored on a user's computer). Their access is controlled by the system administrator. Communication between the user's browser and HAN application is encrypted.

Disaster Recovery and Information Technology Continuity

It is critical that public health agencies and facilities develop an information technology (IT) component as part of their disaster plan to mitigate the risks that could affect their ability to deliver public health services. The disaster plan should include arrangements for both clinical and business applications and detail a plan for recovery in the event of a disaster. The plan should be tested every 6 months to ensure that it is functional and viable. The test of the plan should be documented and the documentation retained.

The IT disaster plan should address the basic needs of the organization in maintaining continuity of operations and at a minimum include the following:

Prevention: A plan for protecting agency assets and identifying and managing the risks to the core activities of the organization

○ Inventory of critical forms, magnetic media, hardware, software, equipment, and supplies

- Development and maintenance of a vendor contact list
- List of critical organization applications
- Written vendor agreements
- Description of emergency recovery team roles and responsibilities
- Agreements with off-site data processing facilities in the event of an emergency

Response: Protocols for managing the crisis and its short- or long-term interruptions in agency operations

- Procedures to notify employees and partners and to escalate response activities
- Backup procedures and data recovery procedures

Recovery: Recovery of all operations.

Restoration: Repair and restoration of facilities and organizational operations

Chapter 7

Essentials of Disaster Planning

Although disasters are often unexpected, disaster planning can anticipate the common problems encountered and tasks required following large-scale emergencies. This chapter highlights the federal requirements and guidance for planning and discusses the principles of disaster planning, constraints on being able to plan, planning for various types of disasters, common tasks of disaster response, components of a disaster preparedness plan, key considerations in surge capacity, delivery of care under extreme conditions, and exercises to practice the plan.

Public Health Role

- Use traditional planning principles in preparing for the delivery of public health and health care services during the impact and postimpact phases
- Participate as full partners with the emergency management community in disaster response and recovery
- Participate in the development of and serve as an integral part of a community's disaster preparedness plans
- Participate in organizing all health partners in the community
- Coordinate efforts with state and federal planners

Planning Is Required

Planning has been an essential component of the emergency management field for decades. The devastating aftermath of Hurricane Katrina in 2005 led to legislation requiring enhanced planning and the development of capabilities to improve the medical and public health response to future disasters. Federal guidance discussed in this chapter includes the Pandemic and All-Hazards Preparedness Act (PAHPA) and the National Health Security Strategy (NHSS). As defined in Chapter 3, capabilities are the operational capacity and ability to execute preparedness tasks. Capabilities-based planning examines how this operational capacity can be built into a plan and identifies the skills required to execute the needed preparedness tasks.

PAHPA requires that health care facilities, including hospitals and mental health facilities, trauma care, and emergency medical service systems, develop plans to:

- Strengthen medical management, treatment capabilities, medical evacuation and fatality management
- Ensure the rapid distribution and administration of medical countermeasures

- Ensure effective utilization of public and private medical assets and integration with federal assets
- Protect health care workers and first responders from workplace exposures during public health emergencies

To do this, PAHPA requires public health organizations to develop and sustain essential profession-specific capabilities for federal, state, local, and tribal governments for the following:

- Monitoring and containment of disease

  ○ Situational awareness through detection, identification, and investigation domestically and abroad
  ○ Containment through isolation, quarantine, social distancing, and decontamination

- Risk communication and public preparedness
- Rapid distribution and administration of medical countermeasures

The NHSS[1] identifies capabilities for the provision of medical and public health services. The three key provisions are the following:

- Restore the public health, medical, and behavioral health infrastructure

  ○ Rebuild the medical and public health systems
  ○ Provide services even when critical infrastructure is affected (e.g., utilizing alternate care sites, supplementing the medical workforce with personnel from outside the community or jurisdiction)

- Mitigate hazards to health and public health facilities and systems

  ○ Reduce risks, including environmental toxins
  ○ Mitigate hazards by conducting risk assessments and developing detailed action plans to reduce vulnerabilities

- Enhance network of support services for long-term recovery

  ○ Build local response networks to aid in immediate response and long-term recovery in neighborhoods
  ○ Provide alternate options for service delivery

In March 2011, the Centers for Disease Control and Prevention (CDC) published guidance for state and local planners preparing to meet the needs of their

[1]U.S. Department of Health and Human Services (HHS). 2009. *National Health Security Strategy of the United States of America.* Washington, DC: HHS. Available at: http://www.phe.gov/preparedness/planning/authority/nhss/strategy/documents/nhss-final.pdf.

communities in a public health crisis. CDC identified 15 core capabilities grouped into six categories that describe the skills and capacity that each public health organization should have. The six categories are biosurveillance, community resilience, countermeasures and mitigation, incident management, information management, and surge management. The capabilities, definitions, and functions are identified in Appendix E. The complete standards include tasks, performance measures, and resource elements (available at http://www.cdc.gov/phpr/capabilities/Capabilities_March_2011.pdf).

Finally, the NHSS (as discussed in Chapter 3) includes 1 goal and several objectives to meet the public health and medical requirements. Maintaining and sustaining vital public health and medical services during a health emergency are addressed in:

- Goal 2 (strengthen and sustain health and emergency response systems)
- Strategic Objective 5 (ensure timely and effective communications)
- Strategic Objective 3 (ensure situational awareness)
- Strategic Objective 4 (foster integrated, scalable health care delivery systems that can incorporate surge capacity)

Federal Planning

Federal planning aims to fulfill the responsibilities of the Department of Health and Human Services (HHS) under both the National Response Framework and the requirements of relevant Homeland Security Presidential Directives (HSPDs). The principles in this chapter will be common to all planning activities even if some federal planning activities are revised under the policy development for Presidential Decision Directive (PDD) 8 (discussed in Chapter 3).

Federal planning for public health preparedness is organized into 4 areas:

- Federal Emergency Support Function 8 (ESF-8)
- Regional emergency coordination (REC)
- State and local preparedness
- Chemical, biological, radiological/nuclear (CBRN)

Federal Emergency Support Function 8

Those planning to carry out ESF-8 tasks develop playbooks for the operational response needed for each of the National Planning Scenarios (discussed later in this chapter). This planning is done so that HHS can fulfill its responsibilities under the National Response Framework. Once established, the specifics of the playbooks are integrated into HHS's response operations and those of the agencies that support ESF-8 activities.

Regional Emergency Coordination

The Regional Emergency Coordinators (REC) represent the Assistant Secretary for Preparedness and Response (ASPR) at the same ten regions used for other federal agencies around the country. They work closely with governmental and private sector health and emergency management officials to maintain high levels of preparedness in their region. The RECs collaborate with governmental, tribal, and private sector authorities to integrate everyone's plans for a comprehensive response to natural disasters, terrorist incidents, and other public health or medical emergencies.

State and Local

State and local planners develop policy and plans for state and local emergency preparedness and integrate their plans with federal planning. These planners meet regularly with the CDC, other HHS divisions, and the U.S. Department of Homeland Security to assure that preparedness activities are integrated across programs. State and local planners are also responsible for identifying performance measures and evaluating the preparedness of the systems receiving federal funding to enhance interoperable communications and surge capacity. This funding is available through the Health Care System Preparedness Cooperative Agreement Program administered by the ASPR. States are accountable for their preparedness outcomes through the evaluation processes led by state and local planners.

Chemical, Biological, Radiological/Nuclear

Chemical, Biological, Radiological/Nuclear (CBRN) planners provide subject matter and operational expertise for the development of CBRN-related playbooks and the procurement of countermeasures. CBRN planners work with interagency partners to develop tools to support the response to events involving CBRN. These tools include clinical algorithms and geocoding of response locations. CBRN planners also provide strategic direction during a response to CBRN.

Principles of Disaster Planning

Along with their differences, disasters have similarities in that certain problems and tasks occur repetitively and predictably. On the other hand, disasters differ not only quantitatively but also qualitatively from common daily emergencies. Thus, effective disaster response involves much more than an extension of routine emergency response (i.e., mobilization of more personnel, facilities, equipment, or supplies). Understanding the planning process and the lexicon of emergency management increases the effectiveness of public health professionals.

Effective disaster plans are based on empirical knowledge of how people actually behave in disasters. Plans are easier to change than is human behavior, so disaster plans should be based on what people are likely to do rather than on the expectation that the public will behave "according to the plan." Plans must be flexible and easy to change as a result of the breadth and diversity of laws, organizations, populations, technologies, hazards, resources, and personnel involved in disaster response. When developing plans, it is crucial to establish partnerships within the community so that agencies formulate an interactive plan that maximizes the available resources.

Disaster planning should focus on a local response with federal and state support. In any major natural disaster, the main rescue effort will most likely be executed by local authorities during the first 48 to 72 hours to ensure a timely response for the severely injured (e.g., those trapped in a collapsed building). Thus, disaster plans must be acceptable to the elected officials, the departments that will implement them, and those whom the plan is intended to benefit. Plans should be widely disseminated among all those involved and should be exercised regularly as discussed later in this chapter.

Because response to disasters is resource intensive and requires the broadest combination of skills, no single entity has the breadth needed for comprehensive planning. Planners should establish relationships with a variety of stakeholders who can contribute to the plan by understanding their agency's assets, capabilities, and limitations and their familiarity with the needs of the community. Groups and individuals who understand vulnerable populations should be involved in all stages of the planning process so that their needs can be integrated into each component of the community's plan. The emergency plan can include an annex which specifically addresses the actions to be taken to protect those with functional needs. Community planning should include mutual aid agreements and memorandums of under-standing regarding procedures for sharing resources during emergencies.

Similarly, disaster plans should provide for some authority at the lowest levels of the organization, since workers in the trenches must make many decisions during the impact and immediate postimpact phases. Disasters often present decision-making demands that exceed the bureaucratic capacities and information-processing abilities of the day-to-day management structure. Disaster plans that require all decisions to be made from the top down do not optimize the resources of the organization.

Increased Need for Planning

With the rising occurrence and mounting damage associated with natural and technological events, the increasing threat of terrorism, and the federal regulations requiring the capabilities of public health professionals, public health agencies should give priority to planning for disasters. No region of the United States is free from disaster risk. In fact, the effects of natural disasters escalate each year as a result of increases in population and development in vulnerable areas (such as coastal areas, flood plains, seismic fault lines, wilderness areas). At the same time, emerging and resident infectious disease, immigration, imported goods, rapid international transportation, and terrorism increase the potential for technological disasters and epidemic spread of disease. Finally, the economic health of the United States affects both the number of persons displaced (e.g., the homeless, the working poor) and recovery following disaster.

Constraints on Ability to Respond

Trends in health care reimbursement and delivery interfere with efforts by health care facilities to prepare for disasters. First, while federal grants are available for some health care institutions, decreasing reimbursement reduces the likelihood that facilities and community providers will allocate funds for disaster preparedness. Even if the budgetary allocations are adequate, fewer resources are available for the delivery of unusual services. For example, fewer supplies may be available for disaster response because hospitals and other health facilities have eliminated the local warehousing of supplies and instead reorder as needed. The trend to outsource services (laundry, kitchen, security) reduces the availability of important resources that would be needed postimpact. With shorter inpatient lengths of stay and greater use of ambulatory care, hospitals have reduced the number of available beds; with fewer beds, there are fewer available staff. The availability of beds postimpact will be further complicated by the trend toward hospitalizing sicker patients who require more intensive care, so fewer patients will be ready for discharge to create room for victims seriously injured in the disaster. Finally, while the focus on delivering care in nonhospital settings has increased, a parallel effort to ensure disaster readiness in nonhospital health care locations is neither universal nor carried out at the same level.

Planning for Various Disasters

Two strategies for disaster planning include the agent-specific and the all-hazards approaches. In agent-specific planning, communities only plan for threats most likely to occur in their regions (e.g., earthquakes, hurricanes, floods, tornadoes). For example, planning for earthquakes, floods, and wildfires will be more useful in California than would planning for hurricanes and tornadoes. Further, officials and taxpayers are more likely to be motivated by what are perceived locally as the most viable threats.

With the all-hazards approach to disaster planning, the level of preparedness is maximized for the effort and expenditures involved. Since many disasters pose similar problems and similar tasks, an all-hazards approach involves planning for the common problems and tasks that arise in the majority of disasters.

Assistant Secretary for Preparedness and Response Playbooks

The office of the ASPR has developed playbooks so that states and localities will know how to integrate their planning with the federal response. The playbooks available cover hurricanes, aerosolized anthrax, and radiological dispersal devices, and others are being developed. Each playbook addresses the core functions within emergency response of the incident command system (ICS), logistics, planning, and response for each type of event. Further, each describes the federal operational activities conducted under ESF-8. Such activities include providing for life-saving emergency medical care, restoration of the public health and medical infrastructure, evacuating and returning patients, providing veterinary medical assistance, managing fatalities, and providing for all human services needs, including those of vulnerable populations.

Each playbook contains the following five major sections:

- Scenario
- Concept of Operations

- Action Steps/Issues
- Pre-Scripted Mission Assignment Subtasks
- Essential Elements of Information

These playbooks highlight the key decision points, actions, capabilities and assets that may be required to support response to a specific type of emergency. Further, they identify how all federal partners carry out the ESF-8 when called to support a state response. As living documents, the playbooks will be periodically updated as the consequences of some disasters result in changes to current planning or policy decisions evolve. (The playbooks are available at http://www.phe.gov/preparedness/planning/playbooks/Pages/default.aspx).

Prior to the signing of PDD-8, HHS was also developing hazard-specific playbooks for each of the 15 National Planning Scenarios (see Chapter 3 for the complete list).[2] Following the nuclear events in Japan in March 2011, the ASPR highlighted a playbook to guide state and local planners in a medical response to a nuclear detonation (available at http://www.phe.gov/Preparedness/planning/playbooks/stateandlocal/nuclear/Pages/default.aspx).

Common Tasks of Disaster Response

Twelve tasks address the problems that are likely to occur in most disasters, as summarized below.

- *Interorganizational coordination* is critical and is discussed in Chapters 2 and 3.
- *Sharing information among organizations* is complicated by the amount of equipment needed and the number of people involved. During the impact and postimpact phases, two-way radios (also known as *walkie-talkies*) might be the only reliable form of communications across distances. Even if landline, cellular, or wireless telephone systems are not damaged, they are generally congested or overloaded.
- *Resource management*—the distribution of supplemental personnel, equipment, and supplies among multiple organizations—requires a process to identify which resources have arrived or are in transit and to determine where those resources are most needed. Once a security perimeter has been established at the disaster site, a check-in or staging area is usually established outside this boundary. Each staging area has a manager who has radio contact with the incident command post or emergency operations center. Law enforcement or security personnel are usually notified to refer all responders or volunteers to the closest check-in area. There, personnel will be logged in, briefed on the situation, given an assignment, and provided with a radio, communications frequency, or hardware to link them to the broader response effort.
- When advance warnings are possible, *evacuation from areas of danger* can be the most effective lifesaving strategy in a disaster. The warning process is complex and

[2]Planners should follow the policy development for PDD-8 to see whether there is an impact to the identified scenarios.

requires precise communication among numerous agencies. A threat must be detected and analyzed to assess the specific areas at risk as well as the nature of that risk. Warnings should be delivered in such a manner that the population at risk will take the threat seriously and take appropriate action based on the warning. Detection and assessment are usually the responsibility of one agency (e.g., the National Weather Service, flood districts, dam officials). The decision to order an evacuation is the responsibility of other organizations (such as the sheriff's office), and the dissemination of the warning is the responsibility of a third group (such as commercial television or radio stations). The public tends to underestimate risks and downplay warnings if messages are ambiguous or inconsistent. Factors that enhance the effectiveness of warnings include the credibility of the warning source, the number of repetitions (especially if emanating from multiple sources), the consistency of message content across different sources, the context of the warning (e.g., a visible gas cloud or odor accompanying warnings about a hazardous substance leak), the inclusion of information that allows recipients to determine whether they are personally in danger (e.g., details on location or track), the inclusion of specific information on self-protective actions, and invitations from friends or relatives to take shelter.

- *Search and rescue* is an important aspect of postdisaster response. In many disasters, casualties are initially treated in the field, and this process influences their entry into the health care system. To the extent that search and rescue is uncoordinated, the flow of patients through the Emergency Medical Services (EMS) system and the health care system is also uncoordinated. Several characteristics of disaster search and rescue create problems amenable to improvement through organizational planning. Most disaster search and rescue, particularly in the immediate postimpact period, is not initiated by trained emergency personnel but by the spontaneous efforts of untrained bystanders who happen to be in the area. Care of patients also becomes complicated when the disaster occurs across jurisdictional boundaries or involves emergency responders from many agencies (private ambulance providers; municipal first responders; and county, state, federal agencies).

- *Using both mass and social media* to deliver warnings to the public and to educate the public about the avoidance of health problems in the aftermath of a disaster— such as food and water safety, injury prevention through chain saw safety, avoidance of nail punctures, and monitoring carbon monoxide exposure from charcoal and unvented heaters—can be an effective public health tool.

- *Triage*, derived from the French verb *trier* or to sort, is a method of assigning priorities for treatment and transport for injured citizens. Untrained personnel and bystanders who may do the initial search and rescue often bypass established field triage and first aid stations because they do not know where these posts are located or because they want to get the victims to the closest hospital.

- In most domestic disasters, several medical resources can handle the *casualty distribution*. Often, the closest hospitals receive the majority of patients, while other hospitals await casualties that never arrive. Transport decisions made by untrained volunteers are difficult to control. Established protocols between EMS and area hospitals will ensure the more even distribution of casualties.

- *Patient tracking* is complicated by the fact that most persons evacuating their homes do not seek lodging in public shelters where their presence will be registered by the Red Cross. Tracking the location of victims is further obfuscated because no single agency serves as a central repository of information about the location of victims from area hospitals, morgues, shelters, jails, or other potential locations. Tracking of the injured is also confounded because most patients get to hospitals by means other than ambulance, leaving EMS with an incomplete record of injuries. When hospitals themselves are damaged, the evacuation of hospitalized patients further complicates tracking where victims might be located.

- *Caring for patients* when the health care infrastructure has been damaged requires careful advance planning. Following natural disasters, hospitals should plan to care for greater numbers of minor injuries than for major trauma. Substantial numbers of patients seeking hospital care do so because of chronic medical conditions rather than trauma, caused in part by damage or loss of access to usual sources of primary medical care. Persons often evacuate their homes without prescription medications or underestimate how long they will be prevented from returning home. In addition, many injuries are sustained not during the disaster impact but during rescue or cleanup activities. Hospitals, urgent care centers, home health care agencies, pharmacies, and dialysis centers must make appropriate plans to ensure that their facilities will not be damaged or disabled in a disaster and that they have backup arrangements for the care of their patients postimpact. This includes providing backup supplies of power and water; building structures resistant to wind, fire, flood, and seismic hazards; maintaining essential equipment and supplies that will be damaged by earthquakes or other disasters; supplying surge protection and data backup for computers with patient accounts, charts, or pharmacy information; making plans for alternative office, business, or clinical sites for displaced local health care resources (physicians, pharmacists, radiology); and developing plans to relocate the site of home health care to sites to which the patients have temporarily relocated.

- The *management of volunteers and donations* is a common problem in disasters. Disaster planning often focuses on the mobilization of resources, when not infrequently more resources arrive than are actually needed, requested, or expected. Procedures should be established to manage massive amounts of resources. First, planners should expect large numbers of donations and unsolicited volunteers (such as spontaneous civilian bystanders, family members, neighbors, coworkers, other survivors). Second, planners should channel public requests for aid to a locality outside the immediate disaster area where resources can be collected, organized, and distributed without disrupting ongoing emergency operations.

- Plan for *organized improvisation* in response to the disruption of shelter, utilities, communication systems, and transportation. Regardless of the level of preplanning, disasters will require some unanticipated tasks. Public health officials must develop the capacity, mutually agreed upon procedures, and training to participate in the community's coordinated, multiorganizational response to unexpected problems.

Components of a Plan

A regional plan will identify the potential jurisdictions that could be affected by a disaster and the corresponding agencies with assigned disaster response and recovery responsibilities. Such a plan will bring together the chief executives and operational leaders of these agencies, initiate a process of joint coordination and situation assessment, identify likely types of disasters, establish communication channels for sharing information, and create a standard protocol to assess the scope of damage, injuries, deaths, and secondary threats.

Baseline Assessment

To develop a regional plan, public health agencies must first work with the emergency management sector to determine the demographic profile of the community and assess:

- the health status and health risks of the community
- the types of assistance required by various populations during an emergency
- the condition of health care facilities
- the protection of vital records
- the potential requirements for public shelters
- available resources for alternative emergency and primary care
- the availability of and procedures for obtaining state and federal assistance

Efforts to assess the health condition of the community must examine the following:

- Prevalent disease and persons with functional needs who will need assistance related to evacuation and continuity of care
- Ability of the affected population to obtain prescription medications
- Building safety and ability to protect victims from injury, the elements, and hazardous material release
- Ability to maintain air quality, food safety, sanitation, waste disposal, vector control, and water systems

Hospitals, urgent care centers, physician offices, outpatient medical clinics, psychiatric clinics, dialysis centers, pharmacies, assisted living and residential facilities for the aged or disabled, and home health care services must have the capacity to meet patient needs and to ensure continuity of power, communications, water, sewer, and waste disposal during disaster situations. Data processing and exchange of patient information will be particularly important in the postimpact and recovery phases.

Disaster plans must take into account the availability of alternate treatment facilities when any or all of these locations are closed. Public health departments should work with hospitals and community providers to develop a plan for providing both routine care and continuity of care for victims experiencing acute exacerbations of chronic medical problems such as asthma, emphysema, diabetes, and hypertension. If the normal source of care for these individuals is not available and no alternative plan is communicated to the public, patients could be expected to seek care from overburdened hospital emergency departments. Following Hurricane Andrew, for example, more than 1000 physician offices were destroyed or significantly damaged, greatly adding to hospital patient loads. Furthermore, provisions for alternative sources of care may continue long after responders from outside the area have returned home. Two years after Hurricane Katrina, seven hospitals were not operating and 50% of the pre-hurricane hospital beds were no longer available.

In addition, plans should be developed for patients in hospitals, in residential care facilities (e.g., long-term care, assisted living, psychiatric treatment, rehabilitation), and living independently with functional needs who may need to be evacuated and placed elsewhere. Plans should also be made to maintain poison control hotlines and to continue home health care services (including dialysis, intravenous antibiotics, visiting nurse services, medical supply) at sites to which patients have been relocated.

Public health departments must collect background data on requirements for the medical needs, lodging, water, sanitation, and feeding arrangements for both victims and rescue and relief personnel. Plans for the management of resources—including directing incoming responders and volunteers to designated check-in or staging areas and determining what resources are present, available, or committed to the incident—should be established in advance. Assignments regarding which tasks will be coordinated or implemented by which agency or individual worker must be designated. This is particularly true for responsibilities that cross functional, geographic, or jurisdictional boundaries and for tasks for which no single person or agency has clear-cut statutory or contractual responsibility. Priorities for resource distribution, cost sharing, acquisition, training, and coordination must be set jointly and disseminated widely.

Finally, public health officials should ensure that the disaster preparedness plan identifies state and federal assistance programs (e.g., Robert T. Stafford Disaster Relief and Emergency Assistance Act of 1988 [Stafford Act], as explained in Chapter 3) for reimbursement and establishes procedures to verify that full reimbursement for disaster-related health care has been recovered.

Identifying Available Resources

Disaster response may call for the use of resources (personnel, equipment, supplies, information) that do not commonly reside in one location or under the jurisdiction of one agency. The ability to reduce morbidity and mortality in the early hours after disaster has struck may depend on locating resources that are not commonly used in response to routine emergencies or are in short supply. A comprehensive plan should establish procedures for locating specialty physicians, search dogs, specialized devices for locating trapped victims in the rubble of collapsed buildings, tools for cutting through and lifting heavy reinforced concrete blocks, dialysis centers or equipment to treat crush injury, laboratories to rapidly analyze hazardous chemicals or biological agents, radiation detection instruments, confined-space rescue teams, and hazardous materials response teams with appropriate protective gear.

Surge Capacity

Surge capacity is the ability to treat a large increase in the number of persons requiring treatment and specimens for analysis, or to conduct the necessary assessments following an emergency event. As a primary tenet, governments at all levels must first ensure that public health agencies have the manpower and resources to handle their core mission and responsibilities on a daily basis, or they will not have the capacity to provide services when a surge is needed during emergencies.

The principles of *capacity planning management* are used in industry to determine how much production capacity is needed, under which conditions and where capacity needs to be increased, and how that increase will be structured. In response to a disaster, health care systems often have to expand their configuration to care for those affected by the incident. Dr. Boaz Tadmor, former chief medical officer for the Home Front Command in Israel, has said that in times of disaster, the organization of the response is more important than the delivery of patient care. Surge capacity requires regional systems that are resilient and flexible to respond effectively to an emergency.

Increasing the capacity of a community's public health and health care system requires the connectedness of health departments, hospitals, and community agencies. For example, in an event involving infectious disease, the burden on the public health system is dependent on many factors, including the nature of the event, the demography and prevalence or incidence of disease in the local population, and the projected spread of the infection. The ability to care for patients will vary according to demand for services and the available staff, equipment, space, antibiotics, and other medical supplies. Community organizations and institutions may need to provide services such as housing for quarantine. With incidents involving biological, chemical, or "dirty bomb" exposures, communities are likely to experience *triage inversion,* in which the least injured patients present first while the most severely injured are extricated at the scene. In this type of scenario, the contaminated victims may appear for care before hospitals have received information from the scene. Thus preparations for surge capacity involve protecting hospitals from contamination and ensuring a mechanism for EMS to quickly communicate to hospitals so that they can set up the decontamination expeditiously.

Surge Capacity Planning

To estimate the potential requirements for increased personnel, assets, and other resources, a community has to inventory available sites of inpatient and ambulatory medical and mental health care; public health agencies; the volume, location and services delivered; and the geographic area served. In addition, the community should survey organizations that serve vulnerable populations that might have functional needs. Once the capacity assessment is complete, coordination with community and regional resources is essential. As an example, when space is needed for any service, alternatives are schools, gymnasiums, military facilities (e.g., National Guard facilities), and conversion of existing space, such as hotels. The need for having this planning in place is highlighted by the problems following Hurricane Katrina when the organizations that had previously provided services to 45,000 people with functional needs could not agree on the nature of their clients' requirements.

Projections for increasing capacity can be determined by estimating the following:

- Potential types of casualties and care needed by the type of incident (e.g., highly infectious biological event versus single location blast event)
- Volume, intensity, and differing rates of morbidity and mortality among projected patients
- Impact of demographics,
- Current services by location
- Knowledge and skill mix of current staffing
- Available treatment and triage on-site at the incident
- How much care can be delivered by primary care physicians, such as caring for the "worried well"
- Alternative sources for capacity (e.g., mutual aid agreements, Medical Reserve Corp)
- Expected time frame, length of the response, and work schedules
- Types of public health and health care services to be added or increased based on these estimates

Scheduling should allow for care or services to be provided over the entire projected length of a response so that staff is not "burnt out" within the first 6 hours. Capacity assessments might indicate that an agency needs to realign staffing assignments by shifting staff from one venue to another or from one location within an agency or facility to another. The same assessment is required for equipment and other resources. Once staffing projections are identified, plans should provide for training of surge staff in the following:

- Their role and responsibilities in the response
- The chain of command within the organization in which they will report
- Reporting protocols and any legal responsibility to report
- Clinical recognition of diseases (i.e., signs and symptoms) where indicated

Delivering Care Under Extreme Conditions

When planning for a disaster, health departments and health care facilities will initially prepare for the delivery of conventional medical care by sharing local, regional, and federal resources; developing strategies to conserve, reuse, adapt, and substitute supplies; and calling upon alternative care systems and facilities (e.g., home and community-based care).

However, the ability to provide conventional care could be hampered by the following:

- Loss of services, including power or water
- Inadequate supplies and pharmaceuticals
- Loss of infrastructure and medical records
- Shortage of personnel, including specialists and essential staff
- Surge in the number of patients seeking care, including those unaffected by the disaster such as women giving birth
- Need for coordination among health care systems that are competing for scarce resources
- Communication barriers
- Need for enhanced security

As these conditions deteriorate during a catastrophic disaster or incident, it is assumed that the provision of conventional health services will evolve into contingency care. When the growing demand for services cannot be met by the available resources, crisis standards for care may need to be initiated. When crisis standards are implemented, the needs of individual patients are set aside in order to distribute the greatest good for the greatest number of patients.

Crisis standards of care are formally declared by a state government and involve a substantial change in the organization of services and delivery of health care. A formal declaration to institute crisis standards of care legally protects health care providers as they allocate scarce medical resources and dramatically alter the operations at their facilities. Many states have executive orders that governors can sign when needed. Further, during a declared disaster, a waiver of requirements under Section 1135 of the Social Security Act suspends penalties for noncompliance with the Health Insurance Portability and Accountability Act of 1996 and Emergency Medical Treatment and Labor Act regulations (available at http://www.idph.state.il.us/h1n1_flu/NEA_and_1135waivers.pdf). Planning for situations where crisis standards of care are needed will fortify a community's ability to respond in the most difficult circumstances.

Crisis standards of care should be formulated with strong ethical underpinnings and be fair, equitable, involve collaboration between the community and providers in a formalized process, and authorize providers to carry out necessary and appropriate actions and interventions in response to emergencies under laws which support the standards. Chapter 14 discusses ethical considerations in more depth. Crisis standards should

- Be consistent across states with clear indicators, triggers, and lines of responsibility
- Ensure attention to the needs of vulnerable and functional needs populations
- Adhere to ethical norms when making choices regarding the allocation of scarce health care resources
- Legally protect providers and institutions by adjusting scopes of practice for licensed or certified health care practitioners

- Ensure consistency in the implementation of these standards through advisory committees which develop clinical guidance and protocols

Exercises, Drills, and Training

The existence of a written emergency response plan does not ensure that it will be used or that the plan will be effective if needed. Exercises and drills are used to test the effectiveness of plans. Ideally, local public health and health care facilities are integrated into a communitywide plan that is exercised and evaluated at least once every 12 months. When all of the agencies that will be called upon to respond to a disaster, including public health, have participated in the plan's development, they are more likely to ensure that the full needs of the community can be met and that individual organizations are not overburdened as a result of poor planning. In addition, health departments, hospitals, and other public health agencies should perform stand-alone exercises to ensure that their plans are effective.

Because disasters often cross political, geographic, functional, and jurisdictional boundaries, exercises and training are most effective when carried out on a multiorganizational, multidisciplinary, multijurisdictional basis. Coordination is also facilitated when participants are familiar with the skills, level of knowledge, and dependability of other responders upon whom they may one day need to rely. The full-scale exercise will often involve prehospital as well as hospital response.

Exercises are used to improve planning. The *test-exercise cycle* begins with an assumption about how agencies will function in a response. Following training, an objective for an exercise is developed. The exercise is organized and conducted. An evaluation occurs and the plan is revised based on the evaluation. Responders are then retrained for the revised plan.

The Preparedness Directorate of the Department of Homeland Security (DHS) established a program with standardized methodology and terminology for preparedness exercises. The Homeland Security Exercise and Evaluation Program (HSEEP) provides tools and resources, such as the Evaluation Guides, to help jurisdictions and organizations test their plans and identify and remedy vulnerabilities prior to a real incident. Any jurisdiction that receives funding from DHS to conduct an exercise is required to follow HSEEP. To be considered HSEEP compliant, four performance requirements must be satisfied:

- Conduct an annual workshop for training and planning exercises and develop and maintain a multiyear training and exercise plan
- Plan and conduct exercises following HSEEP guidelines (Volumes I–III)
- Develop and submit a properly formatted after-action report/improvement plan (AAR/IP) (format in HSEEP, Volume III)
- Track and implement corrective actions identified in AAR/IP

Table 32 identifies the types of activities that public health could practice in either agency-specific or communitywide exercises.

Table 32. Public Health Activities for Disaster Plan Exercises

Category	Activities
Preparedness	Develop mutual aid networks for your community
Response	Escalate a response by activating federal resources and response Request, receive, and distribute medications, supplies, or equipment (such as ventilators) from the Strategic National Stockpile Distribute pharmaceuticals for treatment or prophylaxis Implement ring or mass vaccinations Activate social distancing, including isolation and quarantine Implement evacuation and sheltering in place Import health professionals from neighboring states Provide for requirements of functional needs populations
Delivery of health care	Care for mass casualties, including care for burns or other trauma Conduct decontamination Provide mental health support for responders, survivors, and other community members Coordinate among the various health care systems in the community or region
Communication	Activate the area Health Alert Network Operate a Joint Information Center Communicate with the public about health risks and protective behaviors
Operations into policy	Translate epidemiological investigations into policy, operational/management, and public communications actions
Dealing with remains	Set up a mass mortuary

Adapted from Public Health Emergency, Office of the Assistant Secretary for Preparedness and Response. 2007. *Public Health Emergency Response: A Guide for Leaders and Responders*. Chapter 9. Conducting exercises for preparedness. Washington, DC: Department of Health and Human Services. Available at: http://www.phe.gov/emergency/communication/guides/leaders/Documents/freo_section09.pdf.

Types of Exercises

HSEEP has identified two types of exercises, which are identified in Table 33: discussion based (i.e., seminars, workshops, tabletop exercises) or operations-based (i.e., games, drills, functional exercises, and full-scale exercises).

Vulnerable Populations

A cadre of people with functional needs have been involved as developers, trainers, and participants in emergency management training. Public health professionals should partner with these individuals and the organizations that serve them when developing exercises and training for responders. These individuals can

- Assist in the development of plans that consider functional needs.
- Identify weaknesses and gaps in plans.
- Articulate emergency needs within their communities.
- Build awareness about functional needs when a community prepares for emergencies.
- Facilitate collaboration, coordination, and communication between responding agencies and those with functional needs.

Those responsible for integrating the needs of vulnerable populations into exercises and exercise programs should fully understand what the various groups would need by including representatives from these groups as active participants in exercises. People with disabilities and different vulnerabilities can help identify issues and provide ideas for effective solutions. To ensure their active participation, transportation to and from the exercise and facilities where the exercises are conducted should be fully accessible. In addition, communication about and instructions during the exercises should be varied so all understand. Communities should not include young children as participants in exercises, because they may not be able to distinguish between an exercise and an actual event.

When an AAR/IP is developed, the specific functional needs communities should be asked to provide feedback on and potential solutions to gaps that were identified in the exercise. For additional training, the Federal Emergency Management Agency's Emergency Management Institute offers independent study courses (IS 197.EM Functional Needs Planning Considerations for Emergency Management and IS 197.SP Functional Needs Planning Considerations for Service and Support Providers, which were to be revised in 2011; available at http://www.training.fema.gov/index.asp).

Table 33. Homeland Security Exercise and Evaluation Program Exercises

Type	Use or Purpose	How Conducted
	Discussion-Based Exercises	
	Used as starting point Usually emphasize existing plans, policies, agreements, and procedures Used to familiarize agencies and personnel with current and expected capabilities	Led by facilitators
Seminars	Orient participants or provide an overview Good starting when developing or making changes to plans and procedures	Informal discussions led by a presenter
Workshops	Used to determine objectives, develop scenarios, and define evaluation criteria for exercise Produce new standard operating procedures, emergency operations plans, multiyear plans, or improvement plans	Focus on achieving or building a product (such as a draft plan or policy) Participant interaction is increased
Tabletop exercises: Basic	Evaluation of group's problem-solving, handling of personnel contingencies, message interpretation, information sharing, interagency coordination, and achievement of specific objectives Key personnel discuss hypothetical scenarios in an informal setting	Situation established by the scenario materials remains constant Players apply their knowledge and skills to a list of problems presented by the leader/moderator Problems are discussed as a group Leader summarizes the resolutions
Tabletop exercises: Advanced		Pre-scripted messages alter the original scenario Moderator introduces problems one at a time in various formats (message, simulated telephone call, videotape, etc.) Participants discuss issues raised by the simulated problem, applying appropriate plans and procedures

(*continued on next page*)

Table 33. (*continued*)

Type	Use or Purpose	How Conducted
Games (simulations)	Simulation of operations involving teams; uses rules, data, and procedures in an actual or real-life situation Explore decision-making processes and the consequences of those decisions	Computer-generated scenarios and simulations Internet-based, multiplayer games
Operations-Based Exercises		
	Validate the effectiveness of plans, policies, agreements, and procedures Clarify roles and responsibilities Identify gaps in resources needed to implement plans and procedures Improve individual and team performance	Actual reaction to simulated intelligence Response to emergency conditions Mobilization of apparatus, resources, and/or networks Commitment of personnel, usually over an extended period of time
Drills	Validate a single, specific operation or function in a single agency or organizational entity Provide training on new equipment Develop or validate new policies or procedures Practice and maintain current skills	Coordinated, supervised activity Narrow focus measured against established standards Immediate feedback Realistic environment
Functional exercises	Validate and evaluate individual capabilities, multiple functions, activities within a function, or interdependent groups of functions Simulates the reality of operations by presenting complex and realistic problems in a highly stressful, time-constrained environment	Activation and simulated activity of all sections of the ICS Test disaster plan in simulated field conditions Participants include players, simulators, controllers, and evaluators

(*continued on next page*)

Table 33. (*continued*)

Type	Use or Purpose	How Conducted
Full-scale exercises	Validate many facets of preparedness Responders get to know each other and their roles, gain experience working with the community's plan, and understand what must be done—thus enhancing their ability to rely on each other's activities Implement and analyze plans, policies, procedures, and cooperative agreements Presents complex and realistic problems that require critical thinking, rapid problem-solving, and effective responses Test the mobilization of all or as many as possible of the response components using principles of the National Incident Management System	Scripted scenario with built-in flexibility to allow updates to drive activity Conducted in real time in stressful, time-constrained environment that closely mirrors actual events Personnel and resources are mobilized and deployed to the scene where they conduct activities as if a real incident had occurred Multiagency, multijurisdictional, multiorganizational Participants include responder, controller, evaluator, and victims

Adapted from Homeland Security Exercise and Evaluation Program. 2007. *Terminology, Methodology, and Compliance Guidelines.* HSEEP Exercise Types. Washington, DC: Department of Homeland Security. Available at: https://hseep.dhs.gov/support/HSEEP_101.pdf.

Chapter 8

Environmental and Occupational Health Issues

Maintaining environmental health is essential to preventing disease following disasters. Because of the complexity of environmental issues, there is seldom a single environmental health specialist responsible for all of the environmental problems that follow a disaster. In complex large-scale disasters and disasters in urban areas, it is common for numerous governmental agencies and consultants at all levels to be pulled together to coordinate an environmental response. This chapter addresses public health interventions to ensure proper sanitation and waste disposal, maintain safety of water and food supplies, feed and ensure adequate heating and shelter for large numbers of people, provide for worker safety including those with disabilities, protect workers through use of personal protective equipment (PPE), protect against air contamination, handle human remains, and control vector populations.

Public Health Role

- Provide technical assistance in addressing environmental threats and hazards
- Contain or remove sources of environmental contamination, or evacuate people to ensure that they are no longer exposed to the hazard
- Conduct quantitative monitoring of environmental services, including environmental sampling, ensuring the replacement or repair of existing sanitary barriers and waste management
- Provide guidance, education, and assurance of safe water, safe food, and safe shelter to compensate for disrupted sanitary environments
- Ensure that people have sufficient cooking utensils, equipment, and fuel to cook and store food safely
- Inspect temporary housing, mass feeding centers, drinking water distribution, and waste disposal
- Provide commercial toilets and handwashing stations
- Supervise construction of latrines, if toilets not available
- Protect worker safety by ensuring the use of protective measures and by monitoring illness and injury to inform modifications in the use of protective measures
- Provide regular advisories to the public and the medical community

Reducing Exposure to Environmental Hazards

Disrupted environments have variable effects on health depending on the presence of endemic disease, the susceptibility and habits of the population, and the availability of protective measures. The types of disease most often spread, such as respiratory infections and diarrhea, are those that have a short transmission cycle and incubation period and are widespread.

Public health professionals can use three major approaches to reduce exposure to environmental hazards: instituting measures of control, establishing multiple barriers, and providing distance between the hazard and populations at risk.

> **Instituting Measures of Control:** Certain hazards move through the environment and cause harm to humans. Public health professionals can control disease by preventing the hazard from being released or occurring, by preventing the transport of the hazard, or by preventing people from being exposed to the hazard. For example, malaria control involves a three-pronged approach of draining stagnant water to prevent mosquito breeding, spraying for mosquitoes to prevent the transport of pathogens, and diminishing exposure by encouraging the use of treated bed netting and insect repellent.
>
> **Establishing Multiple Barriers:** Since no single environmental measure is fail-safe, redundant barriers must be set up between hazards and populations. Multiple sanitary barriers provide redundant protection where, for example, public health professionals protect surface water used for drinking. If on a given day, any of the redundant measures are not functioning, the others will reduce the hazard. Most waterborne outbreaks in the United States occur when multiple barriers fail simultaneously. Protection from environmental hazards depends on awareness of risk, diligence in surveillance, and investment in multiple barriers to keep the risk to populations low.
>
> **Providing Distance Between Hazards and Populations:** In general, the distance needed to protect a population from exposure to a hazardous substance varies according to the volume and nature of the hazardous substance. The greater the distance existing between a hazard and a population, the greater the amount of time before an inadvertent release of the hazardous material reaches the populated area. With a longer time delay, the release is more likely to be detected in time for the population to take protective measures. Since most pollutants degrade or disperse over distance, providing space between hazardous materials and populations may by itself reduce human exposure.

Environmental Surveillance

Three conditions should be monitored to estimate the number of individuals whose environment is affected by a disaster: access to excreta disposal facilities, water consumption, and the percentage of people consuming safe water.

> **Access to Excreta Disposal Facilities:** Public health officials must assess the number of people per latrine to determine the relative availability of latrines and

the amount of sharing required. To estimate people per latrine, conduct a walk-through survey or interview people. For those who indicate that they have a family latrine, ask how many people are in their family and if they share the latrine with anyone else. If families are using communal latrines, calculate sanitation coverage as the number of latrines divided by the number of people using them. Where people continue to live in dwellings in which not all toilets are functional, monitor the fraction of households with a functioning toilet or latrine as a proxy for sanitation coverage.

Water Consumption: Water consumption depends both on water availability and the population's ability to obtain the water. Bucket shortages, security concerns, and long lines can all prevent plentiful sources from being fully utilized. Public health officials must survey the population and estimate water consumption by asking for a 24-hour recall of water use, or by monitoring how much water is collected at the various sources and dividing this by the number of people being served. Water consumption is defined in terms of gallons or liters per person per day.

Percentage of People Consuming Safe Water: In settings where groundwater supplies at wells or springs are determined to be safe to drink, monitor the fraction of people obtaining water from the safe sources versus unsafe sources. Public health workers should monitor the percentage of people who are getting safe water when it is being collected; remembering that collecting water from a safe source does not assure that the water is safe at the time of ingestion. With piped systems, workers must collect samples at household taps throughout the system, with a collection scheme such that each sample represents a similar number of people (e.g., one sample per 10,000 people). The fraction of water samples that are safe corresponds to the fraction of people whose water arrives safely at the point where the water is collected.

Sanitation During Disaster Situations

Sewage systems are a network of pipes that carry wastes away from a population. Sewers often become flooded or clogged during hurricanes, earthquakes, and floods. Hurricanes or other storms may cause untreated sewage to be washed into waterways. Clogged sewer lines may also cause waste to spill into the environment at locations where it is likely to expose large numbers of people to biological or chemical hazards. Typically, problems within sewage networks are mitigated by pumping or rerouting the sewage, which may not be possible following a disaster. Public health officials should document the location of bypass valves, confirm that they are functional and that auxiliary pumping capacity exists, and have an operational plan for storm events as part of a disaster preparedness program.

Where sanitation systems are destroyed, one of the first activities should be the reestablishment of a system of latrines, since containing human excreta is the most protective environmental measure that can be taken following a disaster. When defecation fields are required, their location must be thoughtfully planned. Proper spaces for defecation fields must be set aside and located away from water sources and downhill from living quarters. Latrines should be built before the population arrives at a relocation site. Importantly, to ensure personal hygiene, paper, water, and soap must be made readily available in or near the latrine, especially where diarrheal diseases and dysentery are likely to occur.

The World Health Organization recommends the provision of one pit latrine per family. Where that is not possible, both the United Nations High Commission for Refugees and United Nations International Children's Education Fund have set a maximum target of 20 people per latrine. To the extent possible, households should not share latrines or toilets. Efforts should be made to build separate latrines for men and women or separate latrines for children. Privacy screens should be constructed. Establishing one latrine per household, rather than sharing latrines, will increase the likelihood that the facilities will be kept clean. With mortality and morbidity rates among displaced populations often higher in the first days and weeks following an event, it is essential to persuade everyone to use the latrines that have been set up.

To increase use of latrines by young children, two approaches may be useful. First, educate child care providers about proper handling of children's feces and the importance of washing their hands after cleaning the child or handling the child's feces. Second, establish excreta disposal facilities that are child friendly (e.g., well lit, have an opening smaller than that used in adult latrines).

Public health information officers should promote handwashing, particularly after defecating and before preparing food to protect against fecal-oral illnesses. Educational messages should be short, relate to the route by which disease may be transmitted, and focus on behaviors that are key to the prevention of fecal-oral illness. Public health workers should likewise establish a simple monitoring component to assure that increased handwashing (or other preventive behavior) is actually occurring.

Ensuring Water Safety

Providing people with more water is more protective against fecal-oral pathogens than is providing people with cleaner water. Public health officials should work closely with the agencies that are monitoring the availability of water. Estimate water consumption at least weekly during the postimpact phase. Measure water consumption by what people receive, not what the water operators produce. Water consumption can be measured through sampling, such as household interviews, or by the actual collection of water at watering points.

Attempts should be made to provide each family with their own water bucket to reduce the risk of illness. The average water consumption should be 3.9 gallons (15 liters) per day or more, with no one consuming less than 5 liters or 1 gallon per person per day. The World Health Organization recommends 4.2 to 5.2 gallons (16 to 20 liters) per day. A 3- to 5-day supply of water (5 gallons per person) should be stored for food preparation, bathing, brushing teeth, and dishwashing. Where residents are preparing supplies in advance of a disaster, such as earthquake-prone California, they should store water in sturdy plastic bottles with tight fitting lids. Stored water should be located away from the storage of toxic substances and should be changed every 6 months.

Water for Drinking and Cooking

Safe drinking water includes bottled, boiled, or treated water. Residents should drink only bottled, boiled, or treated water until the supply is tested and found safe. They must be instructed not to use contaminated water to wash dishes, brush teeth, wash and prepare food, or make ice. All bottled water from an unknown source must be boiled or treated before use. To kill harmful bacteria and parasites, residents should bring water to a rolling boil for 1 minute. Water may also be treated with chlorine or iodine tablets or by mixing six drops (1/8 teaspoon) of unscented household chlorine bleach (5.25% sodium hypochlorite) per gallon of water. Mix the solution thoroughly, and let stand for about 30 minutes. This treatment will not, however, kill parasitic organisms.

The United Nations High Commission for Refugees considers water with less than 10 fecal coliforms per 100 milliliters to be reasonably safe, whereas water with more than 100 fecal coliforms is considered unsafe. Contaminated water sources should not be closed until equally convenient facilities become available.

It may be necessary to transport safe drinking water to the disaster site by truck. Trucks that normally carry gasoline, chemicals, or sewage should not be used to transport water. Trucks should be inspected and cleaned and disinfected before being used for water transportation because they may be contaminated with microbes or chemicals. Containers, such as bottles or cans, should be rinsed with a bleach solution before reusing them. Do not rely on untested devices for decontaminating water.

Water Supply

There are three sources of water: groundwater, surface water, and rainwater. Groundwater, although generally of higher quality microbiologically, is relatively difficult to access because it is located within the earth's crust. Surface waters, found in lakes, ponds, streams and rivers, have predictable reliability and volume and are relatively easy to gather but are generally microbiologically unsafe and require treatment. Rainwater is seldom used because collection is unreliable.

Collecting and Treating Surface Water

Once collected, water quality deteriorates over time. The handling and storing of water is the main determinant in water safety. When water is collected in buckets, it should be chlorinated either in the home or by health workers at the point of collection. Residents should be instructed to add an initial dose of 2.5 milligrams per liter of chlorine to the bucket so that after 30 minutes, at least 0.5 milligrams per liter of free chlorine remains in the water. People should be encouraged to wait for 30 minutes after chlorination before consuming water to allow for adequate disinfection to occur. The dipping of water from household storage buckets causes considerable contamination. To maintain clean stored water, residents should add a chlorine residual.

With a piped system, typically chlorine levels are adjusted to assure that 0.2 to 0.5 milligrams per liter of free chlorine is in the water at the tap level where it is collected. During times of outbreaks or in systems where there are broken distribution pipes, workers should aim to have 0.5 to 1.0 milligrams per liter of free chlorine.

To prevent cross-contamination, water utilities in consultation with health officials should increase the pressure in the water pipes and increase the level of residual chlorine. Pressure can be augmented by increasing the rate of pumping into the system, by cutting down on water wastage, or by closing off sections of the distribution system. Because cross-contamination usually occurs in unknown locations in a distribution system, the chlorine residual must be kept high throughout the network. Monitoring of chlorine should be done throughout the system, and the dose put into the system should be set so that there is free chlorine in at least 95% of locations.

Accessing and Treating Groundwater

To collect spring water without contamination, workers should build a collection basin that has an outflow pipe constructed at or just below the point where the water comes to the surface. To prevent contamination in wells, they can build a skirt around the opening of the well or a plate sealing off the surface at the top of the well.

Water should be disinfected when household water contamination is high, when there is a high risk of a waterborne outbreak, or when the groundwater is of poor quality. Chlorine can be used in buckets when the water is collected or stored at people's homes. To chlorinate wells, use a chlorination pot or the method of shock chlorination described next.

A chlorination pot includes a small container, such as a 1-liter soda bottle, with a few holes punched in it. This container is filled with a chlorine powder and gravel mixture and placed inside a larger vessel (such as a 4-liter milk jug or a clay pot) that also has holes punched in it. The chlorine disperses from the double layered pot slowly. The number and size of holes in the vessels control the disinfectant dose and must be tailored to match a specific well volume and withdrawal rate. Invariably, the first water drawn in the morning will have an offensively high level of chlorine, and if a well has hours of very high use, the dose may become too low. Thus, pot chlorination schemes are not widely used, and should not be commenced during the acute phase of a crisis when a lack of time and attention will prevent proper monitoring and adjustment of the chlorine levels.

Shock chlorination is conducted by adding 5 to 10 milligrams per liter to the water in a well and allowing it to sit unused for a period of hours. The first water drawn from the well after the disinfection period is discarded, and normal use is subsequently resumed. When a well is drawing from safe groundwater but has been contaminated by people or an unusual event (such as a major rainstorm), shock chlorination can eliminate a transient threat to water quality. Shock chlorination does not provide chlorinated water to the people in their homes because after the first few hours of use after treatment, little or no residual chlorine will remain in the drawn water.

Disinfecting Wells

The Centers for Disease Control and Prevention (CDC) has recommended procedures for disinfecting wells following an emergency. Before any chlorine is added,

- All power sources should be turned off.
- Those in the field should wear protective gear including shoes or boots with thick rubber soles, rubber gloves, water apron, and protective face gear (such as goggles or a face shield).
- The area around the well should be cleared of any hazards including debris or downed electrical wires.
- The well should be checked for gases and vapors.

To disinfect bored or dug wells, use Table 34 to calculate how much liquid bleach to use. To determine the exact amount of bleach required, multiply the amount of disinfectant needed (according to the diameter of the well) by the depth of the well. For example, a well 5.0 feet in diameter requires approximately 4.5 cups of bleach per foot of water. If the well is 30 feet deep, multiply 4.5 by 30 to determine the total cups of bleach required (135 cups). Add this total amount of disinfectant (in this case, 135 cups ÷ 16 cups per gallon = 8 gallons and 7 cups of bleach) to about 10 gallons of water. Splash the mixture around the wall or lining of the well. Be certain the disinfectant solution contacts all parts of the well. Seal the well top. Open all faucets, and pump water until a strong odor of bleach is noticeable at each faucet. Then stop the pump and allow the solution to remain in the well

Table 34. Bleach Required to Disinfect a Bored or Dug Well

Depth of Water	Diameter of Well					
	0.5 foot	1 foot	2 feet	3 feet	4 feet	5 feet
10 feet	.5 cups	1.75 cups	7 cups	1 gal	1.75 gal	2.75 gal
20 feet	1 cup	3.5 cups	14 cups	2 gal	3.5 gal	5.5 gal
30 feet	1.5 cups	5.25 cups	1.25 gal	3 gal	5.25 gal	8.25 gal
40 feet	2 cups	7 cups	1.75 gal	4 gal	7 gal	11 gal
50 feet	2.5 cups	8. 75 cups	2.25 gal	5 gal	8.75 gal	13.75 gal

Note: Use only unscented household liquid chlorine bleach; amounts are approximate—goal is to achieve chlorine concentration of 100 milligrams per liter; gal = gallon; 1 cup = 8 fluid ounces; 1 gallon = 16 cups.

Adapted from Centers for Disease Control and Prevention (CDC). 2011. Disinfecting Wells After a Disaster. Table 1. Approximate amount of bleach for disinfection of a bored or dug well. Atlanta, GA: CDC. Available at http://www.bt.cdc.gov/disasters/wellsdisinfect.asp.

overnight. The next day, operate the pump by turning on all faucets, continuing until the chlorine odor disappears. Adjust the flow of water faucets or fixtures that discharge to septic systems to a low flow to avoid overloading the disposal system.

It is important to boil water from the well (rolling boil for 1 minute) until the well water is tested and found to be safe. Before use, wait 7 to 10 days after the chlorine has been added and then test after all traces of chlorine have been washed from the system.

Emergency Basic Services

During catastrophic events, all basic services may need to be reestablished. Where the infrastructure to provide safe water and food is not intact, interim measures must be established to provide services until systems are fully operational. In catastrophic circumstances, public health officials may issue orders to boil water, warn about foods that may have spoiled during electrical outages, or announce where potable water will be provided.

Boil Water Order

Through the Safe Drinking Water Act, Congress requires the U.S. Environmental Protection Agency (EPA) to regulate contaminants that may be health risks and that may be present in public drinking water supplies. The EPA sets legal limits on the levels of certain contaminants in drinking water and establishes the water-testing schedules and methods that water systems must follow. The rules also list acceptable techniques for treating contaminated water. The Safe Drinking Water Act gives individual states the opportunity to set and enforce their own drinking water standards so long as the standards are at least as strong as the EPA's national standards. Most states and territories directly oversee the water systems within their borders.

The Total Coliform Rule sets legal limits for total coliform levels in drinking water and specifies the type and frequency of testing to determine if legal limits are exceeded. Coliforms are a broad class of bacteria that live in the digestive tracts of humans and many animals. The presence of coliform bacteria in tap water suggests that the treatment system is not working properly or that a problem exists in the pipes. Exposure to coliform can cause gastroenteritis, which is characterized by diarrhea, cramps, nausea, and vomiting.

Coliforms cannot be found in more than 5% of the samples tested each month. If more than 5% of the samples contain coliforms, water system operators must report this violation to the state and the public. If a sample tests positive for coliforms, the system must collect a set of repeat samples within 24 hours. When a routine or repeat sample tests positive for total coliforms, it must also be analyzed for fecal coliforms and *Escherichia coli*, which are coliforms directly associated with fresh feces. A positive result to this last test signifies an acute Maximum Contaminant Level (MCL) violation, which necessitates rapid state and public notification as a result of its direct health risk.

Following a disaster that may compromise a community's water supply, those responsible for monitoring water safety may use the regular water-sampling plan or make modifications, depending on the severity and geographic location of concern. When a decision has been made that water sampled from one or more sites exceeds the MCL and poses a threat to the public's health, a decision may be made to issue a boiled water order or advisory.

The EPA issued a revised set of Drinking Water Standards and Health Advisories in 2009. With few exceptions, the health advisory values have been rounded to one significant figure. The Surface Water Treatment Rule requires systems using surface water or groundwater under the direct influence of surface water to disinfect and filter their water or meet criteria for avoiding filtration so that these contaminants are controlled at the levels summarized in Table 35. The MCL goal refers to the maximum level of a contaminant in drinking water at which no known or anticipated adverse effects occur and that allows for an adequate margin of safety. These are nonenforceable public health goals. The MCL, which is an enforceable standard, identifies the maximum permissible level of a contaminant in water that is delivered to any user of a public water system. Treatment technique is an enforceable procedure or level of technical performance that public water systems must follow to ensure control of a contaminant.

Public Notice Templates

The EPA has developed templates that can be used by water suppliers to ensure that the notice that they provide is complete. The templates can be found in the EPA's Revised Public Notification Handbook. The notification handbook (available at http://water.epa.gov/lawsregs/rulesregs/sdwa/publicnotification/upload/PNrevisedPNHandbook March2010.pdf) provides guidance on how to communicate effective public notice. These public notice templates can be downloaded from the EPA Web site (available at http://water.epa.gov/lawsregs/rulesregs/sdwa/publicnotification/compliancehelp_templates.cfm). Because some states have different requirements for identifying violations or for the wording of any notice, check with your state.

Food Defense and Safety

Governments are concerned about food contamination as a terrorist act because it does not require much technical skill or an extensive organization to cause widespread public health consequences. Protecting food from intentional contamination is known as *food defense*. Risk of contamination can occur at any point, including growing, manufacturing, transportation, and distribution. Contamination of the food supply is a risk to supermarkets, restaurants, and other food establishments, and food distribution centers and warehouses. Threats to food can occur as follows:

- Unintentional contamination (food-borne illness, outbreaks)
- Deliberate contamination (explosive or spray devices, food tampering)
- Transportation accidents (train, truck)
- Natural disasters (fires, floods, hurricanes, tornadoes)
- Building events (explosions, ammonia leaks)
- Hoaxes

Table 35. Drinking Water Contaminants

Microorganisms	Maximum Contaminant Level Goal (mg/L)	Maximum Contaminant Level or Treatment Technique	Potential Health Effects From Ingestion of Water	Source of Contaminant in Drinking Water
Cryptosporidium spp.	–	Filter to remove 99%	Gastrointestinal disease	Human and animal fecal waste
Giardia lamblia	0	99.99% killed or inactivated	Giardiasis, a gastroenteric disease	Human and animal fecal waste
Heterotrophic plate count (HPC)	N/A	≤500 bacterial colonies per milliliter	HPC has no health effects but can indicate how effective treatment is at controlling microorganisms	N/A
Legionella spp.	0	Use treatment technique for *Giardia*	Legionnaire's disease (pneumonia)	Found naturally in water, multiplies in heating systems
Total coliforms	0	≤5.0% samples total coliform-positive in a month. Every sample with total coliforms must be analyzed for fecal coliforms. No fecal coliforms are permitted.	Used as an indicator that other potentially harmful bacteria may be present	Human and animal fecal waste
Turbidity	N/A	Turbidity (cloudiness) must be ≤5 nephelometric turbidity units (NTU)	Turbidity has no health effect but can interfere with disinfection and provide a medium for microbial growth. It may indicate the presence of microbes.	Soil runoff
Viruses	0	99.99% killed/inactivated	Gastrointestinal disease	Human and animal fecal waste

Adapted from U.S. Environmental Protection Agency (EPA). 2009. Drinking Water Standards and Health Advisories. Microbiology Table, p. 11. Washington, DC: EPA. Available at http://water.epa.gov/action/advisories/drinking/drinking_index.cfm; and Centers for Disease Control and Prevention (CDC). 2009. Fact Sheet for Healthy Drinking Water: Drinking Water Treatment Methods for Backcountry and Travel Use. Atlanta, GA: CDC. Available at http://www.cdc.gov/healthywater/pdf/drinking/Backcountry_Water_Treatment.pdf.

Three federal agencies are responsible for ensuring food safety and defense: the U.S. Food and Drug Administration (FDA), the U.S. Department of Agriculture (USDA), and the Department of Homeland Security (DHS).

FDA: Oversees domestic and imported food, animal drugs, feeds and veterinary devices. Working closely with state and local food safety officers, the FDA conducts scientific evaluations to analyze potential hazards, identifies points of potential hazard, and establishes preventive measures.

USDA: Oversees ongoing inspection of foods to ensure they are safe and accurately labeled, enforces sanitary requirements through monitoring and surveillance, and samples for harmful zoonotic diseases.

DHS: The CDC reports and tracks food outbreaks and works with state and local health officers to investigate and control disease. The EPA evaluates levels of pesticides and herbicides. The U.S. Customs and Border Protection monitors imported food.

The key public health task is to distinguish between intentional and unintentional outbreaks. Communities should have food defense plans as part of their emergency response action plan. The food defense plan should include procedures for identifying food-borne illness, food recalls, and food safety following natural disasters or pandemics.

Food Safety

Improper food storage is associated with *Bacillus cereus, Clostridium perfringens, Salmonella spp., Staphylococcus aureus,* and group A *Streptococcus.* Lack of handwashing and personal hygiene are associated with shigellosis, hepatitis A, gastroenteritis, and giardiasis. Three food-handling techniques are a major source of food-borne illness following disaster: improper storage, inadequate cooking, and poor personal hygiene. In addition to careful handwashing, cooking utensils must be washed in boiled or treated water before being used.

Stored Food

When preparing for disasters, residents should store at least a 3-day supply of food. Canned foods and dry mixes will remain fresh for about 2 years when stored in a cool, dry, dark place away from ovens or refrigerator exhausts at a temperature of 40 to 60°F. Residents should date all food items and use or replace food before it loses freshness. Food items should be heavily wrapped or stored in airtight containers above the ground to both prolong shelf life and to protect it from insects and rodents. Cans that bulge at the ends or that leak should be discarded.

Refrigerated Food

Ideally, meat, poultry, fish, and eggs should be refrigerated at or below 40°F. Refrigerators, without power, will keep foods cool for about 4 hours if left unopened. Block or dry ice can be added to refrigerators if the electricity is off longer than 4 hours. Perishable food in the refrigerator or freezer should be used before stored food. Unrefrigerated cooked foods should be discarded after 2 hours at room temperature regardless of appearance. Only foods that have a normal color, texture, and odor should be eaten.

Frozen Food

Frozen food is safe when stored at or below 0 °F. When a freezer is full, food will be safe for 2 days. When a freezer is half full, food may be safe up to 24 hours. Twenty-five pounds of dry ice will keep a 10-cubic-foot freezer below freezing for 3 to 4 days. Dry ice freezes everything it touches and must be handled with dry, heavyweight gloves to avoid injury. Thawed food can usually be eaten or refrozen if it is still refrigerator cold or if it still contains ice crystals. Any food that has been at room temperature for 2 hours or more or that has an unusual odor, color, or texture should be discarded.

Flooded Food Supplies

Discard all food not stored in a waterproof container. Undamaged, commercially canned foods can be saved by removing the can labels, thoroughly washing the cans, and then disinfecting them with a solution consisting of 1 cup of bleach in 5 gallons of water. Cans should be relabeled, including expiration date, with a nonerasable marker. Food containers with screw caps, snap lids, crimped caps (soda pop bottles), twist caps, flip tops, and home canned foods cannot be disinfected. Only preprepared canned baby formula that requires no added water should be used for infants.

Table 36 provides tips for safe food handling; Table 37 lists foods that cannot be salvaged following loss of power or exposure to contaminated water.

Table 36. Measures for Ensuring Food Safety

Step	Hazard	Action
Supply/purchase	Contamination of raw foodstuffs	Obtain foods from reliable supplier
		Specify conditions for production and transport
	Contamination of ready-to-eat foods	Purchase foods from reliable supplier
Receipt of food	Contamination of high-risk foods with pathogens	Control temperature and time of transport
Storage	Further contamination	Store foods in closed container or wrapped
		Control pests
	Growth of bacteria	Control temperature and duration of storage, rotate stock

(continued on next page)

Table 36. (*continued*)

Step	Hazard	Action
Preparation	Further contamination, via hands or in other ways	Wash hands before handling food
		Prevent cross-contamination via surfaces, cooking utensils
		Separate cooked foods from raw foods
		Use boiled water, especially if food won't be cooked again
	Growth of bacteria	Limit exposure of food to room temperature
Cooking	Survival of pathogens	Make sure that food is cooked thoroughly (i.e., all parts have reached at least 165°F)
Cooling and cold holding	Growth of surviving bacteria or their spores, production of toxins	Cool food as quickly as possible to temperatures below 40°F (for example, place foods in shallow trays and cool to chill temperatures)
		Avoid overfilling the refrigerator or cold storage room
		During long periods of cold storage, monitor the temperature fluctuations by occasional measurement
	Contamination from various sources	Cover food properly, avoid all contact with raw foods and nonpotable water
		Use clean utensils to handle cooked food
Hot holding	Growth of surviving bacteria or their spores, production of toxins	Ensure that food is kept hot (i.e., above 140°F)
Reheating	Survival of bacteria	Ensure that the food is thoroughly reheated
Serving	Growth of bacteria, spores, production of toxins	Ensure that leftovers, or foods prepared in advance, are thoroughly reheated
	Contamination	Prevent contact with raw foods, unclean utensils, and nonpotable water
		Do not touch food with hands
		Serve food when it is still hot

Adapted from Wisner B, Adams J, editors. 2002. *Environmental Health in Emergencies and Disasters: A Practical Guide*. Table 9.1. Control measures for ensuring food safety, p. 150. Geneva: World Health Organization.

Table 37. Food Products That Should Be Destroyed

Food Type	Incident Type	Examples
Produce	Flood, loss of electricity	Lettuce, celery, cabbage
Packaged foods	Flood	In bags: coffee, tea, flour, cereals, beans, grains, sugars, nuts Paper- or cellophane-wrapped candles, cereals, breads, cakes, chewing gum, etc. Ice cream and dairy products Spices Salt, sugar, dried milk, powdered eggs, etc.
	Fire, extreme heat	Look for charred labeling or other package damage
Screw-top or crimped-cap containers with drinks	Flood	Canned soft drinks, beer, wine, and other liquor products
Frozen foods	Flood, loss of electricity	Partially or completely thawed; if properly stored in adequate refrigeration, can be sold as "freshly thawed"
Refrigerated foods	Loss of electricity	Should be discarded if temperature above 40 °F for 4 hours or more Eggs whether frozen or in shell Fish and seafood products
Open barrels	Flood	Sauerkraut or pickles
Glass or plastic containers with cork stoppers	Flood	Catsup, vinegar, condiments; syrup, molasses, honey
Glass containers with anchor-type vacuum-packed tops	Flood	Must be completely cleaned and sanitized Home canned goods must be destroyed
Various	Fire, smoke damage, exposure to chemicals used in fire prevention, aerosols, insecticides	Meats, oil products (including better) produce

Adapted from Houston Department of Health and Human Services, City of Houston. 2005. Food Surveillance and Salvage Following Disasters. Houston, TX: City of Houston. Available at http://www.houstontx.gov/health/Food/food-surv.htm.

Feeding Large Numbers of Displaced People

Food requirements can be estimated by assessing the effect of the disaster on food supplies and the number of people who are without food. Seasonal variations may affect the availability of food. Estimates of food requirements should be calculated for 1 week and 1 month: 16 metric tons (35,273.6 pounds) of food are needed for 1000 people for 1 month, and 2 cubic meters (70.6 cubic feet) of space are needed to store 1 metric ton of food. Table 38 lists the elements needed to feed a large number of displaced persons.

Food Safety Monitoring

At the CDC, the Foodborne Diseases Active Surveillance Network, known as *FoodNet*, is a Web-based system which identifies the sources and monitors the burden of new and emerging food-borne diseases. As a collaborative project of the CDC's Emerging Infections Program (EIP), ten EIP sites, the USDA, and the FDA, FoodNet uses active surveillance to strengthen the ability of state and local health departments to detect and respond to food-borne outbreaks. Public health officials contact laboratory directors to find new cases of food-borne diseases and report these

Table 38. Elements Needed at Mass-Feeding Stations

Water supplies

Toilets for staff and others: at least 1 toilet for every 50 people

Handwashing facilities: at food handler stations and near toilets

Facilities for liquid wastes from kitchens: grease trap or strainer is a must

Facilities for solid wastes from kitchens: dispose in rubbish bins which are tightly covered

Basins, tables, chopping blocks: thoroughly disinfect with strong chlorine solution after each meal

Facilities for dishwashing: separate basins for washing, eating, and cooking

Adequate materials for cooking/refrigeration: prepare food sufficient for one meal

Layout to prevent cross-contamination: adequate space and separation of raw food and animal products

Adequate serving pieces: use disposables if no facilities to thoroughly wash and rinse

Control of rodents and other pests: use traps for flies, screen kitchen areas, dispose of sullage and waste; never place rodenticides on surfaces used for food preparation

Food safety information: place posters in full view by those in the food preparation areas

Adapted from Wisner B, Adams J, editors. *Environmental Health in Emergencies and Disasters: A Practical Guide.* 2002. Box 9.2. Facilities needed at mass-feeding centres. p. 155. Geneva: World Health Organization.

cases electronically to the CDC. Because most food-borne infections cause diarrheal illness, FoodNet focuses on persons who have a diarrheal illness. FoodNet could be used to detect and monitor the emergence of food-borne disease secondary to disaster or related to intentional poisoning.

Mass Care Shelters

Emergency Support Function (ESF) 6 provides guidance on the delivery of what are known as *mass care* services. Local governmental agencies, including human services and the health department, coordinate with the American Red Cross and other voluntary agencies in the provision of mass care. This type of assistance is provided through temporary shelters, fixed or mobile feeding stations, and direct distribution of relief supplies.

Local public health professionals may be involved in the following:

- Selection of the shelter site
- Organization and layout of shelter
- Assuring food safety
- Assuring adequate safe water for drinking and food preparation
- Provision of toilets, sinks for handwashing, soap, disposable towels, showers, and laundry
- Ensuring proper management of wastewater and solid waste
- Protecting indoor air quality (e.g., temperature control, humidity, odors, dust).
- Identifying and assuring general safety
- Monitoring housekeeping and cleaning
- Identifying and controlling vector/pest-related concerns
- Monitoring outside grounds (playgrounds, debris, and physical hazards)
- Monitoring and intervening in operations of shelter (for example, address needs of people in long lines)

Table 39 provides information about the physical requirements of shelters.

Control Strategies for Epidemic Diarrheal Diseases

Diarrheal diseases are a common problem following natural disasters. Environmental measures and education campaigns should be specific to the fecal-oral disease public health officials seek to protect against.

Cholera

Public health bulletins must instruct residents to consume only chlorinated or boiled fluids and to eat only hot, cooked foods or peeled fruits and vegetables. Emphasize handwashing in food preparation and before eating. During a cholera outbreak, ensure that the water being consumed is chlorinated. Where chlorination is not possible, order the boiling of water or the addition of a lemon per liter. Acidic sauces added to foods, such as tomato sauce, can provide some protection against food-borne cholera.

Table 39. Shelter Requirements

	Provision	Requirement
Spacing	Toilets	One toilet for every 20 people
	Showers	One shower for every 15 people
	Handwashing	One handwashing fixture with clean water for every 15 people. Hand sanitizers are not a replacement for handwashing fixtures
	Cots/beds	Minimum floor space of 30 square feet per person, spaced 3 feet apart, alternating head-to-toe
	Ventilation	40 to 50 cubic feet of air space per person
Waste management	Containers	One 30-gallon plastic container per ten people Containers should have plastic liner bags and lids and be emptied daily
	Sharps container	Approved sharps containers at designated areas Arrange for approved medical waste transporter to collect, transport, and dispose of sharps
Food and food equipment safety	Food storage, preparation, handling, and distribution	Follow local food safety guidelines
	Dishwashing	At least one dishwashing machine for baby bottles, nipples, and pacifiers
	Refrigerators	Dedicate refrigerator(s) for storage of baby formulas and opened baby foods Equip refrigerators with thermometers and keep temperatures at or below 40 °F
Housekeeping	Cleaning	All floors should be mopped or vacuumed daily
Insect and rodent control	Food	No food in sleeping areas of shelter
	Reporting	Alert staff and residents to immediately report insect or rodent sightings or droppings
	Integrated pest management program	Should be developed and implemented by pest control specialist

(continued on next page)

Table 39. (*continued*)

	Provision	Requirement
	Prevention	Screen all openings with at least 16 mesh screen materials and close any crawl spaces with wire mesh
Soiled linen and clothing	Hampers	Provide hampers for soiled towels and other clothing
	Procedures	Provide residents with procedures for handling soiled and clean linen (e.g., with posters in shower rooms or other strategic locations)
Child care facilities	Diaper changing	Provide posters near diaper changing stations with sanitary procedures
	Sanitary supplies	Provide sanitary wipes, disposable diaper changing pads, sanitizing solution, and handwashing facilities at each diaper changing station
	Other supplies	All lotions, creams, and ointments applied to children's skin should be dispensed from single-use containers or containers designated for use on an individual child.
	Safety	All electrical outlets should be covered by protective caps or similar child safety devices
Toilet and shower facilities	Supplies	Provide soap dispensers with soap, paper towel dispensers with paper towels, and trash receptacles at handwashing stations
	Signage	Provide handwashing signs in relevant languages at handwashing stations
	Safety	Provide watertight, slip-resistant floors in all lavatories and showers
General safety	Maintenance	Follow local building code regulations
		Fire exits must comply with local fire code regulations

Adapted from Golob BR. 2007. *Environmental Health Emergency Response Guide*. Hopkins, MN: Twin Cities Metro Advanced Practice Center. Available at http://www.cdc.gov/nceh/ehs/Docs/EH_Emergency_Response_Guide.pdf.

Typhoid Fever

As with cholera, residents must be told to consume only chlorinated or boiled fluids and to eat only hot, cooked foods or peeled fruits and vegetables. Public health officials must ensure that the water supply is chlorinated and emphasize handwashing in food preparation and before eating. Workers must also ensure that infected residents do not prepare food for others for 3 months after the onset of their symptoms.

Shigella

Public health campaigns must educate residents about a comprehensive personal hygiene program. Public health workers must provide soap and lots of water and promote handwashing, the chlorination of water, and the proper handling and heating of food. Educational efforts should be focused in households where cases have occurred because secondary cases within households are common.

Hepatitis A

Water is the main route of transmission during major outbreaks. The most common form of fecal-oral hepatitis, hepatitis A, is transmitted by food and other routes. Control measures should therefore concentrate on the chlorination of water. Since pregnant women are particularly vulnerable, special efforts should be made to educate them and help them carry out personal and food hygiene.

Heating and Shelter

Provision of sufficient shelter following disaster prevents, depending on weather conditions, hypothermia, frostbite, malaise, heatstroke, and dehydration.

In cold climates, higher caloric intake is required to maintain the same activity level. For each degree below 68 °F, about 1% more calories are required. If a house is 50 °F, residents will require 10% more food intake to sustain their activity level. Public health interventions following cold weather disasters include making high-energy foods available, providing blankets and sleeping bags, distributing plastic sheeting to cover windows and unused doorways, encouraging the sharing of a heated place by several people or households, and instructing residents of multistory buildings to heat the same room, allowing heat lost from one floor to augment heat in the room above. Educational messages should warn people about the signs of carbon monoxide poisoning and provide instructions to check for gas leaks.

In warmer climates, sheeting should be provided to keep people dry during rainstorms and to provide shade in the daylight.

Worker Health and Safety

The collapse of a building or the occurrences of a large fire are two environmental events in which worker safety is of great concern. Workers can be exposed to hazards from the release of contaminants or from construction safety issues. Other occupational hazards at disaster sites include excessive noise, contaminated dust, heat stress from working in a hot climate or wearing PPE, cold stress from working in a cold environment for an extended period, working in confined spaces, injuries from dust or flying debris, and exposure to blood and body fluids. Workers may come in contact with plants that cause contact dermatitis or be potentially exposed to infectious disease when responding to disasters that occur in regions where such disease is endemic. In addition, workers are potentially exposed to chemicals and other toxic agents when a disaster involves their release.

Morbidity and Mortality

Depending upon the hazard, workers may experience traumatic injuries from falls; puncture wounds, lacerations, or abrasions; temporary hearing loss or difficulty communicating with coworkers; irritation or injury of eyes, nose, throat, or lungs; heat exhaustion and cramps to heatstroke; hypothermia or frostbite; entrapment or death by asphyxiation, constriction, or crushing; infections from exposure to blood-borne pathogens; and symptoms related to toxic agent exposures including death.

Public Health Interventions

In advance of traveling both domestically and internationally to respond to disasters, all personnel should take precautions to ensure their health and safety. In addition to the general guidelines provided below, the CDC provides guidance on necessary preventive measures for specific travel destinations (available at http://wwwnc.cdc.gov/travel/content/relief-workers.aspx).

All routine immunizations should be up to date:

- Tetanus/diphtheria vaccine or booster
- Polio booster if traveling to a polio-endemic or epidemic area (see http://www.polioeradication.org).
- Measles for those who do not have documented immunity
- Influenza vaccine
- Hepatitis B
- Hepatitis A

Specific vaccinations or protective actions are required when traveling to areas where the following are endemic:

- Japanese encephalitis (vaccination with the full course of immunization completed at least 10 days before departure and access to medical care during this 10-day period)
- Rabies
- Yellow fever
- Typhoid

- Cholera (although cholera vaccine is not available in the United States, the vaccine must be obtained before the worker arrives in the area where outbreaks of cholera are known)
- Malaria prophylaxis

Detailed information about preventive actions against traveler's diarrhea, insect and snake bites, environmental hazards, and extremes in temperature is available online (at http://wwwnc.cdc.gov/travel/cpntent/relief-workers.aspx).

Worker Safety

The National Response Framework includes an annex entitled "Worker Safety and Health Support," which outlines the national and regional assistance that will be provided to protect workers. These services vary, based upon the scope, complexity, and hazards associated with the incident, and can include the following:

- Identify and assess the health and safety hazards at the incident site and in the environment
- Assess resources needed to protect workers and identification of available sources
- Provide technical expertise in industrial hygiene, occupational safety and health, structural collapse engineering, safety engineering, radiation safety, biological and chemical agent response, and occupational medicine
- Create and implement a site-specific health and safety plan
- Monitor and manage through on-site identification, evaluation, analysis, and mitigation of personal exposure to hazards
- Assist in development, implementation, and monitoring the PPE program
- Coordinate collection and management of exposure and accident/injury data
- Coordinate and provide worker training related to specific incidents
- Assist with development and distribution of educational materials on preventing and mitigating hazards

Federal Guidance

To minimize worker injury in disaster response and recovery, planning is essential. Numerous standards have been developed to protect the health and safety of workers who are responding during disasters. The Occupational Safety and Health Administration (OSHA) issued a National Emergency Management Plan that clarifies procedures and policy for OSHA's national and regional offices during responses to nationally significant incidents (e.g., a presidential declaration, the activation of the Federal Response Framework, or a request for assistance from DHS). The National Emergency Management Plan requires that each OSHA region develop a Regional Emergency Management Plan coordinating federal and state plans. Further, it outlines logistical and operational procedures to ensure the health and safety of emergency responders and recovery workers. Where response activities are provided by contractors, communities should review their contracts to ensure that full protection is provided by both the contractors and any subcontractors who would be involved in search and rescue and/or recovery activities.

OSHA has published the "Principal Emergency Response and Preparedness Requirements and Guidance," which summarizes the requirements to protect workers in emergencies. This guidance includes the requirements of the Hazardous Waste Operations and Emergency Response (HAZWOPER), Process Safety Management (PSM), and a fire prevention plan, and also references the emergency planning and response requirements in many other OSHA standards. The PSM standard requires employers to establish a program to prevent injuries in chemical emergencies and to implement an emergency action plan (EAP). HAZWOPER and EAPs are discussed below.

HAZWOPER (OSHA 29 CFR 1910.120) is a useful framework for organizing the protection of those responding to a disaster. Among the requirements relevant to disaster response and recovery, HAZWOPER requires (1) extensive safety and health training, including instruction in decontamination for personnel, equipment, and hardware, response required by levels A, B, and C and establishing appropriate decontamination lines, and donning and doffing of protective equipment; (2) the development of and implementation of a written safety and health program; (3) a medical surveillance program; (4) an effective site safety and health plan; (5) an emergency response plan and procedures; (6) provision of recommended sanitation equipment; (7) development of work practices to minimize employee risk from site hazards; (8) safe use of engineering controls, equipment, and relevant new safety technology or procedures; (9) establishing methods of communication including those used while wearing respiratory protection; and (10) provision of PPE.

Community disaster plans for small businesses should include EAPs that provide for worker safety. An employer must review their organization's EAP with each employee when the plan is developed, an employee is initially assigned to a job, the employee's responsibilities under the plan change, or the plan is changed. An EAP must have the following minimum elements:

- Be in writing, kept in the workplace, and available to employees for review (An employer with ten or fewer employees may communicate the plan orally)
- Procedures for reporting a fire or other emergency
- Procedures for emergency evacuation, including exit route and assignments
- Procedures to be followed by employees who remain to operate critical plant operations before they evacuate
- Procedures to account for all employees after evacuation
- Procedures to be followed by employees performing rescue or medical duties
- The name or job title of every employee who is responsible for providing more information about the plan, including an explanation of employee duties under the plan
- A working employee alarm system

- Designated and trained employees who assist in the safe and orderly evacuation of other employees

OSHA's Employee Emergency Plans and Fire Protection Plans (29 CFR 1910.38) include EAP requirements that are also applicable to the protection of rescue workers. These additional requirements include (1) use of various types of fire extinguishers; (2) first aid, including cardiopulmonary resuscitation; (3) the requirements of the OSHA blood-borne pathogens standard; (4) chemical spill control procedures; (5) use of self-contained breathing apparatus (SCBA); (6) use of other PPE; (7) search and emergency rescue procedures; (8) emergency communication; and (9) hazardous materials emergency response in accordance with 29 CFR 1910.120. In addition to employers' providing these measures, workers must be trained in their use. Finally, it is important to ensure that subcontracts, where used, provide the same protections for their workers.

Protecting Workers With Disabilities

The Americans With Disabilities Act of 1990 requires employers who have an emergency evacuation plan to include actions that protect people with disabilities. Employers must also implement OSHA standards that require consideration of employees with disabilities in the development of their EAP.

The Office of Disability Employment Policy, at the U.S. Department of Labor, provides the following recommendations for implementing workplace emergency preparedness procedures for people with disabilities:

- When developing a plan, ask employees for their input
- Workers with disabilities should take responsibility for their safety by offering their ideas and input
- Develop the plan in consultation with local fire, police, and emergency departments, and community-based organizations
- Plan should be periodically revised and updated to reflect changes in technology, personnel, and procedures
- Plan should address the following:

  - Evacuation after the day shift ends
  - Method to identify visitors with special needs
  - Detailed method for communicating with hearing-impaired workers when they are away from their work areas
  - Be easy to read and understandable

- Plan should be distributed in a format accessible to all employees and be incorporated into standard operating procedures

  - Drills should be performed regularly and encompass the needs of workers with disabilities

Alerting Hearing-Impaired Employees

Although employees typically receive notification of an emergency through auditory devices, hearing-impaired workers may have difficulty understanding what is communicated over a public address (PA) system. A PA system is ineffective in communicating emergencies if the alarm interferes with or drowns out voice announcements. OSHA's Employee Alarm Systems standard (29 CFR 1910.165) requires that an alarm system be able to alert all employees and be heard above ambient noise. Strobe lights or similar lighting and tactile devices meet the standard for hearing-impaired employees. Visual alarms must be installed so that hearing-impaired persons can see them. The Underwriters Laboratories Standard for Emergency Signaling Devices for the Hearing-Impaired (UL 1971) establishes criteria for systems used for emergency notification.

A range of alerting device options is available to alert those with severe to profound hearing loss or mild hearing impairment. The hearing-impaired employees or an occupational audiologist can help determine the device or combination of devices that work best for their particular situation. Some alerting device options include the following:

- Exit signs set to flash when an emergency alarm sounds
- Strobe lights or vibrating alarm signals
- Visual or vibrating alarm signals at the employee's workstation
- Vibrating pagers worn by hearing-impaired workers
- Vibrating watches or other type of body alarm worn by hearing-impaired workers
- Two-way vibrating pagers for text messages
- Hearing dogs trained to alert the hearing-impaired worker
- Buddy systems in which a coworker alerts a hearing-impaired worker
- Amplified telephone ring signaler to alert the worker to a phone ringing
- A modem that converts the personal computer into a telecommunications device for the deaf (text telephone; TTY)
- Instant messaging or e-mail pop-up
- A flashlight provided to hearing-impaired individuals for signaling their location in the event they are separated from the rescue team or buddy

Personal Protective Equipment

Safety equipment, such as PPE, must meet the criteria contained in the OSHA standards or described by a nationally recognized standards producing organization. HAZWOPER 1910.120(c)(5)(i, iii) requires that PPE shall be

> provided and used during initial site entry which will provide protection to a level of exposure below permissible exposure limits and published exposure levels for known or suspected hazardous substances and health hazards. . . . If the preliminary site evaluation does not produce sufficient information to identify the hazards or suspected hazards of the site an ensemble providing equivalent to Level B PPE shall be provided as minimum protection, and direct reading instruments shall be used as

appropriate for identifying [immediately dangerous to life or health] IDLH conditions.

National Institute of Occupational Safety and Health (NIOSH) Publication No. 2009-132, "Recommendations for the Selection and Use of Respirators and Protective Clothing for Protection Against Biological Agents" (available at http://www.cdc.gov/niosh/docs/2009-132), provides additional guidance in the event of a terrorist attack involving biologicals. Table 40 lists the four types of PPE and their uses.

Although OSHA requires that employers are responsible for ensuring that their employees have adequate respiratory protection, depending on the size and location of the disaster, state and local departments of health (DOHs) may be responsible for

Table 40. Levels of Personal Protective Equipment

Level	Use	Apparatus
Level A	Greatest level of skin, respiratory, and eye protection is required	Fully encapsulated self-contained breathing apparatus (SCBA); Disposable protective suit, gloves, and boots (depending on suit construction, may be worn over totally encapsulating suit)
Level B	Highest level of respiratory protection is necessary, but with a lesser level of skin protection	Encapsulated SCBA Hooded chemical-resistant clothing (overalls and long-sleeved jacket; coveralls; one- or two-piece chemical-splash suit; disposable chemical-resistant overalls)
Level C	The concentration(s) and type(s) of airborne substance(s) are known and criteria for using air purifying respirators are met	Full-face or half-mask, air purifying respirators (National Institute of Occupational Safety and Health approved) Hooded chemical-resistant clothing (overalls; two-piece chemical-splash suit; disposable chemical-resistant overalls)
Level D	The atmosphere contains no known hazard Work functions preclude splashes, immersion, or the potential for unexpected inhalation of or contact with hazardous levels of any chemicals	Work uniform with standard precautions (gloves, mask)

Adapted from Occupational Safety and Health Administration (OSHA). 1994. OSHA Regulation Standard 29 CFR 1926.65. Appendix B. General Description and Discussion of the Levels of Protection and Protective Gear. Washington, DC: OSHA. Available at http://www.osha.gov/pls/oshaweb/owadisp.show_document?p_table=STANDARDS&p_id=10653.

assessing initial safety and health practices at the site of the disaster and for providing the initial distribution of PPE. An appropriate respirator program involves medical screening, fit testing, and training. Training includes instructing the workers on how to wear, clean, and maintain the respirators. Employees exposed to accidental chemical splashes, falling objects, flying particles, unknown atmospheres with inadequate oxygen or toxic gases, fires, live electrical wiring, or similar emergencies need PPE, including the following:

- Safety glasses, goggles, or face shields for eye protection
- Properly selected and fitted respirators
- Hard hats and safety shoes for head and foot protection
- Whole body coverings (chemical suits, gloves, hoods, and boots for protection from chemicals)
- Body protection for abnormal environmental conditions such as extreme temperatures

Effective emergency communication is vital. A system should be established to account for personnel once workers have been deployed or evacuated, with a person in the control center responsible for notifying police or emergency response team members of persons believed missing. Management should provide emergency alarms and ensure that workers know how to report emergencies within the response activities. Handout materials need to be developed that are simple to read. Key ideas can be listed on a card, such as site safety rules or the use of PPE. The card can be laminated so that it can be posted on equipment used in the rescue or recovery.

Finally, a mechanism is needed to monitor environmental exposures of the community and of response workers. The establishment of a worker injury and illness surveillance system will permit the generation of daily injury reports which can guide the modification of prevention measures and the types of PPE needed. More specific information is available in the Occupational Safety and Health Standards (Title 29, Code of Federal Regulations, Part 1910), which are the OSHA General Industry Standards (available at http://www.osha.gov/pls/oshaweb/owas-tand.display_standard_group?p_toc_level=1&p_part_number=1910).

Air Contaminants

Many disasters result in potential exposure to airborne substances, such as smoke, dust, or other contaminants. The EPA has established standards about particulate exposures which direct public health actions. Those at increased risk from exposures to contaminants include pregnant women and their unborn children, children, the elderly, those with chronic conditions such as heart disease and asthma, and workers. Table 41 shows the EPA particulate standards.

DOHs are responsible for monitoring the air immediately after an event occurs when there is a public health concern. DOH reviews the numerous air quality, debris sample, and personal air monitoring tests that other agencies may perform. Sometimes

Table 41. U.S. Environmental Protection Agency Particulate Standards

	Inhalable Coarse Particles	Fine Particles
Level of concern	150 μg/m^3 for PM$_{10}$ over a 24-hour period	35 μg/m^3 for PM$_{2.5}$ over a 24-hour period
Annual exposure	Revoked	15.0 μg/m^3

Adapted from U.S. Environmental Protection Agency (EPA). 2006. Particulate Matter: PM Standards Revision—2006. Washington, DC: EPA. Available at http://www.epa.gov/pm/naaqsrev2006.html.

federal agencies, such as the Agency for Toxic Substances and Disease Registry or the EPA, or the local department of environmental protection will be involved in the study of air and dust samples. These samples will be compared with standards, such as indoor air quality standards, to determine potential health effects. Exposures following disasters can also be measured by outdoor air monitors. One example, BioWatch, the system to monitor biological releases, is discussed in Chapter 11.

Depending on the disaster, the community may need instruments that provide instantaneous readings, because of the length of time it takes to get a laboratory analysis. Data should inform use of PPE and actions public health officials can take such as advising a community that it is safe to reenter homes and businesses. HAZWOPER provides guidance by requiring an ongoing air monitoring program for workers that should guide public health actions on air monitoring. Public health response should include monitoring the air with test equipment that permits direct reading for conditions immediately dangerous to life or health and other conditions that may cause death or serious harm (e.g., combustible or explosive atmospheres, oxygen deficiency, toxic substances). NIOSH and the CDC have developed guidance on the installation of filtration and air cleaning systems that can protect building environments from airborne agents. A full description is beyond the scope of this book, but more information is available through the publications included in the reference section.

Careful thought should go into communicating information about the risks from potential air contaminants to the public (discussed more fully in Chapter 6). DOHs should develop advisories that can be communicated both to the public and to rescue personnel on air quality issues and on practical information about the particular hazards posed by the disaster. Examples include the advisories that the New York City Health Departments posted about using wet methods, such as wet mopping or high-efficiency particulate vacuum, after the World Trade Center collapses in 2001.

Recovery and Handling of Human Remains

When establishing a temporary mortuary, look for a secure building which has the capacity for a reception room, a viewing room, a place for storing bodies at 39°F, and rooms for records and personal effects. Mortuary personnel should wear gloves and protective clothing and wash thoroughly with a disinfectant soap. Mortuary supplies include stretchers, leather gloves, rubber gloves, overalls, boots, caps, soap, cotton cloth and disinfectants, property bags, body bags and labels, wheeled trolleys to transport bodies, and plastic sheeting for the floor. In the United States it is common to use ice skating rinks, where available, to store remains and refrigerator trucks to transport the bodies. When setting up a facility for the identification of bodies, the World Health Organization recommends 2187 square yards (1828.6 square meters) for 1000 unidentified bodies.

When a disaster involves the recovery of human body parts, there is no threat of a general outbreak of infectious disease. Workers are at risk of viral or bacterial infection if they cut themselves with an object contaminated with blood, body fluids, or tissue, or if these materials touch the rescuers' eyes, nose, mouth, or areas of broken skin. Bad odors coming from decomposing bodies are not harmful.

Rescue workers who expect that they might have direct contact with human remains should be advised to do the following:

- Wear heavy-duty waterproof gloves to protect against injury from sharp environmental debris or bone fragments; a combination of a cut-proof inner glove and a latex or similar outer layer is preferable
- Use eye protection and respirators equipped with OVAG (organic vapor/acid gas) cartridges to protect eyes, nose, and mouth from splash exposures and noxious odors; where OVAG protection is not available, workers can use a plastic face shield or a combination of eye protection and a surgical mask
- Wear protective garments to protect skin and clothes
- Immediately wash hands with soap and water after removing gloves
- Use alcohol-based hand sanitizers only when hands are not visibly soiled
- Promptly care for any wounds received while handling remains, including a tetanus booster

Integrated Pest Management

Vector control is always important for the prevention of communicable disease, but becomes even more important when there is the potential for increased spread of disease caused by the breakdown in environmental controls following disaster. The most effective way to control vector-borne disease is to establish sanitary disposal of waste as soon as possible. Where vector-borne disease is known to be endemic, control programs should be accelerated in the postimpact phase of a disaster. The principles of integrated pest management are to eliminate breeding sites, to eliminate food, and to control harborage (where pests can live). A community vector control program includes several components:

- Collect and dispose of garbage as soon as possible
- Educate the public about rat and mosquito control
- Eliminate mosquito breeding sites by overturning receptacles, covering swimming pools, and draining or covering other stagnant water sources
- Reduce rat population and spread by closing up cracks in walls and bringing cats to chase the rats
- Store food in enclosed, protected areas

In flooded areas, rats will search for dry places to hide. Rats and other vectors can feed off dead animals and other organic waste. Therefore, animal carcasses should be sprinkled with kerosene to protect them from predatory animals.

Chapter 9

Behavioral Health Strategies

ost victims and workers in disasters respond normally to an abnormal situation. However, disasters can affect both short-term and long-term mental health when they destroy people's homes, their livelihoods, and the lives of loved ones. The long-term psychosocial effects of disasters are mitigated by understanding what is likely to occur and preplanning the management strategy. Many people may need support services in the immediate aftermath of a disaster and some will need long-term services. By knowing who is at greater risk, behavioral health professionals can triage and more closely monitor those at higher risk. This chapter reviews the psychosocial affects of natural and technological disasters, how communities and individuals can develop resilience, the interventions needed for special populations (e.g., children, older adults, emergency workers), the impact of cultural background, and the considerations of post-traumatic stress disorder (PTSD) and trauma work. Building upon that foundation, the chapter lays out a plan for organizing services for mental and substance-use conditions, including assistance center and patient locator systems.

Public Health Role

- Help restore the psychological and social functioning of individuals and the community
- Reduce the occurrence and severity of adverse behavioral health outcomes caused by exposure to natural and technological disasters through prevention, assessment, and response
- Help speed recovery and prevent long-term problems by providing information about normal reactions to disaster-related stress and how to handle these reactions
- Provide practical, concrete services that address shelter, food, and employment issues
- Coordinate with medical providers to assist in the identification and referral of those in their practices who could benefit from further behavioral health intervention
- In communities where services for mental and substance-use conditions are organized separately from public health, assure that coordination occurs as part of community planning

Psychosocial Impacts of Disaster

Living through the experience of a disaster can have profound psychosocial effects and can alter social structure. The type of disaster predicts the level of psychological injury. Natural disasters have the lowest level, followed by events resulting from human error, whereas violence and terrorism have the biggest impact. When planning a response to or delivering services in the aftermath of a disaster, public health professionals must consider the wide range of responses among victims and responders.

Disasters are very stressful, disruptive experiences that affect the entire community and can be life-changing. However, two thirds of those who have experienced a disaster do not suffer long-term effects. Human behavior in emergencies generally adapts to meet immediate needs, with people behaving within their usual patterns pre- and postdisaster. The challenge of dealing with a disaster can also result in positive responses by both individuals and communities. Residents typically work together and support one another as they rebuild their lives and their communities. Residents of disaster-stricken areas tend to exhibit prosocial behaviors, are proactive in remediating the effects of the event, and are willing to help one another in their recovery. People generally provide assistance to one another and support those managing the response to the emergency. Volunteer activity increases at the time of the impact and continues throughout the postimpact period. Many disaster tasks are carried out spontaneously by civilian bystanders (such as family, friends, coworkers, neighbors) rather by trained emergency or relief personnel. The abilities of adjusting to the circumstances and taking positive actions are examples of resilience. We know that resilient individuals and communities recover sooner.

In terms of morbidity, the social and psychosocial impacts of a disaster can greatly add to and often outlast the physical injuries. The social and psychosocial effects of disasters can last months, years, or an entire lifetime. People who are involved in disasters, as either victim or responder, may experience a wide variety of stress symptoms. These symptoms can have the broadest range of emotional, physical, cognitive, and interpersonal effects. In some disaster situations, victims recover quickly without long-lasting effects. In others, victims and responders suffer major problems with mental and substance-use conditions both immediately and for years after the event. They may have lost loved ones, need to adjust to new role changes, need to clean and repair property, or move from their home and neighborhood. In addition, peer support may be lost or victims may find that their peers are drinking more in response to stress.

Individual factors can influence one's psychological response. In addition to genetic vulnerabilities, an individual's prior history (e.g., child abuse, previous traumatic experience, experience of multiple stressors, prior psychological disorder, or none of these) and the family's emotional health and ability to provide support can all make an individual more or less vulnerable to long-term psychological difficulties.

The severity of one's exposure is a risk factor for adverse psychosocial outcomes. One's proximity to the events; specific stressors, such as losing a loved one, being injured or seeing a family member injured, having your life threatened, or losing your home or community can all have significant effects on behavioral health. Loss of social support, particularly for those who are displaced from their home or community, lose their usual routine, or experience the death of significant others, will negatively influence an individual's ability to adapt.

Both victims and responders experience a disaster as a crisis. Unusual events exacerbate the trauma, as there may be deaths of family or friends, injuries, job difficulties, illness, loss of personal belongings, and disruption of the regular routine. Initially, people feel numbness rather than panic. Those who experience a disaster want to talk about it with everyone who will listen. Victims may exhibit anger toward "the system," such as a perceived slow response by responding agencies. In time, everyone attempts to return to a normal routine, but delays in achieving normalcy impede emotional recovery.

Some predictors of potential long-term dysfunction can be managed. Both children and adults show a dose–response reaction to disaster threats—the greater the exposure, the greater the difficulties. Fortunately, the mobilization of support can offset the impact of the severity of exposure. People who receive high levels of support are helped in dealing with the serious impacts of the disaster experience.

Resilience

The mental health of a community following a disaster is dependent, in part, on the community's preparedness: their organizational response, ability to protect those who are impacted from harm, and ability to provide needed assistance. The impact of disasters on individuals and on the larger community is also influenced by their resilience.

Developing resilience, the capacity of individuals and community to adapt following devastating disasters, has become a foundation of disaster preparedness and effective response. The capacity to adapt is affected by the types, timing, and levels of support received. Although disasters often bring numerous losses, there are also opportunities for individual growth and improvements in the community. For example, Greensburg, Kansas, established itself as a futuristic model "green" town by building a new school at LEED (Leadership in Energy and Environmental Design) platinum standards after a tornado devastated the entire town.

Resilience for individuals varies in each phase of a disaster. When the disaster first strikes, an individual's capacity to adapt is dependent on their level of individual preparedness, household preparedness, and the individual's ability to manage by themselves. Those who are better prepared, by having an emergency plan and stored food and water, for example, are better able to adjust. During the response, resilience is dependent on working with other members of the community to plan and carry out tasks. Through institutional planning, communities enhance their resilience by having mechanisms to mobilize residents and volunteers. As the response continues, the adaptive capacity of communities is reflected in their effective working with manpower and resources external to the community.

The capacity of a community to adapt is dependent on having both the necessary volume and diversity of resources to cope with any disruption and the systems and skills to coordinate and utilize those resources. Communities with fewer resources are less resilient because they are less able to cope with the loss of those resources. Resilient communities have the capacity to anticipate, prepare for emergencies, and plan for the future. Resilient communities involve their residents in the process of responding and recovering; they believe that individual preparedness is a public responsibility and that residents are partners who multiply the community's capacity to respond. Emergency planners bring the members of resilient communities into the process and assimilate and coordinate their perspectives within the emergency plan.

Communities are more resilient when social capital holds a community together. Individuals with large social networks are more resilient than are those acting alone, because of their collective resources. For example, the larger one's social network, the more likely the person will receive information about protective actions to take during an emergency. Furthermore, those who have networks and relationships before an emergency can more rapidly mobilize necessary resources and support. To increase resilience, people in a community must be engaged in preparedness activities for themselves, their households, and their communities. In addition, responders should work to advance the development of naturally occurring social supports postimpact and during recovery.

Normal Reaction to Abnormal Situations

In general, the transient reactions that people experience after a disaster, such as grief and stress reactions, represent a normal response to a highly abnormal situation. The goal is to assist individuals and communities experiencing transient dysfunction to return to their predisaster levels of functioning.

Victims of a disaster should be viewed as normal persons, capable of functioning effectively, who have been subjected to severe stress and may be showing signs of emotional strain. Mild-to-moderate stress reactions during the emergency and in the early postimpact phases of a disaster are highly prevalent among survivors, families, community members, and rescue workers. Although some individuals may exhibit symptoms of extreme stress, these reactions generally do not lead to chronic problems. However, public health professionals should not ignore common stress reactions. Counselors may find that the marital problems that families have previously been working on are heightened following a disaster. Mental health professionals can help speed recovery and prevent long-term problems by providing information about normal reactions and educating victims about ways to handle those reactions.

A portion of the population will suffer more serious, persistent symptoms. Although most individuals exposed to traumatic events and disasters recover and do not suffer prolonged psychiatric illness, some exhibit behavioral change or develop physical or psychiatric illness. Troublesome reactions can result from exposure to both natural and technological disasters and can include depression, alcohol abuse, anxiety, somatization disorder, domestic violence, difficulties in daily functioning, and PTSD. Although less serious reactions, insomnia and anxiety may also be experienced by disaster victims and workers.

The following are common to all who experience a disaster:

- Concern for basic survival
- Grief over loss of loved ones and loss of important possessions

- Fear and anxiety about one's physical safety and that of loved ones
- Sleep disturbances, including nightmares and flashbacks from the disaster
- Concerns about relocation, potentially crowded living conditions, and being separated from support system
- Need to talk about events and feelings associated with the disaster
- Need to feel part of the community and its disaster recovery efforts

Behavioral Health Morbidity and Mortality

Adults and children manifest symptoms of distress differently. Disasters can have emotional, cognitive, physical, and interpersonal effects. For adults, the initial emotional response is usually shock and disbelief. This lasts from a few minutes to a few hours. Behavior is dazed or stunned. For the next several days, victims are willing to follow directions and are grateful for assistance. They may feel guilty for surviving.

In the next several weeks, victims will likely seek out others who were affected and participate in group activities of recovery. This activity is often followed by despair and depression. Victims can experience flashbacks, anger, emotional numbing, or dissociation, perceiving their experience as "dreamlike." Cognitive effects can include impaired memory, concentration, and decision-making ability. Interpersonal relationships can become strained. Some victims worry about their futures and blame themselves. Furthermore, victims may increase their use of alcohol and over-the-counter sleep aids.

In the long term, there is a risk of decreased self-esteem and self-sufficiency. Some victims experience intrusive thoughts and memories. Physical effects can include sleep disturbances leading to insomnia and fatigue. Some victims and responders experience hyperarousal or a "startle" response. There can be somatic complaints such as headaches, gastrointestinal problems, reduced appetite, and decreased libido. Finally, disasters can have profound and widespread interpersonal effects such as alienation, social withdrawal, increased conflict within relationships, and both vocational and school impairment.

Symptoms of Distress

Those most at risk for psychosocial impacts are children, older adults, people with serious mental illness, families of people who die in a disaster, and responders. Different age groups are vulnerable to stress in different ways. Most people do not see themselves as needing services for mental and substance-use conditions following disaster and will not voluntarily seek out such services.

Children

Although a disaster affects everyone in the community, children are a particularly vulnerable group and require special attention and programs to avoid a traumatic experience. Children look to caregivers for support—parents, peers, and teachers will be the first responders to children in the preimpact and impact phases of disaster.

For children, a key protective factor is their family. When a mother is resilient and adapts to the events, a child also adapts. This is especially true for children younger than 6 years old. For teenagers however, their peer group is more influential. Because a child has a strong initial reaction does not mean that he or she will not recover. As families and social support are the primary protective factors, it is best to provide postdisaster counseling with families together.

Helping children will likely involve working closely with teachers and schools. The goal for those intervening with children is to help them integrate the experience and to reestablish a sense of security and mastery. Children who are most at risk are those who have lost family members or friends, who had a previous experience with a disaster, or who have preexisting family or individual crises. Children may not be able to describe their fears, which is a normal reaction stimulated by real events. Fear can outlast the event and can persist even if no physical injury occurred. Exposure to repeated media coverage can increase and prolong symptoms.

Preschool children needing extra help may appear withdrawn or depressed, or they may not respond to directed attention or to attempts to draw them out. They may exhibit thumb-sucking, bed-wetting, fears of darkness or animals, clinging to parents, night terrors, incontinence or constipation, speech difficulties, or changes in appetite. Preschoolers are vulnerable to disruptions in their environment, are affected by the reactions of their family, and are disoriented by changes to their regular schedule. Quickly reestablishing their regular schedule for eating, playing, and going to bed is important. Other interventions to help preschoolers include reenactment of the events in play (for example, with fire trucks, dump trucks, ambulances), nonverbal activities such as drawing, and games that involve touching (Ring Around the Rosie; London Bridge; Duck, Duck, Goose). Verbal reassurance, physical comforting, frequent attention, expressions regarding loss of pets or toys, and sleeping in the same room as their parents may be helpful as well, because it should be temporary.

Children aged 5 to 11 years may exhibit irritability, whining, clinging, aggressive behavior, competition for parent's attention, night terrors or nightmares, fears of darkness, withdrawal from peers, and avoidance, disinterest, or poor concentration in school. Interventions for this age group include patience and tolerance, play sessions with adults and peers, discussions with adults and peers, relaxed expectations, structured free time with activities, and rehearsal of safety measures for the future. Children in this age group who reenact the events over and over and who have ongoing intrusive thoughts should be referred for evaluation.

Children aged 11 to 14 years can experience sleep disturbances, changes in appetite, rebellion at home, physical complaints, and problems with or less interest in school activities. At this age, children may benefit from encouraging the resumption of normal routines, organizing groups with peers, engaging in group discussions about the disaster, relaxing expectations temporarily, taking on structured responsibilities, and receiving additional attention as needed.

Children aged 14 to 18 years may exhibit psychosomatic symptoms, disturbances of sleep and appetite, hypochondriasis, changes in energy level, apathy, decline in interest in the opposite sex (or same sex if that is their norm), irresponsible or delinquent behavior, fewer struggles for emancipation from parents, and poor concentration. Junior- and senior-high school–aged children may become disoriented (for example, confused regarding their name, town, the date), despondent, agitated, restless, severely depressed and withdrawn, unable to make simple decisions, and unable to carry out daily activities. These children may also pace, appear pressured, hallucinate, become preoccupied with one idea or thought, engage in self-mutilation, abuse drugs or alcohol, experience significant memory gaps, and become delusional or suicidal. Interventions include encouraging participation in community reclamation, resumption of social activities, discussion of experience with peers, reducing expectations temporarily, and discussion of experience with family. Adolescent activities should end on a positive note, such as talk of heroic acts, helping the community, and preparing for the next time. Small groups could develop a plan to help the community rehabilitate. Adolescents who begin or increase risk-taking activities (for example, substance abuse is common) should be referred for evaluation.

Finally, disaster plans can help protect the welfare of children by ensuring that all buildings where children congregate have written plans for all-hazards evacuation, for the relocation and reunification of children with their families or caregivers, and for the care of children with functional needs.

Older Adults

Older adults are in the highest risk group following a disaster. Generally, older adults have fewer support networks, limited mobility, and preexisting illness. In addition, disasters can trigger memories of other traumas experienced earlier in life. Older persons worry about their deteriorating health and needing to be institutionalized, and as a result may conceal the full extent of their physical problems. Research has shown that this population experiences a higher proportion of personal injury or loss because they often live in places more vulnerable to damage. Since they experience a greater loss of mobility, their independence and self-sufficiency are harmed because they are less able to rebuild their homes, businesses, and other losses following a disaster. Living in assisted living or long-term care facilities may involve built-in supports that protect older adults.

Responders

Those whose job is to respond to disasters have physically demanding work that is tiring, may interrupt sleep patterns, and may expose them to hazards which are life threatening or have potential long-term health risks. Response tasks, such as search and rescue, expose responders to mutilated bodies and mass destruction. Their role as a help provider is also stressful. Some responders experience feelings similar to those experienced by the victims. They can be irritable, finding fault with things that never bothered them before. They can be suspicious and resent authority. They can be concerned for their own safety and the safety of their children. Responders can be stressed by their working environment, particularly in the presence of understaffing of their units, overwork, and conflicts with other professionals. Responders may face anxiety about their competence, are more affected by the impact of sights and smells, and can also struggle to balance family responsibilities and work demands in the face of an emergency.

Some responders may develop a condition known as critical incident stress syndrome. This syndrome must be recognized and treated because critical incident stress lowers group morale, increases absenteeism, interferes with mutual support, and adversely affects home life. The symptoms include deterioration in sense of well-being, exhaustion, depression, hostility, lost tolerance for victims, dread of new encounters, guilt, helplessness, or isolation. Burnout is often recognized by looking for either detachment or overinvolvement.

Cultural Considerations

With the population of the United States becoming increasingly more diverse, public health professionals can develop more effective behavioral health programs by understanding how people's ethnicity and culture impact responses to disaster. People's reactions to disaster, their ability to adapt, and their receptivity to assistance and services for mental health and substance-use vary according to their cultural traditions. Reactions to and recovery from disasters is influenced by one's ethnocultural background and the inherent life experience and values embedded in that background. The role of the family and who makes decisions also varies. In some cultures, elders and extended family play a significant role, whereas in others nuclear families make the decisions. Behavioral health services following disasters are most effective when victims receive assistance that is consistent with their cultural beliefs as well as their needs.

Community is especially important for racial/ethnic minority groups. As discussed in the section on resilience, intact communities provide strong social support. A community that is disrupted and fragmented is less able to provide the needed support, and this loss of social support can dramatically affect one's ability to adapt and recover. Refugees to the United States may have experienced a previous loss of social support, making them more vulnerable following repeated losses. Further, racial/ethnic minority groups may be severely impacted where socio-economic conditions cause the community to live in housing that is vulnerable to many disasters.

American Indian and Alaska Native tribes are federally recognized sovereign nations; thus, disaster response involves working with multiple agencies within the tribes and with all levels of government. In addition, tribes may work together to receive assistance and services. The Stafford Act provides that a state government must request a presidential disaster declaration on behalf of a tribe. Before a disaster declaration, responding agencies can work directly with a tribe to meet their needs using existing resources. Table 42 describes different aspects of daily life in which cultural customs should be considered by those providing disaster services to diverse populations.

Table 42. Cultural Views That Can Impact Response and Recovery

Communication: Culture influences how people express their feelings and what feelings are appropriate to express. The inability of both verbal and nonverbal communication can make both parties feel alienated and helpless.

Personal Space: Spatial requirements can be similar among people in a given cultural group. One person might touch or move closer to another as a friendly gesture, whereas someone from a different culture might consider such behavior invasive. Disaster crisis counselors must look for clues to a survivor's need for space, such as moving their chair back or stepping closer.

Social Organization: Understanding the influences of beliefs, values, and attitudes will enable the disaster worker to more accurately assess a survivor's reaction to the events. A survivor's answers to questions about hobbies and social activities can lead to insight into his or her life before the disaster.

Time: Perceptions of time may be altered during a disaster. Diverse cultures may view time differently, including their interpretations of the overall concept of time. Social time may be measured in terms of "dinner time," "worship time," or "harvest time." It is important to set time frames that are meaningful or realistic.

Environmental Control: Some people believe that events occur because of some external factor—luck, chance, fate, will of a higher being, or the control of others. These views can affect a person's response to disaster and the types of assistance needed. Those who feel that events and recovery are out of their control may be pessimistic about recovery, whereas those who believe that they personally can affect events may be more willing to take action.

Adapted from Athey J, Moody-Williams J. 2003. *Developing Cultural Competence in Disaster Mental Health Programs: Guiding Principles and Recommendations*. Table 2-2. Important considerations when interacting with people of other cultures. Washington, DC: U.S. Department of Health and Human Services, Substance Abuse and Mental Health Service Administration.

Post-Traumatic Stress Disorder

PTSD is a prolonged stress response associated with impairment and dysfunction. PTSD is a process, not a singular reaction or experience. How an individual perceives and experiences the disaster is a more salient factor in developing PTSD than the events themselves. PTSD usually appears within 3 months of the trauma but may surface months or years later. The duration of the disorder varies. Not all traumas cause PTSD. Sometimes the symptoms of PTSD disappear over time, and sometimes PTSD persists for many years. Post-traumatic disorders are best understood as a failure to recover. The seven factors which increase the likelihood of developing PTSD include being a young child, being female, lacking social supports, having a history of psychiatric disorder, having previously experienced a traumatic event, experiencing a panic attack at the time of the event, and experiencing stressful events subsequent to the event.

Although PTSD has been the subject of considerable research in recent years, other serious problems that can develop after a disaster include acute stress disorder, major depression, generalized anxiety disorder, and substance abuse. Acute stress disorder is characterized by post-traumatic stress symptoms lasting at least 2 days but not longer than 1 month following the trauma. In the long term, individuals who have experienced a disaster suffer more from depression than they do from PTSD. Finally, alcohol abuse can increase by 5 to 7% following a disaster.

Criteria for Post-Traumatic Stress Disorder[1]

A diagnosis of PTSD, as listed in the *Diagnostic and Statistical Manual of Mental Disorders (DSM-IV)*, requires that several criteria be met. PTSD symptoms can be acute, chronic, or delayed in their onset.

The first criterion relates to the nature of the traumatic event and the response it evokes:

> The person has been exposed to a traumatic event in which both of the following were present: (1) the person experienced, witnessed, or [has] been confronted with an event or events that involved actual or threatened death or serious injury, or a threat to the physical integrity of self or others . . . [and] (2) the person's response involved intense fear, helplessness or horror . . . (p. 209).

The second criterion relates to the reexperiencing of the traumatic event:

> The traumatic event is persistently reexperienced in one (or more) of the following ways: (1) recurrent and intrusive distressing recollections of the event . . . (2) recurrent distressing dreams of the event . . . (3) acting or feeling as if the traumatic event were recurring . . . (4) intense psychological distress at exposure to internal or external cues that symbolize or resemble an aspect of the traumatic event; (5) physiological reactivity on exposure to internal or external cures that symbolize or resemble an aspect of the traumatic event (pp. 209–210).

The third criterion relates to avoidance, that is, the person avoiding things that remind him or her of the traumatic event:

> Persistent avoidance of stimuli associated with the trauma and numbing of general responsiveness (not present before the trauma), as indicated by three (or more) of the following: (1) efforts to avoid thoughts, feelings or conversations associated with the trauma; (2) efforts to avoid activities, places or people that arouse recollections of the trauma; (3) inability to recall an important aspect of the trauma; (4) markedly diminished interest or participation in significant activities; (5) feeling of detachment or estrangement from others; (6) restricted range of affect (e.g., unable to have love feelings); (7) sense of a foreshortened future . . . (p. 211).

---

[1]Diagnostic criteria from *Diagnostic and Statistical Manual of Mental Disorders*. 1994. Washington, DC: American Psychiatric Association:209-211.

The fourth criterion relates to the person experiencing increased arousal after the traumatic event:

> Persistent symptoms of increased arousal (not present before the trauma), as indicated by two (or more) of the following: (1) difficulty falling asleep; (2) irritability or outbursts of anger; (3) difficulty concentrating; (4) hypervigilance; (5) exaggerated startle response (p. 211).

The fifth criterion relates to the duration of the symptoms just described. In particular, for a diagnosis of PTSD to be made, the duration of the symptoms in the second, third, and fourth criteria must exceed one month.

Finally, the disturbance must cause "clinically significant distress or impairment in social, occupational or other important areas of functioning."

Post-Traumatic Stress Disorder Risk Factors/Predictors

Several factors can help predict which individuals might be at risk for PTSD. The nature or severity of the trauma the person has experienced plays a major role. Higher-risk scenarios potentially leading to long-term adjustment problems include exposure to life-threatening situations, having a loved one die, loss of home and belongings, exposure to toxic contamination, and exposure to terror, horror, or grotesque sights such as multiple casualties. Additional risk factors relate to life events before the disaster; a history of prior exposure to trauma, concurrent stressful life events, and lack of social support all predispose to PTSD.

Family members of trauma victims and family members of disaster workers may also develop PTSD and related symptoms. Spouses and domestic partners should be included in debriefing, education programs, and treatment programs as indicated.

Ethnocultural Issues in Post-Traumatic Stress Disorder

Rates of PTSD or other disaster-related impairment can differ among groups of different race/ethnicity, as a result of culturally varying perceptions of what constitutes a traumatic experience as well as individual and social responses to trauma. PTSD has been detected in traumatized cohorts from very different ethnocultural backgrounds, and victims from all groups who meet PTSD diagnostic criteria have shown a similar clinical course and response to treatment. Assessments of the stress reaction of all individuals who have experienced a disaster should be carried out in a culturally sensitive manner, accounting for factors that may be unknown. Major depression, generalized anxiety disorder, and substance abuse are well documented after exposure to trauma and disasters. When planning interventions and developing programs, including members of the group in the planning and delivery of services and incorporating cultural aspects from the group's background will help give a sense of empowerment and result in better outcomes.

Natural Disasters and Technological Disasters

The similarities and differences between technological and natural disasters are the degree to which the events are felt to be preventable and controllable. The two types of disasters have in common the immediate threat and the potential for ongoing disruption. However, they differ with regard to whether someone can be blamed for the event and whether it could have been prevented. People understand that humans have little control over nature and that some geographic locations are more prone to some natural disasters than are others. By contrast, they believe people can control technology and thus feel a greater sense of a loss of control with technological events, since these events could have presumably been prevented.

Residents who are victimized by technological disasters may have their stress exacerbated by knowing that their tragedy was caused by other human beings. Technological disasters of the same magnitude as natural disasters generally cause more severe problems with mental and substance-use conditions, because it is harder in the former case to achieve psychological resolution and to move on. During the nuclear disaster that followed the earthquake and tsunami in Japan in March 2011, the Japanese people were upset because they had been led to believe that their nuclear reactors were designed to prevent damage from earthquakes. Although many people initially doubted the official version of events, they became angrier when they learned that the government had issued inaccurate information.

For several reasons, technological disasters present complex challenges for public health professionals. First, unlike the community cohesiveness that occurs after natural disasters, communities are often in conflict after an environmental disaster. Where the disaster involves contaminants that are usually invisible, great uncertainty often exists as to the risks of exposure. Contaminants may not have dispersed evenly, resulting in very different perceptions of the events by people living in the same community. Victims of technological disasters often feel unsure about the long-term risks. Because of this ambiguity and insecurity, neighbors can become bitterly divided, and their support networks may be irreversibly damaged. Worse, residents of affected communities can be stigmatized by society as a result of the unknown risks of their exposure.

Technological disasters often cause chronic uncertainty and distress. Unlike natural disasters, which generally have a low point after which things can be expected to improve, in disasters involving chemicals and radiation, those affected often do not know when all of the recovery activities will resolve. Uncertainty continues about the chronic health effects of exposure to invisible contaminants. Furthermore, long-term consequences, such as cancer, may take years to develop. Events that have a beginning and an end, such as tornadoes or hurricanes, allow the process of recovery to begin. Technological disasters do not have this defined timeline, and as a result, the psychological threat can be continual and chronic.

Following a technological disaster, psychophysiological symptoms are prevalent, along with chronic stress and demoralization. Psychological effects may result from either direct exposure or reaction to mitigation activities. Exposure to chemicals often does not result in a large number of exposed seeking immediate medical treatments. Here, concerns are long term. Information about the level of exposure or contamination may not be available for some time. Loss of social support and status can cause stress, especially if evacuation is required. These symptoms can manifest as physical complaints, can lead to increased morbidity of chronic diseases, such as hypertension, and can lead to medical problems attributable to the earlier exposure but appearing later in life. Groups at high risk for psychological health effects from environmental exposures include older persons living alone, mothers with young children, evacuees, responders, and persons with previous mental disorders. The following causes of stress can follow major environmental exposures[2]:

- Acute stress reaction
- Worry about long-term health effects
- Uncertainty about long-term effects
- Housing and job security
- Media siege
- Somatic complaints
- Stigma and social rejection
- Cultural pressures
- Inadequate medical follow-up and compensation

Terrorism

People who have experienced terrorist events, either as a victim or a relative of a victim, can suffer some psychological impairment. Prevalence varies by the specific events, differences in population involved, and nature of the events. Those most likely to be affected are those who were injured, first responders exposed to trauma, and those who were already at risk to develop psychological symptoms.

Individuals who experience violence through terrorism tend to be angrier about what has happened than are those who have experienced other kinds of disasters. Those who have uncontrolled anger and rage which persists over time can predictably have the worst outcome psychologically.

Resilience and Recovery Intervention Model

Although disasters affect a whole community or region, individuals do not all react in the same manner. Many individuals might need assistance, but not everyone will benefit from the same type of aid. The challenge is identifying those who need more support and proactively delivering those services. Despite being traumatized, many who survive find themselves having a life experience that makes them feel stronger.

Increasing an individual's and a community's capacity to adapt requires an identification and implementation of protective actions. Several strategies can be

---

[2]Adapted from Baxter PJ. 2002. Public health aspects of chemical catastrophes. In: Havenaar JM, Cwikel JG, Bromet EJ, editors. *Toxic Turmoil: Psychological and Societal Consequences of Ecological Disasters.* New York, NY: Kluwer Academic/Plenum.

implemented by community officials to foster the development of psychological body armor. These include the following:

- Be ready to support the community by all sectors of society including government, nonprofit, and business sector
- Develop perception of credible and competent leadership
- Provide practical preparation by establishing realistic expectations
- Develop stress management and coping skills through preparatory training
- Train civilian volunteers in basic skills, capacities, and an understanding of their responsibility
- Build redundancy into support systems, preparedness plans, and community capacity
- Ensure effective communication with accurate information, reassurance, direction, motivation, and a sense of connectedness
- Promote the development of social support and solid group structures
- Build the perception of an ability to organize, take action, and view stressful events as challenges which can be overcome
- Foster positive awareness and insight, positive memories of those who have died

Interventions to help people return to normal functioning include the following:

- Get people to a safe place and help them understand that they are safe
- Use media to inform the public about risks and provide calming assurance
- Provide accurate information from a trusted source about danger and options for action
- Furnish needed resources
- Provide needed care for medical, mental, and substance-use conditions

Resilience for Children and Families

Following Hurricane Katrina, many lessons were learned about helping children and families adapt to the tremendous losses that they experienced. To foster child and family resilience, community officials and others involved in the response to an event should do the following:

- Promote control, empowerment, and normalcy
- Reunite families as quickly as possible
- Help families recognize strengths and resources
- Assist the integration of those evacuated into the community
- Encourage proactive measures to cope with change and losses
- Provide ready access to basic human needs
- Treat individuals with dignity and respect
- Be sure that those with functional needs are assisted in the most appropriate way possible

Organizing Disaster Behavioral Health Services

Section 416 of The Robert T. Stafford Disaster Relief and Emergency Assistance Act of 1988 (Public Law 100-707; available at http://www.fema.gov/pdf/about/

stafford_act.pdf) establishes legislative authority for the president to provide training and services to alleviate behavioral health problems caused or exacerbated by major disasters. The Act reads as follows:

> Crisis Counseling Assistance and Training. The President is authorized to provide professional counseling services, including financial assistance to State or local agencies or private mental health organizations to provide such services or training of disaster workers, to survivors/victims of major disaster in order to relieve mental health problems caused or aggravated by such major disaster or its aftermath. (42 U.S.C. 5183; p. 47)

Federally, the Crisis Counseling Assistance and Training Program (commonly referred to as the Crisis Counseling Program) is managed by the Federal Emergency Management Agency (FEMA) in cooperation with the Center for Mental Health Services. Their *Training Manual for Mental Health and Human Service Workers in Major Disasters* (2nd edition) is available online (at http://www.mentalhealth. samhsa.gov/publications/allpubs/adm90-538/default.asp), and should be used as a guide for establishing community programs and training personnel.

What Services Are Needed

The organization for and delivery of behavioral health services should be part of a community's overall disaster plan to avoid the difficult task of recruiting and orienting masses of volunteers in the chaos immediately following a disaster. Before developing the community plan for behavioral services, it is useful to consider the range and types of services that might be required. Table 43 describes the types of behavioral services that are likely to be required in a major disaster. Although the services needed may vary with the nature of the event, such as type of disaster, severity, and time of year, in previous events a pattern of social and counseling services has been required.

Survey of Existing Services

With potential postdisaster needs understood, a community can map those against the resources available to determine whether a community can handle these extra services or whether additional capacity is needed. The behavioral health community should gather a compendium of available resources, including experts in critical areas (e.g., post-traumatic stress disorder, children's behavioral health, death and dying), and identify where gaps exist. The list should include the credentials and emergency contact information for the available resources, the location of specialized treatment and outreach services in the community (such as employee assistance programs, housing, restoration of utilities), and be updated regularly.

Table 43. Community Behavioral Services Needed Following a Disaster

- Adult, adolescent, and child services

- Assessments, crisis interventions, evaluations, and referrals

- Bereavement counseling

- Business counseling

- Crisis counseling

- Debriefing groups for health care and emergency workers

- Drop-in crisis counseling

- Emergency services in medical emergency departments

- Family support center

- Individual and group counseling

- Mobile mental and substance-use crisis teams

- Multidisciplinary services to designated community sites (police precincts, fire departments, temporary business locations)

- Multilingual services

- Outpatient behavioral health services and counseling

- Ongoing support groups

- Outreach to schools for students, parents, and teachers

- Outpatient services

- School presentations

- Short-term treatment

- Telephone triage

- 24-hour emergency psychiatric service

- 24-hour crisis hotline

- Walk-in services

- Weekly support groups

Staffing

With the increased interest and training that has been initiated in every behavioral health discipline since the 2001 attack on the World Trade Center buildings, it is likely that larger communities can bring together a sufficient cadre of local behavioral health responders. It is advantageous, where possible, to establish a core of trained and credentialed culturally competent professionals from the providers within a community. The advantage of using local providers is that they are knowledgeable about and work with local resources, local customs, existing organizations, and support networks on a daily basis. In the initial stages, victims are interested in getting relief for practical, concrete problems, such as loss of shelter or business interruptions, and volunteers from outside the community may not have information to match the local resources with the need. Further, in a major disaster, it will be an additional strain to divert staff to train out-of-town volunteers about the community.

However, where there are identified service gaps in a community and when the need exceeds the capacity, the behavioral health community may need to expand its capacity because of an anticipated surge in those needing both short- and long-term services. The number of behavioral health professionals needed will vary by existing resources. Further, in the weeks and months during recovery, when volunteers have gone, programs need to be instituted for those individuals who need long-term behavioral health intervention.

Those conducting the needs assessment to determine the number of behavioral health providers required should look at the demographics of the community, the magnitude and scope of the disaster, the potential number of subgroups affected within the community and the number of individuals within those groups, the cultural issues of those subgroups, and the potential behavioral health resources available. Deployment of behavioral health staff will depend on the number of people affected and the circumstances of the event, but as a guide communities have previously activated 40 behavioral health professionals per 250 victims.

When behavioral health resources from outside the community are likely to be required, advance planning should be carried out. Agency managers should establish memorandums of understanding with other organizations which address use of multiagency providers and community providers, roles and boundaries of each agency, plans for deployment and delivery of service by type of service, and establishment of a chain of command for services for both concrete and behavioral and substance-use conditions following a disaster. When developing these memorandums, coordination with the state or local office of emergency management is needed to ensure that the plan conforms to the community's broader emergency management plans. Finally, reimbursement for delivering behavioral health services will likely be funded through a federal contract with the state department of mental health, which will in turn contract with the local department, which will contract with local agencies.

Immediately after a disaster, there is often an infusion of volunteer professionals from outside the community offering their assistance. The registration and orientation of the behavioral health volunteers who arrive from outside the impacted region is a time-consuming task. A mechanism for incorporating and credentialing these volunteer providers should be worked out in advance with local behavioral health agencies and the various responding organizations.

Community emergency response plans provide for the Red Cross to deliver disaster services. If response to a significant disaster is projected to exceed resources, the local Red Cross chapter alerts the state chapter, which alerts the national system. The national Red Cross determines if the response will be regional or national. When the Red Cross gets activated, it issues a call to respond to all chapters in that area. Although the Red Cross views all disasters as local, with municipal or county governments initiating response, in large-scale disasters activation may start before any official call is made. When the Red Cross mental health unit is activated, the local department of mental health is responsible for coordinating services delivered, although there will be close coordination with the Red Cross.

Mental health volunteers through the Red Cross are all credentialed or licensed professionals in the states in which they practice. Each chapter of the Red Cross is responsible for verifying the background of behavioral health volunteers, including receiving a copy of their professional license. These volunteers are trained in a 2-day, 16-hour course to provide crisis intervention with clients and modified defusing and debriefing for response workers. Another national nonprofit organization which identifies psychiatrists and credentials them before they arrive is Disaster Psychiatry Outreach.

Organizing Culturally Sensitive Services

To include culture considerations in behavioral health plans following disasters, service providers need specialized knowledge, skills, and attitudes. The agency organizing the culturally sensitive services needs appropriate policies and structures to offer supportive care to diverse populations. The Center for Mental Health Services has published guidelines stating that workers need to have the following traits to be competent in carrying out services to diverse populations: Behavioral health workers must value diversity, have the capacity for cultural assessment, be aware of cross-cultural dynamics, develop cultural knowledge, and adapt service delivery to reflect an understanding of cultural diversity.

Those who need assistance may distrust offers of help from persons who are not part of their group, and may be more willing to accept help if they are working with those of similar backgrounds. The availability of trained bilingual and bicultural staff is key to success. If indigenous workers are not available, agencies should work to recruit staff from other agencies or jurisdictions with the same racial or ethnic background and language skills as those affected by the disaster. It is preferable to work with trained translators rather than family members such as children, because of the importance of preserving a parent's role in the family and general privacy concerns regarding behavioral health issues.

In addition, because some groups may not be familiar with the mechanisms required to apply for assistance, those working directly with disaster victims should ensure that their description of facts, policies, and procedures are understood and properly interpreted. Disaster information and application procedures should be translated into the primary spoken languages of the communities in the catchment area and also be available in recordings that can be viewed.

To develop a culturally competent behavioral health plan, planners must perform the following:

- Assess and understand the makeup of the communities to be served
- Identify the needs of the communities that are associated with culture
- Know about institutions (formal and informal) within the communities that can provide diverse behavioral health services
- Establish working relationships in advance with organizations, service providers, and cultural leaders and gatekeepers who are trusted by diverse communities
- Anticipate and identify solutions to culturally related difficulties that may arise in delivering disaster services

Delivery of Services

Cultural background can influence how and whether an individual seeks help, uses natural support networks, and relies on their customs and traditions to deal with trauma, loss, and healing. Individuals from cultures that believe traumatic events have spiritual causes may be less receptive to help. In many cultures, individuals reach out to family, friends, or cultural leaders before seeking help from government or nonprofit agencies. They prefer to receive services from familiar community groups. Places of worship also function as an important support in ethnic communities. Further, some refugee groups, fearing deportation, may be reluctant to seek services.

Different cultural groups experience the phases of a disaster differently. There are cultural variations in the expression of emotion, the manifestation and description of psychological symptoms, traditions about death and burial, and views about counseling. For example, Hispanics are more likely than are non-Hispanics to seek information about disasters from social networks and to believe the information received through these networks. In some cultures, age also can affect how an individual responds, with the old and young responding differently. The old and young may have different needs in identifying with and functioning in cross-cultural environments. Finally, different cultures handle grief in different ways. Helping a community carry out their usual burial rituals can facilitate the return to normal functioning.

If a community remains intact, their cultural norms, traditions, and values will provide support. However, if a community is devastated, the usual cultural mechanisms can be overwhelmed and unable to meet the extraordinary demands. Behavioral health programs should work to expedite the rebuilding of the cultural community. In Asian American and Pacific Islander cultures, the individual does not exist apart from the group, so it is crucial to strengthen family relationships and their connection to the community.

Death Notification

In preparing for catastrophic disasters with many deaths, it is important to establish protocols in advance to ensure smooth coordination. Legally, notification of death is the task of the medical examiner, who may extend that duty to local law enforcement. The Red Cross prefers that behavioral health professionals from the community sit with law enforcement officials when they speak to families about the death of loved ones. Behavioral health coordination with local law enforcement should outline how the two disciplines will work together as survivors file reports for missing persons, review death lists, and engage in DNA collection.

Staff Training

As part of the management plan for assessment, referral, and treatment, social service agencies should provide general information (such as fact sheets, contact information for resources and consultants) to all staff members. Similar documents can also be distributed to the public at the reception desk, waiting rooms, and cafeteria. Agencies should provide facts about expected normal responses to the media spokespersons so that they can educate the community about issues related to grief and loss and explain the role of the mental health and behavioral response within the emergency. They should establish a toll-free hotline for the community, including 24-hour, 7-day coverage. Coordination with other behavioral health providers in the community (including hospitals, community mental health centers, youth services organizations, and group homes) should be part of the plan. The behavioral health services plan must ensure that culturally competent providers will be available to meet the needs of their community both in the crisis period immediately after the disaster and in the months and years that follow. Finally, provisions should include a transition period for the staff and agencies involved in delivering services, as these individuals will personally need time to reenergize and recover from their experience before they can go back to business as usual.

A community may not have a plan for providing behavioral health services. When determining whether to establish behavioral health and psychosocial services, seven criteria have been suggested[3] for evaluating the need to develop these services. These criteria include the following:

- The role of epidemiology and community concerns in determining the prevalence of health and mental and substance-use conditions
- Predictability, rapidity of onset, duration of the crisis, and severity of the problems
- Adequacy of resources
- Sustainability
- Political and ethical acceptability
- Cultural sensitivity
- Effectiveness

Table 44 summarizes the steps in establishing disaster services for mental and substance-use conditions.

---

[3]Speckhard A. 2002. Voices from the inside: psychological response from toxic disasters. In: Havenaar JM, Cwikel JG, Bromet EJ, editors. *Toxic Turmoil: Psychological and Societal Consequences of Ecological Disasters*. New York, NY: Kluwer Academic/Plenum.

Table 44. Establishing Disaster Behavioral Health Services

1. Establish a Disaster Behavioral Health Preparedness Committee whose membership represents administrative, environmental, allied behavioral health, and community agency interests

2. Establish an organization chart to manage emergencies

3. Establish objectives of disaster behavioral health services, including definition of roles and responsibilities

4. Establish procedures for emergency response

5. Establish procedures for evaluation of mental status and distribution of psychiatric drugs and assisted treatment for substance abuse

6. Incorporate procedures into community's disaster plan

7. Develop memorandums of understanding between each organization and other key agencies within the community (e.g., Red Cross, community agencies, medical examiner, law enforcement)

8. Train behavioral health staff in disaster behavioral health plan, roles, and responsibilities

9. Prepare education materials preassembled for distribution

10. Schedule regular mock exercises with outside review

11. Regularly review and update emergency plan, including evaluation of resources and potential impediments to implementation

Adapted from Department of Veterans Affairs (VA). 1997. *Disaster Mental Health Services: A Guidebook for Clinicians and Administrators*. Washington, DC: VA.

Setting Up Family Assistance Centers

In large-scale disasters, one of the first activities is the establishment of a central place where victims and their families can go for relief. Communities might consider establishing two distinct assistance centers: one for the victims, their families, and friends, and one for the responders and caregivers. These centers are multipurpose, established to meet the needs of a broad group of people, and are intended to bring all of the agencies or services that a family needs to deal with to one location. As part of a community's disaster plan, two elements should be identified in advance: location with adequate space, and personnel.

The first component is the identification of a location with adequate space so that these centers do not have to be relocated once they are open. Sufficient space is needed for all of the functions, and private space must be carefully thought out to minimize retraumatization. Table 45 describes the type of services that might be provided at a family assistance center.

Table 45. Services Provided at Family Assistance Centers

- Child care

- Crisis counseling

- Death certificate processing

- Disaster Medicaid

- Distribution of gifts and donations received

- Emergency financial assistance

- Employment assistance

- Family reunification

- Food stamps

- Follow-up phone calls to recipients of crisis counseling

- Health and medical assistance, including pharmaceuticals and durable medical equipment

- Housing assistance

- Immigration services

- Legal assistance

- Meals for victims, families, responders, and caregivers

- Medication assessments

- Personal care items

- Phone banks

- Relief application assistance through FEMA

- Small Business Association loans

- Stress management for relief workers

- Training for FEMA interpreters

- Transportation

- Workers' compensation

The organization of the space must accommodate desks or areas where each of these activities can occur. It is possible that need evolves in catastrophic disasters and that more space and services are required than initially thought. Dedicated areas should be designated where private conversations can occur and where a drop-in center, much like a surgical waiting room, can be an environment for social support. The child care center should be located away from places where there might be strong emotional reactions. The assistance centers can provide ample food and drink to the families and staff who use them, since families needing multiple services may spend many hours at the center. Staffing decisions should consider how many shifts will be needed and the number of people simultaneously served at each agency table. At the family assistance center set up following the 2001 World Trade Center collapse, the assignment of behavioral health staff ranged from 8 to 30 per shift.

Following disasters where there has been a great loss of life, some family members may wish to visit the center repeatedly, whereas others may not. To help those who prefer less contact, when establishing the registration process try to identify all of the things that families would need to bring to register a missing family member. This registration list should include legal documentation (birth certificate, driver's license, social security card, marriage license) and sources of scientific information (hair samples, dental records) used for DNA testing and victim identification when necessary. Expect variability in family reactions, their behavior, and how much families hear of what is said to them.

Especially following disasters where a prolonged search and rescue operation is necessary, the assistance center for responders and caregivers will provide food and drink, showers, sleeping cots, changing rooms, and debriefing areas. These should be located in close proximity to where the disaster occurred, whereas the family assistance center should be located in a different, more distant part of the community.

The second component is the designation of personnel (by title and organization) who will serve as the administrators of this center once it is opened. An advance agreement on leadership is essential to avoid spending time establishing the management scheme while trying to set up the assistance centers.

In planning for the establishment of assistance centers, it is useful to consider who the users will be. In planning for the delivery of services, it is important to have preestablished protocols for the delivery of basic crisis intervention, medical intervention (e.g., prescriptions), making referrals to psychiatry for prescriptions, and providing services to those needing immediate attention. Table 46 lists the types of individuals who may use these centers.

Patient Locator System

After a disaster resulting in many injuries and deaths, the most pressing behavioral health needs are those of family and friends wanting to know what happened to their loved ones, employers wanting to track their employees, and authorities wanting to account for people who are missing. When telephones do not function, the ability to

Table 46. Types of Individuals Using Family Assistance Centers

- Family members of the deceased

- Those displaced from or who lost housing

- Workers who lost jobs

- Those whose business was interrupted

- Those who experienced prior trauma, have preexisting mental health, or substance abuse conditions

- Those who lost financial and social supports

- Responders and other caregivers

contact hospitals may be impeded. Even if loved ones can connect, hospital operators only have the names of those admitted to their facility. In incidents such as these, the need for a patient locator system is paramount. Although people want to know the information immediately, it may take several days to get the system running if it is not in place in advance. If no preexisting system is in place, hospitals will likely fax emergency department logs to a central collection point and volunteers will need to sort through the logs and organize a database. Importantly, there will be numerous legal hurdles to overcome because of privacy concerns.

To establish a patient locator system in advance, several steps are necessary. A Web site or placeholder on a Web site of a central authority, such as the state department of health should be created. Every hospital should be able to log in, and using Public Health Information Network messaging standards, securely upload patient information to create a database searchable by match. Reportable information should include patients who present at each emergency department, including unidentified patients and those who come into a unit (e.g., a burn unit) and cannot speak. Data may not be precise, so it is better to include the name and age of all patients and sort the list later. Each list should identify the hospital and provide contact information. In time, the list will get cleaned as names of patients whose visits were unrelated to the disaster are removed. To ensure patient privacy, the lists should be constructed so that those using the list search by typing in a name and seeking a match rather than scrolling through names. The plan for the patient locator system should include daily printing and posting of the identified list at the family assistance center(s). Plans for the system should include hospital switchboard training so those answering the phone can explain how the system is set up and how to provide information about patients who were treated and released, within the guidelines of the Health Insurance Portability and Accountability Act of 1996.

Public Health Intervention

Natural Disasters

The delivery of psychosocial services following a disaster strongly emphasizes the principle of prevention using a multifaceted, multilevel approach aimed at helping individuals, groups, and the community as a whole. Most of the early work will be the provision of concrete services to psychologically normal people who are under stress, such as information about available services, how to get insurance benefits or loans, assistance with applications at government agencies, health care, child care, transportation, and other routine needs. Public health workers should initiate counseling as a preventive measure and encourage open communication. Some of the most important ways of helping may be simply listening and indicating interest or concern.

If evacuation is required, responders should keep families together and try to keep support systems intact. Workers can also help in rebuilding support networks as quickly as possible. During the short- and long-term recovery phases, public health and human service professionals must visit community sites where survivors are involved in the activities of their daily lives. Such places include neighborhoods, schools, shelters, disaster application centers, meal sites, hospitals, churches, community centers, and other central locations. Among the services typically provided after disaster are telephone help lines, information and referral services, literature on the emotional effects of disaster, facilitation of self-help, support groups, crisis counseling, public education through the media, information sessions for community groups, grief support services, and advocacy services. Behavioral health workers are important members of the teams who help workers cope with the recovery and identification of dead bodies, and communicate positive identification to families, significant others and domestic partners.

Encouraging parents to reduce their children's exposure to the media is important, as is encouraging them to talk about their experiences. This reduction in exposure includes graphic images on television, newspapers, and computers. In addition, it is important to reach out not only to those directly involved, but also to those with indirect exposure (having a friend who knew someone who was killed or injured). Further, it is important to ensure that trauma and grief counseling interventions are included in a community's disaster plan.

Technological Disasters

There is evidence to suggest that the most advantageous intervention with communities exposed to a technological disaster is to establish open communication with the community. Because of the potential spread of toxic agents in environmental disasters, planning should be regional. It is important to establish cooperation among public health, medical, media, and advocacy groups as part of everyday practice around environmental issues, so that if a technological disaster strikes a community, good working relationships are already in place. Part of the plan should include training service workers to have a basic understanding of the technical aspects of environmental contamination, as well as the needs of the community in these complex situations.

Interdisciplinary cooperation is needed among psychologists, social workers, and educators. As in natural disaster, initial programs should offer practical assistance with concrete services—advice, shelter, clothing, and referral to medical care and evaluation. Care should be coordinated among the breadth of health, mental health, and social service agencies and educational institutions. The community will need a broad range of social needs—family counseling, support groups, day care, play therapy, information services, and health education. Immediately after the incident or release, it is important to provide accurate health information, assure the availability of physical exams, provide supportive counseling, and prepare specialized materials to help the entire community understand and deal with the situation.

Throughout the disaster relief effort, several general management strategies should be followed:

- Show clear decision-making in actions so victims feel that the designated leaders are active in the response
- Issue warnings with instructions of specific actions to take
- Plan ahead for necessary resources, with call-up procedures in place
- Tailor activities and services provided in the aftermath of disaster to the community being served and involve them in the development and delivery of services
- Target psychosocial services toward psychologically normal people responding normally to an abnormal situation.
- Identify persons at risk for severe psychological or social impairment caused by their experience of the disaster

Chapter 10

Vulnerable Populations

Individuals whose age, health, physical limitations, or lack of resources place them at greater risk of harm during emergencies require dedicated attention to ensure that their needs are met. This chapter defines the populations that are at risk and considered vulnerable, provides an overview of federal guidance on emergency preparedness for at-risk populations, and describes disaster planning councils, the training of response personnel and planning for vulnerable communities, the use of registries to ensure continuity of services, specific strategies for protecting vulnerable groups, steps to ensure individual preparedness, preparedness in shelters, ensuring accessible communications and preparedness in buildings, and the gathering and maintenance of emergency health information.

Public Health Role

- Ensure that communities include vulnerable groups and the organizations that serve them in the planning process
- Ensure that community preparedness plans accommodate the needs of vulnerable populations
- Educate the community about actions that can be taken to protect vulnerable individuals and groups in times of emergency
- Coordinate vulnerability-specific preparedness efforts in health care delivery sites, shelters, and distribution centers

Who Is at Risk?

The Pandemic and All-Hazards Preparedness Act (PAHPA; Section 2814) requires that emergency planning include the needs of "at-risk" populations. In their definition, the Assistant Secretary for Preparedness and Response (ASPR) and the U.S. Department of Health and Human Services (HHS) followed the description of "at risk" populations found in the National Response Framework (NRF) and added two categories (indicated in the list below by an asterisk). Thus, the public health definition of "at-risk" individuals is those who "Before, during, and after an incident, . . . may have additional needs in one of more of the following functional areas":

Maintaining Independence: Need support to be independent in daily activities when support is lost in a disaster. Includes loss of durable medical equipment and essential supplies.

Communication: Cannot receive or respond to emergency information. Includes ability to hear announcements, see directional signage, and understand how to get assistance.

Transportation: Cannot drive because of disability or do not have transportation. May include accessible vehicles equipped with lifts or oxygen.

Supervision: Require supervision to make decisions, including unaccompanied children and individuals with psychiatric conditions, cognitive impairment, or Alzheimer's.

Medical Care: Not self-sufficient and need trained medical care to manage unstable, terminal, or contagious conditions. Includes taking vital signs and providing intravenous therapy, tube feeding, dialysis, oxygen and suction administration, wound management, and the operation of electrically powered, life-sustaining equipment.

In addition to those specifically defined in the PAHPA statute (children, pregnant women, senior citizens, and others who have functional needs during a public health emergency), other at-risk groups include those with the following:

- Disabilities
- Limited proficiency in English or non–English speakers
- Transportation disadvantages
- Chronic medical disorders*
- Pharmacological dependency*

The ASPR supports the national Advisory Committee on At-Risk Individuals and Public Health Emergencies, which focuses on public health emergencies as they relate to at-risk individuals. In addition, the Federal Emergency Management Agency (FEMA) appoints a Disability Coordinator to provide guidance on planning requirements and direct emergency management activities for individuals with disabilities. FEMA has established the Office of Disability Integration and Coordination (ODIC), which advises FEMA, serves as liaison to the Department of Homeland Security (DHS) and other federal partners, and implements the Post-Katrina Emergency Management Reform Act of 2006 (PKEMRA). ODIC has posted extensive resources on its Web site (available at http://www.fema.gov/about/odic).

People With Disabilities

The National Organization on Disability defines individuals with disabilities as persons who have a physical or mental impairment that limits their major life activities, who have an ongoing or chronic physical or mental condition, or who are regarded by the community as disabled even without such a condition.

According to the 2010 U.S. Census, 56.4 million Americans (20% of the population) have a disability, including 1.8 million unable to see words in print; 4 million who require assistance with dressing, eating, or bathing; 28 million with hearing loss, of which 1 million are unable to hear conversations; 3.3 million older than age 14 years who use a wheelchair; and 10 million who require the use of canes, crutches, or walkers for at least 6 months. Furthermore, there are over 4000 adult day care centers in the United States and about 800,000 people in assisted living facilities. These statistics may not account for the additional segment of the population with chronic illnesses that would inhibit their ability to function in a disaster situation. Following disaster, chronic illnesses are aggravated by the loss of both medications and access to care, and the secondary impacts resulting from loss of power (e.g., nonfunctioning nebulizers, oxygen therapy, suction devices), increasing the potential number of those needing special assistance.

National Guidance

Key federal documents provide direction that is helpful in planning for vulnerable populations. The NRF defines the term *functional needs populations* and addresses specific issues regarding these populations in the appropriate operational protocols. The National Incident Management System stresses the importance of the accessibility of emergency communications, effective outreach to functional needs populations, and the addition of a special-needs advisor within the incident command structure. FEMA and the DHS Office for Civil Rights and Civil Liberties developed a guidance document, *Accommodating Individuals with Disabilities in the Provision of Disaster Mass Care, Housing, and Human Services* (available at http://www.fema.gov/oer/reference). The DHS Grants Program includes planning for functional needs populations (available at http://www.fema.gov/government/grant/hsgp/index.shtm). In addition, eight federal laws prohibit discrimination in emergency preparedness and response on the basis of disability:

- Americans With Disabilities Act of 1990 (ADA)
- Robert T. Stafford Disaster Relief and Emergency Assistance Act of 1988 (Stafford Act)
- PKEMRA
- Rehabilitation Act of 1973
- Fair Housing Act of 1968
- Architectural Barriers Act of 1968
- Individuals With Disabilities Education Act of 1975
- Telecommunications Act of 1996

These statutes apply in activities of preparation, notification, evacuation and transportation, sheltering, first aid and medical services, temporary lodging and housing, transition back to community, and cleanup. Two key regulations are discussed next.

American With Disabilities Act Guidance

Preparedness for disasters should include specific safeguards to ensure the safety of those with disabilities both in the workplace and in the community. The ADA (Public Law 101-336, July 26, 1990) mandates "reasonable accommodation" or assuring the same level of safety and utility for people with disabilities and other limitations as that provided to the entire population. The ADA provides a process to determine if individuals with disabilities have been discriminated against or denied services because of their disability, including the emergency preparedness activities of a community. The process involves a complaint filed with the U.S. Department of Justice, followed by an investigation, mediation, litigation, or suit.

The ADA Accessibility Guidelines (ADAAG), which primarily cover new construction and alterations, include specifications for accessible means of egress (ADAAG 4.1.3[9], 4.3.10), emergency alarms (ADAAG 4.1.3[14], 4.28), and signage (ADAAG 4.1.3[16], 4.30). State and local governments have additional ADA requirements, including the provision of auxiliary aids and services, the acquisition or modification of equipment or devices, appropriate adjustment or modification of training materials or policies, the provision of qualified readers or interpreters, and other similar accommodations. In addition, 47 CFR Section 79.2 obliges distributors of video programming to make emergency information accessible to people with hearing disabilities or vision loss. The Interagency Coordinating Council on Emergency Preparedness and Individuals with Disabilities, part of DHS, ensures that the federal government provides needed services to individuals with disabilities during disasters.

Post-Katrina Emergency Management Reform Act

On October 4, 2006, Congress passed the PKEMRA in response to the deficiencies in the federal government's response to Hurricane Katrina. Although PKEMRA revamped the federal government's overall approach to managing preparedness, key sections required improving preparedness and response for individuals with disabilities. In PKEMRA, the term *individual with a disability* is defined by reference to section 3(2) of ADA. Key sections include the following:

Section 689(a) requires FEMA to "develop guidelines to accommodate individuals with disabilities" including accessibility of shelters, recovery centers, first aid stations, mass feeding areas, portable pay phone stations, portable toilets, and temporary housing.

Section 689(c) amends the Stafford Act and provides temporary housing assistance to individuals with disabilities whose residence is rendered "inaccessible" as a result of a major disaster.

Section 689(e) amends the Stafford Act to require FEMA to coordinate with state and local governments in the planning for population groups with limited English proficiency; to ensure that information is made available in formats that can be understood; and to develop and maintain an informational clearinghouse of model language assistance programs and best practices.

Section 689(a) amends Section 308(a) of the Stafford Act to prohibit discrimination on the basis of "disability and English proficiency."

In addition, PKEMRA required that services be provided so that individuals with disabilities can maintain their health, safety, and independence in a shelter whose residents are from the general population. Known as *Functional Needs Support Services* (FNSS), these regulations call for the provision of accessible supplies and services, including the following:

- Reasonable modification to policies, procedures, and practices
- Durable medical equipment
- Consumable medical supplies
- Personal assistance services
- Other goods and services as needed

Table 47 identifies some national standards that provide guidance in preparedness and response activities for at-risk populations.

Disaster Planning Councils for Vulnerable Populations

Ideally, planning for people with disabilities occurs at both the total community and the individual levels. As part of community planning, one strategy is to organize a disaster planning council for vulnerable populations. In coordination with emergency management, public health professionals can reach out to the organizations that represent the breadth of individuals who meet the ASPR/HHS definition of vulnerable individuals. The planning group should identify what is needed during a disaster, what strategies can be used to address those needs, and which agency or group will be responsible for providing which services. Planning councils for vulnerable populations should always include persons for whom specific equipment and procedures are intended to ensure that the solutions will work as well as provide confidence to those who need them. Effective planning requires the utilization of multiple methods, as the needs of vulnerable groups are both broad and varied. Furthermore, an important part of the task is to inform the various groups of vulnerable individuals about a community's specific disaster plans that apply to them.

Disaster planning councils should include governmental agencies, community providers, community-based organizations (CBOs), advocacy groups, congregate living centers, and the local affiliate of national advocacy and disability organizations, where available. Because the definition of the individuals at risk is so broad, communities might develop sections, such as school-based councils, to address the specific needs of a particular group. Disaster planning councils should be an essential part of a community's emergency response network, ensuring that the segment of the vulnerable population that the CBOs serve is prepared. When forming the council, leaders from various segments of the vulnerable population in the community should be located who will know the issues and agencies that need to be addressed. These leaders, often known as *advocates*, can help to identify both the groups that represent only their community and the organizations that represent the interests of more than one vulnerable group. Table 48 lists examples of the potential groups who could participate in a planning council, though the names of these groups may vary by locale and region of the country. Because the official names of different types of organizations may not be the same in every community, public health professionals

Table 47. National Standards in Preparedness and Response for At-Risk Populations

Organization	Guidance Name	What It Does	Source
Federal Emergency Management Agency (FEMA)	Comprehensive Preparedness Guide 301 (CPG-301): Emergency Management Planning Guide for Special-Needs Populations	Helps governments develop emergency plans for people with functional needs Addresses planning considerations for range of hazards, security, and emergency functions Provides general guidelines for developing a governmental household pet and service animal plan	http://www.fema.gov/pdf/media/2008/301.pdf
American With Disabilities Act (ADA) and ADA Amendments Act (2008)	ADA Amendments Act	Requires equal access to all government programs Broadened scope of the definition of *disability* Allows people with functional needs to seek protection under ADA, including all disaster plans developed for a community under Title II	http://www.ada.gov
ADA guide	Making Community Emergency Preparedness and Response Programs Accessible to People with Disabilities	Provides guidance for making local emergency preparedness and response programs accessible to people with disabilities	http://www.usdoj.gov/crt/ada/emergencyprep.htm
1986 Superfund Amendment and Reauthorization Act (SARA), Title III	Local emergency planning committees (LEPCs)	Directs the creation and membership of LEPCs	http://www.epa.gov/emergencies/content/epcra/epcra_plan.htm#LEPC
The Joint Commission	Emergency Management Standards of The Joint Commission	Oversees standard setting for health care facilities and accredits health care facilities	http://www.jointcommission.org

(continued on next page)

Table 47. (*continued*)

Organization	Guidance Name	What It Does	Source
National Fire Protection Association (NFPA)	NFPA 99, 1600	Recommends safety codes and standards for the prevention of fires and other hazards	http://www.nfpa.org
Federal Communications Commission	Emergency Alert System (EAS) Rules (47 CFR Part 11) Closed-Captioning Rules (47 CFR § 79)	Regulations regarding both EAS and closed-captioning	http://www.fcc.gov
FEMA	Guidance on Planning Integration of Functional Needs Support Services Needs in General Population Shelters	Provides guidance for the implementation of practices so that individuals with disabilities can maintain their health, safety, and independence in a shelter whose residents are from the general population.	http://www.fema.gov/pdf/about/odic/fnss_guidance.pdf

Adapted from National Organization on Disability. 2009. *Functional Needs of People With Disabilities: A Guide for Emergency Managers, Planners and Responders.* Washington, DC: National Organization on Disability Emergency Preparedness Initiative; and BCFS Health and Human Services. 2010. *Guidance on Planning for Integration of Functional Needs Support Services in General Population Shelters.* Washington, DC: Federal Emergency Management Agency. Available at: http://www.fema.gov/pdf/about/odic/fnss_guidance.pdf.

Table 48. Potential Members of a Planning Council for Vulnerable Populations

Government Agencies	Community Providers	Advocacy Groups
Mayor's office or county executive Committee on People With Disabilities	Visiting Nurse Service	National Association of the Deaf
	Meals on Wheels	Hearing Loss Association of America
	Residential and assisted living facilities	Telecommunications for the Deaf, Inc.
Department of health and/or mental health	Home health agencies	National Organization on Disability
Board of education	Ambulette and paratransit businesses	Local chapters of the American Foundation for the Blind and Council for the Blind
Departments of rehabilitation and aging	After-school programs	Alliance for Technology Access
Department of social services and regional centers	Easter Seals United Cerebral Palsy	Parent Teacher Association
		Center for Independent Living Center

can work with an umbrella organization such as the United Way to identify which groups are present and active in a locale.

The disaster planning council can determine the specific plans, equipment, resources, and response activities required to ensure the safety of vulnerable individuals during and in response to a disaster. Disaster plans for vulnerable populations should specify the assignment of personnel, identify specialized equipment needed, and include information on the location of and availability of necessary assets. As part of preparedness activities, disaster planning councils can submit proposals to foundations to establish pre-disaster agreements so that, in an emergency, need for replacement equipment, medications, assistive devices, and the numerous other needs of vulnerable populations can be quickly met.

Communities should designate a coordinator for vulnerable populations who can work as part of the council and serve as liaison with CBOs. The council can identify specific responsibilities that would be carried out by community and institutional providers in cooperation with advocacy-specific groups as part of a community's emergency response. Most importantly, members of the planning council have to be trained in developing a disaster plan for their organizations, their role and responsibilities as part of the overall community plan, and how to communicate and serve clients during an emergency.

Training

Training is necessary for response personnel so they are equipped and skilled in using assistive equipment to aid individuals with disabilities during emergencies. In addition, the members of vulnerable groups need to know what to do in a disaster. Building on the materials developed by the Red Cross on sheltering and evacuation and emergency planning for people with disabilities and other needs, the council can establish educational tools and work with the community to conduct "train-the-trainer" sessions about the creation of accessible facilities and services; transportation, lifting, or carrying; accessible communications and assistance, developing personal support networks, home preparation, preparation of Go Packs (discussed later in this chapter), and assistance animals.

Community Plans for Vulnerable Populations

A community's plan should provide for guidance to its constituent organizations on improving preparedness for vulnerable populations in their homes and where they work, attend school, conduct activities of daily living, and receive services. A broad range of organizations provide service to these groups. Because the abilities and needs vary from one at-risk group to another, it is important to develop emergency procedures that are specific to each group. For example, the range of disabilities that would impact one's ability to respond in a disaster is broad and whereas some disabilities are permanent, others are temporary. Both permanent conditions (such as arthritis) and temporary conditions (sprained ankle, broken leg) can limit one's ability to respond in a disaster. Planning is complicated because an otherwise able-bodied person may have what is called a *situational disability* because of the environment in which an emergency occurs. For example, many people would not be able to walk down a stairway of hundreds of steps in a high-rise building.

Specific planning should account for all who meet the at-risk definition, including people with learning and developmental disabilities, people with medical impairments (such as asthma, emphysema, and other respiratory disorders; cardiac conditions; cerebral palsy; communication disorders; pregnancy; psychiatric disorders; seizure disorders; strokes), people with mobility impairments (including arthritis, broken legs, paraplegia, and sprained ankles, as well as wheelchair users), and people with sensory disabilities (visually impaired or blind, hard of hearing or deaf). Even if some people with these disabilities perform well in a drill, they may experience problems in an actual emergency.

Because individuals with disabilities are often connected through CBOs, home health care organizations, and health care providers, it is important to train these groups to communicate and provide direct services to their clients in times of emergency. CBOs, community centers, and programs at which individuals with disabilities spend time or receive services can distribute information about preparedness in their newsletters. Liaison relationships should be established with local social service departments to work out procedures for contacting clients in an affected disaster area. CBOs should encourage those with vulnerabilities to assess their own needs during a disaster and develop contingency plans. Disease registries, particularly those that actively collect longitudinal case information, are another source for locating those who are at risk. Once registered, preparedness information can be mailed to those on the list and in-person consultation can be offered.

Registries

As part of community planning, public health can work with CBOs to help create internal organizational registries of vulnerable individuals. These registries help emergency management organizations understand how many individuals are at risk in the community and the range of types of problems that these individuals may encounter in a disaster. Once the registries are developed, public health works with the local Office of Emergency Management to determine what services may be needed during a disaster.

Registries enable communities to develop specific disaster plans that include the necessary resources and response for vulnerable individuals. Experience in previous disasters has demonstrated the need for preestablished procedures which facilitate the approval of and payment for medication and the replacement of durable medical equipment, such as wheelchairs, respirators, hearing aids, and other adaptive devices. This includes preestablished arrangements with designated pharmacies for the provision of pharmaceuticals on an emergency basis. Where communities set up a registry of individuals who are dependent on power for life-saving equipment, these persons can be registered with utility companies for priority to have services reconnected. This accommodation is sometimes called a *lifeline service*. Disaster plans could oblige utility companies to provide immediate notification to persons who are dependent on life-sustaining electrical equipment if they are aware that power is going to be reduced. Further, arrangements could be made for the priority restoration of power to those persons dependent on adaptive equipment.

For communities that maintain these registries and distribute them to appropriate government departments and local emergency management teams, it is difficult to keep them current, and there may be concerns about privacy. Individuals should be asked to register annually, with periodic contact to determine whether they still need the registry's services. Information should be collected about alternative contacts for the registrant during the day, as many individuals provide their home address to the registry but could be at school, work, or elsewhere when a disaster occurs. Registries should not be used as the definitive list for first responders, as participation in registries is voluntary, and not everyone who potentially requires assistance during a disaster will enroll.

Developing comprehensive registries for vulnerable populations may be labor intensive; several strategies can be used to minimize effort. A jurisdiction can target a registry to a segment or segments of the population. For example, a jurisdiction might choose to register individuals who will require evacuation or transportation assistance during a disaster. Communities may limit registries to individuals living in their own homes, as the needs of individuals living in congregate settings, including group homes and other residential facilities, are known. The organization that manages these facilities should be encouraged to participate in community planning and develop preparedness arrangements for their specific population. Finally, in some communities, Citizen Corps volunteers have helped gather information by going door to door to register individuals who have previously identified themselves as having functional needs.

Historically, vulnerable groups have been reluctant to sign on to registries because of a concern about privacy. The Health Insurance Portability and Accountability Act's (HIPAA's) privacy rule permits covered entities (such as health care organizations and providers) to disclose information for public health purposes. Registry databases should be stored on a secure server with steps taken to protect the information, and this safeguard of privacy should be shared with registrants. Further, transportation and social service providers are not likely to be subject to the privacy rule and may be permitted to disclose information about the individuals they serve.

Specific Strategies

Vulnerable individuals should know where to go if they need shelter, transportation, and support services; keep needed assistive devices and equipment nearby; know their evacuation options; and repeatedly practice their plan. This section highlights preparedness tips specific to the needs of particular vulnerable groups. Table 49 summarizes basic preparedness steps for vulnerable individuals.

Blind

Both people who are blind or partially sighted (and their service animal, defined below) are likely to need to be led to safety during a disaster. Some people who are blind or visually impaired may be reluctant to evacuate when the request comes from a stranger, and responders should be prepared to provide assurance of safety. Further, service animals could become confused or disoriented in a disaster and responders should receive training on handling these dogs.

Service animals should be permitted to stay in emergency shelters with their owners. Section 36.104 of Title 3 of the ADA specifies that a service animal is "any guide dog, signal dog, or other animal individually trained to do work or perform tasks for the benefit of an individual with a disability." Section 36.302(c) requires public accommodations to modify policies, practices, and procedures to accommodate the use of service animals. In addition to guide dogs, this can include hearing dogs, seizure alert dogs, mobility dogs, and others. A service animal is not required to have any special certification or identification. The local emergency management office will have more information.

Children

Of the U.S. population, almost 25% are children who have functional needs during disasters. Children who are injured require pediatric-specific equipment, drug preparations, and delivery systems. Children who do not have parents or guardians present medicolegal challenges. A meta-analysis of 160 samples of disaster victims revealed that over the long term, only middle-aged women who are caregivers fare worse than children who have experienced a disaster. Disaster planning for children must be family centered and meet the needs of families who may have health care challenges. Since children spend much of their day in school, public and private schools need to be included in a community's emergency preparedness activities so that schools integrate with local response systems. Hospitals should include pediatric issues in their facility disaster plans and drills.

Table 49. Basic Preparedness Steps for Vulnerable Individuals

Disability/Special Need	Steps for Preparedness
Alzheimer's patients	Be listed in the emergency registry Wear an identification bracelet or necklace Carry papers with information about behaviors Carry contact information for family, friends, physician
Bedbound individuals	Have an emergency transportation plan Stock supplies of daily care items (e.g., bed pans, adult diapers, linens)
Diabetics	Store special dietary foods Stock testing supplies Stock insulin supplies that do not require refrigeration Wear medical emblem on bracelet or necklace
Dialysis patients	Ensure dialysis facility knows where to find patient Start emergency diet as soon as aware of emergency situation Ensure that no one uses dialysis access for fluid or medication Make arrangements for dialysis at the evacuation destination Do not use disinfected water for dialysis Wear medical emblem on bracelet or necklace
Hearing impaired persons	Verify that the necessary equipment is available, or make special arrangements to receive warnings and communicate needs
Mobility impaired persons	Arrange for special assistance to get to a shelter Keep information readily available that details the proper way to transfer or move someone in a wheelchair and the best exit routes
Non–English-speaking individuals	May need assistance planning for and responding to emergencies Include community and cultural groups in preparedness efforts
Oxygen-dependent persons	Stock oxygen supplies (including power source) Stock extra water for oxygen condensers
Individuals without vehicles	Make arrangements for transportation
Individuals with special dietary needs	Stockpile an adequate emergency food supply

Adapted from Federal Emergency Management Agency (FEMA). 2010. Are You Ready? Washington, DC: FEMA. Available at: http://www.fema.gov/areyouready/emergency_planning.shtm; and University of Florida IFAS Extension. Disaster Planning Tips for Senior Adults. Gainesville, FL: University of Florida. Available at: http://www.edis.ifas.ufl.edu/pdffiles/fy/fy62000.pdf.

In 2008, Congress authorized the formation of the National Commission on Children and Disasters to ensure that children's needs are considered in disaster plans at all levels of government. Before being terminated in April 2011, the Commission issued a report that recommended more than 30 improvements in emergency preparedness and response for children (available at http://www.ahrq. gov/prep/nccdreport/nccdreport.pdf). The 2010 report also included standards for the care of children in shelters, reflected in Appendix Q. At shelters, children need safety, nutrition, waste disposal, protection against infectious disease, and stress management. Those setting up shelters should protect children from hazardous materials, trip hazards, and adult predators. All medication should be secured from access by children. Finally, the frail elderly should be protected from unruly children.

FEMA established the Children's Working Group in 2009 to guarantee that federal planning in emergency management includes the needs of children. The Lessons Learned Information Sharing service working with the National Commission on Children and Disasters and the FEMA Children's Working Group, created the Children and Disasters resource page to consolidate guidance documents, training programs, and lessons learned from exercises and real-world incidents involving children (available at https://www.llis.dhs.gov/DynamicPage.do? pageTitle=ChildrenandDisastersEX).

Deaf and Hard of Hearing

People with hearing loss should

- Stockpile and maintain extra batteries for hearing aids, text telephone (TTY) devices when used, and light phone signalers.
- Store hearing aids in a secured place so they can be easily found if a disaster occurs. Hearing aids will be difficult to replace or fix immediately after a major disaster.
- Install both audible and visual smoke alarms with at least one alarm that is battery operated.
- Determine how to communicate with emergency personnel by interpreter (if available), or by paper and pen (which should be stored).
- Carry preprinted messages such as "I speak American Sign Language (ASL) and need an ASL interpreter."
- Determine which broadcasting systems will have continuous news that is captioned or signed. Captioned radio, known as HD radio, is available in many areas of the United States. HD radio transmits text, pictures, and graphics.

The Community Emergency Preparedness Information Network (CEPIN) project was developed by Telecommunications for the Deaf and Hard of Hearing, Inc. (TDI) to strengthen the country's emergency preparedness efforts for people who are deaf and hard of hearing. Through CEPIN, TDI developed a course, AWR-186: Emergency Responders and the Deaf and Hard of Hearing Community, to help responders understand the complex communication issues faced during a disaster by people who are deaf or hard of hearing. The course also provides people who are deaf and hard of hearing with the information and skills needed to prepare for, respond to, and recover from disasters. Information about the course is available online (at http://www.cepintdi.org/course-offerings/awr-186).

Finally, people with hearing loss have developed their own volunteer teams through the Community Emergency Response Team (CERT) program. Community planners should check with their local CERT teams to determine whether this resource is locally available.

Life Support Systems

People who depend on life support systems (such as dialysis, respirator, oxygen, suction, intravenous pump, or infusion therapy) can enhance their preparedness by the following:

- Secure life support equipment so that it is not damaged by falling.
- Determine alternative facilities and providers who could help if the home system becomes inoperable or their provider cannot provide service.
- Register with the local utility company as a customer dependent on powered life support systems.
- Identify and arrange for alternative power sources that could provide electrical service for 5 to 7 days if needed.
- Consider purchasing a generator.
- Determine whether manually operated equipment can be used.
- Determine whether the equipment can be powered from a vehicle battery and obtain necessary equipment for the hookup.
- Regularly test and charge stored batteries.
- Be aware of battery life and be sure to have enough charged batteries to provide power for 5 to 7 days.
- Those using breathing machines should have a 3-day supply of oxygen, tubing, solutions, and medications.
- Oxygen users should determine whether a reduced flow rate can be used. If possible, record the revised flow numbers on the equipment for easy reference.
- If necessary, post "Oxygen in Use" signs in the home so that responders are immediately aware of this.
- Keep the shutoff switch for oxygen equipment close by to enable a quick turnoff in case of emergency.

Older Adults

Older adults are vulnerable during a disaster because they may

- Be dependent on wheelchairs, canes, or walkers to get around and unable to climb stairs as a result of impaired physical mobility.
- Have chronic health conditions that

- ○ Can be exacerbated by exposure to conditions associated with many disasters, such as lack of safe food and water, extreme heat or cold, stress, or exposure to infection.
- ○ Require an emergency plan that accommodates medical devices and medications.
- ○ Could make them prone to adverse medical events if essential medications and/ or individualized medication regime (e.g., insulin, blood thinners, psychotropic drugs) or special diets are not available during an emergency.
- ○ Could make them experience additional confusion and fear (for example, people with dementia who are unable to take their medications).

- Be prone to heat stress and require adequate hydration.
- Be dependent on caretakers and may not have a support system.
- Lose their place to live and retirement security if the disaster destroys their home.
- Lack sufficient income or other resources to enable preparations for disasters and to respond and adapt when they occur.
- Be sensory impaired (hearing or sight) or cognitively impaired with difficulty understanding information or following directions.
- Feel overwhelmed by a disaster because they have difficulty moving around, standing in line, or sleeping on a low cot in a noisy shelter.
- Have difficulties evacuating if they no longer drive or do not own a vehicle.
- Be reluctant to evacuate and leave behind lifelong possessions.
- Be worried about their pets.
- Be reluctant to accept assistance.
- Fear institutionalization or loss of independence.
- Perceive the task of rebuilding their lives as too much, leading to depression.
- Be physically less able to go through the steps needed to meet basic needs following a disaster.

Locally, organizations providing aging services should help older adults develop personal preparedness plans. Further, all sectors of the aging services network should participate in their community or state's preparedness and response planning. Where a community needs additional federal resources following a disaster, money is available for services to older adults. The Older Americans Act of 1965, reauthorized in 2006, enables HHS's Administration on Aging to reimburse state agencies on aging for additional expenses incurred following a presidentially declared disaster. These funds can be used for outreach, counseling, food, cleaning of homes, emergency transportation, and medications for the elderly.

Special Medical Needs

Where applicable, people with special medical needs should

- Have a 7-day supply of all medications.[1]
- Store medications in one location in their original containers.

[1]After the tragic events in Japan in March of 2011, U.S. emergency planners suggest that to prepare for the catastrophic disasters, people should plan to be self-sufficient for at least 7 days.

- Have a list of all medications: name of medication, dose, frequency, and the name of the doctor who prescribed it.
- Have a 7-day supply of bandages, ostomy bags, or syringes.
- Determine whether an infusion pump has a battery backup and how long it would last without power.
- Learn about manual infusion techniques in case of a power outage.
- Attach written operating instructions to all equipment.
- Have a "Go Pack" ready at all times.
- Have copies of vital medical papers such as insurance cards, advanced directive, power of attorney.
- Discuss disaster plans with their home health care provider.
- Keep a contact list of providers and vendors for all equipment and supplies.

Personal Support Networks

Community plans should encourage all at-risk individuals to develop a network of relatives, friends, or coworkers who can check on and assist them in an emergency. These are often referred to as *personal support networks* (PSNs). PSNs help vulnerable individuals evaluate their homes, prepare for a disaster by identifying and gathering the resources they'll need, and provide emergency assistance through a redundant set of people who know the individual's needs. Vulnerable individuals may need to organize more than one PSN (e.g., for home, school, and workplace), depending on where their time is spent. For example, if there are at least three people at each location where an at-risk individual regularly spends time, these individuals may be assured that there is redundancy in the plan. The members of each PSN should have a written list of what the individual needs as well as copies of medical information, medical or disability-related supplies and special equipment list, evacuation plans, relevant emergency documents, and a personal disaster plan. Prearranged plans detailing the circumstances for when and how the members of the network will contact the person with a medical vulnerability or disability are essential. Members of a PSN should be provided with written instructions and trained in the location of the person's keys, the operation and movement of any adaptive or durable equipment used, locating their medical supplies, familiarity with any service animal, and needed personal care. Table 50 identifies basic elements of a personal assessment that will guide the plans worked out with the PSN. The personal assessment is best based on the environment after the disaster, individual capabilities, the individual's limitations, and the lowest anticipated level of functioning.

Go Packs

Everyone should prepare a "Go Pack." A Go Pack is an individualized portable kit (preferably housed in a waterproof plastic box) that is prepared in advance. For those on medications, it should include at least 7 days of medication stored at the recommended temperature, rotated every week to ensure it hasn't exceeded its expiration date. For others, the Go Pack may include an extra cane, hearing aid

Table 50. Elements of a Personal Assessment

- List personal needs and resources
- Evaluate activities of daily living
  - Assistance needed with personal care
  - Use of adaptive equipment to get dressed
- Assess needs if water service or hot water cut off for several days
- Identify equipment needed for personal care (shower chair, tub-transfer bench)
- Identify adaptive feeding devices and need for special utensils to prepare or eat food independently
- Arrange for continuation of electricity-dependent equipment (dialysis, electrical lifts)
- Plan for getting around if the disaster causes debris in home
- Plan for specially equipped vehicle or accessible transportation
- Practice evacuating a building in the community or at home
- Locate and plan for finding mobility aids and equipment necessary for service animal
- Evaluate ramp access
- Plan for care of service animal (provide food, shelter, veterinary attention) during and after a disaster
- Arrange for another caregiver for the service animal if unable to care for it

batteries, a walker, a ventilator, lightweight emergency evacuation chair, augmentative communication equipment, insulin supplies, and food and water for a guide dog. This procedure was very effective in New York City after September 11, 2001, because it ensured that life-saving medication was available even when pharmacies were not. Note that some states will not permit patients on Medicaid to receive more than a 30-day supply of medication; it is important to check local state rules and determine what is allowable. Finally, if the individual receives Social Security benefits, the Go Pack should include a copy of the most recent award letter.

Shelters and Distribution Centers

In working with the community, public health can do a great deal to help vulnerable populations prepare for evacuating from home during emergencies. At-risk individuals should be encouraged to plan how to get out of their home, work, or any building where they receive services, in the event of an emergency. Since some roads may be closed or blocked in a disaster, they should plan for two evacuation routes. These individuals should be encouraged to assemble a Go Pack as discussed above and store extra food, water, and supplies for any service animals.

Public health should work with the Red Cross to develop a list of all ADA-suitable shelters that can accommodate wheelchair access, larger restroom facilities, and service animals, and communicate those locations to the advocacy groups and providers who deliver services to the elderly and disabled. The U.S. Department of Justice has developed an ADA Checklist for Emergency Shelters that details the accommodations that must be made at facilities used to provide shelter during emergencies. These guidelines can be found online (at http://www.ada.gov/pcatoolkit/chap7shelterchk.htm).

The level of medical oversight that will be provided at each shelter must be determined as part of community planning. Planners must determine whether there will be different classes of shelters (for example, medical management, mixed populations). With advance planning, it will be possible to ensure that the highly specialized medical needs of those using the shelter will be properly identified and addressed. Plans for shelters and distribution centers should provide for accessible and adequate electrical outlets so that adaptive equipment, such as battery-powered wheelchairs, light talkers, computers, and respirators, can be operated. Emergency running lights should be installed along floors. Preestablished procedures for shelters should include prior arrangements with providers of durable medical equipment that can loan, repair, or replace adaptive equipment (e.g., battery chargers, wheelchairs) following a disaster. Hotlines should include and publish TTY numbers.

Distribution centers for forms, food stamps, and hotel vouchers must meet the ADA standard of accessibility. Physical access must be assured at the facility, in waiting lines, restrooms, and telephones. Educational and informational materials prepared for distribution in these shelters should be prepared in Braille, large print, languages other than English, and audiocassette tape formats, because the ADA requires that written materials used in disaster response be available in multiple formats upon request. Materials for home use should include formats with an assistive computer device such as text to speech.

Phone communication following a disaster must be accessible for those who are deaf or hard of hearing, as required by the ADA. The use of TTY is waning as more people are using a video relay service (VRS). With VRS, the worker at the hotline would need to be able to use ASL. The deaf and hard of hearing may also use a video relay interpreter or captioned telephone (CapTel) which are both similar to a voice phone call, discussed more in the Specific Tools section below. In addition, as many deaf and hard of hearing are using pagers or phones to send e-mail or text messages, agencies providing services during a disaster should be equipped to communicate via this technology.

Some community plans may incorporate alternative procedures to those who cannot access a shelter, such as the direct delivery of food and water. Another solution is to establish a process where community residents can access information and complete applications on the Internet, by phone, TTY, or e-mail.

Communication

Emergency communication should be accessible for people with disabilities, limited English proficiency, and to members of diverse cultures. Although regulatory requirements specify the ways that emergency communications are to occur, public health should include targeted strategies to reach out to different populations. People who are deaf or hard of hearing cannot hear audible alerts sent via radio, television, or sirens. Individuals who are blind or have low vision may not be aware of visual cues, such as flashing lights or emergency information scrolling on television screens.

Emergency alerts and warnings should be provided in languages other than English on public access channels and in cooperation with non-English radio and television stations. Some communities with high rates of limited English proficiency use bilingual staff or interpreters at radio and television stations to communicate information.

Vulnerable populations may need targeted education about the meaning of alerts and warnings. For example, some individuals who are blind may not be aware that an audible beep from a television signals that an emergency alert message is streaming as text across the bottom of the television screen, or that the listener should turn on a radio for more information.

Technology used to communicate with vulnerable populations should be exercised regularly, and emergency plans should include redundant methods to provide a general notification for the community. Deaf, hard-of-hearing, and blind populations can be reached via closed-captioning, qualified sign language interpreters, Braille, text messaging, TTY, large print, and audiotape.

For the benefit of individuals with cognitive disabilities, the most pertinent information should be repeated frequently using a simple vocabulary. Pictorial representations can provide quick and easily understood instruction to many individuals including children, individuals with limited English proficiency, and some with cognitive disabilities.

Title II of the ADA provides that residents of a community must be able to contact emergency management agencies by alternative means such as TTY or VRS capabilities. Providers of VRS and internet protocol relay need to provide ten-digit telephone numbers to subscribers so that their emergency calls automatically route to the call center responsible for answering calls to a community's emergency telephone number, also known as the Public Safety Answering Point dispatcher. TTY allows persons with hearing loss to send and receive text messages using the telephone. Technology improvements now allow consumers to make digital wireless calls with TTY-compatible handsets. In locations where not available, TTY users can place 911 emergency calls using wireless phone service, analog phone service, or telecommunications relay service (TRS). (More information is available online at http://www.fcc.gov/cgb/consumerfacts/ttywireless.html).

Compliance With the Emergency Captioning Rules

The Federal Communications Commission (FCC) rules require broadcasters and cable operators to make local emergency information accessible to persons who are deaf or hard of hearing and to persons who are blind or have visual disabilities as part of a community's emergency plan. For public health, this means that emergency information must be provided both aurally and in a visual format. All information being communicated through video programming distributors (broadcasters, cable operators, satellite television services, and other multichannel video programming distributors) must meet this standard. Television stations can be helpful in broadcasting both text and audible emergency information to all their viewers.

Accessibility of Emergency Information Required

The FCC requires that for persons who are deaf or hard of hearing, emergency information provided in the audio portion of programming must include either closed-captioning or other methods of visual presentation, such as open captioning, *crawls*, or scrolls that appear on the screen. No emergency information should block the closed-captioning, and closed-captioning should not block any emergency information provided in any other manner. For persons whose vision is impaired, emergency information must be made accessible when provided in both the video portion of a regularly scheduled newscast, or in a special newscast that interrupts regular programming. The oral description of emergency information must be included in the main audio portion of the broadcast. Emergency information provided in the video portion of any newscast through *crawling* or *scrolling* must also be accompanied by an aural tone. This tone alerts persons with any vision impairment that the broadcaster is providing emergency information, and that the viewer should turn on another source, such as a radio, for more information.

The delivery of emergency information must meet this standard for weather warnings and watches, community emergencies (e.g., discharge of toxic gases, widespread power failures, industrial explosions, civil disorders, school closings), and scheduling changes for school buses caused by any of these conditions. Information must be communicated about the specifics of the emergency, how to respond, if the community will be evacuated, the location of shelters, and how to shelter in place. Educational announcements made during and immediately after disasters such as earthquakes or tornadoes should encourage those with disabilities to check for hazards at home, since items that have moved can cause injury or block an escape path for someone with limited mobility. Finally, announcements should inform those with chronic medical conditions to bring their medication(s) and medical supplies when they evacuate.

Some local news stations provide captions when broadcasting information on weather emergencies, such as tornadoes. An alternative source of notification is a National Oceanic and Atmospheric Administration (NOAA) weather radio, which displays a short text message describing the nature of any emergency declared in the area. Weather radios can be indefinitely left on in standby mode. These radios are silent until an emergency is declared, at which time they sound an alarm and broadcast a spoken message concerning the emergency. Strobe lights and bed vibrators are available as attachments for people who cannot hear the alarm, and most models display text messages.

The CDC developed a series of video clips using ASL for public service announcements. Closed-captioned video clips using ASL are available on the CDC

Emergency Web page (at http://www.emergency.cdc.gov/disasters/hurricanes/psa.asp). These clips cover broad topics, including preparing for a storm, cleanup, coping, safe food and water, and prescription drugs.

Specific Tools

A receiver system for NOAA Weather Radio (NWR) is specifically available to provide an alert for the deaf and hard of hearing. NWR embeds nonverbal information in its broadcasts to provide warnings of life-threatening events. The warnings are delivered via connected vibrators, bed shakers, pillow vibrators, or strobe lights.

With SAME (specific area message encoding) technology, NWR receivers can be programmed to set off an alarm for specific events (e.g., tornado, flash flood) and specific jurisdictions. Basic NWR receiver and systems are available with SAME technology and external alarm devices. These NWR receivers can be connected to existing home security alerting systems, similar to a doorbell or smoke detector. In more complex installations where wireless or wired remote modules are used, installation requires a connection to a device that allows the remote placement of alarms. Such alarms may require external power from batteries or modular power supplies. Ready-to-use systems are marketed by Silent Call Communications (available at http://www.silentcall.com/catalog/contact_us.php) and Harris Communications (available at http://www.harriscomm.com).

Other devices that can be connected to external alarms require the skills of an electronics technician and are manufactured or sold by several companies, including Radio Shack, Midland, Uniden, and First Alert.

Finally, several technologies are available to assist the deaf and hard of hearing when communicating by telephone. The TRS is provided by telephone companies at no cost to the user; the costs of providing TRS are reimbursed from either a state or a federal fund. In addition, a form of TRS known as *video relay* enables people who use ASL to communicate with voice telephone users through video equipment. Another system, CapTel, works like any other telephone for people with hearing loss. Using CapTel technology, users can listen to the caller and the system translates the voice into text so that the user can read the written captions in a display window.

Transportation

Accessible transportation must be available for evacuation before, during, and after a disaster. As part of both community and facility planning, managers should ensure the availability of vehicles with wheelchair lifts or ramps. Although a community's emergency fleet can be assumed to be available to respond, redundant arrangements to use nonemergency vehicles should also be included in disaster plans, since it is likely that the number of specially equipped vehicles will be limited and thus not available or in service elsewhere. The Federal Highway Administration report, *Evacuating Populations With Special Needs*, provides best practices and tools for transporting vulnerable populations during evacuations. The report, which includes a checklist for officials and transportation providers, is available online (at http://www.ops.fhwa.dot.gov/eto_tim_pse/publications/index.htm).

Building Preparedness for Individuals With Disabilities

To develop an evacuation plan that accounts for both staff and visitors with disabilities, organizations and buildings should develop an emergency committee whose first task is to understand general evacuation issues. The evacuation committee might meet with the building management; local fire department, police, and HAZMAT personnel; a manufacturer of evacuation equipment; and other agencies and groups with evacuation interests involving persons with disabilities and other vulnerable users. In addition to identifying the individuals who regularly work in a building, preparations should be made for visitors who may require assistance. Furthermore, the committee should identify and train personnel who can properly lead individuals to safety who need assistance. Conducting regular drills and assessing performance are as essential to the evacuation plan as they are to the larger community preparedness plan.

It is useful to assess the number of employees and their types of vulnerabilities and to meet with disabled individuals to discuss their preferences for evacuation as part of the committee process. The U.S. Equal Employment Opportunity Commission has stated that federal disability discrimination laws do not prevent employers from obtaining and appropriately using information necessary for a comprehensive emergency evacuation plan. Employers may ask employees to self-identify if they will require assistance in the event of an evacuation due to a disability or medical condition. This list, which will be essential if emergency evacuation is necessary, should be updated at least annually. Employers may obtain this information at three different times: after making a job offer, but before employment begins; during periodic surveys of all employees, when the employer indicates that self-identification is voluntary; and by asking employees with known disabilities if they will require assistance in the event of an emergency. An employer should inform and ensure individuals that the information is confidential and shared only with those who have responsibilities under the emergency evacuation plan. An employer may ask individuals who indicate a need for assistance because of a medical condition to describe the type of assistance needed. An employer can distribute a memo that includes a form requesting information from employees. The employer may also have individual follow-up conversations when necessary to obtain more detailed information. The ADA has provisions requiring employers to maintain confidentiality about employee medical information. In the event of an evacuation, employers can share medical information, including the type of assistance an individual needs, with safety personnel, medical professionals, emergency coordinators, floor captains, colleagues who are part of the employee's personal support network, building security officers who need to confirm that everyone has been evacuated, and other nonmedical personnel who are responsible for ensuring safe evacuation under the employer's emergency evacuation plan.

Detection

The detection of some hazards (such as fires) often occurs through systems which function automatically. Automatic systems (e.g., with strobes, horns) must be compliant with the ADA updated regulations and the Underwriters Laboratories Standard for Emergency Signaling Devices for the Hearing Impaired (UL Standard 1971). This standard requires that signaling devices alert those with hearing loss through the use of light, vibrations, and air movement. Where facilities use manual devices that require pulling, codes require that these pull stations be mounted at a height of 48 to 54 inches so that an individual seated in a wheelchair could reach the alarm.

Notification

Plans need to include a process of informing all building occupants that emergency action is needed. Because emergencies often disrupt technology, it is important to have low-tech solutions with built-in redundancy. Although special considerations might be needed for those with disabilities, plans should consider the community in general, because everyone benefits from improved notification systems.

The ADAAG provides specifications for emergency alarms so that they are accessible to persons with disabilities, including those with sensory impairments (ADAAG 4.1.3[14], 4.28). Where emergency alarm systems are provided, they must meet criteria that address audible and visual features. It is important to install multiple systems because events may cause one or another system to fail. For example, audible signs may not be distinguishable above the sound of alarms, the signs may not be heard or distinguishable from siren alarms, or without electricity, the systems may not be operable. Further, interpreters must be provided where indicated.

Since audible instructions delivered via emergency paging systems are not effective for the hard of hearing or deaf, visual strobes with high-intensity flashing lights should be used to notify these individuals that the alarm has sounded. The ADAAG specifications for visual appliances address intensity, flash rate, mounting location, and other characteristics. Audible alarms installed in corridors and lobbies can be heard in adjacent rooms, but a visual signal can be observed only within the space it is located. Visual alarms are required in hallways, lobbies, restrooms, and any other areas for general and common use, such as meeting and conference rooms, classrooms, cafeterias, employee break rooms, dressing rooms, examination rooms, and similar spaces. Alternatively, visual instructions can be provided through television monitors, scrolling text, or pagers that vibrate. As example, closed-circuit TV magnifiers consist of a camera which takes the picture of a printed page and displays the enlarged image on a television monitor. Finally, low-level signage should be placed 6 to 8 inches above the floor as a supplement to required exit signs placed higher on the wall, because exit signs are usually located over exits or near the ceiling and can become obscured by smoke.

Tactile and Audible Signage

The ADAAG 4.1.3(16), 4.30 requires that certain types of building signs be tactile and use both raised and Braille characters. This is intended to include signs typically placed at doorways, such as room and exit labels, because doorways provide a tactile cue to locating signs. Tactile specifications also apply to signs used to label the function of rooms and to the floor level designations provided in stairwells. Examples include signs labeling restrooms, exits, and rooms and floors designated by numbers or letters. The ADAAG also addresses informational and directional signs. These types of signs are not required to be tactile but must meet criteria for legibility, such as character size and proportion, contrast, and sign finish.

Braille signs, commonly found as raised patterns of dots on elevator control panels, have been installed in many buildings to assist people who are visually impaired. The usefulness of these panels is limited, because the person must be at the location of the Braille signs to feel them. Plans should include an alternative way to provide directional guidance to exits, such as audible directional signage.

Audible directional, or remote, signage, is a device used to inform those with visual impairments about their environments. Audible instructions are transmitted by low-power radio waves or infrared beams. Small receivers, carried by the individuals, pick up these signals and are equipped with a voice that announces directions (e.g., "the exit is ten steps from the front desk") or a word identifying where they are (e.g., "stairway," "elevator"). One example of audible signs is Talking Signs, which provide those who are blind with the information that helps them navigate in the environment. These signs "speak" by sending information from installed infrared transmitters. Handheld receivers pick up information from the transmitters and give verbal directions to those carrying them. Alternatively, some devices include a two-part, battery-operated smoke detector and transmitter that are attached to a wall and a companion vibrator device which is either placed on a desk or held in the hand. The vibrator is activated when a smoke detector transmits a signal to the receiver.

Preparedness at the Building Level: Evacuation

Moving people to safe areas is an important part of any disaster response, especially in tall buildings. Although contingency plans should be developed for providing evacuation assistance for all building occupants, there will always be someone in such buildings who will need special assistance in any emergency in which evacuation is required. Further, unique evacuation problems are created where the elderly or disabled live or work on higher floors in high-rise buildings.

The methods of accommodation and the choice of assistive devices should be discussed with those needing them. When assisting persons with vision impairments, a building's emergency plans should provide for announcing one's presence when entering the area, grasping the elbow of the person requiring assistance for guidance, and describing what he or she will be doing, including the mention of stairs, doorways, narrow passages, and ramps. Someone should remain with such an individual until he or she is safe.

There may be different procedures or preferences among local fire departments regarding evacuation procedures for persons with disabilities, but many evacuation plans will include the use of evacuation chairs for those needing assistance. These devices are designed with rollers, treads, and braking mechanisms that enable a person to be transported down stairs with the assistance of another individual. For additional information, planners should check with the local fire, police, or HAZMAT department.

Following an inventory of the number of employees requiring assistance and estimating the number of visitors to the building, it will be possible to determine how many evacuation chairs are needed. Decisions may be made to also stock heavy gloves to protect individuals' hands from debris when pushing their manual wheelchairs, a patch kit to repair flat tires, and extra batteries for those who use motorized wheelchairs or scooters. Staff should be trained on the use of evacuation chairs, through viewing the training videotape provided by the manufacturer as well as receiving on-site training from the manufacturer. When buildings conduct mandated fire drills, part of their exercise should test the ability to evacuate those with disabilities. Drills should focus on the use of evacuation and other assistive devices and occur on all shifts so that evening and night staff are familiar with the procedures and their responsibilities. Drills also provide an opportunity for individuals requiring assistance to practice transferring into and out of the evacuation chairs. It is important to practice evacuation procedures with blocked exits and service animals such as guide dogs, who accompany their owners during the evacuation. Drills can include the use of protective gear, such as booties made of Velcro for service animals to wear when evacuating from fire or walking over glass. (See Chapter 7 for more on drills and exercises.)

In planning for people with limited mobility, such as in residential institutions, there may be scenarios where sheltering in place is the best plan, even temporarily. Disaster plans should include the designation of several offices as waiting areas where individuals using wheelchairs or mobility devices and others can report and await assistance from the fire department, as is required in new construction (ADAAG 4.1.3[9], 4.3.11). Known as *areas of rescue assistance* or *areas of refuge*, in new construction these spaces must meet specifications for fire resistance and ventilation and are often incorporated into the design of fire stair landings, but can be provided in other recognized locations meeting the design specifications, including those for fire and smoke protection. An exception is provided for buildings equipped with sprinkler systems that have built-in signals used to monitor the system's features. In older buildings, offices designated as areas of refuge can be located at different parts of the building (e.g., front, back). Each designated area of refuge should have a preprinted sign requesting rescue assistance, a window, supplies that enable individuals to block smoke from entering the room from under the door, respirator masks, and a telephone and two-way radio (areas of rescue assistance must include two-way communication devices so that users can communicate about evacuation assistance). Employees should be instructed to post rescue signs in the window to alert the fire department of their location. The location of these waiting areas should be communicated to the local fire department.

Evacuation Equipment

The ability to evacuate during an emergency is highly dependent on one's mobility. The types of equipment discussed here are not meant to be all inclusive, as experimental equipment is continuously being developed and improved. Wheelchair users are one group with mobility limitations. Because wheelchairs are frequently fitted to the specific physical needs of the user, those evacuated will need to have their own chairs returned to them if they are separated during the evacuation.

Several types of evacuation or fold-up chairs allow for people to be moved up or down stairs, and can be permanently installed within stairways to accommodate wheelchair users or stored near emergency exits. In one type, the person transfers or is transferred from the wheelchair to a portable chair. These chairs are designed to move down stairs on special tracks equipped with friction braking systems, rollers, or other devices which control the speed of descent. With another device, the wheelchair user rolls onto the transporter and the wheelchair is secured to the device as it descends. In addition, there are chairs that can be rolled down stairs. Table 51 describes examples of devices that can be used to evacuate individuals who need assistance. Contact information for the manufacturers of these devices is found in Appendix R.

Carrying Techniques

Wheelchair users are trained in special techniques to transfer from one chair to another. There are two techniques for carrying people in an emergency: the cradle lift and the swing or chair carry. The cradle lift is preferred when the person to be

Table 51. Assistive Devices for Evacuation

Evac+Chair	Weighs 18 pounds and has a 300-pound carrying capacity
Evacu–Trac	Designed so passenger's weight propels it down the stairs, and has a 360-pound carrying capacity
Ferno Rescue Seat, Evacuation Chairs	Adjustable and portable devices enable easy maneuvering through confined spaces with a 350-pound carrying capacity
LifeSlider	Flat-bottomed, toboggan-like device that slides down stairs, around landings, through small doorways, around inside corners, and across pavement
Rescue Chairs	Designed to go up and down stairs with a 300-pound carrying capacity
Scalamobil	Battery-operated portable stair climber, attaches to most manual folding wheelchairs, and has a 264-pound carrying capacity

carried has little or no arm strength. It is also safer if the person being carried weighs less than the carrier. In the cradle carry, the person needing assistance is sitting and the carrier bends his knees and places one arm under the person's legs and the other arm around the person's back. The person being carried puts an arm over the shoulder of the carrier. The carrier lifts up with the person in front of him or her.

For the swing or chair carry, a two-person technique, the carriers stand on opposite sides of the individual. They take the arm of the person and wrap it around each of their shoulders. Each carrier grasps their partner's forearm at the small of the back of the person being carried. They reach under the person's knees and grasp the wrist of the carry partner's other hand. Both partners lean in close to the person and lift on the count of three. The carriers should continue pressing into the person being carried for additional support.

Service Animals

In preparation for any emergency, those who have service animals should ensure that the animal's identification tags, licenses, and vaccinations are current, and that the tags display the owner's contact information and an out-of-town contact. Public health should work with the community to identify and list the shelters that are set up for service animals. Owners should prepare a supply kit for the animal which includes bowls for water and food, food, plastic bags, a toy, a collar, and an extra leash or harness.

Plan Implementation and Maintenance

After the final evacuation plan is written, a copy should be distributed to all company employees and key personnel. In addition, evacuation drills should be regularly performed to make sure all employees are familiar with the plan. To ensure that accommodations continue to be effective, the plan should be integrated into the standard operating procedures, practiced, and accommodations updated periodically. In addition, a system for reporting new hazards and accommodation needs should be developed; a relationship with local fire, police, and HAZMAT departments should be maintained; and new employees should be made aware of the plan. Finally, all accommodation equipment used in emergency evacuation should be inspected and maintained in proper working order.

Emergency Health Information

Everyone who has a diagnosis that may impact emergency treatment should always carry information about their health needs and emergency contacts, updated twice a year, with a copy given to a family member and a friend or neighbor. This emergency health information lets others know about their medical condition or disability if they are unable to provide information. For those with disabilities, this information should detail special equipment and supplies that they use, such as hearing aid batteries; detailed information about the specifications of their medication regime, including current prescription names and dosages, shelf life, and temperature at which it should be stored; and the names, addresses, and telephone numbers of doctors and pharmacists.

Emergency health information should be kept in emergency supply kits, wallets (behind driver's license or official identification card), and wheelchair packs. A MedicAlert tag or bracelet identifies the type of disability or medical condition and includes a toll-free number for an office at which the wearer's current medication and diagnosis are on file. MedicAlert bracelets are available at pharmacies. Figure 4 provides a template for collecting a person's emergency health information.

Finally, a copy of the checklist in Figure 5 should be distributed to personnel who are responsible for creating, reviewing, maintaining, practicing, and revising emergency plans.

Emergency Health Information		Date:		Updated:	
Name					
Address		City		State	Zip
CONTACT METHOD	HOME			WORK	
Phone:	Cell:		Fax:		E-mail:
Birth Date	Blood Type		Social Security No.		
Health Plan		Individual #		Group #	
Emergency Contact:					
Address		City		State	Zip
CONTACT METHOD	HOME			WORK	
Phone:	Cell:		Fax:		E-mail:
Primary Care Provider:					
Address		City		State	Zip
Phone:	Cell:		Fax:		E-mail:
Disability/conditions:					
Medications and dose:					
Allergies:					
Immunizations		Dates			
Communication/Devices/Equipment/Other:					

Figure 4. Emergency Health Information

Reprinted with permission from Kailes JI. 1998. *Be a Savvy Health Care Consumer, Your Life May Depend on It!* Playa del Rey, CA: June Isaacson Kailes. Available at: http://www.jik.com/resource.html.

Date Completed	Activity
	Assure that a relationship is established with the local fire department that includes the following: • Fire department reviews the plan at least once a year • Fire department receives a copy of a current log containing names and locations of all people needing assistance • The plan is coordinated and practiced with the fire department
	Practice plans through regular drills
	Know how to get to all exits and practice it as part of regular drills
	Practice using evacuation devices
	Practice dealing with different circumstances and unforeseen situations, such as blocked paths or exits
	Ensure that shift workers and others who are at the site after typical hours (e.g., cleaning crews, evening meeting coordinators) are included in drills
	Plans should include the following: • People who are at the site on a regular basis • People who are at the site outside of typical working hours • How visitors, guests, and customers with small children who require extra time to evacuate will be assisted • Specific dates for revisions and updates
	Orient all people to the plan
	Plan dissemination: • Have people read the plan? • Have people been oriented to the plan? Placing plans in a drawer or even a prominent place on a bookshelf is as good as burying them. • Is the plan distributed and reviewed with all people at the site? • Do people get a copy of the plan in a usable format (Braille, large print, text file, and cassette tape, or in appropriate formats for non–English speakers and people who have poor reading skills)? • Are these formats always updated when the plan is revised?
	Assure that people know how to report safety hazards (e.g., fire extinguishers that need servicing, exits which are not kept clear, furniture and other items that block barrier-free passages)

Figure 5. Disability-Related Action Items for Emergency Plan Coordinators

Reprinted with permission from Kailes JI. 2002. Emergency Evacuation Preparedness: Taking Responsibility for Your Safety: A Guide for People With Disabilities and Other Activity Limitations. Pomona, CA: Center for Disability Issues and the Health Professions, Western University of Health Sciences. Available at: http://www.wvdhsem.gov/other_docs/emergency_evacuation.pdf.

Chapter **11**

Public Health Response to Emerging Infections and Biological Incidents

Natural disasters visibly impact environments, leaving behind visceral images of destruction. Infectious disease and super-lethal microorganisms, or biological agents, can spread through the air without being visible. These invisible threats pose special concerns and response requirements for health departments and health care systems. Although fighting the spread of infectious disease is a core competency of public health professionals, the timely availability of medical teams and resources in an emergency may be inadequate if the public health infrastructure is not maintained at a sufficient level. Responding to a biological attack or event requires careful coordination between governmental departments and agencies that don't necessarily work together in the daily practice of their professions (e.g., law enforcement and medicine). Both scenarios require a carefully planned response utilizing many of the principles discussed in this chapter and other chapters in the book. This chapter reviews the response to pandemic influenza, unknown disease, covert and overt threats, categories of bioterrorism agents, and the public health and medical response required at the federal, regional, and community levels.

Public Health Role

- Develop and use multidisciplinary protocols for collaboration among state and local public health agencies, community hospitals, academic health centers, community health care providers, laboratories, professional societies, medical examiners, emergency response units, manufacturers of safety and medical equipment, the media, government officials, and federal agencies such as the U.S. Office of the Assistant Secretary for Preparedness and Response, the Centers for Disease Control and Prevention (CDC), and the Agency for Toxic Substances and Disease Registry
- Establish specific criteria for monitoring emerging infections and activate surveillance systems that can quickly identify emerging or reemerging diseases, closely monitor unexplained morbidity and mortality caused by infectious disease, and improve surveillance for flulike illness
- Increase lab capacity, educate microbiologists about reporting, and establish communication linkages with the Laboratory Response Network (LRN) for the rapid evaluation and identification of biological agents
- Develop and activate diagnostic clinical and treatment protocols that are communicated to the medical community which improve rapid reporting of suspect cases, unusual clusters of disease, and unusual manifestations of disease

- Plan for and respond, where necessary, to reduce the morbidity and mortality from pandemic influenza or a biological incident by stockpiling antibiotics, preparing multilingual patient information, developing contingency plans for social distancing and quarantine, and developing community plans for the delivery of medical care to large numbers of patients, as well as to those who are not ill but seek medical treatment for reassurance and who are known as the *worried well*
- Utilize and expand access to the Health Alert Network (HAN)
- Develop contingency plans, with the local medical examiner, for mass mortuary services, including plans for the utilization of Federal Disaster Medical Assistance Teams and Disaster Mortuary Operational Response Teams
- Train all health organizations required to deliver care
- Communicate emergency instructions, prevention, control, and treatment information
- Resolve legal issues related to public health authority in emergencies

Response to Unknown Disease

With global climate change, globalization of commerce, inadvertent transport of vectors, zoonotic disease, and antigenic shift, it is inevitable that the U.S. public health system will continue to confront serious diseases that are not common today. Furthermore, although pandemic influenza may overwhelm our health care delivery systems and incidents involving CBRNE[1] (chemical, biological, radiological, nuclear, and high-yield explosives) may involve many victims and damage to buildings and other property, these emerging infections and incidents are dissimilar to typical disasters in several ways. A major difference between natural disasters and an event involving an infectious disease is the widespread health impact. Officials may not recognize that an incident is underway until several casualties, outbreaks of infection, or multiple releases have occurred. The scope of the incident may expand geometrically and affect multiple jurisdictions, as victims unknowingly spread infection or carry the agent to health care facilities and across geographic areas. The fear of the unknown may generate concern from the public, resulting in larger numbers of worried well than of actual victims. The workings of the typical response team could be disrupted as the scope of events requires expansion of the emergency response personnel who normally work together.

Depending on the emerging infection or type of agent used, there may be a shortage of any of a number of medical resources including intensive care unit (ICU) beds, ventilators and other critical care needs, and antibiotics and antiviral agents. If a release of a contagious disease, such as smallpox, occurs, several patients will likely appear in emergency rooms with rash illness that hopefully will be reported to authorities as suspected smallpox. Nontraditional treatment centers may need to be established on short notice. There is potentially a high demand for mortuary or

---

[1]CBRNE include chemical (cyanide, incapacitating agents, pulmonary agents, vesicants), biological (bacteria, virus, toxins), radiological, nuclear (detonation or "dirty" explosives), and high-yield explosives (rapid release of gas and heat) agents. This chapter focuses primarily on the public health preparedness and response to biological agents, although many of the principles discussed in this book will apply to preparedness for other agents.

funeral services and social and counseling services. Unlike morbidity and mortality associated with natural disasters, demands on medical care in each community are likely to be prolonged as the illness spreads among the population. The need for home care may increase if the elderly and other high-risk and vulnerable populations can't or won't leave their homes to receive care for chronic medical conditions because of the threat of exposure to infectious disease. In addition to surveillance and activating the participation of other agencies, public health officials may initiate actions to protect the community, including social distancing, quarantine, and immunization. Further, the fire and safety workforce may be reduced in number and overwhelmed if first responders, who normally are the main core of personnel on the scene of an incident, become ill from early or repeated exposure to communicable disease. Finally, communities will need to be self-sufficient for potentially prolonged periods if resources cannot be diverted from other geographic areas because of regional spread.

Unlike the response to an overt chemical event for which fire, police, or hazardous material units are the first responders, the public health department is charged with identifying infectious disease in a community. This response to emerging infections and bioterrorism requires an interdependent working relationship among local, state, and federal agencies and among community clinicians, emergency responders, and local public health personnel. Once a plan is in place, the public health response to unknown disease outbreaks has five components: detection of unusual events, investigation and containment of potential threats, organization of care, laboratory capacity, and coordination and communication.

Pandemic Influenza

Preparing for the uncommon, but potentially devastating, occurrence of pandemic influenza is a national strategy for the United States. Before discussing pandemic influenza, it is important to understand seasonal influenza. Seasonal influenza, which occurs annually between late fall and early spring, is a common but frequently serious disease known as *flu*. Because flu can be transmitted by those who are infected but asymptomatic, the virus spreads from person to person rapidly, and public health agencies may notice simultaneous outbreaks across a region. Most people have some immunity to the circulating virus, either from previous infections or from vaccination, and recover relatively quickly. However, for groups at higher risk for complications from flu, including the very young, the very old, the immunocompromised, and those with chronic illnesses, even seasonal influenza can cause serious complications (pneumonia or death). During a typical flu season in the United States, more than 200,000 people are hospitalized and approximately 36,000 persons die as a result of having contracted the virus.

Pandemic flu occurs on average every three to four decades when a new strain of the flu emerges. Pandemic influenza can be thought of as the flu on steroids, because in previous pandemics influenza caused significantly more morbidity and mortality. When pandemics occur, they are followed by multiple waves after the initial outbreak, overwhelming public health and health care systems that have not made adequate preparation.

Three groups of influenza viruses (A, B, and C) can cause illness in humans, but only group A viruses cause major epidemics or pandemics. The two major antigenic components of influenza A viruses (hemagglutinin [H] and neuraminidase [N]) are continually undergoing changes, known as *drift*. When drift occurs, these changes in antigenic structure cause illness in individuals because immunity from prior infections does not protect them from getting sick when exposed to the changed virus. Drift can result in annual epidemics. Pandemics of influenza arise when a reassortment, or *antigenic shift*, of the H and N components occurs. In this antigenic shift, humans, birds, or swine are simultaneously infected with two different influenza A viruses, resulting in a new or *novel* strain against which no one has immunity.

Most people have some immunity to seasonal influenza strains because they have circulated in previous years. By contrast, during pandemics, there is little natural immunity to the circulating novel strain. As a result, the virus can spread easily from person to person increasing the number of unexpected deaths.

Three major pandemics occurred in the last century. The 1918 influenza pandemic caused more than 600,000 deaths in the United States and up to 50 million deaths worldwide. Although subsequent pandemics in 1957 and 1969 were less deadly, the number of excess U.S. deaths was in the tens of thousands. In addition to high morbidity and excess mortality, influenza pandemics have also been accompanied by social and economic disruption. Thus the challenge of reducing the severity of pandemics is a critically important responsibility for public health professionals.

Twenty-First-Century Influenza Strains

From 2003 to 2006, an avian influenza strain (H5N1) caused widespread disease among birds and spread to humans. Although H5N1 did not spread extensively among humans, it was associated with high case-fatality rates, and there was concern that the virus might become more easily transmissible among humans. Before that could happen, there was worldwide spread of a novel influenza strain found in swine (H1N1).

Swine influenza (swine flu) is a common respiratory disease caused by the type A influenza virus that typically infects pigs. In 2009, a novel swine flu virus spread worldwide in humans. Before the spring of 2009, swine flu had only occurred periodically in the United States. The 1976 outbreak, first noticed in Fort Dix, New Jersey, prompted more than 40 million people to be vaccinated. In September 1988, a previously healthy 32-year-old pregnant woman died from pneumonia after being infected with swine flu. Between December 2005 and February 2009, 12 people were diagnosed with swine flu in just ten U.S. states.

The virus that circulated in 2009 was a new subtype of A/H1N1 not previously detected in swine or humans to which many people had no preexisting immunity. This contagious virus, which spread among humans around the world, killed nearly 13,000 and sickened more than 60 million in the United States alone. In this pandemic, the H1N1 virus dominated other seasonal influenza viruses. Most strikingly, the severest cases occurred more often in younger age groups (reversing the usual seasonal influenza pattern). As part of the response, health departments around the country implemented their pandemic influenza plans, the CDC provided national guidance, and the Strategic National Stockpile (SNS) released antiviral drugs, personal protective equipment (PPE), and respiratory protection devices.

In the postpandemic phase, H1N1 had spread to all countries around the globe, all age groups in many countries developed some immunity to the new virus, no large or unusual outbreaks occurred in the summer of 2010, and seasonal influenza was again causing illness in many countries. It is expected that the H1N1 virus will continue to circulate for many years and cause variable illness.

Stages of a Pandemic

In 2005, the World Health Organization (WHO) distributed a preparedness plan for global influenza which defines the stages of a pandemic, outlines the role of the WHO, and makes recommendations for national measures before and during a pandemic. This plan guides worldwide efforts to minimize the impact of each phase of the pandemic. The six phases that occur during the interpandemic, pandemic alert, and pandemic periods are described in Table 52.

The United States prepares and initiates a national response based on the pandemic phases tracked by the WHO. The CDC is involved in the global preparedness effort by supporting WHO activities and maintaining cooperative agreements for surveillance in other countries. The U.S. Department of Health and Human Services (HHS) pandemic flu Web site provides comprehensive information and planning tools as reference for public health agencies and providers across the United States.

The HHS Pandemic Influenza Plan provides guidance for pandemic influenza preparation and response to local and state health departments and health care providers. (The full plan can be found online at http://www.hhs.gov/pandemicflu/plan.) Part 1 of the plan outlines the key roles of HHS and its agencies in providing public health and medical support in the event of a pandemic. Part 2, Public Health Guidance for State and Local Partners, provides detailed guidance to local and state health departments in 11 key areas:

1. Pandemic influenza surveillance
2. Laboratory diagnostics
3. Health care planning
4. Infection control
5. Clinical guidelines
6. Vaccine distribution and use
7. Antiviral drug distribution and use
8. Community disease control and prevention
9. Managing travel-related risk of disease transmission
10. Public health communications
11. Workforce support: psychosocial considerations and information needs

Part 3 details each HHS agency's operational plans, including specific roles and responsibilities in the event of a pandemic.

Table 52. World Health Organization Pandemic Phases

	Phase	Characteristics
Interpandemic period	1	No new influenza virus subtypes have been detected in humans. An influenza virus subtype that has caused human infection may be present in animals. If present in animals, the risk of human infection or disease is considered to be low.
	2	No new influenza virus subtypes have been detected in humans. However, a circulating animal influenza virus subtype poses a substantial risk of human disease.
Pandemic alert period	3	Human infection(s) with a new subtype, but no human-to-human spread, or at most rare instances of spread to a close contact.
	4	Small cluster(s) with limited human-to-human transmission, but spread is highly localized, suggesting that the virus is not well adapted to humans.
	5	Larger cluster(s) but human-to-human spread still localized, suggesting that the virus is becoming increasingly better adapted to humans, but may not yet be fully transmissible (substantial pandemic risk).
Pandemic period	6	Pandemic: increased and sustained transmission in general population.
Postpandemic period		Return to the interpandemic period (Phase 1).

Adapted from World Health Organization (WHO). 2005. HHS Pandemic Influenza Plan. Table C-1. Summary of WHO global pandemic phases. Geneva: WHO. Available at: http://www.hhs.gov/pandemicflu/plan/appendixc.html.

Lessons Learned

During the last century, important lessons were learned about pandemics that should be incorporated into public health preparedness for the next pandemic[2]:

- Pandemics are unpredictable, with great variation in mortality, severity of illness, and patterns of spread
- Consistently, the number of cases will exponentially increase very quickly, and hospitals need to be prepared for a sudden surge in patients needing medical care
- The capacity of the virus to cause severe disease in the very young and elderly will determine the pandemic's impact
- Pandemics occur in waves; subsequent waves can be more severe if the virus mutates to a more virulent form, or the second wave reaches those more at risk of severe disease causing fatal complications

[2]Adapted from WHO. 2005. Avian Influenza: Assessing the Pandemic Threat. Geneva, Switzerland: WHO. Available at: http://www.who.int/csr/disease/influenza/H5N1-9reduit.pdf.

- Virological surveillance is key to rapidly confirming the onset, alerting health services, isolating and characterizing the virus, and making it available to vaccine manufacturers
- Most pandemics originate in Asia, where surveillance for both influenza among animals and clusters of unusual respiratory disease in humans provides an early warning
- Public health interventions have delayed but not stopped the spread of past pandemics, and quarantine and travel restrictions have shown little effect, but the temporary banning of public gatherings and closure of schools are potentially effective measures
- Delaying the spread of the virus is important, because with fewer people ill, medical and other essential services are more likely to be maintained
- Vaccination during a pandemic must be sufficient and timely
- Countries that manufacture vaccine will be the first to receive it
- As pandemics have been most severe in later waves, there is an extension of the time needed to produce more vaccine for high-risk populations; successive waves may begin as quickly as a month later
- Although a community's experience in administering yearly vaccination to large groups of people can reduce excess mortality because of their skill at the logistics of vaccination, regions should expect a sudden surge of many sick people and a high demand for medical care during a pandemic

Public Health Planning and Preparedness for Pandemic Flu

Local and state health departments have developed plans to prepare for and respond to a pandemic influenza. Preparing for a pandemic requires both internal and communitywide planning. When a novel strain of flu virus emerges, it is unlikely that there will be time to manufacture sufficient vaccine for the new strain. As a result, responders (first responders, public health, and health care professionals) could become ill. A prolonged outbreak will occur over months, impacting the continuity of operations of essential services. Planning for a pandemic should assume that there will be a significant decrease in the available workforce. Regional and federal assets, such as ventilators, may not be available because of both demand and the difficulty of transporting them with reduced manpower.

HHS[3] identifies the primary strategies for combating influenza as the following:

- Vaccination
- Treatment of infected individuals and prophylaxis of exposed individuals with influenza antiviral medications
- Implementation of infection control and social distancing measures

Carrying out these tasks requires epidemiology and surveillance, planning mass vaccination (including the receipt of the vaccine, distribution to a broad spectrum of

---

[3]U.S. Department of Health and Human Services (HHS). 2007. *Community Strategy for Pandemic Influenza Mitigation*. Washington, DC: HHS. Available at: http://www.flu.gov/professional/community/commitigation.html.

vaccination sites, monitoring doses, and the administration of the vaccination process); the delivery and distribution of antiviral countermeasures; community mitigation through social distancing and quarantine; communicating to the public; and confirmatory laboratory diagnostics.

When response to a pandemic begins, decisions will be made about the use of antiviral medications because of the expected time delays in the availability of effective vaccination for mass immunization. Additional decisions on how to protect the public using social distancing and quarantine will be made. All decisions will be based on scientific data, ethical considerations, public opinion on protective measures and their impact on society, and common sense. Table 53 describes interventions and mitigation strategies that can be used when effective vaccine against the novel virus is either unavailable or insufficient. Additional information on infection control measures is available online (at http://www.pandemicflu.gov).

Key public health tasks include robust surveillance and laboratory testing. Laboratories will be required to handle a surge of specimens and to verify as required that their testing algorithms are adequate. In an era of technology, traditional "shoe leather" investigative methods will be required for contact tracing. Health departments should prepare by vetting the legality of procedures for isolation and quarantine in advance of any outbreak. The distribution of vaccine and antiviral medications will be a massive undertaking and coordination with the SNS will be required. Procedures should be in place for (1) acquiring and taking delivery of the drugs, (2) prioritizing which populations will receive available drugs, (3) tracking the distribution and use of supplies, (4) conducting mass vaccination clinics, and (5) tracking adverse events caused by vaccination. If vaccination to a novel virus requires two doses of vaccine to achieve maximum immunity, health departments should develop a plan for tracking and recalling individuals who receive a novel flu vaccine. As part of planning, health departments should determine how they will communicate about behaviors that reduce risk, such as social distancing, handwashing, and respiratory etiquette. Further, planning should include communications about seeking care and about vaccine or antiviral distribution. The following lists key behaviors for preventing the spread of flu:

✓ Cover nose and mouth with a tissue when coughing or sneezing
✓ Dispose of tissues in the trash after use
✓ Wash hands with soap and water, especially after coughing or sneezing
✓ Clean hands with alcohol-based hand sanitizers
✓ If sick with influenza, stay home from work or school and limit contact with others to avoid infecting them
✓ Avoid touching eyes, nose, or mouth with unwashed hands
✓ Stay away from those who are sick
✓ Stay away from settings where large groups have gathered when there is illness in the community
✓ Clean frequently touched surfaces often (e.g., door knobs, hand rails)
✓ Get an influenza vaccine every year

Table 53. Interventions and Mitigation Strategies, by Pandemic Severity Index

Interventions by Setting	Pandemic Severity Index		
	1	2 and 3	4 and 5
Home			
Many sick individuals who are not critically ill may be managed safely through voluntary isolation at home combined with use of antiviral treatment as available and indicated	Recommend	Recommend	Recommend
Voluntary quarantine of household members in homes with sick persons	Generally not recommended	Consider short-term implementation	Recommend plus antiviral prophylaxis to household contacts where national policy advises
School			
Social distancing by dismissal of students from schools and school-based programs	Generally not recommended	Consider ≤4 weeks	Recommend ≤12 weeks; actual duration may vary depending on transmission in the community
Closure of child care centers			
Reduce social contacts and community meetings			
Workplace/Community Social Distancing			
Encouraging alternatives to in-person meetings (e.g., teleconferences)	Generally not recommended	Consider	Recommend
Modify contact at work via telecommuting and staggered schedules			
Postpone or cancel public gatherings where large groups will congregate			

Note: Interventions are used in combination with other infection control measures, including hand hygiene, cough etiquette, and personal protective equipment such as face masks.

Generally not recommended = where consequences for entire populations outweigh the benefits, unless there is a compelling rationale for specific populations or jurisdictions; Consider = part of a prudent planning strategy; also consider characteristics of the pandemic locally, nationally, and globally (e.g., age-specific illness rate, geographic distribution, magnitude of adverse consequences); Recommended = important component of the planning strategy.

Adapted from U.S. Department of Health and Human Services (HHS). 2007. *Community Strategy for Pandemic Influenza Mitigation.* Table 2. Summary of the community mitigation strategy, by pandemic severity. Washington, DC: HHS. Available at: http://www.flu.gov/professional/community/commitigation.html.

Collection, Storage, Processing, and Testing of Flu Specimens

In 2009, the CDC issued interim guidance on the appropriate collection, storage, processing, and testing of specimens for patients with suspected novel H1N1 virus infection. This detailed guidance is now archived (and available at http://www.cdc.gov/h1n1flu/specimencollection.htm) and the information can guide planning. All facilities which collect specimens during an outbreak should check the CDC Web site for any updates.

In the case of H1N1, the novel influenza A virus was confirmed in persons with an influenzalike illness by a laboratory test (real-time reverse transcription test, real-time polymerase chain reaction test, or viral culture). Although isolating the novel influenza virus helps diagnose the infection, lab results may not be returned quickly enough for timely management of clinical symptoms. Furthermore, in 2009, a negative viral culture did not rule out infection with the H1N1 virus.

Because the duration of viral shedding with novel influenza A/H1N1 virus is unknown, the CDC estimated the duration of viral shedding based upon the behavior of seasonal influenza virus. They assumed that infected persons shed the virus and were potentially infectious from the day prior to the onset of illness until the fever resolved, or up to 7 days from the onset of illness.

Clinicians can test for suspected cases of novel H1N1 by obtaining an upper respiratory specimen. Preferred respiratory specimens should be collected as soon as possible after the onset of illness and include nasopharyngeal swab, nasal aspirate, or a combined nasopharyngeal swab with oropharyngeal swab. A nasal swab or oropharyngeal swab is acceptable. An endotracheal aspirate, bronchoalveolar lavage, or sputum specimens should also be collected from intubated patients.

Respiratory specimens should not be kept longer than 4 days. Specimens should be placed in sterile viral transport media and immediately placed on ice or cold packs or at 4°C (refrigerator) for transport to the laboratory. Clinical specimens should be shipped on wet ice or cold packs in appropriate packaging. All specimens should be labeled clearly and include all information requested by each state's public health laboratory. Suspected case specimens shipped from the state public health laboratory to the CDC should include all information required for submitting seasonal influenza surveillance isolates or specimens.

For more details, see recommended infection control guidance for persons collecting clinical specimens in clinical settings (available at http://www.osha.gov/Publications/OSHA_pandemic_health.pdf) and for laboratory personnel (available at http://www.cdc.gov/h1n1flu/guidelines_labworkers.htm).

Infection Control

The CDC has published infection control recommendations for suspected or confirmed H1N1 patients for which treatment involves aerosol-generating procedures, potentially spreading the virus via droplets in the air. These aerosol-generating activities include the collection of clinical specimens, inserting or removing of endotracheal tubes, giving nebulizer treatments, performing bronchoscopy, and cardiac pulmonary resuscitation or emergency intubation. Once medically cleared, fit-tested, and trained for respirator use, medical personnel should wear a fit-tested disposable N95 respirator when entering the patient's room. All hospital personnel should follow hand hygiene practices by washing with soap and water or using hand sanitizer immediately after removing gloves and other equipment and after any contact with respiratory secretions. Any personnel providing care to or collecting clinical specimens should wear disposable nonsterile gloves, gowns, and eye protection (such as goggles). Information on comprehensive respiratory protection programs and fit-test procedures can be accessed online (at http://www.osha.gov/SLTC/etools/respiratory).

Other infection control procedures include the following:

- Patients should be placed in a single-patient room with the door kept closed or an airborne infection isolation room with negative pressure, and suctioning, bronchoscopy, or intubation should be performed in a procedure room with negative-pressure air handling
- The ill person should wear a surgical mask when outside of the patient room and should be encouraged to wash hands frequently and follow respiratory hygiene practices
- Routine cleaning and disinfection strategies performed during influenza seasons can be used for the environmental management of swine flu (more information can be found online at http://www.cdc.gov/ncidod/dhqp/gl_environinfection.html)
- Standard, droplet, and contact precautions should be used for all patient care activities, and maintained for 7 days after the onset of illness or until symptoms have resolved

Preparedness for Vulnerable Populations

Because flu is a highly contagious respiratory disease that spreads quickly and exponentially, it is critical that preparedness for influenza involve all populations, including those with vulnerabilities that increase their risk during a pandemic. In addition to the large population already identified in Chapter 10 as at risk from other disasters, many factors such as access to treatment, health literacy, immigration status, and spoken language may increase the number of people who are vulnerable during an influenza pandemic. Immigrants and refugees are vulnerable to pandemic influenza as a result of a high prevalence of chronic disease that predisposes them to complications from flu, low rates of seasonal flu vaccination, and numerous social, linguistic, and economic barriers to accessing and using preventive measures. Many immigrants work in low-paying jobs without benefits such as sick leave; this discourages them from staying home when ill. They may also live in crowded conditions, making it difficult to isolate a sick family member. In addition, there are millions of undocumented persons living in the United States who may not follow advice for preventive immunization or other actions that could expose them to potential deportation. Some may lack the experience to understand how to carry out the preventive actions being recommended. Some might experience cross-cultural misunderstanding, which acts as a barrier and reduces their ability to take preventive measures or get timely medical care. Further, vulnerability is increased for those who lack the funds to stockpile medications and supplies, lack adequate health insurance, or are not aware of or can't take preventive measures because of limited emotional and financial resources.

Communication and Response

Ideally, the public acts as a partner with government officials in taking actions that will prevent infectious disease from spreading in the community. An effective partner must receive and understand the messages being communicated and accept the actions being recommended. To reach diverse groups, targeted communication and response strategies need to be developed that address any potential concerns about receiving vaccination, taking antiviral medications, staying home from work, or potential reprisal for coming forward to seek vaccination or treatment. As discussed in Chapter 6, officials should strengthen their partnerships with trusted members of a targeted population and involve them in development of both the communication strategy and the messages during the prepandemic period. The first step is collaboration between public health agencies and the various communities that might be vulnerable. Possible participants include community health centers, school-based clinics, primary care practices, and home health care workers. Faith- and community-based organizations may be helpful in working with immigrants in adopting preventive behaviors, such as cough etiquette and the use of face masks and respirators. Members of vulnerable communities should also be asked to participate in their community's pandemic planning and preparedness activities.

Since pandemic influenza is likely to occur over a period of months or years and to appear and abate in waves, one challenge will be to get the public to trust and act upon messages that might evolve. As a pandemic progresses, public uncertainty may grow; specific strategies should be developed with the targeted communities to deal with any doubts. The public will look to officials to quickly respond to their concerns about the risks inherent in the rapid spread of infection or in any proposed preventive actions. What is communicated should be personally relevant (for example, expressed in the spoken language of the targeted communities) and reflect a group's cultural beliefs and views about the risk. Communications about unanticipated complications should be timely and ongoing. When mass immunization is being given, providers of mobile clinical vans can reach out and work with the various agencies that serve the targeted communities.

Chemical or Biological Warfare

The global recognition of the potential peril from bioterrorism is highlighted by the increase in terrorist activity around the world. With increased terrorist activity, the likelihood of a chemical or biological warfare (CBW) attack is also growing. Of the 15 National Planning Scenarios discussed in Chapter 3, almost one third are centered on biological attacks indicating the degree to which this threat is taken seriously. Because the public health and health sectors would have difficulty containing a massive outbreak caused by an intended spread of infectious disease, it is important to understand CBW and be prepared to respond should it occur.

Overt and Covert Releases

Detection of an intentional release of CBW may occur in several different ways. Overt releases of CBW are those where a threat assessment is possible before a response is initiated, because the threat is announced. Some announced threats are hoaxes. Public health officials should assume that potential hoaxes are in fact real when threats are accompanied by increased morbidity or mortality, even if the microorganisms have not been confirmed. Communities may choose a limited response to hoaxes based on a sophisticated analysis of the situation and a relatively easy resolution of the incident.

Covert releases are those without prior warning in which a biological agent presents as illness in the community and for which traditional surveillance methods are needed to detect the agent. With covert releases, patients fall ill or die from unknown causes or unusual origins. Covert dissemination of a biological agent in a public place will probably not have an immediate impact because of the incubation period of the disease, resulting in a delay between exposure and onset.

The covert release of a contagious agent or the appearance of a highly infectious illness has the potential for multinational spread prior to detection. Release in a transportation hub or in a mobile population could disseminate a highly contagious agent such as smallpox across borders before the epidemic is recognized. As person-to-person contact continues, successive waves of transmission could carry infection to other localities around the globe. In a very short time, public health authorities would be asked to determine that an attack has occurred, identify the organism, and prevent more casualties through prevention strategies (e.g., mass vaccination, prophylactic treatment, or universal precautions and quarantine). The ability to detect covert releases depends on enhancing public health infrastructure and increasing the skills of front-line medical practitioners so they recognize and report suspicious syndromes.

Critical Biological Agents

The CDC has identified three major categories of high-priority agents: A, B, and C. (More information is available at http://emergency.cdc.gov/agent/agentlist-category.asp.) The CDC advises that

High-priority agents include organisms that pose a risk to national security because they

- can be easily disseminated or transmitted from person to person;
- result in high mortality rates and have the potential for major public health impact;
- might cause public panic and social disruption; and
- require special action for public health preparedness.

Category A

Category A is a list of the nine highest priority agents. Although the occurrence of these diseases is relatively infrequent, their impact is high because of the speed with which they spread. The agents on the Category A list pose a risk to national security because they can be easily disseminated or transmitted person to person; cause high mortality, with the potential for major public health impact; could cause public panic and social disruption; and require special action for public health preparedness.

Bacillus anthracis

Anthrax, an acute bacterial disease affecting the skin, chest, or intestinal tract is considered to be a highly efficacious biological warfare agent, because it forms spores (providing stability in aerosol form), is relatively easy to disseminate using off-the-shelf technology, and is frequently fatal if inhaled. Its incubation period is 1 to 7 days, but postexposure disease is possible up to 60 days later. Transmission from person to person is very rare.

Clostridium botulinum

Botulism is poisoning by a toxin produced by a common environmental organism that can be easily cultured from soil. Victims of the toxin often require intensive supportive medical care. Food-borne botulism results from ingesting contaminated food. Botulism in wounds occurs when the organism grows in a deep wound and forms toxin, which is carried to the bloodstream. Intestinal botulism occurs mostly in infants, less than 1 year old, from the ingestion of spores which grow in their intestines. The case-fatality rate for infants is less than 1%.

The public health response to botulism is complicated. If paralysis occurs in a large number of individuals, the short supply of respiratory intensive care beds and ventilators will not be enough. The immunoglobulin used in the routine treatment of both wound and food-borne botulism can be lifesaving if given early, but is limited in both supply and availability. Public health preparedness requires a major stockpiling effort to cover possible bioterrorism response needs resulting from botulism.

Variola major

Smallpox, for which dissemination requires person-to-person transmission, is highly contagious in unimmunized populations and has a mortality rate as high as 35%. Smallpox has a cycle time of 10 to 14 days, an attack rate of up to 90%, and a secondary attack rate among the unvaccinated of 50%.

Yersinia pestis

Pneumonic plague is a respiratory-acquired illness that is spread from person to person through sneezing or coughing. It is diagnosed by culturing bacteria from sputum, blood, spinal fluid, or infected glands. Pneumonic plague is almost 100% fatal if not treated quickly. Bubonic plague is the form characterized by severely swollen and infected lymph nodes in the groin or axilla, called *buboes*. Plague occurs as an enzootic disease of rodents in the United States, making it relatively easy to obtain an isolate for use as a terrorist agent. Infected rats and their fleas transfer bacterial infection to animals and humans through bites or via scratches from infected cats. Symptoms occur 2 to 7 days after exposure. If untreated, bubonic plague has a 50 to 60% mortality.

Francisella tularensis

Tularemia is a zoonotic bacterial disease with varying clinical manifestations related to the route of transmission. It can be transmitted from rabbit, tick, or fly bites, or by handling infected animal carcasses. Tularemia can also be disseminated in water. Tularemia is not transmissible person to person. In aerosol form, the organism produces a severely debilitating pneumonia with a lower mortality rate than anthrax. The incubation period, related to strain, can range from 1 to 14 days but is commonly 3 to 5 days.

Filoviruses and Arenaviruses

Two filoviruses, Ebola hemorrhagic fever and Marburg hemorrhagic fever, and two arenaviruses, Lassa fever and Machupo, complete Category A.

Category B

Category B agents are considered the second highest priority because they are moderately easy to disseminate, cause moderate morbidity and low mortality, and require specific enhancements of the CDC's diagnostic capacity as well as enhanced disease surveillance. Category B agents include the following:

- Brucellosis (*Brucella* species)
- Epsilon toxin of *Clostridium perfringens*
- Glanders (*Burkholderia mallei*)
- Melioidosis (*Burkholderia pseudomallei*)
- Psittacosis (*Chlamydia psittaci*)
- Q fever (*Coxiella burnetii*)
- Ricin toxin from *Ricinus communis* (castor beans)
- Staphylococcal enterotoxin B
- Typhus fever (*Rickettsia prowazekii*)
- Viral encephalitis (alphaviruses; e.g., Venezuelan equine encephalitis, eastern equine encephalitis, western equine encephalitis)

A subset of Category B agents includes pathogens that are food- or waterborne. These pathogens include but are not limited to the following:

- *Salmonella* species
- *Shigella dysenteriae*
- *Escherichia coli* O157:H7
- *Vibrio cholerae*
- *Cryptosporidium parvum*

Category C

Category C, the third-highest-priority agents, include emerging pathogens that could be engineered for mass dissemination because of their availability; ease of production and dispersion; and potential for high morbidity, mortality, and public health impact. Preparedness for Category C agents requires ongoing research to improve disease detection, diagnosis, treatment, and prevention. Category C agents include emerging infectious diseases such as Nipah virus and hantavirus.

Table 54 summarizes the information contained in the current CDC fact sheets on known bioterrorism agents.

Biological Incident Response Plan

Chapter 7 describes general principles that apply to disaster planning for natural hazards or technological events. Tasks related to threats from biological agents that require similar preparation include interorganizational coordination, sharing information, resource management, triage, casualty distribution, using the media to communicate to the public, and patient tracking. Because of the potential for the rapid spread of disease, however, planning to mitigate the impacts of emerging infections or biological agents relies heavily on skills that are uniquely those of public health and health care systems, and include additional functions that are not normally included in a community's comprehensive emergency plan.

Federal Planning and Response Overview

The federal response to bioterrorism or to a naturally occurring disease outbreak with a known or novel pathogen is found in the Biological Incident Annex (BIA), a document which supplements the National Response Framework. BIA describes federal actions, roles, and responsibilities in response to a human disease outbreak of known or unknown origin. The federal actions described in BIA can occur whether or not there has been a presidential Robert T. Stafford Disaster Relief and Emergency Assistance Act of 1988 (Stafford Act) declaration or the secretary of Health and Human Services has declared a public health emergency. The response actions in the BIA include detection and assessment of threat through disease surveillance and environmental monitoring, procedures for identifying and notifying the population(s) at risk, laboratory testing, procedures for joint investigation and response, controlling any possible epidemic, augmenting local public health and medical services, and recovery activities.

Table 54. Bioterrorism Agent Summary

	Inhalational Anthrax	Brucellosis	Botulism	Tularemia	Pneumonic Plague	Smallpox	Viral Hemorrhagic Fever
Infective dose	8000-50,000 spores	10-100 organisms	0.001 g/kg (type A)	10-50 organisms	<100 organisms	10-100 particles	1-10 particles
Incubation	1-6 days	5-60 days	6 hours to 10 days	1-21 days	2-3 days	7-17 days	4-21 days
Duration	3-5 days	Weeks to months	24-72 hours	~2 weeks	1-6 days	~4 weeks	7-16 days
Mortality untreated	~100%	~5%*	1st case 25% Subsequent cases 4% Overall 5-10%	33%	40-70%	*Variola minor:* <1% *Variola major:* 20-50%	53-88%
Mortality treated	~40%	<1%	1st case 25% Subsequent cases 4% Overall 5-10%	<4%	5%	*Variola minor:* <1% *Variola major:* 20-50%	53-88%
Person-to-person transmission†	No	No	No	No	Yes (high)	Yes (high)	Yes (moderate)
Isolation precautions‡	Standard	Standard	Standard	Standard	Droplet§	Airborne§	Airborne and contact§

(continued on next page)

Table 54. (continued)

	Inhalational Anthrax	Brucellosis	Botulism	Tularemia	Pneumonic Plague	Smallpox	Viral Hemorrhagic Fever
Persistence	40 years in soil	10 weeks in water/soil	Weeks in food/water	Months in moist soil	1 year in soil	Very stable	Unstable

Adapted from National Center for Preparedness, Detection, and Control of Infectious Diseases, Division of Bioterrorism Preparedness and Response. 2007. General Fact Sheets on Specific Bioterrorism Agents. Atlanta, GA: Centers for Disease Control and Prevention. Available at: http://www.bt.cdc.gov/bioterrorism/factsheets.asp.

*Endocarditis accounts for the majority of brucellosis-related deaths.

†For inhalational anthrax, brucellosis, botulism, or tularemia, no evidence of person-to-person transmission exists; for pneumonic plague, for 72 hours following initiation of appropriate antimicrobial therapy or until sputum culture is negative; for smallpox, approximately 3 weeks, which usually corresponds with the initial appearance of skin lesions through their final disappearance, though most infections during the first week of rash via inhalation of virus released from oropharyngeal-lesion secretions of the index case; for viral hemorrhagic fever, varies with virus but at minimum, all of the duration of illness and for Ebola/Marburg, transmission via semen may occur up to 7 weeks after clinical recovery.

‡Graner JS. 1996. Guidelines for isolation precautions in hospitals. The Hospital Infection Control Practices Advisory Committee. *Infect Control Hosp Epidemiol.* 17:53–80; and *Am J Infect Control.* 24:24–52.

§In addition to standard precautions that apply to all patients.

Planning Assumptions

A biological incident may be identified in multiple jurisdictions concurrently causing public health and medical emergencies at numerous sites. Contemporaneous biological incidents require a highly coordinated response between numerous agencies at all levels of government and with the private sector across many jurisdictions. The biological incident may also affect other countries, necessitating extensive coordination with the international health community. Finally, local officials may be the first to identify the threat or disease outbreak.

Federal Response

HHS leads the federal effort for the public health and emergency medical planning, and the response to a biological terrorism attack or naturally occurring outbreak. This outbreak could result from either a known or novel pathogen, including an emerging infectious disease. HHS also provides guidance on the proper handling of materials related to a disease outbreak, and collaborates with other federal departments and agencies to determine the level of public health and medical response required. If environmental contamination occurs, HHS also collaborates with the U.S. Environmental Protection Agency. The Department of Homeland Security coordinates all nonmedical activities, and the Federal Bureau of Investigation (FBI) coordinates the investigation of any suspected criminal activities. In addition, for a significant outbreak of zoonotic disease or human food-borne pathogen, HHS collaborates with the U.S. Department of Agriculture (USDA). Finally, the Laboratory Response Network (LRN) tests samples for the presence of biological threat agents and the original samples may be sent to the CDC for confirmation of LRN analyses.

Once notified that there is a credible threat of a biological incident or a disease outbreak, HHS assembles the agency partners who provide support under Emergency Support Function 8. Officials from the impacted jurisdiction(s) are involved in the coordination of assessment and response activities. Their task is to assess the situation and determine the appropriate public health and medical actions. An investigation into intentional biological threats or incidents will likely require the initiation of a joint criminal and epidemiological investigation. The FBI would coordinate criminal investigation activities with appropriate state, local and federal partner agencies, such as DHS, HHS, and USDA.

The first task following notification is to identify the affected population and the geographic scope of the incident. Figure 6 shows the flow of communication when the public health system is the first to learn that a bioterrorism event has occurred. The local public health system initiates appropriate measures for everyone affected, including first responders and other workers engaged in incident-related activities. These measures may include mass vaccination or prophylaxis for populations at risk but not yet exposed, including exposure from secondary transmission or through environmental contact. The public health and medical response also includes the following:

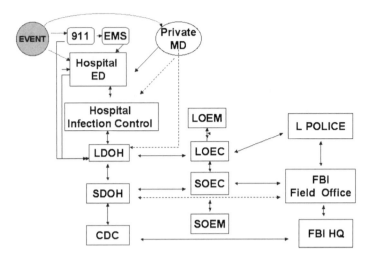

Figure 6. When Medicine or Public Health Identifies an Event

CDC = Centers for Disease Control and Prevention; **ED** = emergency department; **EMS** = Emergency Medical Services; **FBI** = Federal Bureau of Investigation; **HQ** = headquarters; **L Police** = local police; **LDOH** = local Department of Health; **LOEC** = local Emergency Operations Center; **MD** = medical doctor; **LOEM** = local Office of Emergency Management; **SDOH** = state Department of Health; **SOEC** = state Emergency Operations Center; **SOEM** = state Office of Emergency Management.

- Targeted epidemiological investigation (e.g., contact tracing)
- Dissemination of key safety information and necessary medical precautions
- Intensified syndromic surveillance with health care settings, provider offices, laboratory test orders, school absences, over-the-counter pharmacy sales, unusual increase in sick animals, wildlife deaths, or decreased commercial fish yields
- Organization and potential deployment of federal public health and medical response assets (e.g., personnel, medical, and veterinary supplies, SNS, and the National Veterinary Stockpile)

Controlling the Epidemic

HHS will assist public health and medical authorities with epidemic surveillance and coordination in the affected region and will assess whether increased surveillance is needed in locales not initially involved in the outbreak. If necessary, HHS will notify public health officials in the additional jurisdictions.

HHS makes recommendations regarding the need for isolation, quarantine, or shelter in place to prevent the spread of disease. Using the legal authorities of a state or locality, the governor of an affected state implements isolation, quarantine, or social-distancing requirements. Under tribal legal authorities, the leader of a recognized tribe may also order a curfew, isolation, social distancing, and quarantine. Federal actions to prevent interstate spread are authorized in Title 42 of the U.S. Code, 42 CFR Parts 70 and 71, and 21 CFR Part 1240.

Although DHS coordinates the release of public messages regarding a biological incident, public health and medical messages to the public should be communicated by a recognized health authority (e.g., the U.S. surgeon general). Table 55 lists the numerous agencies that cooperate in responding to a biological incident.

Regional Planning

Regional planning can improve a community's response in preventing the spread of disease. Regional agreements should specify how coordination will work, including roles, chain of command, reimbursement, distribution of scarce resources,

Table 55. Cooperating Agencies in a Biological Incident

Department of Agriculture

Department of Commerce

Department of Defense

Department of Energy

Department of Homeland Security

Department of the Interior

Department of Justice

Department of Labor

Department of State

Department of Transportation

Department of Veterans Affairs

Environmental Protection Agency

General Services Administration

U.S. Agency for International Development

U.S. Postal Service

Red Cross

Adapted from Federal Emergency Management Agency (FEMA). 2008. Biological Incident Annex, National Response Framework. Washington, DC: FEMA. Available at: http://www.fema.gov/pdf/emergency/nrf/nrf_BiologicalIncidentAnnex.pdf.

information management strategies, and the maintenance, inventory, and supply of response equipment.

Following a bioterrorism attack, a community needs the following:

An emergency management program: A comprehensive plan, coordination with emergency management and health sectors, training, and drills

Personnel: Clinicians, public health officials, logisticians, and pharmacists

Material: Pharmaceuticals, isolation facilities, sites for mass vaccination, PPE, decontamination showers, and supplies with backup for mass care

Monitoring and providing information: Prevention guidelines, home care instructions for patients, and information regarding characteristics of the infectious agent to aid decision-making about quarantine, isolation, social distancing, and evacuation

Communication system: Redundant equipment tested regularly

Security: Identification badges, restricted vendor access, security patrol, access control for entire facility, mail handling procedures

Financial support for each of the above

At the local or regional level, public health preparation for a biological incident can be modeled after planning paradigms for pandemic influenza because many biological agents present as flulike illness. A planning committee should be established with key representatives from the health and public health, emergency management, and public safety sectors. This committee is responsible for establishing an overall command and control structure (see Chapter 3 on incident command); overseeing the prevention, planning, response, and recovery activities; and ensuring that a jurisdiction's plan is developed, reviewed, and revised when needed. Because the response to a biological incident will require cooperation from a broad variety of community groups, it is important to identify who the stakeholders are and solicit their support. Participation from the community should involve personnel knowledgeable about communicable disease and immunization, hospitals, laboratories, specialists in information systems, the media, citizen band radio groups, social service agencies, the Red Cross, law enforcement, fire and emergency medical services, the medical community, the medical examiner and coroner, funeral directors, local utilities, local veterinary facilities capable of handling affected animals, and local government officials, among others. The planning committee will ask that stakeholders develop the components of the plan for which they have expertise.

Local health departments interested in obtaining "Project Public Health Ready" recognition need to develop comprehensive all-hazards preparedness and response plans, develop the capacity to respond within their workforce, and demonstrate the department's readiness through exercises or response to actual events. Each year's planning guidance for local public health agencies is available online from the National Association of County and City Health Officials (NACCHO). (The Project Public Health Ready is available at http://www.naccho.org/topics/emergency/pphr/index.cfm).

Communities or regions should plan for three levels of response to an incident involving biological agents. Examples of this three-tiered approach include separate plans for incidents with up to 100 victims, for incidents with 100 to 10,000 victims, and for incidents with more than 10,000 victims. An important part of each plan will be the logistics of obtaining and distributing vaccines and antibiotics. Plans should identify the location of local or federal depositories, designate distribution sites, and establish priorities for distribution. Stockpiles will most likely be flown into commercial airports or trucked from private vendors. A protocol must be established for off-loading antibiotics and supplies, and a site located for repackaging the materials into smaller units. In addition, a system must be established for ensuring that the antibiotics are used before their shelf life expires. If a push pack is predeployed in anticipation of an event, permission is required to open it.

Planning for surge capacity[4] should consider higher estimates for the morbidity and mortality resulting from a release of highly contagious agents such as smallpox or pneumonic plague. (Surge capacity planning is discussed in Chapter 7.) Attempts should be made to direct patients to alternative sites and away from hospitals which could become quickly overwhelmed. To assure adequate staffing, prepare contingency plans for replacements for essential personnel, such as reassignment of personnel from nonessential programs within the local agencies, or calling up retired personnel or private-sector personnel with relevant expertise. Establish a protocol for the protection of public safety personnel early in the outbreak through inoculation or the distribution of PPE. Further, to ensure the maintenance of a healthy workforce, those wearing PPE in order to decontaminate victims can only remain in PPE for about 15 minutes. Multiple teams need to be trained and these responders should be required to prehydrate themselves. Although estimates vary widely for those who might seek care because they think they are sick, a comprehensive plan should arrange to triage a large number of unaffected patients who are the worried well. In major metropolitan regions, a conservative estimated ratio of worried well to affected patients has been as high as 30 to 1, yet more than 30,000 people nationwide received prophylaxis for anthrax in 2001, far exceeding this ratio. Large numbers of potential patients would require the rapid establishment of alternative care facilities. Because patients have been found to seek health care from locations at which they regularly receive care, alternative care facilities should be set up as close in proximity to hospitals as possible.

Public Health Community Plan for Biological Incident Response

Many of the activities for response to a novel influenza virus or other emerging disease and to a bioterrorism attack are similar. In addition to a description of a unified command and control, a management structure, and responsibilities (including protocols for coordinating activities of the health sector with those of the emergency management sector), a public health community plan for biological incidents includes the following:

---

[4]The CDC has developed software to assist local planners in estimating the potential impact of large flu outbreaks that can be adapted to planning for bioterrorism events. The software can be downloaded online (available at http://www.2.cdc.gov/od/fluaid/default.htm).

- Protocols for large-scale outbreak investigation and infection control which detail duties of personnel
- Notification and response protocols for suspected and confirmed cases
- Protocols for field decontamination and transfer to hospitals
- Assessment of staffing and maintenance of health care and essential community functions during periods of high absenteeism, including outreach criteria, guidelines for worker safety, and training needs
- Protocols on the handling of laboratory specimens to ensure rapid diagnostic testing including collection, transfer and laboratory confirmation of samples, safe disposal, labeling, and appropriate chain of custody of samples related to suspected terrorism and referrals to reference or national laboratories, as well as whether laboratory reports require the attention of the local public health department
- Assessment of facility needs, type/availability/location of drugs, vaccines, beds, and equipment
- Stockpiling and monitoring of expiration dates of pharmaceutical inventories for a range of potential agents
- Plans for mass medical care
- Resolution of legal issues
- Protocols for both external communication to the public and internal communication among those coordinating the response
- Measures to assure environmental decontamination, biosafety, arrangements for mass burials, and mortuary management
- Protocols for management of mental health issues
- Coordination with civic organizations and other volunteers to provide food, medical, and other essential support for persons confined to their homes
- Baseline data with scheduled updates on the following:

  ○ Hospital admissions
  ○ Acute bed occupancy
  ○ ICU bed occupancy
  ○ Emergency room visits for infection
  ○ Ambulatory department utilization
  ○ Influenza-like illness
  ○ Flu cases in patient billing and emergency department visit data
  ○ Unexplained deaths
  ○ Unusual syndromes in ambulatory patients
  ○ 911 calls
  ○ Diarrheal disease
  ○ Weekly sales of antidiarrheal medicine from a regional distributor
  ○ Daily number of stool samples submitted to labs
  ○ Daily incidence of gastrointestinal illness in nursing home populations
  ○ Calls to poison control centers
  ○ Antibiotic and other pharmaceutical supplies
  ○ Total number of respirators
  ○ Workforce and school absenteeism

Initial tasks during an infectious disease emergency include:

- Activate response plan, public health OEC, and ICS
- Interface with appropriate state and federal counterparts
- Activate communications plan: disseminate information on the infectious disease emergency, prevention, and control
- Increase surveillance at hospitals and clinics
- Initiate vaccine/pharmaceutical distribution if appropriate
- Coordinate activities with neighboring jurisdictions
- Notify key government officials and legislators of the need for additional resources where needed

Table 56 summarizes the supplies and antidotes that should be stockpiled and monitored for a response to a range of potential agents.

Defining, Detecting, and Responding to Biological Events

A possible bioterrorism event includes one of the following:

- A single, definitively diagnosed or strongly suspected case of an illness caused by a recognized bioterrorism agent occurring in a patient without a plausible explanation for his or her illness
- A cluster of patients presenting with a similar clinical syndrome with either unusual characteristics (age distribution), or unusually high morbidity or mortality without an obvious etiology or explanation
- An unexplained increase in the incidence of a common syndrome above seasonally expected levels

Table 56. Supplies and Antidotes for Potential Chemical or Biological Warfare Agents

Agent	Supplies Needed
Bacterial agents	Ciproflaxin, doxycycline, penicillin, chloramphenicol, and azithromycin
Botulinum toxin	Mechanical respiratory ventilators and associated supplies
Burn/vesicants	Sterile bandages, intravenous fluids, and broad spectrum antibiotics
Cyanide	Cyanide antidote kits containing amyl nitrate, sodium nitrate, and sodium thiosulfate
Lewisite	British anti-lewisite, nerve agent atropine, pralidoxime chloride, and diazepam
Radiological exposure	Potassium iodide
All	Resuscitation equipment and supplies, vasopressors

A biological event or emerging disease would most likely present as one of the above, with initial detection likely to take place at the local level. Because most agents that could be used for biological agents have incubation periods, an attack may not be apparent until days or even weeks after the attack has occurred. During the early stages of illness, many related diseases have vague, nonspecific symptoms making them difficult to differentiate from numerous naturally occurring diseases. Primary health care providers in the local medical community may be the first to recognize unusual disease caused by a covert attack, with state and local health departments most likely to initiate a communitywide response. A potential biological incident might be a group of patients with a similar clinical syndrome with unusual characteristics, such as age distribution, unusually high morbidity or mortality without obvious explanation for the illness, unusual concurrence of geographic exposure, unusual disease not previously found in the region, a case of inhalation anthrax or smallpox, or unexplained increase in a common syndrome above seasonally expected levels (e.g., cluster flu epidemic in summer with negative virology, food poisoning without a single source).

Veterinarians should be encouraged to report suspicious illness in their patients. The beginning of the West Nile epidemic in the United States was marked by the avian veterinarian at the Bronx Zoo, New York, reporting birds dying around the time that a community physician called the New York City Department of Health and Mental Hygiene about an unusual cluster of meningitis cases.

Because accurate diagnosis of diseases caused by the most likely bioterrorism agents may be delayed because of the initial flulike presentation and the several days needed for positive laboratory identification, public health officials cannot depend on passive surveillance systems. Labor-intensive active surveillance requires outreach and can be costly, but will be essential in identifying when the flu is not "the flu." Flu-like symptoms usually come on suddenly and may include the following:

- High fever
- Headache
- Tiredness/weakness (can be extreme)
- Dry cough
- Sore throat
- Runny nose
- Body or muscle aches
- Diarrhea and vomiting (more common in children)

A full mobilization of public health efforts includes sending suspected samples to reference laboratories for rapid confirmation of bioterrorism agents, deploying active surveillance and epidemiological teams to identify the source of initial exposure (e.g., review charts of suspected patients), ensuring appropriate isolation and universal precautions where indicated, initiating treatment and prophylaxis to reduce morbidity and mortality, assessing geographic spread, identifying unexpected features of the outbreak, and the launching of preestablished communication protocols among many medical community and emergency management agencies and between government and the public. The public health team should be organized to respond to potential biological, chemical, or radiological events and include professionals from multiple disciplines, such as laboratory scientists, emergency management, emergency medical technicians and paramedics, environmental health scientists, epidemiologists, hazardous material response teams, health physicists, industrial hygienists, infectious disease specialists, medical examiners, occupational health physicians, public health laboratory designees, toxicologists, and veterinarians.

An effective surveillance system will be able to rapidly track changes in disease trends, be based on clinical syndromes, and be generated by data that are collected continually, reviewed daily, and remain geographically representative. An alert in these systems prompts an epidemiological investigation to determine if there is an outbreak and to identify the potential microbial etiology and the source of transmission. Sources of data for biological and emerging disease include the following:

- Biosurveillance
- Hospital reports (admissions to ICUs of previously healthy persons with unexplained febrile illnesses)
- Infectious disease and laboratory reports
- Diagnostic categories with trends and unusual patterns from emergency departments
- Outbreaks in institutional settings (e.g., nursing homes)
- Workforce and school absenteeism
- Prescription and over-the-counter medication sales
- Animal outbreaks and deaths
- Police and emergency medical services reports
- Geographic analyses of 911 calls categorized by disease syndrome (e.g., codes for difficulty breathing, respiratory distress, and other markers for influenza-like disease)

Although medical examiner reports are useful, a 2- to 3-day delay often occurs between the time of death and the filing of the death certificate. In addition, it is difficult to identify clusters using death certificates. Optimally, electronic death reporting can be instituted so that this information is more timely. In addition, epidemiologists will want to examine environmental factors such as food, the presence of vectors (e.g., ticks, fleas, flies, rodents, cats, mosquitoes, bats), and trends in animal populations and food crops.

Early detection of a covert release is designed to occur through autonomous detection systems, which include focused active surveillance and diagnostic laboratory testing. In the environmental surveillance system known as BioWatch, vacuum cleaner–like machines, operating both indoors and outdoors, continuously collect air samples. BioWatch may detect the presence of a biological agent in the environment. This detection triggers environmental sampling; samples are tested in public health laboratories 7 days a week. In addition, clinical surveillance is intensified to rule out or confirm an incident. If confirmed, the early detection through environmental surveillance systems such as BioWatch prompts a mobilized response by public health, health care institutions, and law enforcement before too many clinical cases are identified.

Active Surveillance and Epidemiological Investigations

To activate a rapid surveillance, materials must be prepared in advance. Essential tools include preplanned instruments of generic questions designed to determine case and risk exposure, a sampling strategy, a centralized database with fields defined, and a mechanism to call up and deploy teams to conduct the surveillance around the clock. The instrument might pose questions about location of residence and work, usual commuter routes, and a detailed diary of the patient's activities during the incubation period of the suspected agent.

If there is a confirmed bioterrorism event, health departments will be responsible for tracking the cases and performing epidemiological investigations to determine the source and sites of exposure. Public health officials will implement active hospital-based and enhanced passive surveillance, including hard-to-reach populations (such as the homeless), contact tracing similar to that used for measles or syphilis, and coordination with local poison control centers. This information will be essential in determining who else might have been exposed and will require prophylaxis. Epidemiological investigations will help identify the determinants, distribution, and frequency of disease in both human and animal populations. Epidemiology will detect possible vector control requirements and the likelihood of secondary spread. These investigations will be coordinated with neighboring health departments as well as interstate and international agencies.

Mass Medical and Mortuary Care

In addition to baseline surveys that provide information about a community's capacity to care for patients exposed to bioterrorism agents, guidelines are needed for the care of exposed patients. Community care guidelines should include distributing protocols and disease-specific information to the health care community on identifying cases, medical management of those exposed, initiating mass medical care including triage and surge capacity with trained personnel, turning shelters or schools into hospitals, establishing patient isolation in many locations including homes, distributing pharmaceuticals to large numbers of the population, transporting patients, and mortuary care.

Managing the media and keeping the general public accurately informed is a crucial component of a mass care plan. Communication is accomplished with providers through HAN, broadcast alerts, and communication hotlines. Consider establishing three separate hotlines: one for physicians, one for persons requiring the services at a point of distribution (POD) center, and one for the general public with staff being given prepared scripts to answer questions. Use the media to issue warnings to the public and for public service announcements on how to prevent exposures and distinguish symptoms, control measures, who may need antibiotics, and local effects of disease.[5]

---

[5]The CDC has established notification procedures for state and local public health officials, available at http://emergency.cdc.gov/ eMContact/Protocols.asp.

A plan for mass antibiotic prophylaxis or immunization of the population should include the following:

- Description of the decision-making process that would be used to initiate a mass immunization campaign
- Method of identifying the affected population
- Adjustable distribution plans to provide vaccine or antibiotics to high-priority target groups and the general population where there is a severe vaccine shortage, moderate vaccine shortage, or an adequate vaccine supply
- Plans for moving a pharmaceutical stockpile to distribution points
- Designated personnel who will manage the arrival, distribution, and local dissemination of vaccines and antibiotics, ensure the smooth flow of clients into POD, and translate when needed, including sign language
- Plans for the storage, transportation, and handling of pharmaceuticals; one refrigerated tractor trailer would be adequate to handle the storage of 12 million doses of vaccine
- Clinical algorithm and preprinted instruction sheets for different prophylactic regimens, including procedures for immunization of differing age groups
- Procedures for record keeping and strict accountability, including a log for recording the manufacturer, lot number, expiration date, and quantity of vaccine received and distributed in compliance with federal vaccine administration guidelines
- Plans for the availability of protective clothing by personnel
- Plans for ensuring community participation
- Development of information sheets in all relevant languages (templates for influenza are available online at http://www.dhss.mo.gov/InterventionMICA/Immunizations/CampaignsandPromotions/index_5.html; the Immunization Action Coalition is also a useful resource, available at http://www.immunize.org)
- Regional coordination of proposed pharmaceutical distribution plan
- Procedures for monitoring compliance with medication protocols, symptoms or illness attributable to the vaccine, illness following immunization attributable to vaccine failure, and adverse events

Hospitals

For both pandemic influenza and releases of biological agents, hospitals should prepare for a dramatic increase in patients visiting the emergency department and requiring hospitalization. Even a mild pandemic could produce a dramatic increase in demand for inpatient and ICU beds and ventilators. With high attack rates, assume staff absenteeism will be high, resulting in limited availability of critical resources. Hospital preparations should address the following:

- Surge capacity
- Management of triage, volunteers, and home care
- Infection control guidelines
- Resource allocation
- Mass mortality
- Support for staff and their families
- Management and tracking of hospital resources

Although hospitals are required to have a disaster plan to be accredited by The Joint Commission, a sequence of stand-alone facility plans do not prepare a community to respond to a biological incident. The hospitals in a community or region must coordinate their efforts, including the transport of patients, the ordering and stockpiling of supplies and pharmaceuticals, communications during the event, handling of bodies, and other major tasks. The coordination of resources is all the more important as more hospitals practice "just-in-time" delivery of supplies and pharmaceuticals. Designating the delivery of services to certain hospitals in advance (e.g., limiting high-cost specialty care to those hospitals with the most experience in treating severely injured patients) and formalizing protocols for coordination between prehospital and hospital care (e.g., establishing protocols for first responders to rapidly transport patients) have been shown to contribute to improved patient outcomes. The regional plan should ensure that all hospitals participate in multihospital drills.

Hospitals plans for responding to a large infectious disease outbreak include provisions for triaging large numbers of patients in the emergency department, patient decontamination and patient overflow, increasing bed capacity, calling in additional staff, and establishing isolation units on short notice, including airborne, contact, and universal precautions. Staff should be educated about their specific roles in the hospital incident command system (HICS) and instructed to continue with their regular duties if they are not involved in the hospital's own incident command structure. Hospital staff should know whom to notify if they are the first to learn about the event, what questions to ask (e.g., where is it and what is happening), and how to use universal precautions. Multilingual information sheets and consent forms should be prepared. In addition, instructional sheets on the methodology for administering vaccines should be ready for use.

Hospital plans establish the medical protocols that will be followed, the stockpiling and distribution of medications or vaccines, and whether to set up community-based mass prophylaxis clinics. If a patient presents where the providers suspect an infectious disease, at a minimum the emergency department protocol should include the following:

- Contacting the department of health with specifics of the case
- Rapid screening of individuals in waiting room
- Checking for supply of isolation equipment, particulate respirators, isolation rooms for negative pressure
- Triage and isolation in negative-pressure rooms for those with known contact with the index case or with fever or suspicious rash
- Contacting hospital infection control and disease experts
- Standard precautions, including fit-tested N95 or N100 masks
- Rapid screening and gathering of contact information for all in waiting area

Point of Distribution

When large numbers of persons require prophylaxis by medication or vaccine, it is necessary to establish a POD. POD activities include registration, triage, taking swab samples, medical evaluation or screening, dispensing antibiotics or vaccine, reassuring the worried well, briefing clients about the infectious disease and POD operations, collecting information for surveillance or investigative purposes, transferring persons to a medical facility (when needed), counseling, managing client flow, and maintaining security. Preplanning is essential because once an event occurs necessitating mass distribution of medication, there is little time between the decision to open a POD and the initiation of operations. Prior arrangements should be made with other community agencies and medical volunteers so that issues of credentialing, medical-legal responsibility, and reimbursement are worked out in advance.

Experience, such as that of the New York City Department of Health and Mental Hygiene, suggests that the services within PODs may be organized or function differently depending on the type and scope of event. Allocate sufficient time to ensure that supplies have arrived and trained staff are ready before opening a POD. Adequate staffing is essential, including a dedicated physician in charge, liaison, supplies coordinator, and clinic manager. To provide antibiotic prophylaxis to up to 10,000 persons in 72 hours, approximately 50 to 55 persons per shift are needed for round-the-clock coverage in 12-hour shifts. In selecting a site for a POD, choose a place convenient to members of the community who have to use it and be large enough to distribute antibiotics or vaccine to the necessary population. To dispense antibiotics to 500 to 10,000 persons over a 72–hour period, a space of at least 2500 square feet is needed. Establishing good communication is critical from the incident command center to POD, from the health department to the public, and from the health department to community medical providers. When events do not indicate immunizing or prophylaxing large segments of the population, it will be necessary to establish a plan for triaging the worried well. Figures 7 and 8 show schemata of a model POD layout.

When an event involves bioterrorism—a criminal act—law enforcement agencies require separate space for investigation away from the POD to minimize concerns about confidentiality. The FBI and CDC developed a guide which describes the role of public health and law enforcement in these investigations.

Point of Distribution Functional Areas

A typical POD includes space for these types of functions (Figures 7 and 8):

> **Screening station:** Verify eligibility; provide writing tools, information sheets, epidemiologic interview forms, law enforcement interview forms, and medical record forms
>
> **Client registration:** Logbook or spreadsheet on a laptop, or data entry screens and wireless connections to an on-site server
>
> **Triage area:** Assess if persons go to the dispensing station, need to be medically evaluated, or need further evaluation and transfer to a health care facility; provide printed material (e.g., medication fact sheets, epidemiological interviews); staff at triage: physicians, nurses, and physician assistants
>
> **Briefings** on risks of exposure, symptoms, and side effects of antibiotics

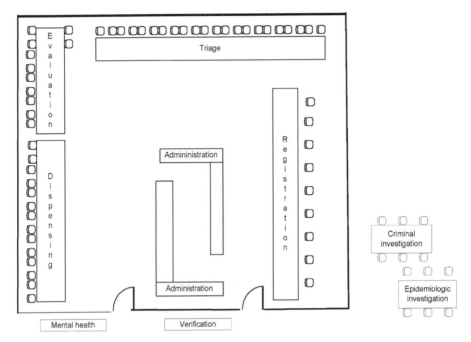

Figure 7. Template POD Layout: Reception Area

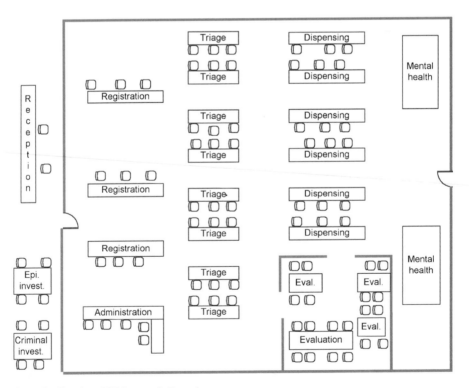

Figure 8. Template POD Layout: Delivery Area

Specimens collection as needed (e.g., nasal swabs)

Dispensing station for antibiotic distribution. Staff: nurses, physicians, pharmacists

Counseling staff: mental health, medical advisors, and public health educators at POD entrance, near POD exit, and as consultation for referring persons to hotlines and Web sites

Security at the entrance, exit, and pharmaceutical supplies

Clerical area for medical charting

Space for filling out forms and conducting interviews

The box below lists key information collected in a medical chart at a POD.

POD MEDICAL CHART

Use a two-sided, one-sheet, self-administered questionnaire as a medical chart, limited to information relevant to the rapid distribution of antibiotics (similar medical record for pediatrics) which includes the following:

Contact information:
    Address
    Telephone numbers
    Emergency contacts
Signed consent form for testing and treatment
Brief medical history:
    Presence or absence of current symptoms
    Relevant drug allergies
    Use of specific medications known to interact with drugs of choice
    (e.g., doxycycline or ciprofloxacin for anthrax) and pregnancy status
Place to document:
    Specimen collection
    Dispensing and receipt (or refusal) of antibiotics/vaccine
    Antibiotic/vaccine lot numbers

Adapted from Blank S, Moskin LC, Zucker JR. 2003. An ounce of prevention is a ton of work: mass antibiotic prophylaxis for anthrax: New York City, 2001. *Emerg Infect Dis.* (serial online) June. Available at: http://www.cdc.gov/ncidod/eid/vol9no6/03-0118.htm.

Laboratory Response Network

The LRN was established in 1999 by the Association of Public Health Laboratories, the CDC, and the FBI to assist in the U.S. response to biological and chemical terrorism. The LRN is now an integrated national and international network of about 169 biological and 54 chemical laboratories with the capacity to respond to acts of CBW, emerging infectious diseases, and other public health threats and emergencies. These laboratories produce high-confidence test results that are the basis for threat analysis and intervention by both public health and law enforcement authorities.

LRN includes the following types of labs:

- Federal (the CDC, U.S. Army Medical Research Institute for Infectious Diseases [USAMRIID], and other federally run facilities)
- State and local public health laboratories
- Military
- Food testing (the Food and Drug Administration and the USDA, state food testing laboratories)
- Environmental (testing water and other environmental samples)
- Clinical (local hospitals and other larger clinical laboratories)
- Veterinary (the USDA [animal testing], veterinary diagnostic laboratories)
- International (labs in Canada, the United Kingdom, Australia, and Mexico)

The LRN supports surveillance and epidemiological investigations by identifying disease, providing direct and reference services, and conducting environmental, rapid, and specialized testing. Five of the major threats (botulism, plague, anthrax, tularemia, and poxvirus illnesses) occur naturally in the United States, and specimens for these diseases are routinely evaluated by public health laboratories. In addition, the standard techniques for detecting bacterial agents (gram stain, culture on selective media, visual colony morphology, growth after heat shock, and confirmatory methods using phage and direct immunofluorescence) are well recognized for establishing definitive diagnoses. Methods such as isolation in cell culture, inoculation of animals, direct fluorescence, and electron microscopy are considered definitive methods in virology.

The personnel who work in public health laboratories are highly skilled and familiar with following complex identification algorithms. The procedures used can be readily adapted to environmental samples that might be collected after an overt threat, or in the attribution of the source of a sample. Further, the public health laboratories are all certified under the Clinical Laboratory Improvement Act of 1967 as employing appropriate quality assurance and quality control procedures. Although definitive identification requires a few days, preliminary results can be available in hours. In particular, the minimum response time for a definitive negative result with a rapidly growing organism such as anthrax may be 16 hours. Slower growing organisms or complex procedures may take 48 hours or more. Furthermore, many methods require a fixed facility with traditional lab techniques not readily adaptable to a field situation.

The Laboratory Response Network for Biological Terrorism Preparedness has three levels of organization designated as sentinel, reference, or national. Designation depends on the types of tests a laboratory can perform and how it handles infectious agents to protect workers and the public. Membership in the LRN is not automatic. State lab directors determine the criteria and whether public health labs in their states should be included in the network. In addition to regulatory requirements, prospective reference labs must have the equipment, trained personnel, properly designed facilities, and must demonstrate testing accuracy.

Sentinel labs (formerly Level A) represent the thousands of hospital-based clinical labs that are on the front lines. In an unannounced or covert bioterrorism attack, sentinel labs could be the first to identify a suspicious specimen and screen out a presumptive case during routine patient care. A sentinel laboratory's responsibility is to recognize, rule out, and refer a suspicious sample to the right reference lab. Laboratory personnel use Bio Safety Level 2 (BSL) techniques for agents that can cause human disease, but with limited potential for human transmission.[6]

Reference labs (formerly Levels B and C) can perform tests to detect and confirm the presence of a threat agent. Approximately 90% of the U.S. population lives within 100 miles of a reference lab. These labs ensure a timely local response in the event of a terrorist incident or other emergency. Rather than having to rely on confirmation from labs at the CDC, reference labs are capable of producing conclusive results. Reference labs can be city, county, or major state public health laboratories that perform direct fluorescence or phage testing such as molecular diagnostics. Using BSL 3 techniques for agents that may be transmitted by the respiratory route and can cause serious infection, reference labs have the safety and proficiency to confirm and characterize susceptibility and to probe, type, and perform toxigenicity testing.

National laboratories (formerly Level D) are part of the CDC and USAMRIID and can perform research on and development of new techniques that are disseminated to other levels of the network. National labs have unique resources to handle highly infectious agents and are responsible for definitive high-level characterization (seeking evidence of molecular chimeras) or identifying specific agent strains. The CDC and USAMRIID national labs, operating at BSL 4, handle the most dangerous agents which have the highest risk of life-threatening disease, are transmitted by as aerosols and for which there is no vaccine or treatment.

If a covert event occurs that is not recognized immediately, the incidence of disease in the community would trigger public health to submit samples to the laboratory and report to the surveillance network. With an announced threat or an overt event, the situation would be reported to the FBI, which would in turn determine what level of laboratory is required and transport samples to the nearest appropriate laboratory resource in the network. Figure 9 shows the chain of events if law enforcement is the first to recognize an event.

Legal Issues

As legal authority varies from state to state, it is necessary for public health to investigate specific state laws regarding emergency preparedness. Legal questions that may arise regarding the powers of the health commissioner upon a declaration of emergency must be clarified and include the following:

---

[6]Laboratory personnel use work practices and safety equipment in a facility designed to minimize exposures to infectious agents. This combination of containment practices is known as Bio-Safety Level (BSL). The CDC has specified 4 levels of containment which range from the lowest (BSL level 1) to the highest (BSL level 4).

- The ability to remove legal barriers relative to dispensing of medicines
- Licensing of out-of-state physicians and nurses
- Transfer of patients between hospitals during the emergency
- Emergency credentialing of providers who are not credentialed through the federal response
- Isolation, quarantine, social distancing, blockade, zone perimeters, requisitions, curfews, governance, restricted access, and due process under different scenarios
- The power to define diseases deemed dangerous to public health
- Control and prevention
- Reportable disease
- The liability of hospitals in the reporting of information
- The process of declaring a state of emergency in a locale

Public health authorities should identify who has the authority, what criteria must be met, what legal mechanism must be followed, and who is responsible for enforcement. Once the legal mechanism is defined, contingency plans to quarantine patients and protocols for implementation and enforcement should be established. Finally, although the Health Insurance Portability and Accountability Act Privacy Rule regulates how "covered entities" use and disclose "protected health information" (PHI), PHI disclosures without patient authorization may occur if the disclosure was required by law, authorized by the individual, for treatment purposes, or to legally authorized public health entities for public health activities. Public health activities include surveillance, investigation, and intervention.

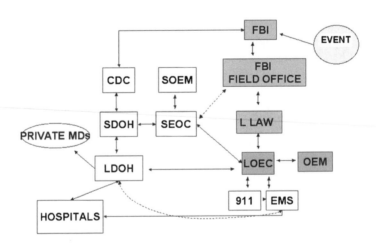

Figure 9. When Law Enforcement Identifies an Event

CDC = Centers for Disease Control and Prevention; EMS = Emergency Medical Services; FBI = Federal Bureau of Investigation; L Law = local law enforcement; LDOH = local Department of Health; LOEC = local Emergency Operations Center; MDs = medical doctors; OEM = Office of Emergency Management; SDOH = state Department of Health; SOEC = state Emergency Operations Center; SOEM = state Office of Emergency Management.

Chapter 12

Public Health Considerations in Recovery and Reconstruction

D isaster preparedness plans must also consider the long-term process of recovery and reconstruction. This chapter examines the three postimpact phases of disaster and the priorities in planning for each. Particular attention is paid to providing services immediately postimpact, such as shelters, and caring for those with functional and medical needs.

Public Health Role

- Restore the public health and health care delivery infrastructures
- Organize communitywide programs for delivery of health care and public health services, including functional needs and medical shelters
- Provide community education to enhance public awareness (e.g., injury control), aid community adjustment, form the basis for future disaster mitigation, and educate the community about likely health risks and how to deal with them
- Assess health needs in the community to determine necessary services to meet the long-term physical and behavioral health needs of affected populations

Principles of Disaster Recovery and Reconstruction

The federal government is obligated to assist states and localities as provided for in the Robert T. Stafford Disaster Relief and Emergency Assistance Act of 1988 (Stafford Act). The National Response Framework includes an annex, Emergency Support Function 14: Long-Term Community Recovery Annex (available at http://www.fema.gov/pdf/emergency/nrf/nrf-esf-14.pdf), that describes the federal role in recovery and designates the lead agency for each task. With federal support, local people must set the priorities and direct the use of resources.

Factors that influence recovery planning and policy include the accuracy of needs assessments, intense pressure by citizens to rebuild as soon as possible, the amount of time and resources allocated to problem solving and recovery, and the many and often conflicting preferences of affected groups. Community participation is essential for planning the recovery and reconstruction phase, because local residents better understand their own needs and the problems that create those needs. Residents should be the direct beneficiaries of recovery projects, since they will be responsible for monitoring development that continues after relief workers have left.

In planning each activity, aid agencies and the community must consider both short- and long-term positive and negative impacts. For example, aid should be provided in such a way that allows people to stay at home when possible, continue their normal lives, and resume normal activities when possible. Integrated recovery programs may include work schemes to repair community facilities that pay residents cash to replace lost possessions. This injection of money will stimulate local markets and help speed recovery. To aid recovery further, loans or grants can be made available to small businesses.

Phases of Recovery and Reconstruction

Three phases categorize the types of activities which occur postimpact in the affected community: emergency, transition or recovery, and reconstruction. During the emergency phase, activity focuses on saving lives through search and rescue, first aid, emergency medical assistance, and overall disaster assessment. Efforts immediately begin to repair critical facilities, restore communications and transportation networks, and, in some cases, to evacuate residents from areas still vulnerable to further disaster.

During the transition or recovery phase, people return to work, repair damaged buildings and infrastructure, and initiate other actions that allow the community to return to normal as soon as possible. Victims begin their emotional recovery and some may experience depression or post-traumatic stress disorder (see Chapter 8). External assistance is provided in the form of cash and credit. Construction projects and other types of job creation are the most appropriate types of aid.

During the recovery phase, priorities include the assurance of adequate shelter, medical services, infrastructure, utilities, business, economic activity, and social networks. Congress set restrictions on reimbursements available to states and localities after a disaster. In the event that an exception is made to previously set limits, it is very important that agencies involved in response and recovery can account for all resources lost in a disaster and all funds spent in recovery, regardless of how miniscule the amounts. Without documentation, opportunities for reimbursement may be lost.

The reconstruction phase is characterized by physical reordering of communications, utilities, roads, and the general physical environment. Residents repair or rebuild their housing, and agricultural activities resume. Reconstruction may span years, especially for the restoration of housing and other buildings.

The timing of each phase varies with the nature of the disaster, its location, and the capacity of the affected community to mend. This process often occurs in four stages, which are not necessarily sequential. Different parts of a community can be moving forward at different paces, depending on the extent of devastation and resources available. The stages are as follows:

- Emergency response (i.e., debris removal and provision of temporary housing)
- Restoration of public services (i.e., electricity, water, and telephone)
- Replacement and reconstruction of capital stock

- Initiation of improvements and reconstruction that stimulate economic growth and local development

Factors affecting recovery time include the environment (e.g., risk of secondary disasters, availability of communications, general economy); the economy (cash flow, cost and supply of materials); technical aspects (availability of technical assistance, existence of conflicts in technical advice, ability to reuse salvaged materials, process of dealing with irrelevant aid); politics (public rejection of recovery plans, bureaucracy in government and other responding agencies, efforts by interest groups to channel aid to rebuild their areas first); and community motivation.

Postdisaster Assessments

Needs assessments conducted postimpact provide the information required to begin recovery. Emergency needs are more apparent than are long-term needs, and long-term needs vary over time. Communication about the findings and the next steps must be established between responding jurisdictions and organizations and those affected by the disaster.

The first step in such an assessment is to assess community capacities and vulnerabilities, including physical environment (such as intact infrastructure and resources), social conditions (such as existing organizations and support networks), and the population's attitude toward recovery and their motivation to recover. Needs are determined by visiting representative areas, talking to selected groups in affected communities, and conducting rapid health assessments (see Chapter 5). When possible, needs should be quantified (e.g., percentage of families without running water, number of patients served by pharmacies that were destroyed), even if the number is determined by extrapolation. Public health workers should highlight gaps in the community's emergency response which impact public health and health care services. Once the baseline capacities and vulnerabilities have been assessed, this information must be continuously gathered and reevaluated to determine progress toward recovery and identify what remains to be done.

Reestablishing Local Business and Economic Activity

When reestablishing lost infrastructure, communities should take the opportunity to make improvements and reduce future vulnerability to disaster. Local efforts can influence the pace, location, type, density, design, and cost of redevelopment. In addition to providing guidance on disaster-resistant building techniques, community leaders can aid reconstruction by ensuring optimal urban planning, permitting families to rebuild housing according to their tastes and incomes, and financing the delivery of electricity, water, and sewer lines.

A major disaster usually causes a decline in income and employment, thus reducing the resources of the population at the time of its greatest need. This income reduction reduces the tax base when increased government resources are most needed. Jobs, economic activity, and reestablishing schools give people a sense of return to normalcy. Jobs, economic growth, and housing repair influence long-term recovery more than do immediate disaster relief efforts.

Social Environment

To aid in social recovery, local leaders must be familiar with basic family structure, economic patterns, governmental structure, religious affiliations, customs and practices, and power relationships within their community before disaster strikes. Each community has a variety of internal social structures that help individuals and families through difficult periods. Coping mechanisms exist at the level of the individual, family, community, and region. Effective intervention after a disaster requires an understanding of these coping mechanisms.

Strengthening horizontal community ties provides a means of redevelopment and preparation for future disasters. In some cases, the disaster may provide an opportunity for the community to work together in ways it previously has not, resulting in a stronger community—and a stronger sense of community—than existed before the crisis.

Emphasis on reestablishing community means that where options exist, leaders should choose the option that strengthens or maintains the community. For example, disaster recovery plans should avoid building camps or large shelters whenever possible and instead provide aid in such a way that people can stay at home or in their neighborhoods, which will allow residents to rely on preexisting social connections and promote resumption of normal activities.

Incorporating Disaster Preparedness Into Recovery

Vulnerability assessments require a review of land use based on postdisaster needs. Vulnerability assessments can also be used to predict the effects (both positive and negative) of redevelopment by projecting the impact of anticipated changes. The assessment of vulnerabilities should be used to avoid or reduce negative outcomes from future disasters. Encouraging communities to rebuild and commit to their communities in the long term requires attracting investment and demonstrating that the community has worked to reduce the negative impact if disaster recurs. For example, if housing is needed following a flood, a vulnerability assessment can tell officials where to build new houses to reduce the risk of damage from future flooding. Reconstruction should use improved designs and standards that reduce the vulnerability of structures. Reconstruction may also involve the erection of structures to reduce future mortality, such as hurricane shelters, and to detect possible events, such as early warning systems.

Shelters

While securing permanent shelter is a top priority, postimpact shelter may be provided as emergency or temporary housing. Emergency or temporary shelters should be located in a facility capable of withstanding a disaster and that has communication capabilities, power, running water, and an area to care for those who have functional needs. The ideal general population shelter would have separate zones for registering residents, conducting physical examinations, offering mental and behavioral health treatment, childcare, sleeping, eating, and recreation. All shelters must comply with state and local codes and all standards related to accessibility. When selecting a shelter location, if the chosen facility has features that are inaccessible, a plan must be in place to make the shelter accessible before use.

When establishing an emergency shelter, the Red Cross allocates 40 square feet per person for sheltering longer than 72 hours. Routes through the shelter and around cots must be accessible to people using wheelchairs, crutches, or walkers. People who use wheelchairs, lift equipment, service animals, and personal assistants can require up to 100 square feet. Accessible cots must be available. An accessible cot is 17 to 19 inches high (without a mattress) and at least 27 inches wide. It can hold 350 pounds and is constructed with flexible head and feet positioning. If the accessible cot has side rails, the rails must be movable so that a wheelchair user can access the cot. Red Cross shelters do not permit pets but do allow service animals (such as seeing eye or hearing dogs).

Functional Needs Support Services

A body of federal law[1] mandates that people with disabilities have equal opportunities in disaster response and recovery, including support services for individuals with functional needs. Historically, shelters may not have met the standards of the Americans With Disabilities Act for accessible design (28 CFR Part 36), resulting in difficulties in providing appropriate care to those with access and functional needs.

The Federal Emergency Management Agency (FEMA) has issued guidelines (FEMA Guidance)[2] to help communities plan to meet the access and functional needs of vulnerable populations within general population shelters. The FEMA guidance recommends activities, known as *Functional Needs Support Services* (FNSS), which change the way general population shelters have traditionally been established and operated. FNSS is defined as "services that enable children and adults to maintain their usual level of independence in general population shelters." The services include reasonable modifications to policies, procedures, and practices, and the provision of durable medical equipment (DME), consumable medical supplies (CMS), personal assistance services (PAS), and other goods and services as needed. DME is medical equipment used in the home to aid in a better quality of living, and is a benefit included in most insurance plans including Medicaid and Medicare. CMS are nondurable supplies and items that enable activities of daily living. PAS are services provided to assist children and adults with activities of daily living (e.g.,

---

[1]Stafford Act; Post-Katrina Emergency Reform Act, Section 689; and Title VIII of the Civil Rights Act of 1968 (Fair Housing Act) as amended.

[2]FEMA. 2010. *Guidance on Planning for Integration of Functional Needs Support Services in General Population Shelters.* Washington, DC: FEMA. Available at: http://www.fema.gov/pdf/about/odic/fnss_guidance.pdf. This publication includes Guidance, Operational Tools, and Appendices.

bathing, eating, toileting). The regulatory foundation for FNSS is found in the Americans With Disabilities Act of 1990, the Rehabilitation Act of 1973, and the Fair Housing Act of 1968. A new FEMA course (replacing GS197 and entitled "Integrating Access and Functional Needs into Emergency Planning, Response, and Recovery") provides details on implementation and will be offered in 2011.

Planning the Shelters

Public health professionals should be involved in planning for shelters, as they bring skills and knowledge that can facilitate the appropriate preparations for the broadest health needs of the community. Specialized shelters which can provide medical care following a disaster are scarce resources. Where feasible, communities should plan for the integration of FNSS in general population shelters to preserve this precious medical resource for those who truly need it. With better planning, more people can be safely accommodated in general population shelters. Some elements of FNSS are already in place. Currently, the Red Cross operates a health services unit that is responsible for replacing medications and other items at general population shelters.

Even with the integration of FNSS, there will still be the need for medical shelters. The responsibility for setting up medical shelters following a disaster varies from state to state—sometimes it lies with the local health department, sometimes a private agency. Medical shelters may be co-located with general population shelters. Planners can use processes identified in Chapters 4, 5, and 10 for the estimation and identification of the medical and functional needs of a community's residents. Advance identification of endemic medical needs in the region will facilitate the development of a system to triage patients who require medical shelters when the disaster strikes. If plans are in place when evacuation is required, officials can notify residents through emergency alerts and direct them to the appropriate shelter (medical or general population) with the supplies and resources to match their needs.

Planning for Functional Needs Support Services

When planning for the integration of FNSS in general population shelters, communities should coordinate with stakeholders, including the following:

- Individuals requiring FNSS
- Agencies and organizations that provide FNSS
- Advocates for FNSS
- Providers of DME, CMS, PAS, and communication services

These stakeholders can help identify the types of DME and CMS that may require emergency replacement. Table 57 lists typical DME and CMS items.

FEMA recommends that planning includes arrangements for a credentialed team that assesses the needs of children and adults who have access or functional needs when they arrive at a shelter. The Functional Assessment Service Team

Table 57. Typical Durable Medical Equipment and Consumable Medical Supplies

Durable Medical Equipment	Consumable Medical Supplies
Blood glucose monitors	Blood-testing strips
Continuous positive airway pressure (CPAP) machines	Bandages and dressings
Crutches	Catheters and electrodes
Hospital beds	Forceps
Knee braces	Gloves
Orthotics and prosthetic devices	Plasters and bandage grips
Oxygen tents	Swabs
Nebulizers	Syringes and needles
Walkers	Wooden tongue depressors
Wheelchairs	

(FAST)[3] is a program developed in California that determines what resources are necessary to support identified needs in a general population shelter and enable them to maintain their independence. FAST members may come from governmental agencies or community-based organizations that have broad experience working with individuals with disabilities. FAST members should be knowledgeable about the services required and the vendors who can supply the needs of this population quickly. Memorandums of understanding should be established in advance with the individuals or organizations that will participate in FAST.

FEMA guidelines also change the staffing patterns in shelters. General population shelters will now include assistants for personal care, communications support for those with hearing or visual impairments, and translators. Shelters should prepare to track the numerous providers who may deliver services. The list includes the following:

- Communication (interpreters, computer services, and TTY)
- FNSS equipment (DME and CMS)
- Food services (including special diets)

[3]FAST is a California-only model. More information can be found online (at http://www.dss.cahwnet.gov/dis/res/pdf/AppendixB.pdf). Another model is used in Louisiana through their Louisiana Volunteers in Action (LAVA) program (information available at https://www.lava.dhh.louisiana.gov).

- Medical staffing (e.g., on-site nursing, dental, pharmaceutical)
- Personal assistance (basic personal care and activities of daily living)
- Resource suppliers (e.g., blood sugar monitoring, dialysis, oxygen, power source)
- Service animals (veterinarians)
- Transportation (such as paratransit)

To care for those who arrive at a shelter without DME, supplies, or medications but who need them, planners should arrange for the provision and maintenance of equipment and supplies through memorandums of understanding. The list should include the needs of children and adults with and without disabilities who have access and functional needs. Appendices 3 and 4 of the FEMA guidance provide a sample list of the estimated DME and CMS needed in a shelter for 100 people for 1 week. A readiness contract has been executed so that DME will be available for presidentially declared disasters. The Homeland Security Grant Program may be a source of funding to purchase equipment needed to meet these needs (available at http://www.dhs.gov/xopnbiz/grants).

Medications

State and local laws differ about the storage, preparation, administration, documentation, and disposal of medications. Planners should consult with state and local authorities to determine if and how they can obtain, store, and dispense medications in a general population shelter. To ensure that shelter residents have access to medications, agreements should be established with pharmacies to supply needed medications to shelters. Table 58 describes key medication considerations in general population shelters.

Medical Shelters

Disaster victims who cannot be evacuated to a general population shelter include those with certain health or medical conditions, such as an infectious disease requiring isolation, a serious injury, or intensive postsurgical care. Although community planning may vary, patients for whom a medical shelter is appropriate may include those who require infusion therapy, complex sterile dressing changes, hyperalimentation, intensive care, or life support equipment. Medically complex, unstable, and terminally ill patients with "do not resuscitate" orders should be cared for in a hospital-level setting where possible.

For these patients, communities may choose to continue establishing plans for alternative care facilities referred to as *medical shelters*. These facilities may be associated with a hospital so that persons requiring medical management but not hospital-level care can be safely housed. Bedridden and total-care patients who go to medical shelters must bring a responsible caregiver and not actually require a hospital bed. Medical shelters are generally intended to operate for a limited period (1 to 4 days). Plans should detail how bedridden patients will be moved if additional evacuation is necessary (e.g., using flatbed trucks).

Table 58. Medication Considerations in General Population Shelters

Procedure or Program	Considerations
Filling prescriptions	Chain pharmacies may have information about a shelter resident's medications in a centralized site away from the disaster location
Storage	Residents are usually responsible for safeguarding, storing, and administering their own medication If refrigeration is needed or residents can't self-medicate, keep prescription medications in locked container used only for storing medications at first aid station
Disposal	All medications kept at first aid station should be returned to residents at discharge Needles or hypodermic syringes with needles attached must be disposed of in biohazard containers
Emergency Preparedness Assistance Program, a joint program of Federal Emergency Management Agency and the Department of Health and Human Services	Provides a 30-day supply of pharmaceuticals and durable medical equipment (DME) lost in disaster, or lost or damaged in transit to the designated shelter facility Permits pharmacies to process claims for prescription medications and limited DME for uninsured individuals from area with presidential disaster declaration

Adapted from Federal Emergency Management Agency (FEMA). 2010. *Guidance on Planning for Integration of Functional Needs Support Services in General Population Shelters*. p. 34. Washington, DC: FEMA. Available at: http://www.fema.gov/pdf/about/odic/fnss_guidance.pdf.

For patients needing the services provided in medical shelters, public health officials are advised to make arrangements with providers and hospitals as part of global community planning. In the event of natural disasters such as hurricanes, earthquakes, and tornadoes, hospitals may be damaged or may receive large numbers of severely injured patients, necessitating the discharge of stable medical patients and the inability to handle medical patients whose conditions have become acute.

Protocols and Procedures

Communities should establish protocols for staff assistance and procedures for triage, supportive care, and universal precautions (e.g., no smoking, proper handling of body fluids and medical waste, continuous monitoring of patients by caregivers). Nurses and other staff at medical shelters can offer supportive care while patients and their caregivers manage routine needs. Caregivers focus on helping with activities of daily living, administering medications, and providing oxygen and other medical support. Medical shelter nurses offer supervision and assistance, if needed, when patients or caregivers assume responsibility for their own procedures.

The community plan must anticipate medical staffing requirements, including the types of personnel (medical director, nurses, emergency medical technicians, social workers, and support staff), credentialing process, scheduling, and on-site recruitment, registration, and supervision of volunteers. Plans for medical shelters must ensure cultural and linguistic competence among staff members. Protocols must be established for admitting and registering patients and caregivers and for acquiring and storing supplies. Staff members must be capable of handling a range of medical and nursing requirements, including labor in pregnant women, violent situations, and deaths. Procedures for closing down the medical shelter and relocating patients as needed must be established as part of the overall plan.

Dialysis Centers

Individuals who require dialysis need to know what to do in an emergency. Dialysis centers should develop a plan for each patient. This plan should include prepared statements or messages which communicate the circumstances that make the centers unavailable to provide care. Centers should provide the names, locations, and contact information for available treatment facilities. Finally, if no other dialysis centers are operating, patients should receive detailed directions on the procedures they should follow to stretch the time before another dialysis treatment is needed.

Chapter 13

Evaluation Methods for Assessing Public Health and Medical Response to Disasters

E valuating disaster response is essential for preparedness planning. This chapter addresses the principles involved in comprehensive and objective assessment of disaster plans and how they are implemented and provides details on how to develop effective evaluation tools.

Public Health Role

- Conduct systematic reviews of public health and medical aspects of disaster response to improve efforts to reduce morbidity and mortality
- Use professionally recognized measures of process and outcome to monitor public health and medical programs and to direct resources in all phases of disaster response and recovery

Evaluation in Disasters

Emergency management has traditionally been a response-oriented field. As a result, advancements in practice do not often come from scientific evaluation. Emergency preparedness and response have improved through analysis of what are known as *after action reports*, application of institutional knowledge, establishment of guidelines and protocols, and self-initiation by thinking "it *can* happen to me."

Most fields advance by incorporating scientific evidence of what works. In emergency response, one can't evaluate how well things have gone or identify areas for improvement through experimentation, such as through the use of case-control studies. However, public health is a science-based field, and public health principles can be applied to the evaluation of disaster preparedness and response in a manner that will advance practice. The Pandemic and All-Hazards Preparedness Act of 2006 mandated that research centers conduct evaluations to improve public health preparedness and response. Preparedness and Emergency Response Research Centers were established at designated schools of public health in 2008. Their research should yield evidence of best practices that can be applied to improve the structure, capabilities, and performance of public health systems in preparation for and response to disasters.

Evaluation Methods

Evaluation has several purposes, the most fundamental of which is to determine the extent to which an organization, program, or unit achieves its clearly stated and measurable objectives in responding to a disaster. Evaluations are used to adjust disaster plans, focus practice drills and preparedness, improve planning for rapid assessment and management of daily response operations, provide input for the refinement of measures of effectiveness, and collect data for hypothesis-driven research. Evaluations often provide objective information for managers to formulate and revise policy through a retrospective and descriptive design for capturing information. Administrators can improve their management of health care systems affected by disasters by drawing information systematically from a variety of sources. For example, collecting information from broad categories of personnel and lay informants could be used in lieu of probability sampling. Evaluation of disaster response cannot always use experimental or quasi-experimental design for data collection or analysis unless evaluation teams are in place and have prepared methods and instruments, because the exact timing of most disasters cannot be predicted.

Disaster evaluation research seeks to obtain information that can be used in preparation for future disasters by

- Developing profiles of victims and types of injuries to inform the revision of existing or preparation of enhanced disaster plans (e.g., disaster epidemiology).
- Assessing whether program adjustments can reduce disability and save lives (e.g., effectiveness of community collaborations).
- Determining whether better methods to organize and manage a response exist, including the use of resources in a relief effort (i.e., effectiveness of Incident Command Systems and Emergency Operations Center, improvements in drills and exercises, and reaching diverse audiences with critical information about emergencies).
- Determining best practices (e.g., effectiveness of preparedness and emergency response systems, improvements in training).
- Identifying measures that can be implemented to reduce harm to communities and residents (e.g., communications to vulnerable populations).
- Assessing the long-term physical and emotional effects of a disaster on individuals and communities (e.g., ability to prepare for and respond to mental and behavioral health needs of victims and responders).

Evaluations should examine the structure of the public health and health care system's response to the disaster, the allocation of medical and public health resources, the sequence of events, the impact of the program at each stage, issues that arose during the public health and health care system's response to the disaster, the limitations of the response, and policy lessons. Key steps in developing and implementing an evaluation plan[1] include:

- Defining goals of what is being evaluated
- Selecting measures
- Determining how the data will be collected
- Collecting and reviewing the data

[1]Adapted from RAND Corporation. 2010. Enhancing Public Health Emergency Preparedness for Special Needs Populations: A Toolkit for State and Local Planning and Response. Chapter 8. Arlington, VA: RAND Corp. Available at: http://www.rand.org/pubs/technical_reports/2009/RAND_TR681.pdf.

Designing Evaluation Studies

A structured evaluation, which might look at preparedness activities and how participants carry them out or the capacity to conduct rapid surveillance, must begin before the disaster occurs. If evaluating a disaster response, the evaluators would assess equipment needs, strategies for medical and public health interventions, and the chain of command among participating response organizations. Internal and external communication methods and participants should also be examined. All personnel who participate in disaster response must be evaluated for the timing and execution of duties in relation to their planned assignments and actual implementation in the field.

Define Goals and Measures

Evaluations begin by reviewing the disaster response plan and its measurable objectives. Without measurable objectives, a disaster response plan cannot be evaluated. To ensure accurate measurement, the first step is to identify the core outcome that is desired. For example, when evaluating a center that is distributing mass vaccination, the focus of the evaluation might be the efficiency of operations (how many people received vaccination per hour), the communication during operations (what types of methods were used to communicate with individuals who are visually or hearing impaired), or the actual distribution process (actions taken to prepare, vaccinate, and discharge).

Once the specific goals are defined, determining how to measure them is the next important step. Continuing with the previous example, to measure how many people received vaccination per hour, each consent form could be time stamped. Other goals could result in requiring users to sign a log to collect information about the equipment or using interpreters to communicate with individuals who are visually or hearing impaired. The distribution process for vaccination could be described through interviews at each step. The key is to follow the principles of research methods as vigorously as possible given the events.

Data Collection

During the impact and postimpact phases of a disaster, a record of important medical, environmental, and social events is usually created and searchable in journalistic features, photographs, videos, official records, recollections of partici-pants, and other reports. To study these events, information must be obtained from a variety of informants, documents, and records. Thorough preplanning of the evaluation is essential to ensure that the evaluation will yield valid findings. Multidisciplinary teams must design studies, collect data, and interpret the findings. A typical postimpact team consists of a physician, emergency medical services specialist, social or behavioral scientist, epidemiologist, and disaster management specialist. This research team should hold daily debriefings to discuss issues and problems related to the implementation of the evaluation protocol.

Although record keeping during a disaster is difficult and gaps in the record will often occur, some written accounting on a case-by-case basis is usually available. Public health officials can look for data in hospital E-codes, electronic health records, emergency department records, field station logs, and autopsy reports. Impressions of patient treatment can be made by reviewing available patient records, supplemented by interview data. Other sources of evaluation data include journalistic accounts and interviews with injured survivors, public health and medical professionals, search and rescue personnel, relief workers, lay bystanders, and disaster managers.

For interviews, a series of questions designed to probe the effectiveness of the disaster relief operation can be incorporated into an administered questionnaire. In such a questionnaire questions should be structured, calling for a fixed response, although a small number of open-ended questions can provide useful information. In addition, medical record abstract forms can be used to collect hospital and autopsy data. The data should be validated by cross-checking multiple sources.

Conducting an Evaluation

In the process of conducting an evaluation, assessments are directed for five domains of activity: structure, process, outcomes, response adequacy, and costs.[2] The following sections describe each domain and provide sample questions that might be asked in order to evaluate the response to a disaster involving a large number of casualties.

Structure

Evaluation of structure examines how the medical and public health response was organized, what resources were needed, and what resources were available. Questions used to evaluate structure for the response to mass casualty incidents may include the following:

- Were ambulances, hospital emergency departments, and critical care units sufficiently equipped and supplied to meet the demands of the disaster?
- Were sufficient numbers of properly trained staff available, especially volunteers, first responders, ambulance personnel, emergency department nurses, critical care physicians, and communications staff?
- Did staff receive prior training in methods specific to the provision of public health and medical care during a disaster?
- Did the communications system have sufficient capacity, flexibility, and backup capabilities during the disaster for both internal and external communications?
- How were patients transported to the hospital? To what extent was the ambulance system overloaded? What equipment shortages were experienced?
- How well did the following functions operate during the impact and postimpact phases: resource management (e.g., dispatch, coordination with emergency

---

[2]The Agency for Healthcare Research and Quality provides a model to evaluate hospital disaster drills designed to identify specific weaknesses that can be improved to strengthen hospital preparedness (available at http://www.ahrq.gov/research/hospdrills/index.html).

medical services and public services), medical supervision, and communication among hospitals, mobile units, and other services?

Process

Process assessments identify how the system (both medical and public health components) functioned during the impact and postimpact, how well individuals were prepared, and what problems occurred. The process questions should be sorted into those that probe the operation of the disaster response system and those that assess the process of treating patients. Process questions to ask for a mass casualty incident include the following:

- Were medical staff available during the search and rescue of patients? How soon after the response was initiated did they arrive?
- Did medical staff trained in detection and extrication possess the skills and knowledge required to perform their functions during the disaster?
- Were medical staff trained in detection and extrication able to apply their medical knowledge under disaster conditions? What factors, if any, prevented optimum performance?
- How effectively was the triage function performed? What, if any, factors interfered?
- Was there adequate control over the management and deployment of resources during the postimpact response? Was responsibility for decision-making clear? Were appropriate decisions made concerning the process of patient triage, transfer, and treatment?
- What first aid was provided to victims, by whom, and when? Was this appropriate and effective?
- How were patients transferred from the scene of the disaster to treatment sites?
- Did effective coordination and communication among agencies occur?
- How did the hospital respond to the volume of patients?
- How did volunteers function? Was their participation supportive, or did it interfere with the treatment of patients? What controls, if any, were exercised?
- Did any compromises in standard medical care occur? Were these compromises necessary and acceptable?
- Was the public prepared to act appropriately when the disaster occurred? Should the plan to provide public education and information be modified to facilitate a future public health or medical response?

Outcomes

Outcomes assessments identify what was and was not achieved as a result of the medical and public health response. This assessment focuses on the impact of care provided to patients during the disaster. Outcome assessment can be achieved using either implicit or explicit criteria through a review of patient records. If implicit standards and criteria are used, a panel of critical care and emergency care specialists can review a sample of patient records and make judgments about the appropriateness of treatment related to patient outcomes. If explicit standards and criteria are employed, the reviewer uses written guidelines to determine the adequacy of treatment. Forms for summarizing patient treatment and outcome data should be developed well in advance of their use, and evaluated for completeness after use to assess a disaster response. Data to be collected should include, at a minimum, the following:

- Personal characteristics of patient (such as age, sex, residence)
- Medical condition/status prior to injury
- Principal diagnosis, secondary diagnosis, type of injury
- Body location of injury (extremities, back, chest, head, neck, abdomen)
- Whether (and what) prehospital care was provided and by whom
- Method of transportation to hospital
- Hospital treatment provided
- Patient status on discharge
- Cause of death, if applicable

Response Adequacy

Assessing the adequacy of the disaster response examines the extent to which the response systems were able to meet the needs of the community during the disaster. The analysis of the adequacy of the response is valuable in planning for future disasters. The main concern is, *overall, how much death and disability occurred that could have been prevented?* To assess this dimension of the response for a mass casualty incident, information should be obtained about the following:

- To what extent was the prehospital system able to function as designed?
- What types of victims were cared for and what types were the hospital and prehospital systems unable to treat? For what reasons?
- How many victims were transported to more than one hospital because of limitations in hospital beds, intensive care beds, supplies, or staff?
- How effectively did hospitals cooperate to distribute patients to share the burden of treatment and to refer patients in need to specialty care?

Costs

Disaster response costs can be measured in several ways: the total cost of the relief effort, the cost per each life saved, the cost for various subsystems that operated during the response phase, and the costs of preparedness. Questions to ask include the following:

- What were each of the previously defined costs?
- What portion did the state pay? The federal government? The local community?
- How well did the local community capture reimbursable costs?
- Did the cost of the program correlate with the benefits to the community?

Chapter 14

Ethical Considerations in Public Health Emergencies

W hy are ethics important in times of emergencies? Many ethical decisions should be determined before an emergency occurs, or our ability to provide the fairest treatment may be hindered. Not considering the ethical implications of how public health services are to be delivered can have serious consequences for society. The consequences of not ensuring ethical considerations when establishing processes for emergency preparedness and response can lead to the loss of public trust, confusion about roles and responsibilities, and low staff morale. The continuing disruption of many victims' lives following Hurricane Katrina is an example of a lack of ethical planning.

Historically, disasters have had a more catastrophic impact on developing countries where infrastructure is poor or nonexistent and resources are not always well organized. For those countries, international preparedness to care for vulnerable populations is commonplace. The United States confronted the necessity of ethical planning during the aftermath of Hurricane Katrina and the subsequent flooding. The elderly and the poor were disproportionately affected by this catastrophic storm. Although planners had evacuation plans for the region, many elderly and poor residents lacked the resources to evacuate the coastal regions before the hurricane struck land. The elderly, who are often frail, isolated, or afraid to leave everything they own, accounted for nearly half of the deaths from the storm and its aftermath.

The next pandemic is likely to present situations for which chosen public health strategies, such as isolation and quarantine, could benefit the public but infringe upon individual liberties. The closure of public areas can slow the spread of disease but runs counter to the principles of free association, free commerce, and free travel. Although the federal government has developed stockpiles and is organizing the capacity to create a workforce surge, it is likely that the availability of medical personnel, equipment, and supplies will be limited. Limited resources could result in some individuals receiving care and others not. Without planning that has included careful deliberation of ethical considerations, public health care workers may find themselves forced to deny treatment to patients without guidance, policy, or protocol in the middle of an emergency response. The ethical dilemma faced by medical personnel who found themselves providing care without adequate resources in isolated health care facilities after the post-Katrina flooding is an example of what professionals must grapple with in the absence of protocols.

In order to assure public safety, public health may have to make difficult decisions that affect individuals but benefit the community, region, or country. During an emergency, clinical decision-making by triage is based on the principle of the common good—what is best for the greatest number of individuals. Those who are affected are more likely to cooperate if they know that public health workers' actions are based on ethical principles. Good planning may minimize the need for tough choices if adequate resources and effective arrangements are in place before a disaster strikes. Even with good planning, using ethical principles to predetermine the criteria that will be used in any triage process, and having a protocol to follow, can relieve individual workers from the burden of making these decisions while trying to deliver care.

Developing an ethical framework as part of a community's emergency response plan can

- Improve the quality and management of care during a surge.
- Establish a uniform and fair allocation of resources.
- Minimize legal liability for providers.
- Increase clinician compliance with triage protocols.

What Are the Ethical Principles That Apply to Emergencies?

Preparing for emergencies has inherent ethical goals, including the protection of the lives and health of those impacted. To accomplish these goals during a disaster, it may be necessary to limit the individual freedom inherent in U.S. culture in order to do the most good for the community. Response to public health emergencies often requires the setting of priorities, rationing of supplies or care, and triage of the services to be performed. Any of these may necessitate the use of coercive measures that override individual liberty and property rights.

The Humanitarian Charter, first drafted in 1997 by a group of nongovernmental organizations (NGOs) and the International Red Cross and Red Crescent, identified minimum standards for disaster assistance. This guidance is based on principles of international humanitarian law, international human rights law, refugee law, and the Code of Conduct for the International Red Cross and Red Crescent and NGOs in Disaster Relief (available at http://www.ifrc.org/Docs/idrl/I259EN.pdf). The core principles assert that populations impacted by disaster have the right to protection and assistance. As emergency planners have come to understand that disasters disproportionately affect those who are most vulnerable and that the poorest communities may need help the most because they have fewer resources, it is particularly important that planning includes special consideration for vulnerable populations. It is important to recognize the differing needs of vulnerable groups, to understand how they are affected in different disaster contexts, and to formulate a response accordingly.

Public health ethics are based on a set of principles that will ensure fairness and respect for all individuals even when it is necessary to adopt utilitarian methods during an emergency. Guidelines for ethical decisions during disasters include the following:

Reasonableness: Responders can provide a rationale for taking actions to address the health and public health needs of the community based on science, evidence, practice, experience, and principles

Responsiveness: Health care workers will do as much as possible to limit harm to patients because of the lack of necessary resources and will revise and revisit decisions as the crisis unfolds

Fairness: Health care resources need to be allocated fairly as the benefits and burdens of the emergency will be shared equally among the affected community. With anticipated limited resources, the fair distribution of resources is not directed by what is best for the individual, but rather by the principle of "the greater good of the community"

Respect for person: Every person impacted by a disaster should be treated and believe that they will be treated fairly, justly, and with dignity

Solidarity: To ensure that members of our society care for each other, each person must consider the greater good of one's family and the community rather than one's own self interest

Accountability based on openness and transparency: Those impacted by a disaster want assurance that their leaders are making ethical decisions throughout the crisis. Their confidence is based in part on whether all affected stakeholders are able to examine the information that was used to make decisions

Principles for ethical practice in public health were codified by the Public Health Leadership Society in 2002 following a "town hall" assembly at the 2000 American Public Health Association Annual Meeting in Boston, Massachusetts. Many of the highlighted values are delineated in a document called *Principles of Public Health Ethics* and are applicable during a public health emergency. Table 59 describes some of these ethical principles and how each applies to public health emergencies.

Ethical Decisions to Be Made

Judgments that determine the deployment and allocation of resources are made both in preparation for and in response to emergencies. Public health professionals are trained to take actions that reduce harm and promote the health and safety of communities, and inherently understand how ethical principles are incorporated into preparedness and response activities. Seven tasks identified by the University of North Carolina Gillings School of Global Public Health highlight the decision areas for which ethical considerations should be incorporated into the decision process.

1. Coordination and collaboration. Responders from diverse professional backgrounds, whose motivation and perception of the tasks may conflict, need to work together in a regional response. Use of the National Incident Management System reduces the opportunity for ethical differences by establishing a clear and mutual understanding of how services will be organized and delivered.

2. Decision-making. While some response activities are planned, the unpredictability of events results in decisions being made in real time and reality may not be anything like what was expected. As a result, those in charge determine priorities, policies,

Table 59. The Application of Ethics to Public Health Emergencies

Ethical Principle	Impact/Action in Emergencies
Prevent adverse health outcomes by addressing fundamental causes of disease	Emergencies can disrupt and destroy the protective barriers that ensure health.
Respect the rights of individuals in the community	Public health response should be equitable in a public health emergency. Restrictions should be necessary, relevant, and proportional.
Ensure input from community members in development and evaluation of policies, programs, and priorities	Solidarity and trust are essential in ethical response, such as in vetting an emergency response plan with the community. For example, the U.S. Department of Health and Human Services conducted town hall meetings when developing vaccine allocation guidelines.
Ensure that basic resources and conditions necessary for health are accessible to all, including disenfranchised community members	Apply fairness principle by ensuring that preparedness and response activities reach all who are affected.
Provide information needed for decisions on policies or programs	Actions that impinge on liberty may be required but should be clearly explained.
Conduct public health actions in a timely manner with information and resources at hand	Ethical decisions can be made in an emergency with limited information when a delay in additional information can lead to greater harm.
Incorporate a variety of approaches that anticipate and respect diverse values, beliefs, and cultures in the community	In an emergency, public health agencies need to communicate with all who live in the impacted area.
Protect the confidentiality of information	Individual privacy may be compromised during emergency conditions.
Build the public's trust and the institution's effectiveness through collaboration and affiliation	Confidence in the choice being made requires transparency and careful communication.

Adapted from Public Health Leadership Society. 2002. *Principles of the Ethical Practice of Public Health*. Version 2.2. Washington, DC: American Public Health Association. Available at: http://www.apha.org/NR/rdonlyres/1CED3CEA-287E-4185-9CBD-BD405FC60856/0/ethicsbrochure.pdf.

and protocols in an accelerated time frame, and a course of action may be determined without the best or necessary information.

3. Protection and response of emergency responders. Disaster response can be dangerous work. Employers have an ethical duty not to put responders in danger, both physically and psychologically. Health workers also have a duty to provide care, especially during an infectious disease outbreak. It is likely that responders and organizations will have conflicting duties, such as medical providers to their patients and their families, even when they are clear on their duties and responsibilities.

4. Informing the public. When possible, public health informs the public of preventive actions preimpact, during the emergency, and postimpact. The public needs to receive timely and accurate information in order to mitigate harm.

5. Resource constraints. In many emergencies, an expected surge in demand for health and public health services stresses resources. Even with the deployment of stockpiles and volunteers, difficult decisions that are ethically challenging may need to be made about whether potentially limited resources (e.g., ventilators) will be made available and to whom. The lack of resources increases the urgency of making ethical decisions.

6. Isolation and quarantine. To limit the spread of infectious disease, public health professionals use a strategy called *social distancing*, where distance or a barrier is established between individuals. Social distance techniques that limit mobility, such as isolation and quarantine, can be considered constraints of civil liberty. Other prevention strategies are mechanical (e.g., requesting that individuals wear personal protective equipment such as masks). Sometimes it may be necessary to restrict liberty in the interest of protecting the public's health. Fortunately, public health professionals have been preparing for emergencies that require social distancing and have had the opportunity to discuss strategies to reduce the spread of infection.

7. Timeliness and responsiveness. Because public health emergencies require accelerated actions in a condensed time frame, it may not be possible to prevent negative health effects.

How to Use the Ethical Process

Decisions during the planning stage should be based on the ethical values discussed previously. The values to be considered include the following:

- Professional duty to provide care
- Every patients' right to receive needed medical care equally
- Any restrictions to individual liberty should be necessary and relevant to protect the common good
- Protection of individual privacy when possible
- Proportional actions to restrict individual liberty as necessary to benefit the community
- Support provided to those facing a disproportionate risk of disease or injury
- Communication and collaboration across systemic and institutional boundaries should reflect solidarity
- Allocating resources should be done using ethical behavior and decision-making

In planning for emergencies, it is important and necessary to build trust with the community before an emergency occurs. Ensuring that public health workers and health care providers know and adhere to the tenets of public health ethics makes it more likely that the community will accept necessary decisions. Through transparent communication and participation in decisions, members of a community can be assured that public health decisions are made fairly. Obtaining the cooperation of the public is a critical goal of preparedness. Although public health officials can use legal remedies during an emergency, it is far better to gain the cooperation and collaboration of a population by their acceptance of the actions being taken.

The Centers for Disease Control and Prevention describe a process for making ethical determinations in their Public Health Law 101 course. The three-step process includes analyzing the ethical issues, evaluating the ethical dimensions, and justifying a decision. In thinking through these steps, public health workers should look to the professional code of ethics for guidance. Table 60 identifies the tasks involved in each step.

Table 60. Analysis of Tasks Involved in Ethical Decision-Making

Analyze Ethical Issues	Evaluate Ethical Dimensions	Justify Decision
Identify stakeholders and their particular interest	Identify moral norms and moral considerations	Present sufficient reasons for course of action
Understand inherent public health risks and potential harms	Action produces balance of benefits over harms	Base actions on moral norms, ethical principles, professional codes, and history
Identify public health goals	Benefits and burdens are distributed fairly	Goal is likely to be accomplished
Identify any legal authority being questioned	Affected groups had opportunity to participate in decision	Probable benefits outweigh any moral infringements
Identify any precedence or historical context	Action respects individual's autonomy, liberty, and privacy	Action is least restrictive and intrusive
Identify alternative courses of action	Action respects professional roles and values	Public justification for action or policy exists that is acceptable to those most affected
Professional code of ethics provides guidance	Ethical principles provide guidance	By following ethical principles, guarantee fairness

BASICS

Common Terms Used in Disaster Preparedness and Response

Accessible—having the legally required elements to ensure that individuals with a wide variety of disabilities can enter and use places, programs, services, and activities.

Adaptive equipment—equipment that helps a person move, groom, or eat independently such as mobility aids, grooming aids, feeding aids, and similar devices used to offset functional limits.

Advanced life support—provided by paramedics; includes much more sophisticated diagnosis of patient conditions followed by protocol–driven, on-site initial medical treatment for conditions that will receive definitive treatment in hospitals.

Alarm procedure—alerting every concerned party as part of disaster management; various optical and acoustical means of alarm are possible: flags, lights, sirens, radio, telephone.

All-hazards—grouping all types of emergencies together for purposes of preparedness and response; types of hazards include natural disasters, accidental human actions, terrorism, or any chemical, biological, radiological, nuclear, or explosive accident.

Analysis-epidemiologic measures—descriptive statistics, specific disease and death rates, secular trends, tests for sensitivity, and predictive value positive, if appropriate.

Antemortem—information about a dead or missing person that can be used for identification.

Antigen—any substance (such as a toxin or enzyme) that stimulates an immune response in the body (particularly the production of antibodies).

Antigenic drift—mutational changes in viruses that occur, rendering immune responses against previous strains ineffective and enabling the virus's spread throughout a partially immune population; occurs in both influenza A and influenza B viruses.

Antigenic shift—sudden shift in viral proteins in influenza A, through a recombination of the genomes of two strains, that produces a novel virus; usually results in a pandemic or a worldwide epidemic.

Assessments—short- and long-term "snapshots" of disaster situations which help with decisionmaking and enhance monitoring; the goal of conducting assessments is to convey information quickly in order to recalibrate a system's response.

Augmentative communication device—device used to help a person communicate by voice.

Avalanche—sudden slide of a large mass of snow and ice, usually carrying with it earth, rocks, trees, and other debris.

Average throughput time—time from a client's entry into a point-of-distribution site until exit.

Basic life support—noninvasive measures (such as elimination of airway obstruction, cardiopulmonary resuscitation, hemorrhage control, wound care, and immobilization of fractures) used to preserve the lives of unstable patients.

Becquerel (Bq)—unit of nuclear activity that has replaced the curie; 1 Bq represents the amount of radioactive substance for which disintegration occurs per second.

Bioterrorism—unlawful release of biological agents or toxins targeted at humans, animals, or plants with the intent to intimidate or coerce a government or civilian population in furtherance of political or social objectives.

Blast wave—intense over-pressurization impulse created by a detonated high explosive; injuries incurred by such an impulse are characterized by anatomical and physiological changes caused by the direct or reflective over-pressurization force impacting the body's surface. Should be distinguished from the forced super-heated air flow of a "blast wind."

Blindness/visual disability—visual condition that interferes with a person's ability to see, occasionally resulting in a person's complete loss of vision.

Blogs—frequently updated Web site with chronological entries. A **microblog** is a short form of blogging in which users write brief messages up to 140 characters on their Web site.

Cache—predetermined tools, equipment, or supplies stored in a designated location.

Capabilities—the operational capacity and ability to execute preparedness tasks aimed at prevention, mitigation, response, and recovery.

Case—unit of observation in the surveillance system regarding the health condition of interest.

Case definition—standardized criteria used in investigations and comparing potential cases for deciding whether a person has a particular disease or health-related condition; provide the basis for deciding which disaster-specific health conditions should be monitored through an emergency information surveillance system.

Casualty—any person suffering physical or psychological damage as a result of outside violence which leads to death, injuries, or material losses.

Casualty clearing station—collection point for victims in the immediate vicinity of the disaster site at which further triage and basic and advanced life support can be provided.

Catastrophic incident—any natural or man-made incident that results in extraordinary amounts of mass casualties, damage, or disruption.

Centers for independent living—community-based, non-residential organizations that work with people who have disabilities.

Central holding area—location at which ambulances assemble and leave to pick up patients from a casualty clearing station or a neighboring hospital, according to a victim distribution plan.

Closed captions—visual text displays hidden in video signals that are used to display information for those who are deaf or hearing impaired; can be accessed through a television remote control, an onscreen menu, or a special decoder. All televisions with a 13-inch or larger screen manufactured after 1993 have the needed circuitry. Open captions are an integral part of the television picture, like subtitles in a movie, and cannot be turned off. Text that advances very slowly across the bottom of the screen is referred to as a *crawl*; displayed text or graphics that move up and down the screen are said to *scroll*.

Cognitive impairment—medical condition or injury that affects a person's ability to understand spoken or written information.

Communication disability—medical condition or injury that interferes with a person's ability to communicate by using one's voice.

Community profile—characteristics of the local environment prone to natural disasters or technological accidents, including population density, age distribution, roads, railways, waterways, types of dwellings and buildings, and the relief agencies locally available.

Comprehensive emergency management—integrated approach to organizing multiple emergency programs and activities; four phases comprise the "life cycle" of emergency management: mitigation, preparedness, response, and recovery.

Comprehensive Preparedness Guide 101: Producing Emergency Plans—guide that describes the intersection of federal, state, tribal, and local emergency planning.

Contamination—accidental release of hazardous chemical or nuclear materials leading to pollution of the environment and which places humans at risk for exposures, potentially affecting populations externally (skin and mucous membranes), internally (by inhalation or ingestion), or both.

Contingency plan—anticipatory emergency plan to be followed during an expected or eventual disaster, based on risk assessment, availability of human and material resources, community preparedness, and local and international response capability.

Contingency planning—site-specific plan that recognizes a disaster could occur at any time.

Covered entity—defined in the Health Insurance Portability and Accountability Act of 1996 rules as health plans, health care clearinghouses, and health care providers who electronically transmit any health information in connection with transactions for which the U.S. Department of Health and Human Services has adopted standards (generally, those concerning billing and payment for services or insurance coverage).

Covert releases—unannounced releases of a biological agent that present as illness in the community. Since detection of the released agent is dependent on traditional surveillance methods, the potential for large-scale spread is high.

Cracker—individual who uses computer programming to gain unauthorized or illegal access to a computer network or file.

Crisis standards of care—substantial change in the delivery of health care necessitated by a catastrophic disaster and formally declared by a state government; such a declaration legally protects health care providers in the event of scarce medical resource allocation and implementation of alternative operations at their facilities.

Data collection—accumulation of information conducted by various media, such as e-mail or facsimile, or by regular pickup and delivery by an assigned person to an assigned place.

Deafness/hearing disability—medical condition or injury that interferes with a person's ability to hear sounds.

Decontamination—removal of hazardous chemical or nuclear substances from the skin and mucous membranes by showering, washing with water, or rinsing with sterile solutions.

Demobilization—orderly, safe, and efficient return of a resource to its original location and status.

Disability—physical or mental impairment that substantially limits one or more major life activities of an individual.

Disaster—any occurrence (typically a sudden one) that causes damage, ecological disruption, loss of human life, deterioration of health and health services, *and* that exceeds the adjustment capacity of the affected community on a scale sufficient to require outside assistance; may include such events as earthquakes, floods, fires, hurricanes, cyclones, major storms, volcanic eruptions, spills, air crashes, droughts, epidemics, serious food shortages, and civil strife.

Disaster continuum—life cycle of a disaster event; also referred to as emergency management cycle.

Disaster epidemiology—study of disaster-related deaths, illnesses, or injuries in humans and of the factors impacting those events; methods involve identification of risk factors and comparison of affected persons with those not affected. May provide informed advice regarding probable health effects.

Disaster informatics—theoretical and practical aspects of information processing and communication based on knowledge and experience derived from processes in medicine and health care in disaster settings.

Disaster-prone—measure of risk that an individual, community, population, or area faces in regards to a particular hazard or disaster or disaster agent; determined by a history of past events and the risks of new events. Also referred to as *at-risk*.

Disaster recovery center—facility established in a centralized location within or near the disaster area at which victims can apply for disaster aid.

Disaster Severity Scale—the classification of disasters by a number of criteria (radius of disaster site, number of dead, number of wounded, average severity of injuries sustained, impact time, and rescue time), the attribution of a numeric value between 0 (least severe) and 2 (most severe) to each of the variables, and the totaling of all numeric values to provide a number between 0 and 18 that indicates the severity of an event.

Disaster vulnerability—ability to absorb and recover from the effects of an extreme event or situation; varies from one society to another or from one place to another.

Dispatch communications system—system used to assign ambulance personnel and other first responders to respond to persons in need.

Drills—supervised activities designed to test one or more components of an overall emergency management plan; a drill may be a step toward an exercise or may be an actual field response.

Durable medical equipment—certain medical equipment for use in the home, such as walkers, wheelchairs, scooters, and catheters.

Earthquake measures—scales used to measure earthquake intensity or magnitude. Most common are the Richter scale and the Modified Mercalli Intensity (MMI) scale. The MMI scale is a subjective measure of the intensity of an earthquake, whereas the Richter scale is an objective and numerical measurement based on readings taken by seismometers. A correlation between the magnitude and intensity of an earthquake can be made by correlating the measurements of the Richter and MMI scales.

Aftershocks—sequence of smaller earthquakes that can follow a larger-magnitude earthquake by day, months, or years, exacerbating damage.

Intensity—a subjective measure of earthquakes quantified by the MMI scale, which describes the physical effects of an earthquake to a specific location, persons, or man-made structures.

Magnitude—numerical quantity that characterizes earthquakes in terms of the total energy released after adjusting for difference in epicentral distance and focal depth. Magnitude differs from intensity in that magnitude is determined on the basis of instrumental records; whereas intensity is determined on the basis of subjective observations of the damage.

Modified Mercalli Intensity scale—Subjectively applied measurement system that indicates the intensity of an earthquake; a measure of the degree of damage from a particular location. Measurement is denoted by Roman numerals from I to XII. Intensity VI denotes the threshold for potential ground failure, such as liquefaction. Intensity VII denotes the threshold for architectural damage. Intensity VIII denotes the threshold for structural damage. Intensity IX denotes intense structural damage. Intensities X to XII denote various levels of destruction up to total destruction. An earthquake has many intensities, but only one magnitude.

Richter scale—Devised by Charles F. Richter, the Richter scale has a logarithmic formula for calculating the magnitude of earthquake from the instrument readings, and ranges from 0 to excess of 10 in numerical magnitude. Minor earthquakes measure 0–4.9, moderate earthquakes 5–5.9, strong earthquakes 6–6.9, and the most destructive earthquakes 7 and greater. The energy increases exponentially with magnitude; thus, a magnitude 6.0 earthquake releases 31.5 times more energy than a magnitude 5.0 earthquake or approximately 1,000 times more energy than does a magnitude 4.0 earthquake.

Emergencies—any occurrence which requires an immediate response that may be a result of epidemics, technological catastrophes, strife, or other natural or man-made causes.

Emergency Management Assistance Compact—congressionally ratified organization that facilitates interstate mutual aid by establishing written agreements regarding liability and reimbursement.

Emergency Medical Services System—organizational structure that includes prehospital (public access, dispatch, emergency medical technicians/paramedics, and ambulance services) and in-hospital (emergency departments, hospitals, and other definitive care facilities and personnel) support for victims of emergencies who require medical support.

Emergency medical technicians—commonly referred to as EMTs; emergency medical responders trained to identify and field-treat the most common medical emergencies and injuries, and to provide medical support to victims while en route to the hospital.

Emergency Support Functions—standardized concepts of resource management used by the federal government to organize and provide assistance following an emergency.

Emergency Support Function Annexes—describe the missions, policies, structures, and responsibilities of federal agencies in response to an emergency.

Emergency Support Function 6: Mass Care—concept that includes the tasks of sheltering, feeding, emergency first aid, family reunification, and distribution of emergency relief supplies to disaster victims; the National Response Framework designates the Red Cross as the primary agency responsible for this function.

Emergency Support Function 8: Public Health and Medical Services—basis of federal preparedness, response, and recovery actions in regards to the health needs of disaster victims; coordinated by the Office of the Assistant Secretary for Preparedness and Response. The lead agency is the Department of Health and Human Services.

Epidemic—occurrence of a number of cases of a disease, known or suspected to be of infectious or parasitic origin, that is unusually large or unexpected for the given place and time. A **threatened epidemic** occurs when the circumstances are such that a specific disease may reasonably be anticipated to occur in unusually large or unexpected numbers.

Evacuation—organized removal of people from dangerous or potentially dangerous areas.

Evacuation assistive equipment—equipment or devices used to help people leave a building in an emergency.

Evaluation—detailed review of a program; purpose is to determine whether the program met its objectives, to assess its impact on the community, and to generate "lessons learned" for the design of future projects; conducted during the program, at the completion of important milestones, or at the end of a specific period.

Evaluation research—application of scientific methods to assess the effectiveness of programs, services, or organizations designed to improve health or prevent illness.

Exposure surveillance—search for exposure variable. In disaster settings, exposure may be based on physical or environmental properties of the disaster event.

Exposure variable—characteristic of interest, also known as risk factor or predictor variable.

Famine Early Warning System—established by the U.S. Agency for International Development to monitor climate and meteorology, availability of food in the market, and morbidity related to nutrition to predict the occurrence of famine.

Far-field—following a nuclear accident at a nuclear plant, the area outside the immediate (or near-field) vicinity in which effects of the incident are still noticeable.

Federal Coordinating Officer—person appointed by the Federal Emergency Management Agency (FEMA) following a presidential declaration of a severe disaster or of an emergency to coordinate federal assistance. He or she initiates immediate action to assure that federal assistance is provided in accordance with the disaster declaration, any applicable laws or regulations, and the FEMA–state agreement. The Federal Coordinating Officer is also the senior federal official appointed in accordance with the provisions of Public Law 93–288 (the Stafford Act), as amended, to coordinate the overall consequence management response and recovery activities and to represent the president by coordinating the administration of federal relief activities in the designated disaster area. Additionally, the Federal Coordinating Officer is delegated responsibilities and performs those for the FEMA director as outlined in Executive Order 12148 and those responsibilities delegated to the FEMA regional director in the Code of Federal Regulations, Title 44, Part 205.

Federal On-Scene Commander—official designated upon the activation of the Joint Operations Center who ensures appropriate coordination of the U.S. government's overall response with federal, state, and local authorities. The On-Scene Commander maintains this role until the U.S. attorney general transfers the lead federal agency role to FEMA.

Federal-to-federal support—coordination of additional assistance, such as interagency or intra-agency reimbursable agreements, in accordance with the Economy Act of 1933 or other applicable authorities.

First responder—local police, fire, and emergency medical personnel who arrive first on the scene of an incident and take action to save lives, protect property, and meet basic human needs.

Food defense—protection of food products from intentional adulteration by biological, chemical, physical, or radiological agents.

Food safety—protection of food products from unintentional contamination.

Functional model of public health response in disasters—paradigm for identifying disaster-related activities for which each core area of public health has responsibility; interface between the core components of professional public health training and the matrix of emergency management functions; relation between the framework of activities defined by the emergency management community and public health practice.

Functional needs populations—formerly referred to as "special needs populations," populations whose members may have additional needs before, during, and after an emergency, including but not limited to maintaining independence, communication, transportation, supervision, and medical care. May include those with disabilities or living in institutionalized settings, the elderly, children, persons from non-native cultures, those with limited English proficiency or who are non–English speaking, or who are transportation disadvantaged.

Functional needs support services—services that enable individuals to maintain their independence in a general care shelter.

Fujita scale—classification system used to measure the strength of tornadoes; assesses the damage caused by the tornado after it has passed over a man-made structure. The scale ranges from F0 (breaks tree branches with winds 40–72 mph) to F5 (steel reinforced concrete structures badly damaged with winds 261–318 mph). (An F6 tornado has been classified but is considered inconceivable with winds at 319–379 mph.)

Geographic Information System[1]—commonly referred to as GIS; a collection of computer hardware, software, and geographic data for capturing, storing, updating, manipulating, analyzing, and displaying all forms of geographically related information.

Access rights—privileges given to a user for reading, writing, deleting, and updating files on a disk or tables in a database. Access rights are stated as "no access," "read only," and "read/write."

Address—point stored as an "x,y" location in a geographic data layer, referenced with a unique identifier.

Address geocoding—Assigning "x,y" coordinates to tabular data such as street addresses or zip codes so they can be displayed as points on a map.

Altitude—elevation above a reference datum, usually sea level, of any point on the earth's surface or in the atmosphere, or the z value in a three-dimensional coordinate system.

Area chart—chart that emphasizes the difference between two or more groups of data; for example, the changes in a population from one year to the next. The area of interest is usually shaded in a different color.

Attribute—information about a geographic feature in a GIS, generally stored in a table and linked to the feature by a unique identifier.

Base data—map data over which other information is placed.

Basemap—map depicting geographic features used for locational reference and often including a geodetic control network as part of its structure.

[1]Reprinted with permission from Kennedy H, editor. 2001. *Dictionary of GIS Terminology*. Redlands, CA: ESRI Press.

Cell—smallest square in a grid. Each cell usually has an attribute value associated with it.

Clean data—data that are free from error.

Connectivity—how geographic features in a network of lines are attached to one another functionally or spatially.

Database—includes data about the spatial locations and shapes of geographic features recorded as points, lines, areas, pixels, and grid cells, as well as their attributes.

Data dictionary—set of tables containing information about the data stored in a GIS database, such as the full names of the attributes, meanings of codes, scale of source data, accuracy of locations, and map projections used; also referred to as metadata.

Geocode—code representing the location of an object, such as an address, census tract, postal code or "x,y" coordinates.

Global Positioning System—commonly referred to as GPS, a constellation of 24 satellites developed by the U.S. Department of Defense, that orbit the earth at an altitude of 20,200 kilometers (12,552 miles) and transmit signals that allow a receiver anywhere on earth to calculate its own location. GPS is used for navigation, mapping, surveying, and other applications for which precise positioning is necessary.

Hierarchical database—database that stores related information in a structure similar to that of a tree, where records can be traced to parent records which in turn can be traced to a root record.

Lookup table—tabular data file that contains additional attributes for records stored in an attribute table.

Managed data—data which has been standardized, compared with U.S. postal street data, verified, and corrected so that it precisely identifies locations of each address.

Overlay—superimposed series of two or more maps registered to a common coordinate system, either digitally or on a transparent material, in order to show the relationships between features that occupy the same geographic space.

Raster—spatial data model of rows and columns of cells that share the same value representing geographic features.

Relational database—data stored in tables that are associated with shared attributes, which can be arranged in different combinations.

Shapefile—vector file format for storing location, shape, and attributes of geographic features; stored in a set of related files and contains one feature class.

Spatial analysis—study of the locations and shapes of geographic features and the relationships between them; traditionally includes overlay and contiguity analysis, surface analysis, linear analysis, and raster analysis.

Unmanaged data—commercially available data that provides household level information without an extensive effort to ensure that the coordinates match the physical address.

Vector—data structure used to represent linear geographic features. Features are made of ordered lists of "x,y" coordinates and represented by points, lines, or polygons; points connect to become lines, and lines connect to become polygons. Attributes are associated with each feature (as opposed to a raster data structure, which associates attributes with grid cells).

Golden hour—principle that a victim whose airway, breathing, or circulation is erratic must be stabilized as soon as possible or within one hour following injury or he or she will die.

Governor's Authorized Representative—individual empowered by a governor who executes documents for disaster assistance on behalf of the state, represents the governor in the Unified Coordination Group, coordinates the disaster assistance program for states, and helps identify state's critical information needs.

Hardiness—psychological state, characterized by belief that one can exert control over events, viewing stressful events as challenges that can be overcome, and strong commitment and purpose.

Hazard—probability of the occurrence of a disaster caused by a natural phenomenon (such as earthquake, tropical cyclone), failure of man-made sources of energy (nuclear reactor, industrial explosion), or uncontrolled human activity (conflicts, overgrazing).

Hazard identification and risk assessment—process to identify hazards and associated risk likely to occur in a specified region or environment (e.g., earthquakes, floods, industrial accidents).

Hazard surveillance—assessment of the occurrence of, distribution of, and the secular trends in levels of hazards (e.g., toxic chemical agents, physical agents, biomechanical stressors, as well as biological agents) responsible for disease and injury.

Impact phase—phase during a disaster event when activities of warning and preparedness occur.

Incident—occurrence or event, natural or human-caused, that requires an emergency response to protect life or property.

Catastrophic incidents—comparable with presidentially declared major disasters.

Incident Action Plan—written document developed by the Incident Commander or the planning section of the Incident Command System that details actions that will be conducted through the Incident Command System in response to an incident; developed for specific time periods, referred to as *operational periods*, based on the needs of the incident. The Incident Commander is responsible for overseeing and implementing the plan.

Incident Command System—model for command, control, and coordination of a response that provides a means to coordinate the efforts of individual agencies.

Area Command—activated when complexity of the incident requires oversight of multiple incidents for which multiple incident management teams are involved.

Branch—organizational level having functional or geographic responsibility for major parts or incident operations. The Incident Commander may establish geographic branches to resolve span-of-control issues or may establish functional branches to manage specific functions (e.g. law enforcement, fire, emergency medical).

Chain of command—series of command, control, executive, or management positions in hierarchical order of authority.

Command—act of directing, ordering, or controlling by virtue of explicit statutory, regulatory, or delegated authority.

Division—organizational level with responsibility for operations within a defined geographic area; the organizational level between single resources, task forces or strike teams, and the branch level.

Emergency Operations Center—location where department heads, government officials, and volunteer agencies coordinate the response to an emergency event.

Function—one of the five major activities in the Incident Command System: Command, Operations, Planning, Logistics, and Finance/Administration.

Group—organizational level having responsibility for a specified functional assignment at an incident (e.g., perimeter control, evacuation, fire suppression); managed by a group supervisor.

Incident Commander—person with overall authority and responsibility for conducting incident operations and managing all incident operations.

Integrated communications—system using a common communications plan, standard operating procedures, clear text, common frequencies, and common terminology.

Resource management—functional area that maximizes use, consolidates control, reduces communication barriers, provides accountability, and ensures safety for personnel.

Section—organizational level with responsibility for a major functional area of the incident; located organizationally between branches and the Incident Commander.

Sizeup—problem identification and an assessment of the possible consequences; is initially the responsibility of the first officer to arrive at the scene, but continues throughout the response to update continually the nature of the incident, hazards that are present, the size of the affected area, whether the area can be isolated, if a staging area is needed and the best location, and where to establish entrance and exit routes for the flow of personnel and equipment.

Span of control—number of individuals that one supervisor manages; a manageable span of control for one supervisor ranges between three to seven resources, with five being optimal.

Staging area—place where resources are kept awaiting assignment.

Strike team—group of resources of the same size and type.

Task force—combination of single resources assembled for a particular operational need, with common communications and a leader.

Top-down—command function that is established by the first arriving officer, who becomes the Incident Commander.

Unified Area Command—command system established when incidents under an Area Command are multijurisdictional.

Unified Command—within an Incident Command System, used when more than one agency has incident jurisdiction or when incidents cross political jurisdictions. Agencies work together through the designated members of the Unified Command to establish a common set of objectives and strategies and a single Incident Action Plan.

Unity of command—concept that each person within an organization reports to only one designated person.

Incident Command Post—field location at which the primary response functions are performed.

Incident Coordination Plan—plan approved and published by the Emergency Management Group for the support of response operations.

Incident management—way in which incidents are managed across all Department of Homeland Security activities, including prevention, protection, response, and recovery.

Incident Management Assistance Team—interagency nationally- or regionally-based team composed of subject-matter experts and incident management professionals from multiple federal departments and agencies.

Integrated recovery programs—balanced recovery programs that respond to a variety of community needs; characterized by stimulation of activity in various sectors, sequencing of activities at appropriate times, and the use of both indirect and direct methods.

International assistance—assistance provided by one or more countries or international and voluntary organizations to a country in need, usually for development or for an emergency. The four main elements of assistance within the international community are: intergovernmental agencies such as the United Nations and the European Union, nongovernmental organizations, the International Red Cross, and bilateral agreements.

Interoperable communications—ability to exchange and use information through different types of equipment.

Isolation—sequestration of symptomatic patents either in their home or in the hospital so that they will not infect others.

Joint Field Office—temporary federal facility that provides a central location for the coordination of federal, state, tribal, and local governments and private-sector and nongovernmental organizations with primary responsibility for response and recovery.

Joint Information Center—interagency hub that coordinates and disseminates information for the public and media concerning an incident.

Jurisdiction—an agency's legal responsibilities and authority.

Jurisdictional agency—agency having jurisdiction and responsibility for a specific geographical area or function.

Landslide—the most common and wide-spread type of ground failure that is characterized by massive and more or less rapid toppling, sliding, falling, spreading, or flowing of soil and rock down unstable slopes.

Latrines—holes in the ground, usually with a covering platform and privacy wall, designed to capture and contain excreta; may be dug as a trench with multiple platforms across it, or can be a solitary pit with a self-standing structure.

Limited English proficiency—classification of persons who have a limited ability to read, speak, write, or understand English who may be entitled to language assistance in order to access a particular type of service, benefit, or encounter.

Liquefaction—when wet soil behaves like liquid and temporarily loses bearing strength; occurs mainly in young, shallow, loosely compacted, water-saturated sand and gravel deposits when subjected to ground shaking;

Logistician—individual skilled at calculating and arranging for the various tasks involved in moving and providing personnel, supplies, and so on as part of a response.

Long-term evolution—next-generation wireless technology for mobile broadband networks that provides high bandwidth and accelerates the transfer of information.

Long-term recovery—process of recovery that may continue for months or years, depending on the severity and extent of the damage sustained.

Loss—range of adverse consequences impacting communities and individuals that includes but is not limited to damage; decrease in economic value, function, natural resources, or ecological systems; environmental impact; health deterioration; mortality; and morbidity.

Major disaster—under the Robert T. Stafford Disaster Relief and Emergency Assistance Act of 1988, any natural catastrophe or, regardless of cause, any fire, flood, or explosion in the United States that, in the determination of the president, causes damage of sufficient severity and magnitude to warrant major federal disaster assistance to supplement the efforts and available resources of states and local governments.

Man-made or technological disasters—technological events that are not caused by natural hazards but that occur in human settlements, such as fire, chemical spills and explosions, and armed conflict.

Mass casualty incident—incident that generates a large number of patients in a relatively short period, usually as the result of a single occurrence, such as an aircraft accident, hurricane, flood, or earthquake, that exceeds the local capacity to respond.

Measures of biological effects—human health effects that indicate impacts of disasters, including but not limited to age-specific injury and death rates, laboratory typing of organisms, biochemical testing of exposures to toxic chemicals, and anthropometric measurements, such as height-to-weight ratios.

Measures of physical effects—used to indicate magnitude of disaster; examples include the height of a river above flood stage, the level of pollutants in air after forest fire; and the level of toxic chemicals in drinking water or sediment.

Measuring environmental hazards—assessment of the occurrence, distribution, and trends in the level of environmental hazards responsible for disease and injury; examples of hazards include biomechanical stressors, biological agents, and toxic chemicals.

Medical coordination—coordination between prehospital and hospital phases of medical care; characterized by simplification and standardization of materials and methods utilized.

Mission assignment—work order issued to another federal agency directing completion of a specific task or provision of a service in anticipation of, or in response to, a presidential declaration of a major disaster or emergency.

Mitigation—measures taken to reduce the harmful effects of a disaster by attempting to limit impacts on human health and economic infrastructure.

Mobile Web sites—Web sites designed to display on mobile devices, such as smartphones, capable of accessing the Internet.

Mobility disability—medical condition or injury that impedes a person's ability to move.

Mobilization—process and procedures used for activating, assembling, and transporting all resources that have been requested to respond to or support an incident.

Monitoring—process of observing response and recovery programs to determine performance by measuring them against their stated objectives; used to identify bottlenecks and obstacles that cause delays or require reassessment.

Mortality data—information regarding the number of deaths caused by a disaster; used to assess the magnitude of an event, evaluate the effectiveness of disaster preparedness and the adequacy of warning systems, and identify high risk groups for contingency planning.

Mortality surveillance—process that identifies the number of deaths caused by a disaster and the key information regarding those deaths; such information is collected through disaster mortuary teams, medical examiners, coroners, hospitals, nursing homes, and funeral homes.

Multiagency coordination group—team of administrators or their representatives authorized to commit agency resources and funds that coordinates decisionmaking and allocation of resources, establishes the disaster priorities, and provides strategic guidance and direction to support incident management.

Multiagency coordination system—mechanism for assisting agencies and organizations during a response by coordinating prioritization, critical resource allocation, communications systems integration, and information coordination.

Multijurisdictional incident—incident requiring action from multiple agencies that each have jurisdiction to manage certain aspects of the incident. In the Incident Command System, these incidents will be managed under Unified Command.

Mutual aid and assistance agreement—written or oral agreement between and among agencies, organization, or jurisdictions that provides a mechanism to quickly obtain emergency assistance in the form of personnel, equipment, materials, and other associated services.

National Operations Center—primary national hub for coordination of disaster response operations across the federal government; provides the secretary of Homeland Security and other principals with information necessary to make national-level incident management decisions.

National Planning Scenarios—scenarios that depict the range of potential emergencies as the basis for coordinated federal planning, training, and exercises.

National Preparedness Guidelines—guidance for national preparedness that provides a systematic approach for prioritizing preparedness efforts across the United States.

National Preparedness Vision—concise statement of the core preparedness goal for the United States.

National Response Coordination Center—component of the National Operations Center that serves as the primary operations center responsible for national incident response, recovery, and resource coordination.

National Response Framework—document which provides the key principles, roles, and structures that organize national response to disasters; how all partners coordinate by applying these principles; and defines circumstances in which the federal government has a larger role.

National Voluntary Organizations Active in Disaster—consortium of more than 30 national organizations active in disaster relief that provide capabilities to assist in incident management and response efforts at all levels. During major incidents, the consortium typically sends representatives to the National Response Coordination Center to represent the voluntary organizations and assist in response coordination.

Natural disasters—rapid, acute onset phenomena with profound effects, such as earthquakes, floods, tropical cyclones, tornadoes.

Natural–technological disasters—natural disasters that create technological emergencies, such as urban fires resulting from seismic motion or chemical spills resulting from floods.

Nongovernmental organization—organization that works cooperatively with governmental agencies to provide relief services to disaster victims, including specialized services to disabled persons.

Outcome surveillance—monitoring for a health outcome or event of interest, usually illness, injury, or death.

Outcome variable—health event, usually illness, injury, or death; also known as response variable, dependent variable, or effect variable.

Overt release—announced release of a biological agent, by terrorists or others; this type of release often allows treatment before the onset of disease.

Pandemic—epidemic over a wide geographic area or one that affects a large proportion of the world's population.

Paramedic—highly-trained EMT capable of providing advanced life support functions to victims in a disaster or emergency setting.

Paratransit—transportation services used by the mobility impaired or transportation disadvantaged. Includes taxis, carpools, vanpools, minibuses, jitneys, demand-responsive bus services, and specialized bus services.

Personal assessment—Written list of what an individual needs and the resources for meeting those needs following a disaster

Personal assistance services—formal and informal services provided by paid personnel, personal attendants, friends, family, and volunteers that enable those in general population shelters to maintain their usual level of independence.

Personal space—area immediately surrounding a person, including the objects within that space.

Personal support network—group of people who help those with disabilities at home, school, workplace, volunteer site, or any other location; can include roommates, relatives, neighbors, friends, and coworkers. Such a network must know that individual's capabilities and needs, be able to check if an individual needs assistance, and be able to help within minutes.

Phases of the functional model—model composed of six phases that correspond to the type of activities that public health professionals are involved in preparing for in the event of a disaster.

PHIN Messaging System—message transport system that allows secure data transmission over the Internet.

Planning—working cooperatively with other disciplines in advance of a disaster event to initiate prevention and preparedness.

Podcast—Web-based audio or video file that users download to portable listening devices.

Point of distribution—area established in which mass distribution of antibiotics or vaccine is performed and patients are registered, are triaged, have swab samples taken, are medically evaluated, and are provided with antibiotics or vaccine.

Postdisaster surveillance—conducted by health authorities primarily to monitor health events, detect sudden changes in disease occurrence, follow long-term trends of specific diseases, identify changes in agents and host factors for the diseases of interest, and recognize changes in health practices for treating relevant diseases.

Postimpact phase—period after a disaster event when activities of response and recovery occur.

Power-dependent equipment—equipment that requires electricity to operate.

Predictive value positive—ability to detect that cases considered positive have the health event being assessed under surveillance.

Preimpact phase—period before a disaster strikes during which activities of mitigation or prevention occur.

Preparedness—aggregate of all measures and policies taken by humans before an event occurs that allows mitigation of the impact caused by the event through responses to the impact of the event; includes contingency plans and responses, warning systems, evacuation, relocation of dwellings, stores of food and water, temporary shelter, energy, management strategies, disaster drills and exercises, and laying a framework for recovery; also includes prevention, mitigation, and readiness.

Prepositioned resources—resources moved to an area near the expected incident site in response to anticipated resource needs.

Pre-scripted mission assignment—mechanism used by the federal government to facilitate a rapid response of federal resources. Pre-scripted mission assignments identify resources or capabilities that federal departments and agencies, through various emergency support functions, commonly provide during incident response.

Presidential (Decision) Directives—U.S. government policy decisions on foreign affairs and national security that occur after the National Security Council gathers facts, conducts analyses, determines alternatives, and presents policy choices to the president for decision.

Prevention—primary, secondary, and tertiary efforts to avert a disaster; includes the activities that are commonly thought of as "mitigation" in the emergency management model, and in public health terms, refers to actions that may prevent further loss of life, disease, disability, or injury.

Primary prevention—averting occurrence of deaths, injuries, or illnesses related to a disaster event (e.g., evacuation of a community in a flood-prone area, sensitizing warning systems for tornadoes and severe storms).

Secondary prevention—mitigating health consequences of disasters (e.g., use of carbon monoxide detectors when operating gasoline-powered generators after loss of electric power after ice storms, employing appropriate occupant behavior in multistory structures during earthquakes, building a "safe room" in dwellings located in tornado-prone areas); may be instituted when disasters are imminent.

Tertiary prevention—minimizing the effects of disease and disability among the already ill; employed in persons with preexisting health conditions and in whom the health effects from a disaster event may exacerbate those health conditions. Examples include appropriate sheltering of persons with respiratory illnesses and those prone to such conditions, particularly the elderly and young children, from haze and smoke originating from forest fires, and sheltering elderly who are prone to heat illnesses during episodes of extreme ambient temperatures.

Principal Federal Official—may be appointed to serve as the secretary of Homeland Security's primary representative in the federal management of catastrophic or unusually complex incidents.

Public access system—911 emergency telephone system by which the public notifies the authorities that a medical emergency exists.

Public health surveillance—ongoing and systematic collection, analysis, and interpretation of health data used for planning, implementing, and evaluating public health interventions and programs; used to determine the need for public health action and to assess the effectiveness of programs.

Quarantine—separation of asymptomatic persons who may have been exposed to infection from the general community.

Radiation

Acute radiation exposure—single large dose or a series of lesser but substantial doses over a short period.

Acute radiation syndrome—radiation illness associated with an acute radiation exposure.

Alpha particle—positively charged subatomic particle consisting of two protons and two neutrons, identical with the nucleus of the helium atom; the most energetic alpha particle is incapable of penetrating the skin.

As Low As Reasonably Achievable (ALARA)—concept and administrative program meant to keep workers' exposures to ionizing radiation "as low as reasonably achievable." This specific action program, which takes economic and social factors into account, is expected to reduce collective medical and occupational doses (person-rems) while maintaining an individual worker's dose at 10 percent or less of the dose limits contained in 10 CFR 20.

Background radiation—ionizing radiation that is a natural part of a person's environment; primarily, cosmic rays and that emitted by natural materials.

Beta particle—charged particle that is ejected from the nucleus of an atom; it has a mass and charge equal in magnitude to that of the electron.

Buffer zone—intermediate area between a radioactively contaminated zone and the rest of a "clean" building.

Cytogenetic dosimetry—estimation of radiation dose based on typical radiation-induced chromosomal aberrations as calibrated against standard exposures.

Film bandage—type of personal radiation monitor, or dosimeter, that records the extent of one's radiation exposure by means of sensitized photographic film.

Gamma ray—high-energy radiation of short wavelength emitted during the radioactive decay of many radioactive elements. Similar in properties to X-rays, gamma rays are of nuclear origin, whereas X-rays are formed by the excitation of orbital electrons.

High-level radiation dose—defined as being from 150 to 350 rems, per the National Council on Radiation Protection and Measurements Report No. 64.

International Commission on Radiological Protection—group, founded in 1928, whose function is to recommend international standards for radiation protection.

Ionizing radiation—form of radiation which is able to cause a neutral atom or molecule to gain or lose orbital electrons and thereby acquire a net electrical charge.

Isotope—one of two or more atoms with the same atomic number (and thus, similar chemical properties) but with different atomic weights and somewhat different physical properties.

Low-level radiation dose—generally considered for occupational purposes to be less than 5 rems per year, or 20 rems of a single dose, of uniform whole body radiation.

National Council on Radiation Protection and Measurements—nonprofit corporation chartered by Congress in 1964 to develop information and recommendations for the United States regarding radiation protection and measurements.

Personal monitor—device for measuring a person's exposure to a physical or chemical agent in the environment, such as radiation; information on the dose-equivalent of ionizing radiation to biological tissue is derived from film badges, ionization chambers, and thermoluminescent devices; determinations based on whole-body counting and analysis of biological specimens; and area monitoring and special surveys. Also referred to as a personnel dosimeter or monitor.

Rad—special unit for an absorbed dose of ionizing radiation.

Radionuclide—radioactive nuclide.

Rem—"radiation equivalent, man"; a special unit of dose equivalent based on biological effect and numerically equal to the absorbed dose in rad units multiplied by a modifying factor; however, for simplicity and for the types of radiation most often encountered environmentally, it is numerically equivalent to both the rad and Roentgen.

Roentgen (R)—special unit of radiation exposure based on measurement in air or before radiation strikes the body.

Sealed source—radioactive store that is contained within an impervious and durable package so as to prevent contact with or release and dispersal of the radioactive items.

Thermoluminescent dosimeter—personnel monitor in which orbital electrons are displaced or trapped within a crystal such as manganese-activated calcium or lithium fluoride as a result of the crystal's exposure to ionizing radiation; when the crystal is later heated to a certain point, the stored energy of the electron displacement is released as light, which is then measured and related to radiation dose.

Transuranic elements—those elements with an atomic number greater than 92, or heavier than uranium (e.g., americium and plutonium); all are radioactive and not naturally occurring.

Radio bands—collection of neighboring frequencies allocated on different bands. Each two-way radio is designed for a specific band and will not work on other bands.

Rapid needs assessment—collection of techniques (epidemiologic, statistical, anthropological) designed to provide information about an affected community's needs after a disaster.

Readiness—links preparedness to relief; reflects the current capacity and capability of organizations involved in relief activities.

Real Simple Syndication (RSS) feeds—message that notifies users when a Web site is updated.

Reasonable accommodation/modification—any change to the rules, policies, procedures, or environment that enables an individual with a disability to participate. A requested accommodation is unreasonable if it poses an undue financial or administrative burden or a fundamental alteration in the program or service.

Recovery—actions for returning the community to normal after an emergency but before the reconstruction phase, including the stimulation of community and government cohesion and involvement, such as repair of infrastructure, damaged buildings, and critical facilities; has policy, political, and social implications that are both short and long term.

Red Cross—general term used for one or all the components of the worldwide organization active in humanitarian work. The official overall name is the International Red Cross and Red Crescent Movement, which has three components: the International Committee of the Red Cross, which acts mainly in conflict disasters as a neutral intermediary in hostilities and for the protection of war victims; the League of the Red Cross and Red Crescent Societies, which serves as the international federation of the National Societies and is active in non-conflict disasters and natural calamities; and the individual National Red Cross or Red Crescent Society of every country.

Regional Response Coordination Center—multiagency coordination center in a FEMA region staffed by emergency support personnel in anticipation of a serious incident in the region or immediately following an incident; operates under the direction of the FEMA Regional Administrator and is responsible for coordinating federal regional response efforts with state and local efforts.

Rehabilitation or reconstruction—efforts to reconstruct a system or infrastructure to the level which existed before an emergency through long-term development; during this time, attempts should be made to construct a system or infrastructure using the positive aspects of the previous system while at the same time attempting to correct the past problems and add improvements as a "reconstruction plus" approach.

Relief—period in which attention is focused on saving lives via such actions as search and rescue, first aid, and restoration of emergency communications and transportation systems, and attention to immediate care and basic needs of survivors, such as food, clothing, and medical or emotional care.

Report format—instrument on which surveillance data are reported.

Reporting unit for surveillance—institution which provides information for the surveillance system, such as a hospital, clinic, health post, mobile health unit, or other unit determined after a case is defined.

Representativeness—accuracy of data in measuring the occurrence of a health event over time and its distribution by person and place.

Resilience—ability of a community or its members to rapidly and effectively rebound from events that are psychologically or behaviorally unsettling.

Resistance—ability of community or its members to resist clinical distress, impairment, or dysfunction associated with the range of disasters; psychological/behavioral immunity to distress and dysfunction.

Resource description framework—standard model for data interchange on the Web.

Response—phase of a disaster that encompasses relief and recovery and addresses the short-term, direct effects of an incident; includes immediate actions to save lives, protect property, and meet basic human needs; includes both the delivery of services and the management of activities.

Risk assessment—systematic process used to determine the likelihood of adverse effects in a population following exposure to a specified hazard; endpoints or consequences depend on the hazard and include damage, loss of economic value, loss of function, loss of natural resources, loss of ecological systems, environmental impact, and deterioration of health, mortality, and morbidity. The major components of a risk assessment include hazard identification and analysis and vulnerability analysis and answer the questions, What can happen? How likely are each of the possible outcomes? and When the possible outcomes happen, what are the likely consequences and losses? Risk is frequently presented as a probability estimate. Risk assessment is now a key planning tool for overall disaster management, especially prevention and mitigation activities. Risk is frequently depicted by the following useful formula (although the association is not strictly arithmetic): risk = hazard × vulnerability.

Risk indicator—descriptor that briefly denotes a risk that may cause a disaster.

Risk management—public process of deciding what to do when risk assessments indicate that risk, or the chance of loss, exists. Risk management encompasses choices and actions for communities and individuals (e.g., prevention, mitigation, preparedness, and recovery) that are designed to stop increasing the risk to future elements that will be placed at risk to hazards, start decreasing the risk to existing elements already at risk, and continue planning ways to respond to and recover from an extreme situation or catastrophic event.

Saffir-Simpson Hurricane Wind scale—used to alert the public about the possible intensity of a hurricane. The scale categorizes a hurricane's intensity on a 1-to-5 scale to give an estimate of the potential property damage and flooding expected along the coast where the hurricane makes landfall. In general, damage from the hurricane increases by a factor of four for every category increase.

Secure Digital—memory card format used in portable devices.

Self-efficacy—psychological state characterized by the belief that one can organize and carry out necessary tasks to reach a goal.

Service animal—specially-trained animal used by a disabled person to help with daily living; these animals are allowed by law to accompany their owners anywhere they go.

Short-term recovery—process of recovery that is immediate and overlaps with response; includes such actions as providing essential public health and safety services, restoring interrupted utilities, reestablishing transportation routes, and providing food and shelter for those displaced by a disaster. Although called "short term," some of these activities may last for weeks.

Situational awareness—ability to identify, process, and comprehend the critical elements of information about an incident.

Social capital—connections within and between social networks that provide access to resources; social relationships that have productive benefits.

Social distancing—range of measures used to impede the spread of infectious disease in a community; does not involve quarantine but can reduce contact between persons, such as closing schools or prohibiting large gatherings.

Social networking sites—online communities in which users interact and exchange information.

Social vulnerability—susceptibility of individuals or organizations to the adverse impacts that accompany disasters.

Specific Area Message Encoding—protocol used to encode the Emergency Alert System for broadcast stations in the United States.

Stafford Act—formally known as the Robert T. Stafford Disaster Relief and Emergency Assistance Act of 1988, P.L. 93-288, as amended, this act describes the programs and processes by which the federal government provides disaster and emergency assistance to state and local governments, tribal nations, eligible private nonprofit organizations, and individuals affected by a declared major disaster or emergency. The act covers all hazards, including natural disasters and terrorist events.

State Coordinating Officer—individual appointed by the governor to coordinate state disaster assistance efforts with those of the federal government. The State Coordinating Officer plays a critical role in managing state response and recovery operations following Stafford Act declarations.

Stockpile—a store of material, medicines, and other supplies needed for emergency relief in disaster that is kept in a specific place.

Stress—physical, mental, or emotional strain or tension.

SUMA—also known as "supply management program"; computer-based system developed by the Pan-American Health Organization that provides a mechanism for sorting, classifying, and preparing an inventory of relief supplies sent to a disaster-stricken country.

Support annexes—describe how federal departments and agencies, the private sector, volunteer organizations, and nongovernmental organizations coordinate and execute the common support processes and administrative tasks required during any type of incident.

Surge capacity—health care system's ability to rapidly expand and deliver services beyond what is required during normal care.

Surveillance—ongoing and systematic collection, analysis, and interpretation of health data essential to the planning, implementation, and evaluation of public health practice, closely integrated with the timely dissemination of data to those who need to know; includes both data collection and monitoring disease.

Target capabilities list—defined specific capabilities that all levels of government should possess in order to respond effectively to incidents.

Technological hazard—potential threat to humans caused by technological factors (e.g., chemical release, nuclear accident, dam failure); natural hazards can trigger technological hazards.

Telecommunications Relay Service—telephone service that uses operators, called communications assistants, to facilitate telephone calls between people with hearing and speech disabilities and voice telephone users.

Text messaging—short messages exchanged between mobile devices.

Tiger team—military term for a group that probes security to find weaknesses that can be remedied.

Timeliness—how quickly information can be made available.

Toxicological disaster—serious environmental pollution and illness caused by the massive accidental escape of toxic substances into the air, soil, or water.

Toxin—substance secreted by certain living organisms that are capable of causing harmful effects in other organisms.

Transportation to definitive medical care—use of ground ambulances, helicopters, boats, and snow cats for transport of patients to a higher level of medical care, usually at a hospital.

Traumatic stress—somewhat undefined category of stress caused by events and circumstances that are both extreme and outside of the realm of everyday experiences; this type of stress is often the result of dangerous, overwhelming, and sudden events and typically causes fear, anxiety, withdrawal, and avoidance in persons who experience them.

Triage—selection and categorization of disaster victims for appropriate treatment according to the degree of severity of illness or injury and the availability of medical and transport facilities.

Tsunami—oceanic tidal wave generated by an underwater upheaval such as an earthquake or volcanic eruption. Waves move out in all directions over many miles, causing great destruction.

Tsunami run-up—measurement of the height of the water when a peak in the tsunami wave travels onto shore, much like very strong and fast-moving tides.

Unified Coordination Group—comprised of specified senior leaders representing identified jurisdictions which provides leadership within a Joint Field Office; typically consists of the Principal Federal Official (if designated), Federal Coordinating Officer, State Coordinating Officer, and senior officials from other entities with primary statutory or jurisdictional responsibility and significant operational responsibility for an aspect of an incident.

Victim—person who has been affected by a disaster. There are three classes of victims: primary victims, who are affected by the physical impact of the disaster; secondary victims, who reside within an affected community or on the border of an affected area and suffer economic loss as a result of the disaster or actions taken by relief operations; and tertiary victims, who are indirectly affected and who may live in the same country but not necessarily in the affected area.

Victim distribution—plan established to define transport and distribution of victims among neighboring hospitals according to their hospital treatment capacity; the plan often involves avoiding the hospital nearest the disaster site since walking victims will overcrowd it.

Video relay—form of telecommunications service that enables people who are deaf, hard of hearing, or have speech disabilities who use American Sign Language to communicate with voice telephone users through video equipment rather than through typed text.

Virtual private network—network that uses a public telecommunication infrastructure, such as the Internet, to provide remote offices or individual users with secure access to their organization's network.

Voluntary agency—nonprofit, nongovernmental, private association maintained and supported by voluntary contributions that provides assistance in emergencies and disasters.

Volunteer—any individual accepted to perform services without compensation.

Vulnerability—susceptibility of a given element to a given adverse event at a given intensity; the factors that influence vulnerability include demographics, age and resilience of the built environment, technology, social differentiation and diversity, regional and global economies, and political arrangements.

Vulnerability analysis—assessment of an exposed population's susceptibility to the adverse health effects of a given hazard.

Warning—indication that a severe weather event is presently happening, is going to happen, or has been observed on radar.

Watch—indication that a severe weather is threatening and may occur in an area; a watch indicates that citizens should listen to the radio or watch television for information and advice.

White hat tools—security tools used to protect systems.

Widgets—small software applications on a Web page or program that have a specific function (e.g. clocks, event countdowns, auction-tickers, stock market tickers, flight arrival information, daily weather alerts).

WiFi—trademark of the Wi-Fi Alliance that manufacturers use to brand products that belong to a class of wireless local area network.

Worried well—individuals who are not ill but seek medical treatment for reassurance.

Common Acronyms Used in Disaster Preparedness, Response and Recovery

AAR/IP	After-Action Report/Improvement Plan
ACIP	Advisory Committee on Immunization Practices
ACPHP	Academic Center for Public Health Preparedness
ADA	Americans With Disabilities Act
ADS	Automatic Detection System
AED	Automated External Defibrillator
AHRQ	Agency for Healthcare Research and Quality
ALS	Advanced Life Support
AMA	American Medical Association
APHL	Association of Public Health Laboratories
ARC	American Red Cross
ASPR	Assistant Secretary for Preparedness and Response
ASTHO	Association of State and Territorial Health Officials
ATSDR	Agency for Toxic Substances and Disease Registry
AVA	Anthrax Vaccine Adsorbed
AVRP	Anthrax Vaccine Research Program
BARDA	Biomedical Advanced Research and Development Authority
BLS	Basic Life Support
BSL	Biosafety Level
CAP	Common Alerting Protocol
CAT	Crisis Action Team
CBO	Community-Based Organization
CBRN	Chemical, Biological, Radiological/Nuclear
CCP	Casualty Collection Point
CCRF	Commissioned Corps Readiness Force
CDC	Centers for Disease Control and Prevention
CDRG	Catastrophic Disaster Response Group
CEPPO	Chemical Emergency Preparedness and Prevention Office
CERCLA	Comprehensive Environmental Response, Compensation, and Liability Act
CFR	Code of Federal Regulations
CHI	Consolidated Health Informatics
CINC	Commander-in-Chief
CLIA	Clinical Laboratory Improvement Act
CMAS	Commercial Mobile Alert System
CMHS	Center for Mental Health Services

CMS	Consumable Medical Supplies
CMT	Crisis Management Team
CONPLAN	Concept of Operations Plan
COOP	Continuity of Operations (Plan)
CPHP	Centers for Public Health Preparedness
CPR	Cardiopulmonary Resuscitation
CRC	Crisis Response Cell
CSG	Counterterrorism Security Group
CSTE	Council of State and Territorial Epidemiologists
CWA	Clean Water Act
DAE	Disaster Assistance Employee
DCO	Defense Coordinating Officer
DFO	Disaster Field Office
DFSG	Disaster Financial Services Group
DHS	U.S. Department of Homeland Security
DMAT	Disaster Medical Assistance Team
DME	Durable Medical Equipment
DMORT	Disaster Mortuary Response Team, National Disaster Medical System
DPO	Disaster Psychiatry Outreach
DRC	Disaster Recovery Center
DRM	Disaster Recovery Manager
DWI	Disaster Welfare Inquiry
EAP	Emergency Action Plan
EAS	Emergency Alert System
EBS	Emergency Broadcast System
EC	Emergency Coordinator
ECS	Emergency Communications Staff/System
EEI	Essential Elements of Information
EICC	Emergency Information and Coordination Center
EIS	Epidemic Intelligence Service
EISO	Epidemic Intelligence Service Officer
ELR	Electronic Laboratory-Based Reporting
EMAC	Emergency Management Assistance Compact
EMG	Emergency Management Group
EMS	Emergency Medical Services
EMT	Emergency Medical Technician
EOC	Emergency Operations Center
EPA	Environmental Protection Agency
EPAP	Emergency Prescription Assistance Program
EPI-x	Epidemic Information Exchange
EPO	Epidemiology Program Office
ERC	Emergency Response Coordinator
ERCG	Emergency Response Coordination Group
ERT	Emergency Response Team
ERT-A	Emergency Response Team – Advance Element

ESAR-VHP	Emergency Service Advanced Registration of Volunteer Healthcare Providers
ESF	Emergency Support Function
EST	Emergency Support Team
FAA	Federal Aviation Administration
FACT	Family Assistance Center Team
FAST	Functional Assessment Service Team
FBI	Federal Bureau of Investigation
FCC	Federal Communications Commission/Federal Coordinating Center
FCO	Federal Coordinating Officer
FDA	Food and Drug Administration
FECC	Federal Emergency Communications Coordinator
FEMA	Federal Emergency Management Agency
FERC	FEMA Emergency Response Capability
FESC	Federal Emergency Support Coordinator
FHWA	Federal Highway Administration
FMO	Financial Management Office
FMS	Federal Medical Station
FNS	Food and Nutrition Service
FNSS	Functional Needs Support Services
FRCM	FEMA Regional Communications Manager
FRERP	Federal Radiological Emergency Response Plan
FRP	Federal Response Plan
GAR	Governor's Authorized Representative
GIS	Geographic Information System
GMPCS	Global Mobile Personal Communication System
GPMRC	Global Patient Movement Requirements Center
GSA	General Services Administration
HAN	Health Alert Network
HAZMAT	Hazardous Material
HAZWOPER	Hazardous Waste Operations and Emergency Response Standard
HET-ESF	Headquarters Emergency Transportation - Emergency Support Function
HHS	U.S. Department of Health and Human Services
HICPAC	Healthcare Infection Control Practices Advisory Committee
HICS	Hospital Incident Command System
HIFI	High Frequency
HIPAA	Health Insurance Portability and Accountability Act
HIRA	Hazard Identification and Risk Assessment
HLT	Hurricane Liaison Team
HPP	Hospital Preparedness Program
HQUSACE	Headquarters, U.S. Army Corps of Engineers
HRSA	Health Resources and Services Administration
HSAS	Homeland Security Advisory System
HSPD	Homeland Security Presidential Directive
HUD	U.S. Department of Housing and Urban Development
HWC	Health and Welfare Canada

IAEA	International Atomic Energy Agency
IAP	Incident Action Plan
ICC	Interagency Coordinating Committee on Emergency Preparedness and Individuals with Disabilities
ICP	Incident Command Post
ICPAE	Interagency Committee on Public Affairs in Emergencies
ICRC	International Committee of the Red Cross
ICS	Incident Command System
IMAT	Incident Management Assistance Team
IMS	Incident Management System
IMSurT	International Medical Surgical Team
IPAWS	Integrated Public Alert and Warning System
IRAT	Immediate Response Assessment Team
IRCT	Incident Response Coordination Team
IT	Information Technology
JCAHO	Joint Committee on Accreditation of Health Care Organizations
JFO	Joint Field Office
JIC	Joint Information Center
JIS	Joint Information System
JOC	Joint Operations Center
JPAKS	Joint Patient Assessment Tracking System
LRAT	Logistical Response Assistance Team
LRN	Laboratory Response Network
LTE	Long-Term Evolution
MAC	Multi-Agency Coordination
MACS	Multi-Agency Coordination System
MANETS	Mobile Ad Hoc Network
MARS	U.S. Army Military Affiliate Radio System
MASF	Mobile Aeromedical Staging Facility
MERC	Mobile Emergency Response Support
MMWR	*Morbidity and Mortality Weekly Report*
MOA	Memorandum of Agreement
MOU	Memorandum of Understanding
MRC	Medical Reserve Corps
MRE	Meals Ready to Eat
MSEHPA	Model State Emergency Health Powers Act
NACCHO	National Association for City and County Health Officials
NBC	Nuclear, Biological, Chemical
NCBDDD	National Center on Birth Defects and Developmental Disease
NCC	National Coordinating Center
NCCDPHP	National Center for Chronic Disease Prevention and Health Promotion
NCEH	National Center for Environmental Health
NCHS	National Center for Health Statistics
NCHSTP	National Center for HIV, STD, and TB Prevention
NCID	National Center for Infectious Disease

NCIPC	National Center for Injury Prevention and Control
NCP	National Contingency Plan (National Oil and Hazardous Substances Pollution Contingency Plan)
NCS	National Communications System
NCS/DCA-OC	National Communications System/Defense Communication Agency–Operations Center
NDMOC	National Disaster Medical Operations Center
NDMS	National Disaster Medical System
NDMSOSC	National Disaster Medical System Operations Support Center
NECC	National Emergency Coordination Center
NEDSS	National Electronic Disease Surveillance System
NEIS	National Earthquake Information Service
NEMP	National Emergency Management Plan
NFDA	National Funeral Directors Association
NGO	Nongovernmental organization
NHPP	Division of National Healthcare Preparedness Program
NHSN	National Healthcare Safety Network
NHSS	National Health Security Strategy
NIC	NIMS Integration Center
NICC	National Infrastructure Coordinating Center
NIFCC	National Interagency Fire Coordination Center
NIH	National Institutes of Health
NIMH	National Institutes of Mental Health
NIMS	National Incident Management System
NIOSH	National Institute for Occupational Safety and Health
NIP	National Immunization Program
NLTN	National Laboratory Training Network
NNRT	National Nurse Response Team
NOAA	National Oceanic and Atmospheric Administration
NOC	National Operations Center
NPD	National Preparedness Directorate
NPLT	National Pharmacy Logistics Teams
NPPTL	National Personal Protective Technology Laboratory
NPRT	National Pharmacy Response Team
NRC	Nuclear Regulatory Commission
NRCC	National Response Coordinating Center
NRF	National Response Framework
NRT	National Response Team
NSEP	National Security Emergency Preparedness
NSF	National Strike Force
NTIA	National Telecommunications and Information Administration
NTSP	National Telecommunications Support Plan
NTU	Nephelometric Turbidity Units
NVOAD	National Voluntary Organizations Active in Disaster
NVRT	National Veterinary Response Team

NWR	National Oceanic and Atmospheric Administration Weather Radio
NWS	National Weather Service
OAMCG	Office of Acquisition Management, Contracts and Grants
OCHAMPUS	Office of Civilian Health and Medical Program of the Uniformed Services
OCR	Office of Civil Rights
OEP	Office of Emergency Preparedness
OET	Office of Emergency Transportation
OFDA	Office of U.S. Foreign Disaster Assistance
OFPA	Office of Financial Planning and Analysis
OFRD	Office of Force Readiness and Deployment
OHS	Office of Health and Safety
OIG	Office of Inspector General
OPEO	Office of Preparedness and Emergency Operations
OPHPR	Office of Public Health Preparedness and Response
OPLAN	Operations Plan
OPP	Office of Policy and Planning
OSC	On-Scene Coordinator
OSEP	Office of Security and Emergency Preparedness
OSG	Office of the Surgeon General
OSHA	Occupational Safety and Health Administration
OTPER	Office of Terrorism Preparedness and Emergency Response
OVAG	Organic Vapor/Acid Gas
PAHO	Pan-American Health Organization
PAHPA	Pandemic and All-Hazards Preparedness Act
PAS	Personal Assistance Services
PDA	Preliminary Damage Assessment
PFO	Principal Federal Official
PHA	Public Health Advisor
PHEMCE	Public Health Emergency Countermeasure Enterprise
PHEP	Public Health Emergency Preparedness
PHI	Protected Health Information
PHICS	Public Health Incident Command System
PHIN	Public Health Information Network
PHPPO	Public Health Practice Program Office
PIO	Public Information Officer
PKEMRA	Post-Katrina Emergency Management Reform Act
POD	Point of Distribution
PPACA	Patient Protection and Affordable Care Act
PPE	Personal Protective Equipment
PSAP	Public Safety Answering Points
PTSD	Post-Traumatic Stress Disorder
PVO	Private Voluntary Organization
PVS	Pre-Event Vaccination System
RACES	Radio Amateur Civil Emergency Services
RD	Regional Director

RDC	Office of Research and Development Coordination
RDF	Resource Description Framework
REACT	Radio Emergency Associated Communication Team
REC	Regional Emergency Coordinator
RECC	Regional Emergency Communications Coordinator
RECP	Regional Emergency Communications Plan
REP	Regional Evacuation Point
RET	Regional Emergency Transportation
RETCO	Regional Emergency Transportation Coordinator
RFA	Request for Assistance
RHA	Regional Health Administrator
RISC	Regional Inter-Agency Steering Committee
RRC	Ready Reserve Corps
RRCC	Regional Response Coordinating Center
RSS	Really Simple Syndication
SAME	Specific Area Message Encoding
SAMHSA	Substance Abuse and Mental Health Services Administration
SAP	Select Agent Program
SAR	Search and Rescue (National Urban)
SARA	Superfund Amendments and Reauthorization Act
SCBA	Self-Contained Breathing Apparatus
SCC	Secretary's Command Center
SCO	State Coordinating Officer
SD	Secure Digital
SEMO	State Emergency Management Office
SFLEO	Senior Federal Law Enforcement Officer
SHO	Senior Health Official
SO	Senior Official
SLPP	State and Local Preparedness Program
SLPS	State and Local Programs and Support Directorate
SNS	Strategic National Stockpile
SOC	Secretary's Operations Center
SOP	Standard Operating Procedure
SUMA	Supply Management System
SVP	Smallpox Vaccination Program
TARU	Technical Advisory Response Unit
TCL	Target Capabilities List
TED	Training, Education, and Demonstration Package
TOPOFF	Top officials
TRPLT	Terrorism Response and Preparation Leadership Team
TTY	Text Telephone
UC	Unified Command
UCG	Unified Coordination Group
UNDRO	United Nations Disaster Relief Organization
UNHCR	United Nations High Commission for Refugees

UNICEF	United Nations International Children's Education Fund
USACE	U.S. Army Corps of Engineers
USAID	U.S. Agency for International Development
USCG	U.S. Coast Guard
USDA	U.S. Department of Agriculture
USGS	U.S. Geological Survey
USPHS	U.S. Public Health Service
US&R	Urban Search and Rescue
VA	U.S. Department of Veterans Affairs
VAERS	Vaccine Adverse Effects Reporting System
VANET	Vehicular Ad-Hoc Network
VHA	Veterans Health Administration
VIG	Vaccinia Immune Globulin
VMAT	Veterinary Medical Assistance Team
VMI	Vendor Managed Inventory
VOAD	Voluntary Organizations Active in Disaster
VPA	Volunteer Protection Act
VPN	Virtual private network
VRS	Video relay service
WHO	World Health Organization
WISER	Wireless Information for Emergency Responders
XML	Extensible Markup Language
24-7	Twenty-four hours a day/seven days a week

The Language of Disasters, Emergencies, Hazards, and Incidents

Numerous terms are used to describe disasters. These terms include "domestic disaster," "natural disaster," "major disaster," "incident," and "catastrophic incident." These terms are derived from two documents: the Stafford Act (major disaster, natural disaster, and domestic disaster) and the National Response Framework (NRF; incident and catastrophic incident). In addition, the term "emergency" is also used and defined by the NRF Resource Center as

> Any incident, whether natural or manmade, that requires responsive action to protect life or property. Under the Robert T. Stafford Disaster Relief and Emergency Assistance Act, an emergency means any occasion or instance for which, in the determination of the President, Federal assistance is needed to supplement State and local efforts and capabilities to save lives and to protect property and public health and safety, or to lessen or avert the threat of a catastrophe in any part of the United States.

The terms in the Stafford Act were developed before the attacks of September 11, 2001, whereas the terms from the NRF were developed after the attacks.

Disasters and Hazards

As used in the Stafford Act, a disaster has already occurred and has caused significant damage. As defined by the NRF, a hazard is "something that is potentially dangerous or harmful, often the root cause of an unwanted outcome." The earthquake that struck Japan on March 11, 2011, was a disaster, although earthquakes in general are hazards. A major disaster is defined as

> Any natural catastrophe or, regardless of cause, any fire, flood, or explosion, in any part of the United States, which in the determination of the President causes damage of sufficient severity and magnitude to warrant major disaster assistance under [the Stafford Act] to supplement the efforts and available resources of States, local governments, and disaster relief organizations in alleviating the damage, loss, hardship, or suffering caused thereby.

Incidents

The NRF uses the term "incident" in a broader and more inclusive manner than it uses the terms "disaster" and "emergency." According to the NRF, an incident is "an occurrence or event, natural or human-caused, that requires an emergency response to protect life or property." As defined, thousands of incidents across the United States occur every year. Most do not involve public health and are handled by first responders. Only a small number are of the magnitude that requires federal assistance, including catastrophic incidents.

Catastrophic incidents are comparable with presidentially-declared major disasters and are described as

> Any natural or man-made incident, including terrorism, that results in extraordinary levels of mass casualties, damage, or disruption severely affecting the population, infrastructure, environment, economy, national morale, and/or government functions.

The NRF includes a Catastrophic Incident Annex that can only be implemented by the secretary of the Department of Homeland Security or a designee. The annex covers both natural and man-made disasters that do significant harm and which overwhelm the response capabilities of local and state governments.

Details of the Two Documents

Full Name	Robert T. Stafford Relief and Emergency Act of 1988 (as amended)	National Response Framework
Short Name	Stafford Act or 42 USC §§ 5121-5206	NRF
Date	1988, effective May 1989	January 2008
Creator	U.S. Congress	U.S. Department of Homeland Security
Purpose	"To provide an orderly and continuing means of assistance by the Federal Government to State and local governments in carrying out their responsibilities to alleviate the suffering and damage which result from ... disasters."	"To establish a comprehensive, all-hazards approach to domestic across a spectrum of activities, including prevention, preparedness, response, and recovery."
Lead Agency	Federal Emergency Management Agency	U.S. Department of Homeland Security

From Federal Emergency Management Agency (FEMA). 2008. Robert T. Stafford Disaster Relief and Emergency Assistance Act. Washington, DC: FEMA. Available at: http://www.fema.gov/pdf/about/stafford_act.pdf.; and FEMA. 2008. National Response Framework. Washington, DC: FEMA. Available at: http://www.fema.gov/pdf/emergency/nrf/nrf-core.pdf; and Federal Emergency Management Agency National Response Framework Resource Center. Available at: http://www.fema.gov/emergency/nrf/glossary.htm#E.

STANDARDS

Key Elements of a Public Health Preparedness Program

System Characteristics

- Resiliency, capacity to maintain continuity of activities
- Ability to effectively manage the response to a disaster
- Ability to recover or return to normal as quickly as possible

Advance Preparedness

- Identify hazards and vulnerabilities to inform planning
- Conduct advanced planning for emergencies and build capabilities necessary for coordinated and effective response
- Integrate planning so local, state, and federal partners in emergency management and public health know how they will work together during disaster response

  - Community determines gaps in local assets
  - Plan compares available assets to likely needs
  - Community, state, and federal partners identify what gaps will be filled by state or federal resources
  - Regularly exercise plans to test roles and responsibilities and to ensure integration of all responding agencies and organizations

- Develop an integrated Incident Command System for decision-making and response capability, which clearly defines and assigns individual and agency roles and responsibilities in all sectors, at all levels of government, and with all individuals
- Develop capacity to deliver essential services

  - Identify critical resources for public health emergency response and arrange for delivery of these resources throughout the supply chain

- Ensure reliable communication systems

  - Ensure capability to provide accurate and credible information to the public in culturally appropriate ways
  - Ensure capacity and reliability of health information infrastructure

- Develop capacity for early detection and identification of health threats

  ○ Maintain and improve systems to monitor, detect, and investigate potential hazards (environmental, radiological, toxic, or infectious)
  ○ Ensure laboratory capacity

- Develop community mitigation strategies (e.g., isolation and quarantine, social distancing) and countermeasure distribution strategies
- Identify and address issues of legal authority and liability barriers in monitoring, preventing, or responding to a public health emergency

Coordinated Rapid-Response Capability

- Use an integrated Incident Command System for decision-making and response capability
- Identify nature of disaster and public health concerns via surveillance, epidemiological investigation, and laboratory diagnosis
- Deliver essential services (i.e., mass health care) post-impact to the affected community
- Implement prevention and containment strategies

  ○ Implement community mitigation strategies and distribute appropriate countermeasures
  ○ Educate and mobilize the public by rapidly providing accurate and credible information in culturally appropriate ways

- Distribute essential resources needed for public health interventions

Trained Workforce

- Develop and maintain a public health and health care workforce that has the skills and capabilities needed in a public health emergency
- Train, recruit, and develop public health leaders who can mobilize resources, engage the community, develop interagency relationships, and communicate with the public

Accountability and Quality Improvement

- Test operational capabilities through real public health events, drills, and exercises
- Develop financial systems to track resources used and services delivered to ensure adequate and timely reimbursement

Adapted from Nelson C, Lurie N, Wasserman J, Zakowski S. 2007. Conceptualizing and defining public health emergency preparedness. Am J Public Health. 97(Supplement 1):S9–S11.

Public Health Preparedness Capabilities: National Standards for State and Local Planning

Capability Definitions, Functions, and Associated Performance Measures

Capability 1: Community Preparedness

Definition

Community preparedness is the ability of communities to prepare for, withstand, and recover—in both the short and long term—from public health incidents. By engaging and coordinating with emergency management; health care organizations (private and community-based); mental/behavioral health providers; community and faith-based partners; and state, local, and territorial governments, public health's role in community preparedness is to do the following:

- Support the development of public health, medical, and mental/behavioral health systems that support recovery
- Participate in awareness training with community and faith-based partners on how to prevent, respond to, and recover from incidents of public health significance
- Promote awareness of and access to medical and mental/behavioral health resources that help protect the community's health and address the functional needs (e.g., communication, medical care, independence, supervision, transportation) of at-risk individuals
- Engage public and private organizations in preparedness activities that represent the functional needs of at-risk individuals as well as the cultural and socioeconomic, demographic components of the community
- Identify those populations that may be at higher risk for adverse health outcomes
- Receive and integrate the health needs of populations who have been displaced as a result of incidents that have occurred in their own or distant communities (e.g., improvised nuclear device or hurricane)

Functions and Associated Performance Measures

This capability consists of the ability to perform the functions listed below. At present, there are no Centers for Disease Prevention and Control (CDC)–defined performance measures for these functions.

Function 1: Determine risks to the health of the jurisdiction

Function 2: Build community partnerships to support health preparedness

Function 3: Engage with community organizations to foster public health, medical, and mental/behavioral health social networks

Function 4: Coordinate training or guidance to ensure community engagement in preparedness efforts

Capability 2: Community Recovery

Definition

Community recovery is the ability to collaborate with community partners (e.g., health care organizations, business, education, and emergency management) to plan and advocate the rebuilding of public health, medical, and mental/ behavioral health systems to a level of functioning comparable with pre-incident levels at a minimum and improved levels where possible.

This capability supports National Health Security Strategy Objective 8: Incorporate Post-Incident Health Recovery Into Planning and Response. Post-incident recovery of the public health, medical, and mental/behavioral health services and systems within a jurisdiction is critical for health security and requires collaboration and advocacy by the public health agency for the restoration of services, providers, facilities, and infrastructure within the public health, medical, and human services sectors. Monitoring the public health, medical and mental/behavioral health infrastructure is an essential public health service.

Functions and Associated Performance Measures

This capability consists of the ability to perform the functions listed below. At present, there are no CDC-defined performance measures for these functions.

Function 1: Identify and monitor public health, medical, and mental/behavioral health system recovery needs

Function 2: Coordinate community public health, medical, and mental/behavioral health system recovery operations

Function 3: Implement corrective actions to mitigate damages from future incidents

Capability 3: Emergency Operations Coordination

Definition

Emergency operations coordination is the ability to direct and support an event or incident with public health or medical implications by establishing a standardized, scalable system of oversight, organization, and supervision consistent with jurisdictional standards and practices and with the National Incident Management System.

Capability Definitions, Functions, and Associated Performance Measures

Functions and Associated Performance Measures

This capability consists of the ability to perform the functions listed below. Associated CDC-defined performance measures are also listed below.

Function 1: Conduct preliminary assessment to determine need for public activation

Function 2: Activate public health emergency operations

Measure 1: Time for pre-identified staff covering activated public health agency incident management lead roles (or equivalent lead roles) to report for immediate duty. Performance Target: 60 minutes or less

Function 3: Develop incident response strategy

Measure 1: Production of the approved Incident Action Plan before the start of the second operational period

Function 4: Manage and sustain the public health response

Function 5: Demobilize and evaluate public health emergency operations

Measure 1: Time to complete a draft of an After Action Report and Improvement Plan

Capability 4: Emergency Public Information and Warning

Definition

Emergency public information and warning is the ability to develop, coordinate, and disseminate information, alerts, warnings, and notifications to the public and incident management responders.

Functions and Associated Performance Measures

This capability consists of the ability to perform the functions listed below. Associated CDC-defined performance measures are also listed below.

> **Function 1:** Activate the emergency public information system
> **Function 2:** Determine the need for a joint public information system
> **Function 3:** Establish and participate in information system operations
> **Function 4:** Establish avenues for public interaction and information exchange
> **Function 5:** Issue public information, alerts, warnings, and notifications
>
>> Measure 1: Time to issue a risk communication message for dissemination to the public

Capability 5: Fatality Management

Definition

Fatality management is the ability to coordinate with other organizations (e.g., law enforcement, health care, emergency management, medical examiner/coroner) to ensure the proper recovery, handling, identification, transportation, tracking, storage, and disposal of human remains and personal effects; certify cause of death; and facilitate access to mental/behavioral health services to the family members, responders, and survivors of an incident.

Functions and Associated Performance Measures

This capability consists of the ability to perform the functions listed below. At present, there are no CDC-defined performance measures for these functions.

> **Function 1:** Determine role for public health in fatality management
> **Function 2:** Activate public health fatality management operations
> **Function 3:** Assist in the collection and dissemination of antemortem data
> **Function 4:** Participate in survivor mental/behavioral health services
> **Function 5:** Participate in fatality processing and storage operations

Capability 6: Information Sharing

Definition

Information sharing is the ability to conduct multijurisdictional, multidisciplinary exchange of health-related information and situational awareness data among federal, state, local, territorial, and tribal levels of government and the private sector. This capability includes the routine sharing of information as well as issuing of public health alerts to federal, state, local, territorial, and tribal levels of government and the private sector in preparation for, and in response to, events or incidents of public health significance.

Capability Definitions, Functions, and Associated Performance Measures

Functions and Associated Performance Measures

This capability consists of the ability to perform the functions listed below. At present, there are no CDC-defined performance measures for these functions.

> **Function 1:** Identify stakeholders to be incorporated into information flow
> **Function 2:** Identify and develop rules and data elements for sharing
> **Function 3:** Exchange information to determine a common operating picture

Capability 7: Mass Care

Definition

Mass care is the ability to coordinate with partner agencies to address the public health, medical, and mental/behavioral health needs of those impacted by an incident at a congregate location. This capability includes the coordination of ongoing surveillance and assessment to ensure that health needs continue to be met as the incident evolves.

Functions and Associated Performance Measures

This capability consists of the ability to perform the functions listed below. At present, there are no CDC-defined performance measures for these functions.

> **Function 1:** Determine public health role in mass care operations
> **Function 2:** Determine mass care needs of the impacted population
> **Function 3:** Coordinate public health, medical, and mental/behavioral health services
> **Function 4:** Monitor mass care population health

Capability 8: Medical Countermeasure Dispensing

Definition

Medical countermeasure dispensing is the ability to provide medical countermeasures (including vaccines, antiviral drugs, antibiotics, antitoxins) in support of treatment or prophylaxis (oral or vaccination) to the identified population in accordance with public health guidelines and recommendations.

Functions and Associated Performance Measures

This capability consists of the ability to perform the functions listed below. Associated CDC-defined performance measures are also listed below.

Function 1: Identify and initiate medical countermeasure dispensing strategies

Function 2: Receive medical countermeasures

Function 3: Activate dispensing modalities

   Measure 1: Composite performance indicator from the Division of Strategic National Stockpile in CDC's Office of Public Health Preparedness and Response

Function 4: Dispense medical countermeasures to identified population

   Measure 1: Composite performance indicator from the Division of Strategic National Stockpile in CDC's Office of Public Health Preparedness and Response

Function 5: Report adverse events

Capability 9: Medical Materiel Management and Distribution

Definition

Medical materiel management and distribution is the ability to acquire, maintain (e.g., cold chain storage or other storage protocol), transport, distribute, and track medical materiel (e.g., pharmaceuticals, gloves, masks, ventilators) during an incident and to recover and account for unused medical materiel, as necessary, after an incident.

Capability Definitions, Functions, and Associated Performance Measures

Functions and Associated Performance Measures

This capability consists of the ability to perform the functions listed below. Associated CDC-defined performance measures are also listed below.

Function 1: Direct and activate medical materiel management and distribution

   Measure 1: Composite performance indicator from the Division of Strategic National Stockpile in CDC's Office of Public Health Preparedness and Response

Function 2: Acquire medical materiel

   Measure 1: Composite performance indicator from the Division of Strategic National Stockpile in CDC's Office of Public Health Preparedness and Response

Function 3: Maintain updated inventory management and reporting system

Measure 1: Composite performance indicator from the Division of Strategic National Stockpile in CDC's Office of Public Health Preparedness and Response

Function 4: Establish and maintain security

Measure 1: Composite performance indicator from the Division of Strategic National Stockpile in CDC's Office of Public Health Preparedness and Response

Function 5: Distribute medical materiel

Measure 1: Composite performance indicator from the Division of Strategic National Stockpile in CDC's Office of Public Health Preparedness and Response

Function 6: Recover medical materiel and demobilize distribution operations

Measure 1: Composite performance indicator from the Division of Strategic National Stockpile in CDC's Office of Public Health Preparedness and Response

Capability 10: Medical Surge

Definition

Medical surge is the ability to provide adequate medical evaluation and care during events that exceed the limits of the normal medical infrastructure of an affected community. It encompasses the ability of the health care system to survive a hazard impact and maintain or rapidly recover operations that were compromised.

Functions and Associated Performance Measures

This capability consists of the ability to perform the functions listed below. At present, there are no CDC-defined performance measures for these functions.

Function 1: Assess the nature and scope of the incident
Function 2: Support activation of medical surge
Function 3: Support jurisdictional medical surge operations
Function 4: Support demobilization of medical surge operations

Capability 11: Nonpharmaceutical Interventions

Definition

Nonpharmaceutical interventions are the ability to recommend to the applicable lead agency (if not public health agency) and implement, if applicable, strategies for disease, injury, and exposure control. Strategies include the following:

- Isolation and quarantine
- Restrictions on movement and travel advisory/warnings
- Social distancing
- External decontamination
- Hygiene
- Precautionary protective behaviors

Capability Definitions, Functions, and Associated Performance Measures

Functions and Associated Performance Measures

This capability consists of the ability to perform the functions listed below. At present, there are no CDC-defined performance measures for these functions.

Function 1: Engage partners and identify factors that impact nonpharmaceutical interventions
Function 2: Determine nonpharmaceutical interventions
Function 3: Implement nonpharmaceutical interventions
Function 4: Monitor nonpharmaceutical interventions

Capability 12: Public Health Laboratory Testing

Definition

Public health laboratory testing is the ability to conduct rapid and conventional detection, characterization, confirmatory testing, data reporting, investigative support, and laboratory networking to address actual or potential exposure to all-hazards. Hazards include chemical, radiological, and biological agents in multiple matrices that may include clinical samples, food, and environmental samples (e.g., water, air, soil). This capability supports routine surveillance, including pre-event or pre-incident and postexposure activities.

Functions and Associated Performance Measures

This capability consists of the ability to perform the functions listed below. Associated CDC-defined performance measures are also listed below.

Function 1: Manage laboratory activities

Measure 1: Time for sentinel clinical laboratories to acknowledge receipt of an urgent message from the CDC Public Health Emergency Preparedness (PHEP)-funded Laboratory Response Network biological (LRN-B) laboratory

Measure 2: Time for initial laboratorian to report for duty at the CDC PHEP-funded laboratory

Function 2: Perform sample management

Measure 1: Percentage of Laboratory Response Network (LRN) clinical specimens without any adverse quality assurance events received at the CDC PHEP-funded LRN-B laboratory for confirmation or rule-out testing from sentinel clinical laboratories

Measure 2: Percentage of LRN nonclinical samples without any adverse quality assurance events received at the CDC PHEP-funded LRN-B laboratory for confirmation or rule-out testing from first responders

Measure 3: Ability of the CDC PHEP-funded Laboratory Response Network chemical (LRN-C) laboratories to collect relevant samples for clinical chemical analysis, package, and ship those samples

Function 3: Conduct testing and analysis for routine and surge capacity

Measure 1: Proportion of LRN-C proficiency tests (core methods) successfully passed by CDC PHEP-funded laboratories

Measure 2: Proportion of LRN-C proficiency tests (additional methods) successfully passed by CDC PHEP-funded laboratories

Measure 3: Proportion of LRN-B proficiency tests successfully passed by CDC PHEP-funded laboratories

Function 4: Support public health investigations

Measure 1: Time to complete notification between CDC, on-call laboratorian, and on-call epidemiologist

Measure 2: Time to complete notification between CDC, on-call epidemiologist, and on-call laboratorian

Function 5: Report results

Measure 1: Percentage of pulsed field gel electrophoresis (PFGE) subtyping data results for *E. coli* O157:H7 submitted to the PulseNet national database within 4 working days of receiving isolate at the PFGE laboratory

Measure 2: Percentage of PFGE subtyping data results for *Listeria monocytogenes* submitted to the PulseNet national database within 4 working days of receiving isolate at the PFGE laboratory

Measure 3: Time to submit PFGE subtyping data results for *Salmonella* to the PulseNet national database upon receipt of isolate at the PFGE laboratory

Measure 4: Time for CDC PHEP-funded laboratory to notify public health partners of significant laboratory results

Capability 13: Public Health Surveillance and Epidemiological Investigation

Definition

Public health surveillance and epidemiological investigation is the ability to create, maintain, support, and strengthen routine surveillance and detection systems and epidemiological investigation processes, as well as to expand these systems and processes in response to incidents of public health significance.

Functions and Associated Performance Measures

This capability consists of the ability to perform the functions listed below. Associated CDC-defined performance measures are also listed below.

Function 1: Conduct public health surveillance and detection

Measure 1: Proportion of reports of selected reportable diseases received by a public health agency within the jurisdiction-required time frame

Function 2: Conduct public health and epidemiological investigations

Measure 1: Percentage of infectious disease outbreak investigations that generate reports

Measure 2: Percentage of infectious disease outbreak investigation reports that contain all minimal elements

Measure 3: Percentage of acute environmental exposure investigations that generate reports

Measure 4: Percentage of acute environmental exposure reports that contain all minimal elements

Function 3: Recommend, monitor, and analyze mitigation actions

Measure 1: Proportion of reports of selected reportable diseases for which initial public health control measure(s) were initiated within the appropriate time frame

Function 4: Improve public health surveillance and epidemiological investigation systems

Capability 14: Responder Safety and Health

Definition

The responder safety and health capability describes the ability to protect public health agency staff responding to an incident and the ability to support the health and safety needs of hospital and medical facility personnel, if requested.

Functions and Associated Performance Measures

This capability consists of the ability to perform the functions listed below. At present, there are no CDC-defined performance measures for these functions.

Function 1: Identify responder safety and health risks
Function 2: Identify safety and personal protective needs
Function 3: Coordinate with partners to facilitate risk-specific safety and health training
Function 4: Monitor responder safety and health actions

Capability 15: Volunteer Management

Definition

Volunteer management is the ability to coordinate the identification, recruitment, registration, credential verification, training, and engagement of volunteers to support the jurisdictional public health agency's response to incidents of public health significance.

Functions and Associated Performance Measures

This capability consists of the ability to perform the functions listed below. At present, there are no CDC-defined performance measures for these functions.

Function 1: Coordinate volunteers
Function 2: Notify volunteers
Function 3: Organize, assemble, and dispatch volunteers
Function 4: Demobilize volunteers

From Office of Public Health Preparedness and Response. 2011. *Public Health Preparedness Capabilities: National Standards for State and Local Planning.* Atlanta, GA: Centers for Disease Control and Prevention. Available at: http://www.cdc.gov/phpr/capabilities/Capabilities_March_2011.pdf.

RESPONSIBILITIES AND CAPABILITIES

Emergency Support Function 8: Public Health and Medical Services

Purpose

Emergency Support Function (ESF) 8—Public Health and Medical Services provides the mechanism for coordinated federal assistance to supplement state and local resources in response to a public health and medical disaster, potential or actual incidents requiring a coordinated federal response, and a developing potential health and medical emergency. This annex includes responding to medical needs associated with mental health, behavioral health, and substance abuse considerations of incident victims and response workers. Services also cover the medical needs of members of the "at-risk" or "special needs" population described in the Pandemic and All-Hazards Preparedness Act and in the National Response Framework (NRF) Glossary, respectively. It includes a population whose members may have medical and other functional needs before, during, and after an incident.

Capabilities

Public Health and Medical Services includes behavioral health needs consisting of both mental health and substance abuse considerations for incident victims and response workers and, as appropriate, medical needs groups defined in the core document as individuals in need of additional medical response assistance, and veterinary and animal health issues.

ESF-8 involves supplemental assistance to state, tribal, and local governments in the following core functions:

- Assessment of public health/medical needs
- Health surveillance
- Medical care personnel
- Health/medical/veterinary equipment and supplies
- Patient evacuation
- Patient care
- Safety and security of drugs, biologics, and medical devices
- Food safety and security
- Agriculture safety and security

- All-hazard public health and medical consultation, technical assistance, and support
- Behavioral health care
- Public health and medical information
- Vector control
- Potable water/wastewater and solid waste disposal
- Mass fatality management, victim identification, and decontaminating remains
- Veterinary medical support

Members

ESF Coordinator:	Department of Health and Human Services (HHS)
Primary Agency:	HHS
Support Agencies:	Department of Agriculture
	Department of Defense
	Department of Energy
	Department of Homeland Security
	Department of the Interior
	Department of Justice
	Department of Labor
	Department of State
	Department of Transportation
	Department of Veterans Affairs
	Environmental Protection Agency
	General Services Administration
	U.S. Agency for International Development
	U.S. Postal Service
	American Red Cross

Concept of Operations Overview

The secretary of HHS leads the ESF-8 response. ESF-8, when activated, is coordinated by the Assistant Secretary for Preparedness and Response (ASPR). Once activated, ESF-8 functions are coordinated by the Emergency Management Group (EMG) through the secretary's Operation Center. During the initial activation, HHS coordinates audio and video and conference calls with the ESF-8 supporting departments and agencies, and public health and medical representatives from state, tribal and local officials, to discuss the situation and determine the appropriate initial response actions.

HHS alerts and requests supporting organizations to provide a representative to the EMG to provide liaison support.

HHS may designate a Senior Health Officer to serve as the senior federal health official at the Joint Field Office (JFO).

Regional ESF-8 staff are ready to rapidly deploy, as the Incident Response Coordination Team Advance (IRCT-A), to provide ESF-8 support to the affected location. As the situation matures, the IRCT-A will receive augmentation from HHS and partner agencies to transition into a full IRCT capable of providing the full range of ESF-8 support, including medical command and control.

The regional ESF-8 staff includes representatives to staff the Regional Response Coordination Center and JFO, as required, on a 24-hour basis for the duration of the incident.

From Federal Emergency Management Agency (FEMA). 2008. Overview ESF and Supporting Annexes Coordinating Federal Assistance In Support of the National Response Framework. Washington, DC: FEMA. Available at: http://www.fema.gov/pdf/emergency/nrf/nrf-overview.pdf.

Original Target Capabilities List

Common Capabilities

Planning
Communications
Community Preparedness and Participation
Risk Management
Intelligence and Information Sharing and Dissemination

Prevention Capabilities

Information Gathering and Recognition of Indicators and Warning
Intelligence Analysis and Production
Counter-Terror Investigation and Law Enforcement
Chemical, Biological, Radiological, Nuclear, and Explosives Detection

Protection Capabilities

Critical Infrastructure Protection
Food and Agriculture Safety and Defense
Epidemiological Surveillance and Investigation
Laboratory Testing

Response Capabilities

On-Site Incident Management
Emergency Operations Center Management
Critical Resource Logistics and Distribution
Volunteer Management and Donations
Responder Safety and Health
Emergency Public Safety and Security
Animal Disease Emergency Support
Environmental Health
Explosive Device Response Operations
Fire Incident Response Support
Weapons of Mass Destruction and Hazardous Materials
Response and Decontamination

Citizen Evacuation and Shelter-in-Place
Isolation and Quarantine
Search and Rescue (Land-Based)
Emergency Public Information and Warning
Emergency Triage and Prehospital Treatment
Medical Surge
Medical Supplies Management and Distribution
Mass Prophylaxis
Mass Care (Sheltering, Feeding and Related Services)
Fatality Management

Recovery Capabilities

Structural Damage Assessment
Restoration of Lifelines
Economic and Community Recovery

Adapted from U.S. Department of Homeland Security (DHS). 2007. Target Capabilities List: A Companion to the National Preparedness Guidelines. Washington, DC: DHS. Available at: http://www.fema.gov/pdf/government/training/tcl.pdf.

MANAGEMENT STANDARDS

The Joint Commission 2010 Emergency Management Hospital Standards

As of 2010, The Joint Commission designated the importance of the accreditation requirements for emergency management in health care organizations by organizing them in a consolidated chapter and renumbering them. The hospital standards are as follows:

Chapter: Emergency Management

Standard: EM.01.01.01: The hospital engages in planning activities prior to developing its written Emergency Operations Plan. Note: An *emergency* is an unexpected or sudden event that significantly disrupts the organization's ability to provide care, or the environment of care itself, or that results in a sudden, significantly changed or increased demand for the organization's services. Emergencies can be either human-made or natural (such as an electrical system failure or a tornado), or a combination of both, and they exist on a continuum of severity. A *disaster* is a type of emergency that, due to its complexity, scope, or duration, threatens the organization's capabilities and requires outside assistance to sustain patient care, safety, or security functions.

Rationale: An emergency in a health care organization can suddenly and significantly affect demand for its services or its ability to provide those services. Therefore, the organization needs to engage in planning activities that prepare it to form its Emergency Operations Plan. These activities include identifying risks, prioritizing likely emergencies, attempting to mitigate them when possible, and considering its potential emergencies in developing strategies for preparedness. Because some emergencies that impact an organization originate in the community, the organization needs to take advantage of opportunities where possible to collaborate with relevant parties in the community.

Elements of Performance (EP)[1]:
1. The hospital's leaders, including leaders of the medical staff, participate in planning activities prior to developing an Emergency Operations Plan.

---

[1]The reader will notice that the numbering of these standards (Elements of Performance) is not necessarily consecutive. The Joint Commission previously used a convention by which the numbering of standards signified the type of organization (hospital, long-term care, behavioral) to which the standards applied. Where a number is skipped, the standards are not intended for that type of organization, in this case hospitals.

2. The hospital conducts a hazard vulnerability analysis (HVA) to identify potential emergencies that could affect demand for the hospital's services or its ability to provide those services, the likelihood of those events occurring, and the consequences of those events. The findings of this analysis are documented. (See also EM.03.01.01, EP 1; IC.01.06.01, EP 4) Note 1: Hospitals have flexibility in creating either a single HVA that accurately reflects all sites of the hospital, or multiple HVAs. Some remote sites may be significantly different from the main site (for example, in terms of hazards, location, and population served); in such situations a separate HVA is appropriate. Note 2: If the hospital identifies a surge in infectious patients as a potential emergency, this issue is addressed in the "Infection Prevention and Control" (IC) chapter.

3. The hospital, together with its community partners, prioritizes the potential emergencies identified in its hazard vulnerability analysis (HVA) and documents these priorities. Note: The hospital determines which community partners are critical to helping define priorities in its HVA. Community partners may include other health care organizations, the public health department, vendors, community organizations, public safety and public works officials, representatives of local municipalities, and other government agencies.

4. The hospital communicates its needs and vulnerabilities to community emergency response agencies and identifies the community's capability to meet its needs. This communication and identification occur at the time of the hospital's annual review of its Emergency Operations Plan and whenever its needs or vulnerabilities change. (See also EM.03.01.01, EP 1)

5. The hospital uses its hazard vulnerability analysis as a basis for defining mitigation activities (that is, activities designed to reduce the risk of and potential damage from an emergency). Note: Mitigation, preparedness, response, and recovery are the four phases of emergency management. They occur over time: Mitigation and preparedness generally occur before an emergency, and response and recovery occur during and after an emergency.

6. The hospital uses its hazard vulnerability analysis as a basis for defining the preparedness activities that will organize and mobilize essential resources. (See also IM.01.01.03, EPs 1-4)

7. The hospital's incident command structure is integrated into and consistent with its community's command structure. Note: The incident command structure used by the hospital should provide for a scalable response to different types of emergencies. (The National Incident Management System (NIMS) is one of many models for an incident command structure available to health care organizations. The NIMS provides guidelines for common functions and terminology to support clear communications and effective collaboration in an emergency situation. The NIMS is required of hospitals receiving certain federal funds for emergency preparedness.)

8. The hospital keeps a documented inventory of the resources and assets it has on site that may be needed during an emergency, including, but not limited to, personal protective equipment, water, fuel, and medical, surgical, and medication-related resources and assets. (See also EM.02.02.03, EP 6)

Standard: EM.01.01.01: The hospital engages in planning activities prior to developing its written Emergency Operations Plan. Note: An emergency is an unexpected or sudden event that significantly disrupts the organization's ability to provide care, or the environment of care itself, or that results in a sudden, significantly changed or increased demand for the organization's services. Emergencies can be either human-made or natural (such as an electrical system failure or a tornado), or a combination of both, and they exist on a continuum of severity. A disaster is a type of emergency that, due to its complexity, scope, or duration, threatens the organization's capabilities and requires outside assistance to sustain patient care, safety, or security functions.

Rationale: An emergency in a health care organization can suddenly and significantly affect demand for its services or its ability to provide those services. Therefore, the organization needs to engage in planning activities that prepare it to form its Emergency Operations Plan. These activities include identifying risks, prioritizing likely emergencies, attempting to mitigate them when possible, and considering its potential emergencies in developing strategies for preparedness. Because some emergencies that impact an organization originate in the community, the organization needs to take advantage of opportunities where possible to collaborate with relevant parties in the community.

Elements of Performance:
1. The hospital's leaders, including leaders of the medical staff, participate in planning activities prior to developing an Emergency Operations Plan.
2. The hospital conducts a hazard vulnerability analysis (HVA) to identify potential emergencies that could affect demand for the hospital's services or its ability to provide those services, the likelihood of those events occurring, and the consequences of those events. The findings of this analysis are documented. (See also EM.03.01.01, EP 1; IC.01.06.01, EP 4) Note 1: Hospitals have flexibility in creating either a single HVA that accurately reflects all sites of the hospital, or multiple HVAs. Some remote sites may be significantly different from the main site (for example, in terms of hazards, location, and population served); in such situations a separate HVA is appropriate. Note 2: If the hospital identifies a surge in infectious patients as a potential emergency, this issue is addressed in the "Infection Prevention and Control" (IC) chapter.
3. The hospital, together with its community partners, prioritizes the potential emergencies identified in its hazard vulnerability analysis (HVA) and documents these priorities. Note: The hospital determines which community partners are critical to helping define priorities in its HVA. Community partners may include other health care organizations, the public health department, vendors, community organizations, public safety and public works officials, representatives of local municipalities, and other government agencies.
4. The hospital communicates its needs and vulnerabilities to community emergency response agencies and identifies the community's capability to meet its needs. This communication and identification occur at the time of the hospital's annual review of

its Emergency Operations Plan and whenever its needs or vulnerabilities change. (See also EM.03.01.01, EP 1)

5. The hospital uses its hazard vulnerability analysis as a basis for defining mitigation activities (that is, activities designed to reduce the risk of and potential damage from an emergency). Note: Mitigation, preparedness, response, and recovery are the four phases of emergency management. They occur over time: Mitigation and preparedness generally occur before an emergency, and response and recovery occur during and after an emergency.

6. The hospital uses its hazard vulnerability analysis as a basis for defining the preparedness activities that will organize and mobilize essential resources. (See also IM.01.01.03, EPs 1-4)

7. The hospital's incident command structure is integrated into and consistent with its community's command structure. Note: The incident command structure used by the hospital should provide for a scalable response to different types of emergencies. (The National Incident Management System (NIMS) is one of many models for an incident command structure available to health care organizations. The NIMS provides guidelines for common functions and terminology to support clear communications and effective collaboration in an emergency situation. The NIMS is required of hospitals receiving certain federal funds for emergency preparedness.)

8. The hospital keeps a documented inventory of the resources and assets it has on site that may be needed during an emergency, including, but not limited to, personal protective equipment, water, fuel, and medical, surgical, and medication-related resources and assets. (See also EM.02.02.03, EP 6)

Standard: EM.02.01.01: The hospital has an Emergency Operations Plan. Note: The hospital's Emergency Operations Plan (EOP) is designed to coordinate its communications, resources and assets, safety and security, staff responsibilities, utilities, and patient clinical and support activities during an emergency (refer to Standards EM.02.02.01, EM.02.02.03, EM.02.02.05, EM.02.02.07, EM.02.02.09, and EM.02.02.11). Although emergencies have many causes, the effects on these areas of the organization and the required response effort may be similar. This "all hazards" approach supports a general response capability that is sufficiently nimble to address a range of emergencies of different duration, scale, and cause. For this reason, the Plan's response procedures address the prioritized emergencies but are also adaptable to other emergencies that the organization may experience.

Rationale: A successful response effort relies on a comprehensive and flexible Emergency Operations Plan that guides decision making at the onset of an emergency and as an emergency evolves. Although the Emergency Operations Plan can be formatted in a variety of ways, it must address response procedures that are both applicable to the hospital's likely emergencies and adaptable in supporting key areas (such as communications and patient care) that might be affected by emergencies of different causes.

Elements of Performance:

1. The hospital's leaders, including leaders of the medical staff, participate in the development of the Emergency Operations Plan.

2. The hospital develops and maintains a written Emergency Operations Plan that describes the response procedures to follow when emergencies occur. (See also EM.03.01.03, EP 5) Note: The response procedures address the prioritized emergencies but can also be adapted to other emergencies that the hospital may experience. Response procedures could include the following: Maintaining or expanding services; Conserving resources; Curtailing services; Supplementing resources from outside the local community; Closing the hospital to new patients; Staged evacuation; Total evacuation.

3. The Emergency Operations Plan identifies the hospital's capabilities and establishes response procedures for when the hospital cannot be supported by the local community in the hospital's efforts to provide communications, resources and assets, security and safety, staff, utilities, or patient care for at least 96 hours. Note: Hospitals are not required to stockpile supplies to last for 96 hours of operation.

4. The hospital develops and maintains a written Emergency Operations Plan that describes the recovery strategies and actions designed to help restore the systems that are critical to providing care, treatment, and services after an emergency.

5. The Emergency Operations Plan describes the processes for initiating and terminating the hospital's response and recovery phases of an emergency, including under what circumstances these phases are activated. Note: Mitigation, preparedness, response, and recovery are the four phases of emergency management. They occur over time: Mitigation and preparedness generally occur before an emergency, and response and recovery occur during and after an emergency.

6. The Emergency Operations Plan identifies the individual(s) who has the authority to activate the response and recovery phases of the emergency response.

7. The Emergency Operations Plan identifies alternative sites for care, treatment, and services that meet the needs of the hospital's patients during emergencies.

8. If the hospital experiences an actual emergency, the hospital implements its response procedures related to care, treatment, and services for its patients.

Standard: EM.02.02.01: As part of its Emergency Operations Plan, the hospital prepares for how it will communicate during emergencies.

Rationale: The hospital maintains reliable communications capabilities for the purpose of communicating response efforts to staff, patients, and external organizations. The hospital establishes backup communications processes and technologies (for example, cell phones, landlines, bulletin boards, fax machines, satellite phones, Amateur Radio, text messages) to communicate essential information if primary communications systems fail.

Elements of Performance:

1. The Emergency Operations Plan describes the following: How staff will be notified that emergency response procedures have been initiated.

2. The Emergency Operations Plan describes the following: How the hospital will communicate information and instructions to its staff and licensed independent practitioners during an emergency.

3. The Emergency Operations Plan describes the following: How the hospital will notify external authorities that emergency response measures have been initiated.

4. The Emergency Operations Plan describes the following: How the hospital will communicate with external authorities during an emergency.

5. The Emergency Operations Plan describes the following: How the hospital will communicate with patients and their families, including how it will notify families when patients are relocated to alternative care sites.

6. The Emergency Operations Plan describes the following: How the hospital will communicate with the community or the media during an emergency.

7. The Emergency Operations Plan describes the following: How the hospital will communicate with suppliers of essential services, equipment, and supplies during an emergency.

8. The Emergency Operations Plan describes the following: How the hospital will communicate with other health care organizations in its contiguous geographic area regarding the essential elements of their respective command structures, including the names and roles of individuals in their command structures and their command center telephone numbers.

9. The Emergency Operations Plan describes the following: How the hospital will communicate with other health care organizations in its contiguous geographic area regarding the essential elements of their respective command centers for emergency response.

10. The Emergency Operations Plan describes the following: How the hospital will communicate with other health care organizations in its contiguous geographic area regarding the resources and assets that could be shared in an emergency response.

11. The Emergency Operations Plan describes the following: How and under what circumstances the hospital will communicate the names of patients and the deceased with other health care organizations in its contiguous geographic area.

12. The Emergency Operations Plan describes the following: How, and under what circumstances, the hospital will communicate information about patients to third parties (such as other health care organizations, the state health department, police, the FBI).

13. The Emergency Operations Plan describes the following: How the hospital will communicate with identified alternative care sites.

14. The hospital establishes backup systems and technologies for the communication activities identified in EM.02.02.01, EPs 1-13.

17. The hospital implements the components of its Emergency Operations Plan that require advance preparation to support communications during an emergency.

Standard: EM.02.02.03: As part of its Emergency Operations Plan, the hospital prepares for how it will manage resources and assets during emergencies.

Rationale: The hospital that continues to provide care, treatment, and services to its patients during emergencies needs to determine how resources and assets (that is, supplies, equipment, and facilities) will be managed internally and, when necessary, solicited and acquired from external sources such as vendors, neighboring health care providers, other community organizations, state affiliates, or a regional parent company. The hospital should also recognize the risk that some resources may not be available from planned sources, particularly in emergencies of long duration or broad geographic scope, and that contingency plans will be necessary for critical supplies. This situation may occur when multiple hospitals are vying for a limited supply from the same vendor.

Elements of Performance:
1. The Emergency Operations Plan describes the following: How the hospital will obtain and replenish medications and related supplies that will be required throughout the response and recovery phases of an emergency, including access to and distribution of caches that may be stockpiled by the hospital, its affiliates, or local, state, or federal sources.
2. The Emergency Operations Plan describes the following: How the hospital will obtain and replenish medical supplies that will be required throughout the response and recovery phases of an emergency, including personal protective equipment where required.
3. The Emergency Operations Plan describes the following: How the hospital will obtain and replenish non-medical supplies that will be required throughout the response and recovery phases of an emergency.
4. The Emergency Operations Plan describes the following: How the hospital will share resources and assets with other health care organizations within the community, if necessary. Note: Examples of resources and assets that might be shared include beds, transportation, linens, fuel, personal protective equipment, medical equipment, and supplies.
5. The Emergency Operations Plan describes the following: How the hospital will share resources and assets with other health care organizations outside the community, if necessary, in the event of a regional or prolonged disaster. Note: Examples of resources and assets that might be shared include beds, transportation, linens, fuel, personal protective equipment, medical equipment, and supplies.
6. The Emergency Operations Plan describes the following: How the hospital will monitor quantities of its resources and assets during an emergency. (See also EM.01.01.01, EP 8)
9. The Emergency Operations Plan describes the following: The hospital's arrangements for transporting some or all patients, their medications, supplies, equipment, and staff to an alternative care site(s) when the environment cannot support care, treatment, and services. (See also EM.02.02.11, EP 3)

10. The Emergency Operations Plan describes the following: The hospital's arrangements for transferring pertinent information, including essential clinical and medication-related information, with patients moving to alternative care sites. (See also EM.02.02.11, EP 3)

12. The hospital implements the components of its Emergency Operations Plan that require advance preparation to provide for resources and assets during an emergency.

Standard: EM.02.02.05: As part of its Emergency Operations Plan, the hospital prepares for how it will manage security and safety during an emergency.

Rationale: N/A

Elements of Performance:

1. The Emergency Operations Plan describes the following: The hospital's arrangements for internal security and safety.

2. The Emergency Operations Plan describes the following: The roles that community security agencies (for example, police, sheriff, National Guard) will have in the event of an emergency.

3. The Emergency Operations Plan describes the following: How the hospital will coordinate security activities with community security agencies (for example, police, sheriff, National Guard).

4. The Emergency Operations Plan describes the following: How the hospital will manage hazardous materials and waste.

5. The Emergency Operations Plan describes the following: How the hospital will provide for radioactive, biological, and chemical isolation and decontamination.

7. The Emergency Operations Plan describes the following: How the hospital will control entrance into and out of the health care facility during an emergency.

8. The Emergency Operations Plan describes the following: How the hospital will control the movement of individuals within the health care facility during an emergency.

9. The Emergency Operations Plan describes the following: The hospital's arrangements for controlling vehicles that access the health care facility during an emergency.

10. The hospital implements the components of its Emergency Operations Plan that require advance preparation to support security and safety during an emergency.

Standard: EM.02.02.07: As part of its Emergency Operations Plan, the hospital prepares for how it will manage staff during an emergency.

Rationale: To provide safe and effective patient care during an emergency, staff roles are well defined in advance, and staff are oriented in their assigned responsibilities. Staff roles and responsibilities may be documented in the Plan using a variety of formats (for example, job action sheets, checklists, flowcharts). Due to the dynamic nature of emergencies, effective training prepares staff to adjust to changes in patient volume or acuity, work procedures or conditions, and response partners within and outside the hospital.

Elements of Performance:
2. The Emergency Operations Plan describes the following: The roles and responsibilities of staff for communications, resources and assets, safety and security, utilities, and patient management during an emergency.
3. The Emergency Operations Plan describes the following: The process for assigning staff to all essential staff functions.
4. The Emergency Operations Plan identifies the individual(s) to whom staff report in the hospital's incident command structure.
5. The Emergency Operations Plan describes how the hospital will manage staff support needs (for example, housing, transportation, incident stress debriefing).
6. The Emergency Operations Plan describes how the hospital will manage the family support needs of staff (for example, child care, elder care, pet care, communication).
7. The hospital trains staff for their assigned emergency response roles.
8. The hospital communicates, in writing, with each of its licensed independent practitioners regarding his or her role(s) in emergency response and to whom he or she reports during an emergency.
9. The Emergency Operations Plan describes how the hospital will identify licensed independent practitioners, staff, and authorized volunteers during emergencies. (See also EM.02.02.13, EP 3; EM.02.02.15, EP 3) Note: This identification could include identification cards, wristbands, vests, hats, or badges.
10. The hospital implements the components of its Emergency Operations Plan that require advance preparation to manage staff during an emergency.

Standard: EM.02.02.07: As part of its Emergency Operations Plan, the hospital prepares for how it will manage staff during an emergency.

Rationale: To provide safe and effective patient care during an emergency, staff roles are well defined in advance, and staff are oriented in their assigned responsibilities. Staff roles and responsibilities may be documented in the Plan using a variety of formats (for example, job action sheets, checklists, flowcharts). Due to the dynamic nature of emergencies, effective training prepares staff to adjust to changes in patient volume or acuity, work procedures or conditions, and response partners within and outside the hospital.

Elements of Performance:
2. The Emergency Operations Plan describes the following: The roles and responsibilities of staff for communications, resources and assets, safety and security, utilities, and patient management during an emergency.

3. The Emergency Operations Plan describes the following: The process for assigning staff to all essential staff functions.
4. The Emergency Operations Plan identifies the individual(s) to whom staff report in the hospital's incident command structure.
5. The Emergency Operations Plan describes how the hospital will manage staff support needs (for example, housing, transportation, incident stress debriefing).
6. The Emergency Operations Plan describes how the hospital will manage the family support needs of staff (for example, child care, elder care, pet care, communication).
7. The hospital trains staff for their assigned emergency response roles.
8. The hospital communicates, in writing, with each of its licensed independent practitioners regarding his or her role(s) in emergency response and to whom he or she reports during an emergency.
9. The Emergency Operations Plan describes how the hospital will identify licensed independent practitioners, staff, and authorized volunteers during emergencies. (See also EM.02.02.13, EP 3; EM.02.02.15, EP 3) Note: This identification could include identification cards, wristbands, vests, hats, or badges.
10. The hospital implements the components of its Emergency Operations Plan that require advance preparation to manage staff during an emergency.

Standard: EM.02.02.09: As part of its Emergency Operations Plan, the hospital prepares for how it will manage utilities during an emergency.

Rationale: Different types of emergencies can have the same detrimental impact on an organization's utility systems. For example, brush fires, ice storms, and industrial accidents can all result in a loss of utilities required for care, treatment, services, and building operations. Organizations, therefore, must have alternative means of providing for essential utilities (for example, alternative equipment at the hospital; negotiated relationships with the primary suppliers; provision through a parent entity; Memoranda of Understanding (MOU) with other organizations in the community). Hospitals should determine how long they expect to remain open to care for patients and plan for their utilities accordingly. Because some emergencies may be regional in scope or of long duration, organizations should not rely solely on single source providers in the community. Where possible, hospitals should identify other suppliers outside of the local community in case the communities' infrastructure is severely compromised and unable to support the hospital.

Elements of Performance:
2. As part of its Emergency Operations Plan, the hospital identifies alternative means of providing the following: Electricity.
3. As part of its Emergency Operations Plan, the hospital identifies alternative means of providing the following: Water needed for consumption and essential care activities.
4. As part of its Emergency Operations Plan, the hospital identifies alternative means of providing the following: Water needed for equipment and sanitary purposes.

5. As part of its Emergency Operations Plan, the hospital identifies alternative means of providing the following: Fuel required for building operations, generators, and essential transport services that the hospital would typically provide.

6. As part of its Emergency Operations Plan, the hospital identifies alternative means of providing the following: Medical gas/vacuum systems.

7. As part of its Emergency Operations Plan, the hospital identifies alternative means of providing the following: Utility systems that the hospital defines as essential (for example, vertical and horizontal transport, heating and cooling systems, and steam for sterilization).

8. The hospital implements the components of its Emergency Operations Plan that require advance preparation to provide for utilities during an emergency.

Standard: EM.02.02.11: As part of its Emergency Operations Plan, the hospital prepares for how it will manage patients during emergencies.

Rationale: The fundamental goal of emergency management planning is to protect life and prevent disability. The manner in which care, treatment, and services are provided may vary by type of emergency. However, certain activities are so fundamental to patient safety (this can include decisions to modify or discontinue services, make referrals, or transport patients) that the organization should take a proactive approach in considering how they might be accomplished. The emergency triage process will typically result in patients being quickly treated and discharged, admitted for a longer stay, or transferred to a more appropriate source of care. A disaster may result in the decision to keep all patients on the premises in the interest of safety or, conversely, in the decision to evacuate all patients because the facility is no longer safe. Planning for clinical services must address these situations accordingly, particularly in the face of escalating events or in potentially austere care conditions.

Elements of Performance:

2. The Emergency Operations Plan describes the following: How the hospital will manage the activities required as part of patient scheduling, triage, assessment, treatment, admission, transfer, and discharge.

3. The Emergency Operations Plan describes the following: How the hospital will evacuate (from one section or floor to another within the building, or, completely outside the building) when the environment cannot support care, treatment, and services. (See also EM.02.02.03, EPs 9 and 10)

4. The Emergency Operations Plan describes the following: How the hospital will manage a potential increase in demand for clinical services for vulnerable populations served by the hospital, such as patients who are pediatric, geriatric, disabled, or have serious chronic conditions or addictions.

5. The Emergency Operations Plan describes the following: How the hospital will manage the personal hygiene and sanitation needs of its patients.

6. The Emergency Operations Plan describes the following: How the hospital will manage its patients' mental health service needs that occur during an emergency.

7. The Emergency Operations Plan describes the following: How the hospital will manage mortuary services.

8. The Emergency Operations Plan describes the following: How the hospital will document and track patients' clinical information.

11. The hospital implements the components of its Emergency Operations Plan that require advance preparation to manage patients during an emergency.

Standard: EM.02.02.13: During disasters, the hospital may grant disaster privileges to volunteer licensed independent practitioners. Note: A disaster is an emergency that, due to its complexity, scope, or duration, threatens the organization's capabilities and requires outside assistance to sustain patient care, safety, or security functions.

Rationale: N/A

Elements of Performance:

1. The hospital grants disaster privileges to volunteer licensed independent practitioners only when the Emergency Operations Plan has been activated in response to a disaster and the hospital is unable to meet immediate patient needs.

2. The medical staff identifies, in its bylaws, those individuals responsible for granting disaster privileges to volunteer licensed independent practitioners.

3. The hospital determines how it will distinguish volunteer licensed independent practitioners from other licensed independent practitioners. (See also EM.02.02.07, EP 9)

4. The medical staff describes, in writing, how it will oversee the performance of volunteer licensed independent practitioners who are granted disaster privileges (for example, by direct observation, mentoring, medical record review).

5. Before a volunteer practitioner is considered eligible to function as a volunteer licensed independent practitioner, the hospital obtains his or her valid government-issued photo identification (for example, a driver's license or passport) and at least one of the following: A current picture identification card from a health care organization that clearly identifies professional designation; A current license to practice; Primary source verification of licensure; Identification indicating that the individual is a member of a Disaster Medical Assistance Team (DMAT), the Medical Reserve Corps (MRC), the Emergency System for Advance Registration of Volunteer Health Professionals (ESAR-VHP), or other recognized state or federal response organization or group; Identification indicating that the individual has been granted authority by a government entity to provide patient care, treatment, or services in disaster circumstances; Confirmation by a licensed independent practitioner currently privileged by the hospital or by a staff member with personal knowledge of the volunteer practitioner's ability to act as a licensed independent practitioner during a disaster.

6. During a disaster, the medical staff oversees the performance of each volunteer licensed independent practitioner.

7. Based on its oversight of each volunteer licensed independent practitioner, the hospital determines within 72 hours of the practitioner's arrival if granted disaster privileges should continue.

8. Primary source verification of licensure occurs as soon as the disaster is under control or within 72 hours from the time the volunteer licensed independent practitioner presents him- or herself to the hospital, whichever comes first. If primary source verification of a volunteer licensed independent practitioner's licensure cannot be completed within 72 hours of the practitioner's arrival due to extraordinary circumstances, the hospital documents all of the following: Reason(s) it could not be performed within 72 hours of the practitioner's arrival; Evidence of the licensed independent practitioner's demonstrated ability to continue to provide adequate care, treatment, and services; Evidence of the hospital's attempt to perform primary source verification as soon as possible.

9. If, due to extraordinary circumstances, primary source verification of licensure of the volunteer licensed independent practitioner cannot be completed within 72 hours of the practitioner's arrival, it is performed as soon as possible. Note: Primary source verification of licensure is not required if the volunteer licensed independent practitioner has not provided care, treatment, or services under the disaster privileges.

Standard: EM.02.02.15: During disasters, the hospital may assign disaster responsibilities to volunteer practitioners who are not licensed independent practitioners, but who are required by law and regulation to have a license, certification, or registration. Note: While this standard allows for a method to streamline the process for verifying identification and licensure, certification, or registration, the elements of performance are intended to safeguard against inadequate care during a disaster.

Rationale: N/A

Elements of Performance:

1. The hospital assigns disaster responsibilities to volunteer practitioners who are not licensed independent practitioners only when the Emergency Operations Plan has been activated in response to a disaster and the hospital is unable to meet immediate patient needs.

2. The hospital identifies, in writing, those individuals responsible for assigning disaster responsibilities to volunteer practitioners who are not licensed independent practitioners.

3. The hospital determines how it will distinguish volunteer practitioners who are not licensed independent practitioners from its staff. (See also EM.02.02.07, EP 9)

4. The hospital describes, in writing, how it will oversee the performance of volunteer practitioners who are not licensed independent practitioners who have been assigned disaster responsibilities. Examples of methods for overseeing their performance include direct observation, mentoring, and medical record review.

5. Before a volunteer practitioner who is not a licensed independent practitioner is considered eligible to function as a practitioner, the hospital obtains his or her valid government-issued photo identification (for example, a driver's license or passport) and one of the following: A current picture identification card from a health care organization that clearly identifies professional designation; A current license, certification, or registration; Primary source verification of licensure, certification, or registration (if required by law and regulation in order to practice); Identification indicating that the individual is a member of a Disaster Medical Assistance Team (DMAT), the Medical Reserve Corps (MRC), the Emergency System for Advance Registration of Volunteer Health Professionals (ESAR-VHP), or other recognized state or federal response organization or group; Identification indicating that the individual has been granted authority by a government entity to provide patient care, treatment, or services in disaster circumstances; Confirmation by hospital staff with personal knowledge of the volunteer practitioner's ability to act as a qualified practitioner during a disaster.

6. During a disaster, the hospital oversees the performance of each volunteer practitioner who is not a licensed independent practitioner.

7. Based on its oversight of each volunteer practitioner who is not a licensed independent practitioner, the hospital determines within 72 hours after the practitioner's arrival whether assigned disaster responsibilities should continue.

8. Primary source verification of licensure, certification, or registration (if required by law and regulation in order to practice) of volunteer practitioners who are not licensed independent practitioners occurs as soon as the disaster is under control or within 72 hours from the time the volunteer practitioner presents him- or herself to the hospital, whichever comes first. If primary source verification of licensure, certification, or registration (if required by law and regulation in order to practice) for a volunteer practitioner who is not a licensed independent practitioner cannot be completed within 72 hours due to extraordinary circumstances, the hospital documents all of the following: Reason(s) it could not be performed within 72 hours of the practitioner's arrival; Evidence of the volunteer practitioner's demonstrated ability to continue to provide adequate care, treatment, or services; Evidence of the hospital's attempt to perform primary source verification as soon as possible.

9. If, due to extraordinary circumstances, primary source verification of licensure of the volunteer practitioner cannot be completed within 72 hours of the practitioner's arrival, it is performed as soon as possible. Note: Primary source verification of licensure, certification, or registration is not required if the volunteer practitioner has not provided care, treatment, or services under his or her assigned disaster responsibilities.

Standard: EM.03.01.01: The hospital evaluates the effectiveness of its emergency management planning activities.

Rationale: The risks and hazards facing an organization or an area of the organization may change over time. The scope or goals of the hospital's planning activities may evolve in response to changes in the organization, its structure, patient population, community planning partners, or a number of other factors. Such changes can have an impact on the hospital's response capabilities, including decisions about its inventory of resources and assets needed during an emergency. The hospital conducts an annual review of its planning activities to identify such changes and support decision making regarding how the hospital responds to emergencies.

Elements of Performance:
1. The hospital conducts an annual review of its risks, hazards, and potential emergencies as defined in its hazard vulnerability analysis (HVA). The findings of this review are documented. (See also EM.01.01.01, EPs 2 and 4)
2. The hospital conducts an annual review of the objectives and scope of its Emergency Operations Plan. The findings of this review are documented.
3. The hospital conducts an annual review of its inventory. The findings of this review are documented.

Standard: EM.03.01.03: The hospital evaluates the effectiveness of its Emergency Operations Plan.

Rationale: The organization conducts exercises to assess the Emergency Operations Plan's appropriateness; adequacy; and the effectiveness of logistics, human resources, training, policies, procedures, and protocols. Exercises should stress the limits of the plan to support assessment of the organization's preparedness and performance. The design of the exercise should reflect likely disasters but should test the organization's ability to respond to the effects of emergencies on its capabilities to provide care, treatment, and services.

Elements of Performance:
1. As an emergency response exercise, the hospital activates its Emergency Operations Plan twice a year at each site included in the plan. Note 1: If the hospital activates its Emergency Operations Plan in response to one or more actual emergencies, these emergencies can serve in place of emergency response exercises. Note 2: Staff in freestanding buildings classified as a business occupancy (as defined by the Life Safety Code) that do not offer emergency services nor are community designated as disaster-receiving stations need to conduct only one emergency management exercise annually. Note 3: Tabletop sessions, though useful, are not acceptable substitutes for these exercises. (The Life Safety Code is a registered trademark of the National Fire Protection Association, Quincy, MA. Refer to NFPA 101-2000 for occupancy classifications.)
2. For each site of the hospital that offers emergency services or is a community-designated disaster receiving station, at least one of the hospital's two emergency response exercises includes an influx of simulated patients. Note 1: Tabletop sessions, though useful, cannot serve for this portion of the exercise. Note 2: This portion of the

emergency response exercise can be conducted separately or in conjunction with EM.03.01.03, EPs 3 and 4.

3. For each site of the hospital that offers emergency services or is a community-designated disaster receiving station, at least one of the hospital's two emergency response exercises includes an escalating event in which the local community is unable to support the hospital. Note 1: This portion of the emergency response exercise can be conducted separately or in conjunction with EM.03.01.03, EPs 2 and 4. Note 2: Tabletop sessions are acceptable in meeting the community portion of this exercise.

4. For each site of the hospital with a defined role in its community's response plan, at least one of the two emergency response exercises includes participation in a community-wide exercise. Note 1: This portion of the emergency response exercise can be conducted separately or in conjunction with EM.03.01.03, EPs 2 and 3. Note 2: Tabletop sessions are acceptable in meeting the community portion of this exercise.

5. Emergency response exercises incorporate likely disaster scenarios that allow the hospital to evaluate its handling of communications, resources and assets, security, staff, utilities, and patients. (See also EM.02.01.01, EP 2)

6. The hospital designates an individual(s) whose sole responsibility during emergency response exercises is to monitor performance and document opportunities for improvement. Note 1: This person is knowledgeable in the goals and expectations of the exercise and may be a staff member of the hospital. Note 2: If the response to an actual emergency is used as one of the required exercises, it is understood that it may not be possible to have an individual whose sole responsibility is to monitor performance. Hospitals may use observations of those who were involved in the command structure as well as the input of those providing services during the emergency.

7. During emergency response exercises, the hospital monitors the effectiveness of internal communication and the effectiveness of communication with outside entities such as local government leadership, police, fire, public health officials, and other health care organizations.

8. During emergency response exercises, the hospital monitors resource mobilization and asset allocation, including equipment, supplies, personal protective equipment, and transportation.

9. During emergency response exercises, the hospital monitors its management of the following: Safety and security.

10. During emergency response exercises, the hospital monitors its management of the following: Staff roles and responsibilities.

11. During emergency response exercises, the hospital monitors its management of the following: Utility systems.

12. During emergency response exercises, the hospital monitors its management of the following: Patient clinical and support care activities.

13. Based on all monitoring activities and observations, the hospital evaluates all emergency response exercises and all responses to actual emergencies using a multidisciplinary process (which includes licensed independent practitioners).

14. The evaluation of all emergency response exercises and all responses to actual emergencies includes the identification of deficiencies and opportunities for improvement. This evaluation is documented.

15. The deficiencies and opportunities for improvement, identified in the evaluation of all emergency response exercises and all responses to actual emergencies, are communicated to the improvement team responsible for monitoring environment of care issues. (See also EC.04.01.05, EP 3)

16. The hospital modifies its Emergency Operations Plan based on its evaluation of emergency response exercises and responses to actual emergencies. Note: When modifications requiring substantive resources cannot be accomplished by the next emergency response exercise, interim measures are put in place until final modifications can be made.

17. Subsequent emergency response exercises reflect modifications and interim measures as described in the modified Emergency Operations Plan.

Required Elements of Risk Assessment

The 2010 edition of the National Fire Protection Association (NFPA) 1600 *Standard on Disaster/Emergency Management and Business Continuity Programs* defines the required elements of a risk assessment. Standard 5.4 states that a risk assessment should be conducted "to identify strategies for prevention and mitigation," "evaluate the potential effects of regional, national, or international incidents that could have cascading impacts," and "gather information to develop plans for response, continuity, and recovery." Although all of the events below do not necessarily meet the definition of a disaster, the full list is included for reference regarding the NFPA 1600 standard and what it includes.

Risk assessments should identify, evaluate and monitor the vulnerability of the following:

- Health and safety of persons in the affected area at the time of incident (injury and death)
- Health and safety of personnel responding to the incident
- Continuity of operations
- Property, facilities, assets, and critical infrastructure
- Delivery of the entity's services
- Supply chain
- Environment
- Economic and financial condition
- Regulatory and contractual obligations
- Reputation of or confidence in the entity

The risk assessment should be done for the following hazards:

Natural Hazards			Human-Caused Events		
Geological	Meteorological	Biological	Accidents	Intentional	Technological
Earthquake	Flood, flash flood, seiche, tidal surge	Emerging diseases (plague, smallpox, anthrax, West Nile virus, foot and mouth disease, severe acute respiratory syndrome, bovine spongiform encephalopathy)	Hazardous material spill, release	Terrorism (explosive, chemical, biological, radiological, nuclear, cyber)	Central computer, mainframe, server, software, application failure
Tsunami	Drought	Animal, insect infestation or damage	Explosion, fire	Sabotage	Ancillary support equipment hazards
Volcano	Fire		Transportation	Civil disturbance, public unrest, mass hysteria, riot	Telecommunications failure
Landslide, mudslide, subsidence	Snow, ice, hail, sleet, avalanche		Building, structural collapse	Enemy attack, war	Energy/power/utility failure
Glacier, iceberg movement	Extreme temperatures		Energy/power/utility failure	Insurrection	
	Lightning strikes		Fuel, other resource shortage	Strike or labor dispute	
	Famine		Air or water pollution, contamination	Disinformation	
	Geomagnetic storm		Water control structure failure	Criminal activity (vandalism, arson, theft, fraud, embezzlement, data theft)	
			Economic depression, inflation, financial system collapse	Electromagnetic pulse	
			Communication system interruptions	Physical or information security breach	
			Misinformation	Workplace, school, university violence	
				Product defect, contamination	
				Harassment, discrimination	

The following are methodologies and techniques for risk assessment:

Methods and Techniques	Functions
What-if	Identify specific hazards or hazardous situations that could result in undesirable consequences Relies on knowledgeable individuals familiar with the area, operations, and processes Value dependent on team and questions asked
Checklist	Specific list of items used to identify hazards and hazardous situations Compare current or projected situations with accepted standards Value dependent on checklist quality and assessor experience and credentials
What-if/checklist	Combines what-if and checklist techniques Uses strengths of both techniques What-if questions are developed and checklists fill in any gaps Value dependent on team and the questions asked
Hazard and operability study	Requires interdisciplinary team that is very knowledgeable of the areas, operations, and processes to be assessed Thorough, time consuming, and costly approach Value depends on team qualifications and experience, quality of reference material available, ability of team to function as a team, and strong, positive leadership
Failure mode and effects analysis	Examines each element in system individually and collectively Determines effect when one or more elements fail Bottom-up approach: elements are examined and effect of failure on overall system is predicted Small interdisciplinary team required Best suited for assessing potential equipment failures Value dependent on credentials of team and scope of system to be examined
Fault-tree analysis	Top-down approach: undesirable event is identified and range of potential causes identified Value dependent on competence in using the fault-tree analysis process, on credentials of team, and depth of team's analysis

Adapted from National Fire Protection Association (NFPA). 2009. NFPA 1600 *Standard on Disaster/ Emergency Management and Business Continuity Programs*, 2010 Edition. Section 5.4 and Annex A. Quincy, MA: NFPA. Available at: http://www.nfpa.org/assets/files/PDF/NFPA16002010.pdf.

MORBIDITY

Common Food-Borne Diseases Caused by Bacteria

The following table will be helpful when public health professionals require a quick reference to comparative information about food-borne diseases caused by bacteria. Professionals can consult this table to review the clinical symptoms for common food-borne diseases, the typical foods associated with each disease, and specific prevention and control measures.

Disease (Causative Agent)	Principal Symptoms	Typical Foods	Prevention and Control Measures
Food poisoning (*Bacillus cereus*)	Diarrhea, cramps, occasional vomiting	Meat products, soups, sauces, vegetables	Cook all potential food sources thoroughly, serve at correct temperature, cool rapidly
Food poisoning, emetic (*B. cereus*)	Nausea, vomiting, sometimes diarrhea and cramps	Cooked rice, pasta	Minimize hot holding times
Botulism food poisoning (heat-labile toxin of *Clostridium botulinum*)	Fatigue, weakness, double vision, slurred speech, respiratory failure, sometimes death	Type A and B: vegetables, fruits, meats, fish and poultry products, condiments; Type E: fish and fish products	Purchase commercially processed foods, serve foods sautéed or infused with oils, promptly discard leftovers
Botulism food poisoning: infant infection (heat-labile toxin of *C. botulinum*)	Constipation, weakness, respiratory failure, sometimes death	Honey, soil	Do not feed honey to infants
Campylobacteriosis (*Campylobacter jejuni*)	Diarrhea, abdominal pain, fever, nausea, vomiting	Infected food source, animals	Cook animal foods thoroughly, cool rapidly, avoid cross-contamination, use pasteurized milk

(*continued on next page*)

(*continued*)

Disease (Causative Agent)	Principal Symptoms	Typical Foods	Prevention and Control Measures
Food poisoning (*Clostridium perfringens*)	Diarrhea, cramps, rarely nausea and vomiting	Cooked meat, poultry	Cook animal foods thoroughly, cool rapidly, avoid cross-contamination
Food-borne infections, enterohemorrhagic (*Escherichia coli*)	Watery, bloody diarrhea	Raw or uncooked beef, raw milk	Cook animal foods thoroughly, cool rapidly, avoid cross-contamination
Food-borne infections, enteroinvasive (*E. coli*)	Cramps, diarrhea, fever, dysentery	Raw foods	Teach food handlers good hygiene practice, have food handlers wear gloves, minimize holding time
Food-borne infections, enterotoxigenic (*E. coli*)	Profuse watery diarrhea, sometimes cramps, vomiting	Raw foods	Teach food handlers good hygiene practice, have food handlers wear gloves, minimize holding time
Listeriosis (*Listeria monocytogenes*)	Meningoencephalitis, stillbirths, septicemia or meningitis in newborns	Raw milk, cheese, vegetables	Use pasteurized milk, cook foods thoroughly
Salmonellosis (*Salmonella species*)	Diarrhea, abdominal pain, chills, fever, vomiting, dehydration	Raw, undercooked eggs; raw milk, meat and poultry	Cook animal foods thoroughly, minimize hot holding time, chill food rapidly, avoid cross- contamination
Shigellosis (*Shigella species*)	Diarrhea, fever, nausea, sometimes vomiting, cramps	Raw foods	Cook animal foods thoroughly, minimize hot holding time, chill food rapidly, avoid cross- contamination

(*continued on next page*)

(*continued*)

Disease (Causative Agent)	Principal Symptoms	Typical Foods	Prevention and Control Measures
Staphylococcal food poisoning (heat-stable enterotoxin of *Staphylococcus aureus*)	Nausea, vomiting, diarrhea, cramps	Ham, meat, poultry products; cream filled pastries; whipped butter, cheese	Restrict food handlers with skin lesions or respiratory infections from handling food
Streptoccocal food-borne infection (*Streptococcus pyogenes*)	Various, including sore throat, erysipelas, scarlet fever	Raw milk, deviled eggs	Use pasteurized milk, teach food handlers good hygiene practice, chill foods rapidly
Food-borne infections (*Vibrio parahaemolyticus*)	Diarrhea, cramps, sometimes nausea, vomiting, fever headache	Fish and seafood	Cook fish and seafood thoroughly, minimize hot holding time

Reprinted from Owen AL, Splett PL, Owen GM. 1999. *Nutrition in the Community: The Art and Science of Delivery Services*, 4th ed. Boston, MA: WCB McGraw Hill.

Diseases Affecting Displaced Persons During and After Disasters

Disease	Symptoms	Environmental Risk Factors	Possible Health Hazards
Acute upper respiratory tract infections	Symptoms of common cold; for pneumonia, chest pain and pain between shoulder blades	Crowding, poor hygiene	Influenza and pneumonia can result in severe complications in groups at risk
Cholera	Fever, severe liquid diarrhea, abdominal spasms, vomiting, rapid weight loss, dehydration	Contaminated drinking water or food or poor sanitation	Dehydration, especially in children; dark color of urine, dry tongue, leathery skin
Diarrhea	Watery stools at least three times per day; fever, nausea, or vomiting	Contaminated drinking water or food or poor sanitation	Dehydration, especially in children; dark color of urine, dry tongue, leathery skin
Diphtheria	Inflamed and painful throat, coughing	Crowding, poor hygiene	A secretion is deposited in the respiratory tract which can lead to asphyxiation
Heat stress	Elevated body temperatures, nausea, vomiting, headache	Excessive temperatures	Coma
(Viral) hepatitis A	Nausea, slight fever, pale-colored stools, dark-colored urine, jaundiced eyes and skin	Poor hygiene	Long-term disabling effects
Malaria	Painful muscles and joints, high fever with chills, headache, possible diarrhea and vomiting	Breeding of *Anopheles* mosquitoes in stagnant water bodies	Disease may rapidly become fatal unless medical care provided during the first 48 hours

(*continued on next page*)

(*continued*)

Disease	Symptoms	Environmental Risk Factors	Possible Health Hazards
Measles	Fever and catarrhal symptoms, followed by maculopapular rash	Crowding, poor hygiene	High fatality rate
Meningococcal meningitis	Infected persons may show no symptoms for a considerable time; headache, fever, and general malaise suggest diagnosis when symptoms are epidemic	Crowding	Only fatal if untreated in early stage; neurological problems in survivors
Rabies	Fatigue, headache, disorientation, paralysis, hyperactivity	Bite from infected animal host	Fatal if untreated
Shigella dysentery	Diarrhea with blood in stool, fever, vomiting, abdominal cramps	Contaminated drinking water or food, poor sanitation, poor hygiene	Case fatality rate may be high
Tetanus	Muscle spasms, starting in the jaws and extending to rest of body over several days	Poor hygiene, injury	Fatal
Typhoid fever	Initial symptoms are similar to malaria; diarrhea, prolonged fever, and delirium are occasional symptoms	Contaminated drinking-water or food or poor sanitation	Without appropriate medical care, can lead to fatal complications in a few weeks
Louse-borne typhus	Prolonged fever, headache, body pains	Unhygienic conditions leading to lice infestations	Potentially fatal without treatment

Adapted from Wisner B, Adams J, eds. 2002. *Environmental Health in Emergencies and Disasters.* Table 11.1. Control measures for ensuring food safety. p. 170. Geneva, Switzerland: World Health Organization.

FIRST AID

First Aid and Emergency Supply Kits

Basic items that should be assembled and stored in case of emergency include water, food, a first aid kit, tools, and supplies, and special medications and supplies when indicated. First aid supplies should be stored in a fireproof, waterproof box that is easy to carry. As with a first aid kit, all items described below should be inspected regularly and replaced when no longer useable. Important medical information and most prescriptions can be stored in the refrigerator and rotated every 6 months. In addition, copies of important papers (e.g., contact information, copies of most recent social security award letter [if applicable], drivers' license, insurance policies, medical plan cards, name and phone number of physician, social security card, personal phone book) should be secured and put in a safe place.

Water

Store 1 gallon per person per day in plastic containers. Maintain a 7 day supply that is replaced every 6 months.

Food

Store a 7 day supply of non-perishable food for each person. Rotate the food supply every 6 months.

- Baby formula, food
- High energy foods-nutrition bars, nuts, peanut butter, trail mix
- Juices: canned, boxed, powdered or crystallized
- Milk: boxed, powdered or canned
- Ready-to-eat canned or dried meats, fruits, and vegetables
- Soups, bouillon cubes, or dried soups
- Vitamins

First Aid Kit

- Ace bandages
- Adhesive tape roll
- Alcohol swabs (individually wrapped)
- Antacid
- Antibiotic ointment
- Antidiarrheal medicine

- Antiseptic or hydrogen peroxide
- Aspirin and nonaspirin tablets
- Assorted sizes of safety pins
- Cleansing agent or soap
- Cold packs
- Cotton-tipped swabs
- Dressings
- Emetic (to induce vomiting)
- Eye drops or eye wash
- Hyperallergenic adhesive tape
- Latex gloves
- Laxative
- Moist towelettes
- Needle
- Prescriptions and any long-term medications
- Rolled gauze
- Rubbing alcohol
- Safety razor blade
- Snake bite kit
- Sterile adhesive bandages (assorted sizes)
- Thermometer
- Tweezers

Other First Aid Supplies

- Bar soap
- First aid book
- Needle and thread
- Paper cups
- Pocket knife
- Scissors
- Small plastic bags
- Splinting materials
- Sunscreen

Sanitation Kit

- Disinfectant
- Facial tissues
- Household bleach
- Personal hygiene items (e.g. sanitary napkins)
- Plastic garbage bags, ties
- Soap, liquid detergent
- Toilet paper, moist towelettes

Home Survival Tools and Supplies

- Adhesive labels
- Aluminum foil
- Ax
- Battery-operated radio
- Batteries in various sizes
- Blankets or sleeping bags
- Broom
- Candles
- Cash or traveler's checks, coins
- Change of clothing
- Compass
- Disposable dust masks
- Facial tissues
- Fire extinguisher (multipurpose, dry chemical type)
- Flashlight
- Food and water for pets
- Garden hose (for siphoning and firefighting)
- Hammer
- Knife
- Manual can opener
- Map of the area
- Medicine dropper
- Mess kits or disposable plates, cups, and utensils
- Needles, thread
- Nylon cord
- Paper, pencil
- Patch kit and can of seal-in-air
- Plastic bucket with tight lid (for indoor toilet)
- Plastic sheeting
- Plastic storage bags and containers
- Pliers
- Recreational supplies for children and adults
- Rope for towing or rescue
- Safety goggles
- Scissors
- Screwdriver
- Shovel
- Signal flare
- Spray paint
- Sturdy shoes
- Tape, such as duct tape
- Tent
- Thick work gloves
- Toilet paper

- Tools (e.g., crowbar, hammer, nails, pliers, screwdriver, wood screws, adjustable wrench)
- Utility knife
- Water-proof matches or in a waterproof container
- Whistle

Car Survival Kit

- Blankets
- Bottled water
- Change of clothes
- Coins for telephone calls
- Duct tape
- Emergency signal device (light sticks, battery-type flasher, reflector)
- Fire extinguisher (multipurpose, dry chemical type)
- First aid kit and manual
- Flashlight and batteries
- Food (nonperishable items such as nutrition bars, trail mix)
- Heavy work gloves
- Jumper cables
- Local map and compass
- Moist towelettes
- Paper and pencils
- Rope for towing and rescue
- Small bag or backpack to carry items
- Small mirror
- Sturdy shoes or work boots
- Toilet paper
- Tools (e.g., pliers, adjustable wrench, screwdriver)
- Whistle

Workplace Survival Kit

- Blanket
- Bottled water
- Essential medications
- Extra pair of eyeglasses or contact lens solution
- Flashlight
- Food (nonperishable items such as nutrition bars, trail mix)
- Jacket or sweatshirt
- Portable battery-operated radio and batteries
- Small first aid kit
- Small mirror
- Sturdy shoes
- Whistle

Disability-Related Supplies and Special Equipment List

- Cane(s)
- Crutches
- Dentures
- Dialysis equipment
- Dressing device
- Eyeglasses
- Eating utensils
- Flow rate regulator
- Grooming utensils
- Hearing device
- Monitors
- Ostomy supplies
- Oxygen
- Sanitary supplies
- Suction equipment
- Urinary supplies
- Walker
- Wheelchair
- Wheelchair repair kit
- Writing device

AT-RISK POPULATIONS

Community Planning Network for At-Risk Populations

The following agencies, organizations, and institutions should be involved in disaster planning for at-risk populations:

- Emergency management agencies
- Citizen Corps Councils and program partners (Community Emergency Response Teams, Medical Reserve Corps, fire corps, Volunteers in Police Service, and Neighborhood Watch groups)
- Local emergency planning committees
- First responders (i.e., police, fire and rescue, Emergency Medical Services)
- Metropolitan Medical Response System
- Government and nongovernment disability agencies
- Developmental disabilities networks and service providers
- Protection and advocacy agencies
- Departments of aging and social services
- Hospitals and hospices
- Culturally or language-based community groups
- Voluntary organizations active in disaster such as the Red Cross and Salvation Army
- Health departments
- Departments of education
- Health and human services agencies (including child welfare)
- Human services information and referral services
- Housing and Urban Development (HUD) or other rent-subsidized multifamily complexes
- HUD or otherwise subsidized non-licensed supervised living facilities
- Nursing homes
- Media
- Home health care organizations
- Medical service and equipment providers (including durable medical equipment providers)
- Pharmaceutical providers
- Agencies on alcohol and drug addiction
- Job and family service agencies
- Vocational rehabilitation agencies
- Independent living centers
- Behavioral health and mental health agencies

- Commissions on the deaf and hard of hearing and the blind and visually impaired
- Governor's committees on individuals with functional needs and disabilities
- Translation and interpretation service agencies
- Transportation service providers (including those with accessible vehicles)
- Utility providers
- Colleges and universities
- Faith-based organizations
- Schools
- Child care facilities (both center-based and home-based)
- Veterinary resources
- Individuals with functional needs

Adapted from Federal Emergency Management Agency (FEMA). 2010. Developing and Maintaining Emergency Operations Plans. Comprehensive Preparedness Guide (CPG) 101. Version 2.0. WDC: FEMA. Available at: http://www.fema.gov/pdf/about/divisions/npd/CPG_101_V2.pdf.

Protection and Disposal of Medical Devices and Safe Drug Use After a Natural Disaster

The following are a series of guidelines to ensure that medical devices are maintained and remain useable after a natural disaster.

General Safety

- Keep device and supplies clean and dry.
- Notify the local public health authority to request evacuation prior to adverse weather events.
- Check all power cords and batteries to make sure they are not wet or damaged by water. If electrical circuits and electrical equipment have gotten wet, turn off the power at the main breaker.
- Maintain the device in an area with good lighting (e.g., refilling the insulin pump, checking the glucose meter).
- Keep the device in as clean and secure a location as possible.
- Always check the device for pests before use.

Power Outage

- Register with the electric company and fire department as a user who is dependent on a medical device that needs power (e.g., ventilator, apnea monitor).
- Determine if the device can be used with batteries or a generator.
- Locate a generator if possible.
- Do not plug a power cord in an electrical outlet if the cord or the device is wet.
- When power is restored, check to make sure the settings on the medical device have not changed or reset to a default.

Water Contamination

Some medical devices and equipment, such as dialyzers or intravenous pumps, require safe water for their use, cleaning, and maintenance. Disasters involving water, such as hurricanes or flooding, can contaminate the public water supply. Public announcements will be made about the safety of the municipal water supply. In an emergency situation, to ensure that water is safe for use with medical devices:

- Use only bottled, boiled, or treated water until the water supply is tested and found safe.
- If available water cannot be verified as having come from a safe source, it should be boiled or treated before use.
- Boiling water, when practical, is the preferred way to kill harmful bacteria and parasites. Bringing water to a rolling boil for 1 minute will kill most organisms.
- When boiling water is not practical, water can be treated with chlorine tablets, iodine tablets, or unscented household chlorine bleach (5.25% sodium hypochlorite). Follow the directions on the packaging for chlorine or iodine tablets. If household bleach is being used and if the questionable water is clear, add 1/8 teaspoon (~0.75 mL) of bleach per gallon of water; if the water is cloudy, add 1/4 teaspoon (~1.50 mL) of bleach per gallon. Mix the solution thoroughly and let it stand for about 30 minutes before using it. Keep in mind that treating water with chlorine tablets, iodine tablets, or liquid bleach will not kill parasitic organisms.
- Use a bleach solution to rinse water containers before reusing them.
- Use water storage tanks and other types of containers with caution because storage tanks and previously used cans or bottles may be contaminated with microbes or chemicals.

Sterility

- When performing medical procedures, maintain a clean environment by using bleach, alcohol, or a disinfectant in the area in which you are working (e.g., catheter changes, dressing changes, suctioning).
- Check sterile packaging to make sure it is dry and intact (e.g., sterile gauze). If the packaging is wet or damaged, do not use the product inside.
- When purchasing supplies, always check the packaging to make sure it hasn't been damaged.

Reuse of Medical Devices

- Do not reuse a medical device designed for a single use. If you need to reuse a device intended for multiple uses (e.g., infusion tubing, syringes), the device must be cleaned and disinfected or sterilized according to the device manufacturer's instructions. Devices should not be boiled unless explicitly allowed on the product label or instructions for use.
- To clean, disinfect, or sterilize a medical device or its components, make sure the water source is safe first before proceeding.

Heat and Humidity

- Heat and humidity can have an effect on home diagnostic test kits, rendering test results inaccurate. The owner's manual provides instructions to determine if a test kit is working properly.
- Before using a blood glucose meter, check the meter and test strip package insert for information on use during unusual heat and humidity. Store and handle the meter and test strips according to the instructions. Perform quality-control checks to make sure that the home glucose testing is accurate and reliable.

- To protect a device from heat and humidity:

  - Use a dry cloth to wipe off the device regularly.
  - Keep the device out of direct sunlight.
  - Enclose medical products in plastic containers to keep them dry.
  - Use dry ice or instant cold packs to keep devices cool.
  - Do not use disposable devices that are wet.

Adapted from Food and Drug Administration (FDA). 2011. FDA Offers Tips about Medical Devices and Hurricane Disasters. Washington, DC: FDA. Available at: http://www.fda.gov/medicaldevices/safety/emergencysituations/ucm055987.htm.

Checking Medical Devices for Contamination

In determining which medical devices should be discarded, the owner must assess each product's current condition and potential safety risks (as described below). For additional information, see Food and Drug Administration advice about medical devices that have been exposed to unusual levels of heat and humidity (available at http://www.fda.gov/MedicalDevices/Safety/EmergencySituations/ucm056086.htm).

- Electrical or electronic equipment (e.g. blood pressure measurement devices, glucose meters and digital thermometers)

  - Check packaging for water damage. If the package got wet, the product inside could be damaged or contaminated. Discard the device if the packaging is wet or if it shows signs of having been wet (such as water stains or discoloration).

- Packaged devices, supplies, and test kits

  - Check packaging for water damage, signs of mold or breaks in the package seals. If the package got wet, the product inside could be contaminated. Discard the device if the packaging is wet or if it shows signs of having been wet (such as water stains or discoloration), has mold growth on it, or if the package is torn or damaged in any way that could break its seal.
  - Determine whether and how long the package was exposed to unusually high room temperatures. Many test kit reagents are temperature-sensitive and could perform unreliably if exposed to unusually high storage temperatures for an extended period of time. Discard packaged test kits if the facility had unusually high room temperatures for more than 24 hours.
  - Examples: bandages and gauzes, feminine hygiene products, urinary incontinence pads, contact lens supplies, eye drops, glucometers and test strips, pregnancy tests, fertility prediction tests, glycated hemoglobin test kits, urine dipsticks, drugs-of-abuse tests, pH measurement devices, sperm detection devices, home Protime meters and strips to measure prothrombin time, HIV and hepatitis sample collection kits.

- Refrigerated products (e.g., laboratory reagents, sterilants, and disinfectants)

  ○ Determine whether the refrigerators in which the products were stored were without power. Because refrigerated devices and supplies could perform unreliably if they were exposed to unusually high temperatures in storage, discard refrigerated devices and supplies if the refrigerator storing them was without power for more than 8 hours.

Adapted from Food and Drug Administration (FDA). 2011. Emergency Situations (Medical Devices): Disposal of Contaminated Devices. Washington, DC: FDA. Available at: http://www.fda.gov/ MedicalDevices/Safety/EmergencySituations/ucm055974.htm.

Protection of Drugs

Concerns about the efficacy or safety of a particular product should be addressed with a pharmacist, health care provider, or the manufacturer's customer service department, but the below guidelines are a general set of parameters for the protection of drugs:

- Drugs exposed to excessive heat, such as fire

  ○ When lifesaving medication in its original container looks normal, it can be used until a replacement is available.

- Drugs exposed to unsafe water

  ○ All drugs—even those in their original containers—should be discarded if they have come into contact with flood or contaminated water.

- Lifesaving drugs exposed to water

  ○ When lifesaving drugs may not be readily replaced, if the container is contaminated but the contents appear unaffected—if the pills are dry—the pills may be used until a replacement can be obtained. However, if a pill is wet, it is contaminated and should be discarded.

- Reconstituted drugs

  ○ For children's drugs that require water to reconstitute, the drug should only be reconstituted with purified or bottled water. Liquids other than water should not be used to reconstitute these products.

- Drugs that need refrigeration

  ○ For drugs that require refrigeration (e.g., insulin, somatropin, and drugs that have been reconstituted), the drug should be discarded if electrical power has been off for a long time. If the drug is absolutely necessary to sustain life (e.g., insulin) it may be used until a new supply is available.

○ Temperature-sensitive drugs should be replaced with a new supply as soon as possible. For example, insulin that is not refrigerated has a shorter shelf life than the labeled expiration date.

○ If a contaminated product is considered medically necessary and would be difficult to replace quickly, contact a health care provider (e.g., physician, poison control, health department) for guidance.

Adapted from Food and Drug Administration (FDA). 2011. Emergency Preparedness: Safe Drug Use After a Disaster. Washington, DC: FDA. Available at: http://www.fda.gov/Drugs/EmergencyPreparedness/ ucm085200.htm.

Appendix O

Emergency Power Planning for People Who Use Electricity- and Battery-Dependent Assistive Technology and Medical Devices

This emergency power–planning checklist is for people who use electricity- and battery-dependent assistive technology and medical devices. Electricity- and battery-dependent devices include breathing machines (e.g., respirators, ventilators), power wheelchairs and scooters, and oxygen, suction, or home dialysis equipment. Some of this equipment is essential to the independence of those who use it, while other equipment is vital to sustaining life. Persons who are dependent on electricity- and battery-powered equipment (and those responsible for their care) should use the checklist on the pages following to make power-backup plans. Review and update this checklist every 6 months.

The following are Internet sources for more information:

Title	Web Site
Disaster Resources for People With Disabilities, Disability-Related Organizations and Emergency Managers and Planners	June Isaacson Kailes, Disability Policy Consultant home page (http://www.jik.com/disaster.html)
Tips for People With Activity Limitations and Disabilities	Emergency Survival Program home page (http://www.espfocus.org)
General Preparedness Tips for People With Disabilities	Disaster Preparedness for People With Disabilities page (http://www.redcross.org/www-files/Documents/pdf/Preparedness/Fast%20Facts/Disaster_Preparedness_for_PwD-English.pdf)
Generator Buying Advice	Generator Buying Advice featured video page (http://www.consumerreports.org/cro/video-hub/home-garden/tools-power-equipment/generator-buyingadvice/17037617001/5030179001)
Hazards of Portable Generators	Consumer Product Safety Commission Safety Alert, Portable Generator Hazards page (http://www.cpsc.gov/cpscpub/pubs/portgen.html)

Adapted from: Kailes JI. 2009. Emergency Safety Tips for People Who Use Electricity and Battery-Dependent Devices. Available at: http://www.jik.com.

Date Completed	Does Not Apply	*Planning Basics*
		Create a plan for alternative sources of power.
		Read equipment instructions and talk to equipment suppliers about backup power options.
		Get advice from local power company regarding type of backup power planned.
		Regularly check backup or alternative power equipment to ensure it will function during an emergency.
		Ensure many other people know how to operate equipment and use backup systems (see below, Establish a Support Team).
		Keep a list of alternate power providers.
		Ask nearby police and fire departments and hospital if they can be used in the event that personal backup systems fail.
		Label all equipment with name, address, and phone number. Attach simple and clear laminated instruction cards to equipment.
		Keep copies of lists of serial and model numbers of devices, as well as important use instructions in a waterproof container in the emergency supply kit.
Date Completed	Does Not Apply	*Life-Support Device Users*
		Contact power and water companies about needs for life-support devices in advance of a disaster.
		Contact the customer service department of your utility companies to ask to be put on a "priority reconnection service" list, if possible.
		Keep in mind that even if you are on the "priority reconnection service" list, power could still be out for many days following a disaster, so maintain power backup options for equipment.
		Let local fire department know about your dependency on life-support devices.
		All ventilator users should keep a bag-valve mask handy.
		If you receive dialysis or other medical treatments, ask your providers what to do in case of emergency.

Note. A 2000- to 2500-watt gas-powered portable generator can power a refrigerator and several lamps. (A refrigerator needs to run only 15 minutes per hour to stay cool if the door is kept closed. Therefore, it can be unplugged to allow operation of other devices.)

Date Completed	Does Not Apply	*Oxygen Users*
		Check with health care provider to determine if you can use a reduced flow rate in an emergency to extend the life of the system. Record on your equipment the approved reduced flow numbers so that you can easily refer to them.
		Be aware of oxygen safety practices: • Avoid areas where gas leaks or open flames may be present. • Post "Oxygen in Use" signs. • Always use battery powered flashlights or lanterns rather than gas lights or candles when oxygen is in use. • Keep the shut-off switch for oxygen equipment nearby in case of emergency.
Date Completed	**DoesNot Apply**	*Generator Users*
		Determine whether use of a generator is appropriate and realistic.
		Operate generators in open areas to ensure good airing.
		Safely store fuel (note this can be challenging when living in an apartment) and a siphon kit.
		Test it occasionally to make sure it will work when needed.
		Some generators can connect to the existing home wiring systems; always contact utility company regarding critical restrictions and safety issues.
Date Completed	**Does Not Apply**	*Rechargeable Batteries*
		Check with vendor/supplier to find alternative ways to charge batteries (e.g., connecting jumper cables to a vehicle battery, using a converter that plugs into a vehicle's cigarette lighter)
		If primary mode of transportation is a motorized wheelchair or scooter, store a lightweight manual wheelchair for emergency use.
		If your survival strategy depends on storing batteries, closely follow a recharging schedule.
		Know the working time of any batteries necessary for systems.
		When possible, choose equipment that uses batteries easily purchased from nearby stores.
Date Completed	**Does Not Apply**	*Other Backup Plans*
		When power is restored, check to make sure the settings on medical device have not changed.

Cultural Competence Checklist

Competencies	Tasks
Recognize the importance of culture and respect diversity.	Complete a self-assessment to determine your own beliefs about culture. Assess capabilities of counselors to understand and respect the values, customs, beliefs, language, and interpersonal style of the disaster survivor. Seek evidence of personnel respect for the importance of verbal and nonverbal communication, space, social organization, time, and environment controls within various cultures.
Maintain a current profile of the cultural composition of the community.	Develop and periodically update a community profile that describes composition of race, ethnicity, age, gender, religion, refugee and immigrant status, housing status, income and poverty levels, percent living in rural and in urban areas, unemployment rate, language and dialects, literacy level, and number of schools and businesses. Include information about values, beliefs, social and family norms, traditions, practices, politics, and historic racial relations or ethnic issues. Gather information in consultation with community cultural leaders who represent and understand local cultural groups.
Recruit disaster workers who are representative of the community or service area.	Review community profile when recruiting volunteers and recruit from the ethnic and cultural groups impacted by the disaster. If workers are not available from the impacted groups, recruit from similar backgrounds and spoken language. Assess workers' personal attributes, knowledge, and skills.
Provide ongoing cultural competence training to staff and volunteers.	Include language and sign interpreters and temporary staff.

(*continued on next page*)

(continued)

Competencies	Tasks
Ensure that services are accessible, appropriate, and equitable.	Identify and take steps to overcome resistance to use services. Identify and take steps to eliminate service barriers. Involve representatives of diverse cultural groups in program committees, planning boards, policy-setting bodies, and decision-making.
Recognize the role of help-seeking behaviors, customs, and traditions and natural support networks.	Identify cultural patterns that may influence help-seeking behavior. Build trusting relationships and rapport with disaster survivors. Recognize that survivors may find the procedures used in providing emergency assistance and traditional relief confusing or difficult. Recognize customs and traditions for healing, trauma, and loss and identify how these influence an individual's receptivity to and need for assistance. Acknowledge cultural beliefs about healing and recognize their importance to disaster survivors. Help survivors establish rituals and organize culturally appropriate anniversary activities. Recognize that outreach efforts focused only on the individual may not be effective for those whose cultures are centered around family and community. Determine who is significant in survivor's families and social networks.
Involve community leaders and organizations representing diverse cultural groups as cultural brokers.	Collaborate with trusted leaders (e.g., spiritual leaders, clergy and teachers). Invite organizations representing cultural groups to participate in program planning and service delivery. Collaborate with community-based organizations to communicate with cultural groups they represent. Identify ways to work with informal culture-specific groups. Coordinate with other public and private agencies in your cultural outreach.

(continued on next page)

(*continued*)

Competencies	Tasks
Ensure that services and information are culturally and linguistically competent.	Identify indigenous workers who speak the language of the survivors; use interpreters only when necessary.
	Identify trained interpreters who share the survivors' background.
	Determine the dialect of the survivor before asking for an interpreter.
	Assess the level of acculturation on the interpreter relative to the survivors.
	Establish a plan to provide written materials in relevant languages at the literacy level of the target population.
	Provide means to reach people who are deaf or hard of hearing.
	Consult with cultural groups to determine the most effective outreach.
	Use existing resources (e.g., multicultural television and radio stations) to enhance outreach.
Assess and evaluate the program's level of cultural competence.	Continuously assess the program.
	Involve representatives of various cultural groups in the evaluation.
	Communicate evaluation findings to key informants and cultural groups engaged in the program.

Adapted from Substance Abuse and Mental Health Services Administration, U.S. Department of Health and Human Services (HHS). 2003. Developing Cultural Competence in Disaster Mental Health Programs. Washington, DC: HHS. Available at: http://www.hhs.gov/od/documents/CulturalCompetence_FINALwithcovers.pdf.

Standards and Indicators for Disaster Shelter and Temporary Respite Care for Children

The following guidelines are intended to ensure that children have a safe and secure environment during and after a disaster:

- Typically, a parent, guardian, or caregiver will be the primary resource for their children, 18 years old and younger.
- When children are not with parents or guardians, local law enforcement personnel and local child protective and welfare services should be contacted to help reunite families.
- Children should be sheltered together with their families or caregivers.
- Families should have a designated area apart from the general shelter population.
- Family areas should have direct access to bathrooms.
- Parents, guardians, and caregivers are to be notified that they should accompany their children when they use the bathrooms.
- Space should be set aside for family interaction which provides:

  ○ Reduction of a child's repeated exposure to news coverage of the disaster.
  ○ Age-appropriate toys, with play supervised by parents, guardians, or caregivers.

- Regular cleaning and disinfecting of shared environmental surfaces with a bleach solution or similar commercial product, including diaper changing surfaces, communal toys, sinks, toilets, doorknobs, and floors. Local health department authorities can provide information about infection control.
- Staff will refer children who show signs of illness to on-site or local health services personnel for evaluation. Parents will be asked for consent.
- Staff will refer children who show signs of emotional stress to on-site or local health services personnel for evaluation. Parents will be asked for consent.
- Age-appropriate and nutritious food (including baby formula and baby food) and snacks should be available and offered to children.
- Diapers should be available for infants and children. Infants and toddlers need up to 12 diapers a day.
- Age-appropriate blankets should be available.
- A private and safe space for breastfeeding women should be available (e.g., curtained-off area or provision of blankets for privacy).
- Basins and supplies for bathing infants should be readily available.

Those caring for children may benefit from a period during which they are temporarily relieved of that responsibility. This temporary respite should be provided in a secure, supervised, and supportive location in which children have a play experience. This may be located in a disaster recovery center, assistance center, shelter, or other service delivery site. Parents, guardians, or caregivers are required to stay on site or designate an on-site adult to be responsible for their children. The following standards and indicators apply to the provision of temporary respite care:

- Temporary respite care for children is provided in a safe, secure environment following a disaster.
- The location, hours of operation, and other information about temporary respite care for children is provided and be easy for parents, guardians, and caregivers to understand.
- The site follows all applicable local, state, and federal laws, regulations, and codes.
- The area is fully accessible to all children.
- The area has enclosures or dividers to protect children from hazards and ensure that children are supervised in a secure environment.
- The area is located close to restrooms and a source of drinking water and hand-washing or hand-sanitizing stations are available in the area.
- Procedures are in place to sign children in and out of the area and ensure that children are only released to the person or persons listed on their registration form.
- Attendance records, registration forms, and injury or incident report forms include identifying information, parent, guardian, or caregiver names and contact information, information about allergies, and other special needs; this information must be provided, maintained, and available to staff at all times.
- Toys and materials in the area are safe and age-appropriate.
- All shelter staff members receive training and orientation and undergo a satisfactory criminal and sexual offender background check prior to working in the shelters. Spontaneous volunteers are not permitted. While working, staff must visibly display proper credentials at all times.
- At least two adults are present at all times. No child should be left alone with one adult who is not his or her parent, guardian, or caregiver.
- All staff members must be aged 18 years or older and the supervisor must be aged 21 years or older.
- An evacuation plan is developed with a designated meeting place outside the center. The evacuation plan should be posted and communicated to parents, caregivers, and guardians when registering their children.
- The child-to-staff ratio is appropriate to the space available and to the ages and needs of the children in the area at any given time.

Adapted from National Commission on Children and Disasters. 2010. *2010 Report to the President and Congress*. Appendix B: Standards and Indicators for Disaster Shelter Care for Children. AHRQ Publication No. 10-M037. Rockville, MD: Agency for Healthcare Research and Quality.

Manufacturers of Emergency Evacuation Devices and Emergency Products

AOK Global Products, Ltd.
940 Grand Blvd., Unit D
Deer Park, NY 11729
Toll free: (800) 649-4265
Direct: (631) 242-1642
Web site: http://www.rescuechair.com

Concept Development Associates, Inc.
PO Box 6772
Santa Rosa, CA 95406
Toll free: (877) 760-0868
E-mail: info@cda-designs.com
Web site: http://www.safetychairs.net

Evac+Chair
3000 Marcus Ave., Suite #3E6
Lake Success, NY 11042
Direct: (516) 502-4240
E-mail: sales@evac-chair.com
Web site: http://www.evac-chair.com

Ferno-Washington, Inc.
70 Weil Way
Wilmington, OH 45177
Toll free: (800) 733-3766
Web site: http://www.ferno.com

Frank Mobility Systems, Inc.
1003 International Drive
Oakdale, PA 15071
Toll free: (888) 426-8581
Fax: (724) 695-3710
E-mail: info@frankmobility.com
Web site: http://www.frankmobility.com

Garaventa Accessibility
P.O. Box 1769
Blaine, WA 98231
Toll free: (800) 663-6556
E-mail: productinfo@evacu-trac.com
Web site: http://www.garaventalift.com

LifeSlider, Inc.
25553 61st Road
Arkansas City, KS 67005
Toll free: (888) 442-4543
Fax: (620) 442-2320
E-mail: aaron@lifeslider.com
Web site: http://www.lifeslider.com

MAX-Ability, Inc.
1275 Fourth Street, Suite 304
Santa Rosa, CA 95404
Toll free: (800) 577-1555
Direct: (707) 575-5558
Web site: http://www.max-ability.com/evac.html

Stryker EMS
3800 E. Centre St.
Portage, MI 49002
Toll free: (800) 784-4336
Direct: (269) 324-6566
Web site: http://www.ems.stryker.com

INFECTIOUS DISEASE AND CBRNE

Maintaining and Managing the Vaccine Cold Chain

Table 1. Vaccine Storage Temperature Requirements

Temperature	Instructions	Vaccine
35 °F–46 °F (2 °C–8 °C)	Do not freeze or expose to freezing temperatures. Set temperature at mid- range (40 °F). Use a continuous temperature monitor that gives a visual record of the temperature fluctuations in the refrigerator. Contact state or local health department or manufacturer for guidance on vaccines exposed to temperatures above or below the recommended range.	Diphtheria, tetanus, or pertussis-containing vaccines Haemophilus conjugate vaccine Hepatitis A and hepatitis B vaccines[a] Inactivated polio vaccine Measles, mumps, and rubella vaccine (MMR) in the lyophilized (freeze-dried) state[b] Meningococcal polysaccharide vaccine Pneumococcal conjugate vaccine Pneumococcal polysaccharide vaccine Trivalent inactivated influenza vaccine Smallpox vaccine Anthrax Vaccine Absorbed[c]
≤5 °F (−15 °C)	Maintain in continuously frozen state with no freeze/thaw cycles. Contact state or local health department or manufacturer for guidance on vaccines exposed to temperatures above the recommended range.	Live attenuated influenza vaccine Varicella vaccine

Adapted from Centers for Disease Control and Prevention (CDC). 2003. Notice to readers: guideline for maintaining and managing the vaccine cold chain. Table 1. Vaccine storage temperature requirements. *MMWR.* 52(42):1023-1025; CDC. 2003. Guidelines for smallpox vaccine packing and shipping. Atlanta, GA: CDC. Available at: http://www.bt.cdc.gov/agent/smallpox/vaccination/pdf/packing-shipping.pdf; Bioport Corporation. 2002. Biothrax product insert. Available at: http://www.biothrax.com.

[a]ActHIB (Aventis Pasteur, Lyon, France) in the lyophilized state is not expected to be affected detrimentally by freezing temperatures, although no data are available.
[b]MMR in the lyophilized state is not affected detrimentally by freezing temperatures.
[c]Biothrax (Emergent Bio Solutions, Rockville, MD) is not to be used after expiration date given on the package.

Table 2. Comparison of Thermometers Used to Monitor Vaccine Temperatures

Thermometer Type	Advantages	Disadvantages
Standard fluid-filled	Inexpensive and simple to use Thermometers encased in biosafe liquids can reflect vaccine temperatures more accurately	Less accurate (+/−1℃) No information on duration of out of specification exposure No information on min/max temperatures Cannot be recalibrated Inexpensive models might perform poorly
Min-max	Inexpensive Monitors temperature range	Less accurate (+/−1℃) No information on duration of out of specification exposure Cannot be recalibrated
Continuous chart recorder	Most accurate Continuous 24-hour readings of temperature range and duration Can be recalibrated at regular intervals	Most expensive Requires most training and maintenance

Adapted from Centers for Disease Control and Prevention. 2003. Notice to readers: guideline for maintaining and managing the vaccine cold chain. Table 2. Vaccine storage temperature requirements. *MMWR.* 52(42):1023–1025.

Key Elements of an Effective Biological Response

- Rapid detection of the outbreak or presence of a biological agent
- Rapid dissemination of key safety information, appropriate personal protective equipment, and necessary medical precautions
- Swift identification and confirmation of the biological agent
- Identification of the population at risk
- Determination of how the agent is transmitted, and how efficiently
- Determination of susceptibility to prophylaxis and treatment
- Definition of the public health and medical services, human services, and mental health implications
- Control and containment of spread of the infection when possible, and use of mitigation strategies when containment is not possible (e.g., influenza pandemic)
- Identification of the law enforcement implications and assessment of the threat
- Augmentation of local public health and medical resources
- Protection of the population through appropriate public health and medical actions
- Dissemination of information to enlist public support and provide risk communication assistance to responsible authorities
- Assessment of environmental contamination and cleanup, decontamination, and proper disposal of bioagents that persist in the environment
- Consultation on the safety of drinking water and food products which are directly or environmentally exposed (e.g., animals, crops, plants and trees, marine life)
- Tracking and preventing secondary disease outbreak
- Administration of countermeasures when appropriate

Adapted from: National Response Framework. 2008. Biological Incident Annex. Washington, DC: Federal Emergency Management Agency. Available at: http://www.fema.gov/pdf/emergency/nrf/nrf_ BiologicalIncidentAnnex.pdf.

Incident Commander's Considerations for Managing Nuclear, Biological, and Chemical Incidents

Element of Command	Operational Considerations	Response
Scene safety	Responder protection Secondary devices Shelter-in-place versus evacuation	Crew rotation

Command, control, and
   communication
	Initial warning
	Incident Command Post
	   location
	Evidence preservation and
	   collection
	Airspace restriction
		Apparatus approach
		Communication capabilities
		Management
		Transition to unified command

Medical support	Control patient's fear and modesty Casualty transport	Control patient's movement On-scene treatment
Decontamination	Casualty decontamination Water source for decontamination	Decontaminate the site Decontaminate site's run-off
Media and public information	Overwhelming response	Information control
Resource management	Available resources	Additional resources

International Nuclear and Radiological Event Scale

The International Nuclear and Radiological Event Scale (INES) below is a tool used when communicating the safety significance of reported nuclear and radiological incidents and accidents to the media and the public. The scale can be applied to any event associated with nuclear facilities, as well to as the transport, storage, and use of radioactive material and radiation sources. INES is not intended for naturally occurring phenomena, such as radon.

Level	Event Description
1 (anomaly)	Minor problems with safety; does not involve spread of contamination or overexposure of members of the community.
2 (incident)	Significant failure of safety provisions resulting in exposure of a worker to a dose exceeding statutory limit, exposure of a member of the public in excess of 10 mSv,* or significant contamination within the facility in areas where not expected by design. Requires corrective action.
3 (serious incident)	Exposure in excess of 10 times the statutory annual limit for workers, nonlethal health effects (e.g., burns), or severe contamination within the facility in areas where not expected by design with a low probability of significant public exposure.
4 (accident local consequences)	Minor release of radioactive material unlikely to result in implementation of planned countermeasures other than local food controls, at least one death from radiation, or release of significant quantities of radioactive material with a high probability of significant public exposure.

(continued on next page)

(continued)

Level	Event Description
5 (accident with wider consequences)	Limited release of radioactive material likely to require implementation of countermeasures, significant damage to reactor core, release of large quantities of radioactive material with high probability of significant public exposure, could be caused by accident or fire, several deaths from radiation (e.g., the 1979 accident at Three Mile Island).
6 (serious accident)	Significant release of radioactive material likely to require full implementation of planned countermeasures (e.g., the 1957 accident at Kyshtym, Soviet Union).
7 (major accident)	Major release of radioactive material with widespread health and environmental effects requiring implementation of planned and extended countermeasures (e.g., the 1986 accident at Chernobyl and the 2011 crisis at Japan's Fukushima plant).

*A sievert (Sv) is a unit of "dose equivalent" radiation. One sievert is a large dose as the recommended Threshold Limit Values (TLVs) established by the American Conference of Governmental Industrial Hygienists is an average annual dose of 0.05 Sv or 50 millisievert (mSv) for occupational exposures. The term *rem* is more commonly used in the United States. 1 rem equals 0.01 Sv, which equals 10 mSv. The International Commission on Radiological Protection recommends an annual dose limit of 1 mSv for the general public.

The effects of being exposed to large doses of radiation at one time vary with the dose. As examples:

10 Sv—Risk of death within days or weeks
1 Sv—Risk of cancer later in life (5 in 100)
100 mSv—Risk of cancer later in life (5 in 1000)
50 mSv—TLV for annual dose for radiation workers in any 1 year
20 mSv—TLV for annual average dose, averaged over 5 years

Adapted from International Atomic Energy Agency. 2008. International Nuclear and Radiological Event Scale. Available at: http://www.iaea.org/Publications/Factsheets/English/ines.pdf.

Site Safety Checklist

- Assign key personnel and alternates responsible for site safety.
- Describe risks associated with each operation conducted.
- Confirm that personnel are adequately trained to perform jobs.
- Assign key person to handle volunteers.
- Describe the protective clothing and equipment to be worn by personnel during site operations.
- Describe site-specific medical surveillance requirements.
- Describe needed air monitoring, personnel monitoring, and environmental sampling.
- Describe actions to be taken to mitigate existing hazards (e.g., containment) to make the work environment less hazardous.
- Define site control measures (e.g., secure the area) and include a site map.
- Establish decontamination procedures for personnel and equipment.
- Establish site access and exit control requirements.
- Establish site food, water, shelter, and sanitation requirements.
- Establish site electrical safety requirements.
- Perform exit interviews or surveys regarding adverse health outcomes and exposures during the response.
- Identify those responders who should receive medical referral and possible enrollment into a long-term medical surveillance program, based on concerning exposures or signs and symptoms of physical or emotional ill health.

National Institute for Occupational Safety and Health. 2010. *Suggested Guidance for Supervisors at Disaster Rescue Sites.* Atlanta, GA: Centers for Disease Control and Prevention. Available at: http://www.cdc.gov/niosh/topics/emres/emhaz.html.

RESOURCES AND REFERENCES

Information Technology Security Checklist

The list below was originally published in February 2002 by *Government Technology* magazine. Today, numerous resources are available to provide guidance in securing an organization's information technology (IT) infrastructure. One of them, U.S. Security Awareness, is a nonprofit organization that collects and publishes information about IT security. Links to a variety of information about security auditing programs and materials can be found on their Web site (at http://www.ussecurityawareness.org/highres/infosec-auditing.html). The materials on these sites offer the most current thinking on what should be reviewed in IT security. Because the opinions offered are diverse, the original list is presented as a foundation.

Policy and Organization

- Set up overall information security policy with executive oversight and support.
- Develop an enterprise-wide approach to planning to include all stakeholders.
- Appoint an enterprise information security officer with authority, independence, and budget.
- Appoint or establish external security auditors to ensure compliance with established information security policies and program objectives.
- Appoint information security managers at the agency or departmental level that report to the enterprise information security officer.
- Create an information security handbook covering information that everyone needs to know.
- Develop staff training and awareness procedures and ensure these are implemented.
- Set policy for handling sensitive and confidential data by appropriate information classification and retention schemes.

Prevention and Detection

Physical Security Procedures

- Make computer rooms secure with appropriate locks, password controls, and user and visitor log-in systems.
- Deploy dropped ceilings and raised floors to protect hardware and network wiring with appropriate environmental monitoring systems or mechanisms.
- Install fire detection and containment equipment and establish safety and evaluation procedures. Adopt a no-smoking policy.

- Ensure networking equipment is secure in a separate room (not in the janitorial closet).
- Install restraints, if appropriate, on equipment for earthquake protection.
- Protect equipment from flooding, storms, or area-specific weather threats.

Staff Security Procedures

- Check new staff references and perform background checks.
- Keep staff informed of new security regulations and their role in enforcement.
- Set agreements with vendors to check the backgrounds of their employees.
- Train staff to watch for suspicious activity and provide appropriate reporting procedures.
- Train supervisors to watch for possible employee problems and ensure that corrective action plans are in place.

Overall Information Security Controls

- Provide a framework for ensuring that risk assessments are understood and that mitigating controls are implemented.
- Inventory all equipment and network access points—including employees and contractors that have remote access to network infrastructure—to ensure that security protocols are known and enforced.
- Ensure that only authorized software programs are implemented and that a consistent change control process is in place.
- Restrict the ability of one individual to independently perform a task without detection. Ensure separation of duties.
- Protect sensitive programs from tampering and misuse—especially if they support multiple applications—and have alarms in place for violation notification.
- Ensure that computer-dependent and, as necessary, disaster recovery procedures are in place and frequently tested.

Software Controls

- Adopt information security policies for new software development, testing, and production implementation.
- Set information security guidelines for developing new systems.
- Use system development life cycle, including information security and auditing standards.
- Adopt standard procedures for obtaining security patches from software developers and post in a centralized area to ensure access and validity.
- Restrict the use of system tools on both test and production environments.

Overall Administrative and Operations Information Security Controls

- Keep an up-to-date inventory of hardware and software for disaster recovery and business continuity planning.
- Information owners should review user privileges on a regular basis.

- Account for dial-in accounts to ensure they are authorized.
- Establish and maintain comprehensive disaster recovery and business continuity plans with every stakeholder.
- Conduct random information security checks using white-hat tools.
- Establish procedures for dealing with computer crime to include handling of information for forensic and evidence value.

Intrusion and Detection Planning

- Perform penetration audits using "tiger teams" who are trained on how to locate and exploit system and network vulnerabilities.
- Conduct a business impact analysis to ensure resources are recoverable as the business needs require.
- Deploy an intrusion detection system that both detects and notifies appropriate staff.
- Install appropriate virus detection software.
- Deploy appropriate firewall technology.
- Ensure passwords are strong; use one-time passwords, deploy tokens, or biometric authentication when required.
- Turn off unneeded network services.

Recovery and Continuity

- Develop and test a robust business continuity plan.
- Ensure that contingency planning and incident response teams are enabled in the event of unplanned outages or breached systems.
- Make sure staff involved in recovery efforts is well trained and that secondary personnel are available.
- Enable hot and cold recovery sites where the business case justified return on investment.
- Practice recovery and continuity plans frequently.
- Keep the plans up to date as risks change.

Reprinted with permission from the Center for Digital Government. General technology information on best practices is available at http://www.centerdigitalgov.com.

Principles of the Ethical Practice of Public Health

1. Public health should address principally the fundamental causes of disease and requirements for health, aiming to prevent adverse health outcomes.
2. Public health should achieve community health in a way that respects the rights of individuals in the community.
3. Public health policies, programs, and priorities should be developed and evaluated through processes that ensure an opportunity for input from community members.
4. Public health should advocate and work for the empowerment of disenfranchised community members, aiming to ensure that the basic resources and conditions necessary for health are accessible to all.
5. Public health should seek the information needed to implement effective policies and programs that protect and promote health.
6. Public health institutions should provide communities with the information they have that is needed for decisions on policies or programs and should obtain the community's consent for their implementation.
7. Public health institutions should act in a timely manner on the information they have within the resources and the mandate given to them by the public.
8. Public health programs and policies should incorporate a variety of approaches that anticipate and respect diverse values, beliefs, and cultures in the community.
9. Public health programs and policies should be implemented in a manner that most enhances the physical and social environment.
10. Public health institutions should protect the confidentiality of information that can bring harm to an individual or community if made public. Exceptions must be justified on the basis of the high likelihood of significant harm to the individual or others.
11. Public health institutions and their employees should engage in collaborations and affiliations in ways that build the public's trust and the institution's effectiveness.
12. Public health institutions and their employees should engage in collaborations and affiliations in ways that build the public's trust and the institution's effectiveness.

From Public Health Leadership Society. 2002. Principles of the Ethical Practice of Public Health. Version 2.2. Washington, DC: APHA. Available at: http://www.apha.org/NR/rdonlyres/1CED3CEA-287E-4185-9CBD-BD405FC60856/0/ethicsbrochure.pdf.

List of Offices of the Federal Emergency Management Agency

Region 1: Connecticut, Maine, Massachusetts, New Hampshire, Rhode Island, Vermont
J.W. McCormack Post Office and Court House, Room 442
Boston, MA 02109-4595
(617) 223-9450

Region 2: New Jersey, New York, Puerto Rico, Virgin Islands
26 Federal Plaza, Room 1337
New York, NY 10278-0002
(212) 225-7209

Region 3: Delaware, District of Columbia, Maryland, Pennsylvania, Virginia, West Virginia
One Independence Mall, 6th Floor
615 Chestnut Street
Philadelphia, PA 19106-4404
(215) 931-5608

Region 4: Alabama, Florida, Georgia, Kentucky, Mississippi, North Carolina, South Carolina, Tennessee
3003 Chamblee-Tucker Road
Atlanta, GA 30341
(770) 220-5200

Region 5: Illinois, Indiana, Michigan, Minnesota, Ohio, Wisconsin
536 South Clark Street, 6th Floor
Chicago, IL 60605
(312) 408-5501

Region 6: Arkansas, Louisiana, New Mexico, Oklahoma, Texas
Federal Regional Center
800 N. Loop 288
Denton, TX 76201-3698
(817) 898-5104

Region 7: Iowa, Kansas, Missouri, Nebraska
2322 Grand Blvd, Suite 900
Kansas City, MO 64108-2670
(816) 283-7061

Region 8: Colorado, Montana, North Dakota, South Dakota, Utah, Wyoming
Denver Federal Center
Building 710, Box 25267
Denver, CO 80225-0267
(303) 235-4812

Region 9: American Samoa, Arizona, California, Guam, Hawaii, Nevada, Commonwealth of the Northern Mariana Islands, Federated States of Micronesia, Republic of the Marshall Islands
1111 Broadway
Suite 1200
Oakland, CA 94607-4052
(510) 627-7100

Region 10: Alaska, Idaho, Oregon, Washington
Federal Regional Center
130 228th Street, S.W.
Bothell, WA 98021-9796
(206) 487-4604

Useful Internet References and Resources

General

Agency for Healthcare Research and Quality Development of Models for Emergency Preparedness, Personal Protective Equipment, Decontamination, Isolation/ Quarantine, and Laboratory Capacity
• http://www.ahrq.gov/research/devmodels

Disaster Response Tools and Resources
• http://www.ahrq.gov/path/katrina.htm

Hospital Preparedness Exercises Resources
• http://www.ahrq.gov/prep/hospex.htm

Public Health Emergency Preparedness
• http://www.ahrq.gov/prep

Surge Capacity
• http://www.ahrq.gov/prep

Agency for Toxic Substances and Disease Registry
• http://www.atsdr.cdc.gov
• http://www.atsdr.cdc.gov/HEC/primer.html

ToxFAQs, Toxic Substances Portal
• http://www.atsdr.cdc.gov/toxfaqs/index.asp

Medical Management Guidelines for Acute Chemical Exposures
• http://www.atsdr.cdc.gov/MMG/index.asp

American Academy of Child and Adolescent Psychiatry
• http://www.aacap.org

American Academy of Experts in Traumatic Stress
• http://www.aaets.org

American Hospital Association
• http://www.aha.org/aha_app/issues/Emergency-Readiness/index.j

American Medical Association Disaster Medicine Journal
• http://www.ama-assn.org/ama/pub/news/news/new-publisher-dmphp.shtml

American Public Health Association
• http://www.apha.org

   Get Ready
   • http://www.getreadyforflu.org/newsite.htm

American Psychiatric Association
• http://www.psych.org/search.aspx?SearchPhrase=disaster

American Radio Relay League, HAM Radio Association and Resources
• http://www.arrl.org/www.arrl.org

   Radio Amateur Civil Emergency Service Regulations
   • http://www.usraces.org
   • http://edocket.access.gpo.gov/cfr_2002/octqtr/47cfr97.407.htm

American Red Cross
• http://www.redcross.org

   Disaster Online Newsroom
   • http://newsroom.redcross.org

   National Blog
   • http://www.facebook.com/redcross

   Shelter Map (Web version)
   • http://app.redcross.org/nss-app

   Shelter App (iPhone)
   • http://itunes.apple.com/us/app/american-red-cross-shelter/id419258261?mt=8

   Social Media Handbook
   • http://sites.google.com/site/wharman/social-media-strategy-handbook

   Twitter
   • http://twitter.com/redcross

American Veterinary Medical Association Disaster Preparedness
• http://www.avma.org/disaster/default.asp
• http://www.avma.org/disaster/vmat/default.asp

Anthrax Vaccine Information
• http://www.anthrax.osd.mil

Armed Forces Institute of Pathology
• http://www.afip.org

Armed Forces Radiobiology Research Institute
• http://www.afrri.usuhs.mil

Army Bibliography
• http://www.carlisle.army.mil/usawc/dclm/family/fac6bib.doc

Association for Infection Control Practitioners
• http://www.apic.org

Association of State and Territorial Health Officials
• http://www.statepublichealth.org

Bioterrorism Resources
• http://www.usuhs.mil/med/milmedgoalsbio.htm
• http://www.moxietraining.com

California Emergency Management Agency
• http://www.oes.ca.gov

Caltech Earthquake Engineering Research Library Technical Reports
• http://caltecheerl.library.caltech.edu

Canadian Centre for Emergency Preparedness
• http://www.ccep.ca

CANUTEC (HAZMAT Transport Canada)
• http://www.tc.gc.ca/eng/canutec/menu.htm

Centers for Disease Control and Prevention
• http://emergency.cdc.gov

  Biosafety
  • http://www.cdc.gov/biosafety
  • http://www.cdc.gov/od/ohs/biosfty/bmbl4/bmbl4toc.htm

  Bioterrorism Agents
  • http://www.bt.cdc.gov/agent/agentlist.asp

  Emergency Preparedness and Response
  • http://www.bt.cdc.gov

Emerging Infectious Disease Journal
• http://www.cdc.gov/ncidod/EID/index.htm

Environmental Health Shelter Assessment Tool
• http://www.bt.cdc.gov/shelterassessment

Morbidity and Mortality Weekly
• http://www.cdc.gov/mmwr

National Center for Infectious Diseases Publications Online
• http://www.cdc.gov/ncidod/publicat.htm

Preparation and Planning
• http://www.bt.cdc.gov/planning/index.asp

Strategic National Stockpile
• http://www.bt.cdc.gov/stockpile

Center for Earthquake Research and Information at University of Memphis
• http://www.ceri.memphis.edu

Center for Food Safety and Applied Nutrition, US Food and Drug Administration
• http://www.fda.gov/Food/default.htm

"Bad Bug Book," Foodborne Pathogenic Microorganisms and Natural Toxins
Handbook, FDA
• http://www.fda.gov/Food/FoodSafety/FoodborneIllness/Foodborne
IllnessFoodbornePathogensNaturalToxins/BadBugBook/default.htm

(James Martin) Center for Nonproliferation Studies
• http://cns.miis.edu

Chemical and Biological Weapons Resource Page
• http://cns.miis.edu/cbw

CBS News Disaster Links
• http://www.cbsnews.com/digitaldan/disaster/disasters.shtml

Centre for Research on the Epidemiology of Disasters
• http://www.cred.be

Coast Guard Command Center
• http://www.uscg.mil/hq/commandcenter/opcen.asp

Counterterrorism Training and Resources for Law Enforcement
• http://www.counterterrorismtraining.gov

Crisis Commons
• http://crisiscommons.org

Defense Threat Reduction Agency
• http://www.dtra.mil

DisasterAssistance.gov (portal for disaster victims)
• http://www.disasterassistance.gov/daip_en.portal

Disaster Center
• http://www.disastercenter.com

> Bibliography on Terrorism
> • http://www.disastercenter.com/terror.htm

Disaster News Network
• http://www.disasternews.net

Disaster Recovery Yellow Pages
• http://www.rothstein.com/data/dr119.htm

Disaster Research Center, University of Delaware
• http://www.udel.edu/DRC

Disasters Roundtable of the National Academies
• http://dels-old.nas.edu/dr

Earthquakes
• http://earthquake.usgs.gov

Emergency Management Assistance Compact Operations
• http://www.emacweb.org/?305

Emergency Management Forum
• http://www.emforum.org

Emergency Nutrition Network
• http://www.ennonline.net

Emergency System for Advance Registration of Volunteer Health Professionals
• http://www.phe.gov/esarvhp/Pages/about.aspx

Environmental Protection Agency, Emergency Management
• http://www.epa.gov/emergencies/index.htm

Federal Emergency Management Agency (FEMA)
• http://www.fema.gov

Bibliography for Emergency Management
• http://training.fema.gov/EMIWeb/edu/docs/Wayne's%20Bibliography.doc

Comprehensive Preparedness Guide 101
• http://www.fema.gov/about/divisions/cpg.shtm

Declaration Process Fact Sheet
• http://www.fema.gov/media/fact_sheets/declaration_process.shtm

Emergency Management Competencies and Curriculum
• http://training.fema.gov/EMIWeb/edu/EMCompetencies.asp

Federal Response Framework, Emergency Support Function #8 Public Health and Medical Services Annex
• http://www.fema.gov/pdf/emergency/nrf/nrf-esf-08.pdf

FEMA for Kids
• http://www.fema.gov/kids

Flood Insurance Manual
• http://www.fema.gov/nfip/manual.htm

Library of Reference Documents
• http://www.fema.gov/library

National Incident Management System
• http://www.fema.gov/pdf/emergency/nims/NIMS_core.pdf

National Response Framework Resource Center
• http://www.fema.gov/emergency/nrf
• http://www.fema.gov/emergency/nrf/index.htm
• http://www.fema.gov/emergency/nrf/responsepartnerguides.htm

Public Assistance Grant Program
• http://www.fema.gov/government/grant/pa/index.shtm

State Offices and Agencies of Emergency Management
• http://www.fema.gov/about/contact/statedr.shtm

Target Capabilities List
   Original
   • http://www.fema.gov/pdf/government/training/tcl.pdf

Updated User's Guide
• http://www.iaem.com/committees/governmentaffairs/documents/
TargetCapabilitiesUserGuide_17February2009.pdf

Terrorism Training
• http://www.fema.gov/pdf/government/grant/bulletins/info249a.pdf

What is Disaster Assistance
• http://www.fema.gov/assistance/process/individual_assistance.shtm

Field Operations Guide, Coast Guard
• http://www.ecy.wa.gov/programs/spills/response/oilspillfog.pdf

Fire Administration
• http://www.usfa.dhs.gov

Fire and Explosion Planning Matrix
• http://www.osha.gov/dep/fire-expmatrix/index.html

First Responders in the Field
• http://www.remm.nlm.gov/remm_FirstResponder.htm

FloodSmart.Gov
• http://www.earthsat.com/wx/flooding/index.html
• http://www.floodsmart.gov

Food and Drug Administration Disaster Procedures
• http://www.fda.gov/ICECI/Inspections/IOM/ucm122554.htm

FoodSafety.Gov
• http://www.foodsafety.gov

Gender and Disasters Network
• http://www.gdnonline.org

Geological Survey
• http://www.usgs.gov

Global Emerging Infections Surveillance and Response System
• http://www.geis.fhp.osd.mil
• http://www.first-search.com/geis.fhp.osd.mil.htm
• http://www.afhsc.mil/geis

Government Emergency Telecommunications Service
• http://gets.ncs.gov

Hazardous Materials Training and Links
- http://www.usfa.dhs.gov/fireservice/subjects/hazmat

Health Library for Disasters
- http://helid.desastres.net

Hospital Incident Command System
- http://www.emsa.ca.gov/hics/default.asp
- http://www.emsa.ca.gov/HICS/files/Guidebook_Glossary.doc

Hurricane Watch Net
- http://www.hwn.org

Infectious Disease Society of America
- http://www.idsociety.org

International Association of Emergency Managers
- http://www.iaem.com

International Critical Incident Stress Foundation
- http://www.icisf.org

International Federation of the Red Cross and Red Crescent Societies
- http://www.ifrc.org

International Network of Crisis Mappers
- http://www.crisismappers.net

International Rescue Committee
- http://www.theirc.org

International Society for Traumatic Stress Studies
- http://www.istss.org/Home.htm

Inventory and Assessment of Databases Relevant for Social Science Research of Terrorism
- http://www.loc.gov/rr/frd/pdf-files/inventory_04.pdf

Johns Hopkins Office of Critical Event Preparedness and Response
- http://www.hopkinsmedicine.org/emergencymedicine/divisions/CEPAR.html

Joint Electronic Library (military search engine for federal laws, regulations, and documents relating to emergency management)
- http://www.dtic.mil

Lawrence Livermore National Laboratory Global Security Principal Directorate
• http://www.llnl.gov/nai/rdiv/rdiv.html

Lessons Learned Information Sharing System
• https://www.llis.dhs.gov/index.do

Medical Reserve Corps
• http://www.medicalreservecorps.gov/HomePage

Mental Health Field Manual
• http://disaster.efpa.eu/ddl.php/d875ea9eef038e5cb683f0eaae2a62b4/?dkey=
d875ea9eef038e5cb683f0eaae2a62b4

Medical Management of Radiology Casualties Handbook, U.S. Army
• http://www.afrri.usuhs.mil/www/outreach/pdf/2edmmrchandbook.pdf

Medical Management of Biological Casualties Handbook, U.S. Army Medical
Research Institute of Infectious Diseases (USAMRIID)
• http://www.usamriid.army.mil/education/bluebookpdf/USAMRIID%20BlueBook
%206th%20Edition%20-%20Sep%202006.pdf

Medical Management of Chemical Casualties Handbook, USAMRIID
• https://www.rke.vaems.org/wvems/Libraryfiles/Dis/E_04.pdf

National Association of Community Health Centers, Developing and Implementing
an Emergency Management Plan for Your Health Center
• http://www.nachc.org/client/documents/publications-resources/rm_11_05.pdf

National Association of County and City Health Officials, Preparedness
• http://www.naccho.org/search/index.cfm?q=Preparedness&site=
naccho&searchbutton.x=4&searchbutton

  Public Health Preparedness
  • http://www.naccho.org/topics/emergency

  Toolbox
  • http://www.naccho.org/toolbox/index.cfm?v=4&id=116&topicname=
  Surveillance

National Association of School Psychologists
• http://www.nasponline.org

National Association of Social Workers
• http://www.socialworkers.org/pressroom/events/911/disasters.asp

National Environmental Health Association
• http://www.neha.org/index.shtml

National Fire Protection Association
• http://www.nfpa.org/assets/files/PDF/NFPA16002010.pdf

National Center for Post-Traumatic Stress Disorder
• http://www.ptsd.va.gov

National Emergency Management Association
• http://www.nemaweb.org/home.aspx?CFID=416185&CFTOKEN=187804

National Emergency Response and Rescue Training Center
• http://teexweb.tamu.edu/nerrtc

National Hurricane Center
• http://www.nhc.noaa.gov

National Institutes of Health
• http://www.nih.gov

   Library
   • http://nihlibrary.nih.gov/Pages/default.aspx

National Institute on Mental Health
• http://www.nimh.nih.gov

National Institute for Occupational Safety and Health
• http://www.cdc.gov/niosh

   Disaster Site Management
   • http://www.cdc.gov/niosh/topics/emres/sitemgt.html

   Pocket Guide to Chemical Hazards
   • http://www.cdc.gov/niosh/npg

   Publications and Products
   • http://www.cdc.gov/niosh/pubs/all_date_desc_nopubnumbers.html

National Library of Medicine
• http://www.nlm.nih.gov

   PUBMED
   • http://www.ncbi.nlm.nih.gov/pubmed

TOXNET, Toxicology Data Network
- http://toxnet.nlm.nih.gov

National Oceanic and Atmospheric Administration
- http://www.cpc.noaa.gov

Hydrologic Services
- http://www.nws.noaa.gov/os/water/tadd

National Weather Service
- http://www.nws.noaa.gov
- http://www.weather.gov/view/nationalwarnings.php

Real-Time Monitoring of Hurricane Potential for Atlantic Ocean
- http://www.cpc.noaa.gov/products/hurricane

Real-Time Monitoring of Hurricane Potential for Tropical East Pacific Ocean
- http://www.cpc.noaa.gov/products/Epac_hurr/index.shtml

Real-Time Tracking of Tornado Touch Downs
- http://www.tornadopaths.org

Weather Radio
- http://www.nws.noaa.gov/nwr

Winter Storms: The Deceptive Killers
- http://www.nws.noaa.gov/om/brochures/winterstorm.pdf

National Organization for Victim Assistance
- http://www.trynova.org

National Response Center, U.S. Coast Guard
- http://www.nrc.uscg.mil/nrchp.html
- http://www.nrc.uscg.mil/index.html

National Response Team
- http://www.nrt.org

National Safety Council
- http://www.nsc.org/Pages/Home.aspx

National Technical Information Service
- http://www.ntis.gov

National Voluntary Organizations Active in Disaster
• http://www.nvoad.org

Natural Hazards Center, University of Colorado
• http://www.colorado.edu/hazards

   Quick Response Research Program
   • http://www.colorado.edu/hazards/research/qr

Office of Foreign Disaster Assistance
• http://www.usaid.gov/our_work/humanitarian_assistance/disaster_assistance
• http://www.globalcorps.com/ofda.html

   Field Operations Guide, Version 4
   • http://www.usaid.gov/our_work/humanitarian_assistance/disaster_assistance/
   resources/pdf/fog_v4.pdf

   Mitigation Practitioner's Handbook
   • http://www.usaid.gov/policy/ads/200/hbkoct18.pdf

Overview of Stafford Act Support to States
• http://www.fema.gov/pdf/emergency/nrf/nrf-stafford.pdf

Pan-American Health Organization (PAHO)
• http://new.paho.org
• http://new.paho.org/disasters/newsletter

   PAHO Humanitarian Supply Management System
   • http://www.disaster-info.net/SUMA

Presidential Decision Directives
• http://www.fas.org/irp/offdocs/direct.htm

Refugee Health Information Network
• http://rhin.org/search/search_results.asp?zoom_query=Disaster%20Planning

Regional Disaster Information Center Latin American and the Caribbean (CRID)
• http://www.crid.or.cr/crid/ing/index_ing.html

ReliefWeb
• http://www.reliefweb.int/rw/dbc.nsf/doc100?OpenForm

Rural EMS and Trauma Technical Assistance Center
• http://www.remsttac.org

State Emergency Management Listing
• http://www.emergencymanagement.org/stat

State Health Department Listing
• http://www2a.cdc.gov/phtn/sites.asp

Southern California Earthquake Center
• http://www.scec.org

Stimson Center, Pragmatic Steps for Global Security
• http://www.stimson.org

Substance Abuse and Mental Health Services Administration
• http://www.mentalhealth.samhsa.gov/cmhs

Surge Capacity
• http://www.dtic.mil/ndia/2003terrorism/barb.pdf

United Nations High Commissioner for Refugees
• http://www.unhcr.org/cgi-bin/texis/vtx/home

U.S. Army Medicine
• http://www.armymedicine.army.mil

    Medical Research Institute of Chemical Defense
    • https://ccc.apgea.army.mil/links.htm

    Medical Research Institute of Infectious Diseases
    • http://www.usamriid.army.mil/index.htm
    • http://www.usamriid.army.mil/biodefenselinks.htm

    Public Health Command
    • http://phc.amedd.army.mil/Pages/default.aspx

U.S. Department of Defense, Chemical and Biological Defense Programs
• http://www.acq.osd.mil/cp

    Dictionary of Military and Associated Terms
    • http://www.dtic.mil/doctrine

U.S. Department of Health and Human Services
• http://www.hhs.gov

    HHS Archive
    • http://archive.hhs.gov/drugs

Disaster Information Management Research Center
• http://phpreparedness.nlm.nih.gov/tools.php

U.S. Department of Health and Human Services, Public Health Emergency Responders, Clinicians, and Practitioners
• http://www.phe.gov/preparedness/responders/Pages/default.aspx

National Disaster Medical System
• http://www.phe.gov/Preparedness/responders/ndms/Pages/default.asp

Public Health and Medical Services Support
• http://www.phe.gov/Preparedness/support/medicalresponse/Pages/default.aspx

Public Health Emergency, Hospital Preparedness Program
• http://www.phe.gov/SearchCenter/Pages/Results.aspx?k=hospitals
• http://www.phe.gov/preparedness/planning/hpp/Pages/default.aspx

Public Health Emergency, Medical Surge Capacity Capability
• http://www.phe.gov/Preparedness/support/mscc/Pages/default.aspx

Public Health Service Act, Legal Authority and Related Guidance
• http://www.phe.gov/Preparedness/planning/authority/Pages/default.aspx

Public Health Services Commissioned Corps
• http://www.usphs.gov

Public Health Services Commissioned Corps, Emergency Response
• http://www.usphs.gov/aboutus/emergencyresponse.aspx

U.S. Department of Homeland Security, Preparedness, Response and Recovery
• http://www.dhs.gov/files/prepresprecovery.shtm

Computer Emergency Readiness Team
• http://www.us-cert.gov

Preparedness, Response, and Recovery
• http://www.dhs.gov/files/prepresprecovery.shtm

State Contracts and Grant Award Information
• http://www.dhs.gov/xgovt/grants/index.shtm

U.S. Department of Transportation, Emergency Response Guidebook (First Responder's Guide for HAZMAT Operations)
• http://www.phmsa.dot.gov/hazmat/library/erg

Developing a Hazardous Materials Exercise Program: A Handbook for State and Local Officials
• http://ntl.bts.gov/DOCS/254.html

HazMat Safety Community
• http://phmsa.dot.gov/hazmat

University of Wisconsin Disaster Management Center
• http://dmc.engr.wisc.edu

World Health Organization (WHO)
• http://www.who.int/en

Weekly Epidemiological Record
• http://www.who.int/wer/en

Electronic Newsletters, Periodicals, and Publications

Air University Index to Military Periodicals
• http://www.dtic.mil/dtic/aulimp

Chemical and Biological Information Analysis Center Newsletter
• https://www.cbrniac.apgea.army.mil/Pages/default.aspx

CDC Public Health Law News
• http://www2a.cdc.gov/phlp/cphln.asp

Clinical Infectious Disease
• http://www.journals.uchicago.edu/toc/cid/current

Digital Communities
• http://www.govtech.com

Disaster Medicine
• http://www.ama-assn.org/ama/pub/physician-resources/public-health/center-public-health-preparedness-disaster-response/journal-disaster-medicine-public-health-preparedness.shtml

Disaster Medicine and Public Health Preparedness
• http://www.dmphp.org

Disaster Prevention and Management
• http://www.emeraldinsight.com/products/journals/journals.htm?id=dpm

Disaster Recovery Journal
• http://www.drj.com

Disasters
• http://pdm.medicine.wisc.edu

Dispatch, The Chemical and Biological Arms Control Institute
• http://www.cbaci.org/dispatch.htm

Electronic Journals for Disaster Studies
• http://www2.lib.udel.edu/subj/disasters/ej.htm

Emerging Infectious Diseases, CDC, National Center for Infectious Diseases
• http://www.cdc.gov/ncidod/EID/index.htm

Emergency Information Infrastructure Partnership Newsletter
• http://www.emforum.org

Emergency Management
• http://www.emergencymgmt.com

Emergency Medical Services World
• http://www.emsworld.com

Emergency Preparedness Information Exchange (EPIX)
• http://www.osh.net/directory/emerg_mang/index.htm

Environmental Hazards
• http://www.sciencedirect.com/science/journal/17477891

FEMA HAZUS News
• http://www.fema.gov/plan/prevent/hazus/hz_news.shtm

Government Technology
• http://www.govtech.com

HealthNet News
• http://www.healthnet.org/e-newsletters

Homeland Defense Journal
• http://old.library.georgetown.edu/newjour/h/msg02773.html

International Journal of Mass Emergencies and Disasters
• http://www.ijmed.org

The Journal of Homeland Defense
• http://www.homelanddefense.org

The Journal of Homeland Security
• http://www.homelandsecurity.org/journal/index.cfm

Medicine and Global Survival Magazine
• http://www.healthnet.org

Morbidity and Mortality Weekly Report, CDC
• http://www.cdc.gov/mmwr

National Fire and Rescue Magazine
• http://www.mondotimes.com/2/topics/5/society/36/4684

Natural Hazards
• http://www.springerlink.com/content/102967

Natural Hazards Observer
• http://www.colorado.edu/hazards/o

The Nonproliferation Review
• http://cns.miis.edu/npr

OSHA *Job Safety and Health Quarterly Magazine*:
• http://www.osha.gov/html/jshq-index.html

Prehospital and Disaster Medicine
• http://pdm.medicine.wisc.edu

ProMED Digest
• promed-digest-Owner@promed.isid.harvard.edu

Risk Analysis
• http://www.springerlink.com/content/112113
• http://onlinelibrary.wiley.com/journal/10.1111/(ISSN)1539-6924

GIS Web Sites

Community Vulnerability Assessment Tool
• http://www.csc.noaa.gov/products/nchaz/startup.htm

Data Sources on the Internet
• http://geo.arc.nasa.gov/sge/health/links/links.html

Duke University Library, Sites With a Variety of GIS Data
• http://library.duke.edu/research/subject/guides/gis/data.html

ESRI, Inc.
• http://www.esri.com
• http://training.esri.com/gateway/index.cfm

FEMA Mapping and Analysis Center
• http://www.gismaps.fema.gov

Geographic Information Systems, CDC
• http://www.cdc.gov/gis
• http://www.cdc.gov/gis/training.htm

Geoplace.com
• http://www.geoplace.com/ME2/Default.asp

GIS Data Depot
• http://data.geocomm.com

Special Population Planner
• http://sourceforge.net/projects/spc-pop-planner

WHO HealthMapper
• http://www.who.int/health_mapping/tools/healthmapper/en/index.html

Procedures, Protocols, and Response Resources

All the Virology on the Web
• http://www.virology.net/garryfavwebbw.html

Decontamination, Commercial Resources
• http://www.nbcindustrygroup.com/index03.htm

EPA, National Response System
• http://www.epa.gov/ceppo/web/content/nrs

Hazardous Materials Information Resource System
• http://www.dscr.dla.mil/ExternalWeb/UserWeb/aviationengineering/HMIRS

Incident Command System, U.S. Coast Guard
• http://www.uscg.mil/auxiliary/training/ics100.asp

Joint Information Center Guide
• http://www.fbcoem.org/external/content/document/1528/257624/1/ JICBestPractices.pdf

Medline Plus: Disaster Preparation and Recovery
• http://www.nlm.nih.gov/medlineplus/disasterpreparationandrecovery.html

Public Health Image Library
• http://phil.cdc.gov/phil/home.asp

Wildland Fire Links
• http://www.wildlandfire.com/links.htm

Vulnerable Populations References and Resources

Children

AHRQ—Pediatric Terrorism and Disaster Preparedness
• http://www.ahrq.gov/research/pedprep/pedchap10.htm

Children and Disasters, American Academy of Pediatrics
• http://www.aap.org/disasters/pediatricians.cfm
Emergency Information Form, American Academy of Pediatrics
• http://www.aap.org/advocacy/epquesansw.htm

National Commission on Children and Disasters
• http://www.childrenanddisasters.acf.hhs.gov

Pediatric Disaster Tool Kit, New York City Department of Health and Mental Hygiene
• http://www.nyc.gov/html/doh/html/bhpp/bhpp-focus-ped-toolkit.shtml

Elderly

AARP
• http://www.aarp.org

Administration on Aging, Emergency Preparedness, and Response
• http://www.aoa.gov/AoARoot/Preparedness/index.aspx

Disaster Assistance
• http://www.aoa.gov/aoaroot/Preparedness/Resources_Network/manual/disaster_assist_manual.aspx

Disaster Preparedness for Seniors by Seniors
• http://www.redcross.org/services/disaster/0,1082,0_9_,00.html

Disaster Preparedness Guide for Elders
• http://elderaffairs.state.fl.us/english/pubs/EU/EU2010/Disaster%20Guide%202010_WEB%20.pdf

Disaster Supply Kit
• http://elderaffairs.state.fl.us/english/disaster.php

Emergency Preparedness Checklist
• http://www.fema.gov/pdf/library/epc.pdf

Emergency Preparedness Tips for Older Adults
• http://www.healthinaging.org/public_education/emergency_tips.php

(A) Health Guide for the Public in Disaster Planning and Recovery
• http://www.wvdhhr.org/oehs/disaster-readiness-response-folder/DisasterPlanning_HealthGuide_%20large%20print.pdf

Just in Case: Emergency Readiness for Older Adult and Caregivers
• http://www.aoa.gov/AoA_Programs/HCLTC/Caregiver/docs/Just_in_Case030706_links.pdf

Maintaining a Healthy State of Mind for Seniors
• http://www.redcross.org/preparedness/cdc_english/mentalhealth-6.asp

Mental Health: A Guide for Older Adults
• http://health.nashville.gov/PDFs/MHandAgingdirectoryA.pdf

Nursing Homes Emergency Preparedness: Questions Consumers Should Ask
• http://www.theconsumervoice.org/sites/default/files/advocate/Emergency-Preparedness.pdf

Preparing Makes Sense for Older Americans
• http://www.ready.gov/america/_downloads/older_americans.pdf

Ready America, Older Americans
• http://www.ready.gov/america/getakit/seniors.html

Tips for Seniors and People With Disabilities: Establish a Personal Support Network
• http://www.redcross.org/services/disaster/beprepared/mobileprogs.html

The Role of Long-Term Care Ombudsmen in Nursing Home Closures and Natural Disasters
• http://www.ltcombudsman.org/issues/emergency-preparedness

General

Access Board
• http://www.access-board.gov

Accommodating Individuals With Disabilities in the Provision of Disaster Mass Care, Housing, and Human Services Reference Guide, FEMA
• http://www.fema.gov/oer/reference/index.shtm

American Association of People With Disabilities
• http://www.aapd-dc.org

Americans With Disabilities Act (ADA)
• http://www.ada.gov/pubs/ada.htm

  An ADA Guide for Local Governments: Making Community Emergency Preparedness and Response Programs Accessible to People With Disabilities
  • http://www.ada.gov/emergencyprepguide.htm

At-Risk Populations and Pandemic Influenza, Planning Guidance for State, Territorial, Tribal, and Local Health Departments, Association of Territorial and Health Officials
• http://cms.calema.ca.gov/WorkArea/DownloadAsset.aspx?id=737

Braille and ADA Signage
• http://askjan.org/cgi-win/OrgQuery.exe?Sol231

Center for an Accessible Society
• http://www.accessiblesociety.org

Center for Disability and Special Needs Preparedness
• http://www.disabilitypreparedness.org

Center for Disability Issues and the Health Professions
• http://www.cdihp.org/products.html#eeguide

Closed caption video clips using American Sign Language
• http://www.bt.cdc.gov/disasters/hurricanes/psa/prescription_asl.asp

Community Emergency Preparedness Information Network
• http://www.cepintdi.org

Coping With Disaster: A Guide for Families and Others who Support Adults With Cognitive Disabilities
- http://www.temple.edu/cprep/Library/Disabilities_resource_06.06.doc
- http://www.qualitymall.org/directory/dept1.asp?deptid=72

Cross-Agency Government Web Site Devoted to Disaster Preparedness
- http://www.disasterhelp.gov

Disability Disaster Information
- http://www.floridadisaster.org/disabilities.htm

Disability Preparedness Resource Center
- http://disabilitypreparedness.gov

Disaster Preparedness for People With Disabilities
- http://www.disability911.com

Easter Seals S.a.f.e.t.y. First Evacuation Program
- http://www.easterseals.com/site/PageServer?pagename=ntl_safety_first%20_evacuation

Emergency Access Rules, Federal Communications Commission (FCC)
- http://hraunfoss.fcc.gov/edocs_public/attachmatch/DA-02-1852A1.pdf

Emergency Evacuation Planning Guide for People With Disabilities, National Fire Protection Association
- http://www.nfpa.org/assets/files//PDF/Forms/EvacuationGuide.pdf

Emergency Evacuation Plans
- http://askjan.org/media/emergency.html

Emergency Planning and Special Needs Populations, FEMA Emergency Management Institute
- http://training.fema.gov/index.asp

Emergency Power Planning for People Who Use Electricity and Battery Dependent Assistive Technology and Medical Devices
- http://www.jik.com/disaster-individ.html#Guides

Emergency Preparedness and People With Disabilities. U.S. Department of Labor, Office of Disability Employment Policy
- http://www.dol.gov/odep/programs/emergency.htm

Emergency Preparedness, National Association of the Deaf
- http://www.nad.org/issues/emergency-preparedness

Emergency Procedures for Employees With Disabilities in Office Occupancies
- http://www.usfa.dhs.gov/downloads/pdf/publications/fa-154.pdf
- http://askjan.org/media/emergency.html
- http://www.usfa.dhs.gov/downloads/txt/publications/fa-154.txt

Emergency Warnings: Notification of Deaf or Hard of Hearing People
- http://tap.gallaudet.edu/emergency/nov05conference/EmergencyReports/NADEmergency.doc

Employers' Guide to Including People With Disabilities in Emergency Evacuation Plans, Job Accommodation Network
- http://askjan.org/media/evacchecklist.html

Equal Employment Opportunity Commission (EEOC), Fact Sheet on Obtaining and Using Employee Medical Information as Part of Emergency Evacuation Procedures
- http://www.eeoc.gov/facts/evacuation.html

Evacuation Preparedness Guide, Center for Disability Issues in the Health Professions
- http://www.cdihp.org/evacuation/toc.html

Evacuee Support Planning Guide, FEMA P-760/Catalog No. 09049-2 July 2009
- http://www.fema.gov/pdf/government/evacuee_support_guide.pdf

Guidance on Planning for Integration of Functional Needs Support Services in General Population Shelters, FEMA
- http://www.fema.gov/pdf/about/odic/fnss_guidance.pdf

Guidance on Planning and Responding to the Needs of People With Access and Functional Needs
- http://www.oes.ca.gov/WebPage/oeswebsite.nsf/Content/CF550341643F892B8825749B0080867F?OpenDocument

Guide to Disaster Preparedness for People With Disabilities, American Red Cross/FEMA
- http://www.redcross.org/images/pdfs/preparedness/A4497.pdf

Health Care Language Services Guide
- https://hclsig.thinkculturalhealth.hhs.gov/default.asp

Inclusive Preparedness Center
- http://inclusivepreparedness.org

June Kailes
- http://www.jik.com/disaster.html

Lift and Carry
- http://www.cert-la.com/liftcarry/Liftcarry.pdf

Lighthouse International
• http://www.lighthouse.org

Limited English Proficiency Resources
• http://www.lep.gov/resources/resources.html

Mass Care and Shelter Plan: Functional Needs Annex, City of Oakland, California
• http://www.dralegal.org/downloads/cases/CFILC/Draft_MassCareandShelterPlan.pdf

National Council on Disability
• http://www.ncd.gov

National Institute on Disability and Rehabilitation Research
• http://www.ed.gov/about/offices/list/osers/nidrr/about.html

OK WARN: Weather Alert Remote Notification for the Deaf and Hard of Hearing.
NOAA National Severe Storms Laboratory
• http://www.nssl.noaa.gov/edu/safety/pagers.html

Other Languages, CDC
• http://www.cdc.gov/other/languages

People With Disabilities and Other Access and Functional Needs, FEMA
• http://www.fema.gov/plan/prepare/specialplans.shtm

Persons With Disabilities, Federal Communications Commission
• http://www.fcc.gov/pshs/special-needs.html

Prepare Now
• http://www.preparenow.org

Preparedness Information for Seniors, American Red Cross
• http://www.redcross.org/museum/prepare_org/seniors/srsforsrs.htm

Preparing for Disaster for People With Disabilities and Other Special Needs
• http://www.fema.gov/pdf/library/pfd_all.pdf

Public Health Workbook to Define, Locate and Reach Special, Vulnerable, and
At-Risk Populations in an Emergency, CDC
• http://www.bt.cdc.gov/workbook/pdf/ph_workbookFINAL.pdf

Ready Campaign, DHS
• http://www.ready.gov

Ready New York for Seniors and People With Disabilities, New York City Office of Emergency Management
• http://www.nyc.gov/html/oem/html/ready/seniors_guide.shtml

Resources on Emergency Evacuation and Disaster Preparedness
• http://www.access-board.gov/evac.htm

Saving Lives: Including People With Disabilities in Emergency Planning, National Council on Disability
• http://www.ncd.gov/newsroom/publications/2005/saving_lives.htm

Tactile Graphics and Maps
• http://askjan.org/cgi-win/OrgQuery.exe?Sol401

Telecommunications Relay Services
• http://www.nidcd.nih.gov/health/hearing/telecomm.asp

The Pediatrician and Disaster Preparedness, Policy Paper, American Academy of Pediatrics
• http://aappolicy.aappublications.org/cgi/reprint/pediatrics;117/2/560.pdf

ThisAbled
• http://www.thisabled.com
• http://www.thisabled.com/health-and-wellness/142-you-can-survive-a-disaster-seriously

Visual and Tactile Alerting Devices
• http://www.ilr.cornell.edu/edi/hr_tips/article_1.cfm?b_id=2&view_all=true

United Spinal Association
• http://www.unitedspinal.org

Why and How to Include People With Disabilities in Your Planning Process, Nobody Left Behind
• http://www.nobodyleftbehind2.org/findings/why_and_how_to_include_all.shtml

Web Accessibility Initiative Resources, W3C
• http://www.w3.org/WAI/Resources/#gl

References and Readings

Bioterrorism and Emerging Diseases

Blank S, Moskin LC, Zucker JR. 2003. An ounce of prevention is a ton of work: mass antibiotic prophylaxis for anthrax: New York City, 2001. *Emerg Infect Dis.* 9:615–622.

Bravata DM, McDonald KM, Owens DK, et al. 2004. Regionalization of bioterrorism preparedness and response. Evidence Report/Technology Assessment: Number 96. Rockville, MD: Agency for Healthcare Research and Quality.

Centers for Disease Control and Prevention (CDC). 2005. *Preparation and Planning for Bioterrorism Emergencies.* Atlanta, GA: CDC.

Centers for Disease Control and Prevention. 2001. Considerations for distinguishing influenza-like illness from inhalational anthrax. *MMWR Morbid Mortal Wkly Rep.* 5044:985–986.

Centers for Disease Control and Prevention. 2003. Notice to readers: guidelines for maintaining and managing the vaccine cold chain. *MMWR Morbid Mortal Wkly Rep.* 5242:1023–1025.

Fenner F, Henderson DA, Arita I, et al. 1988. *Smallpox and Its Eradication.* Geneva, Switzerland: World Health Organization:1–276.

Henderson DA, Inglesby TV, Bartlett JG, et al. 1999. Smallpox as a biological weapon: medical and public health management. *JAMA.* 281:1735–1745.

Henderson DA, Inglesby TV, Bartlett JG, et al. 1999. Smallpox as a biological weapon. *JAMA.* 281:2127–2137.

Henderson DA, Inglesby TV, O'Toole TO. 2002. *Bioterrorism: Guidelines for Medical and Public Health Management.* Chicago, IL: American Medical Association.

Henderson DA. 1999. Smallpox: clinical and epidemiologic features. *Emerg Infect Dis.* 5:537–539. Available at: http://www.bt.cdc.gov/bioterrorism/prep.asp. Accessed February 28, 2011.

Meehan PJ, Rosenstein NE, Gillen M, et al. 2004. Responding to detection of aerosolized *Bacillus anthracis* by autonomous detection systems in the workplace. *MMWR Recomm Rep.* 53:1–12.

Mina B, Dym J, Kuepper F, et al. 2002. Fatal inhalational anthrax with unknown source of exposure in a 61-year-old woman in New York City. *JAMA.* 2877:858–862.

Murray V, editor. 1990. *Major Chemical Disasters: Medical Aspects of Management (International Congress and Symposium Series).* New York, NY: Royal Society of Medicine Services Limited.

Novick LF, Marr JS, editors. 2001. *Public Health Issues in Disaster Preparedness: Focus on Bioterrorism.* Sudbury, MA: Jones & Bartlett Learning:1–150.

O'Toole T. 1999. Smallpox: an attack scenario. *Emerg Infect Dis.* 5:540–560.

Occupational Safety and Health Administration. 2005. OSHA Best Practices for Hospital–Based First Receivers of Victims From Mass Casualty Incidents Involving the Release of Hazardous Substances. Washington, DC: U.S. Department of Labor. Available at: http://www.osha.gov/dts/osta/bestpractices/html/hospital_firstreceivers.html. Accessed February 28, 2011.

Pepe PE, Rinnert KJ. 2002. Bioterrorism and medical risk management. *Int Lawyer.* 36:9–20.

U.S. Department of Justice; Federal Bureau of Investigation; U.S. Army Soldier Biological Chemical Command. 2003. Criminal and Epidemiological Investigation Handbook. Available at: http://www.ecbc.army.mil/downloads/mirp/ECBC_ceih.pdf. Accessed February 28, 2011.

Wagner MM, Moore AW, Aryel RM, editors. 2006. *Handbook of Biosurveillance.* New York, NY: Elsevier.

Weinstein RS, Alibek K. 2003. *Biological and Chemical Terrorism: A Guide for Healthcare Providers and First Responders.* New York, NY: Thieme Medical.

Pandemic Influenza

Agency for Healthcare Research and Quality (AHRQ). 2004. Community-Based Mass Prophylaxis: A Planning Guide for Public Health Preparedness. Rockville, MD: AHRQ. Available at: http://www.ahrq.gov/research/cbmprophyl/cbmpro.htm. Accessed February 28, 2011.

American College of Emergency Physicians. 2009. National Strategic Plan for Emergency Department Management of Outbreaks of Novel H1N1 Influenza. Washington, DC: U.S. Department of Health and Human Services. Available at: http://www.flu.gov/professional/hospital/nspemergencydept.html.html. Accessed February 28, 2011.

Association of Public Health Laboratories (APHL). 2010. Public Health Laboratories: Diminishing Resources in an Era of Evolving Threats. Silver Spring, MD: APHL. Available at: http://www.aphl.org/aphlprograms/phpr/ahr/Documents/DiminishingResourcesEvolvingThreats.pdf. Accessed February 28, 2011.

Association of State and Territorial Health Officers. 2008. At-Risk Populations in Emergencies: A Review of State and Local Stories, Tools and Practices. Falls Church, VA: International Association of Emergency Managers. Available at: http://www.iaem.com/committees/SpecialNeeds/documents/ASTHOBestPractices.pdf. Accessed February 28, 2011.

Centers for Disease Control and Prevention (CDC). 2009. Abbreviated Pandemic Influenza Plan Template for Primary Care Provider Offices: Guidance From Stakeholders. Atlanta, GA: CDC. Available at: http://www.cdc.gov/h1n1flu/guidance/pdf/abb_pandemic_influenza_plan.pdf. Accessed February 28, 2011.

Centers for Disease Control and Prevention (CDC). 2009. Interim biosafety guidance for all individuals handling clinical specimens or isolates containing 2009–H1N1 influenza A virus novel H1N1, including vaccine strains. Atlanta, GA: CDC.

Available at: http://www.cdc.gov/h1n1flu/guidelines_labworkers.htm. Accessed March 2, 2011.

Centers for Disease Control and Prevention (CDC). 2009. Interim Guidance on Specimen Collection, Processing, and Testing for Patients With Suspected Novel Influenza A H1N1 Virus Infection. Atlanta, GA: CDC. Available at: http://www.cdc.gov/h1n1flu/specimencollection.htm. Accessed March 2, 2011.

Centers for Disease Control and Prevention (CDC). 2010. Interim Guidance on Infection Control Measures for 2009 H1N1 Influenza in Healthcare Settings, Including Protection of Healthcare Personnel. Atlanta, GA: CDC. Available at: http://www.cdc.gov/h1n1flu/guidelines_infection_control.htm. Accessed March 1, 2011.

ESRI. 2009. Geographic Information Systems and Pandemic Influenza Planning and Response. Redlands, CA: ESRI. Available at: http://www.esri.com/library/white-papers/pdfs/gis-and-pandemic-planning.pdf. Accessed March 1, 2011.

Knebel A, Phillips S. 2008. Home Health Care During an Influenza Pandemic: Issues and Resources. Rockville, MD: Agency for Healthcare Research and Quality. Available at: http://www.flu.gov/professional/hospital/homehealth.html. Accessed March 2, 2011.

Lister SA, Redhead CS. 2009. *The 2009 Influenza Pandemic: An Overview.* Washington, DC: Congressional Research Service. Available at: http://assets.opencrs.com/rpts/R40554_20091116.pdf. Accessed March 1, 2011.

Missouri Department of Health and Human Services. 2008. Missouri Strategic National Stockpile H1N1 Response After Action Report. Atlanta, GA: Centers for Disease Control and Prevention. Available at: https://www.llis.dhs.gov/docdetails/details.do?contentID=33191. Accessed March 2, 2011.

Occupational Safety and Health Administration. 2009. Pandemic Influenza Preparedness and Response Guidance for Healthcare Workers. Washington, DC: U.S. Department of Labor. Available at: http://www.osha.gov/Publications/OSHA_pandemic_health.pdf. Accessed March 2, 2011.

Public Health Emergency, Office of the Assistant Secretary for Preparedness and Response. 2007. *Public Health Emergency Response: A Guide for Leaders and Responders.* Chapter 7. Legal and policy considerations. Washington, DC: U.S. Department of Health and Human Services. Available at: http://www.phe.gov/emergency/communication/guides/leaders/Documents/freo_section07.pdf. Accessed March 2, 2011.

U.S. Department of Health and Human Services (HHS). 2008. Federal Guidance To Assist States In Improving State-Level Pandemic Influenza Operating Plans. Washington, DC: HHS. Available at: http://www.flu.gov/professional/states/index.html. Accessed March 1, 2011.

U.S. Department of Health and Human Services (HHS). 2007. Community Strategy for Pandemic Influenza Mitigation. Washington, DC: HHS. Available at: http://www.pandemicflu.gov/professional/community/commitigation.html. Accessed February 28, 2011.

U.S. Department of Health and Human Services (HHS). 2011. Pandemic Influenza Planning Checklist. Washington, DC: HHS. Available at: http://www.cdc.gov/flu/pandemic/pdf/pandemicfluchecklist.pdf. Accessed March 2, 2011.

World Health Organization (WHO). 2005. *Avian Influenza: Assessing the Pandemic Threat.* Geneva, Switzerland: WHO. Available at: http://www.who.int/csr/disease/influenza/H5N1-9reduit.pdf. Accessed February 28, 2011.

World Health Organization (WHO). 2008. *Outbreak Communication Planning Guide.* Geneva, Switzerland: WHO. Available at: http://www.searo.who.int/LinkFiles/CDS_WHO_Outbreak_Comm_Planning_Guide.pdf. Accessed March 2, 2011.

World Health Organization (WHO). 2009. Interim planning considerations for mass gatherings in the context of pandemic H1N1 2009 influenza. Geneva, Switzerland: WHO. Available at: http://www.who.int/csr/resources/publications/swineflu/cp002_2009-0511_planning_considerations_for_mass_gatherings.pdf. Accessed March 2, 2011.

World Health Organization (WHO). 2009. *Pandemic Influenza Preparedness and Response: WHO Guidance Document.* Geneva, Switzerland: WHO. Available at: http://www.who.int/csr/disease/influenza/pipguidance2009/en/index.html. Accessed March 2, 2011.

Care Guidelines and Standards

Brandt M, Brown C, Burkhart J, et al. 2006. Mold prevention strategies and possible health effects in the aftermath of hurricanes and major floods. *MMWR Recomm Rep.* 55:1–27.

Center for Health Policy, Columbia University School of Nursing. 2008. Adapting Standards of Care Under Extreme Conditions: Guidance For Professionals During Disasters, Pandemics and Other Extreme Emergencies. Silver Spring, MD: American Nurses Association. Available at: http://www.nursingworld.org/MainMenuCategories/HealthcareandPolicyIssues/DPR/TheLawEthicsofDisasterResponse/AdaptingStandardsofCare.aspx. Accessed March 1, 2011.

Centers for Medicare and Medicaid Services. 2007. Preparing for Emergencies: A Guide for People on Dialysis. Available at: http://www.rsnhope.org/resources/PreparingforEmergenices.pdf. Washington, DC: U.S. Department of Health and Human Services. Accessed March 2, 2011.

Institute of Medicine. 2009. Guidance For Establishing Crisis Standards of Care for Use In Disaster Situations. Washington, DC: Institute of Medicine. Available at: http://www.iom.edu/Reports/2009/DisasterCareStandards.aspx. Accessed March 2, 2011.

Nolte KB, Hanzlick RL, Payne DC, et al. 2004. Medical examiners, coroners, and biologic terrorism: a guidebook for surveillance and case management. *MMWR Recomm Rep.* 53:1–27.

Occupational Safety and Health Administration (OSHA). 2005. OSHA Best Practices for Hospital–Based First Receivers of Victims From Mass Casualty Incidents Involving the Release of Hazardous Substances. Washington, DC: U.S. Department of Labor. Available at: http://www.osha.gov/dts/osta/bestpractices/html/hospital_-firstreceivers.html. Accessed March 2, 2011.

Phillips S, Knebel A. 2007. Mass Medical Care With Scarce Resources: A Community Planning Guide. Rockville, MD: Agency for Healthcare Research and Quality. Publication No. 07–0001. Available at: http://www.ahrq.gov/research/mce/mceguide.pdf. Accessed March 2, 2011.

Sasser SM, Hunt RC, Sullivent EE, et al. 2009. Guidelines for field triage of injured patients recommendations of the national expert panel on field triage. *MMWR Recomm Rep.* 58:1–35.

The Joint Commission. 2005. Surge Hospitals: Providing Safe Care in Emergencies. Available at: http://ec.europa.eu/echo/files/policies/sectoral/health_2005_providing_safe_care_in_emergencies_jchao.pdf. Accessed March 2, 2011.

U.S. Food and Drug Administration (FDA). 2009. Disposal of Contaminated Devices. Washington, DC: FDA. Available at: http://www.fda.gov/MedicalDevices/Safety/EmergencySituations/ucm055974.htm. Accessed March 2, 2011.

U.S. Food and Drug Administration (FDA). 2009. Medical Devices Requiring Refrigeration. Washington, DC: FDA. Available at: http://www.fda.gov/MedicalDevices/Safety/EmergencySituations/ucm056075.htm. Accessed March 2, 2011.

U.S. Food and Drug Administration (FDA). 2009. Medical Devices that Have Been Exposed to Heat and Humidity. Washington, DC: FDA. Available at: http://www.fda.gov/MedicalDevices/Safety/EmergencySituations/ucm056086.htm. Accessed March 2, 2011.

U.S. Food and Drug Administration (FDA). 2009. Natural Disasters - Effects on Mammography Facilities. Washington, DC: FDA. Available at: http://www.fda.gov/Radiation-EmittingProducts/MammographyQualityStandardsActandProgram/FacilityCertificationandInspection/ucm127723.htm. Accessed March 2, 2011.

U.S. Food and Drug Administration (FDA). 2010. Safe Drug Use After a Natural Disaster. Washington, DC: FDA. Available at: http://www.fda.gov/Drugs/EmergencyPreparedness/ucm085200.htm. Accessed March 2, 2011.

Case Studies

Alson R, Alexander D, Leonard RB, Stringer LW. 1993. Analysis of medical treatment at a field hospital following Hurricane Andrew, 1992. *Ann Emerg Med.* 22:1721–1728.

Bel N. 1993. Triumph over tragedy: emergency response to Hurricane Andrew. *Emergency.* 25:28–31, 66.

Bernstein RS, Baxter PJ, Falk H, et al. 1986. Immediate public health concerns and actions in volcanic eruptions: lessons from Mount St. Helens eruptions, May 18–October 18, 1980. *Am J Public Health.* 76:25–37.

Brandt M, Brown C, Burkhart J, et al. 2006. Mold prevention strategies and possible health effects in the aftermath of hurricanes and major floods. *MMWR Recomm Rep.* 55:1–27.

Brewer RD, Morris PD, Cole TB. 1994. Hurricane-related emergency department visits in an inland area: an analysis of the public health impact of Hurricane Hugo in North Carolina. *Ann Emerg Med.* 23:731–736.

Carr SJ, Leahy SM, London S, et al. 1996. The public health response to the Los Angeles, 1994 earthquake. *Am J Public Health.* 86:589–590.

Centers for Disease Control and Prevention. 1991. Tornado disaster—Illinois, 1990. *MMWR Morb Mortal Wkly Rep.* 40:33–36.

Centers for Disease Control and Prevention. 1992. Rapid health needs assessment following Hurricane Andrew—Florida and Louisiana, 1992. *MMWR Morb Mortal Wkly Rep.* 41:685–688.

Centers for Disease Control and Prevention. 1992. Tornado disaster—Kansas 1991. *MMWR Morb Mortal Wkly Rep.* 41:181–183.

Centers for Disease Control and Prevention. 1993. Comprehensive assessment of health needs 2 months after Hurricane Andrew—Dade County, Florida. *MMWR Morb Mortal Wkly Rep.* 42:434–437.

Centers for Disease Control and Prevention. 1993. Injuries and illnesses related to Hurricane Andrew—Louisiana, 1992. *MMWR Morb Mortal Wkly Rep.* 42:242–244, 249–251.

Centers for Disease Control and Prevention. 1993. Morbidity surveillance following the Midwest flood—Missouri, 1993. *MMWR Morb Mortal Wkly Rep.* 42:797-8.

Centers for Disease Control and Prevention. 1993. Public health consequences of a flood disaster—Iowa, 1993. *MMWR Morb Mortal Wkly Rep.* 42:653–656.

Centers for Disease Control and Prevention. 1994. Rapid assessment of vectorborne diseases during the Midwest flood, United States, 1993. *MMWR Morb Mortal Wkly Rep.* 43:481–483.

Centers for Disease Control and Prevention. 1996. Surveillance for injuries and illnesses and rapid health needs assessment following Hurricanes Marilyn and Opal, September–October 1995. *MMWR Morb Mortal Wkly Rep.* 45:81–85.

Centers for Disease Control and Prevention. 1997. Fatal human plague—Arizona and Colorado, 1996. *MMWR Morb Mortal Wkly Rep.* 46:617–620.

Centers for Disease Control and Prevention. 1998. Community needs assessment and morbidity surveillance following an ice storm—Maine, January 1998. *MMWR Morb Mortal Wkly Rep.* 47:351–354.

Centers for Disease Control and Prevention. 2001. Injury and illness among New York City Fire Department rescue workers after responding to the World Trade Center attacks. *MMWR Morb Mortal Wkly Rep Special Issue.* 51:1–5.

Centers for Disease Control and Prevention. 2002. Community needs assessment of Lower Manhattan residents following the World Trade Center attacks—Manhattan, New York City, 2001. *MMWR Morb Mortal Wkly Rep.* 51:10–13.

Centers for Disease Control and Prevention. 2002. Impact of September 11 attacks on workers in the vicinity of the World Trade Center—New York City. *MMWR Morb Mortal Wkly Rep.* 51:8–10.

Centers for Disease Control and Prevention. 2002. Morbidity and mortality associated with Hurricane Floyd—North Carolina, September-October 1999. *MMWR Morb Mortal Wkly Rep.* 49:369–372.

Centers for Disease Control and Prevention. 2002. Needs assessment following Hurricane Georges—Dominican Republic, 1998. *MMWR Morb Mortal Wkly Rep.* 48:93–95.

Centers for Disease Control and Prevention. 2002. Notice to readers: New York City Department of Health response to terrorist attack, September 11, 2001. *MMWR Morb Mortal Wkly Rep.* 50:821.

Centers for Disease Control and Prevention. 2002. Psychological and emotional effects of the September 11 attacks on the World Trade Center—Connecticut, New Jersey, and New York 2001. *MMWR Morb Mortal Wkly Rep.* 51:784–786.

Centers for Disease Control and Prevention. 2002. Rapid assessment of injuries among survivors of the terrorist attack on the World Trade Center—New York City, September 2001. *MMWR Morb Mortal Wkly Rep.* 51:1–5.

Centers for Disease Control and Prevention. 2002. Tropical Storm Allison rapid needs assessment—Houston, Texas, June 2001. *MMWR Morb Mortal Wkly Rep.* 51:365–369.

Centers for Disease Control and Prevention. 2002. Use of respiratory protection among responders at the World Trade Center site—New York City, September 2001. *MMWR Morb Mortal Wkly Rep.* 51:6–8.

Centers for Disease Control and Prevention. 2003. Cholera epidemic after increased civil conflict—Monrovia, Liberia. June-September 2003. *MMWR Morb Mortal Wkly Rep.* 52:1093–1095.

Centers for Disease Control and Prevention. 2004. Brief report: acute illness from dry ice exposure during Hurricane Ivan—Alabama, 2004. *MMWR Morb Mortal Wkly Rep.* 53:1182–1183.

Centers for Disease Control and Prevention. 2004. Preliminary results from the World Trade Center Evacuation Study—New York City, 2003. *MMWR Morb Mortal Wkly Rep.* 53:815–817.

Centers for Disease Control and Prevention. 2004. Rapid assessment of the needs and health status of older adults after Hurricane Charley—Charlotte, DeSoto, and Hardee Counties, Florida, August 27–31, 2004. *MMWR Morb Mortal Wkly Rep.* 53:837–840.

Centers for Disease Control and Prevention. 2004. Rapid community health and needs assessments after Hurricanes Isabel and Charley—North Carolina, 2003–2004. *MMWR Morb Mortal Wkly Rep.* 53:840–842.

Centers for Disease Control and Prevention. 2005. Carbon monoxide poisoning after Hurricane Katrina—Alabama, Louisiana, and Mississippi, August-September 2005. *MMWR Morb Mortal Wkly Rep.* 54:996–998.

Centers for Disease Control and Prevention. 2005. Health concerns associated with disaster victim identification after a tsunami—Thailand, December 26, 2004–March 31, 2005. *MMWR Morb Mortal Wkly Rep.* 54:349–352.

Centers for Disease Control and Prevention. 2005. Hurricane Katrina response and guidance for health-care providers, relief workers, and shelter operators. *MMWR Morb Mortal Wkly Rep.* 54:877.

Centers for Disease Control and Prevention. 2005. Infectious disease and dermatologic conditions in evacuees and rescue workers after Hurricane Katrina—multiple states, August–September 2005. *MMWR Morb Mortal Wkly Rep.* 54:961–964.

Centers for Disease Control and Prevention. 2005. Rapid health response, assessment, and surveillance after a tsunami—Thailand, 2004–2005. *MMWR Morb Mortal Wkly Rep.* 54:61–64.

Centers for Disease Control and Prevention. 2005. *Vibrio* illnesses after Hurricane Katrina—multiple states, August–September 2005. *MMWR Morb Mortal Wkly Rep.* 54:928–931.

Centers for Disease Control and Prevention. 2006. Assessment of health-related needs after Hurricanes Katrina and Rita—Orleans and Jefferson Parishes, New Orleans Area, Louisiana, October 17–22, 2005. *MMWR Morb Mortal Wkly Rep.* 55: 38–41.

Centers for Disease Control and Prevention. 2006. Brief report: Leptospirosis after flooding of a university campus—Hawaii, 2004. *MMWR Morb Mortal Wkly Rep.* 55:125–127.

Centers for Disease Control and Prevention. 2006. Health concerns associated with mold in water-damaged homes after Hurricanes Katrina and Rita—New Orleans Area, Louisiana, October 2005. *MMWR Morb Mortal Wkly Rep.* 55: 41–44.

Centers for Disease Control and Prevention. 2006. Health hazard evaluation of police officers and firefighters after Hurricane Katrina—New Orleans, Louisiana, October 17–28 and November 30–December 5, 2005. *MMWR Morb Mortal Wkly Rep.* 55:456–458.

Centers for Disease Control and Prevention. 2006. Heat-related deaths—United States, 1999–2003. *MMWR Morb Mortal Wkly Rep.* 55:796–798.

Centers for Disease Control and Prevention. 2006. Monitoring poison control center data to detect health hazards during hurricane season—Florida, 2003–2005. *MMWR Morb Mortal Wkly Rep.* 55:426–428.

Centers for Disease Control and Prevention. 2006. Morbidity surveillance after Hurricane Katrina—Arkansas, Louisiana, Mississippi, and Texas, September 2005. *MMWR Morb Mortal Wkly Rep.* 55:727–731.

Centers for Disease Control and Prevention. 2006. Mortality associated with Hurricane Katrina—Florida and Alabama, August–October 2005. *MMWR Morb Mortal Wkly Rep.* 55:239–242.

Centers for Disease Control and Prevention. 2006. Public health response to Hurricanes Katrina and Rita—Louisiana, 2005. *MMWR Morb Mortal Wkly Rep.* 55:29–30.

Centers for Disease Control and Prevention. 2006. Rapid assessment of health needs and resettlement plans among Hurricane Katrina evacuees—San Antonio, Texas, September 2005. *MMWR Morb Mortal Wkly Rep.* 55:242–244.

Centers for Disease Control and Prevention. 2006. Rapid community needs assessment after Hurricane Katrina—Hancock County, Mississippi, September 14–15, 2005. *MMWR Morb Mortal Wkly Rep.* 55:234–236.

Centers for Disease Control and Prevention. 2006. Rapid needs assessment of two rural communities after Hurricane Wilma—Hendry County, Florida, November 1–2, 2005. *MMWR Morb Mortal Wkly Rep.* 55:429–431.

Centers for Disease Control and Prevention. 2006. Surveillance for early detection of disease outbreaks at an outdoor mass gathering—Virginia, 2005. *MMWR Morb Mortal Wkly Rep.* 55:71–74.

Centers for Disease Control and Prevention. 2006. Surveillance for illness and injury after Hurricane Katrina—three counties, Mississippi, September 5–October 11, 2005. *MMWR Morb Mortal Wkly Rep.* 55:231–234.

Centers for Disease Control and Prevention. 2006. Surveillance in hurricane evacuation centers—Louisiana, September–October 2005 55:32–35.

Centers for Disease Control and Prevention. 2006. Tuberculosis control activities after Hurricane Katrina—New Orleans, Louisiana, 2005. *MMWR Morb Mortal Wkly Rep.* 55:332–335.

Centers for Disease Control and Prevention. 2007. Wildfire-related deaths—Texas, March 12–20, 2006. *MMWR Morb Mortal Wkly Rep.* 56:757–760.

Centers for Disease Control and Prevention. 2008. Carbon monoxide exposures after Hurricane Ike—Texas, September 2008. *MMWR Morb Mortal Wkly Rep.* 58:845–849.

Centers for Disease Control and Prevention. 2008. Monitoring health effects of wildfires using the biosense system—San Diego County, California, October 2007. *MMWR Morb Mortal Wkly Rep.* 57:741–747.

Centers for Disease Control and Prevention. 2009. Guidelines for field triage of injured patients recommendations of the national expert panel on field triage. *MMWR Recomm Rep.* 58:1–35.

Centers for Disease Control and Prevention. 2009. Hurricane Ike rapid needs assessment—Houston, Texas, September 2008. *MMWR Morb Mortal Wkly Rep.* 58:1066–1071.

Centers for Disease Control and Prevention. 2009. Underground coal mining disasters and fatalities—United States, 1900–2006. *MMWR Morb Mortal Wkly Rep.* 57:1379–1382.

Centers for Disease Control and Prevention. 2010. Rapid establishment of an internally displaced persons disease surveillance system after an earthquake—Haiti, 2010. *MMWR Morb Mortal Wkly Rep.* 59;939–945.

Chapman LE, Sullivent EE, Grohskopf LA. 2008. Recommendations for postexposure interventions to prevent infection with Hepatitis B virus, Hepatitis C virus, or human immunodeficiency virus, and tetanus in persons wounded during bombings and other mass-casualty events—United States, 2008. *MMWR Recomm Rep.* 57:1–19.

Clinton JJ, Hagebak BR, Sirmons JG, Brennan JA, et al. 1995. Lessons from the Georgia floods. *Public Health Rep.* 110:684–689.

Combs DL, Parrish RG, McNabb SJ, Davis JH. 1996. Deaths related to Hurricane Andrew in Florida and Louisiana, 1992. *Intl J Epidemiol.* 25:537–544.

Durkin ME, Thiel Jr CC, Schneider JE, de Vriend T. 1991. Injuries and emergency medical response in the Loma Prieta earthquake. *Bull Seismological Soc Am.* 81:2143–2166.

Erikson K. 1976. *Everything in Its Path: Destruction of Community in the Buffalo Creek Flood.* New York, NY: Simon & Schuster.

Federal Communications Commission (FCC). 2008. Emergency Communications During the Minneapolis Bridge Disaster: A Technical Case Study. Washington, DC: FCC. Available at: http://www.fcc.gov/pshs/docs/clearinghouse/references/minneapolis-bridge-report.pdf. Accessed March 2, 2011.

Gautam K. 1998. Organizational problems faced by the Missouri DOH in providing disaster relief during the 1993 floods. *J Public Health Manage Pract.* 44:79–86.

Grace MC, Green BL, Lindy JD, Leonard AC. 1993. The Buffalo Creek Disaster: a 14-year follow-up. In: Wilson JP, Raphael B, editors. *The International Handbook of Traumatic Stress Syndromes.* New York, NY: Plenum Press:441–449.

Green BL, Grace MC, Lindy JD, et al. 1990. Buffalo Creek survivors in the second decade: comparison with unexposed and non-litigant groups. *J Appl Soc Psychol.* 20:1033–1050.

Haynes BE, Freeman C, Rubin JL, et al. 1992. Medical response to catastrophic events: California's planning and the Loma Prieta earthquake. *Ann Emerg Med.* 21:368–374.

Hogan DE, Waeckerle JF, Dire DJ, Lillibridge SR. 1999. Emergency department impact of the Oklahoma City terrorist bombing. *Ann Emerg Med.* 34:160–167.

Johnson WP, Lanza CV. 1993. After Hurricane Andrew: an EMS perspective. *Prehosp Disaster Med.* 82:169–171.

Kerns DE, Anderson PB. 1990. EMS response to a major aircraft incident: Sioux City, Iowa. *Prehosp Disaster Med.* 52:159–166.

Landesman LY. 2001. A department of health learns about its role in emergency public health. In: Rowitz L, editor. *Public Health Leadership: Putting Principles Into Practice.* Gaithersburg, MD: Aspen Publishers: 150–153.

McNabb SJ, Kelso KY, Wilson SA, et al. 1995. Hurricane Andrew–related injuries and illnesses, Louisiana, 1992. *South Med J.* 88:615–618.

Noji EK, Kelen GD, Armenian HK, et al. 1990. The 1988 earthquake in Armenia: a case study. *Ann Emerg Med.* 19:891–897.

Nolte KB, Hanzlick RL, Payne DC, et al. 2004. Medical examiners, coroners, and biologic terrorism: a guidebook for surveillance and case management. *MMWR Recomm Rep.* 53:1–27.

Siders C, Jacobson R. 1998. Flood disaster preparedness: a retrospective from Grand Forks, South Dakota. *J Healthcare Risk Manage.* 18:33–40.

Whitman S, Good G, Donoghue ER, et al. 1997. Mortality in Chicago attributed to the July 1995 heat wave. *Am J Public Health.* 879:1515–1518.

Chemical Accidents

World Health Organization (WHO). 2009. *Manual for the Public Health Management of Chemical Accidents.* Geneva, Switzerland: WHO. Available at: http://www.who.int/environmental_health_emergencies/publications/FINAL-PHM-Chemical-Incidents_web.pdf. Accessed March 1, 2011.

Children

Centers for Bioterrorism Preparedness Planning Pediatric Task Force; New York City Department of Health and Mental Health Pediatric Disaster Advisory Group. 2006. Hospital Guidelines for Pediatrics in Disasters. 2nd ed. Available at: http://www.nyc.gov/html/doh/downloads/word/bhpp/bhpp-focus-ped-toolkit.doc. Accessed March 1, 2011.

Markenson D, Redlener I. 2003. Pediatric Preparedness for Disasters and Terrorism: A National Consensus Conference. Executive Summary. New York, NY: National Center for Disaster Preparedness. Available at: http://www.bt.cdc.gov/children/pdf/working/execsumm03.pdf. Accessed March 1, 2011.

McKennna C. 2010. More states complete disaster planning for children. *Emerg Manage.* August 20. Available at: http://www.emergencymgmt.com/disaster/Disaster-Planning-Children.html. Accessed March 1, 2011.

Norris FH, Friedman MJ, Watson PJ, et al. 2002. 60,000 disaster victims speak: part I: an empirical review of the empirical literature, 1981–2001. *Psychiatry.* 653:207–239.

Weiner DL. 2009. Lessons learned from disasters affecting children. *Ped Emerg Med.* 103:149–152.

Communication

Alcatel-Lucent. 2010. A How-To Guide for LTE in Public Safety. Government Technology. Available at: http://www.cmu.edu/silicon-valley/dmi/files/howto_guide.pdf. Accessed March 1, 2011.

American Medical Association. 1999. Health literacy: report of the Council of Scientific Affairs. *JAMA*. 281:552–557.

Baron G. 2009. Five ways social media is changing emergency management. *Emerg Manage*. October 19. Available at: http://www.emergencymgmt.com/emergency-blogs/crisis-comm/Five-Ways-Social-Media.html. Accessed March 2, 2011.

Bennett P. 1999. Understanding responses to risk: some basic findings. In: Bennett P, Calman K, editors. *Risk Communication and Public Health*. Oxford, England: Oxford University Press:319.

Centers for Disease Control and Prevention (CDC). 2008. Social Media and Your Emergency Communication Efforts. Atlanta, GA, CDC. Available at: http://www.bt.cdc.gov/ercn/01/RiskCommunicatorIssue1article04.asp. Accessed March 2, 2011.

Chess C, Hance BJ, Sandman PM. 1988. *Improving Dialogue With Communities: A Short Guide to Government Risk Communication*. Newark: New Jersey Department of Environmental Protection.

Churchill RE. 1997. Effective media relations. In: Noji EK, editor. *The Public Health Consequences of Disasters*. New York, NY: Oxford University.

Collins H. 2009. Emergency managers and first responders use Twitter and Facebook to update communities. *Emerg Manage*. July 27. Available at: http://www.emergencymgmt.com/safety/Emergency-Managers-and-First.html. Accessed March 2, 2011.

Covello V. 1992. Risk communication, trust, and credibility. *Health Environ Digest*. 61:1–4.

Covello V. 2003. Best practices in public health risk and crisis communication. *J Health Commun*. 8:5–8.

Currie D. 2009. Expert Round Table on Social Media and Risk Communication During Times of Crisis: Strategic Challenges and Opportunities. Washington, DC: American Public Health Association, Booz/Allen/Hamilton, George Washington School of Public Health and Health Services, International Association of Emergency Managers and NAGC.

Federal Communications Commission (FCC). 2010. Amendment of Part 97 of the Commission's Rules Regarding Amateur Radio Service Communications During Government Disaster Drills. Washington, DC: FCC. Available at: http://www.fcc.gov/pshs/eas. Acessed March 2, 2011.

Federal Emergency Management Agency (FEMA). 2009. FEMA and the FCC announce adoption of standards for wireless carriers to receive and deliver emergency alerts via mobile devices [press release]. Washington, DC: FEMA. Available at: http://www.fema.gov/news/newsrelease.fema?id=50056. Accessed March 2, 2011.

Federal Emergency Management Agency (FEMA). 2011. Integrated Public Alert and Warning Systems. Washington, DC: FEMA. Available at: http://www.fema.gov/emergency/ipaws. Accessed March 2, 2011.

Ferguson EW, Sarkisian A, Young F, de Ville de Goyet C. 1995. Telemedicine for national and international disaster response. *J Med Sys*. 19:121–123.

Fischhoff B, Lichtenstein S, Slovic P, Keeney D. 1981. *Acceptable Risk*. Cambridge, Massachusetts: Cambridge University Press.

Koplan J. 2003. Communication during public health emergencies. *J Health Comm*. 8:144–145.

Martchenke J, Rusteen J, Pointer JE. 1995. Prehospital communications during the Loma Prieta earthquake. *Prehosp Disaster Med.* 10:225–231.

McKenna C. 2009. Technology's role in disaster mitigation. *Emerg Manage.* May 22. Available at: http://www.emergencymgmt.com/disaster/Technologys-Role-in-Disaster.html. Accessed March 2, 2011.

Mebane F, Temin S, Parvanta C. 2001. Communicating anthrax in 2001: a comparison of CDC information and print media accounts. *J Health Commun.* 8:50–82.

Moore L. 2010. *The Emergency Alert System EAS and All–Hazard Warnings.* Washington, DC: Congressional Research Service. Available at: http://www.fas.org/sgp/crs/homesec/RL32527.pdf. Accessed March 2, 2011.

Morrisey G, Sechrest T. 1987. *Effective Business and Technical Presentation,* 3rd ed. New York, NY: Addison-Wesley Publishing.

Mullin S. 2002. Communicating risk: closing the gap between perception and reality. *J Urban Health.* 793:296–297.

National Oceanic and Atmospheric Administration (NOAA). 2010. Weather Radio All Hazards home page. Silver Spring, MD: NOAA. Available at: http://www.weather.gov/nwr. Accessed March 2, 2011.

Nichols R. 2010. California to deploy nation's first mass mobile alert system. Government Technology. August 24. Available at: http://www.govtech.com/gt/articles/768874. Accessed March 2, 2011.

Parrott R. 1995. *Designing Health Messages: Approaches From Communication Theory and Public Health Practice.* Thousand Oaks, CA: Sage Publications.

Payne J, Schulte S. 2003. Mass media, public health, and achieving health literacy. *J Health Commun.* 8:124–125.

Pidgeon N, Henwood K, Maguire B. 1999. Public health communication and the social amplification of risks: present knowledge and future prospects. In: Bennett P, Calman K, editors. *Risk Communication and Public Health.* Oxford, England: Oxford University Press.

Pittman E. 2010. Disasters 2.0 conference addresses social media use. *Emerg Manage.* January 28. Available at: http://www.emergencymgmt.com/disaster/Disasters-20-Conference-Social-Media-Use.html. Accessed March 2, 2011.

Pollard W. 2003. Public perceptions of information sources concerning bioterrorism before and after anthrax attacks: an analysis of national survey data. *J Health Commun.* 8:93–103.

Prue C, Lackey C, Swenarski L, Gantt J. 2003. Communication monitoring: shaping CDC's emergency risk communication efforts. *J Health Commun.* 8:35–49.

Public Health Emergency, Office of the Assistant Secretary for Preparedness and Response. 2007. *Public Health Emergency Response: A Guide for Leaders and Responders.* Washington, DC: U.S. Department of Health and Human Services. Available at: http://www.phe.gov/emergency/communication/guides/leaders/Documents/freo-full-print.pdf. Accessed March 2, 2011.

Renn O. 1991. Risk communication the amplification of risk. In: Kasperson R, Stallen P, editors. *Communicating Risks to the Public.* Dordrecht, the Netherlands: Kluwer.

Sutton J. 2009. The public uses social networking during disasters to verify facts, coordinate information analysis, social; media package part 1 of 2. *Emerg Manage.* July 30. Available at: http://www.emergencymgmt.com/safety/The-Public-Uses-Social-Networking.html. Accessed March 2, 2011.

U.S. Department of Homeland Security (DHS). 2005. The System of Systems Approach for Interoperable Communications. Washington, DC: DHS. Available at: http://www.safecomprogram.gov/NR/rdonlyres/FD22B528-18B7-4CB1-AF49-F9626C608290/0/SOSApproachforInteroperableCommunications_02.pdf. Accessed March 2, 2011.

Vander M. 2010. HOW TO: Prepare for Disasters Using Social Media. Mashable. March 9. Available at: http://mashable.com/2010/03/09/prepare-disaster-social-media. Accessed March 2, 2011.

White C, Plotnick L, Kushma J, et al. 2010. An Online Social Network for Emergency Management. Proceedings of the 6th International ISCRAM Conference, Gothenberg, Sweden, May 2009.

Wimberly R. 2010. Getting the word out through notifications, alerts, and warnings. *Emerg Manage.* April 6. Available at: http://www.emergencymgmt.com/safety/Notifications-Alerts-Warnings.html. Accessed March 2, 2011.

Wray RJ, Kreuter MW, Jacobsen J, et al. 2004. Theoretical perspectives on public communication preparedness for terrorist attacks. *Fam Commun Health.* 273:232–241.

Yasin R. 2010. 5 ways social media improves emergency management. *Government Computer News.* 18–23.

Cultural Considerations

Athey J, Moody-Williams J. 2003. Developing Cultural Competence in Disaster Mental Health Programs. Washington, DC: U.S. Department of Health and Human Services, Substance Abuse and Mental Health Service Administration. Available at: http://www.hhs.gov/od/documents/CulturalCompetence_FINALwithcovers.pdf. Accessed March 2, 2011.

Betancourt JR, Green AR, Carrillo JE, Ananeh-Firempong O. 2003. Defining cultural competence: a practical framework for addressing racial/ethnic disparities in health and healthcare. *Public Health Rep.* 1184:293–302.

Montgomery County Advanced Practice Center. 2008. Emergency Preparedness Training Curriculum for Latino Health Promoters. Rockville, MD: Department of Health and Human Services. Available at: http://www.montgomerycountymd.gov/content/hhs/phs/apc/LatinoHealthInitiative/emerg_curriculum_english_0710.pdf. Accessed March 1, 2011.

National Mental Health Information Center. 2008. Tips for Teachers: The Role of Culture in Helping Children Recover From a Disaster. OneStorm. Available at: http://www.onestorm.org/prepare/children/AfterTheStorm/ChildRoleOfCulture.aspx. Accessed March 2, 2011.

Nunez A, Robertson C. 2006. Cultural competence. In: Satcher D, Primes RJ, editors. *Multicultural Medicine and Health Disparities.* New York, NY: McGraw Hill.

Shiu-Thornton ST, Balabis J, Tamayo A, Oberle M. 2007. Disaster preparedness for Limited English Proficient (LEP) communities: medical interpreters as cultural brokers and gatekeepers. *Public Health Rep.* 1224:466–471.

Curriculum

Gebbie KM. 1999. The public health workforce: key to public health infrastructure. *Am J Public Health.* 895:660–661.

Landesman LY. 1993. The availability of disaster preparation courses at US schools of public health. *Am J Public Health*. 8310:1494–1495.

Landesman LY, editor. 2001. *Disaster Preparedness in Schools of Public Health: A Curriculum for the New Century*. Washington, DC: Association of Schools of Public Health.

Qureshi KA, Gershon RRM, Merrill JA, et al. 2004. Effectiveness of an emergency preparedness training program for public health nurses in New York City. *Fam Commun Health*. 273:242–249.

Cyclone

Friedman E. 1994. Coping with calamity: how well does health care disaster planning work? *JAMA*. 27223:1875–1879.

Malilay J. 1997. Tropical cyclones. In: Noji EK, editor. *The Public Health Consequences of Disasters*. New York, NY: Oxford University Press:287–301.

General Disasters

Dynes RR, Tierney KJ, editors. 1994. *Disasters, Collective Behavior, and Social Organization*. Newark: University of Delaware Press.

Earthquake

Alexander D. 1996. The health effects of earthquakes in the mid-1990s. *Disasters*. 203:231–247.

Bissell RA, Pinet P, Nelson M, Levy M. 2004. Evidence of the effectiveness of health sector preparedness in disaster response: the example of four earthquakes. *Fam Commun Health*. 273:193–203.

Frankel DH. 1994. Public health assessment after earthquake. *Lancet*. 343:347–348.

Freeman C. 1990. Casualty estimation and state medical/health response to disasters. In: California Emergency Medical Services Authority, editor. *Workshop on Modeling Earthquake Casualties for Planning and Response Model Definition and User Output Requirements*. Sacramento: California Emergency Medical Services Authority:18–36.

Guha-Sapir D. 1991. Rapid assessment of health needs in mass emergencies: review of current concepts and methods. *World Health Stat Q*. 443:171–181.

Guha-Sapir D. 1993. Health effects of earthquakes and volcanoes: epidemiological and policy issues. *Disasters*. 173:255–262.

Noji EK. 1997. Earthquakes. In: Noji EK, editor. *The Public Health Consequences of Disasters*. New York, NY: Oxford University:135–178.

Environmental Control

Boyce JM, Pittet D, editor. 2002. Guideline for Hand Hygiene in Health Care Settings: Recommendations of the Healthcare Infection Control Practice Advisory Committee of the HICPA/SHEA/APIC/ Hand Hygiene Task Force. Atlanta, GA: Centers for Disease Control and Prevention.

California Conference of Directors of Environmental Health. 2010. *Disaster Field Manual for Environmental Health Specialists.* Cameron Park, CA: California Association of Environmental Health Administrators. Available at: http://www.ccdeh.com/products/24-disasterman/18-disasterman. Accessed March 2, 2011.

Claudio L, Garg A, Landrigan PJ. 2003. Addressing environmental health concerns. In: *Terrorism and Public Health.* Levy BS, Sidel VW, editors. New York, NY: Oxford University Press.

Diaz JH. 2004. The public health impact of global climate change. *Fam Commun Health.* 27:218–229.

Disaster Preparedness Technical Advisory Committee, Community Health Technical Advisory Committee. 2006. *Environmental Health Disaster Preparedness Model Planning Guide.* California Conference of Directors of Environmental Health. Available at: http://www.ccdeh.com/documents/doc_view/67-ccdeh-environmental-health-disaster-preparedness-model-planning-guide-2006. Accessed March 2, 2011.

Esrey SA, Potash JB, Roberts L, Shiff C. 1991. Effects of improved water supply and sanitation on ascariasis, diarrhoea, dracunculiasis, hookworm infection, schistoso-miasis, and trachoma. *Bull WHO.* 69:609–621.

Golob BR. 2007. Environmental Health Emergency Response Guide. Hopkins, MN: Twin Cities Metro Advanced Practice Center. Available at: http://www.cdc.gov/nceh/ehs/Docs/EH_Emergency_Response_Guide.pdf. Accessed March 2, 2011.

Hatch D, Waldman RJ, Lungu GW, Piri C. 1994. Epidemic cholera during refugee resettlement in Malawi. *Int J Epidemiol.* 23:1292–1329.

National Fire Protection Association (NFPA). 2009. NFPA 1600 Standard on Disaster/Emergency Management and Business Continuity Programs, 2010 Edition. Quincy, MA: NFPA. Available at: http://www.nfpa.org/assets/files/PDF/NFPA16002010.pdf. Accessed March 2, 2011.

National Institute for Occupational Safety and Health. 2003. Filtration and Air-Cleaning Systems to Protect Building Environments From Airborne Chemical, Biological, or Radiological Attacks. Washington, DC: Department of Health and Human Services.

National Institute for Occupational Safety and Health. 2003. Guidance for Protecting Building Environments From Airborne Chemical, Biological, or Radiological Attacks. Atlanta, GA: Centers for Disease Control and Prevention. Available at: http://www.cdc.gov/niosh/docs/2003-136/default.html. Accessed March 2, 2011.

Occupational Safety and Health Administration. 2002. Emergency action plans. Washington, DC: U.S. Department of Labor. Available at: http://www.osha.gov/pls/oshaweb/owadisp.show_document?p_id=9726&p_table=STANDARDS. Accessed March 2, 2011.

Occupational Safety and Health Administration. 2006. Hazardous Waste Operations and Emergency Response Standard. Washington, DC: U.S. Department of Labor. Available at: http://www.osha.gov/pls/oshaweb/owadisp.show_document?p_table=standards&p_id=9765. Accessed March 2, 2011.

Peterson AE, Roberts L, Toole M, Peterson DE. 1998. Soap use effect on diarrhea: Nyamithuthu refugee camp. *Int J Epidemiol.* 27: 520–524.

Spears MC, Gregoire M, Spears M. 2007. *Foodservice Organizations: A Managerial and Systems Approach.* 6th ed. New York, NY: Pearson Education.

U.S. Environmental Protection Agency (EPA). 2009. Drinking Water Standards and Health Advisories. Washington, DC: EPA. Available at: http://water.epa.gov/action/advisories/drinking/drinking_index.cfm. Accessed March 2, 2011.

Westphal RG. 2004. Commentary on the public health impact of global climate change. *Fam Comm Health.* 27:230–231.

Wisner B, Adams J, editors. 2002. Control Measures for Ensuring Food Safety From Environmental Health in Emergencies and Disasters. Geneva, Switzerland: World Health Organization.

Epidemic

Manderson L, Aaby P. 1992. An epidemic in the field? Rapid assessment procedures and health research. *Soc Sci Med.* 357:839–850.

Mohamed J. 1999. Epidemics and public health in early colonial Somaliland. *Soc Sci Med.* 48:507–521.

Perrin P. 1996. *War and Public Health: Handbook on War and Public Health.* Geneva, Switzerland: International Committee of the Red Cross.

Toole MJ. 1994. The rapid assessment of health problems in refugee and displaced populations. *Med Global Survey.* 14:200–207.

Toole MJ. 1997. Communicable diseases and disease control. In: Noji EK, editor. *The Public Health Consequences of Disasters.* New York, NY: Oxford University Press: 79–100.

Toole MJ, Waldman R. 1993. Refugees and displaced persons: war, hunger, and public health. *JAMA.* 2705:600–605.

World Health Organization (WHO). 1999. *Rapid Health Assessment Protocols for Emergencies.* Geneva, Switzerland: WHO.

Ethics

Bayer R, Gostin LO, Jennings B, Steinbock B, editors. 2007. *Public Health Ethics: Theory, Policy and Practice.* New York, NY: Oxford University Press.

Centers for Disease Control and Prevention (CDC). Public Health Law 101: A CDC Foundational Course for Public Health Practitioners. Atlanta, GA: CDC. Available at: http://www2a.cdc.gov/phlp/phl101. Accessed March 2, 2011.

Gostin L. 2006. Public health strategies for pandemic influenza: ethics and the law. *JAMA.* 14:1700–1704.

Jennings B. 2008. *Disaster Planning and Public Health.* Garrison, New York: The Hastings Center.

Martin DK. 2007. Making hard choices: the key to health system sustainability. *Practical Bioethics.* 2,3:1,5–8. Available at: http://www.practicalbioethics.org/FileUploads/PB_Rationing.053107.pdf. Accessed March 2, 2011.

Pandemic Influenza Working Group. 2005. Stand on Guard for Thee: Ethical Considerations in Preparedness Planning for Pandemic Influenza. Toronto, Ontario: University of Toronto Joint Centre for Bioethics. Available at: http://www.jointcentreforbioethics.ca/people/documents/upshur_stand_guard.pdf. Accessed April 12, 2011.

Program in Public Health Ethics, Gillings School of Global Public Health. 2010. Public Health Ethics in Disaster Home Page. Chapel Hill, NC: University of North Carolina at Chapel Hill. Available at: http://www.sph.unc.edu/ethics/public_health_ethics_in_ disasters. Accessed March 2, 2011.

Roberts M, Renzo E. Ethical considerations in community disaster planning. In: Agency for Healthcare Research and Quality (AHRQ). *Mass Medical Care With Scarce Resources.* Rockville, MD: AHRQ. Available at: http://www.ahrq.gov/research/mce/ mce2.htm. Accessed March 2, 2011.

Stokowski LA. 2009. Ethical Dilemmas for Healthcare Professionals: Can We Avoid Influenza? Medscape. Available at: http://www.medscape.com/viewarticle/702371. Accessed March 2, 2011.

The Sphere Project. 2011. Humanitarian Charter and Minimum Standards in Disaster Response. Available at: http://www.sphereproject.org. Accessed March 2, 2011.

Thompson AK, Faith K, Gibson JL, Upshu RE. 2006. Pandemic influenza preparedness: an ethical framework to guide decision-making. *BMC Med Ethics.* 7:12.

Wisconsin State Expert Panel on the Ethics of Disaster Preparedness. 2009. Executive Summary: Allocation of Scarce Resources Project. Available at: http://www.wha.org/ disasterPreparedness/scarceResources/ExecSummaryTheAllocationofScarceResources Project.pdf. Accessed March 2, 2011.

Evaluation Methods Applied to Emergencies and Disasters

Bissell R, Pretto E, Angus D, et al. 1994. Post-preparedness medical disaster response in Costa Rica. *Prehosp Disaster Med.* 9:96–106.

Cayton C, Herrmann N, Cole L, et al. 1978. Assessing the validity of EMS data. *J Am Coll Emerg Physicians.* 7:11.

Cayton C, Murphy J. 1986. Evaluation. In: Schwartz G, Safar P, Stone I, et al, editors. *Principles and Practices of Emergency Medicine,* 2nd ed. Philadelphia, PA: WB Saunders:634.

De Boer J. 1997. Tools for evaluating disasters: preliminary results of some hundreds of disasters. *Eur J Emerg Med.* 4:107–110.

Donabedian A. 1980. *The Definition of Quality and Approaches to Its Assessment.* Ann Arbor, MI: Health Administration Press.

Eisenberg M, Bergner J. 1979. Paramedic programs and cardiac mortality: description of a controlled experiment. *Public Health Rep.* 941:80–84.

Gibson G. 1974. Guidelines for research and evaluation of emergency medical services. *Health Serv Rep.* 89:99–111.

Klain M, Ricci E, Safar P, et al. 1989. Disaster reanimatology potentials: a structured interview study in Armenia, I: methodology and preliminary results. *Prehosp Disaster Med.* 42:135–154.

Manni C, Magalini S. 1989. Disaster medicine: a new discipline or a new approach? *Prehosp Disaster Med.* 42:167–70.

McAuliffe W. 1979. Measuring the quality of medical care: process versus outcome. *Mill Mem Fund Q.* 57:119.

Noji EK. 1987. Evaluation of the efficacy of disaster response. *United Natl Disaster Relief Organ News.* July/August:11–13.

Quarantelli EL, Taylor V. 1977. *Delivery of Emergency Medical Services Disasters.* Columbus, OH: Disaster Research Center, Ohio State University:18.

Ricci E. 1985. A model for evaluation of disaster management. *Prehosp Disaster Med.* Suppl 1.

Roy A, Looney G, Anderson G. 1979. Prospective vs. retrospective data for evaluating emergency care: a research methodology. *JACEP.* 8:141.

Succo W, Champion H, Stega M. 1984. *Trauma Care Evaluation.* Baltimore, MD: University Park Press.

Flood

Ali HM, Homeida MMA. 1991. Flood disaster impact on health and nutritional status of the population—Khartoum, Sudan. In: Abu Sin ME. *Disaster Prevention and Management in Sudan.* Khartoum, Sudan: University of Khartoum:82–104.

Malilay J. 1997. Floods. In: Noji EK, editor. *The Public Health Consequences of Disasters.* New York, NY: Oxford University Press:287–301.

Geographic Information Systems

Amdahl G. 2001. *Disaster Response: GIS for Public Safety.* ESRI Press: Redlands, CA.

Cromley EK, McLafferty SL. 2002. *GIS and Public Health.* New York, NY: The Guilford Press.

Enders A, Brandt Z. 2007. Using Geographic Information System technology to improve emergency management and disaster response for people with disabilities. *J Disability Policy Stud.* 17:223–229.

ESRI. 2008. Geographic Information Systems Providing the Platform for Comprehensive Emergency Management. Redlands, CA: ESRI. Available at: http://www.esri.com/library/whitepapers/pdfs/gis-platform-emergency-management.pdf. Accessed March 1, 2011.

Greene RW. 2002. *Confronting Catastrophe: A GIS Handbook.* Redlands, CA: ESRI Press.

Kennedy H, editor. 2001. *Dictionary of GIS Terminology.* Redlands, CA: ESRI Press.

Lang L. 2000. *GIS for Health Organizations.* Redlands, CA: ESRI Press.

McLeod J. 2010. A Risk Too Great: Using Unmanaged GIS Data For Emergency Notification. Nashville, TN: Infocode. Available at: http://www.infocode.com/whitepaper.php. Accessed March 1, 2011.

Skinner R. 2011. Integrating location into hospital and healthcare facility emergency management. *J Healthcare Protection Manage.* 27(1):31–35. Available at: http://www.iahss.org/JOURNALS/iahss_v27i1.pdf.

Handling Dead Bodies

Centers for Disease Control and Prevention. 2005. Guidelines for preventing the transmission of Mycobacterium tuberculosis in health care facilities. *MMWR Morb Mortal Wkly Rep.* 54:RR-17. Available at: http://www.cdc.gov/mmwr/pdf/rr/rr5417.pdf. Accessed March 1, 2011.

Demiryurek D, Bayramoglu A, Ustacelebi S. 2002. Infective agents in fixed human cadavers: a brief review and suggested guidelines. *Anat Rec.* 196.

Gershon RR, Vlahov D, Escamilla JA, et al. 1998. Tuberculosis risk in funeral home employees. *J Occup Environ Med.* 40:497–503.

Healing TD, Hoffman PN, Young SEE. 1995. The infectious hazards of human cadavers. *Commun Dis Rep CDR Rev.* 5:61–68.

Pan American Health Organization (PAHO). 2004. Management of Dead Bodies in Disaster Situations. Washington, DC: PAHO. Available at: http://www.paho.org/English/dd/ped/ManejoCadaveres.htm. Accessed March 1, 2011.

Hospital Preparedness

Delaney KA. 2002. Impact of the threat of biological and chemical terrorism on public safety-net hospitals. *Int Lawyer.* 361:21–28.

Joint Commission on Accreditation of Healthcare Organizations. 2003. Health Care at the Crossroads: Strategies for Creating and Sustaining Community-Wide Emergency Preparedness Systems. Oakbrook Terrace, IL: The Joint Commission. Available at: http://www.jointcommission.org/assets/1/18/emergency_preparedness.pdf. Accessed March 2, 2011.

Landesman LY, editor. 1997. *Emergency Preparedness in the Healthcare Environment.* Oakbrook, IL: Joint Commission of Healthcare Organizations.

Landesman LY, Leonard R. 1993. SARA three years later: physician knowledge and actions in hospital preparedness. *Int J Prehosp Disaster Med.* Jan-Mar:39–44.

Landesman LY, Markowitz SB, Rosenberg SN. 1994. Hospital preparedness for chemical accidents: the effect of environmental legislation on health care services. *Prehosp Disaster Med.* 93:154–159.

Landesman LY. 1994. *Hospital Preparedness for Chemical Accidents: Plant, Technology and Safety Management Series.* Oakbrook, IL: Joint Commission on Accreditation of Healthcare Organizations.

Lewis CP, Aghababiam R. 1996. Disaster planning, part 1: overview of hospital and emergency department planning for internal and external disasters. *Emerg Med Clin North Am.* 14:439–452.

Peters MS. 1996. Hospitals respond to water loss during the Midwest floods of 1993: preparedness and improvisation. *J Emerg Med.* 143:34–50.

Salinas C, Salinas C, Kurata J. 1998. The effects of the Northridge earthquake on the pattern of emergency department care. *Am J Emerg Med.* 163:254–6.

Simon HK, Stegelman M, Button T. 1998. A prospective evaluation of pediatric emergency care during the 1996 Summer Olympic Games in Atlanta, Georgia. *Ped Emerg Care,* 141:1–3.

Information Systems

Butler DL, Anderson PS. 1992. The use of wide area computer networks in disaster management and the implications for hospital/medical networks. *Ann N Y Acad Sci.* 670:20210.

Federal Communications Commission (FCC). [n.d.] Disaster Information Reporting System (DIRS). Washington, DC: FCC. Available at: http://www.fcc.gov/pshs/services/cip/dirs/dirs.html. Accessed March 1, 2011.

O'Carroll PW, Friede A, Noji EK, et al. 1995. The rapid implementation of a statewide emergency health information system during the 1993 Iowa flood. *Am J Public Health*. 854:564–567.

van Bemmel JH, Musen MA, editors. 1997. *Handbook of Medical Informatics*. Houten, the Netherlands: Bohn Stafleu Van Loghum.

Legal

ABA Center on Children and the Law. 2008. *Children, Law, and Disasters: What We Learned From Katrina and the Hurricanes of 2005*. Houston, TX: University of Houston's Center for Children, Law and Policy.

Farber D, Chen J. 2006. *Disasters and the Law: Katrina and Beyond*. New York, NY: Aspen Publishers.

Federal Emergency Management Agency (FEMA). 2007. *Public Assistance Guide*. 2007. Washington, DC: FEMA. Available at: http://www.fema.gov/government/grant/pa/pag07_t.shtm. Accessed March 2, 2011.

Federal Emergency Management Agency (FEMA). 2007. *Public Assistance Policy Reference Manual*. Washington, DC: FEMA. Available at: http://www.fema.gov/pdf/government/grant/pa/policy.pdf. Accessed March 2, 2011.

Federal Emergency Management Agency (FEMA). 2010. *Public Assistance Applicant Handbook*. Washington, DC: FEMA. Available at: http://www.fema.gov/pdf/government/grant/pa/fema323_app_handbk.pdf. Accessed March 2, 2011.

Gostin LO. 2000. *Public Health Law: Power, Duty, Restraint*. Berkeley: University of California Press.

Gostin LO. 2002. Public health law in an age of terrorism: rethinking individual rights and common goods. *Health Aff*. Nov/Dec:216.

Martin W. 2004. Legal and public policy responses of states to bioterrorism. *Am J Public Health*. 947:1093–1095.

McCormick E, editor. 2009. Frequently Asked Questions About Federal Public Health Emergency Law. Atlanta, GA: Centers for Disease Control and Prevention. Available at: http://www2.cdc.gov/phlp/docs/FAQs%20Fed%20PHE%20laws%20101409.pdf. Accessed March 2, 2011.

Misrahi JJ, Foster JA, Shaw FE, Cetron MS. 2004. HHS/CDC legal response to SARS outbreak. *Emerg Infect Dis*. 10:353–355. Available at: http://www.cdc.gov/ncidod/eid/vol10no2/pdfs/03-0721.pdf. Accessed March 2, 2011.

Management

de Ville de Goyet C. 1993. Post disaster relief: the supply-management challenge. *Disasters*. 172:169–176.

Heath SE, Dorn R, Linnabary RD, et al. 1997. Integration of veterinarians into the official response to disasters. *J Am Vet Med Assoc*. 210:349–352.

Henderson AK, Lillibridge SR, Salinas C, et al. 1994. Disaster medical assistance teams: providing health care to a community struck by Hurricane Iniki. *Ann Emerg Med.* 23:726–730.

Landesman LY, Morrow CB. 2008. Roles and responsibilities of public health in disaster preparedness and response. In: Novick LF, Morrow CB, Mays GP, editors. *Public Health Administration: Principles for Population-Based Management*, 2nd ed. Sudbury, MA: Jones and Bartlett Publishers:657–714.

Leaning J, Briggs SM, Chen LC, editors. 1999. *Humanitarian Crises: The Medical and Public Health Response.* Cambridge, MA: Harvard University Press.

Leviton LC, Needleman CE, Shapiro MA. 1998. *Confronting Public Health Risks: A Decision Maker's Guide.* Thousand Oaks, CA: Sage Publications.

Logue JN. 1996. Disasters, the environment, and public health: improving our response. *Am J Public Health.* 869:1207–1210.

Noji EK. 1995. Natural disaster management. In: Auerbach PS, editor. *Management of Wilderness and Environmental Emergencies.* St. Louis, MO: Mosby-Yearbook:644–663.

Pan American Health Organization (PAHO). 2000. *Natural Disasters: Protecting the Public's Health.* Washington, DC: PAHO.

Phreaner D, Jacoby I, Dreier S, McCoy N. 1994. Disaster preparedness of home health care agencies in San Diego County. *J Emerg Med.* 12:811–818.

Sadler A, Sadler B, Webb J. 1997. *Emergency Medical Care: The Neglected Public Service.* Cambridge, MA: Ballinger Publishing Co.

Schultz CH, Koenig KL, Noji EK. 1996. A medical disaster response to reduce immediate mortality after an earthquake. *N Engl J Med.* 334:438–444.

Mental Health

American Psychiatric Association. 2000. *Diagnostic and Statistical Manual of Mental Disorders.* 4th ed. Washington, DC: American Psychiatric Association.

Armenian HK. 2002. Risk factors for depression in the survivors of the 1988 earthquake in Armenia. *J Urban Health.* 793:373–382.

Austin LS, editor. 1992. *Responding to Disaster: A Guide for Mental Health Professionals.* Washington, DC: American Psychiatric Press.

Baum A, Fleming R, Davidson LM. 1983. Natural disaster and technological catastrophe. *Environ Behav.* 153:333–354.

Black D, Newman M, Harris-Hendriks J, Mezey G, editors. 1997. *Psychological Trauma: A Developmental Approach.* London, England: Royal College of Psychiatrists.

Bracht N, editor. 1990. *Health Promotion at the Community Level.* Newbury Park, CA: Sage.

Breslau N, Davis GC, Andreski P, et al. 1991. Traumatic events and posttraumatic stress disorder in an urban population of young adults. *Arch Gen Psychiatry.* 48:216–222.

Carll EK, editor. 1996. *Developing a Comprehensive Disaster and Crisis Response Program for Mental Health: Guidelines and Procedures.* Albany, NY: New York State Psychological Association Disaster/Crisis Network.

DeWolfe D. 2000. *Field Manual for Mental Health and Human Service Workers in Major Disasters.* Washington, DC: U.S. Department of Health and Human Services, Substance Abuse and Mental Health Services Administration.

DeWolfe D. 2000. *Training Manual for Mental Health and Human Service Workers in Major Disasters.* 2nd ed. Washington, DC: Substance Abuse and Mental Health Services Administration. Available at: http://www.kenyoninternational.com/useful_info/US%20Gov%20Training%20Manual%20Mental%20Health%20and%20Human%20Service%20Workers.pdf. Accessed March 2, 2011.

Ehring T, Ehlers A, Cleare AJ, Glucksman E. 2008. Do acute psychological and psychobiological responses to trauma predict subsequent symptom severities of PTSD and depression? *Psychiatry Res.* 161:67–75.

Emergency Services and Disaster Relief Branch, Center for Mental Health Services. 1996. *Responding to the Needs of People With Serious and Persistent Mental Illness in Times of Disaster.* Washington, DC: Substance Abuse and Mental Health Services Administration.

Erikson K. 1995. *A New Species of Trouble: The Human Experience of Modern Disasters.* New York, NY: W.W. Norton.

Everly Jr GS, Mitchell JT. 1997. *Critical Incident Stress Management: A New Era and Standard of Care in Crisis Intervention.* Ellicott City, MD: Chevron Publishing Corporation.

Foa EB, Davidson JR, Frances A, et al. 1999. The expert consensus guidelines series: treatment of posttraumatic stress disorder. *J Clin Psychiatry.* 60:1–76.

Freedy JR, Hobfoll SE, editors. *Traumatic Stress: From Theory to Practice.* New York, NY: Plenum Press.

Fritz CE. 1996. *Disasters and Mental Health: Therapeutic Principles Drawn From Disaster Studies: Historical and Comparative Disaster Series #10.* Newark, DE: Disaster Research Center, University of Delaware.

Fullerton CS, Ursano RJ, editors. 1997. *Post-Traumatic Stress Disorder: Acute and Long-Term Responses to Trauma and Disaster.* Washington, DC: American Psychiatric Press.

Galea S, Ahern J, Resnick H, et al. 2002. Psychological sequelae of the September 11 terrorist attacks in New York City. *N Engl J Med.* 346:982–987.

Galea S, Resnick H, Ahern J, et al. 2002. Posttraumatic stress disorder in Manhattan, New York City, after the September 11th terrorist attacks. *J Urban Health.* 793:340–353.

Gerrity ET, Flynn BW. 1997. Mental Health Consequences of Disasters. In: Noji EK, editor. *Public Health Consequences of Disasters.* Oxford, England: Oxford University Press:101–121.

Ghodse H, Galea S. 2006. Tsunami: understanding mental health consequences and the unprecedented response. *Int Rev Psychiatry.* 18:289–297.

Hartsough DM, Myers DG. 1995. *Disaster Work and Mental Health: Prevention and Control of Stress Among Workers.* Washington, DC: Center for Mental Health Services, Substance Abuse and Mental Health Services Administration, U.S. Public Health Service.

Havenaar JM, Cwikel JG, Bromet EJ, editors. 2002. *Toxic Turmoil: Psychological and Societal Consequences of Ecological Disasters.* New York, NY: Kluwer Academic/Plenum Publishers.

Herman D, Felton C, Susser E. 2002. Mental health needs in New York State following the September 11th attacks. *J Urban Health*. 793:322–331.

Hodgkinson PE, Stewart M. 1998. *Coping With Catastrophe: A Handbook of Post-Disaster Psychosocial Aftercare*, 2nd ed. London, England: Routledge.

Jack K, Glied S. 2002. The public costs of mental health response: lessons from the New York City post-9/11 needs assessment. *J Urban Health*. 793:332–339.

Kasperson RE, Kasperson JX. 1996. The social amplification and attenuation of risk. *Ann Am Acad Political Soc Sci*. 545:95–105.

Kleber RJ, Brom D. 1992. *Coping With Trauma: Theory, Prevention and Treatment*. Amsterdam, the Netherlands: Swets & Zeitlinger.

Kliman J, Kern R, Kliman A. 1982. Natural and human-made disasters: some therapeutic and epidemiological implications for crisis intervention. In: Reuveni U, Speck RV, Speck JL, editors. *Therapeutic Intervention: Healing Strategies for Human Systems*. New York, NY: Human Sciences Press.

Lystad M, editor. 1988. *Mental Health Response to Mass Emergencies: Theory and Practice*. New York, NY: Brunner/Mazel Publishers.

Marsella AJ, Friedman MJ, Gerrity ET, Scurfield RM, editors. 1996. *Ethnocultural Aspects of Post-Traumatic Stress Disorder: Issues, Research, and Clinical Applications*. Washington, DC: American Psychological Association.

McKnight JL, Kretzmann JP. 1990. *Mapping Community Capacity*. Evanston, IL: Center for Urban Affairs and Policy Research, Northwestern University.

Mitchell JT, Everly Jr GS. 1997. *Critical Incident Stress Debriefing: An Operations Manual for the Prevention of Traumatic Stress Among Emergency Service and Disaster Workers Second Edition, Revised*. Ellicott City, MD: Chevron Publishing Corporation.

Myers D. 1994. *Disaster Response and Recovery: A Handbook for Mental Health Professionals*. Rockville, MD: U.S. Department of Health and Human Services, Public Health Service, Substance Abuse and Mental Health Services Administration, Center for Mental Health Services.

National Center for Post–Traumatic Stress Disorders. 2003. Mental-health intervention for disasters. Washington, DC: VA. Available at: http://www.georgiadisaster.info/Healthcare/HC14%20FacititatingResiliency/Link%201%20--%20NCPTSD%20Fact%20Sheet%20on%20MH%20Intervention.pdf. Accessed March 2, 2011.

Neria Y, Galea S, Norris FH, editors. 2009. *Mental Health and Disasters*. New York, NY: Cambridge University Press.

O'Brien LS. 1998. *Traumatic Events and Mental Health*. Cambridge, England: Cambridge University Press.

Pfefferbaum B, Seale TW, McDonald NB, et al. 2000. Posttraumatic stress two years after the Oklahoma City bombing in youths geographically distant from the explosion. *Psychiatry*. 63:358–370.

Quarantelli EL, editor. 1998. *What is a Disaster? Perspectives on the Question*. London, England: Routledge.

Raphael B, Wilson JP. 1993. Theoretical and intervention considerations in working with victims of disaster. In: Wilson JP, Raphael B, editors. *International Handbook of Traumatic Stress Syndromes*. New York, NY: Plenum Press.

Schlenger WE, Caddell JM, Ebert L, et al. 2002. Psychological reactions to terrorist attacks: findings from the national study of Americans' reactions to September 11. *JAMA.* 288:581–588.

Streeter CL, Murty SA, editors. 1996. *Research on Social Work and Disasters.* New York, NY: The Haworth Press.

Stuber J, Fairbrother G, Galea S, et al. 2002. Determinants of counseling for children in Manhattan after the September 11 attacks. *Psychiatric Serv.* 53:815–822.

Substance Abuse and Mental Health Services Administration (SAMHSA). 2003. Mental Health All-Hazards Disaster Planning Guidance. Washington, DC: SAMHSA. Available at: http://www.eird.org/isdr-biblio/PDF/Mental%20health%20all-hazards.pdf. Accessed March 2, 2011.

Taniellan T, Stein B. 2006. Understanding and preparing for the psychological consequences of terrorism. In: Kamien D, editor. *The McGraw-Hill Homeland Security Handbook.* New York, NY: McGraw-Hill. Available at: http://www.rand.org/pubs/reprints/2006/RAND_RP1217.pdf. Accessed March 2, 2011.

Terr LC. 1992. Large-group preventive techniques for use after disaster. In: Austin LS, editor. *Responding to Disaster: A Guide for Mental Health Professionals.* Washington, DC: American Psychiatric Press:81–99.

Ursano RJ, McCaughey BG, Fullerton CS, editors. 1994. *Individual and Community Responses to Trauma and Disaster: The Structure of Human Chaos.* Cambridge, England: Cambridge University Press.

Van der Kolk BA, McFarlane AC, Weisaeth L, editors. 1996. *Traumatic Stress: The Effects of Overwhelming Experience on Mind, Body, and Society.* New York, NY: The Guilford Press.

Van Ommeren M, Saxena S. 2004. *Mental Health of Populations Exposed to Biological and Chemical Weapons.* Geneva, Switzerland: World Health Organization.

Weisaeth L. 1993. Disasters: psychological and psychiatric Aspects. In: Goldberger L, Breznitz S, editors. *Handbook of Stress: Theoretical and Clinical Aspects,* 2nd ed. New York, NY: The Free Press.

Yehuda R, editor. 1998. *Psychological Trauma.* Washington, DC: American Psychiatric Press.

Young BH, Ford JD, Ruzek JI, et al. 1998. *Disaster Mental Health Services: A Guidebook for Clinicians and Administrators.* Menlo Park, CA: National Center for Post–Traumatic Stress Disorders.

Medical Care Delivery

Koenig KL, Schultz CH, editors. 2009. *Koenig and Schultz's Disaster Medicine: Comprehensive Principles and Practices.* New York, NY: Cambridge University Press.

Pointer JE, Michaelis J, Saunders C, et al. 1992. The 1989 Loma Prieta earthquake: impact on hospital patient care. *Ann Emerg Med.* 2110:1228–1233.

Quinn B, Baker R, Pratt J. 1994. Hurricane Andrew and a pediatric emergency department. *Ann Emerg Med.* 234:737–741.

Sabatino F. 1992. Stories of survival. Hurricane Andrew. South Florida hospitals shared resources and energy to cope with the storm's devastation. *Hospitals.* 66:26–30.

Scott S, Constantine LM. 1990. When natural disaster strikes: with careful planning pharmacists can continue to provide essential services to survivors in the aftermath of a disaster. *Am Pharm.* NS3011:27–31.

Morbidity and Mortality

Burkle FM, editor. 1984. *Disaster Medicine.* New Hyde Park, NY: Medical Examination.

McNabb SJ, Kelso KY, Wilson SA, et al. 1995. Hurricane Andrew–related injuries and illnesses, Louisiana 1992. *South Med J.* 886:615–618.

Noji EK, Armenian HK, Oganessian A. 1993. Issues of rescue and medical care following the 1988 Armenian earthquake. *Int J Epidemiol.* 226:1070–1076.

Noji EK. 1993. Analysis of medical needs during disasters caused by tropical cyclones: anticipated injury patterns. *J Trop Med Hyg.* 96:370–376.

Saylor LF, Gordon JE. 1957. The medical component of natural disasters. *Am J Med Sci.* 234:342–362.

Natural Hazards

White GF, Haas JE. 1975. *Assessment of Research on Natural Hazards.* Cambridge, MA: The MIT Press.

White GF. 1974. *Natural Hazards: Local, National, Global.* New York, NY: Oxford University Press.

Zebrowski Jr E. 1997. *Perils of a Restless Planet: Scientific Perspectives on Natural Disasters.* Cambridge, England: Cambridge University Press.

Nutrition

National Voluntary Organizations Active in Disaster (NVOAD). 2010. Multi-Agency Feeding Plan Template. Arlington, VA: NVOAD. Available at: http://www.nvoad.org/index.php/resource-library/documents/doc_details/8-multi-agency-feeding-plan.html. Accessed April 13, 2011.

World Health Organization (WHO). 2000. *The Management of Nutrition in Major Emergencies.* Geneva, Switzerland: International Federation of Red Cross and Red Crescent Societies, United Nations High Commissioner for Refugees, WHO.

Organization of Response

Agency for Healthcare Research and Quality (AHRQ). 2005. Development of Models for Emergency Preparedness, Personal Protective Equipment, Decontamination, Isolation/Quarantine, and Laboratory Capacity. Rockville, MD: AHRQ. Available at: http://www.ahrq.gov/research/devmodels. Accessed March 2, 2011.

Agency for Healthcare Research and Quality (AHRQ). 2007. Disaster Response Tools and Resources. Rockville, MD: AHRQ. Available at: http://www.ahrq.gov/path/katrina.htm. Accessed March 2, 2011.

Assistant Secretary for Preparedness and Response. 2007. Pandemic and All-Hazards Preparedness Act, Progress Report. Washington, DC: U.S. Department of Health

and Human Services. Available at: http://healthyamericans.org/reports/bioterror07/
PAHPAProgressReport.pdf. Accessed March 2, 2011.

Centers for Disease Control and Prevention (CDC). [n.d.] Emergency Preparedness and
Response. Atlanta, GA: CDC. Available at: http://www.bt.cdc.gov/cdcpreparedness/
cphp/index.asp. Accessed March 2, 2011.

Centers for Disease Control and Prevention (CDC). [n.d.] Emergency Preparedness and
Response, Strategic National Stockpile. Atlanta, GA: CDC. Available at: http://
www.bt.cdc.gov/stockpile. Accessed March 2, 2011.

Federal Emergency Management Agency (FEMA). [n.d.] Public Assistance Grant Program.
Washington, DC: FEMA. Available at: http://www.fema.gov/government/grant/pa/
index.shtm. Accessed March 2, 2011.

Federal Emergency Management Agency (FEMA). 2005. Emergency Management
Assistance Compact Operations, Pre–Course Assignment. Washington, DC:
FEMA. Available at: http://www.emacweb.org/?305. Accessed March 2, 2011.

Federal Emergency Management Agency (FEMA). 2010. Developing and Maintaining
Emergency Operations Plans Comprehensive Preparedness Guide (CPG) 101.
Version 2.0. Washington, DC: FEMA. Available at: http://www.fema.gov/pdf/
about/divisions/npd/CPG_101_V2.pdf. Accessed March 2, 2011.

Federal Emergency Management Agency (FEMA). 2008. National Incident Management
System. Washington, DC: FEMA. Available at: http://www.fema.gov/pdf/emergency/
nims/NIMS_core.pdf. Accessed March 2, 2011.

Federal Emergency Management Agency (FEMA). 2008. NIMS Resource Center.
Washington, DC: FEMA. Available at: http://www.fema.gov/emergency/nims/
index.shtm. Accessed March 2, 2011.

Federal Emergency Management Agency (FEMA). 2008. Overview of Stafford Act
Support to States. Washington, DC: FEMA. Available at: http://www.fema.gov/
pdf/emergency/nrf/nrf-stafford.pdf. Accessed March 2, 2011.

Federal Emergency Management Agency (FEMA). 2010. Declaration Process Fact
Sheet. Washington, DC: FEMA. Available at: http://www.fema.gov/media/
fact_sheets/declaration_process.shtm. Accessed March 2, 2011.

Federal Emergency Management Agency (FEMA). 2010. National Response Framework
Resource Center, Response Partner Guides. Washington, DC: FEMA. Available at:
http://www.fema.gov/emergency/nrf/responsepartnerguides.htm. Accessed March 2,
2011.

Federal Emergency Management Agency (FEMA). 2011. What is Disaster Assistance?
Washington, DC: FEMA. Available at: http://www.fema.gov/assistance/process/
individual_assistance.shtm. Accessed March 2, 2011.

HEICS IV National Work Group. 2006. *Hospital Incident Command System Guidebook*.
California State Emergency Medical Services Authority. Available at: http://
www.emsa.ca.gov/HICS/files/Guidebook_Glossary.doc. Accessed March 2, 2011.

Hodge JG, Goskin LO, Vernick JS. 2007. The Pandemic and All–Hazards Preparedness
Act. *JAMA*. 29:1708–1711. Available at: http://jama.ama-assn.org/content/297/15/
1708.full. Accessed March 2, 2011.

Lister S. 2008. Public Health and Medical Preparedness and Response: Issues in the
110th Congress. Washington, DC: Congressional Research Service.

National Fire Protection Association (NFPA). 2009. NFPA 1600 Standard on Disaster/
Emergency Management and Business Continuity Programs, 2010 Edition. Quincy,

MA: NFPA. Available at: http://www.nfpa.org/assets/files/PDF/NFPA16002010.pdf. Accessed March 2, 2011.

Office of the Assistant Secretary for Preparedness and Response. 2011. National Health Security Strategy. Washington, DC: U.S. Department of Health and Human Services. Available at: http://www.phe.gov/Preparedness/planning/authority/nhss/Pages/default.aspx. Accessed March 2, 2011.

Office of the Assistant Secretary for Preparedness and Response. 2011. The Hospital Preparedness Program. Washington, DC: U.S. Department of Health and Human Services. Available at: http://www.phe.gov/preparedness/planning/hpp/pages/default.aspx. Accessed March 2, 2011.

Office of the Civilian Volunteer Medical Reserve Corps. 2010. How to Start an MRC. Washington, DC: U.S. Department of Health and Human Services. Available at: http://www.medicalreservecorps.gov/QuestionsAnswers/ContactingStarting.

Office of the Civilian Volunteer Medical Reserve Corps. 2010. Office of the Civilian Volunteer Medical Reserve Corps Strategic Plan. Washington, DC: U.S. Department of Health and Human Services. Available at: http://www.medicalreservecorps.gov/About/StrategicPlan0910. Accessed March 2, 2011.

Public Health Emergency, Emergency System for Advance Registration of Volunteer Health Professionals (ESAR-VHP). 2011. About ESAR-VHP. Washington, DC: U.S. Department of Health and Human Services. Available at: http://www.phe.gov/esarvhp/Pages/about.aspx. Accessed March 2, 2011.

Public Health Emergency. 2010. Legal Authority and Related Guidance. Washington, DC: U.S. Department of Health and Human Services. Available at: http://www.phe.gov/Preparedness/planning/authority/Pages/default.aspx. Accessed March 2, 2011.

Public Health Emergency. 2010. Medical Surge Capacity Capability. Washington, DC: U.S. Department of Health and Human Services. Available at: http://www.phe.gov/Preparedness/support/mscc/Pages/default.aspx. Accessed March 2, 2011.

Public Health Emergency. 2010. National Health Security Strategy. Washington, DC: U.S. Department of Health and Human Services. Available at: http://www.phe.gov/Preparedness/planning/authority/nhss/Pages/default.asp. Accessed March 2, 2011.

Public Health Emergency. 2010. Pandemic and All Hazards Preparedness Act. Washington, DC: U.S. Department of Health and Human Services. Available at: http://www.phe.gov/Preparedness/legal/pahpa/Pages/default.aspx. Accessed March 2, 2011.

Public Health Emergency. 2010. Public Health and Medical Services Support. Washington, DC: U.S. Department of Health and Human Services.

Public Health Emergency. 2010. Responders, Clinicians and Practitioners. Washington, DC: U.S. Department of Health and Human Services. Available at: http://www.phe.gov/preparedness/responders/Pages/default.aspx. Accessed March 2, 2011.

Trust for America's Health (TFAH). 2002. The Pandemic and All–Hazards Preparedness Act S3678. Washington, DC: TFAH. Available at: http://healthyamericans.org/reports/bioterror06/S3678summary.pdf. Accessed March 2, 2011.

U.S. Department of Health and Human Services. 2010. About the Commissioned Corps Emergency Response. Washington, DC: U.S. Department of Health and Human Services. Available at: http://www.usphs.gov/aboutus/emergencyresponse.aspx. Accessed March 2, 2011.

U.S. Department of Health and Human Services. 2010. U.S. Public Health Service Commissioned Corps home page. Washington, DC: U.S. Department of Health and Human Services. Available at: http://www.usphs.gov. Accessed March 2, 2011.

U.S. Department of Homeland Security (DHS). 2003. National Preparedness Guidelines. Washington, DC: DHS. Available at: http://www.dhs.gov/files/publications/gc_1189788256647.shtm. Accessed March 2, 2011.

U.S. Department of Homeland Security (DHS). 2007. Target Capabilities List: A Companion to National Preparedness Guidelines. Washington, DC: DHS. Available at: http://www.fema.gov/pdf/government/training/tcl.pdf. Accessed March 2, 2011.

Planning

Auf der Heide E. 1996. *Community Medical Disaster Planning and Evaluation Guide.* Dallas, TX: American College of Emergency Physicians.

Auf der Heide E. 1996. Disaster planning, part II: disaster problems, issues, and challenges identified in the research literature. *Emerg Med Clin North Am.* 14:453–480.

Auf der Heide E. 2004. Common misconceptions about disasters: panic, the disaster syndrome, and looting. In: O'Leary M, editor. *The First 72 Hours: A Community Approach to Disaster Preparedness.* Lincoln, Nebraska: iUniverse Publishing.

Auf der Heide E. 2006. The importance of evidence-based disaster planning. *Ann Emerg Med.* 47:34–49.

Dynes RR. 1994. Community emergency planning: false assumptions and inappropriate analogies. *Int J Mass Emerg Disasters.* 12:141–158.

Fong F, Schrader DC. 1996. Radiation disasters and emergency department preparedness. *Emerg Med Clin North Am.* 14:349–370.

Gibbs M, Lachenmeyer JR, et al. 1996. Effects of the AVIANCA aircrash on disaster workers. *Int J Mass Emerg Disasters.* 141:23–32.

Landesman LY. 2004. Forward: does preparedness make a difference? *Fam Commun Health.* 273:186.

Lindell MK, Perry RW. 1992. *Behavioral Foundations of Community Emergency Planning.* Philadelphia, PA: Hemisphere Publishing.

Public Health Emergency, Office of the Assistant Secretary for Preparedness and Response. 2007. *Public Health Emergency Response: A Guide for Leaders and Responders.* Chapter 9. Conducting exercises for preparedness. Washington, DC: U.S. Department of Health and Human Services. Available at: http://www.phe.gov/emergency/communication/guides/leaders/Documents/freo_section09.pdf. Accessed March 2, 2011.

Quarantelli EL. 1991. *Converting Disaster Scholarship Into Effective Disaster Planning and Managing: Possibilities and Limitations.* Newark: Disaster Research Center, University of Delaware.

U.S. Department of Homeland Security (DHS). [n.d.] Homeland Security Exercise and Evaluation Program (HSEEP). Washington, DC: DHS. Available at: http://www.globalsecurity.org/security/systems/hseep.htm. Accessed March 2, 2011.

Waeckerle JF. 1991. Review article: disaster planning and response. *N Engl J Med.* 32:815–821.

Public Health

Lechat MF. 1979. Disasters and public health. *Bull WHO.* 571:11–17.

Noji E, editor. 1997. *The Public Health Consequences of Disaster.* New York, NY: Oxford University Press.

Rosen G. 1993. *A History of Public Health.* Baltimore, MD: Johns Hopkins University Press.

Sidel VW, Onel E, Geiger HJ, et al. 1992. Public health responses to natural and human-made disasters. In: Last JM, Wallace RB, editors. *Maxcy-Rosenau-Last: Public Health and Preventive Medicine.* Stamford, CT: Appleton & Lange:1173–1186.

Radiation

American College of Radiology (ACR). 2011. Radiation Disasters: Preparedness and Response for Radiology. Philadelphia. PA: ACR. Available at: http://www.acr.org/SecondaryMainMenuCategories/BusinessPracticeIssues/DisasterPreparedness/ACRsDisasterPreparednessPrimer/RadiationDisastersPreparednessandResponsefor RadiologyDoc2.aspx. Accessed March 2, 2011.

Armed Forces Radiobiology Research Institute. 2011. Web site. Available at: http://www.usuhs.mil/afrri. Accessed March 2, 2011.

Centers for Disease Control and Prevention (CDC). 2005. Acute Radiation Syndrome: A Fact Sheet for Physicians. Atlanta, GA: CDC. Available at: http://emergency.cdc.gov/radiation/arsphysicianfactsheet.asp. Accessed March 2, 2011.

Centers for Disease Control and Prevention (CDC). 2005. Radio Emergencies Fact Sheet: Acute Radiation Syndrome. Atlanta, GA: CDC. Available at: http://www.bt.cdc.gov/radiation/pdf/ars.pdf. Accessed March 2, 2011.

Chemical Casualty Care Division, U.S. Army Medical Research Institute of Chemical Defense. 2000. *Medical Management of Chemical Casualties Handbook.* 3rd ed. Aberdeen Proving Ground, MD. Available at: http://www.gmha.org/bioterrorism/usamricd/Yellow_Book_2000.pdf. Accessed April 25, 2011.

New York State Department of Health. 2011. Potassium Iodide (KI) and Radiation Emergencies: Fact Sheet. Available at: http://www.health.state.ny.us/environmental/radiological/potassium_iodide/fact_sheet.htm. Accessed March 2, 2011.

Oak Ridge Institute for Science and Education. 2011. Radiation Emergency Assistance Center/Training Site (REAC/TS). Washington, DC: U.S. Department of Energy. Available at: http://www.orau.gov/reacts. Accessed March 2, 2011.

U.S. Food and Drug Administration (FDA). 2001. Guidance: Potassium Iodide as a Thyroid Blocking Agent in Radiation Emergencies. Rockville, MD: FDA. Available at: http://www.fda.gov/downloads/Drugs/GuidanceComplianceRegulatoryInformation/Guidances/ucm080542.pdf. Accessed March 2, 2011.

Rapid Needs Assessment

Brown V, Jacquier G, Coulombier D, et al. 2001. Rapid assessment of population size by area sampling in disaster situations. *Disasters.* 252:164–71.

Guha-Sapir D. 1991. Rapid assessment of health needs in mass emergencies: review of current concepts and methods. *World Health Stat Q.* 44:171–181.

Hlady WG, Quenemoen LE, Armenia-Cope RR, et al. 1994. Use of a modified cluster sampling method to perform rapid needs assessment after Hurricane Andrew. *Ann Emerg Med.* 23:719–725.

International Federation of the Red Cross and Red Crescent Societies. 1993. *Vulnerability and Capacity Assessment.* Geneva, Switzerland: International Federation of Red Cross and Red Crescent Societies.

Lillibridge SR, Noji EK, Burkle Jr FM. 1993. Disaster assessment: the emergency health evaluation of a population affected by a disaster. *Ann Emerg Med.* 22:1715–1720.

Malilay J, Flanders WD, Brogan D. 1996. A modified cluster-sampling method for post-disaster rapid assessment of needs. *Bull World Health Org.* 74:399–406.

World Health Organization (WHO). 1999. *Rapid Health Assessment Protocols for Emergencies.* Geneva, Switzerland: WHO.

World Health Organization (WHO). 2001. *Rapid Assessment of Mental Health Needs of Refugees, Displaced and Other Populations Affected by Conflict and Post-Conflict Situations.* Geneva, Switzerland: WHO.

Yahmed SB, Koob P. 1996. Health sector approach to vulnerability reduction and emergency preparedness. *World Health Stat Q.* 49:172–178.

Recovery

Ball N. 1997. Demobilizing and reintegrating soldiers: lessons from Africa. In: Kumar K, editor. *Rebuilding Societies After Civil War. Critical Roles for International Assistance.* Boulder, CO: Lynne Rienner:85–105.

Berke PR, Kartez J, Wenger D. 1993. Recovery after disaster: achieving sustainable development, mitigation and equity. *Disasters.* 173:93–109.

Cohen R. 1995. *Refugee and Internally Displaced Women: A Development Perspective.* Washington, DC: Brookings Institution.

Cuny F. 1983. *Disasters and Development.* New York, NY: Oxford University Press.

Felton C. 2002. Project Liberty: a public health response to New Yorkers' mental health needs arising from the World Trade Center terrorist attacks. *J Urban Health.* 79:429–433.

Krug EG, Kresnow MJ, Peddicord JP, et al. 1998. Suicide after natural disasters. *N Engl J Med.* 33:373–378.

McDonnell S, Troiano RP, Barker N, et al. 1995. Evaluation of long-term community recovery from Hurricane Andrew: sources of assistance received by population sub-groups. *Disasters.* 19:338–347.

Moore S, Daniel M, Linnan L, et al. 2004. After Hurricane Floyd passed: investigating the social determinants of disaster preparedness and recovery. *Fam Commun Health.* 273: 204–217.

Shrivastava P. 1996. Long-term recovery from the Bhopal Crisis. In: Mitchell JK, editor. *The Long Road to Recovery: Community Responses to Industrial Disaster.* Tokyo, Japan: United Nations University Press:121–147.

Wickramanayake E, Shook GA. 1995. Rehabilitation planning for flood affected areas of Thailand: experience from Phipun District. *Disasters,* 194:348–355.

Resilience

Bach R, Doran R, Gibb L, et al. 2010. Policy challenges in supporting community resilience. Presented at the London Workshop of the Multinational Community Resilience Policy Group. November 4–5, London, England.

Kaminsky M, McCabe OL, Langlieb AM, Everly Jr GS. 2007. An evidence-informed model of human resistance, resilience, and recovery: the Johns Hopkins' outcome-driven paradigm for disaster mental health services. *Brief Treatment Crisis Intervent.* 7:1–11.

Madrid PA, Grant R, Reilly MJ, Redlener NB. 2006. Challenges in meeting immediate emotional needs: short-term impact of a major disaster on children's mental health: building resiliency in the aftermath of Hurricane Katrina. *Pediatrics.* 11:S448–S453.

Masten AS, Obradovic J. 2007. Disaster preparation and recovery: lessons from research on resilience in human development. *Ecology Soc.* 131:9.

Norris FH, Stevens SP. 2007. Community resilience and the principles of mass trauma intervention. *Psychiatry.* Winter:704.

Norris FH, Stevens SP, Pfefferbaum B, et al. 2008. Community resilience as a metaphor, theory, set of capacities, and strategy for disaster readiness. *Am J Commun Psychol.* 411–412:127–150.

Paton D. 2005. Community resilience: integrating hazard management and community engagement. Presented at the International Conference on Engaging Communities. August 14–17, Brisbane, Queensland. Available at: http://www.engagingcommunities 2005.org/abstracts/Paton-Douglas-final.pdf. Accessed April 23, 2011.

Risk Assessment

Centers for Disease Control and Prevention (CDC). 2009. Community Assessment for Public Health Emergency Response (CASPER) Toolkit. Atlanta, GA: CDC.

Malilay J, Henderson A, McGeehin M, Flanders WD. 1997. Estimating health risks from natural hazards using risk assessment and epidemiology. *Risk Analysis.* 17:363–368.

Surveillance

Disaster Surveillance

Glass RI, Noji EK. 1992. Epidemiologic surveillance following disasters. In: Halperin W, Baker EL, editors. *Public Health Surveillance.* New York, NY: Van Nostrand Reinhold:195–205.

Heffernan R, Mostashari F, Das D, et al. 2004. Syndromic surveillance in public health practice, New York City. *Emerg Infect Dis.* 10:858–864.

Lechat MF. 1993. Accident and disaster epidemiology. *Public Health Rev.* 213:243–253.

Lee LE, Fonseca V, Brett KM, et al. 1993. Active morbidity surveillance after Hurricane Andrew, Florida, 1992. *JAMA.* 270:591–594.

Legome E, Robbins A, Rund A. 1995. Injuries associated with floods: the need for an international reporting scheme. *Disasters.* 19:50–54.

Lore EL, Fonseca V, Brett KM. 1993. Active morbidity surveillance after Hurricane Andrew–Florida, 1992. *JAMA.* 270:591–594.

Noji EK. 1997. The use of epidemiologic methods in disasters. In: Noji EK, editor. *The Public Health Consequences of Disasters.* New York, NY: Oxford University Press: 21–36.

O'Connell EK, Zhang G, Legeun F, et al. 2010. Innovative uses for syndromic surveillance. *Emerg Infect Dis.* 16:669–671.

Public Health Emergency, Office of the Assistant Secretary for Preparedness and Response. 2007. *Public Health Emergency Response: A Guide for Leaders and Responders.* Chapter 2. Public health response. Available at: http://www.phe.gov/emergency/communication/ guides/leaders/Documents/freo_section02.pdf. Accessed March 2, 2011.

Western KA.1982. *Epidemiologic Surveillance after Natural Disasters.* Washington, DC: Pan American Health Organization.

Wetterhall SF, Noji EK. 1997. Surveillance and Epidemiology. In: Noji EK, editor. *The Public Health Consequences of Disasters.* New York, NY: Oxford University Press: 37–64.

General Surveillance

Halperin W, Baker Jr EL, Monson RR, editors. 1992. *Public Health Surveillance.* New York, NY: Van Nostrand Reinhold.

Klauke DN, Buehler JW, Thacker SB, et al. 1988. Guidelines for Evaluating Surveillance Systems. *MMWR Morbid Mortal Wkly Rep.* 5:1–18.

Langmuir AD. 1971. Evolution of the concept of surveillance in the United States. *Proc Roy Soc Med.* 64:9–12.

Thacker SB, Berkelman RL. 1988. Public health surveillance in the United States. *Epidemiol Rev.* 10:164–190.

Thacker SB, Berkelman RL, Stroup DF. 1989. The science of public health surveillance. *J Public Health Policy.* 10:187–203.

Thacker SB, Choi K, Brachman PS. 1983. The surveillance of infectious diseases. *JAMA.* 249:1181–1185.

Environmental Public Health Surveillance

Deutsch PV, Adler J, Richter ED. 1992. Sentinel markers for industrial disasters. *Israel J Med Sci.* 288-9:526–533.

Thacker SB, Stroup DF. 1994. Future directions of comprehensive public health surveillance and health information systems in the United States. *Am J Epidemiol.* 140:1–15.

Thacker SB, Stroup DF, Parrish RG, Anderson HA.1996. Surveillance in environmental public health: issues, systems, and sources. *Am J Public Health.* 86:633–638.

Surveillance After Specific Disasters

Centers for Disease Control and Prevention. 1990. Surveillance of shelters after Hurricane Hugo. *MMWR Morb Mortal Wkly Rep.* 39:41–47.

Centers for Disease Control and Prevention. 1992. Rapid assessment following Hurricane Andrew—Florida and Louisiana, 1992. *MMWR Morb Mortal Wkly Rep.* 41:685–688.

Centers for Disease Control and Prevention. 1993. Rapid assessment of vector-borne diseases during the Midwest flood—United States. *MMWR Morb Mortal Wkly Rep.* 43:481–483.

Centers for Disease Control and Prevention. 1994. Coccidioidomycosis following the Northridge earthquake, California, 1994. *MMWR Morb Mortal Wkly Rep.* 43:194–195.

Centers for Disease Control and Prevention. 1996. Deaths associated with Hurricanes Marilyn and Opal—United States, September–October 1995. *MMWR Morb Mortal Wkly Rep.* 45:32–38.

Centers for Disease Control and Prevention. 1996. Surveillance for injuries and illnesses and rapid health–needs assessment following Hurricanes Marilyn and Opal, September–October 1995. *MMWR Morb Mortal Wkly Rep.* 45:81–85.

Centers for Disease Control and Prevention. 1997. Tornado–associated fatalities in Arkansas, 1997. *MMWR Morb Mortal Wkly Rep.* 46:412–416.

Centers for Disease Control and Prevention. 1998. Community needs assessment and morbidity surveillance following an ice storm, Maine, January 1998. *MMWR Morb Mortal Wkly Rep.* 47:351–354.

Malilay J, Guido MR, Ramirez AV, et al. 1996. Public health surveillance after a volcanic eruption: lessons from Cerro Negro, Nicaragua, 1992. *Bulletin PAHO.* 303:218–226.

O'Carroll PW, Friede A, Noji EK, et al. 1995. The rapid implementation of a statewide emergency health information system during the 1993 Iowa flood. *Am J Public Health.* 85:564–567.

Technological Disasters

Baum A. 1987. Toxins, technology, disasters. In: VandenBos GR, Bryant BK, eds, *Cataclysms, Crises, and Catastrophes: Psychology in Action.* Washington, DC: American Psychological Association.

Becker SM. 1997. Psychosocial assistance after environmental accidents: a policy perspective. *Environ Health Perspect.* 105:1557–1563.

Bromet EJ, Parkinson DK, Dunn LO. 1990. Long-term mental health consequences of the accident at Three Mile Island. *Int J Mental Health.* 19:48–60.

Cuthbertson BH, Nigg JM. 1987. Technological disaster and the nontherapeutic community: a question of true victimization. *Environ Behav.* 19:462–483.

Edelstein MR, Wandersman A. 1987. Community dynamics in coping with toxic contaminants. In: Altman I, Wandersman A, editors. *Neighborhood and Community Environments.* Vol 9, Series Human Behavior and Environment: Advances in Theory and Research. New York, NY: Plenum Press.

Edelstein MR. 1988. *Contaminated Communities: The Social and Psychological Impacts of Residential Toxic Exposure.* Boulder, CO: Westview.

Haavenaar JM, Rumyantzeva GM, van den Brink W, et al. 1997. Long-term mental health effects of the Chernobyl disaster: an epidemiologic survey of two former Soviet regions. *Am J Psychiatry.* 154:1605–1607.

International Federation of Red Cross and Red Crescent Societies. 1996. Annex III: The role of the Red Cross and Red Crescent Societies in response to technological disasters. *Int Rev Red Cross.* 310:55–130.

Kroll-Smith JS, Couch SR. 1993. Technological Hazards: Social Responses as Traumatic Stressors. In: Wilson JP, Raphael B, editors. *The International Handbook of Traumatic Stress Syndromes.* New York, NY: Plenum Press:79–91.

Leonard RB. 1993. Hazardous materials accidents: initial scene assessment and patient care. *Aviat Space Environ Med.* June:646–661.

Levitin HW, Siegelson HJ. 1996. Hazardous materials: disaster medical planning and response. *Emerg Med Clinics North Am.* 142:327–348.

Levy K, Hirsch, EF, Aghababian RV, et al. 1999. Radiation accident preparedness: report of a training program involving the United States, Eastern Europe, and the newly independent states. *Am J Public Health.* 89:115–116.

Lillibridge SR. 1997. Industrial disasters. In: Noji EK, editor. *The Public Health Consequences of Disasters.* New York, NY: Oxford University Press:354–372.

Quarantelli EL. 1993. The environmental disasters of the future will be more and worse but the prospect is not hopeless. *Disaster Prev Manage.* 2:11–25.

Volcanic Eruption

Annenberg Media. 2010. Volcanoes: Can We Predict Volcanic Eruptions? Available at: http://www.learner.org/exhibits/volcanoes/entry.html. Accessed March 1, 2011.

Baxter PJ. 1997. Volcanoes. In: Noji EK, editor. *The Public Health Consequences of Disasters.* New York, NY: Oxford University Press.

U.S. Geological Service. 1997. *The Nature of Volcanoes.* Available at: http://pubs.usgs.gov/gip/volc/cover2.html. Accessed March 1, 2011.

U.S. Geological Service. 2011. *Volcano Hazards Program.* Available at: http://volcanoes.usgs.gov. Accessed March 1, 2011.

Vulnerable Populations

At-Risk

Association of Schools of Public Health (ASPH)/Centers for Disease Control and Prevention (CDC). 2007. 2006–2007 ASPH/CDC Vulnerable Populations Collaboration Group Preparedness Resource Kit. Atlanta, GA: CDC. Available at: http://preparedness.asph.org/perlc/documents/VulnerablePopulations.pdf. Accessed April 23, 2011.

Centers for Disease Control and Prevention (CDC). [2010.] Public Health Workbook to Define, Locate, and Reach Special, Vulnerable, and At-Risk Populations in an Emergency. Atlanta, GA: CDC. Available at: http://www.bt.cdc.gov/workbook/pdf/ph_workbookFINAL.pdf. Accessed April 23, 2011.

Cutter SL, Boruff BJ, Shirley WL. 2003. Social vulnerability to environmental hazards. *Soc Sci Q.* 84:242–261.

Federal Emergency Management Agency (FEMA). 2008. Comprehensive Preparedness Guide 301: Special Needs Planning. Interim Emergency Management Planning Guide for Special Needs Populations. Washington, DC: FEMA. Available at: http://serve.mt.gov/wp-content/uploads/2010/10/CPG-301.pdf. Accessed April 23, 2011.

Federal Emergency Management Agency (FEMA). 2011. Preparedness Resources. Washington, DC: FEMA. Available at: http://www.fema.gov/about/odic/preparedness.shtm#1. Accessed March 2, 2011.

Jones NL. 2010. The American With Disabilities Act and Emergency Preparedness and Response. Washington, DC: Congressional Research Service. Available at: http://assets.opencrs.com/rpts/RS22254_20100105.pdf. Accessed March 2, 2011.

Ringel JS, Chandra A, Williams M, et al. 2009. Enhancing Public Health Emergency Preparedness for Special Needs Populations: A Toolkit for State and Local Planning and Response. Technical Reports. Santa Monica, CA: RAND. Available at: http://www.rand.org/pubs/technical_reports/TR681. Accessed March 2, 2011.

Dementia

Alzheimer's Association, RTI International. [n.d.] Disaster Preparedness: Home and Community-Based Services for People With Dementia and Their Caregivers. Research Triangle Park, NC: RT International. Available at: http://www.aoa.gov/AoARoot/Preparedness/Resources_Network/pdf/Toolkit_2_Disaster_Preparedness.pdf. Accessed March 1, 2011.

Dialysis

Centers for Medicare and Medicaid Services. 2007. Preparing for Emergencies: A Guide for People on Dialysis. Available at: http://www.kcercoalition.com/pdf/101501.pdf. Accessed March 1, 2011.

Disabilities

Disability Rights Section, Civil Rights Division. 2007. Americans With Disabilities Act: ADA Checklist for Emergency Shelters. Washington, DC: U.S. Department of Justice. Available at: http://www.ada.gov/pcatoolkit/chap7shelterchk.htm. Accessed March 2, 2011.

Emergency Preparedness Initiative. 2005. Guide on the Special Needs of People With Disabilities for Emergency Managers, Planners and Responders, Revised Edition. New York, NY: National Organization on Disability. Available at: http://www.eadassociates.com/epiguide2005.pdf. Accessed March 2, 2011.

Federal Emergency Management Agency (FEMA). 2010. People With Disabilities and Other Access and Functional Needs. Washington, DC: FEMA. Available at: http://www.fema.gov/plan/prepare/specialplans.shtm. Accessed March 2, 2011.

Fernandez LS, Byard D, Lin CC. 2002. Frail elderly as disaster victims: emergency management strategies. *Prehosp Disaster Med.* 17:67–74.

Kailes JI, Enders A. 2007. Moving beyond special needs: a function–based framework for emergency management and planning. *J Disability Policy Stud.* 17:230–237.

Kailes JI. 2010. Disaster Preparedness for People With Disabilities, Disability-Related Organizations, and Emergency Managers and Planners. Playa del Rey, CA: June

Isaacson Kailes. Available at: http://www.jik.com/disaster.html. Accessed March 2, 2011.

Kailes JI. 2002. Emergency Evacuation Preparedness: Taking Responsibility for Your Safety: A Guide for People With Disabilities and Other Activity Limitations. Pomona, CA: Center for Disability Issues and the Health Professions, Western University of Health Sciences. Available at: http://www.wvdhsem.gov/other_docs/emergency_evacuation.pdf. Accessed March 2, 2011.

National Organization on Disability (NOD). 2009. Functional Needs of People With Disabilities: A Guide for Emergency Managers, Planners and Responders. New York, NY: NOD. Available at: http://nod.org/assets/downloads/Guide-Emergency-Planners.html. Accessed March 2, 2011.

U.S. Access Board. [n.d.] Resources on emergency evacuation and disaster preparedness. Available at: http://www.access-board.gov/evac.htm. Accessed March 2, 2011.

Ethnic Communities

Andrulis DP, Siddiqui NJ, Gantner JL. 2007. Preparing racially and ethnically diverse communities for public health emergencies, *Health Aff.* 265:1269–1279.

Carter-Pokras O, Zambrana RE, Mora SE, Aaby KA. 2007. Emergency preparedness: knowledge and perceptions of Latin American immigrants. *J Health Care Poor Underserved.* 182:465–481.

Evacuation

Kailes JI. 2002. Emergency Evacuation Preparedness: Taking Responsibility for Your Safety: A Guide for People With Disabilities and Other Activity Limitations. Pomona, CA: Center for Disability Issues and the Health Professions, Western University of Health Sciences. Available at: http://www.wvdhsem.gov/other_docs/emergency_evacuation.pdf.

Home Health Agencies

National Association for Home Care and Hospice (NAHCH). 2008. Emergency Preparedness Packet for Home Health Agencies. Washington, DC: NAHCH. Available at: http://www.nahc.org/regulatory/EP_Binder.pdf. Accessed March 1, 2011.

Medical

Kailes JI. [n.d.] Earthquake tips for people who use life support systems. San Francisco, CA: Independent Living Resource Center. Available at: http://www.preparenow.org/eqtlsups.html. Accessed March 1, 2011.

Kailes JI. [n.d.] Earthquake tips for the hearing impaired. San Francisco, CA: Independent Living Resource Center. Available at: http://www.preparenow.org/deaf.html. Accessed March 1, 2011.

Planetree Health Library. [n.d.] People with special medical needs [brochure]. San Jose, CA: Planetree Health Library. Available at: http://www.preparenow.org/pwsmn.html. Accessed March 1, 2011.

Older Adults

Aldrich N, Benson W. 2008. Disaster preparedness and the chronic disease needs of vulnerable older adults. *Preventing Chronic Dis.* 5:A27.

Centers for Disease Control and Prevention (CDC) Healthy Aging Program. [2006.] Disaster Planning Tips for Older Adults and Their Families. Atlanta, GA: CDC. Available at: http://www.cdc.gov/aging/pdf/disaster_planning_tips.pdf. Accessed March 2, 2011.

Fernandez LS, Byard D, Lin CC, et al. 2002. Frail elderly as disaster victims: emergency management strategies. *Prehosp Disaster Med.* 17:67–74.

Gibson MJ. 2006. We Can Do Better: Lessons Learned for Protecting Older Persons in Disasters. Washington, DC: AARP. Available at: http://assets.aarp.org/rgcenter/il/better.pdf. Accessed March 2, 2011.

National Organization on Disability (NOD). [n.d.] Assisting people with disabilities in a disaster. Washington, DC: NOD. Available at: http://www.infinitec.org/live/safety/disaster.htm. Accessed March 2, 2011.

Wilken CS. 2009. Preparing for a Disaster: Strategies for Older Adults. University of Florida Institute of Food and Agricultural Sciences Extension Electronic Data Information Source. Available at: http://edis.ifas.ufl.edu/fy750. Accessed March 2, 2011.

Pandemics

Bouye K, Truman B, Hutchins S, et al. 2009. Pandemic influenza preparedness and response among public-housing residents, single parent families, and low-income populations. *Am J Public Health.* 99:S287–S293.

Groom A, Jim C, LaRoque M, et al. 2009. Pandemic influenza preparedness and vulnerable populations in tribal communities. *Am J Public Health.* 99:S271–S278.

Hutchins S, Truman B, Merlin T, Redd S. 2009. Protecting vulnerable populations from pandemic influenza in the United States: a strategic imperative. *Am J Public Health.* 99:S243–S248.

Truman B, Tinker T, Vaughn E, et al. 2009. Pandemic influenza preparedness and response among immigrants and refugees. *Am J Public Health.* 99:S278–S286.

Vaughn E, Tinker T. 2009. Effective health risk communication about pandemic influenza for vulnerable populations. *Am J Public Health.* 99:S324–S332.

Planning

National Council on Disability (NCD). 2005. Saving Lives: Including People With Disabilities in Emergency Planning. Washington, DC: NCD. Available at: http://www.ncd.gov/newsroom/publications/2005/saving_lives.htm. Accessed March 1, 2011.

Worker Safety

Centers for Disease Control and Prevention (CDC). 2008. Interim Health Recommendations for Workers Who Handle Human Remains After a Disaster.

Atlanta, GA: CDC. Available at: http://www.bt.cdc.gov/disasters/handleremains.asp. Accessed March 2, 2011.

Centers for Disease Control and Prevention (CDC). 2011. Health Recommendations for Relief Workers Responding to Disasters. Atlanta, GA: CDC. Available at: http://wwwnc.cdc.gov/travel/content/relief-workers.aspx. Accessed March 2, 2011.

Golob BR. 2007. Environmental Health Emergency Response Guide. Hopkins, MN: Twin Cities Metro Advanced Practice Center. Available at: http://www.cdc.gov/nceh/ehs/Docs/EH_Emergency_Response_Guide.pdf. Accessed March 2, 2011.

Jackson BA, Peterson DJ, Bartis JT, et al. 2002. Protecting Emergency Responders: Lessons Learned From Terrorist Attacks. Santa Monica, CA: RAND Science and Technology Policy Institute. Available at: http://www.rand.org/pubs/conf_proceedings/2006/CF176.pdf. Accessed March 2, 2011.

Lippy B. 2003. Protecting the health and safety of rescue and recovery workers. In: Levy BS, Sidel VW, editors. *Terrorism and Public Health: A Balanced Approach to Strengthening Systems and Protecting People.* New York, NY: Oxford University Press.

National Institute for Occupational Safety and Health. 2004. *Protecting Emergency Responders,* Vol 3. Safety Management in Disaster and Terrorism Response. Washington, DC: U.S. Department of Health and Human Services. Available at: http://www.cdc.gov/niosh/npptl/guidancedocs/rand.html. Accessed March 2, 2011.

National Institute for Occupational Safety and Health. 2010. Suggested guidance for supervisors at disaster sites. Washington, DC: U.S. Department of Health and Human Services. Available at: http://www.cdc.gov/niosh/topics/emres/emhaz.html. Accessed March 2, 2011.

Occupational Safety and Health Administration. 2003. Personal Protective Equipment. Washington, DC: U.S. Department of Labor. Available at: http://63.234.227.130/Publications/osha3151.pdf. Accessed March 2, 2011.

Occupational Safety and Health Administration. 2004. Principal Emergency Response and Preparedness Requirements and Guidance. Washington, DC: U.S. Department of Labor. Available at: http://www.osha.gov/Publications/osha3122.html. Accessed March 2, 2011.

Occupational Safety and Health Administration. 2005. Workplace Safety and Health Considerations for Hearing-Impaired Workers, Innovative Workplace Safety Accommodations for Hearing-Impaired Workers. Washington, DC: U.S. Department of Labor. Available at: http://www.osha.gov/dts/shib/shib072205.html. Accessed March 2, 2011.

Occupational Safety and Health Administration. 2007. *Emergency Preparedness and Response.* Washington, DC: U.S. Department of Labor. Available at: http://www.osha.gov/SLTC/emergencypreparedness/index.html. Accessed March 2, 2011.

INDEX

U.S. Public Health Service (PHS), 57, 61-62,
    95, 132-133
US&R. *see* Urban Search and Rescue
USACE. *see* U.S. Army Corps of Engineers
USAID. *see* U.S. Agency for International
    Development
USDA. *see* U.S. Department of Agriculture
USGS. *see* U.S. Geological Survey
USPHS. *see* U.S. Public Health Service
Utilities, 6, 9, 11-13, 24, 78, 88, 101t, 104,
    117t, 120, 122, 161, 178, 217, 280,
    296

V

VA. *see* U.S. Department of Veterans Affairs
Vaccination, 29, 80, 98, 168, 192, 255, 261,
    265-266, 269-271, 277, 280, 307
Vaccinations, 98, 168t, 192, 255
    mass, 265-266, 281, 288-291
Variola major. see Smallpox
VEI. *see* Volcanic Explosivity Index
Vendor Managed Inventory (VMI), 65
Ventilation systems, 115
Veterinarians, 61-62, 97, 128, 284-285, 302
Vibrio cholerae, 274
Victim identification, 23, 45, 60, 225
Video relay service (VRS), 246-247
Video relay, 246, 249
Viral encephalitis, 27t, 273
Viral hemorrhagic fever, 27t, 276t
Virtual private network (VPN), 141
VMI. *see* Vendor Managed Inventory
Volcanic eruptions, 8, 15-16
    public health interventions, 16
Volcanic Explosivity Index (VEI), 15
Volunteer Protection Act (VPA), 81
Volunteers, 30, 37, 39, 42, 44, 57, 78, 80-83,
    88, 94, 101, 128, 131, 144, 148, 159,
    160-161, 163, 205, 216-217, 219-220,
    226, 238, 282, 287, 289, 301, 304,
    308-309, 315
    credentialing of, 30, 82
    mental health, 94, 220
VPA. *see* Volunteer Protection Act
VPN. *see* Virtual private network
VRS. *see* Video relay service

Vulnerability analysis, 66, 116, 118
Vulnerability, 2, 22, 33-34, 48, 66, 93, 101, 105,
    113, 116-117, 144, 229, 244, 270, 297-298

W

Warnings, 5, 9, 13, 15, 120, 127, 129-130,
    135, 137, 138, 140t, 141, 159-160,
    228, 240t, 247-249, 286
Waste management, 173, 189
Water safety, 6, 29, 130, 160
    accessing and treating ground, 30
    boil water order, 180-181
    collecting and treating surface, 177-178
Water supply, 3, 25, 38, 66, 180, 191
Water treatment/distribution centers, 115
WCT. *see* Wind Chill Temperature
Weather radios, 248
Well water, disinfecting, 179-180
West Nile virus, 102
    epidemic, 149
WHO. *see* World Health Organization
Whole community, 39, 215
Whole-of-nation, 39
Wi-Fi, 141, 144
Widgets, 132t-133t, 147t
Wildfires, 2t, 17, 68, 113, 158
Wind Chill Temperature (WCT) index, 3
Wind chill, 3
Winter storm warning, 3
Winter storm watch, 3
Worker safety, 38, 75t, 173, 191, 193-194,
    282
World Health Organization (WHO), 91t,
    120, 123, 176, 200, 263, 264t
World Trade Center, 102, 106, 199, 219, 225
Worried well, 165, 260, 281, 289

X

XML. *see* Extensible Markup Language

Y

Yellow fever, 27t, 192
Yersinia pestis. see Pneumonic plague